# Criminal Law
# in Focus

703-302-9793

Aspen Select Series

# Criminal Law in Focus

## Advance Edition

**Alex Kreit**

**Northern Kentucky University Salmon P. Chase College of Law**

To contact Customer Service, e-mail customer.service@wolterskluwer.com, call 1-800-234-1660, fax 1-800-901-9075, or mail correspondence to:

Wolters Kluwer
Attn: Order Department
PO Box 990
Frederick, MD 21705

Printed in the United States of America.

1 2 3 4 5 6 7 8 9 0

ISBN 978-1-4548-8777-5

# About Wolters Kluwer Legal & Regulatory U.S.

Wolters Kluwer Legal & Regulatory U.S. delivers expert content and solutions in the areas of law, corporate compliance, health compliance, reimbursement, and legal education. Its practical solutions help customers successfully navigate the demands of a changing environment to drive their daily activities, enhance decision quality and inspire confident outcomes.

Serving customers worldwide, its legal and regulatory portfolio includes products under the Aspen Publishers, CCH Incorporated, Kluwer Law International, ftwilliam.com and MediRegs names. They are regarded as exceptional and trusted resources for general legal and practice-specific knowledge, compliance and risk management, dynamic workflow solutions, and expert commentary.

*To my sons, Irving and Bennett*

# Summary of Contents

# Table of Contents

# Chapter Three: Property Offenses    **91**

# The Focus Casebook Series

Help students reach their full potential with the fresh approach of the **Focus Casebook Series**. Instead of using the "hide the ball" approach, selected cases illustrate key developments in the law and show how courts develop and apply doctrine. The approachable manner of this series provides a comfortable experiential environment that is instrumental to student success.

Students perform best when applying concepts to real-world scenarios. With assessment features, such as Real Life Applications and Applying the Concepts, the **Focus Casebook Series** offers many opportunities for students to apply their knowledge.

## Focus Casebook Features Include:

**Case Previews and Post-Case Follow-Ups** — To succeed, law students must know how to deconstruct and analyze cases. Case Previews highlight the legal concepts in a case before the student reads it. Post-Case Follow-Ups summarize the important points.

---

**Case Preview**

### *People v. Acosta*

In *People v. Acosta*, the court found there was sufficient evidence to sustain the defendant's conviction for attempted possession of cocaine. The court's opinion sheds additional light on the dangerous proximity test.

As you read the decision, consider the following questions:

1. What is the court's rationale for distinguishing the decision in *Warren*, where the court overturned the defendants' convictions for attempted drug possession on the ground
the crime?

---

**Post-Case Follow-Up**

The court holds that Acosta had "come 'very near' to possessing" cocaine because "the only remaining step between the attempt and the completed crime [was his] acceptance of the proffered merchandise, an act entirely within [Acosta's] control." In light of the holding in *Rizzo*, this outcome might strike some readers as strange since Acosta ultimately decided not to buy the cocaine. To better appreciate the court's holding, it can help to imagine how the dangerous proximity test would apply if the police had entered Acosta's apartment in the middle of the potential drug sale, before Acosta had the opportunity to sample the product and decide whether or not to go through with the purchase. If the police had arrested Acosta at that moment, there is no doubt he would have been guilty of attempted possession of cocaine. In the words of *Rizzo*, once Acosta was in the same room with the seller and the merchandise, "in all reasonable probability the crime would have been committed but for timely

# The Focus Casebook Series

**Real Life Applications** — Every case in a chapter is followed by Real Life Applications, which present a series of questions based on a scenario similar to the facts in the case. Real Life Applications challenge students to apply what they have learned in order to prepare them for real-world practice. Use Real Life Applications to spark class discussions or provide them as individual short-answer assignments.

---

## Ulbricht: *Real Life Applications*

1. Imagine that you are the judge in Ulbricht's case. The case goes to trial, and the jury finds Ulbricht guilty of all of the charges and conduct described in the opinion above. It is now up to you to decide on Ulbricht's sentence. In real life, federal sentencing law (including the Federal Sentencing Guidelines and any applicable mandatory minimum penalty provisions) would restrain the judge's sentencing decision in Ulbricht's case. For purposes of this hypothetical, however, assume that you have free rein to impose whatever sentence you believe is just.
   a. What sentence would you impose in Ulbricht's case? What three factors would be most important to you in reaching your decision?
   b. To what extent, if any, would you consider the legal distinction between single and multiple conspiracies in reaching your sentence? Specifically, would it make a difference to you if Ulbricht was found guilty of a single conspiracy with thousands of Silk Road users or thousands of counts of conspiracy with each Silk Road user?

---

**Applying the Concepts** — These end-of-chapter exercises encourage students to synthesize the chapter material and apply relevant legal doctrine and code to real-world scenarios. Students can use these exercises for self-assessment or the professor can use them to promote class interaction.

## Applying the Concepts

1. Write down a list of the offenses that have been covered in your course. For each offense, identify the *actus reus* element(s) of the offense.

2. Now, identify the *mens rea* element(s) of the offenses on your list. Do any of the offenses appear to have ambiguity about the mental state required for one or more elements of the offense?

3. A federal st
   or other int
   The statute
   of any kind
   Applying th
   defendant h
   lia" to be co

## Criminal Law in Practice

1. About half of all states have adopted the Model Penal Code's default rule regarding *mens rea* or one like it — namely that, "[w]hen the culpability sufficient to establish a material element of an offense is not prescribed by law, such element is established if a person acts purposely, knowingly or recklessly with respect thereto." Model Penal Code § 2.02(3).
   a. Look up whether the state you are in has adopted this provision of the Model Penal Code.
   b. If so, can you find a case issued by a state court in your state where the provision was outcome determinative?
   c. If not, can you find any precedent — either case law or a statute — that guides courts in interpreting the *mens rea* provisions of criminal statutes?

# Preface

## CONTENT SNAPSHOT: CRIMINAL LAW IN FOCUS

Criminal law is one of those rare legal topics that has the ability to capture the public's attention. It can be an exciting, rewarding, and sometimes even heartbreaking area of the law. In practice, criminal law encounters people—both victims and perpetrators—in some of their worst moments. As a law school course, criminal law can feature memorable cases with facts that read like a movie script. But criminal law doctrine can also be quite challenging. Criminal law is notorious for its seemingly endless jurisdictional variations, as well as for its expansiveness in the era of mass incarceration.

With so much jurisdictional variation in the definition of crimes and defenses, it is critical to provide context. *Criminal Law in Focus* clearly describes the most widely followed principles and concepts, alerting students to where there are jurisdictional differences and tensions, and why those differences exist. Using compelling cases that provide a clear application of legal doctrine, the book covers core traditional offenses, like homicide and theft crimes, as well as some offenses that figure prominently in modern practice but which have historically been absent from criminal law classes, like drug possession. The streamlined approach of the Focus Casebook Series also allows for expanded coverage of contemporary issues in criminal law, including the rise of mass incarceration and the persistence of racial disparities in criminal enforcement.

Chapter One, The Purposes of Criminal Law, examines the theories of punishment and related contemporary debate, the unusually high incarceration rates in the U.S., and racial disparities in the criminal justice system.

Chapter Two, Sources and Components of the Criminal Law, provides an overview of the sources of criminal law and the criminal trial process, and introduces the common elements of criminal offenses that recur throughout criminal codes.

Chapter Three, Property Offenses, begins our coverage of individual criminal offenses. It includes coverage of the core theft offenses—larceny, robbery, embezzlement, false pretenses, and extortion—as well as burglary and arson.

Arguably, no single development has had a greater impact on our criminal justice system over the past five decades than the war on drugs. Chapter Four, Drug Offenses, focuses on the crimes of drug possession and drug possession with the intent to distribute.

Chapter Five, Homicide Offenses, unpacks the different degrees of homicide, as well as the doctrine of causation and homicides-by-omission.

Chapter Six, Sex Offenses, focuses on three areas: rape, statutory rape, and laws against child pornography.

Chapter Seven, Attempts, covers the law that governs failed criminal endeavors, with particular attention to the line that separates preparatory acts from conduct that is sufficient to constitute an attempt.

Chapter Eight, Accomplice Liability, explores the legal doctrine and principles of accomplice liability, and the elements required to convict.

Chapter Nine, Conspiracy, examines the elements of the crime of conspiracy and the related doctrine of *Pinkerton v. United States.*

Chapter Ten, Revisiting the Elements of Crimes and Interpreting Criminal Statutes, reviews and more closely examines general principles regarding acts and mental states. It also explores some of the principles that govern the interpretation of criminal statutes.

Chapter Eleven, Affirmative Defenses, addresses the major affirmative defenses: self-defense, duress, necessity, insanity, intoxication, entrapment, and public authority.

A note on editing: The deletion of text from within a sentence or paragraph is indicated by an ellipsis, with the exception of the deletion of in-text citations. To maximize readability, I opted not to use ellipsis where whole paragraphs or the beginning or end of a paragraph have been cut. In a few instances, I have re-ordered paragraphs from the source material to enhance readability. Most in-text citations and almost all footnotes have been deleted. Footnotes that were retained are marked using their original numbering.

# Acknowledgments

I would not have written this casebook if editor Rick Mixter hadn't knocked on my office door several years ago. Our ensuing conversations about pedagogy, criminal law, and more, led me to submit a book proposal. And it would not surprise me if his belief in the project helped smooth things over when I did not meet my original deadline, or the deadline after that, or the deadline after—let's just say, I am grateful to have such an understanding publisher.

Thank you to everyone at Wolters Kluwer and The Froebe Group who worked with me throughout the development and editing process. I am fortunate to have had such a talented and dedicated group of editors. Jess Barmack, Shannon Davis, and Sara Nies all provided valuable suggestions and encouragement; Michelle Humphrey made the permissions process as painless as possible; Kathy Langone, series editor Howard Katz, and Betsy Kenny also all helped in various ways.

I am indebted to my Fall 2020 students at Northern Kentucky University and my Spring 2018 students at Thomas Jefferson School of Law, who endured my typo-ridden draft materials and whose feedback helped make this book better.

Most importantly, I could not have completed this book without the love and support of my family. My sons, Irving and Bennett, pitched in by watching additional episodes of *Super Wings* and *Daniel Tiger's Neighborhood* when I needed to work. My wife, Bridget Kennedy, took on more than her share of pandemic parenting duties during the final editing stages, despite a very busy schedule of her own as a public defender. I am so lucky to be spending my life with someone so incredible and whose dedication to indigent defense is an inspiration to me.

Last, I would like to thank everyone—scholars, practitioners, activists, students, judges, and clients—who has informed my understanding of the criminal law, including the following copyright holders for granting permission to reproduce portions of their work in this book:

Michelle Alexander, "The New Jim Crow." Ohio State Journal of Criminal Law, Vol. 9, No. 1 (2011). Ohio State University, Moritz College of Law. Reprinted with permission.

James Forman, Jr., "Racial Critiques of Mass Incarceration: Beyond the New Jim Crow." New York University Law Review, Vol. 87, No. 1 (2012). New York University. Reprinted with permission from the author.

Angel E. Sanchez, "In Spite of Prison." Harvard Law Review, Vol. 132 (2019). The Harvard Law Review Association. Copyright © 2019.

## IMAGES

Bernhard Goetz speaks in a Bronx courtroom. Charles Arrigo/AP Photo. Copyright © 1987.

Black Lives Matter protest march. Simone Hogan/Shutterstock.com. Copyright © 2020.

George H.W. Bush holds up a bag of crack cocaine during his Address to the Nation on National Drug Control Strategy. Courtesy of the George Bush Presidential Library Foundation (via Wikimedia Commons).

Daniel McNaughton, Insane Murderer. Illustrated London News (1843). Courtesy of the Wellcome Library, London. Licensed under CC BY 4.0.

President Ronald Reagan moments before his assassination attempt on March 30, 1981. Courtesy of the Ronald Reagan Presidential Foundation and Library (via Wikimedia Commons).

U.S. Rep. Bill Janklow leaves the Moody County Courthouse after a second-degree manslaughter conviction. Doug Dreyer/AP/Newscom. Copyright © 2003.

# The Purposes of Criminal Law

Through criminal punishment, we inflict pain on our fellow citizens by taking their property (through fines), their liberty (through imprisonment), and in some cases even their life (through the death penalty). In a speech about criminal justice at the American Bar Association's annual meeting in 2003, former Supreme Court Justice Anthony Kennedy asked attendees to consider the reality of incarceration: "United States Marshalls can recount the experience of leading a young man away from his family to begin serving his time. His mother says, 'How long will my boy be gone?' They say 'Ten years' or '15 years.' Ladies and gentlemen, I submit to you that a 20-year-old does not know how long ten or 15 years is. One day in prison is longer than almost any day you and I have had to endure."

Of course, in order to be sent to prison like the young man in Justice Kennedy's speech, a person must first be convicted of a crime. In some cases, subjecting people to the hardships of criminal punishment may be merited, perhaps even necessary. But most people would agree that criminal law is not a tool for addressing every problem in society. Driving a few miles over the speed limit or littering may be unwelcome behavior, but should we arrest and prosecute people for it? If criminal punishment is not an appropriate response to every objectionable behavior, how should we decide when it *is* warranted? And how should society address concerns about our high incarceration rate and the racial disparities within our criminal justice system?

## A. WHEN IS PUNISHMENT JUSTIFIED?

Why do we punish people? How do we decide when taking away someone's freedom is justified? Beliefs about what kind of conduct should be subject to criminal punishment typically fall into one of two categories: consequentialist and deontological.

## Key Concepts

- What are the theories of punishment?
- How do the theories of punishment shape debates in the criminal law today, such as whether to legalize marijuana?
- Why does the United States have an unusually high incarceration rate?
- How can we address racial disparities in the criminal justice system?

Consequentialist arguments are focused on outcomes. Under the chief consequentialist theory of punishment, **utilitarianism**, punishment is justified if the benefits to society outweigh the costs. This formulation is easy enough to state but difficult to apply. This is because there are a wide range of costs and benefits involved in criminal punishment, and many of the figures depend on predictions about the future (like how many would-be criminals will be deterred by a given law) or involve considerations that are not easily quantifiable (like the emotional pain experienced by a crime victim or by a child of someone who is incarcerated).

Deontological philosophies, like retribution, are not concerned with results. **Retributivists** believe that moral blameworthiness justifies punishment, regardless of any costs or benefits to society. As Immanuel Kant famously put it, "[e]ven if a Civil Society resolved to dissolve itself with the consent of all its members . . . the last Murderer lying in the prison ought to be executed before the resolution was carried out." Immanuel Kant, The Philosophy of Law 198 (1887).

Though there are some who subscribe to only one theory of punishment, in practice, most discussions about when criminal punishment is justified involve a mixture of utilitarian and retributivist arguments. Of course, as a practical matter, legislatures — not legal philosophers — decide what conduct to criminalize (this is discussed further in Chapter 2). Lawmakers do not typically spend a lot of time talking about the theories of punishment. But political discussions around criminal law often tend to track these theories, even if by accident. Having a basic understanding of the main justifications for punishment is therefore important to the study of criminal law. These theories help to shape both the popular and legal discourse about when punishment is justified and how much punishment a person who has committed a crime should receive.

The discussion below provides an overview of the most widely recognized theories of punishment.

## 1. Retribution

Have you ever read a news article about a judge handing down a sentence that you thought was too harsh or too lenient, and said to yourself that the perpetrator of the crime got more or less punishment than she "deserved"? If so, you were using the language of the retributivist. Retributivists believe in the principle of just deserts — that punishment is justified if and when it is deserved, even if the tangible costs of imposing punishment might outweigh the tangible benefits. In this way, retributive theories see punishment as an intrinsic good and an end in itself. Retributivism looks backward at a wrongdoer's conduct to justify punishment, not forward at the consequences of imposing punishment. Among retributivists, there are different views about how best to figure out when punishment is deserved, but common to all retributivist theories "is that they purport to illuminate the attractiveness of punishment without needing to invoke the contingent benefits of the punishment." Dan Markel, *Retributive Justice and the Demands of Democratic Citizenship*, 1 Va. J. Crim. L. 1, 35 (2012).

# 2. Utilitarianism

Utilitarians believe the law should exist to provide a net benefit to society. In the utilitarian outlook, inflicting pain on someone through punishment is undesirable because it decreases happiness. Taking away someone's liberty also imposes a range of costs on society — among other things, it requires the government to expend resources that could be put to other uses, removes the incarcerated person from the labor force, and deprives families of contact with their loved one. Under utilitarianism, punishment is justified if and when its costs are outweighed by the expected benefits in the form of a reduction in crime. Whereas retributivism looks backward at an offender's conduct, utilitarianism is concerned about which policies will achieve the greatest benefit for society in the future. From a utilitarian perspective, criminal punishment aims to achieve the following goals:

## *General Deterrence*

The fear of criminal punishment can provide a **general deterrence** effect. Punishing a person who has already committed a crime may give other would-be offenders a reason not to engage in that same conduct. A politician who votes in favor of a strict sentencing law in order to "send a message to criminals" is likewise motivated by the idea of general deterrence.

## *Individual (or Specific) Deterrence*

In addition to deterring others, punishment might result in **individual (or specific) deterrence** by giving the person punished an incentive to refrain from committing crimes in the future. Imposing punishment might make a person "learn his or her lesson" and decide to abide by the law in order to avoid criminal penalties in the future. *State v. Hopkins*, 168 Wis. 2d 802, 812 (1992).

## *Incapacitation*

General and specific deterrence might be achieved through a number of different forms of punishment, including fines, "shaming" punishments (like being made to stand on a street corner with an embarrassing sign), or even physical punishments (like caning). Imprisonment can serve another potential utilitarian objective: **incapacitation**. When a person is behind bars, she is physically unable to commit additional crimes against the general public (although, of course, incarceration does not prevent her from committing crimes against fellow prisoners). There are steps short of imprisonment, like making a person wear a GPS ankle monitor while on probation, that similarly seek to reduce the risk she will reoffend.

## *Rehabilitation*

Finally, the criminal justice system might benefit society through **rehabilitation**. Providing drug treatment or job training to someone who has committed

## Distinguishing Criminal and Civil Law

What differentiates criminal and civil law? One important distinction is that criminal law is public law. This fact is reflected right in the titles of the cases we will read throughout this book, which bear names like *United States v. Brown*. In a criminal case, the *state* brings the prosecution via attorneys who are paid through tax dollars to represent the community. In torts, contracts, and property cases, by contrast, the plaintiff is typically a private party.

Consider the case of a victim who suffers severe injuries at the hands of a drunken driver. The victim might bring a tort action against the driver to try to recover money damages. But it is up to the state to file criminal charges and prosecute the case. Although the immediate victim may be the person who was injured, the criminal law is meant to vindicate the interests of society as a whole.

The divide between public and private law still does not fully explain what separates criminal law from civil wrongdoing. After all, the state is also responsible for giving out parking tickets. It is tempting to point to incarceration as the dividing line between a parking ticket and a criminal offense. While it is true that many convictions result in incarceration, in plenty of criminal cases the sentence is only a fine. Even if the practical consequences are identical, however, a criminal conviction, unlike a parking ticket, carries the stigma of public condemnation. And this stigma *can* have real-world effects, even if they are only informal. Few employers would care if their employee was caught speeding and given a $250 traffic

a crime might help that person to live a more productive life in the future, thereby benefiting society as a whole. Offenders may not necessarily experience these kinds of responses to crime as punishment. Some drug offenders might be eager and happy to receive drug treatment, for example. As a result, rehabilitation-based strategies are sometimes described as alternatives to traditional punishment. In most cases, however, rehabilitation services are added to traditional punishments, like imprisonment or probation. Notably in this regard, there is evidence that prison may be at cross-purposes with the goal of rehabilitation. See Patrice Villettaz et al., *The Effects on Re-offending of Custodial vs. Non-custodial Sanctions: An Updated Systematic Review of the State of Knowledge*, 11 Campbell Systematic Revs. 1, 7 (2015) (reviewing studies on the effect of incarceration on recidivism and finding "that the rate of re-offending after a non-custodial sanction is lower than after a custodial sanction in most comparisons").

## 3. Applying the Theories of Punishment: *Dudley and Stephens*

Now that we have read a bit about the theories of punishment in the abstract, this section presents a famous case — *The Queen v. Dudley and Stephens* — as a vehicle for thinking more about when punishment is justified.

Before turning to that case, it is helpful to see how the theories of punishment discussed above might fit together. Although retributivist and utilitarian concepts are distinct, they are not necessarily incompatible with one another. As mentioned already, many criminal law theorists and everyday citizens alike hold both retributivist and utilitarian beliefs about punishment.

Indeed, there are few "pure" utilitarians when it comes to criminal law: "No scholarly literature argues for an exclusively consequentialist regime of criminal punishment without regard to individual culpability. Put differently, there is little disagreement that desert is *necessary* to justify punishment. The disagreement instead concerns the sufficiency of desert — whether desert alone is *sufficient* to justify punishment — and the strength of that sufficiency claim — whether desert's sufficiency creates something like a strong presumption to punish or, at the extreme, a State duty to punish." Darryl K. Brown, *Criminal Law Theory and Criminal Justice Practice*, 49 Am. Crim. L. Rev. 73, 76 (2012). One problem with a pure utilitarian theory of punishment is that it might arguably permit the punishment of someone who has not committed a crime for preventive purposes. Some argue that, in an extreme case, a pure utilitarian theory could even justify the framing of an innocent person — for example, if doing so would satisfy society's desire for punishment of an especially heinous crime in a case where the true culprit remained at large. As a result, most proponents of utilitarian theories see blameworthiness as a precondition and constraint on punishment.

ticket. But many employers would be concerned if their employee was convicted of a crime, even if it were just a misdemeanor that resulted in a $250 penalty.

As one commentator put it: "What distinguishes a criminal from a civil sanction and all that distinguishes it . . . is the judgment of community condemnation which accompanies and justifies its imposition." Henry M. Hart, Jr., *The Aims of the Criminal Law*, 23 Law & Contemp. Probs. 401, 404 (1958).

---

**Case Preview**

## *The Queen v. Dudley and Stephens*

The next case, *Dudley and Stephens*, is a law school classic. For decades, the decision has served as the entry point for many, if not most, criminal law classes. The facts of the case are tragic. Four sailors were stranded at sea in the late 1800s. By the time they were rescued, only three of them were still alive. After 20 days at sea, two of the men killed their shipmate who, it appears, was already near death as he was "unable to make any resistance." The three survivors then "fed upon the body and blood" of the deceased until they were unexpectedly rescued four days later. Doctrinally, the court held that necessity is never a defense to murder. But the reason law students continue to read *Dudley and Stephens* today is not for its legal ruling. Instead, the case provides a vehicle for thinking more about the theories of punishment.

As you read the decision, consider the following questions:

**1.** Can you identify which theory (or theories) of punishment the court relies on for its holding?

**2.** Do you personally think the defendants "deserved" punishment, and if so, how much?

**3.** To what extent do you think punishment in this case could further utilitarian goals (general deterrence, specific deterrence, incapacitation, or rehabilitation)? How would you go about weighing any potential benefits against the costs of punishment?

**EXHIBIT 1.1** Newspaper Article About the Shipwrecked Crew

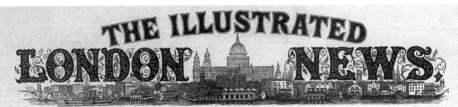

THE LOSS OF THE YACHT MIGNONETTE.—FROM SKETCHES BY MR. EDWIN STEPHENS, THE MATE.

The way in which they stowed themselves in the dinghy.

Sailing before the wind: How the dinghy was managed during the last nine days.

How the dinghy was managed in the heavy weather: with the stern-sheets up aft, and the "sea anchor," made of the water-breaker bed and the head-sheets grating.

# *The Queen v. Dudley and Stephens*
## 14 QBD 273 DC (1884)

LORD COLERIDGE, C.J.

The two prisoners, Thomas Dudley and Edwin Stephens, were indicted for the murder of Richard Parker on the high seas on the 25th of July in the present year. They were tried before my Brother Huddleston at Exeter on the 6th of November, and, under the direction of my learned Brother, the jury returned a special verdict, the legal effect of which has been argued before us, and on which we are now to pronounce judgment.

At the trial before Huddleston, B., at the Devon and Cornwall Winter Assizes, November 7, 1884, the jury, at the suggestion of the learned judge, found the facts of the case in a special verdict which stated "that on July 5, 1884, the prisoners, Thomas Dudley and Edward Stephens, with one Brooks, all able-bodied English seamen, and the deceased also an English boy, between seventeen and eighteen years of age, the crew of an English yacht, a registered English vessel, were cast away in a storm on the high seas 1600 miles from the Cape of Good Hope, and were compelled to put into an open boat belonging to the said yacht. That in this boat they had no supply of water and no supply of food, except two 1 [pound] tins of turnips, and for three days they had nothing else to subsist upon. That on the fourth day they caught a small turtle, upon which they subsisted for a few days, and this was the only food they had up to the twentieth day when the act now in question was committed. That on the twelfth day the remains of the turtle were entirely consumed, and for the next eight days they had nothing to eat. That they had no fresh water, except such rain as they from time to time caught in their oilskin capes. That the boat was drifting on the ocean, and was probably more than 1000 miles away from land. That on the eighteenth day, when they had been seven days without food and five without water, [Dudley and Stephens] spoke to Brooks as to what should be done if no succour came, and suggested that some one should be sacrificed to save the rest, but Brooks dissented, and the boy [Parker], to whom [Dudley and Stephens] were understood to refer, was not consulted. That on the 24th of July, the day before the act now in question, the prisoner Dudley proposed to Stephens and Brooks that lots should be cast who should be put to death to save the rest, but Brooks refused to consent, and it was not put to the boy, and in point of fact there was no drawing of lots. That on that day the prisoners spoke of their having families, and suggested it would be better to kill the boy that their lives should be saved, and Dudley proposed that if there was no vessel in sight by the morrow morning the boy should be killed.

That next day, the 25th of July, no vessel appearing, Dudley told Brooks that he had better go and have a sleep, and made signs to Stephens and Brooks that the boy had better be killed. The prisoner Stephens agreed to the act, but Brooks dissented from it. That the boy was then lying at the bottom of the boat quite helpless, and extremely weakened by famine and by drinking sea water, and unable to make any resistance, nor did he ever assent to his being killed. The prisoner Dudley offered a prayer asking forgiveness for them all if either of them should be tempted to commit a rash act, and that their souls might be saved. That Dudley, with the assent of

Stephens, went to the boy, and telling him that his time was come, put a knife into his throat and killed him then and there; that the three men fed upon the body and blood of the boy for four days; that on the fourth day after the act had been committed the boat was picked up by a passing vessel, and the prisoners were rescued, still alive, but in the lowest state of prostration. That they were carried to the port of Falmouth, and committed for trial at Exeter. That if the men had not fed upon the body of the boy they would probably not have survived to be so picked up and rescued, but would within the four days have died of famine. That the boy, being in a much weaker condition, was likely to have died before them. That at the time of the act in question there was no sail in sight, nor any reasonable prospect of relief. That under these circumstances there appeared to the prisoners every probability that unless they then fed or very soon fed upon the boy or one of themselves they would die of starvation. That there was no appreciable chance of saving life except by killing some one for the others to eat. That assuming any necessity to kill anybody, there was no greater necessity for killing the boy than any of the other three men."

From these facts, stated with the cold precision of a special verdict, it appears sufficiently that the prisoners were subject to terrible temptation, to sufferings which might break down the bodily power of the strongest man, and try the conscience of the best. Other details yet more harrowing, facts still more loathsome and appalling, were presented to the jury, and are to be found recorded in my learned Brother's notes. But nevertheless this is clear, that the prisoners put to death a weak and unoffending boy upon the chance of preserving their own lives by feeding upon his flesh and blood after he was killed, and with the certainty of depriving *him* of any possible chance of survival. The verdict finds in terms that "if the men had not fed upon the body of the boy they would *probably* not have survived," and that "the boy being in a much weaker condition was *likely* to have died before them." They might possibly have been picked up next day by a passing ship; they might possibly not have been picked up at all; in either case it is obvious that the killing of the boy would have been an unnecessary and profitless act. It is found by the verdict that the boy was incapable of resistance, and, in fact, made none; and it is not even suggested that his death was due to any violence on his part attempted against, or even so much as feared by, those who killed him. Under these circumstances the jury say that they are ignorant whether those who killed him were guilty of murder, and have referred it to this Court to determine what is the legal consequence which follows from the facts which they have found.

[And so, we] consider[] the real question in the case — whether killing under the circumstances set forth in the verdict be or be not murder. The contention that it could be anything else was, to the minds of us all, both new and strange, and we stopped the Attorney General in his negative argument in order that we might hear what could be said in support of a proposition which appeared to us to be at once dangerous, immoral, and opposed to all legal principle and analogy. All, no doubt, that can be said has been urged before us, and we are now to consider and determine what it amounts to.

Is there . . . any authority for the proposition which has been presented to us? Decided cases there are none.

The one real authority of former time is Lord Bacon, who, in his commentary on the maxim, "necessitas induct privilegium quoad jura privata," lays down the law as follows: — "Necessity carrieth a privilege in itself. Necessity is of three sorts — necessity of conservation of life, necessity of obedience, and necessity of the act of God or of a stranger. First of conservation of life; if a man steal viands to satisfy his present hunger, this is no felony nor larceny. So if divers be in danger of drowning by the casting away of some boat or barge, and one of them get to some plank, or on the boat's side to keep himself above water, and another to save his life thrust him from it, whereby he is drowned, this is neither [a killing] se defendendo nor by mis-adventure,* but [nevertheless] justifiable." Lord Bacon was great even as a lawyer; but it is permissible to much smaller men, relying upon principle and on the authority of others, the equals and even the superiors of Lord Bacon as lawyers, to question the soundness of his dictum. There are many conceivable states of things in which it might possibly be true, but if Lord Bacon meant to lay down the broad proposition that a man may save his life by killing, if necessary, an innocent and unoffending neighbour, it certainly is not law at the present day.

[T]he learned persons who formed the commission for preparing the Criminal Code** [had this] to say on the subject: —

"We are certainly not prepared to suggest that necessity should in every case be a justification. We are equally unprepared to suggest that necessity should in no case be a defence; we judge it better to leave such questions to be dealt with when, if ever, they arise in practice by applying the principles of law to the circumstances of the particular case."

It would have been satisfactory to us if these eminent persons could have told us whether the received definitions of legal necessity were in their judgment correct and exhaustive, and if not, in what way they should be amended, but as it is we have, as they say, "to apply the principles of law to the circumstances of this particular case."

Now, except for the purpose of testing how far the conservation of a man's own life is in all cases and under all circumstances, an absolute, unqualified, and paramount duty, we exclude from our consideration all the incidents of war. We are dealing with a case of private homicide, not one imposed upon men in the service of their Sovereign and in the defence of their country. Now it is admitted that the deliberate killing of this unoffending and unresisting boy was clearly murder, unless the killing can be justified by some well-recognised excuse admitted by the law. It is further admitted that there was in this case no such excuse, unless the killing was justified by what has been called "necessity." But the temptation to the act which existed here was not what the law has ever called necessity. Nor is this to be regretted. Though law and morality are not the same, and many

---

* *Se defendendo* means in self-defense. By misadventure means accidentally, for example, when "[a] person is doing a lawful act, without any intention of killing, yet unfortunately kills another, as where a person is at work with an ax and the head flies off and kills a bystander." Nev. Rev. Stat. § 200.180. [Footnote by casebook author.]
** This sentence refers to a proposed, but not adopted, criminal code. The 1800s saw a number of attempts to codify the criminal law in England, including through a Royal Commission in the late 1870s. The effort was unsuccessful, however. See, e.g., Sir Leon Radzinowicz & Roger Hood, *Judicial Discretion and Sentencing Standards: Victorian Attempts to Solve a Perennial Problem*, 127 U. Pa. L. Rev. 1288 (1979). [Footnote by casebook author.]

things may be immoral which are not necessarily illegal, yet the absolute divorce of law from morality would be of fatal consequence; and such divorce would follow if the temptation to murder in this case were to be held by law an absolute defence of it. It is not so. To preserve one's life is generally speaking a duty, but it may be the plainest and the highest duty to sacrifice it. War is full of instances in which it is a man's duty not to live, but to die. The duty, in case of shipwreck, of a captain to his crew, of the crew to the passengers, of soldiers to women and children . . . ; these duties impose on men the moral necessity, not of the preservation, but of the sacrifice of their lives for others, from which in no country, least of all, it is to be hoped, in England, will men ever shrink, as indeed, they have not shrunk. It is not correct, therefore, to say that there is any absolute or unqualified necessity to preserve one's life. "Necesse est at eam, non at vivam," is a saying of a Roman officer quoted by Lord Bacon himself with high eulogy in the very chapter on necessity to which so much reference has been made. It would be a very easy and cheap display of commonplace learning to quote from Greek and Latin authors, from Horace, from Juvenal, from Cicero, from Euripides, passage after passage, in which the duty of dying for others has been laid down in glowing and emphatic language as resulting from the principles of heathen ethics; it is enough in a Christian country to remind ourselves of the Great Example whom we profess to follow. It is not needful to point out the awful danger of admitting the principle which has been contended for. Who is to be the judge of this sort of necessity? By what measure is the comparative value of lives to be measured? Is it to be strength, or intellect, or what? It is plain that the principle leaves to him who is to profit by it to determine the necessity which will justify him in deliberately taking another's life to save his own. In this case the weakest, the youngest, the most unresisting, was chosen. Was it more necessary to kill him than one of the grown men? The answer must be "No" —

> "So spake the Fiend, and with necessity,
> The tyrant's plea, excused his devilish deeds."

It is not suggested that in this particular case the deeds were "devilish," but it is quite plain that such a principle once admitted might be made the legal cloak for unbridled passion and atrocious crime. There is no safe path for judges to tread but to ascertain the law to the best of their ability and to declare it according to their judgment; and if in any case the law appears to be too severe on individuals, to leave it to the Sovereign to exercise that prerogative of mercy which the Constitution has intrusted to the hands fittest to dispense it.

It must not be supposed that in refusing to admit temptation to be an excuse for crime it is forgotten how terrible the temptation was; how awful the suffering; how hard in such trials to keep the judgment straight and the conduct pure. We are often compelled to set up standards we cannot reach ourselves, and to lay down rules which we could not ourselves satisfy. But a man has no right to declare temptation to be an excuse, though he might himself have yielded to it, nor allow compassion for the criminal to change or weaken in any manner the legal definition of the crime. It is therefore our duty to declare that the prisoners' act in this case was wilful murder, that the facts as stated in the verdict are no legal justification of the homicide; and to say that in our unanimous opinion the prisoners are upon this special verdict guilty of murder.[1]

The Court then proceeded to pass sentence of death upon the prisoners.

**Post-Case Follow-Up**

*Dudley and Stephens* holds that necessity is no defense to a homicide offense. As we will see in Chapter 11, this principle remains true today. But the real significance of *Dudley and Stephens* is as a test of the justifications of punishment. Toward the beginning of the opinion, the court seems to treat the defendant's argument as frivolous, remarking that the "contention that [Dudley and Stephen's actions] could be anything" but murder "was, to the minds of us all, both new and strange[.]" By the end, however, the court sounds somewhat more sympathetic when it acknowledges that "[w]e are often compelled to set up standards we cannot reach ourselves, and to lay down rules which we could not ourselves satisfy." All these years later, readers continue to debate the question of whether the theories of punishment supported treating Thomas Dudley and Edwin Stephens as murderers.

## Dudley and Stephens: *Real Life Applications*

**1.** The court's finding that Dudley and Stephens were guilty of murder made the penalty, a death sentence, a foregone conclusion. But Dudley and Stephens were never executed. The Crown commuted the sentence to six months' imprisonment. The court appeared to invite the commutation with its observation that if "the law appears to be too severe" it should be left "to the Sovereign to exercise that prerogative of mercy which the Constitution has intrusted to the hands fittest to dispense it." Assume for argument's sake that you agree six months was an appropriate sentence in the *Dudley and Stephens* case. Imagine you are a state legislator rewriting your state's sentencing statutes. What penalty range would you prescribe for the crime of murder? Would you give judges the discretion to impose a sentence as low as six months for defendants convicted of murder in order to account for outlier cases like *Dudley and Stephens*? Or would you try and address the problem of defendants like those in *Dudley and Stephens* in some other way?

**2.** *Dudley and Stephens* makes for a fascinating discussion of legal theory, but it can sometimes seem unconnected to the real world. Few lawyers will ever try a homicide case, let alone a case involving cannibalism and a claim of necessity. Indeed, *Dudley and Stephens* remains an enduring case in part because the facts are so extreme. Thinking through such a challenging case helps to sharpen our

---

[1] My brother Grove has furnished me with the following suggestion, too late to be embodied in the judgment but well worth preserving: "If the two accused men were justified in killing Parker, then if not rescued in time, two of the three survivors would be justified in killing the third, and of the two who remained the stronger would be justified in killing the weaker so that three men might be justifiably killed to give the fourth a chance of surviving."

views about when punishment is justified in the real world and why. With that in mind, think about the following hypothetical cases. Imagine you are a state legislator on a committee tasked with rewriting your state's criminal code. Do you think criminal punishment is warranted in each case? If so, what punishment do you think would be warranted for each defendant and why?

   **a.** *LSD at the concert*: Doris, who has no criminal record, was at a music festival watching the band the Flatbush Zombies perform, when an undercover police officer approached her. The undercover officer struck up a conversation with Doris and, eventually, asked Doris if she knew where to find any drugs. Doris told the undercover officer that she had brought a few hits of LSD to the concert "for personal use" but that she would be glad to share one with the undercover officer. Doris then handed one hit of LSD to the undercover officer. The undercover officer offered Doris some money in exchange, but Doris refused.

   **b.** *Bar room fight*: Ellis, who has no criminal record, was at a bar with some friends one night. Ellis is not usually a heavy drinker. But on this night, Ellis was drowning his sorrows after a bad break-up. By midnight, Ellis had consumed seven alcoholic drinks and was incredibly drunk. Ellis accidentally bumped into Vic, who turned and yelled: "Watch where you're going" and then directed a racial slur at Ellis. In response, Ellis punched Vic in the face, knocking Vic to the ground. A bouncer quickly arrived to break up the fight.

   **c.** *Prior convictions*: Now imagine the defendant in each of the two examples above had a prior conviction for car theft. Would that change your view about whether the conduct should be criminalized or what the appropriate sentence should be? If so, why?

---

## 4. Applying the Theories of Punishment: Marijuana Prohibition

Whatever theory of punishment one subscribes to, retributivists and utilitarians alike generally agree that the conduct covered by most major criminal statutes calls for criminal punishment of some kind. To be sure, there is often strong disagreement about *how much* punishment a robber should receive, including whether or not punishment should include a period of incarceration. But most people support the existence of criminal laws against robbery (or sexual assault or homicide). (The prison abolition movement is discussed later in this chapter.)

The shape of the discourse over public order and vice offenses is much different. Though criminal laws against controlled substances and prostitution are well established, there is a vigorous and ongoing debate over whether this sort of activity should be criminalized at all. Marijuana prohibition provides a particularly notable example. Not too long ago, marijuana legalization was considered to be far outside the political mainstream. The idea that it could actually become law seemed so remote that when President Barack Obama was asked for his thoughts on marijuana legalization in a 2009 online town hall event, he treated the question as a joke. "I don't know what this says about the online audience," President Obama chuckled, before tersely answering that, no, he did not think legalizing marijuana would be "a good strategy to grow our economy." Fast forward three years. On the same night Obama was elected to a second term in November 2012, Colorado and Washington became the first states to pass marijuana ballot measures. All of a sudden, marijuana legalization was no longer a laughing matter. By January 1, 2021, 11 more states — Alaska, Arizona, California, Illinois, Maine, Massachusetts, Michigan, Montana, Nevada, Oregon, and South Dakota — had passed marijuana legalization laws, all but one via ballot initiative. In addition, Washington, D.C. and Vermont have adopted laws allowing people to possess and grow small amounts of marijuana, although commercial distribution and sale remain prohibited. New Jersey voters approved a ballot measure supportive of legalization in 2020, but the implementing legislation required for it to take effect was still in limbo at the start of 2021. (State medical marijuana laws date to 1996, with the passage of California's Compassionate Use Act.)

Marijuana presents a real-world example of the theories of punishment in action. Some supporters of marijuana legalization say that buying and selling marijuana is a "victimless crime," which is another way of making a retributivist argument that the conduct is not sufficiently blameworthy to justify punishment. Other legalization supporters point to utilitarian considerations in support of their positions, like the cost of enforcing marijuana prohibition and the potential tax revenue that might be generated from legalization. Marijuana legalization opponents argue that marijuana use can cause harm to the user and society at large by, for example, increasing the risk of driving under the influence. As a result, they believe that marijuana possession and sale is deserving of punishment and that prohibition provides an overall benefit to society.

Marijuana prohibition also raises questions about whether criminal laws might sometimes result from factors other than the traditional theories of punishment. In an article excerpted later in this chapter, Michelle Alexander argues that the war on drugs has

## The Harm Principle and Just Deserts

The argument that marijuana transactions should not be punished because they are "victimless" is rooted in the harm principle. The harm principle posits that criminal punishment should be reserved for conduct that harms others. John Stuart Mill provided the most well-known and enduring description of the harm principle in his 1859 essay *On Liberty*. In that essay, Mill argued that "the only purpose for which power can be rightfully exercised over any member of a civilized community, against his will, is to prevent harm to others. His own good, either physical or moral, is not a sufficient warrant." Put another way, because harming oneself is not blameworthy conduct, it is not deserving of punishment.

Mill advocated for the harm principle as a limit on the sweep of criminal law. His essay cited the prospect of alcohol prohibition as potentially incompatible with the harm principle, lamenting the fact that "[u]nder the name of preventing intemperance the people of one English colony, and of nearly half the United States, have been interdicted from making any use whatever of fermented drinks."

But does the harm principle really do much to limit the bounds of criminal law? In a 1999 essay, Bernard Harcourt observed that forceful arguments have emerged that many so-called vice offenses that were previously thought to be incompatible with the harm principle actually *do* cause harm to others: "Today, the harm principle is being used increasingly by conservatives who justify laws against prostitution, pornography, public drinking, drugs, and loitering . . . on the basis of harm to others." Harcourt concluded that "[c]laims of harm have become so pervasive that the harm principle has become meaningless: the harm principle no longer serves the function of a critical principle because non-trivial harm arguments permeate the debate." Bernard E. Harcourt, *The Collapse of the Harm Principle*, 90 J. Crim. L. & Criminology 109 (1999). For an argument that the harm principle might still provide a limit to the reach of the criminal law, at least with respect to illegal drug use, see Douglas Husak, *Illicit Drugs: A Test of Joel Feinberg's* The Moral Limits of the Criminal Law, 10 Libertaria (2008).

"little to do with drug crime and much to do with racial politics." Indeed, early criminal laws against marijuana passed in the 1920s and 1930s were fueled by "racial prejudice against both African Americans and Mexicans," with many prohibition advocates of the era using overtly racist language in their advocacy. Steven W. Bender, *The Colors of Cannabis: Race and Marijuana*, 50 U.C. Davis L. Rev. 689, 690 (2016). Stark racial disparities continue to plague marijuana enforcement today. A landmark 2013 report by the American Civil Liberties Union, *The War on Marijuana in Black and White*, found that even though whites and people of color use marijuana at similar rates, a Black person is 3.73 times as likely as a white person to be arrested for possession of marijuana.

Whether you are a supporter or an opponent of marijuana legalization, thinking about the issue through the lens of retributivism and utilitarianism provides additional insight into the theories of punishment.

**Case Preview**

## *State v. Hoseman*

In *Hoseman*, a court was asked to rule on the issue of whether growing marijuana is a victimless crime for purposes of a Wisconsin statute that allows crime victims to seek restitution from criminal defendants during sentencing. By the time the case reached the Court of Appeals, there was little dispute that Hoseman's marijuana growing operation caused significant damage to his landlord's property. The question for the court was whether this fact made the landlord a victim of Hoseman's crime of conspiracy to manufacture marijuana within the meaning of Wisconsin's restitution statute.

As you read the decision, consider the following questions:

1. Why do you think Hoseman was growing marijuana inside of an 1885 Victorian home instead of in an industrial space or on farmland?
2. It is clear that Hoseman caused damage to the Burbeys' home. But were the Burbeys victims of Hoseman's cultivation of marijuana in the same sense that someone whose wallet is stolen is a victim of theft?
3. Do you think Hoseman deserved punishment for his conduct? If so, do you believe the bare fact that he was growing marijuana would justify punishing him, or does he only deserve punishment because of the damage he caused to the home? What do you think would be an appropriate sentence?

# *State v. Hoseman*
## 2011 WI App 88

ANDERSON, J.

Seeking to escape responsibility for damages that rendered an 1885 Victorian home uninhabitable, Michael S. Hoseman appeals from a judgment of conviction in which the court included an order that he pay a $25,000 portion of restitution totaling $106,409.63. Hoseman asserts that the manufacture of marijuana is a "victimless" crime; therefore, he reasons the owners of the residence are not "direct victims" of his criminal conduct. We reject Hoseman's argument and affirm that his unauthorized alterations to the residence in order to construct and operate a hydroponic growing operation were at the heart of the extensive damages that made the residence uninhabitable.

Along with four other individuals, Hoseman was charged with a single count of conspiracy to manufacture between 2,500 and 10,000 grams of marijuana. The charge arose after law enforcement uncovered a sophisticated marijuana growing operation in Walworth county.

The State and Hoseman reached a plea agreement under which Hoseman pled guilty to a lesser charge of conspiracy to manufacture between 200 and 1000 grams of marijuana. The trial court imposed three years' initial confinement and three years' extended supervision. It also tentatively held Hoseman was jointly and severally liable for restitution of $106,409.63 in property damages.

The underlying facts are not in dispute. The growing operation was set up in an 1885 Victorian home owned by Tom and Lisa Burbey. Initially, the Burbeys had the house on the market for sale but without any potential buyers, they decided to rent out the house. Hoseman, posing as the son of co-conspirator John G. Olson, approached the Burbeys seeking to rent the house as a weekend retreat and represented that the long-range plan was to move to the house and purchase it from the Burbeys. After Tom Burbey finalized the lease, he moved to Las Vegas, Nevada, to join his wife.

Olson provided almost $180,000 in capital for the development of the hydroponic growing operation and Hoseman served as the on-scene architect. Two upstairs bedrooms were converted to grow rooms using nutrients from Canada; hydroponic growing equipment purchased from suppliers in California — including buckets, lights, ballasts, fertilizer and a growing medium. Starting with marijuana seeds from Amsterdam, the original fifty plants were cloned to produce 200 plants with a street value of $300,000 to $500,000. To prepare the two grow rooms, blankets covered all the windows and sheets were stapled to the walls to reflect the grow lights. Hoses and electrical wiring ran up the stairs. Fifty-gallon drums that held the nutrients and residual acids from the operation were drained into toilets and sinks. The exhaust gases from the growing operation were vented directly into the house. For security, closed circuit televisions were mounted in the house to provide coverage of the outside lot.

After not receiving rental payments from Hoseman for several months, Tom Burbey returned to Walworth county to begin an eviction action. Upon arriving at the house, he had to break in because the locks had been changed. After discovering the growing operation, Burbey notified law enforcement.

The Burbeys filed a restitution claim for property damage in the amount of $106,409.63. The damage they documented stated that high humidity from the operation encouraged mold and mildew damage to the walls, fixtures, wood and curtains. The huge barrels of chemicals needed for the operation ruined wood floors, carpeting and an antique rug. There were hundreds of staple holes in the walls as the result of stapling reflective sheets. THC resin saturated many surfaces; there was testimony that the "[s]ticky sappy stuff doesn't wash off that sticks to your hands, it leaves your handprint on it when you touch it and smells like marijuana and stinks like marijuana and never goes away." Draining acidic chemicals into the toilets and sinks created stains; the toilets were also stopped up with plant material. Finally, the furnace was not working, resulting in frozen water pipes. In their claim for restitution, the Burbeys asserted that as a result of the damages, their residence was uninhabitable.

After sentencing, Hoseman and his co-conspirators filed a motion demanding an evidentiary hearing on the Burbeys' claim for restitution. When the hearing began, the co-conspirators objected to the court's authority to hear the claim for restitution, insisting that the Burbeys were not victims of a crime.

> Judge, first of all, in a drug case there — in fact, I had a sentencing before you last week where even the state asserted in a drug case there is no victim. Number one, if this were a burglary matter, sexual assault, homicide, something of that nature, then this person could claim to be a victim. This is a civil matter with civil damages, and they have not asserted in any way.

The Burbeys' attorney responded, the house "was not rented to operate a marijuana greenhouse. It was operated as a residential rental. It was a home. They used my clients' house, water, electricity, heat, all of the equipment, the fixtures, everything in my clients' house for that enterprise. That makes my client[s] [] victim[s]."

The trial court denied the motion, holding that the use of the Burbeys' house was a part of the conspiracy to manufacture marijuana. The court concluded that conducting the criminal enterprise in the Burbeys' house made them victims as defined in Wis. Stat. § 950.02(4)(a)(1), entitling them to restitution under Wis. Stat. § 973.20. The court went on to conduct an evidentiary hearing that lasted over two days. At the conclusion of the hearing, the court determined that restitution damages totaled $106,409.63. It set Hoseman's restitution at $25,000, based on his ability to pay during the six-year term of his sentence. Hoseman appeals.

On appeal, Hoseman continues with his theme that the manufacture of marijuana is a "victimless" crime; specifically, he argues that the Burbeys are not victims under Wis. Stat. § 973.20 and are not allowed to receive restitution. He contends that the term "victim" as defined in the statutes is "a person against whom a crime has been committed" and does not include all of those who suffered pecuniary losses caused by a defendant's crime.

The scope of the trial court's authority to order restitution is a question of statutory interpretation. The interpretation of a statute is a question of law which this court reviews de novo.

Restitution is governed by Wis. Stat. § 973.20. It provides, in relevant part:

> When imposing sentence or ordering probation for any crime . . . for which the defendant was convicted, the court . . . shall order the defendant to make full or partial restitution under this section to any victim of a crime considered at sentencing . . . unless the court finds substantial reason not to do so and states the reason on the record. . . .

Because the restitution statute does not define the term "victim," we turn to Wis. Stat. § 950.02(4)(a), which is a related statute. Section 950.02(4)(a)(1) provides that "victim" means "[a] person against whom a crime has been committed."

Case law arising under the restitution statute informs us that there are two components to the question of whether restitution can be ordered. First, the claimant of restitution must be a "direct victim" of the crime. Second, there must be a causal connection between the defendant's conduct and harm suffered by the claimant.

To answer the first component of the analysis, we are required to determine who is "a person against whom a crime has been committed." In *State v. Vanbeek*, 316 Wis. 2d 527, we discussed who is a "direct victim" of a crime. Vanbeek left a bomb scare note in a lunch room threatening to harm school property, forcing the school district to evacuate students and staff to another location. After Vanbeek was found guilty of making a bomb scare, the school district sought restitution, including the salaries and benefits of teachers and staff. We affirmed the circuit court's order for restitution.

In opposing restitution, "Vanbeek argue[d] that the persons occupying the school were the direct victims of his crime, and that the school district was only collaterally impacted." We rejected his attack:

> This argument misses the mark. Vanbeek conveyed a false threat to destroy school district property, which resulted in an evacuation and a direct loss to the school district. There is no doubt that the conduct involved in the crime considered at sentencing — conveying a threat to destroy school district property by means of explosives — was directed at the school district. Vanbeek left the bomb scare note on school district property and the note threatened to destroy school district property.

Hoseman makes an argument similar to Vanbeek's that the Burbeys were not directly impacted by the manufacture of marijuana:

> [T]he defendant was not convicted of any crime related to the damage of property. The offense of manufacturing with intent to deliver THC is not a crime committed against or directed against the homeowners, and thus, under Wisconsin law, the homeowners should not have been awarded restitution under Wis. Stat. § 973.20.

Hoseman . . . relies on *State v. Lee*, 314 Wis. 2d 764, where we held that a police officer who was injured chasing the defendant from the scene of an armed burglary and armed robbery was not a direct victim because he was not the target of the crime of conviction. He argues that *Lee* supports his thesis that because he was not charged with damaging the Burbeys' property, they are not the direct victims of the crime of conviction.

To further support his argument, Hoseman states that "the record does not indicate that there was any direct victim to the crime sentenced upon, in that there was no evidence presented of any purchasers of the defendant's THC product."

The cases Hoseman relies upon are inapposite under the facts of this case; they stand for the proposition that governmental entities are not entitled to restitution for collateral expenses incurred in the normal course of law enforcement. Hoseman is convicted of conspiracy to manufacture marijuana; in furtherance of that conspiracy, Hoseman rented the Burbeys' residence using a ruse, he converted two upstairs rooms into grow rooms for hydroponic growing equipment, he allowed exhaust gases to vent directly into the residence, he ran hoses and electrical wiring up the stairs, and he drained chemicals into the toilets and sinks of the residence. [T]his is not similar to *Lee* where the police officer's injury as collateral damage arising after the crime of conviction was committed. What distinguishes this case from those relied upon by Hoseman is the Burbeys, as owners of the residence, were the direct targets of the conspiracy to manufacture marijuana; it was their residence that was altered and made uninhabitable to further the goal of the conspiracy. If the alterations to the Burbeys' residence had not been made, Hoseman and his co-conspirators could not have manufactured marijuana. The alterations are not collateral to the manufacture of marijuana, they are integral. As the Burbeys' attorney so eloquently argued, the house "was not rented to operate a marijuana greenhouse. It was operated as a residential rental. It was a home. They used my clients' house, water, electricity, heat, all of the equipment, the fixtures, everything in my clients' house for that enterprise. That makes my client[s] [] victim[s]."

Having concluded that the Burbeys were direct victims of the conspiracy to manufacture marijuana, we turn to the second component of our analysis — whether there is a causal connection between the defendant's entire course of conduct and harm suffered by the claimant.

We have previously summarized the extensive damage to the Burbeys' residence that made it uninhabitable and Hoseman does not seriously challenge the inescapable conclusion that the actions taken in furtherance of the conspiracy to manufacture marijuana caused the damage to the residence.

Hoseman's unauthorized alterations to the residence and unauthorized operation of a marijuana growing operation were integral to the damages that rendered the residence uninhabitable. And Hoseman's conduct of turning an 1885 Victorian home into a twenty-first century hydroponic marijuana growing operation was the substantial factor in causing the damages incurred by the Burbeys.

*By the Court.* — Judgment affirmed.

---

**Post-Case Follow-Up**

*Hoseman* holds that the Burbeys were victims of Hoseman's marijuana crime for purposes of the Wisconsin restitution statute. The court goes so far as to describe the Burbeys as "the direct targets of the conspiracy to manufacture marijuana; it was their residence that was altered and made uninhabitable to further the goal of the conspiracy." But was Hoseman's objective in growing marijuana really to cause damage to the home? Putting aside whether you think this was the correct result as a matter of legal doctrine, does the decision change your views about whether or not marijuana crimes are victimless as a matter of moral blameworthiness?

---

# Hoseman: *Real Life Applications*

1. You are Hoseman's attorney. The Wisconsin Supreme Court has granted review of the Court of Appeals' decision and you are starting to outline your opening brief to the court. In one or two paragraphs, what is your argument that the Court of Appeals' holding was incorrect and that the Burbeys weren't really the victims of your client's conduct for purposes of the restitution statute?

2. Now imagine you were the Burbeys' lawyer and your clients called you immediately after discovering the damage to their home. Presumably, if Hoseman had caused all this damage to the Burbeys' home, they could have sued him civilly to recover damages. If you were the attorney for the Burbeys, why might you counsel them to pursue damages under Wisconsin's criminal restitution statute rather than filing a civil lawsuit?

3. The decision in *Hoseman* focuses attention on the question of blameworthiness in the debate over marijuana legalization. Those who object to marijuana criminalization on retributivist grounds might well oppose even the most successful prohibition policy.

   If you believe utilitarian considerations should play a role in determining when punishment is justified, however, your position on marijuana legalization may depend on how well you think the prohibition laws work. Of course, the answer to this question can also be strongly influenced by moral intuitions. Someone who finds marijuana use relatively unobjectionable might think that a reduction in marijuana use rates is worth very little. This person might support a prohibition model only if it dramatically lowered marijuana use at a minimal cost. On the other side of the spectrum, there are those who believe that preventing marijuana use is such a strong moral imperative that they would favor spending large amounts of money to vigorously enforce criminalization laws even if the effort resulted in only a modest decline in use.

   The consequentialist discussion of the merits of marijuana criminalization is inevitably complicated by the wide range of possible objectives and policy options. Even if it were possible to agree on a common objective for our marijuana laws, any attempt to measure their effectiveness would need to account for a number of considerations beyond marijuana use rates. What value, if any, should be placed on principles like individual choice or privacy in a cost-benefit analysis? How should the unintended consequences of marijuana criminalization laws — for example, the violence associated with underground markets — be measured and factored into the assessment? What role should the racist origin of early marijuana laws and racial disparities in modern enforcement play in a utilitarian analysis of marijuana criminalization?

   With so much room for disagreement over how to define and measure costs and benefits in marijuana policy, it should come as no surprise that two people might look at the same set of data and come to different conclusions about what it means. To one person, a 5 percent reduction in marijuana use and availability at a cost of $1 billion might qualify as a resounding success. Someone else might consider that same result to be a dismal failure.

It would be impossible to catalog all of the considerations that might factor into a cost-benefit analysis of marijuana criminalization in this short space. Instead of attempting to do so, imagine you are a legislative aide in a state that is thinking about passing a marijuana legalization law. The state senator you work for has asked you for a list of at least ten factors that you think should be part of any attempt to calculate the costs and benefits of legalizing marijuana. Can you think of ten factors that should be accounted for in a utilitarian analysis of marijuana criminalization and legalization?

## B. PUNISHMENT IN THE UNITED STATES

The first section in this chapter focused on the question of when punishment is justified. Theories like retribution and utilitarianism aim to provide a morally defensible account of punishment. But do these theories fully explain the reality of punishment in the United States today? This section examines mass incarceration, the use of punishment as a tool for social control, the prison abolition movement, and racial disparities in the criminal justice system.

## 1. Mass Incarceration

Since the 1970s, the U.S. criminal justice system has seen a rapid expansion of incarceration. The scope of imprisonment in the United States today is extraordinary. The United States "has five percent of the world's population, but twenty-five percent of the world's prisoners — the highest rate of human caging of any society in the recorded history of the modern world." Alec Karakatsanis, *The Punishment Bureaucracy: How to Think About "Criminal Justice Reform,"* 128 Yale L.J. F. 848, 849-50 (2019). The term **mass incarceration** has come to be used as shorthand for describing this state of affairs.

A full examination of the scope of punishment in the United States and the policy debate that surrounds it is impossible in the context of a Criminal Law course, where the focus is necessarily on legal doctrine. But a basic familiarity with these issues is indispensable to any study of criminal law.

In 2014, the National Research Council published a 464-page report on the "historically unprecedented and internationally unique" rise in imprisonment in the United States. The report's topline findings are striking:

> From 1973 to 2009, the state and federal prison populations . . . rose steadily, from about 200,000 to 1.5 million, declining slightly in the following 4 years. In addition to the men and women serving prison time for felonies, another 700,000 are held daily in local jails.
> The U.S. penal population of 2.2 million adults is the largest in the world. The U.S. rate of incarceration, with nearly 1 of every 100 adults in prison or jail, is 5 to 10 times higher than rates in Western Europe and other democracies.

The Growth of Incarceration in the United States: Exploring the Causes and Consequences 2 (Jeremy Travis, Bruce Western & Steve Redburn eds., 2014).

These figures are eye opening. But, of course, there is disagreement about what they suggest about our approach to punishment. Supporters of the current system argue that our high incarceration rate simply reflects valid penological goals. People in this camp point out, for example, that our crime rate is at near record lows.

On the other hand, many western democracies enjoy crime rates that compare very favorably to our own without incarcerating nearly as many people. Indeed, despite our high incarceration rate, the crime rate in the United States is higher than in many other countries. "Violent crime has reduced markedly in the past few decades[, b]ut America's murder rate is still higher than the average among member countries of the Organization for Economic Cooperation and Development, and about four times the rate in Canada. The number of rapes, adjusted to the size of the population, is four times higher than it is in Denmark. Robberies are more than twice as common as they are in Poland." Annie Lowrey, *Defund the Police: America Needs to Rethink Its Priorities for the Whole Criminal-Justice System*, The Atlantic, June 5, 2020. The high incarceration rate in the United States also requires a significant amount of taxpayer money to maintain — "taxpayers spend $31,286 a year on each incarcerated person, and $12,201 on every primary- and secondary-school student." *Id.* This leaves less money available for social programs, which may help to explain why the United States spends less on them than many peer countries. "The U.S. spends 18.7 percent of its annual output on social programs, compared with 31.2 percent by France and 25.1 percent by Germany. It spends just 0.6 percent of its GDP on benefits for families with children, one-sixth of what Sweden spends and one-third the rich-country average." *Id.*

Recent years have seen growing bipartisan support for reducing incarceration levels. One of the first national politicians to take up the issue of mass incarceration, former United States Senator Jim Webb, argued that "[w]ith so many of our citizens in prison compared with the rest of the world, there are only two possibilities: Either we are home to the most evil people on earth or we are doing something different — and vastly counterproductive." Jim Webb, *Why We Must Fix Our Prisons*, Parade, Mar. 29, 2009. Webb's critique of the criminal justice system was grounded in traditional theories of punishment; other critiques are concerned with principles of equality and justice more broadly.

## 2. Punishment as a Form of Social Control

Retribution and utilitarianism are theories that attempt to explain when punishment is morally justified. They are normative claims about how things ought to be. But do these theories accurately describe how things are? Can they be squared with the phenomenon of mass incarceration?

To understand the motivating factors behind punishment, we may need to look beyond the traditional theories of retribution and utilitarianism — at least in some cases. Another possible explanation for punishment is as a tool for exercising power and control, particularly against politically or socially disfavored groups. Although this might not be a morally desirable objective of punishment, some argue that it better describes at least some aspects of our criminal justice system than retributivism and utilitarianism. For example, in her article *Managerial Justice and Mass Misdemeanors*, Issa Kohler-Hausmann examined the misdemeanor justice system in New York City in the era of stop-and-frisk policing. During that period, New York "pioneered the intentional expansion of misdemeanor arrests as part of a new policing strategy." 66 Stan L. Rev. 611, 614 (2014). Professor Kohler-Hausmann argued that this system had "largely abandoned what I call the adjudicative model of criminal law administration — concerned with adjudicating guilt and punishment in specific cases" in favor of a "managerial model — concerned with managing people over time through engagement with the criminal justice system." *Id.* Rather than aiming "to punish people for specific bad acts," she argued, the system was "largely organized around the supervision and regulation of the population that flows through misdemeanor courts, often with little attention to questions of guilt in individual cases." *Id.* On Professor Kohler-Hausmann's account, this slice of the criminal justice system was based on "a presumption of need for social control over the population brought into misdemeanor court." *Id.* at 627.

In a similar vein, Alec Karakatsanis and others have suggested that control of disfavored groups explains mass incarceration and the U.S. criminal justice system more broadly. Advocates for reducing current levels of incarceration sometimes argue that the system is broken. "But the system is 'broken' only to the extent that one believes its purpose is to promote the well-being of all members of our society. If the function of the modern punishment system is to preserve racial and economic hierarchy through brutality and control, then its bureaucracy is performing well." Karakatsanis, *supra*, at 851. See also Paul Butler, Let's Get Free: A Hip-Hop Theory of Justice (2009) ("Hip-hop suggests that American punishment is not designed mainly to enhance public safety or for retribution against the immoral. Rather, its critique of punishment echoes that of the philosopher Michel Foucault, who argued that prison is designed to encourage a 'useful illegality' that benefits the state by increasing its power.").

## Case Preview

## *Nash v. State*

The case that follows provides a window into some of the factors that drive the extraordinarily high incarceration rate in the United States. The defendant, Willie Nash, was arrested on a misdemeanor charge (the opinion does not disclose the specific offense) and booked into a jail. The officer who booked Nash did not adequately search him (or, possibly, failed to search him at all). As a result, Nash was booked into the jail with his cell phone. The jailers discovered this fact after Nash asked one of them if he could charge his cell phone. Instead of obliging, the jailer confiscated Nash's phone. Nash was then charged with violating a Mississippi statute that makes it a crime for an incarcerated person to possess a cell phone in a correctional facility. Nash was convicted and sentenced to 12 years in prison. The Supreme Court of Mississippi unanimously rejected Nash's argument that the sentence violated the Eighth Amendment's prohibition against cruel and unusual punishment. Justice Leslie D. King wrote a concurring opinion, joined by two other members of the court, to "voice my concern over this case as a whole — it seems to demonstrate a failure of our criminal justice system on multiple levels."

As you read the decision, consider the following questions:

1. Do you believe Nash's prosecution and sentence are justified using the traditional theories of punishment? If so, which theory or theories of punishment support the outcome? If not, what other considerations might explain the decision to prosecute and the penalty in this case?
2. Do you agree with Justice King's argument that the case demonstrates multiple failures of the criminal justice system?
3. When the Mississippi legislature set a sentencing range of 3 to 15 years for the crime Nash was convicted of, do you think they had cases like Nash's in mind?

---

## *Nash v. State*
### 293 So. 3d 265 (Miss. 2020)

MAXWELL, J.

A jury found Willie Nash guilty of possession of a cell phone in a correctional facility. Nash does not appeal the jury's verdict. He only challenges his sentence, twelve years in prison. He claims the twelve-year sentence is grossly disproportionate to the crime and thus violates the Eighth Amendment.

Though harsh, Nash's sentence falls within the statutory range of three to fifteen years. And the judge based his sentencing decision on the seriousness of Nash's crime and evidence of Nash's criminal history. Because Nash has not shown that a threshold comparison of the crime committed to the sentence imposed leads to an inference of gross disproportionality, no further analysis is mandated. We affirm Nash's conviction and sentence.

While confined at the Newton County Jail on a misdemeanor charge, Nash asked a jailer for "some juice." At first, the jailer thought Nash was asking for something to drink. But then Nash slid across a cell phone that he had on his person. The jailer took the phone and gave it to the sheriff's deputy in charge. Nash later denied the phone was his. But when the deputy sheriff unlocked the phone — using the code Nash had given the jailer — he found photos of Nash, as well as a text-message exchange from the day Nash had handed over the phone in jail. The incoming message asked, "WYA" (short for "where you at"), and the outgoing message responded, "in jail."

A jury convicted Nash of possessing a cell phone in a correctional facility in violation of Mississippi Code Section 47-5-193 (Rev. 2015). Any person who violates Section 47-5-193 "shall be guilty of a felony and upon conviction shall be punished by confinement in the Penitentiary for not less than three (3) years nor more than fifteen (15) years . . . ."[1] At Nash's sentencing hearing, the trial judge informed Nash that, while his crime may have seemed insignificant to him, there was a reason possessing a cell phone in a correctional facility "is such a serious charge." The judge also told Nash to "consider yourself fortunate." Based on Nash's prior burglary convictions, he could have been indicted as a habitual offender. This would have subjected him to a fifteen-year sentence to be served day for day. The trial court sentenced Nash below the statutory maximum to a term of twelve years in the custody of the Mississippi Department of Corrections.[2]

Nash filed a motion for new trial challenging the sufficiency of the State's evidence and the trial court's evidentiary rulings. The trial court denied this motion, and Nash appealed.

On appeal, Nash challenges his sentence only. He argues his twelve-year sentence violates the Eighth Amendment of the United States Constitution because it is grossly disproportionate to his crime of possessing a cell phone in jail.

Nash begins his proportionality challenge by asking this Court to recognize "differing degrees of transgression" under Section 47-5-193. Section 47-5-193 prohibits any offender confined to a correctional facility from possessing "any weapon, deadly weapon, unauthorized electronic device, contraband item, or cell phone or any of its components or accessories to include, but not limited to, Subscriber Information Module (SIM) cards or chargers." Nash argues this statute creates "three categories . . . of a descending order in severity." As Nash sees it, possession of weapons is the most serious offense, possession of contraband is less serious, and possession of a cell phone — if not used in criminal activity — is the least serious.

But the statute's language does not support his three-tiered argument. What Nash dubs as the "mere possession of a cell phone" is a specified violation of Section 47-5-193. And the statute subjected him to the same potential punishment as any other violation of Section 47-5-193 — imprisonment for not less than three years and not more than fifteen years.

Nash's twelve-year sentence fell within this statutory range. And "the general rule in this state is that a sentence cannot be disturbed on appeal so long as it does not exceed the maximum term allowed by statute."

There is, however, a very limited and rarely imposed exception to the general rule. "The Eighth Amendment, which forbids cruel and unusual punishments, contains a 'narrow proportionality principle' that 'applies to noncapital sentences.'" *Ewing v. California*, 538 U.S. 11, 20 (2003) (quoting *Harmelin v. Michigan*, 501 U.S. 957, 996-97 (1991) (Kennedy, J., concurring in part and concurring in judgment)).

[Our analysis begins by asking whether] a threshold comparison [of the crime committed to the sentence imposed] leads to an inference of gross disproportionality.

In arguing gross disproportionality, Nash invokes *Davis v. State*, 724 So. 2d 342, 344 (Miss. 1998). In that case, Melissa Davis received the maximum available sentence of sixty years in prison for selling two rocks of cocaine within 1,500 feet of a

---

[1] Nash's conviction also carried a potential fine of up to $25,000. Miss. Code Ann. § 47-5-195. Nash was fined $5,000.
[2] Nash will become parole eligible after serving a quarter of his sentence. Miss. Code Ann. § 47-7-3(1) (Supp. 2019).

church. But on appeal, this Court found no record justification for the trial court's imposing the most severe punishment available. So this Court remanded for the trial judge to conduct proportionality review under *Solem* [*v. Helm*, 463 U.S. 277 (1983)].

In *Ford v. State*, this Court later explained its reasoning in *Davis*. *Ford v. State*, 975 So. 2d 859, 870 (Miss. 2008). The *Ford* Court noted that Davis, a first-time offender, was given the maximum sentence without any seeming justification. "Because the trial judge did not use discretion in and simply opted for the maximum penalty, this Court remanded the cases for reconsideration." By contrast, the sentence in *Ford*, while severe, did not raise the same proportionality concerns. Though Ford was also a first-time offender, she was not given the maximum penalty of twenty years for aggravated assault. And before imposing a seventeen-year sentence, the trial judge "expressed concerns about the severity of the crime."

Here, in contrast to *Davis*, the trial judge did not simply opt for the maximum penalty without justification. Instead, the judge exercised his discretion after reviewing a presentence-investigation report. Similar to *Ford*, the judge emphasized that possession of a cell phone in a correctional facility was a serious charge. And unlike *Davis* and *Ford*, Nash was a documented repeat offender. The judge noted that Nash's prior felony convictions subjected him to fifteen years' imprisonment, to be served day for day, had the State charged him as a habitual offender.

While obviously harsh, Nash's twelve-year sentence for possessing a cell phone in a correctional facility is not grossly disproportionate. *Cf. Tate v. State*, 912 So. 2d 919, 934 (Miss. 2005) (holding a sixty-year sentence for drug distribution, while "certainly harsh," was not grossly disproportionate). The sentence is within the statutory limits. See *Mosley v. State*, 104 So. 3d 839, 842 (Miss. 2012) (holding that sentences totaling 126 years for three drug-possession charges, though severe, did not lead to an inference of gross disproportionality, because the sentences "clearly fall within the statutory limits"). It is also commensurate with other sentences imposed for the same crime. E.g., *Smith v. State*, 275 So. 3d 100, 103 (Miss. Ct. App. 2019) (defendant sentenced as a habitual offender to serve fifteen years, day for day, for possession of a cell phone in a county jail); *Houston v. State*, 150 So. 3d 157 (Miss. Ct. App. 2014) (defendant sentenced to fifteen years, with five suspended, for possession of a SIM card in a correctional facility).

We affirm Nash's conviction and sentence.

Affirmed.

KING, J., specially concurring:

I agree that, with regard to Nash's sentence, this Court has reached the correct result under our caselaw. However, I write separately to voice my concern over this case as a whole — it seems to demonstrate a failure of our criminal justice system on multiple levels.

First, it is highly probable that the Newton County Jail's booking procedure was not followed in Nash's case. An officer at the jail testified that all inmates were strip-searched when booked, although that officer did not book Nash. Yet Nash went into the jail with a large smartphone that would have likely been impossible to hide during a strip search. That officer also testified that all inmates were told during booking that they could not bring phones into the jail. But Nash's behavior was that of a person who did not know this, as he voluntarily showed the officer his phone and asked the officer to charge it for him.

Second, the officer who booked Nash the night before the cell phone incident did not testify at trial. It is consequently unknown whether booking procedures were actually followed in Nash's case. Furthermore, had this officer testified that booking procedures were followed for Nash, he could have been questioned on cross-examination about how he possibly missed a large smartphone during a strip search. It seems problematic to potentially allow someone into the jail with a cell phone, and then to prosecute that person for such action.

Third, I note that Nash's criminal history evinces a change in behavior. Both his previous convictions were for burglary. His last conviction was in 2001, and he was sentenced to serve seven years. So, for approximately eight to ten years,[1] Nash has stayed out of trouble with the law. He has a wife and three children who depend on him. Combining this fact with the seemingly innocuous, victimless nature of his crime,[2] it seems it would have been prudent for the prosecutor to exercise prosecutorial discretion and decline to prosecute or to seek a plea deal. In that same vein, it would have been prudent for the judge to use his judicial discretion in sentencing to sentence Nash to a lesser sentence than that of twelve years.

Cases like Nash's are exactly why prosecutors and judges are given wide discretion. Nash served his time for his previous convictions and stayed out of trouble with the law for many years. He has a wife and three children who rely on him. His crime was victimless, and the facts of the case lend themselves to an interpretation that his crime was accidental and likely caused by a failure in booking procedures. Nash did not do anything nefarious with his phone, and he certainly did not hide his phone from law enforcement. While I do not think this Court can find under the law that the trial court abused its discretion in sentencing, it is a case in which, in my opinion, both the prosecutor and the trial court should have taken a more rehabilitative, rather than punitive, stance.

---

**Post-Case Follow-Up**

This case is presented for the questions it raises about the criminal justice system, and not for its legal holding regarding the Eighth Amendment (a topic that is typically covered in adjudicative criminal procedure and sentencing law courses). Willie Nash's case is in some ways exceptional and in others quite ordinary. Although Nash's 12-year sentence was not so unusually long to convince the Supreme Court of Mississippi to overturn it on Eighth Amendment grounds, it does appear to be an outlier for this kind of offense. According to Nash's attorneys, only two other states — Arkansas and Illinois — permit a sentence of more than ten years for the crime of possessing a cell phone in jail; the maximum sentence is five years in

---

[1] The record does not indicate the date on which Nash was released from jail after serving this sentence.
[2] I do not suggest that possessing a cell phone in a correctional facility is always an innocuous crime. Indeed, those who are serving sentences and have contraband cell phones snuck into jail for them are not committing innocuous acts. However, the facts of this case indicate that Nash's cell phone was simply missed during booking and that he was not secreting it from law enforcement or using it for any nefarious means. He used it simply to communicate to his wife where he was.

36 states and Washington, D.C. See Aaron Morrison, *Mississippi Man Given Extreme 12-Year Sentence for Having a Cell Phone in Jail Asks for Rehearing*, The Appeal, Jan. 23, 2020.

While Nash's exact sentence may not be representative, many aspects of the case are illustrative of the U.S. criminal justice system today. Among other things, Nash's case demonstrates the sprawling and chaotic nature of the system, the importance of prosecutorial discretion in case outcomes, the broad language of many modern criminal statutes, and the severity of sentencing ranges today. (Nash's sentence was longer than most, but the three-year *minimum* sentence for the offense in Mississippi is still quite long.) Perhaps the most mysterious aspect of the case is that, by all appearances, Nash was never even prosecuted for the crime he was arrested for. Why was Nash arrested in the first place? The court says only that it was for a misdemeanor. What happened to the original charge? The court does not say. The unexplained gap between the starting point for this case (an arrest for an unknown misdemeanor that Nash was apparently never convicted of) and the end point (a 12-year sentence for having a cell phone in jail) is emblematic of the coldly bureaucratic operation of the criminal justice system in some cases today.

## Nash: *Real Life Applications*

1. The vast majority of published court opinions in criminal cases are issued after a trial and usually do not discuss the prosecutor's charging decision or what plea negotiations (if any) took place before trial. But as Justice King's concurring opinion in *Nash* suggests, prosecutorial discretion and plea bargaining are both important parts of modern criminal practice. Justice King argued that "it would have been prudent for the prosecutor to exercise prosecutorial discretion and decline to prosecute or to seek a plea deal."
   a. If you had been the prosecutor in *Nash*, would you have declined to prosecute the case?
   b. Now assume that you were the prosecutor assigned to *Nash* and that your boss has decided against declining to prosecute. Although your boss has directed you to pursue the case, you have been given complete discretion over plea negotiations. What kind of plea agreement (if any) would you offer Nash?
   c. Imagine that you were Nash's lawyer and that the prosecutor offered the following deal: Nash will plead guilty to possession of a cell phone in a correctional facility, and in exchange the prosecutor will recommend imposition of the minimum sentence of three years. Would you advise your client to accept or reject this offer?

2. Imagine you are a legislative aide to a state representative in Mississippi. Your boss read about the decision in *Nash* and wants to introduce a bill to amend the statute that Nash was convicted of violating. Specifically, she wants to amend the statute so that it would not apply to cases like Nash's. She has asked you to come up with at least two different options for amending the statute to achieve this goal. What two amendment options would you suggest?

## 3. The Prison Abolition Movement

Many critics of mass incarceration support the imposition of at least some criminal punishment for conduct covered by most major existing criminal statutes — including imprisonment in some cases, although perhaps at reduced lengths. Proponents of prison abolition argue for an approach that abandons incarceration and other forms of penal regulation in favor of other kinds of policy interventions.

In her article *Prison Abolition and Grounded Justice*, 62 UCLA L. Rev. 1156, 1172-73 (2015), Allegra McLeod described prison abolition in this way:

> Criminal punishment organized around incarceration in the United States, as well as incarceration's corollaries (punitive policing, arrest, probation, civil commitment, parole), subject human beings to extreme violence, dehumanization, racialized degradation and indignity, such that prison abolition ought to register as a more compelling call than it has to date. At the same time, the use of imprisonment as a means of achieving collective peace and security, as well as meaningful retributive justice, ought to be called into serious doubt.
>
> Prison abolition seeks to end the use of punitive policing and imprisonment as the primary means of addressing what are essentially social, economic, and political problems. Abolition aims at dramatically reducing reliance on incarceration and building the social institutions and conceptual frameworks that would render incarceration unnecessary. Abolition is not a simple call for an immediate opening or tearing down of all prison walls, but entails an array of alternative nonpenal regulatory frameworks and an ethic that recognizes the violence, dehumanization, and moral wrong inherent in any act of caging or chaining — or otherwise confining and controlling by penal force — human beings. This holds true even in the case of those few people who may pose a severe, demonstrated danger to others and so, as the lesser of two evils, must be convicted and the threat they pose contained.

Although prison abolitionists do not necessarily aim to immediately open the prison doors, they "reject[] . . . the moral legitimacy of confining people in cages." *Id.* at 1164. Some abolitionists allow for the possibility "that there may be, in the end, some people who are so dangerous to others that they cannot live safely among us, those rare persons referred to in abolitionist writings as 'the dangerous few.'" *Id.* at 1168. But, in contrast to those who believe that punishment is justified by retributive and/or utilitarian principles, "an abolitionist ethic recognizes that even if a person is so awful in her violence that the threat she poses must be forcibly contained, this course of action ought to be undertaken with moral conflict, circumspection, and even shame, as a choice of the lesser of two evils, rather than as an achievement of justice." *Id.* at 1171.

The prison abolition movement shares much in common with the movement to defund the police that rose to prominence in the summer of 2020 in the context of protests against police brutality. Amna Akbar discussed the connection between the two movements and some of the history behind the prison abolition movement in *How Defund and Disband Became the Demands*, N.Y. Rev. Books, June 15, 2020.

Professor Akbar explained that the calls of some of the protesters "to defund and disband police have roots in decades of prison abolitionist organizing, which aims to end incarceration and policing in favor of a society grounded in collective care and social provision." *Id.*

> Although calls for defunding and dissolution, rather than reform, may feel new to many, abolitionist organizing against the "prison industrial complex" — which includes prisons, police, and surveillance — goes back more than two decades. The organization Critical Resistance, established in the late 1990s in Berkeley, California, and now with chapters in Oakland, New York, Los Angeles, and Portland, is central to both the organizing work and the dissemination of ideas on which today's campaigns draw. Critical Resistance places its efforts in the history of struggles against enslavement, and identifies slave patrols as the progenitor of US policing. Angela Davis, Ruth Wilson Gilmore, Rose Braz, and Rachel Herzing are among the group's co-founders. Davis's *Are Prisons Obsolete?*, Gilmore's *Golden Gulag*, and Critical Resistance's various handbooks, workshops, and campaigns for prison and police abolition — including against jail expansion and police enforcement of gang injunctions — have become blueprints for organizers across the country.
>
> As organizers were witnessing the failures of reform to produce meaningful change within the criminal legal system, abolitionist experiments across the country made progress. In 2015, a campaign for reparations by Project NIA, We Charge Genocide, Chicago Torture Justice Memorials, and others won redress for black people subject to the Chicago Police Department's decades-long torture program under police commander Jon Burge. The reparations ordinance, adopted by Chicago's City Council, includes free junior college tuition and counseling for survivors and their families, and changes to the public school curriculum to reflect the history of police violence. Mariame Kaba, the founder of Project NIA, explained that the reparations ordinance created "an expansive potential vision of what justice could look like when people are harmed." It disavowed criminal prosecution as a means of gaining redress, and offered an alternate way of providing some measure of justice. It inspired new ways of thinking about campaigns for change.

*Id.* These efforts continued and, "[b]y the beginning of 2020, a growing number of abolitionist and abolitionist-inspired campaigns had taken hold," including coalitions against jail expansions in a number of major cities. *Id.*

Abolitionist organizing helped to lay a foundation for "Defund the Police" to become a rallying cry of some of the anti-police brutality protestors in June 2020. Professor Akbar suggested that, "[w]hile it is unclear whether all those carrying placards emblazoned with today's slogans fully grasp the transformative project of abolition, these mass protests point to a growing understanding that the problem is not police training or inadequate technology. The problem is the institution of policing itself: its power, its origins in enslavement and indigenous dispossession, and its hold on how we conceive of public safety." *Id.* Likewise, prison abolitionists believe that reforming prisons is an inadequate response to mass incarceration. "There is no delusion among abolitionists that we will ever live in a world without conflict or interpersonal violence. Right now our go-to response to all manner of social, political, and economic conflict — whether it is homelessness, domestic violence, migration — is prisons and police. The abolitionist invitation is to investigate these problems with care and particularity, and collectively craft responses that do not rely on violence and punishment." *Id.*

Although the prison abolition movement remains largely outside of the political mainstream, it raises important questions about how to respond to pressing social problems, from violence to substance use disorder.

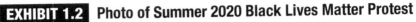

**EXHIBIT 1.2**   **Photo of Summer 2020 Black Lives Matter Protest**

## 4. Racial Disparities in Criminal Enforcement

Appellate court opinions make up the bulk of the assigned reading in most law school courses, and Criminal Law is no exception. Published court decisions make excellent vehicles for learning about and discussing criminal law doctrine. But by design, they capture only a small slice of what happened in the case at hand and focus their attention on the legal issues raised by the parties. Outside of a few areas of the law (such as employment discrimination), the personal characteristics of the parties are seldom relevant to those legal issues. For this reason, most appellate court opinions in criminal cases do not mention the defendant's race, age, or socioeconomic status. Although an individual defendant's race is rarely relevant to the legal issues in a criminal appeal, it is impossible to understand the U.S. criminal justice system without considering the role of race.

In some areas of criminal law, race has driven decisions to make certain conduct a crime (as in the case of early drug criminalization laws, discussed in Chapter 4) or influenced the development of legal doctrine (as in the case of rape law in the late 1800s and early 1900s, discussed in Chapter 6). In other areas, race-neutral laws have sometimes been enforced disproportionately against people of color. Disparities can result from a variety of factors, ranging from differences in local enforcement policies or practices (e.g., more aggressive policing in cities than in suburbs) to conscious or unconscious bias by individual actors within the criminal justice system (e.g., racial profiling in a traffic stop). To be sure, in many individual cases, race may not play any role whatsoever in the outcome. But statistical and anecdotal evidence suggests that, in the aggregate, there are racial disparities in criminal enforcement today. As the Sentencing Project noted in a 2018 report, "African Americans are more likely than white Americans to be arrested; once arrested, they are more likely to be convicted; and once convicted, and they are more likely to experience lengthy prison sentences. African-American adults are 5.9 times as likely to be incarcerated than whites and Hispanics are 3.1 times as likely." The Sentencing Project, Report of the Sentencing Project to the United Nations Special Rapporteur on Contemporary Forms of Racism, Racial Discrimination, Xenophobia, and Related Intolerance 1 (2018).

The role of race in criminal enforcement in the United States is examined in the two articles excerpted below. First, in the following excerpt from her 2011 law review essay, *The New Jim Crow*, Michelle Alexander summarizes the thesis of her influential 2010 book of the same title, in which she argues that "the U.S. criminal justice system functions as a system of contemporary racial control, even as it formally adheres to the principle of colorblindness."

## The New Jim Crow
### Michelle Alexander
### 9 Ohio St. J. Crim. L. 7 (2011)

I find that when I tell people that mass incarceration amounts to a New Jim Crow, I am frequently met with shocked disbelief. The standard reply is: "How can you say that a racial caste system exists? Just look at Barack Obama! Just look at Oprah Winfrey! Just look at the black middle class!"

The reaction is understandable. But we ought to question our emotional reflexes. The mere fact that some African Americans have experienced great success in recent years does not mean that something akin to a caste system no longer exists. No caste system in the United States has ever governed all black people. There have always been "free blacks" and black success stories, even during slavery and Jim Crow. During slavery, there were some black slave owners—not many, but some. And during Jim Crow, there were some black lawyers and doctors—not many, but some. The unprecedented nature of black achievement in formerly white domains today certainly suggests that the old Jim Crow is dead, but it does not necessarily mean the end of racial caste. If history is any guide, it may have simply taken a different form.

Any honest observer of American racial history must acknowledge that racism is highly adaptable. The rules and reasons the legal system employs to enforce status relations of any kind evolve and change as they are challenged. Since our nation's founding, African Americans have been repeatedly controlled through institutions, such as slavery and Jim Crow, which appear to die, but then are reborn in new form—tailored to the needs and constraints of the time.

For example, following the collapse of slavery, the system of convict leasing was instituted—a system many historians believe was worse than slavery. After the Civil War, black men were arrested by the thousands for minor crimes, such as loitering and vagrancy, and sent to prison. They were then leased to plantations. It was our nation's first prison boom. The idea was that prisoners leased to plantations were supposed to earn their freedom. But the catch was they could never earn enough to pay back the plantation owner the cost of their food, clothing and shelter to the owner's satisfaction, and thus they were effectively re-enslaved, sometimes for the rest of their lives. It was a system more brutal in many respects than slavery, because plantation owners had no economic incentive to keep convicts healthy or even alive. They could always get another one.

Today, I believe the criminal justice system has been used once again in a manner that effectively re-creates caste in America. Our criminal justice system functions more like a caste system than a system of crime control.

For those who find that claim difficult to swallow, consider the facts. Our prison system has quintupled for reasons that have stunningly little do with crime. In less than 30 years, the U.S. penal population exploded from around 300,000 to more than 2 million. The United States now has the highest rate of incarceration in the world, dwarfing the rates of nearly every developed country, including highly repressive regimes like China and Iran.

In fact, if our nation were to return to the incarceration rates of the 1970s — a time, by the way, when civil rights activists thought that imprisonment rates were egregiously high — we would have to release four out of five people who are in prison today. More than a million people employed by the criminal justice system could lose their jobs. That is how enormous and deeply entrenched the new system has become in a very short period of time.

As staggering as those figures are, they actually obscure the severity of the crisis in poor communities of color. Professor Loïc Wacquant has argued that the term "mass incarceration" itself is a misnomer, since it implies that nearly everyone has been subject to the new system of control. But, of course that is not the case. The overwhelming majority of the increase in imprisonment has been poor people of color, with the most astonishing rates of incarceration found among black men. It was estimated several years ago that, in Washington, D.C. — our nation's capital — three out of four young black men (and nearly all those in the poorest neighborhoods) could expect to serve time in prison. Rates of incarceration nearly as shocking can be found in other communities of color across America.

So what accounts for this vast new system of control? Crime rates? That is the common answer. But no, crime rates have remarkably little to do with skyrocketing incarceration rates. Crime rates have fluctuated over the past thirty years, and are currently at historical lows, but incarceration rates have consistently soared. Most criminologists and sociologists today acknowledge that crime rates and incarceration rates have, for the most part, moved independently of one another. Rates of imprisonment — especially black imprisonment — have soared regardless of whether crime has been rising or falling in any given community or the nation as a whole.

So what does explain this vast new system of control, if not crime rates? The War on Drugs. The War on Drugs and the "get tough" movement explain the explosion in incarceration in the United States and the emergence of a vast, new racial undercaste. In fact, drug convictions alone accounted for about two-thirds of the increase in the federal system, and more than half of the increase in the state prison population between 1985 and 2000. Drug convictions have increased more than 1000% since the drug war began, an increase that bears no relationship to patterns of drug use or sales.

People of all races use and sell drugs at remarkably similar rates, but the enemy in this war has been racially defined. The drug war has been waged almost exclusively in poor communities of color, despite the fact that studies consistently indicate that people of all races use and sell drugs at remarkably similar rates. This evidence defies our basic stereotype of a drug dealer, as a black kid standing on a street corner, with his pants hanging down. Drug dealing happens in the ghetto, to be sure, but it happens everywhere else in America as well. Illegal drug markets, it turns out — like American society generally — are relatively segregated by race. Blacks tend to sell to blacks, whites to whites, Latinos sell to each other. University students sell to each other. People of all races use and sell drugs. A kid in rural Kansas does not drive to the 'hood to get his pot, or meth, or cocaine, he buys it from somebody down the road. In fact, the research suggests that where significant differences by race can be found, white youth are more likely to commit drug crimes than youth of color.

But that is not what you would guess when entering our nation's prisons and jails, overflowing as they are with black and brown drug offenders. In the United States, those who do time for drug crime are overwhelmingly black and brown. In some states, African Americans constitute 80 to 90% of all drug offenders sent to prison.

I find that many people are willing to concede these racial disparities once they see the data. Even so, they tend to insist that the drug war is motivated by concern over violent crime. They say: just look at our prisons. Nearly half of the people behind bars are violent offenders. Typically this is where the discussion ends.

The problem with this abbreviated analysis is that violent crime is not responsible for the prison boom. Violent offenders tend to get longer sentences than nonviolent offenders, which is why they comprise such a large share of the prison population. One study suggests that the entire increase in imprisonment can be explained by sentence length, not increases in crime. To get a sense of how large a contribution the drug war has made to mass incarceration, consider this: there are more people in prison today just for drug offenses than were incarcerated in 1980 for all reasons. The reality is that the overwhelming majority of people who are swept into this system are non-violent offenders.

In this regard, it is important to keep in mind that most people who are under correctional control are not in prison or jail. As of 2008, there were approximately 2.3 million people in prisons and jails, and a staggering 5.1 million people under "community correctional supervision" — i.e., on probation or parole. Millions more have felony records and spend their lives cycling in and out of prison, unable to find work or shelter, unable to vote or to serve on juries. This system depends on the prison label, not prison time. It does not matter whether you have actually spent time in prison; your second-class citizenship begins the moment you are branded a felon. It is this badge of inferiority — the criminal record — that ushers you into a parallel social universe in which discrimination is, once again, perfectly legal.

How did this extraordinary system of control, unprecedented in world history, come to pass? Most people insist upon a benign motive. They seem to believe that the

War on Drugs was launched in response to rising drug crime and the emergence of crack cocaine in inner city communities. For a long time, I believed that too. But that is not the case. Drug crime was actually declining, not rising, when President Ronald Reagan officially declared the drug war in 1982. President Richard Nixon was the first to coin the term a "war on drugs," but President Reagan turned the rhetorical war into a literal one. From the outset, the war had little to do with drug crime and much to do with racial politics.

The drug war was part of a grand and highly successful Republican Party strategy — often known as the Southern Strategy — of using racially coded political appeals on issues of crime and welfare to attract poor and working class white voters who were resentful of, and threatened by, desegregation, busing, and affirmative action. Poor and working class whites had their world rocked by the Civil Rights Movement. White elites could send their kids to private schools and give them all of the advantages wealth has to offer. But poor and working class whites were faced with a social demotion. It was their kids who might be bused across town, and forced to compete for the first time with a new group of people they had long believed to be inferior for decent jobs and educational opportunities. Affirmative action, busing, and desegregation created an understandable feeling of vulnerability, fear, and anxiety among a group already struggling for survival.

Republican party strategists found that thinly veiled promises to "get tough" on "them" — the racially defined others — could be highly successful in persuading poor and working class whites to defect from the Democratic New Deal Coalition and join the Republican Party. H.R. Haldeman, President Richard Nixon's former Chief of Staff, reportedly summed up the strategy: "[T]he whole problem is really the blacks. The key is to devise a system that recognizes this while not appearing to."

A couple years after the drug war was announced, crack cocaine hit the streets of inner-city communities. The Reagan administration seized on this development with glee, hiring staff who were responsible for publicizing inner-city crack babies, crack mothers, the so-called "crack whores," and drug-related violence. The goal was to make inner-city crack abuse and violence a media sensation that, it was hoped, would bolster public support for the drug war and would lead Congress to devote millions of dollars in additional funding to it.

The plan worked like a charm. For more than a decade, black drug dealers and users became regulars in newspaper stories and saturated the evening TV news — forever changing our conception of who the drug users and dealers are. Once the enemy in the war was racially defined, a wave of punitiveness took over. Congress and state legislatures nationwide devoted billions of dollars to the drug war and passed harsh mandatory minimum sentences for drug crimes — sentences longer than murderers receive in many countries. Many black politicians joined the "get tough" bandwagon, apparently oblivious to their complicity with the emergence of a system of social control that would, in less than two decades, become unprecedented in world history.

Almost immediately, Democrats began competing with Republicans to prove that they could be even tougher on "them." In President Bill Clinton's boastful words, "I can be nicked on a lot, but no one can say I'm soft on crime." The facts bear him out. Clinton's " 'tough on crime' policies resulted in the largest increases in federal and state prison inmates of any president in American history." But Clinton was not satisfied with exploding prison populations. In an effort to appeal to the "white swing voters," he and the so-called "new Democrats" championed legislation banning drug felons from public housing (no matter how minor the offense) and denying them basic public benefits, including food stamps, for life. Discrimination in virtually every aspect of political, economic, and social life is now perfectly legal, once you're labeled a felon.

All of this has been justified on the grounds that getting brutally tough on "them" is the only way to root out violent offenders or drug kingpins. The media images of violence in ghetto communities — particularly when crack first hit the street — led many to believe that the drug war was focused on the most serious offenders. Yet nothing could be further from the truth. Federal funding has flowed to those state and local law enforcement agencies that increase dramatically the volume of drug arrests, not the agencies most successful in bringing down the bosses. What has been rewarded in this war is sheer numbers — the sheer volume of drug arrests.

The results are predictable. People of color have been rounded up en masse for relatively minor, non-violent drug offenses. In 2005, for example, four out of five drug arrests were for possession, only one out of five for sales. Most people in state prison for drug offenses have no history of violence or even of significant selling activity. In fact, during the 1990s — the period of the most dramatic expansion of the drug war — nearly 80% of the increase in drug arrests was for marijuana possession, a drug generally considered less harmful than alcohol or tobacco and at least as prevalent in middle-class white communities as in the inner city.

In this way, a new racial undercaste has been created in an astonishingly short period of time. Millions of people of color are now saddled with criminal records and legally denied the very rights that were supposedly won in the Civil Rights Movement.

None of this is to say, of course, that mass incarceration and Jim Crow are the "same." There are significant differences between mass incarceration and earlier forms of racial control, to be sure. Just as there were vast differences between slavery and Jim Crow, there are important differences between Jim Crow and mass incarceration. Yet all three (slavery, Jim Crow, and mass incarceration) have operated as tightly networked systems of laws, policies, customs, and institutions that operate collectively to ensure the subordinate status of a group defined largely by race. When we step back and view the system of mass incarceration as a whole, there is a profound sense of deja vu. There is a familiar stigma and shame. There is an elaborate system of control, complete with political disenfranchisement and legalized discrimination in every major realm of economic and social life. And there is the production of racial meaning and racial boundaries.

If someone were to visit the United States from another country (or another planet) and ask: "Is the U.S. criminal justice system some kind of tool of racial control?," most Americans would swiftly deny it. Numerous reasons would leap to mind why that could not possibly be the case. The visitor would be told that crime rates, black culture, or bad schools were to blame. "The system is not run by a bunch of racists," the apologist would explain. They would say, "It is run by people who are trying to fight crime." Because mass incarceration is officially colorblind, and because most people today do not think of themselves as racist, it seems inconceivable that the system could function much like a racial caste system.

But more than forty-five years ago, Martin Luther King Jr. warned of the danger of precisely this kind of thinking. He insisted that blindness and indifference to racial groups is actually more important than racial hostility to the creation and maintenance of systems of racial control. Those who supported slavery and Jim Crow, he argued, typically were not bad or evil people; they were just blind. Many segregationists were kind to their black shoe shiners and maids and genuinely wished them well. Even the Justices who decided the infamous Dred Scott case, which ruled "that the Negro had no rights which the white man was bound to respect," were not wicked men, he said. On the whole, they were decent and dedicated men. But, he hastened to add, "They were victims of spiritual and intellectual blindness. They knew not what they did. The whole system of slavery was largely perpetuated by sincere though spiritually ignorant persons."

The same is true today. People of good will — and bad — have been unwilling to see black and brown men, in their humanness, as entitled to the same care, compassion, and concern that would be extended to one's friends, neighbors, or loved ones.

After all, who among us would want a loved one struggling with drug abuse to be put in a cage, labeled a felon, and then subjected to a lifetime of discrimination, scorn and social exclusion? Most Americans would not wish that fate on anyone they cared about. But whom do we care about? In America, the answer to that question is still linked to race. Dr. King recognized that it was this indifference to the plight of African Americans that supported the institutions of slavery and Jim Crow. And this callous racial indifference supports mass incarceration today.

---

The excerpt below, from a law review article by James Forman, Jr., provides a different perspective on the New Jim Crow analogy. Professor Forman argues that while the Jim Crow analogy accurately "highlights how ostensible race-neutral criminal justice policies unfairly target black communities," it "neglects some important truths" about the role of race in mass incarceration.

## *Racial Critiques of Mass Incarceration: Beyond the New Jim Crow*
### James Forman, Jr.
### 87 N.Y.U. L. Rev. 21 (2012)

In the five decades since African Americans won their civil rights, hundreds of thousands have lost their liberty. Blacks now make up a larger portion of the prison population than they did at the time of Brown v. Board of Education, and their lifetime risk of incarceration has doubled. As the United States has become the world's largest jailer and its prison population has exploded, black men have been particularly affected. Today, black men are imprisoned at 6.5 times the rate of white men.

While scholars have long analyzed the connection between race and America's criminal justice system, an emerging group of scholars and advocates has highlighted the issue with a provocative claim: They argue that our growing penal system, with its black tinge, constitutes nothing less than a new form of Jim Crow. The Jim Crow analogy effectively draws attention to the plight of black men whose opportunities in life have been permanently diminished by the loss of citizenship rights and the stigma they suffer as convicted offenders. It highlights how ostensibly race-neutral criminal justice policies unfairly target black communities. In these ways, the analogy shines a light on injustices that are too often hidden from view.

Although the New Jim Crow writers and I agree more often than we disagree, the disagreements matter. I believe that the Jim Crow analogy neglects some important truths and must be criticized in the service of truth. I also believe that we who seek to counter mass incarceration will be hobbled in our efforts if we misunderstand its causes and consequences in the ways that the Jim Crow analogy invites us to do.

[T]he New Jim Crow writers encourage us to view mass incarceration as exclusively (or overwhelmingly) a result of the War on Drugs. But drug offenders constitute only a quarter of our nation's prisoners, while violent offenders make up a much larger share: one-half.

The choice to focus on drug crimes is a natural — even necessary — byproduct of framing mass incarceration as a new form of Jim Crow. One of Jim Crow's defining features was that it treated similarly situated blacks and whites differently. For writers seeking analogues in today's criminal justice system, drug arrests and prosecutions provide natural targets, along with racial profiling in traffic stops. Blacks and whites use drugs at roughly the same rates, but African Americans are significantly more likely to be arrested and imprisoned for drug crimes. As with Jim Crow, the difference lies in government practice, not in the underlying behavior. The statistics on selling drugs are less clear-cut, but here too the racial disparities in arrest and incarceration rates exceed any disparities that might exist in the race of drug sellers.

But violent crime is a different matter. While rates of drug offenses are roughly the same throughout the population, blacks are overrepresented among the population for violent offenses. For example, the African American arrest rate for murder is seven to eight times higher than the white arrest rate; the black arrest rate for robbery is ten times higher than the white arrest rate. Murder and robbery are the two offenses for which the arrest data are considered most reliable as an indicator of offending.

In making this point, I do not mean to suggest that discrimination in the criminal justice system is no longer a concern. There is overwhelming evidence that discriminatory practices in drug law enforcement contribute to racial disparities in arrests and prosecutions, and even for violent offenses there remain unexplained disparities between arrest rates and incarceration rates. Instead, I make the point to highlight the problem with framing mass incarceration as a new form of Jim Crow. Because the analogy leads proponents to search for disparities in the criminal justice system that resemble those of the Old Jim Crow, they confine their attention to cases where blacks are like whites in all relevant respects, yet are treated worse by law. Such a search usefully exposes the abuses associated with racial profiling and the drug war. But it does not lead to a comprehensive understanding of mass incarceration.

Does it matter that the Jim Crow analogy diverts our attention from violent crime and the state's response to it, if it gives us tools needed to criticize the War on Drugs? I think it does, because contrary to the impression left by many of mass incarceration's critics, the majority of America's prisoners are not locked up for drug offenses. Some facts worth considering: According to the Bureau of Justice Statistics, in 2006 there were 1.3 million prisoners in state prisons, 760,000 in local jails, and 190,000 in federal prisons. Among the state prisoners, 50% were serving time for violent offenses, 21% for property offenses, 20% for drug offenses, and 8% for public order offenses. In jails, the split among the various categories was more equal, with roughly 25% of inmates being held for each of the four main crime categories (violent, drug, property, and public order). Federal prisons are the only type of facility in which drug offenders constitute a majority (52%) of prisoners, but federal prisons hold many fewer people overall. Considering all forms of penal institutions together, more prisoners are locked up for violent offenses than for any other type, and just under 25% (550,000) of our nation's 2.3 million prisoners are drug offenders. This is still an extraordinary and appalling number. But even if every single one of these drug offenders were released tomorrow, the United States would still have the world's largest prison system.[102]

Moreover, our prison system has grown so large in part because we have changed our sentencing policies for all offenders, not just drug offenders. We divert fewer offenders than we once did, send more of them to prison, and keep them in prison for much longer. An exclusive focus on the drug war misses this larger point about sentencing choices. This is why it is not enough to dismiss talk of violent offenders by saying that "violent crime is not responsible for the prison boom." It is true that the prison population in this country continued to grow even after violent crime began to decline dramatically. However, the state's response to violent crime — less diversion and longer sentences — has been a major cause of mass incarceration. Thus, changing how governments respond to all crime, not just drug crime, is critical to reducing the size of prison populations.

I am sympathetic to the impulse to avoid discussing violent crime. Like other progressives, the New Jim Crow writers are frustrated by decades of losing the crime debate to those who condemn violence while refusing to acknowledge or ameliorate the conditions that give rise to it. "As a society," [Michelle] Alexander writes, "our decision to heap shame and contempt upon those who struggle and fail in a system designed to keep them locked up and locked out says far more about ourselves than it does about them." Since it is especially difficult to suspend moral judgment when the discussion turns to violent crime, progressives tend to avoid or change the subject.

Avoiding the topic of violence in this manner is a mistake, not least because it disserves the very people on whose behalf the New Jim Crow writers advocate. After all, the same low-income young people of color who disproportionately enter prisons are disproportionately victimized by crime. And the two phenomena are mutually reinforcing.

---

[102] If the 550,000 drug offenders were released, the United States would have 1.75 million prisoners. International comparisons should be made with caution. Nonetheless, using the best available numbers, this would still exceed China's prison population, which stands at 1.57 million. Roy Walmsley, Int'l Ctr. for Prison Studies, King's Coll. London, World Prison Population List 1 (8th ed. 2009), available at http://www.prisonstudies.org/info/downloads/wppl-8th_41.pdf. The Chinese number does not include administrative detention figures, which, if included, would make China the world's largest jailer. *Id.* at 4. The United States, given its smaller population, would still have the highest incarceration rate.

Jim Crow has another distinctive characteristic that threatens to lead us astray when contemplating mass incarceration. Just as Jim Crow treated similarly situated blacks and whites differently, it treated differently situated blacks similarly. An essential quality of Jim Crow was its uniform and demeaning treatment of all blacks. Jim Crow was designed to ensure the separation, disenfranchisement, and political and economic subordination of all black Americans — young or old, rich or poor, educated or illiterate.

Indeed, one of the central motivations of Jim Crow was to render class distinctions within the black community irrelevant, at least as far as whites were concerned. For this reason, it was essential to subject blacks of all classes to Jim Crow's subordination and humiliation. That's why Mississippi registrars prohibited blacks with Ph.Ds from voting, why lunch counters refused to serve well-dressed college students from upstanding Negro families, and why, as Martin Luther King, Jr. recounts in his "Letter from Birmingham Jail," even the most famous black American of his time was not permitted to take his six-year-old daughter to the whites-only amusement park she had just seen advertised on television.

Analogizing mass incarceration to Jim Crow tends to suggest that something similar is at work today. This may explain why many — but not all — of the New Jim Crow writers overlook the fact that mass incarceration does not impact middle- and upper-class educated African Americans in the same way that it impacts lower-income African Americans. This is an unfortunate oversight, because one of mass incarceration's defining features is that, unlike Jim Crow, its reach is largely confined to the poorest, least-educated segments of the African American community. High school dropouts account for most of the rise in African American incarceration rates. [A] black man born in the 1960s is more likely to go to prison in his lifetime than was a black man born in the 1940s. But this is not true for all African American men; those with college degrees have been spared. As Bruce Western's research reveals, for an African American man with some college education, the lifetime chance of going to prison actually decreased slightly between 1979 and 1999 (from 6% to 5%). A black man born in the late 1960s who dropped out of high school has a 59% chance of going to prison in his lifetime whereas a black man who attended college has only a 5% chance. Although we have too little reliable data about the class backgrounds of prisoners, what we do know suggests that class, educational attainment, and economic status are powerful indicators for other races as well. Western estimates that for white men born in the late 1960s, the lifetime risk of imprisonment is more than ten times higher for those who dropped out of high school than for those who attended some amount of college.

The Jim Crow analogy also obscures the extent to which whites, too, are mass incarceration's targets. Since whites were not direct victims of Jim Crow, it should come as little surprise that whites do not figure prominently in the New Jim Crow writers' accounts of mass incarceration. Most who invoke the analogy simply ignore white prisoners entirely. [Michelle] Alexander mentions them only in passing; she says that mass imprisonment's true targets are blacks, and that incarcerated whites are "collateral damage."

Many whites — most of them poor and uneducated — are now behind bars. One-third of our nation's prisoners are white, and incarceration rates have risen steadily even in states where most inmates are white. For some categories of offenses where our laws are especially severe, such as possession of child pornography, most of the defendants are middle-aged white men. Prosecutions for sexually explicit material offenses have risen by more than 400% since 1996. In addition to the dramatic rise in the number of cases filed, the sentences imposed for all child-pornography related offenses have become increasingly severe, rising from an average of 2.4 years in 1996 to almost 10 years in 2008. Moreover, although whites remain relatively underrepresented as drug offenders, the percentage of drug offenders who are white has risen since 1999, while the percentage of drug offenders who are black has declined.

Hispanic prisoners also receive little attention from the New Jim Crow writers, even though they constitute 20% of American prisoners. The fact that quality data on Hispanics in the prison systems is often lacking may be partly to blame for this omission. But it is important to remember that during the Jim Crow years, Hispanics in many jurisdictions were subject to forms of exclusion, segregation, and disenfranchisement not unlike those inflicted on African Americans. And given what we do know about current Hispanic incarceration rates, it is clear that Hispanic prisoners deserve the attention of all who write about the prison system. The Hispanic prison population climbed steadily during the 1990s, to the point where one in six Hispanic males born today can expect to go to prison in their lifetime. The available data suggest that Hispanic incarceration rates are almost double the rates for whites, and many observers believe that these data undercount the true rate at which Hispanics go to prison. Most Hispanic prisoners, like most blacks and whites, are serving time for violent offenses, and about 20% are in prison for drug offenses.

Thus, the data on white and Hispanic prisoners reminds us that while African Americans are incarcerated in numbers grossly disproportionate to their percentage of the overall population, the fact remains that 60% of prisoners are not African American. [A]nyone analyzing mass incarceration must keep that 60% squarely in mind.

## C.  A FIRST-HAND ACCOUNT OF INCARCERATION

Criminal Law courses focus primarily on legal doctrine — the elements of crimes like burglary, larceny, and murder, and of affirmative defenses like self-defense, duress, and insanity. In the cases in this book, courts employ these doctrines to decide whether to affirm or reverse a defendant's conviction. If the conviction is affirmed, the defendant goes on to serve the proscribed sentence — most often, a term of imprisonment.

Few law students or lawyers have experienced incarceration first hand. To better understand this aspect of the criminal justice system, then, it is helpful to consider criminal punishment from the perspective of those who have experienced it.

Some judges make regular prison visits for this purpose. For example, Judge Stephen R. Bough of the United States District Court for the Western District of Missouri has written about how visiting federal prisons has helped to inform his sentencing decisions: "These visits impacted me, as they would anyone. At first, I was a little embarrassed to care about 'these people.' I am the judge; they are federal inmates. But over time, I've realized that all judges care about defendants, even if we show it differently. The implications of imposing a prison sentence are severe, regardless of the length. For me, prison visits, along with the other steps I've taken, help me evaluate what constitutes a sufficient but not greater than necessary sentence." Stephen R. Bough, *Getting to Know a Felon: One Judge's Attempt at Imposing Sentences That Are Sufficient, but Not Greater Than Necessary*, 87 UMKC L. Rev. 25, 32 (2018). "At the end of each day," Judge Bough continued, "each interaction reminds me that felons share more similarities than differences with non-felons." *Id.* at 33. In a similar vein, former federal Judge Mark W. Bennett, who personally visited hundreds of the defendants that he sentenced, found that the "visits have changed me in profound ways. I have a much greater appreciation for the ability of people to make fundamental change in their lives but also understand how hard this is in the prison context. I have great admiration for [Federal Bureau of Prisons] employees from wardens to correctional officers. We all owe them a deep debt of gratitude for their unyielding dedication. These visits have reinforced my views on personal responsibility and change. We are all personally responsible for our past actions and future aspirations. We can receive help from others but ultimately all change must come from within. Finally, the visits have reinforced my belief in the role of hope in all our lives." Mark. W. Bennett, *Reflections on Visiting Federal Inmates*, 94 Judicature 304, 305 (2011).

In the essay that follows, Angel Sanchez shared his "firsthand experiences within the prison system." Sanchez, who was a second-year student at the University of Miami Law School when his essay was published in 2019, was sentenced to a 30-year prison term when he was a teenager in the 1990s. In his essay, Sanchez "bring[s] readers into the lived reality of our prison system — its effects, its contradictions, and its failure to rehabilitate offenders or promote public safety." In the interest of space, the excerpt of Sanchez's essay below omits significant portions of his story, including his journey to law school following his release from prison. Sanchez's essay is just one person's account, of course. As Sanchez himself noted in a portion of the article not excerpted below, "[e]ven though I can speak about many intersecting issues involving prison, my perspective is still limited." Although it is not possible to capture the varied experiences of people in the criminal justice system in this book, the excerpt below provides critically important insight into the reality of incarceration before we begin our study of criminal law doctrine.

### *In Spite of Prison*
**Angel E. Sanchez**
**132 Harv. L. Rev. 1650 (2019)**

How does a former gang-banging, gun-toting Latino serving a thirty-year prison sentence, the product of an elderly uneducated immigrant father and a drug-addicted mother, go from a prison cell to law school? It was not because of prison, but in spite of it.

\* \* \*

"The prosecutor is offering you a plea deal of seven years in juvenile prison, and if you don't take it, they're going to direct file and send you to the adult side. What do you want to do?"

Seven years seemed like an eternity — half of my life at the time to be exact. I was fourteen years old. I tried to process everything.

I responded, "So I either take juvenile prison for, like, forever, or I go to the adult jail where they have honey buns and radios and where I can maybe get a bond?"

To me, the choice was obvious. I refused the so-called offer. With my stomach growling, I went back to my cell, looking forward to the honey buns that I could get in the adult jail. In retrospect, there was something seriously wrong with my fourteen-year-old, shortsighted immaturity in focusing more on honey buns than on my future. I could not appreciate the fact that the rest of my life would be marred by an adult criminal record; in fact, I couldn't have cared less at the time. In my hood, jail was expected, almost like a rite of passage. However, more concerning was the fact that the law permitted prosecuting a fourteen-year-old as an adult, and that all the adults in the courtroom were happily complicit in doing so. Despite the fact that I was offered a juvenile plea indicating that I was still supposedly redeemable, I was quickly waved over to the adult side by laws that now rendered me an irredeemable superpredator.

If the first sentence of this Essay caught your attention, it is likely because it is packed with stereotypes and images that both sensationalize and dehumanize certain populations and justify prisons. The image of a "gang-banging, gun-toting Latino" may drum up enough fear to make us feel like prisons are necessary. Or the idea of uneducated and drug-addicted parents may allow us to focus on family dysfunction (or even cultural pathology), while ignoring deeper societal dysfunctions that need correcting. Even success stories of people who thrive after prison are used to argue that prisons are not bad and are even effective. Our own amazement at those stories, however, shows that deep inside we are aware that prisons are not really expected to make people better.

Professor Angela Davis writes that people find it difficult to imagine a world without prisons, yet they are largely unaware of what goes on inside of prison and believe it is reserved for "evildoers." Personal narratives, therefore, are necessary to shed light on the inhumanity that goes on inside of prison, the social problems that lead to prison, and the humanity of those impacted by prison.

I arrived at Kelsey L. Pharr Elementary in the third grade. I was only eight years old and this was already my fourth elementary school. My father could barely afford rent, so he was forced to look for substandard housing in the hood. The homes were so substandard that we could barely live in them for more than a year: either the landlord failed a housing inspection or the conditions got so bad we had to move. Each time we moved, I had to make new friends at a new school. Ironically, though, making friends became easy because all the schools I attended were practically the same. They were in poor neighborhoods surrounded by drugs and crime. All the boys generally valued the same things: sports, clothes, and a willingness to fight. Focusing too much on grades or being afraid to fight left me ostracized and isolated, so I adjusted. I learned to belong.

In these schools, frustrated teachers told us that if we did not pay attention and behave, we were going to end up homeless or in jail when we grew up, prophecies their very words helped to fulfill. I still remember one of my teachers pointing out a homeless man outside of the school one day and saying to us, "That's what happens to troublemakers." I internalized her comment. I got good grades in class to please my father who weirdly cared a lot about education, but I could not stay out of "trouble." I got into fights when bullied and talked a lot in class.

I was eight years old when I was first taken out of my third-grade class, placed in handcuffs, and given a date to appear in court. That morning was no different from any other. Like most mornings, my father and I woke up late. We rushed to school, barely making it on time. As my father drove away, I saw my friends and joined them as we made our way to class. I quickly learned they were having problems with other kids who had tried to bully one of my friends the day before on his way home from school. Afraid, my friend brought a dinner knife to school, prepared to defend himself. Just as he expected, those kids tried to beat him up again that morning. He pulled out the knife and scared them away. I arrived right after all of this. When I got there, they told me everything that had happened and asked me to hide the knife in my book bag since I had not been around when it happened. I was hesitant but did not want to lose the approval of my friends, which mattered to me in this new school. Once we were in class, the principal showed up and got my friend. My friend told the principal that I had the knife in my book bag, so he came and got me next. I also admitted to everything. The principal told us he was calling the police and that we were going to jail. I remember being eight years old, crying and afraid of what the police would do. When the police arrived, they immediately put us in handcuffs and kept us there until our parents arrived. After a while, I stopped crying. Instead of feeling fear, I became acclimated. I could not change my situation, so I just adjusted to it. In that moment, at eight years of age, for the first time, I accepted — rather than feared — going to jail. The police told our parents that they could take us to jail, but they were going to be nice and give us a notice to appear in court instead. This embarrassed my dad and broke his heart.

I appeared in juvenile court and was suspended before the case was eventually dropped. I was viewed as a problem by school administrators. To my classmates and friends, however, I was popular. I was "bad" and "cool" at the same time.

In middle school, my friends and I began hanging around the older teenagers in our neighborhood. We roamed the few square blocks near our houses without much to do other than smoke weed, make fun of each other, and do dumb things for thrills. At nightfall, we would cross the fence of a nearby school and come together on the basketball courts that gave us a place to call our own. The school was on Tenth Street, so we called ourselves Tenth Street Boys. This would be the start of what law enforcement would later call a gang. At first, we resented the gang label, but as teenagers in search of an identity we eventually embraced it. For a long time, we prided ourselves on not being a gang — we did not have any initiation or leader and were just a group of friends. But after being targeted by known gangs and harassed by the police, we began living up to the label. The harassment by police officers quickly taught us that the police were the biggest gang, the one that was above the law and had the law on its side.

Indeed, my first night in jail came at the hands of a sergeant who slapped me in front of my father and all my friends while we were hanging out on a street corner. That night, we were stopped and frisked as usual. My dad made his way over because he saw all the lights and cop cars on the corner. I was embarrassed. The sergeant called out to me and I responded with an attitude. The sergeant was angry at my response and slapped me across the side of my head saying, "Don't 'what' me!" And as soon as I felt the hit, I instinctively lashed out in rage. In the process, I scratched the sergeant on the arm with the soda can I had in my hand when he slapped me. In a matter of seconds, three officers took control of my undersized thirteen-year-old frame, putting me in a chokehold and punching the wind out of my stomach. They placed me in handcuffs and arrested me for aggravated battery on a law enforcement officer. In that one incident, I learned what is common knowledge in the hood: the police can get away with abusing you while at the same time using the law to arrest you.

This incident pitted me against my father. I could not believe he would allow the police to do this to me in front of him. I did not understand at that time how afraid my dad was and how much he simply wanted me out of jail. As a non-English-speaking immigrant, my dad did not know what to do or where to start. His sense of gratitude for being in this country made him feel as if he had no place to complain. He felt that as an immigrant he was less deserving and that he owed a "thankful to be here" attitude. I now understand this, because as a former felon, I often feel that I must be submissive and deferential whenever given a chance.

Upset at my dad, I ran away as soon as I was released from the juvenile jail. I was determined to go back to the family that understood me, which the law called a gang. My friends were there. Tenth Street was my hood and I was hooked on it.

One of the dope boys who had lots of money (I will call him Marco) let me stay at his house. A couple of other friends who sold drugs for him stayed there too. I felt so at home. We all had fancy clothes and rode around in Marco's fancy cars. I was on top of the world. There was nothing I would not do for this guy — and unfortunately, he knew it. Inside of his house, he would constantly pressure me to smoke weed laced with cocaine until I was finally hooked on it. I knew something was wrong with this, but I did not have the fortitude to say no. Before long, I was holding his drugs and ready to shoot at rival gang members in exchange for a place to stay and the drugs he gave me.

Drive-by shootings around Tenth Street had become an almost-daily occurrence. Friends were getting shot left and right. One of my friends was killed in front of me around that time, when I was fourteen. At one point I was taken hostage, humiliated, and abused at gunpoint by rival gang members. After this incident, I said, "Never again!" I committed to getting my own gun. Ironically, when I should have been more concerned with video games than safety and protection, I traded a Super Nintendo (and sixty dollars) for my first gun at the age of fourteen. With a willingness to use a gun came a sense of safety, respect, and acceptance. Unfortunately, I was an impulsive fourteen-year-old and easily manipulated by older guys. Sure, I was a tragedy waiting to happen, but that is not the same as saying I was inherently dangerous and violent. That is what society said about teenagers like me in the 1990s. I fit the profile of the mythical "super-predator" teenager of the 1990s who allegedly was without conscience and irredeemable. Despite being neither, I nearly became both thanks to these misguided beliefs.

As I mentioned in the beginning of this Essay, I would eventually be treated as a "superpredator" in 1996, at the age of fourteen. My friend and I were on the way to the mall to watch a movie when we got jumped by three older teenagers. I had a gun on me, so I instinctively reached for it and began shooting, hitting one of them in the leg. Afraid, I threw down the gun and tried to run away, before being quickly surrounded, arrested, and taken to juvenile jail. In a matter of weeks, I was declared irredeemable by the prosecutors, prosecuted as an adult, and sent to the Tenth Floor. The infamous Tenth Floor was the place where juveniles were sent when they were tried as adults. It was located on the tenth floor of the main adult jail in Miami. Juveniles were afraid to go there not because of the adult prosecution, but because of the horror of abuse: getting beat down and having one's food and shoes taken were common. Landing in the wrong cell block would get you put on the Tenth Floor diet, in which your food was taken and you were forced to eat scraps left over from other prisoners.

It was never guaranteed that you would end up in the cell safest for you. If you pissed off a guard, they would move you to one of the cells in which you didn't "belong"; it was one of their disciplinary tools. To make matters worse, the cells were overcrowded. There were four inmates in a two-bunk cell. That meant two had to sleep on the floor, and one of those two had to sleep next to the toilet as the others used the bathroom. Sleeping on a bunk instead of the floor was supposed to be determined by order of entry to the cell and by a willingness to fight for it. Whenever someone new came into the cell block, he could challenge you for your bunk. When the odds were against you in the cell block, you had to accept your dehumanized status — sleeping on the floor, having your food taken, and being continuously humiliated. On the other hand, if you were housed with your "kind" and had friends from the streets, then you could avoid the horror stories so long as you fought.

Fortunately for me, I had friends who had finally made it to the Tenth Floor, so instead of fearing it, I now looked forward to the honey buns and radio they had over there. Violence and abuse were the true deterrents that had made me afraid of an adult prosecution. But with that removed, my teenage mind saw no deterrent, at least not the ones intended by the law. I could not appreciate that the rest of my life would be marked by a felony conviction.

After a year in that adult jail, I was released on probation, worse than when I went in. I returned to my hood, popular with my friends and a target to my former enemies. My fifteen-year-old effort at doing "right" was hardly enough. I soon found myself targeted by gang violence. On different occasions, I was jumped, shot at, and sent bleeding to the hospital with a wound that required twenty-eight staples on my head. Before long, I returned to what I knew, and less than ten months after my release, I was rearrested for multiple gang-related shootings and a robbery. This time I would get thirty years in state prison.

It was early August 1999. I sat handcuffed and shackled in a jumpsuit next to others waiting for their cases to be called. Lawyers got up, took the podium, spoke quickly, and moved on to the next case. Everything sounded predetermined, foreign, and rushed — a form of impersonal, assembly-line justice. I was always caught off guard by how quickly the process went, and I barely ever understood what was going on. This time, though, I knew exactly what was going to happen. I had violated my probation and was about to be sentenced for my underlying crime. The probation I had agreed to ten months earlier stipulated that if I violated my release conditions, I would get the top of the sentencing guidelines. Nobody explained what the guidelines were when I was placed on probation, but the maximum sentence they prescribed for my crime was 360 months (thirty years). Since I had violated probation, there was no room for judicial discretion. A machine could have produced the same exact "judicial" results.

My case was called. I stood up as the prosecutor quickly explained that the plea agreement — the one I agreed to as a fifteen-year-old after a year in the adult jail — required a sentence at the top of the guidelines in the event of probation violation. The judge announced that, being bound by the guidelines, he was sentencing me to 360 months in state prison and, just like that, moved on to the next case. In a matter of minutes, I was sentenced to more years than I had been alive. Almost nobody in the courtroom noticed. On my way back to the jail, I began to ask myself how I was supposed to act or feel. I decided to act serious and solemn, but I honestly felt no different inside. I was too young to grasp the severity of my sentence or even the seriousness of my crimes. What did affect me was getting placed in an isolation cell once I got back to the jail. The thirty-year sentence I had just received made me "too dangerous" to be with others. There, in isolation, I fell into a state of depression. In just a matter of days, that solitary confinement cell was affecting me in ways that the thirty-year sentence had not. I told my lawyer that I was ready to accept the plea offers of additional thirty-year sentences running together for my other pending cases. I just wanted to get out of that hell, euphemistically known as the "special housing units." Just days after celebrating my seventeenth birthday, I was back in court for the other cases. Without being old enough to have a career, I was labeled a career offender and sentenced to three more concurrent thirty-year sentences. I was happy to go to prison — just to get out of that isolation cell.[43]

At the reception center, the guards were intent on using strip searches to show us who was in charge. Contraband was not a major concern because we were all coming from a secured facility already. Nevertheless, they yelled and threatened us with confinement and beatings, ready to make an example out of one of us. We were herded into a large cage and made to stand there against the fence. They walked around and screamed at us to take off all our clothes until we all finally stood naked and cold. There I was — an adult in law, but a minor in fact — standing completely naked in front of older guards and dozens of similarly naked prisoners. Instinctively, we covered our private parts. The officers shouted at us to put our hands to the side. It was clear — this was about power, not contraband. Hesitantly, we obeyed. They ordered us to lift our testicles and rub our fingers through our mouths before forcing us to turn around and face the fence. They yelled at us to bend over at the waist, grab our

---

[43] Throughout my time in prison, I witnessed prisoners who had no intentions of killing themselves cut themselves, swallow razors, put feces on themselves, and even attempt to hang themselves simply to get a respite from confinement. Indeed, with few exceptions, the most aberrant behavior I witnessed in prison was always when someone was either in confinement or being sent to confinement.

butt-cheeks, spread them, and cough twice. It had to be loud and in unison, or we would have to repeat it until we got it right. By design, the first time was apparently not loud enough. We were forced to repeat the humiliating act over and over again for what felt like an eternity. With mocking grins, some of the guards yelled when it was over, "Welcome to prison!" I would go on to experience these humiliating power trips repeatedly throughout my twelve years in prison. I wonder if the guards ever stopped to consider (or care) that their power trips were a form of sexual violence or that they returned people to society desensitized and bitter, not better.

After the cavity search, I was given my dormitory assignment. Although I was barely 5′6″ and weighed 130 pounds, I was assigned to the adult side of the prison because I had too much time and my crimes were too serious for me to be classified as a "youthful offender." During intake, some of the other guys were dumbfounded that I was going to the adult side with them because of how little and young I was. They told me that I was lucky because the Latinos were probably going to have my back so long as I was willing to fight and did not come with some questionable reputation from the streets. As I walked into my assigned dorm, I was quickly approached by the Latinos there. I felt interrogated. They asked me if I was Latino, where I was from, and who I knew. As soon as I mentioned some mutual friends from the streets and the county jail, the conversation went from interrogation to acceptance. I breathed a sigh of relief. I was no longer alone in this place. I was so thankful for my streets when I later witnessed how others who did not know anybody and who were unwilling to fight got sexually assaulted, beaten, and extorted.

Each of the nine prisons that I went to over twelve years was filled with physical and psychological violence. Within my first few weeks in prison I was assaulted, not by a prisoner, but by a guard for talking back to him. Thankfully for me, the assault was short-lived, and I did not require medical attention. When it came to guards, I feared the common scenario in which they would beat a prisoner so badly that they had to justify it by lying and charging the prisoner with assaulting them. I spent twelve years avoiding this scenario but saw how it happened to others. [S]ome of my most painful moments in prison — which I am still too ashamed to recount — came from psychological humiliation at the hands of the guards, particularly early in my sentence when I was not courageous enough to stand up to them or late in my sentence when I was too afraid of compromising my release date.

Some of the most respected prisoners that I met were leaders of so-called prison gangs, which I am calling prison groups. Many of them happened to also be college educated because they came from an era over a quarter century ago when college education was still available to prisoners. From them, I learned that I could be feared if I was tough, but respected if I was educated. It was from my so-called prison gang that I got my first books on history, religion, anti-imperialism, and revolutions. The young men around me who were leaders within their prison groups prided themselves not only on being tough, but also on being intellectual. The older men served as mentors to us.

After I earned my GED, there were no other courses available to me, so my education had to come from the prison yard rather than a classroom. I was fortunate to get pointed in the right direction by the older men in my prison group. I learned about the history of groups such as the Nation of Islam, the Young Lords Party, and the

Soledad Brothers. Some of the material I studied provided context for how I ended up in prison. It let me know that I was not inherently bad or the worst of the worst.

The revolutionary material from my prison group ignited my intellectual interest and made me ripe for discovering a passion in the law. One of the men in my prison group happened to be one of the best law clerks in the prison. When I asked for his help on my case, he responded with his rule: I will help you help yourself—I will not do it for you. I accepted. I began going daily to the law library where he worked. I was lost and intimidated. I would read and reread the books he gave me. I could not understand them. I just wanted to sneak out and go back to the prison yard where I did not feel dumb. I could not just leave the law library, however, because I knew he would hold me accountable and not help me with my case.

I knew my friend had done a paralegal course over the mail, so I figured maybe doing the course would help me understand this legal stuff. I told him that my dad would possibly be able to scrape up the twenty-five dollars a month for the course. His eyes lit up. He said that if I enrolled in the course, he would fight to get me a job in the prison law library because they needed somebody who spoke Spanish. During my first day at work, I was surprised by two things: I was given my own desk, and there were no guards harassing or watching us. I remember feeling empowered and free in that moment. I felt responsible for that space and accountable to my friend and the librarian for the job.

It was here, working in the prison law library, that I asked two questions that gave rise to the dream that got me where I am today: Could I be an attorney? And if so, what would it take? I found a case that gave me the answers. A man was imprisoned while attending college in Florida, continued his college education in prison, and went to law school upon release. The bar rejected his application for admission due to his prior convictions, concluding that he did not "meet the standards of conduct and fitness required" to be an attorney. He appealed, and the Florida Supreme Court detailed his journey. The court noted his commitment to continuing his education even while in prison, his attainment of a law degree and a master of laws in taxation, and the recommendations he earned from his professors. The court reasoned that he had shown enough rehabilitation and ordered that he be admitted to the Florida Bar. This was all I needed; it became the blueprint for my journey. From then on I became fixated on getting whatever college education I could in prison. I was determined to go to law school some day despite the fact that my release date was nearly thirty years away: December 30, 2028.

I had no knowledge of how college worked. Nobody in my family had ever completed high school, let alone college. For the first time, I learned that there was a difference between graduate and undergraduate degrees. I was shocked to learn that degrees required dozens of classes—I used to think that they consisted of a single class in a single subject that lasted four years.

I learned from another prisoner about Ohio University, which had a special correspondence program for incarcerated individuals. I figured out how college worked from their brochure. I needed forty courses for a bachelor's degree. Sadly, I could not afford the cost of over $600 per course totaling over $24,000 for a bachelor's degree. My dad could barely budget $20 a week, which was more than most prisoners ever got. I was fortunate, though, because the paralegal school that I was getting my books from for $25 a month began offering associate's degree textbooks. The classes were not regionally accredited and I had to teach myself from the text-books, but that was good enough for me. I was nineteen years old when I got my first ever college textbook. It was one of the happiest moments I could remember. I sat on my prison bunk, proud, thinking to myself, "I'm in college." I was intimidated but excited — this was college, after all. I would later have this same feeling when I arrived at my community college, university, and law school. To my surprise, the material was learnable. I struggled through compounding math without a calcula-tor. I taught myself correct sentence structures (for the first time) and learned how to compose an email even though it would be a decade before I could ever send my first email in 2011. I dissected and engrossed myself in every chapter of every book, taking copious notes.

If there is one thing I hope my story does, it is to highlight the importance of higher education and its transformative power for prisoners. Access to education in prison should not be left to chance and wealth.

I often tell people that every prisoner is learning something in prison, especially young prisoners. The question is, what are they learning? If it is up to prison admin-istrators and guards, it will not be the skills and knowledge taught by higher educa-tion. The prison system's priority is control and security over humanity. Even when education is provided or permitted, it is perceived by most guards as getting in the way of their "job" and viewed by the greater public as coddling prisoners.

In 2000, the Florida Supreme Court in *Heggs v. State* held that the sentencing guidelines under which I had received a thirty-year sentence for violation of proba-tion violated the state constitution. The constitutional guidelines allowed for only a thirteen-year sentence. However, I still had to fight through multiple appeals to with-draw the concurrent thirty-year plea agreements that I had taken for the open cases. I was eventually successful in getting those pleas vacated and received a new sentence of fifteen years followed by ten years of probation. For the first time, the possibility of getting out was no longer a fanciful idea many decades removed, but rather a reality just a few years away.

This was very comforting for my father, whose health was failing, making it impossible for him to make the ten-hour drive to visit me. Fortunately, around the time I was resentenced, I happened to be transferred to a facility near Miami, where he could visit me more easily. During our visits, my father told me how proud he was that I had become a "paralegal" in prison. He reminded me that all he had ever wanted was for me to get an education and become somebody. He said that his only prayer now was to live long enough to see me free someday. But even if he could not, he said he could finally rest in peace because he had lived to see me become educated and knew I was going to get out soon. Six months later, he passed away. I was unable to go to his funeral because I did not have the hundreds of dollars necessary to pay for the correctional transport. This was devastating, as my father was and remains the most important person in my life.

Soon after my father's passing, I was transferred ten hours away from Miami. Contact with my loved ones became strained — no visits, few calls, and barely any letters. Collect calls were inexplicably expensive. Early in my sentence, my mother had sobered up and helped my father financially, which allowed them to make the nearly prohibitively expensive trips to visit me together. Though I argued with my dad about visiting me because of his health and the costs, he believed that family should always visit loved ones whenever they are in a hospital or a prison, so he had to visit me at least on my birthday. As if fearing that I would grow isolated and lonely, he wanted me to know that he was always there for me. Having and recognizing his unconditional love was undoubtedly the most transformational thing in my life. I had taken him for granted as a teenager, but once I matured, I realized how special he was. Many of my friends in prison (including my half-sister, who is in prison today) never had a chance to meet their fathers, yet I had a father who came to every court date, who wrote me letters, who visited me, and who never gave up on me even when people told him he should. He is the person to whom I owe so much. He instilled in me the value of education and scraped up money to buy me my first college textbook (and many more books after that). He preserved my humanity in a place that was determined to destroy it. My success has not been because of prison — it has been because of my father.

## Chapter Summary

- Retributivist theories of punishment hold that punishment is justified if and when it is deserved. Retributivism is backward looking and sees punishment as an intrinsic good. In its most forceful iteration, it holds that morally blameworthy conduct is deserving of punishment even if imposing the penalty would be very costly without producing any tangible benefits.
- Utilitarianism is concerned with costs and benefits. Utilitarianism is forward looking and holds that the law should maximize overall happiness. As a result, utilitarian theories hold that punishment is justified if and when it would produce a net benefit for society.
- In the criminal law, there are four primary potential benefits to punishment that might weigh in the utilitarian calculation. First, punishing one person might keep others from engaging in the same conduct, a concept known as general deterrence. Second, punishment might also result in specific deterrence — making a person suffer might lead him to think twice before breaking the law again in the future. Third, when a person is put in prison, that person is temporarily incapacitated and physically unable to commit crimes against the general public. Finally, punishment could possibly be used to rehabilitate offenders, for example through drug treatment programs.
- The theories of punishment aim to provide a morally defensible account of punishment. But they do not necessarily explain every aspect of our criminal justice system. Challenges like mass incarceration and racial disparities in criminal enforcement raise questions about whether considerations beyond retribution and utilitarianism might be at play in the criminal justice system.
- Mass incarceration refers to the extraordinarily high incarceration rate in the United States today. Although Americans make up only about five percent of the world's population, the United States has about 25 percent of the world's prison population.

■ There are stark racial disparities in the criminal justice system: "African-American adults are 5.9 times as likely to be incarcerated than whites and Hispanics are 3.1 times as likely." The Sentencing Project, Report of the Sentencing Project to the United Nations Special Rapporteur on Contemporary Forms of Racism, Racial Discrimination, Xenophobia, and Related Intolerance 1 (2018).

## Applying the Concepts

1. Consider the real-life case of Cornealious "Mike" Anderson. Anderson, of St. Louis County, Missouri, "was convicted of robbery in 2000 and sentenced to 13 years but was never told when and where to report to prison. He spent the next 13 years turning his life around — getting married, raising three kids, learning a trade. He made no effort to conceal his identity or whereabouts." Then one day, in 2013, "the Missouri Department of Corrections discover[ed] the clerical error that kept [Anderson] free and authorities went to his home and arrested him." CBS News, *Man Who Went to Prison 13 Years Late Ordered Released* (May 5, 2014), https://www.cbsnews.com/news/man-who-went-to-prison-13-years-late-ordered-released/.

   The courts were left to decide whether or not to require Anderson to serve his original 13-year sentence. As you answer the questions below, refer back to the descriptions of the theories of punishment at the start of the chapter.

   a. Assume for purposes of this question that Anderson's 13-year sentence accurately reflected his blameworthiness at the time was imposed. Under a pure retributivist theory of punishment, would Anderson be required to serve his original sentence after he was re-arrested in 2013?

   b. Can you think of any potential benefits that society might realize from punishing Anderson following his re-arrest in 2013? If so, how would you weigh those benefits against the costs of punishment?

   c. Anderson's case also speaks to the issue of mass incarceration. Anderson led a productive, crime-free life for 13 years. But, if not for a clerical error, he would have spent those 13 years behind bars. With Anderson's story in mind, is it possible that a significant number of people serving long sentences in prison could be released safely and would be making beneficial contributions to society if they were free? How should the criminal justice system strike the balance between the possibility that someone who has committed a crime might re-offend and the costs attendant to incarceration?

   d. Anderson ended up spending a little over a year in prison following his re-arrest. Eventually, a judge released Anderson by giving him "credit for the 4,794 days between when he was convicted and when he was arrested last year. The judge also lauded Anderson's exemplary behavior during his 13 years of freedom. 'You've been a good father. You've been a good husband. You've been a good taxpaying citizen of the state of Missouri. That leads me to believe that you are a good and changed man,' he said. 'You're a free man,' [Judge] Brown continued, telling Anderson to go back to his family." Do you think this was the right outcome?

## Criminal Law in Practice

1. You are a legislator drafting a new sentencing law for your state.

   a. What sentence or sentencing range would you set for the following crimes and why: (1) robbery, (2) cocaine possession, (3) cocaine distribution, and (4) resisting arrest? (If you believe one or more of these offenses should not be a crime, which one(s) and why?)

   b. What other factors, if any — for example, a person's criminal history — would you want to try to account for in your sentencing statute?

2. Now, imagine yourself as a prosecutor. How would you go about making charging decisions? Would you always charge the most serious offense available? Or would you try to take other factors into account when making decisions about which crimes to charge a defendant with? If so, what kinds of factors would you consider?

3. As a prosecutor, what steps do you think you could take to help guard against the risk that unconscious biases about a defendant's ethnicity (or other factors like socioeconomic status) might influence your charging and plea negotiation decisions?

4. Refer back to the case of Cornealious "Mike" Anderson from the *Applying the Concepts* section immediately above. You are Anderson's attorney following his re-arrest in 2013. Imagine that the judge decided that Anderson should serve his original 13-year sentence, and that the decision is upheld on appeal. As a result, Anderson's only hope for being released from prison is a commutation from the governor. What points would you focus on in your application for a commutation on behalf of Anderson?

# Sources and Components of the Criminal Law

Chances are, you are reading this book for a course titled, simply, Criminal Law. Criminal Law is also in the title of this book. But the term criminal law is something of a misnomer. Why? Well, consider that each state has its own criminal code, as does the federal government, and that no two criminal codes are exactly alike. As a result, there is no single body of criminal law. Complicating matters further, today's criminal codes cover a vast range of conduct. At the federal level alone, there are literally thousands of criminal offenses — over 4,000 by one recent estimate. So it would be impossible for us to explore every permutation of criminal law in a single book or course. For that reason, most courses narrow the scope of their focus to some of the most noteworthy offenses and affirmative defenses, along with core concepts that recur throughout the criminal law.

Before studying specific crimes and defenses, it is important to understand more about the structure of the criminal law. To that end, this chapter provides an overview of the sources of criminal law, the common elements of crimes, and the criminal trial process.

## A. SOURCES OF CRIMINAL LAW

Today, legislators are responsible for writing the statutes that define crimes. It is then up to the courts to interpret and apply those laws in individual cases. Although the Constitution places some limitations on what conduct may be criminalized, by and large, legislatures are free to define crimes and defenses

## Key Concepts

- What are the sources of criminal law?
- How have the common law and the Model Penal Code influenced today's criminal statutes?
- Criminal offenses are typically divided into elements, each of which must be proven beyond a reasonable doubt to convict. What are the common types of elements of crimes?
- How does the criminal process interact with criminal law doctrine?

**53**

however they like. As a result, there is a good deal of variation from one state's criminal code to the next. Conduct that constitutes murder in one state might result in a conviction for the lesser crime of voluntary manslaughter in another.

It is important to keep the extent of these variations in perspective. For the most part, the similarities in how crimes are defined from one state to the next tend to outweigh the differences. One reason modern criminal codes are often similar from one state to the next is that many of today's crimes have a history that predates the Founding of the United States. English **common law** proscribed arson, burglary, larceny, and so on. When legislatures wrote their first criminal codes, they were heavily influenced by the common law definitions of these crimes. In addition to the common law, the **Model Penal Code** has been an important resource for legislators. Released in 1962, the Model Penal Code was meant to help legislatures modernize and standardize their criminal codes.

To say that criminal statutes are often *similar* across states is not to say they are *identical*. Few, if any, crimes have the same definition in every jurisdiction in the United States. This is due to a number of factors. First, the common law and the Model Penal Code define many crimes and defenses differently from one another. States pick and choose which definition to adopt — the common law, the Model Penal Code, a hybrid, or something else entirely — on a crime-by-crime basis. Second, the criminal law is especially subject to political pressures. One high profile acquittal might lead a legislature to modify the elements of an age-old crime or defense. After President Ronald Reagan's would-be assassin, John Hinckley, Jr., was found not guilty by reason of insanity in 1982, for example, Congress and a number of states passed laws to narrow the insanity defense. Third, not all criminal statutes have their origin in the common law or the Model Penal Code. Lawmakers are constantly adding entirely new crimes to criminal codes. Criminal legislation can result from public outcry about a hot-button issue or simply from the development of a new technology. The invention of the car led to new laws making it a crime to drive while intoxicated. The rise of the personal computer and the Internet gave birth to criminal statutes that target problems like hacking and cyberstalking.

Together, these factors mean that every state's criminal code is unique. If a criminal attorney in California were to read Pennsylvania's criminal code, she would find a lot of overlap in how crimes and defenses are defined. But she would find many important differences as well.

This dynamic also means that students often study more than one definition of a single crime or defense in a Criminal Law course. For any given crime, you might learn about its common law definition, its Model Penal Code definition, another definition entirely, or all of the above. Typically, criminal law professors and casebook authors decide which definitions to cover based on their relative importance. If 45 states have adopted the Model Penal Code's definition of a particular crime and only five still apply the common law's definition, for example, then devoting time to the common law definition may not be worthwhile. This approach gives students a strong foundation in the core principles of criminal law.

The remainder of this section describes the sources of criminal law in greater detail.

# 1. The Common Law

The common law refers to the tradition of judge-made law. It is English in origin and dates back to the reign of King Henry II in the 1100s. The colonists brought the common law system and doctrines with them to the New World. As American courts decided cases of their own, American common law doctrines began to diverge from England's in some respects. Justice Joseph Story described the relationship between American and English common law this way: "The common law of England is not to be taken in all respects to be that of America. Our ancestors brought with them its general principles, and claimed it as their birthright; but they brought with them and adopted only that portion which was applicable to their situation." *Van Ness v. Pacard*, 27 U.S. 137, 144 (1829).

In a pure common law system, judges — not legislatures — are responsible for writing the law. The *Dudley and Stephens* case, covered in Chapter 1, is an example of a common law court decision. Recall that in *Dudley and Stephens*, the court was tasked with deciding whether necessity could be raised as a defense to the crime of murder. There was no statute that defined the defense of necessity, a fact that the court lamented when it noted that "the learned persons who formed the commission for preparing the Criminal Code" had not spoken to the issue. As a result, the court's opinion, as opposed to an act of the legislature, defined the scope of the necessity defense.

Judge-made criminal law continued well after the Founding. Although state legislatures have enacted statutes relating to criminal law throughout our history, until the late 1800s criminal legislation mostly supplemented the power of courts to recognize and apply common law crimes. Beginning in the late 1800s, states began to replace the common law system with comprehensive penal codes that expressly abolished judge-made crimes. For example, California's penal code, adopted on January 1, 1873, provides that "[n]o act or omission, commenced after twelve o'clock noon of the day on which this Code takes effect as law, is criminal or punishable, except as prescribed or authorized by this Code." Cal. Penal Code § 6.

Today, criminal law in the United States is almost exclusively code-based law, written by legislatures and administrative agencies. Subject to exceptions in a few states, courts no longer have the power to create new crimes or to redefine existing crimes, as they once did in the common law era. This does not mean the common law is irrelevant to modern criminal practice, however. To appreciate the continuing significance of the common law in criminal cases, it is important to distinguish the common law method of lawmaking from common law doctrine.

The common law *method* of giving courts the power to define crimes may be dead. But much common law *doctrine* lives on. This is because the authors of the penal codes that replaced the common law method borrowed heavily (either wholesale or with small changes) from common law doctrine in the process of defining and codifying crimes. In addition, several states have expressly incorporated the common law definition of certain crimes into their penal codes in some cases. For example, North Carolina's burglary and arson statutes "do not articulate elements for the crimes, but rather prohibit conduct 'as defined at the common law.' " Carissa Byrne Hessick, *The Myth of Common Law Crimes*, 105 Va. L. Rev. 965, 987 (2019).

In the criminal law setting, when lawyers or law professors say that a jurisdiction follows the common law approach to an issue, they usually mean that the legislature has codified the common law doctrine on that issue.

## 2. The Model Penal Code

The codification of criminal law that began in the late 1800s proceeded without much coordination between states, leaving many state penal codes disorganized. In addition, state legislatures continued to add new crimes to their penal codes in the years and decades after they were first adopted. As a result, by the 1940s, "the vast majority of American criminal codes were in a sorry state. A typical American criminal code at the time was less a code and more a collection of ad hoc statutory enactments, each enactment triggered by a crime or a crime problem that gained public interest for a time." Paul H. Robinson & Markus D. Dubber, *The American Model Penal Code: A Brief Overview*, 10 New Crim. L. Rev. 319, 322-23 (2007).

The American Law Institute (ALI) sought to remedy this problem by promulgating a Model Penal Code. The nonprofit ALI is the same organization that oversees the influential Restatements of Contracts, Property, and Torts, among other subjects. Courts regularly rely on the Restatements to guide their decisions. For criminal law, the ALI decided that a project aimed primarily at legislators would be more worthwhile. The ALI assembled prominent experts, including judges, lawyers, and law professors, to begin work on the Model Penal Code in 1951. Eleven years later, in 1962, the ALI published the final *Proposed Official Draft* of the Model Penal Code.

The Model Penal Code's drafters did not start from scratch or completely reimagine the criminal law. Instead, they built upon existing statutory and common law principles. This was consistent with the project's goal, which was to draft a model code that was "based on the American criminal law at the time it was drafted" while bringing more clarity and stability to an area of the law that, "after centuries of common-law making, had left the criminal law an unprincipled mess." Robinson & Dubber, *supra*, at 332-34. The result was a model code that retained a good deal of common law doctrine, but with many significant changes. For some crimes and defenses, the Model Penal Code and common law definitions are nearly identical. For others, there are importance differences.

The Model Penal Code's drafters were not naïve enough to imagine that state legislatures would adopt their work without modification. Instead, the Code was intended to be a resource for lawmakers interested in reforming their state's criminal codes. Between 1962 and 1983, 34 states recodified their penal codes and "[a]ll of these thirty-four enactments were influenced in some part by the Model Penal Code." *Id.* at 326. Some of these states adopted codes that closely followed the Model Penal Code. Others relied on the Model Penal Code as only one of many resources. None adopted the Model Penal Code wholesale, however. And, as already discussed, every state continues to modify and add to their criminal codes on an ongoing basis.

# 3. Other Sources

For many years, most criminal law casebooks and courses compared the common law and the Model Penal Code doctrine by doctrine. Today, "this bifurcation is outmoded." Anders Walker, *The New Common Law: Courts, Culture, and the Localization of the Model Penal Code*, 62 Hastings L.J. 1633, 1634 (2011). To be sure, both the common law and the Model Penal Code continue to serve as a basis for state codes. In a few areas of the criminal law, there is still a genuine jurisdictional split between states that adhere to the common law definition and those that adhere to the Model Penal Code definition. But in many other areas, the picture is much more fluid. For some crimes and defenses, states have nearly uniformly adopted a single approach — whether based on the common law, the Model Penal Code, or some other source. For other crimes and defenses, there might be three or more definitions that have gained a substantial following in state codes.

One reason for the diversity of approaches to crimes and defenses is that legislatures are not limited to the common law and the Model Penal Code when they define crimes. They have plenty of other sources to draw from. First, and perhaps most important, is their own imaginations. Legislators are free to tinker with or fundamentally rethink any part of their criminal codes as they see fit. Lobbying from concerned citizens and interest groups like District Attorneys Associations or civil liberties organizations can lead lawmakers to reconsider how their state defines a given crime or defense. When this happens, the political process of committee hearings, vote wrangling, and so forth might result in a revised statute with one or more innovations that are unique to that state. Similarly, concerns about a perceived gap in the criminal code can drive lawmakers to create entirely new crimes. And in some states, the power to revise, create, or repeal crimes is not limited to legislators. In states that have a ballot measure process, advocacy groups have the opportunity to change criminal law provisions by popular vote — the trend of state marijuana legalization laws is one example of this.

Second, national interest groups sometimes develop new model statutes pertaining to a particular issue in an effort to spark changes in the law. Organizations like the conservative-leaning American Legislative Exchange

## Ever Expanding Criminal Codes

As noted in the introduction to this chapter, there are over 4,000 criminal offenses at the federal level alone. The proliferation of criminal statutes has resulted in a number of weird and esoteric offenses. In 2014, criminal defense lawyer Mike Chase launched the Twitter account @CrimeADay, devoted to documenting the extensive reach of the federal criminal code. The account gained a popular following and led Chase to write a book, *How to Become a Federal Criminal*, that highlights some of the most ridiculous offenses.

Chase's discussion of a federal statute that makes it a crime to wear a postal uniform if you are not a postal worker humorously illustrates the scope of the criminal law:

> There are only a few clothing choices made criminal by federal statute. One of them is the federal ban on non-postal workers wearing the uniform of a United States letter carrier.
>
> Specifically, 18 U.S.C. § 1730 provides that "whoever, not being connected with the letter carrier branch of the Postal Service wears the uniform or badge which may be prescribed by the Postal Service to be worn by letter carriers, shall be fined . . . or imprisoned not more than six months or both."
>
> By its terms, the statute doesn't require that the uniform wearer do anything nefarious while playing dress-up. The crime is in the wearing. As one federal judge remarked: "The very act of impersonating a letter carrier is by nature an act of deceit." When Americans see those little blue tube socks

strutting down the sidewalk, we want to know we aren't getting duped.

Mike Chase, How to Become a Federal Criminal: An Illustrated Handbook for the Aspiring Offender 16-18 (2019).

Counsel (ALEC) and the progressive-leaning State Innovation Exchange (SIX), to name just two, promulgate and promote draft legislation on a range of issues, including criminal law. In contrast to the Model Penal Code, these model statutes are created by politically minded groups in an effort to try to advance their policy goals. In 2016, for example, ALEC released a model bill titled the Criminal Intent Protection Act, which aimed to reform criminal intent requirements in the states. Sometimes, these model laws become very influential and are adopted by multiple states. Other times, they fail to gain any traction and never become the law in any state. In the case of the Criminal Intent Protection Act, it had not become law in any state as of 2020, although a number of states have adopted similar laws.

Third, apolitical nonprofits sometimes develop model codes that cover discrete areas of criminal law in the spirit of the Model Penal Code. The widely adopted Uniform Controlled Substances Act, which covers drug crimes, provides an example. Promulgated in 1970 by the National Conference of Commissioners on Uniform State Laws, the Uniform Controlled Substances Act was designed to foster consistency between state laws and the then–newly enacted federal Controlled Substances Act. By 1972, more than 30 states had enacted a version of the Uniform Controlled Substances Act. Today, nearly every state's illegal drug statutes are modeled after the Uniform Controlled Substances Act.

## 4. The Role of Courts in Interpreting Statutes

Gone are the days of the common law model of judge-made criminal law. But that does not mean courts have no role in shaping the meaning of criminal statutes. Indeed, this book — like almost every criminal law textbook — relies primarily on court opinions to convey criminal law doctrine. This is partly because court opinions are much richer and more memorable than statutes. But this is also because it is impossible to know the legal effect of a statute without reading the court opinions that have interpreted it.

Even the most meticulously drafted piece of legislation will inevitably contain ambiguities that require court interpretation, and many criminal statutes are not especially well written. Crimes are often defined in relatively broad terms, leaving it to courts to give meaning to key phrases. To take one example, a federal statute substantially increases the sentence for drug distributing "if death or serious bodily injury *results from* the use of such substance." 21 U.S.C. § 841(b)(1)(C) (emphasis added). In some cases, the phrase *results from* is easy enough to apply. But in *Burrage v. United States*, a government expert "could not say whether [the deceased] would have lived had he not taken the heroin, but observed that [the deceased's] death would have been 'very less likely.'" 571 U.S. 204, 207 (2014). Lower courts disagreed about whether or not a death in those circumstances is one that *results from* drug use and so the United States Supreme Court granted certiorari to decide whether the *results from* requirement in the statute "applies when use of a covered drug supplied by the defendant contributes to, but is not a but-for cause of, the victim's death or injury." *Id.* at 885. This is just one of countless examples. If a person writes on her neighbor's front door in a type of chalk that can only be erased using special cleaning supplies, has she *damaged* the front door for purposes of a vandalism statute? Does a law making it a crime to *carry* a firearm in certain circumstances apply to a person who has a firearm in the glove compartment of his car? If the legislature has spoken to the issue directly by defining *damaged* or *carry* in the statute, then that definition will control. But if the legislature has left the terms undefined or ambiguous, then it will be up to the courts to resolve the issue.

The resulting body of case law interpreting criminal statutes is in some ways similar to the common law tradition of judge-made law. When a court of last resort issues an opinion on the meaning of *results from* or *damaged* or *carry*, its ruling is, in a sense, judge-made law. Lower courts will look to the opinion for guidance and rely on it to instruct juries. In this way, court decisions interpreting criminal statutes can be as important a source of criminal law as the statutes themselves, and "result in a type of common law." Hessick, *supra*, at 988. But unlike in the common law tradition, courts are not writing the law from scratch when they interpret statutes, and so their discretion is much more limited. In addition, legislators can always overturn any court decision interpreting a statute by amending the law.

## B. ELEMENTS OF CRIMES: AN OVERVIEW

Every crime is made up of one or more elements—facts that the prosecutor must prove in order to convict a defendant of committing that crime. Crimes vary in their complexity and in their number of elements, but each element of a crime typically falls into one of four categories:

**1.** acts (*actus reus*),
**2.** mental state (*mens rea*),
**3.** causation, and
**4.** attendant circumstances.

As we will see, certain background principles often guide courts in interpreting each of these elements—the definition of a particular mental state is usually the same from one crime to the next, for example. After building a base of knowledge about the major criminal offenses, we will return, in Chapter 10, to explore these background principles in more detail. For now, this section introduces each of these four types of elements.

To better understand each element type, it is useful to have an illustrative statute to use as a reference point. An abridged version of Nebraska's arson statute will serve this purpose. It provides:

> A person commits arson in the first degree if he or she intentionally damages a build-ing . . . by starting a fire . . . when another person is present in the building at the time and . . . the actor knows that fact[.]

Neb. Rev. Stat. § 28-502. Before continuing, take a moment to deconstruct this statute by dividing it into discrete elements. What act(s) does a prosecutor need to prove a person did to convict someone under this statute? What result does a prosecutor need to prove was caused by these acts? What are the additional attendant circumstances required by this statute? Finally, what mental state(s) are required by this statute and how do they interact with the other elements? Keep your answers to these questions in mind as you read the discussion below, which will address each of these issues.

## 1. Act (*Actus Reus*) Elements

Because the law generally does not punish people for thoughts alone, crimes typ-ically include at least one act (*actus reus*) element. The Nebraska arson statute quoted above punishes the act of "starting a fire." If a person intentionally dam-ages a building she knows to be occupied by committing some *other* type of act — spray-painting graffiti onto it, for example — she might be guilty of a crime but it would not be first-degree arson under the Nebraska statute.

Although the act element varies from crime to crime, there is one *actus reus* principle that applies across the criminal code. The *actus reus* of a crime is usu-ally satisfied only by a **voluntary act**, meaning a willed bodily movement. This requirement is easily met in most cases. After all, even accidents usually begin with a volitional act. A person who accidentally starts a fire after leaving the stove on, for example, almost certainly committed a voluntary act when she turned on the stove. Similarly, a person who acts unthinkingly based on habit acts volitionally.

Involuntary acts are rare and tend to involve peculiar situations, such as sleep-walking or hypnosis. The Model Penal Code's definition of involuntary acts is fairly representative. Section 2.01 of the Model Penal Code defines an involuntary act as an act resulting from "a reflex or convulsion; a bodily movement during unconscious-ness or sleep; conduct during hypnosis or resulting from hypnotic suggestion; or a bodily movement that otherwise is not a product of the effort or determination of the actor, either conscious or habitual." Not surprisingly, a criminal lawyer can easily go her entire career without handling a case where the voluntary act doctrine is at issue.

The *actus reus* element of a crime almost always involves an affirmative act, as opposed to a failure to act — referred to in criminal law as an **omission**. This is in part because punishing people for failing to act can present difficult moral and prac-tical line-drawing problems. Imagine a person screaming for help in an apartment building. Two neighbors hear the screams but neither of them takes action. If the person screaming for help ends up dead, it might be tempting to place some blame on the neighbors for failing to call the police. But it is unlikely that they failed to act out of spite. Inaction in a case like this is much more likely to result from hon-estly misjudging the situation or from mistakenly assuming that someone else has already called 911. Punishing the failure to act in this kind of case risks criminalizing the morally blameless. As a result, the default position is that criminal statutes do not create a general legal duty to act and therefore do not punish omissions. Note that this rule means that some people whose inaction seems quite blameworthy may also escape punishment. A bystander who sees an unattended, injured child crying out for help and does nothing would not be guilty of a homicide offense if the child died. This is because, as in the apartment building example, the failure to act in the absence of a recognized legal duty does not give rise to criminal liability.

In some circumstances, the argument for punishing omissions becomes compelling enough to override the general rule against punishing omissions. If a wife hears her husband screaming for help in the other room, for example, the spousal relationship might justify imposing a legal duty to act. Ultimately, of course, it is up to lawmakers and courts to determine when an omission can satisfy the *actus reus* of a particular crime. Legislators have criminalized things like failing to pay taxes or failing to report evidence of child abuse to the police. In addition to these statutory duties, there are a few categories of cases where omissions are regularly criminalized: (1) special relationships, including parents to their children or spouses to one another; (2) a contractual obligation, such as a nursing home's contractual duty to care for its residents; (3) the assumption of care, meaning that a person who starts rendering aid has a duty to continue; and (4) failing to provide assistance after putting someone in harm's way. Returning to the example of a child crying out for help, in contrast to a bystander, a person who owed a legal duty to the child — such as a parent or the child's teacher — could potentially be subject to criminal liability for failing to help the child.

Although legislators have broad discretion to criminalize conduct, the Constitution places some limits on this power. One constitutional restriction on crime creation relates to the act element. The Supreme Court has held that it is unconstitutional to punish someone based on his status alone, as opposed to his acts or omissions.

**Case Preview**

## *Robinson v. California*

In *Robinson*, the United States Supreme Court considered a California statute that made it a crime to "be addicted to the use of narcotics." The Court held the statute unconstitutional because it punished people for their "status" of having an addiction. In doing so, the Justices acknowledged the authority of the state to punish someone for acting on his addiction by possessing or using drugs. Criminalizing the status of being addicted to drugs is different, the Court found, because it would mean that "a person can be continually guilty of this offense, whether or not he has ever used or possessed any narcotics within the State, and whether or not he has been guilty of any antisocial behavior there."

As you read the decision, consider the following questions:

**1.** In light of the fact that the state can constitutionally punish drug possession, what is the practical effect, if any, of the Court's holding?
**2.** Can you think of any reasons, in addition to those discussed by the Court, why punishing "status" offenses might be problematic?

## *Robinson v. California*
### 370 U.S. 660 (1962)

Mr. Justice STEWART delivered the opinion of the Court.

A California statute makes it a criminal offense for a person to "be addicted to the use of narcotics." This appeal draws into question the constitutionality of that provision of the state law, as construed by the California courts in the present case.

The appellant was convicted after a jury trial in the Municipal Court of Los Angeles.

Officer Lindquist testified that he had examined the appellant [and] observed discolorations and scabs on the appellant's arms, and he identified photographs which had been taken of the appellant's arms shortly after his arrest the night before. Based upon more than ten years of experience as a member of the Narcotic Division of the Los Angeles Police Department, the witness gave his opinion that "these marks and the discoloration were the result of the injection of hypodermic needles into the tissue into the vein that was not sterile." He stated that the scabs were several days old at the time of his examination, and that the appellant was neither under the influence of narcotics nor suffering withdrawal symptoms at the time he saw him. This witness also testified that the appellant had admitted using narcotics in the past.

The appellant testified in his own behalf, denying the alleged conversation[] with the police officer[] and denying that he had ever used narcotics or been addicted to their use. He explained the marks on his arms as resulting from an allergic condition contracted during his military service. His testimony was corroborated by two witnesses.

The jury returned a verdict finding the appellant "guilty of the offense charged."

The broad power of a State to regulate the narcotic drugs traffic within its borders is not here in issue. More than forty years ago, in *Whipple v. Martinson*, 256 U.S. 41, this Court explicitly recognized the validity of that power: "There can be no question of the authority of the State in the exercise of its police power to regulate the administration, sale, prescription and use of dangerous and habit-forming drugs . . . . The right to exercise this power is so manifest in the interest of the public health and welfare, that it is unnecessary to enter upon a discussion of it beyond saying that it is too firmly established to be successfully called in question."

Such regulation, it can be assumed, could take a variety of valid forms. A State might impose criminal sanctions, for example, against the unauthorized manufacture, prescription, sale, purchase, or possession of narcotics within its borders. In the interest of discouraging the violation of such laws, or in the interest of the general health or welfare of its inhabitants, a State might establish a program of compulsory treatment for those addicted to narcotics.[7] Such a program of treatment might require periods of involuntary confinement. And penal sanctions might be imposed for failure to comply with established compulsory treatment procedures. Or a State might choose to attack the evils of narcotics traffic on broader fronts also — through public health education, for example, or by efforts to ameliorate the economic and

---

[7] California appears to have established just such a program in §§ 5350-5361 of its Welfare and Institutions Code. The record contains no explanation of why the civil procedures authorized by this legislation were not utilized in the present case.

social conditions under which those evils might be thought to flourish. In short, the range of valid choice which a State might make in this area is undoubtedly a wide one, and the wisdom of any particular choice within the allowable spectrum is not for us to decide. Upon that premise we turn to the California law in issue here.

Although there was evidence in the present case that the appellant had used narcotics in Los Angeles, the jury were instructed that they could convict him even if they disbelieved that evidence. The appellant could be convicted, they were told, if they found simply that the appellant's "status" or "chronic condition" was that of being "addicted to the use of narcotics."

This statute, therefore, is not one which punishes a person for the use of narcotics, for their purchase, sale or possession, or for antisocial or disorderly behavior resulting from their administration. It is not a law which even purports to provide or require medical treatment. Rather, we deal with a statute which makes the "status" of narcotic addiction a criminal offense, for which the offender may be prosecuted "at any time before he reforms." California has said that a person can be continuously guilty of this offense, whether or not he has ever used or possessed any narcotics within the State, and whether or not he has been guilty of any anti-social behavior there.

It is unlikely that any State at this moment in history would attempt to make it a criminal offense for a person to be mentally ill, or a leper, or to be afflicted with a venereal disease. A State might determine that the general health and welfare require that the victims of these and other human afflictions be dealt with by compulsory treatment, involving quarantine, confinement, or sequestration. But, in the light of contemporary human knowledge, a law which made a criminal offense of such a disease would doubtless be universally thought to be an infliction of cruel and unusual punishment in violation of the Eighth and Fourteenth Amendments.

We cannot but consider the statute before us as of the same category. In this Court counsel for the State recognized that narcotic addiction is an illness. We hold that a state law which imprisons a person thus afflicted as a criminal, even though he has never touched any narcotic drug within the State or been guilty of any irregular behavior there, inflicts a cruel and unusual punishment in violation of the Fourteenth Amendment. To be sure, imprisonment for ninety days is not, in the abstract, a punishment which is either cruel or unusual. But the question cannot be considered in the abstract. Even one day in prison would be a cruel and unusual punishment for the "crime" of having a common cold.

We are not unmindful that the vicious evils of the narcotics traffic have occasioned the grave concern of government. There are, as we have said, countless fronts on which those evils may be legitimately attacked. We deal in this case only with an individual provision of a particularized local law as it has so far been interpreted by the California courts.

*Reversed.*

Mr. Justice HARLAN, concurring.

I am not prepared to hold that on the present state of medical knowledge it is completely irrational and hence unconstitutional for a State to conclude that narcotics addiction is something other than an illness nor that it amounts to cruel and unusual punishment for the State to subject narcotics addicts to its criminal law. Insofar as addiction may be identified with the use or possession of narcotics within the State (or, I would suppose, without the State), in violation of local statutes prohibiting such acts, it may surely be reached by the State's criminal law. But in this case the trial court's instructions permitted the jury to find the appellant guilty on no more proof than that he was present in California while he was addicted to narcotics. Since addiction alone cannot reasonably be thought to amount to more than a compelling propensity to use narcotics, the effect of this instruction was to authorize criminal punishment for a bare desire to commit a criminal act.

Accordingly, I agree that the application of the California statute was unconstitutional in this case and join the judgment of reversal.

Mr. Justice CLARK, dissenting.

The Court finds § 11721 of California's Health and Safety Code, making it an offense to "be addicted to the use of narcotics," violative of due process as "a cruel and unusual punishment." I cannot agree.

The majority strikes down the conviction primarily on the grounds that petitioner was denied due process by the imposition of criminal penalties for nothing more than being in a status. This viewpoint is premised upon the theme that § 11721 is a "criminal" provision authorizing a punishment, for the majority admits that "a State might establish a program of compulsory treatment for those addicted to narcotics" which "might require periods of involuntary confinement." I submit that California has done exactly that. The majority's error is in instructing the California Legislature that hospitalization is the *only treatment* for narcotics addiction—that anything less is a punishment denying due process. Section 11721 provides . . . confinement [for a period of not less than 90 days] as treatment for the volitional addicts to whom its provisions apply, in addition to parole with frequent tests to detect and prevent further use of drugs. The fact that § 11721 might be labeled "criminal" seems irrelevant,[1] not only to the majority's own "treatment" test but to the "concept of ordered liberty" to which the States must attain under the Fourteenth Amendment. The test is the overall purpose and effect of a State's act, and I submit that California's program relative to narcotic addicts—including both the "criminal" and "civil" provisions—is inherently one of treatment and lies well within the power of a State.

However, the case in support of the judgment below need not rest solely on this reading of California law. The majority acknowledges, as it must, that a State can punish persons who purchase, possess or use narcotics. Although none of these acts are harmful to society *in themselves*, the State constitutionally may attempt to deter and prevent them through punishment because of the grave threat of future harmful conduct which they pose. Narcotics addiction—including the incipient, volitional addiction to which this provision speaks—is no different. California courts have taken judicial notice that "the inordinate use of a narcotic drug tends to create an irresistible craving and forms a habit for its continued use until one becomes an addict, and he respects no convention or obligation and will lie, steal, or use any

---

[1] Any reliance upon the "stigma" of a misdemeanor conviction in this context is misplaced, as it would hardly be different from the stigma of a civil commitment for narcotics addiction.

other base means to gratify his passion for the drug, being lost to all considerations of duty or social position." Can this Court deny the legislative and judicial judgment of California that incipient, volitional narcotic addiction poses a threat of serious crime similar to the threat inherent in the purchase or possession of narcotics? And if such a threat is inherent in addiction, can this Court say that California is powerless to deter it by punishment?

The argument that the statute constitutes a cruel and unusual punishment is governed by the discussion above. Properly construed, the statute provides a treatment rather than a punishment. But even if interpreted as penal, the sanction of incarceration for 3 to 12 months is not unreasonable when applied to a person who has voluntarily placed himself in a condition posing a serious threat to the State. Under either theory, its provisions for 3 to 12 months' confinement can hardly be deemed unreasonable when compared to the provisions for 3 to 24 months' confinement under § 5355 which the majority approves.

I would affirm the judgment.

Mr. Justice WHITE, dissenting.

If appellant's conviction rested upon sheer status, condition or illness or if he was convicted for being an addict who had lost his power of self-control, I would have other thoughts about this case. But this record presents neither situation.

I do not consider appellant's conviction to be a punishment for having an illness or for simply being in some status or condition, but rather a conviction for the regular, repeated or habitual use of narcotics immediately prior to his arrest and in violation of the California law. As defined by the trial court,[2] addiction *is* the regular use of narcotics and can be proved only by evidence of such use. To find addiction in this case the jury had to believe that appellant had frequently used narcotics in the recent past.

The Court has not merely tidied up California's law by removing some irritating vestige of an outmoded approach to the control of narcotics. At the very least, it has effectively removed California's power to deal effectively with the recurring case under the statute where there is ample evidence of use but no evidence of the precise location of use.

I respectfully dissent.

**Post-Case Follow-Up**

*Robinson* holds that the government may not constitutionally punish a person based on her status alone. By contrast, statutes that punish conduct are constitutional, even if that conduct is closely tied to a person's status. Six years after *Robinson*, the Supreme Court reaffirmed this point in *Powell v. Texas*, 392 U.S. 514 (1968). In *Powell*, the Court rejected a constitutional challenge to a Texas statute that made it a crime

---

[2] The court instructed the jury that, "The word 'addicted' means, strongly disposed to some taste or practice or habituated, especially to drugs. In order to inquire as to whether a person is addicted to the use of narcotics is in effect an inquiry as to his habit in that regard. . . . To use them often or daily is, according to the ordinary acceptance of those words, to use them habitually."

to "get drunk or be found in a state of intoxication in any public place." In contrast to the California statute in *Robinson*, the Court explained, Texas's law criminalized the act of "being in public while drunk on a particular occasion" and not the status of "being a chronic alcoholic."

## Robinson: *Real Life Applications*

1. Although it is unconstitutional to criminalize the status of being addicted to illegal drugs, states may make it a crime to use or possess drugs. Needless to say, people who are active users of an illegal drug will possess that drug on a regular basis. As a result, it might seem as though *Robinson* does not have any practical effect. Imagine you are a defense attorney. Can you think of any ways in which defending a client against charges for the crime of being "addicted to the use of narcotics" might be more difficult than defending against charges of drug possession?

2. Immigration offenses make up a significant percentage of the federal criminal docket. But criminalizing the status of being in the United States without permission seems difficult to square with *Robinson*. Imagine you are a member of Congress. Can you think of a way to draft a statute that would punish people who are inside the United States illegally based on their conduct, as opposed to their status?

## 2. Mental State (*Mens Rea*) Elements

Just as the law does not punish people for thoughts alone, it typically does not punish people for voluntary acts alone, either. Instead, most crimes also include one or more culpable mental state elements, often referred to as the **mens rea** — Latin for "guilty mind" — of the crime. Tying blame to a person's mental state is part of everyday life. As the United States Supreme Court once observed, "[a] relation between some mental element and punishment for a harmful act is almost as instinctive as the child's familiar exculpatory 'But I didn't mean to.'" *Morissette v. United States*, 342 U.S. 246, 250-51 (1952). Consistent with this idea, most criminal statutes punish the "concurrence of an evil-meaning mind with an evil-doing hand." *Id.* at 250.

Returning to the example of Nebraska's first-degree arson law, first presented on page 60, we find two mental state elements. First, "[a] person commits arson in the first degree if he or she *intentionally* damages a building . . . by starting a fire." Neb. Rev. Stat. § 28-502 (emphasis added). Because of this intent requirement, the statute would not apply to a person who inadvertently left the stove on and started a fire. Turning on the stove may have been a voluntary act, but it is not a violation of Nebraska's arson law unless that act was done with the *intent* to damage the building by starting a fire. The mental state portion of Nebraska's statute does not end there. In addition to *intending* to damage a building, a defendant must also have *known* that "another person is present in the building at the time" she starts the fire to be guilty of first-degree arson. *Id.*

Whereas the *actus reus* of a crime is often specific to that offense, the same *mens rea* terms recur throughout the criminal code. Nebraska's arson, theft, and drug distribution laws punish three very different types of acts, but all three include intent as a required mental state. Intent is just one of a handful of mental states that legislators tend to rely on when defining crimes. The others are purpose, knowledge, recklessness, and negligence. In addition to these mental states, there are a few that arise less frequently, such as malice. Of course, lawmakers are not bound by any list of mental states. But in practice, they rarely deviate from the well-established *mens rea* terms.

The definition of a particular mental state is usually the same from state to state and crime to crime. The material in the upcoming chapters will examine each of the most common mental states in more depth, in the context of specific criminal offenses. For now, this section briefly summarizes each of the most common mental states, based on how they are defined in most states.

## Intent

The mental state of intent, which dates back to the common law, is still used in a wide range of criminal statutes. Traditionally, a person acts intentionally either (1) when it is his conscious desire to cause a result or perform an act, *or* (2) "when he knows that the result is practically certain to follow from his conduct, whatever his desire may be as to that result." *United States v. United States Gypsum Co.*, 438 U.S. 422, 445 (1978) (citation omitted). In most cases, the "limited distinction between knowledge and purpose" does not have much practical significance. *Id.* After all, if Dan points a gun at Victor's head and pulls the trigger, Dan is very likely to *both* have the conscious object of causing Victor's death *and* know that it is practically certain his actions will cause Victor's death. Even so, when intent is used in a statute, the most common definition of the term means that the prosecutor needs to prove just one of these two variants to convict.

Occasionally, however, courts or legislatures will define intent more narrowly to include *only* the "conscious object" (i.e., purpose) variant. The narrow interpretation of intent accounts for the fact that the broader definition can reach blameless conduct in certain settings. For example, "a doctor swabbing a wound" may know that she is practically certain to cause a patient pain even though her conscious object is to help the patient, not cause the patient pain. *United States v. Tobin*, 552 F.3d 29, 33 (1st Cir. 2009). When applying the broad definition of intent to a statute is likely to lead to absurd results, courts will often employ the narrower interpretation.

## Purpose

To address ambiguity surrounding the term intent, the Model Penal Code's drafters decided to avoid the term altogether. Instead, the Model Penal Code formally separated the conscious object and knowledge variants of intent into two distinct mental states: purpose and knowledge. Under the Model Penal Code, a person acts purposefully when "it is his conscious object to engage in conduct of that nature or to cause such a result." Model Penal Code § 2.02(2)(a)(i). After being popularized by the Model Penal Code, legislatures have continued to use this mental state in various criminal statutes. Whenever the term appears, it is typically given the definition stated in the Model Penal Code, even in states that have not adopted other portions of the Model Penal Code.

## Knowledge

The mental state of knowledge accounts for the second variant of intent. A person acts knowingly "if he is aware that it is practically certain that his conduct will cause" a particular result. Model Penal Code § 2.02(2)(b)(ii). This definition of knowledge applies when the term is used to describe the actor's mental state with respect to achieving a particular result.

Knowledge has a second, slightly different definition when it is used in connection with an actor's awareness of an existing fact. The Nebraska arson statute includes a requirement that the defendant act with knowledge that "another person is present in the building at the time" of the fire. Neb. Rev. Stat. § 28-502. When used in this way, knowledge means actual awareness of the stated fact or circumstance; mere suspicion that the fact or circumstance might exist is not sufficient.

## Recklessness

In contrast to knowledge, which requires actual awareness of a fact or practical certainty that a result will occur, the recklessness mental state punishes people for consciously disregarding serious risks. The Model Penal Code defines recklessness as follows:

> A person acts recklessly with respect to a material element of an offense when he consciously disregards a substantial and unjustifiable risk that the material element exists or will result from his conduct. The risk must be of such a nature and degree that, considering the nature and purpose of the actor's conduct and the circumstances known to him, its disregard involves a gross deviation from the standard of conduct that a law-abiding person would observe in the actor's situation.

Model Penal Code § 2.02(2)(c). Today, most jurisdictions use the Model Penal Code's definition of recklessness or have adopted one that is very similar.

To get a sense of how this mental state operates, imagine the following altered version of Nebraska's arson statute (the alterations are in strikethrough and underlined text): "A person commits arson in the first degree if he or she ~~intentionally~~ recklessly damages a building . . . by starting a fire . . . ." Now further imagine that one Fourth of July, Dave sets off fireworks five feet from his neighbor Victor's garage, which Dave knows is filled with flammable materials. Although Dave knows that setting off fireworks near flammable material is a significant fire hazard,

he decides to take the risk anyway. Dave's fireworks set Victor's house on fire, causing thousands of dollars in damage. Dave has not intentionally damaged Victor's
house — it wasn't Dave's conscious object to damage Victor's house and Dave was
not practically certain his actions would damage Victor's house — so he could not
be convicted of violating Nebraska's first-degree arson statute. But Dave has acted
recklessly and so might be guilty under the hypothetical altered version of the
arson statute. This is because Dave was aware that setting off fireworks near flammable materials presented a substantial and unjustifiable risk of causing damage to
Victor's house and Dave consciously disregarded that risk.

### Negligence

Criminal negligence and recklessness are very similar in many respects. What distinguishes the two is that negligence can extend to people who do not realize their
conduct involves any risk. Under the Model Penal Code,

> [a] person acts negligently with respect to a material element of an offense when he
> should be aware of a substantial and unjustifiable risk that the material element exists
> or will result from his conduct. The risk must be of such a nature and degree that the
> actor's failure to perceive it, considering the nature and purpose of his conduct and the
> circumstances known to him, involves a gross deviation from the standard of care that
> a reasonable person would observe in the actor's situation.

Model Penal Code § 2.02(2)(d). As with recklessness, most jurisdictions have either
adopted this definition or one that is very similar.

   Whereas recklessness is concerned with conscious risk taking, negligence
applies to people who were not aware their conduct presented a substantial and
unjustifiable risk but "should have been." To appreciate the practical significance
of this distinction, reconsider the fireworks hypothetical from above, except this
time imagine that Dave was not aware that his conduct risked damaging Victor's
home. Maybe Dave had lived a sheltered existence and never learned that fireworks
posed a fire hazard, or maybe Dave was so excited to set off the fireworks that it
genuinely did not occur to him that setting them off so close to Victor's house was
risky. Whatever the reason, if Dave truly did not know that setting off fireworks
presented a substantial risk of damaging Victor's home, he did not act recklessly.
After all, a person cannot consciously disregard a risk that he is unaware of. In this
scenario, Dave did, however, act negligently because a reasonable person in his
situation would have been aware — and so Dave should have been aware — that
lighting fireworks so close to Victor's garage created a substantial risk of causing
damage to the building.

   Is punishing people for inadvertence justifiable? Some commentators argue
that "negligence should be excluded from the scope of penal liability" entirely
because a person who honestly fails to perceive a risk cannot be deterred and cannot be considered morally blameworthy. Jerome Hall, *Negligent Behavior Should
Be Excluded from Penal Liability*, 63 Colum. L. Rev. 632, 634 (1963). Others believe
that punishing people for negligent wrongdoing is perfectly consistent with the

theories of punishment. Even though the threat of punishment may not be able to deter someone who is unaware her conduct presents a risk, it might still have some utilitarian value by incentivizing people to act more carefully in general. From a retributivist perspective, some argue that a person can indeed be culpable for her failure to perceive risk, at least where the failure "stem[s] from a culpable lack of concern for the victim." Samuel H. Pillsbury, *Crimes of Indifference*, 49 Rutgers L. Rev. 105 (1996).

Whether or not the traditional theories of punishment support criminalizing negligent acts, criminal codes continue to include negligence as the applicable mental state for some elements of some offenses. Negligence is less frequently used than the other mental states, however, and some states have a presumption against it. The Model Penal Code, for example, provides that if a statute fails to specify the mental state required for an element of the crime, the mental state of recklessness applies to that element. Model Penal Code § 2.02(3).

In addition to distinguishing criminal negligence from recklessness, it is important not to confuse criminal negligence with civil negligence, which can form the basis for tort liability. The concepts are similar, no doubt. But civil negligence covers a much broader range of conduct than criminal negligence. The civil negligence standard establishes a general legal duty of care based on a cost-benefit analysis that weighs the burden of taking precautions against the probability and gravity of injury. Criminal negligence requires more than a failure to use ordinary care. Instead, criminal negligence involves a "*gross* deviation from the standard of care that a reasonable person would observe" along with a "*substantial* and unjustifiable risk." Model Penal Code § 2.02(2)(d) (emphasis added). As the late former judge and law professor Calvert Magruder is reported to have put it, "if to be ordinarily negligent is to be something of a fool, then to be [criminally] negligent is to be a 'damned fool.'" Michael S. Moore, *Punishing the Awkward, the Stupid, the Weak, and the Selfish: The Culpability of Negligence*, 5 Crim. L. & Phil. 147, 149 (2011) (quoting Judge Magruder).

## Strict Liability

The final *mens rea* term, strict liability, is not a mental state at all. Instead, strict liability refers to the imposition of criminal punishment in the absence of a culpable mental state. In other words, no *mens rea* is required to convict, not even criminal negligence.

Strict liability offenses are controversial because they can punish people who are morally blameless. Among criminal law theorists, strict liability has few defenders. Strict liability crimes are also rare in practice. The overwhelming majority of criminal statutes include a culpable mental state, and there is a presumption against strict liability crimes in almost every jurisdiction.

The two main exceptions are so-called public welfare offenses and statutory rape. The use of strict liability for the crime of statutory rape has its roots in the common law and is covered in Chapter 6. Public welfare offenses are a modern creation that target participants in heavily regulated industries and carry relatively light penalties. In these circumstances, lawmakers sometimes decide to provide for strict liability on the theory that it will incentivize people to be as careful as possible. In some states, for example, selling alcohol to a minor is a strict liability crime. In these jurisdictions, no *mens rea* with respect to the age of the buyer is required — the government only needs to prove that the act of selling alcohol to a minor took place to win a conviction. As a result, a defendant could be convicted of selling alcohol to a minor even if they took every conceivable precaution to try to ensure that the person they were selling to was of age. Selling alcohol to a minor is just one example of a strict liability public welfare offense. Others range from the sale of misbranded drugs to certain environmental offenses.

## Mens Rea *and Statutory Interpretation*

The *mens rea* element(s) of an offense typically modify one or more of the other element(s) of that offense. Consider again the Nebraska arson statute, which provides in part that a person commits arson if "he or she intentionally damages a building . . . by starting a fire." Neb. Rev. Stat. § 28-502. Imagine that Dave intentionally starts a fire in a fire pit in his girlfriend's backyard. A gust of wind carries an ember from the fire to the neighbor's house, causing it to burn down. Has Dave acted with the intent required by Nebraska's statute? No. Dave acted intentionally, but his intent was merely to start a fire. Nebraska's arson statute requires that the defendant starting a fire act with the intent to damage a building. The statute does *not* make it a crime to intentionally start a fire that happens to damage a building.

This brief example highlights that the *mens rea* of a crime does not exist in a vacuum. When we think of the mental state(s) required for a particular crime, we must always be mindful of which element(s) each mental state applies to. "The possible objects of mental states are the actor's conduct, the attendant circumstances, and the result he brings about (or seeks to bring about) by his conduct." Kenneth W. Simons, *Rethinking Mental States*, 72 B.U. L. Rev. 463, 469 (1992).

Because criminal law is statutory, it might be natural to assume that identifying the mental state that applies to each element of an offense would be an easy task. Just

### Can Jurors Effectively Distinguish Between Mental States?

The criminal law asks jurors to determine the defendant's mental state at the time of the alleged crime. But how can jurors know what was in a defendant's mind? In some cases, the jury may have direct evidence in the form of a confession. But often jurors must rely on circumstantial evidence alone.

Complicating matters further, some jurors may have difficulty differentiating the mental states from one another. There has been surprisingly little empirical research on the ability of jurors to distinguish between mental states. But a series of studies by one group of researchers suggests that jurors may not necessarily be capable of consistently distinguishing knowledge from recklessness. In the studies, subjects were given hypothetical fact patterns and asked to apply Model Penal Code mental state definitions in order to rate culpability. The researchers found that "[s]ubjects were able to identify purposeful conduct an impressive 78% of the time, and blameless conduct an even more impressive 88% of the time. They were less good, however, at identifying knowing (50%) and reckless (40%) conduct. These poor results emerged even when subjects were repeatedly instructed on the distinction." Francis X. Shen et al., *Sorting Guilty Minds*, 86 N.Y.U. L. Rev. 1306, 1354 (2011). The authors recommended rethinking the definitions of knowledge and recklessness to make clearer the distinction between the two.

look up the relevant statute and the legislature will have provided a clear answer. Sometimes it is indeed that easy. But where the statutory language is ambiguous, determining which mental state applies to each element of an offense can be quite tricky. This is especially true when lawmakers have omitted any *mens rea* term from a criminal law statute. As already noted above, the Model Penal Code provides that if a statute is silent regarding the mental state required for an element of the crime, the mental state of recklessness applies to that element in the absence of clear legislative intent to the contrary. Model Penal Code § 2.02(3). Roughly half of all states include this provision or one like it as part of their criminal codes. Darryl K. Brown, *Criminal Law Reform and the Persistence of Strict Liability*, 62 Duke L.J. 285, 289 n.8 (2012). Many other jurisdictions have adopted a presumption against strict liability offenses through court precedent. These presumptions do not necessarily mean that a mental state always attaches to every element of a crime, however. Nor do they always provide a clear answer about how to interpret the mental state elements of a given criminal statute. This book returns to the challenge of interpreting criminal statutes in Chapter 10.

## 3. Causation (Results Elements)

Nearly every crime includes an *actus reus* and *mens rea*. By contrast, causation is at issue in only a specific category of offenses: those that include a **results element**.

Many crimes do not include a results element. Consider, for example, a federal statute that makes it a crime to "transmit[] in interstate or foreign commerce any communication containing any threat . . . to injure the person of another." 18 U.S.C. § 875(c). The crime is completed once a defendant transmits a threat with the necessary *mens rea*. There is no additional requirement that the threat to injure actually cause harm to its recipient. Likewise, burglary (as defined at common law and covered in Chapter 3) criminalizes the breaking and entering of the dwelling of another at night with the intent to commit a felony therein. No particular result is required for the offense to be completed. Other offenses that do not incorporate a results element include illegal drug possession, larceny, and attempts.

When a crime does include a results element, the prosecutor must prove that the defendant's acts caused the specified result. The most prominent example, by far, is homicide offenses. To be convicted of a homicide—whether murder or manslaughter—the defendant must have caused the victim's death. If the defendant did not cause the victim's death, then she is at worst guilty of an attempted homicide. Beyond homicides, a wide range of different offenses include a results element. Returning to the abridged version of Nebraska's first-degree arson offense as an example, the statute makes it a crime to "intentionally damage[] a building . . . by starting a fire . . . when another person is present in the building at the time and . . . the actor knows that fact." The results element in this offense is *damage* to a building. If a defendant starts a fire intending to damage an occupied building, he is only guilty of arson under this statute if his actions actually cause damage to the building. As with all statutory language, courts are tasked with interpreting the meaning of results terms like "damage" unless the legislature has provided a definition.

While the definition of results terms can vary by jurisdiction and even by crime — damage might have a different meaning in an arson statute and a vandalism statute, for example — the core legal principles of causation are common to all results elements. To prove causation of a results element in a criminal case, the prosecutor must typically show that the defendant's acts were both a "but-for cause" and a "proximate cause" of the harm. **But-for causation**, also referred to as actual causation, requires the prosecutor to prove that, but for the defendant's acts, the harm would not have occurred when it did. This definition encompasses acts that accelerate the harm. For example, if Victor is in the hospital suffering from a fatal disease and Dan smothers Victor, Dan is a but-for of Victor's death. This is true even if Victor's doctor had just examined him and determined that Victor would be dead of natural causes within the hour. This is because but for Dan's actions, Victor would not have died when he did.

**Proximate cause**, also called legal cause, provides an additional constraint on culpability. The universe of but-for causes is often large and can include acts that are removed from the harm by years or decades. But for Dan's parents, Dan would not have been born and could not have killed Victor, technically making Dan's birth a but-for cause of Victor's death. Proximate cause incorporates a handful of limits, chief among them the intervening causes and foreseeability doctrines. The intervening causes principle holds that certain kinds of intervening acts — a free and deliberate act on the part of the alleged victim, for example — can vitiate the existence of proximate cause by breaking the causal chain between the defendant's act and the harm. The foreseeability principle provides that the harm must have been reasonably foreseeable for there to be proximate cause.

In ordinary criminal cases, causation is rarely a contested issue. This is because it is unusual for a case to involve an intervening actor or give rise to a plausible argument that harm was truly unforeseeable. In the cases where causation does become an issue, however, it often presents tricky legal problems for attorneys and judges. Indeed, in the criminal law setting, "proximate (legal) cause is notorious for its lack of specific standards to guide outcomes." Janice Nadler & Mary-Hunter McDonnell, *Moral Character, Motive, and the Psychology of Blame*, 97 Cornell L. Rev. 255, 299 (2012). Both but-for and proximate cause principles are covered in greater depth in the context of homicide offenses in Chapter 5.

## 4. Attendant Circumstances Elements

In addition to *actus reus*, *mens rea*, and causation, many criminal offenses include one or more attendant circumstances elements. Attendant circumstances "refer to the objective situation that the law requires to exist, in addition to the defendant's act or any results that the act may cause." Model Penal Code § 5.01 cmt. at 301 n.9 (Official Draft and Revised Comments 1985). This is a broad category — something of a catchall that can encompass any element of an offense that is not an act, result, or mental state.

Again, Nebraska's arson statute provides a helpful illustration. Recall that the statute provides: "A person commits arson in the first degree if he or she intentionally damages a building . . . by starting a fire . . . when another person is present in the building at the time and . . . the actor knows that fact[.]" Here, the requirement that "another person [be] present in the building at the time" is an attendant circumstance element. Note that the *mens rea* required for this circumstance is different from the required mental state with respect to causing damage to the building. The statute provides that the defendant must intentionally damage a building and that he must do so with knowledge that another person is present in the building. This is not uncommon. Criminal statutes frequently include more than one mental state, with the *mens rea* required for the act or result differing from that required for the attendant circumstance.

Unlike the other types of criminal law elements, the attendant circumstances category is not governed by any generally applicable principles. When it comes to attendant circumstances, there is nothing akin to the voluntary act requirement, the principles of causation, or the common definitions for mental states. Instead, the legal issues that arise with respect to attendant circumstances are typically specific to the particular offense. The one significant recurring legal problem related to attendant circumstances involves mental states. For whatever reason, it seems that statutes more often fail to specify the mental state required for an attendant circumstance element than for other elements. When this happens, it is up to courts to resolve the ambiguity. In these cases, the outcome is controlled by the principles of statutory interpretation for mental states issues described above and examined further in Chapter 10.

## 5. Affirmative Defenses

As discussed in more detail in the next section, to win a conviction, the prosecutor must prove every element of an offense beyond a reasonable doubt. Even if the prosecution proves each element beyond a reasonable doubt, defendants have one more avenue available to them: affirmative defenses.

Because the law of affirmative defenses is covered in detail in Chapter 11, we will not wade into affirmative defenses doctrine at this point. For present purposes, it is enough to be aware of the role of affirmative defenses in the criminal process. Affirmative defenses rest on the premise that although the defendant's conduct would normally constitute a crime, some other fact excuses or justifies her actions. Intentionally killing another person would normally constitute murder or voluntary manslaughter. But if the perpetrator suffered from a severe mental illness that made her incapable of understanding right from wrong, the law might find her actions excusable under the insanity defense. The criminal law provides for a number of potential affirmative defenses, including self-defense, insanity, duress, and entrapment. Each is addressed in Chapter 11.

## C. THE CRIMINAL CASE PROCESS: A BRIEF OVERVIEW

Criminal Law courses are designed to introduce students to the substance of the criminal law — the definitions of important crimes, affirmative defenses, and so on.

Almost every law school offers a separate course, Criminal Procedure: Adjudication, that is devoted exclusively to the criminal trial process. A third course, Criminal Procedure: Investigation, covers the constitutional rules that pertain to criminal investigations.

Although an in-depth treatment of the criminal process is beyond the scope of this book, a basic understanding of how a case makes its way through the criminal justice system is helpful for learning substantive criminal law. This section outlines the process for adjudicating a criminal prosecution, with special attention to points where the criminal process and substance are most likely to intersect. As you will see in this short overview, the criminal process can sometimes be as or more important to the outcome of a case than criminal law doctrine.

## 1. The Investigation

Every criminal case begins with an investigation. Often, the investigation is so brief—a traffic stop that results in an arrest for driving under the influence, for example—that calling it an investigation might seem a bit strange. But most criminal cases begin this way, with an investigation that lasts a few minutes or maybe an hour or two. A police officer responds to a 911 call or pulls a car over, discovers suspected criminal activity, and makes an arrest. Longer, more resource intensive investigations are usually reserved for certain kinds of offenses: serious crimes, like murder or rape, or crimes that involve complex or hidden activity, like financial crimes or drug conspiracies.

Regardless of the nature and length of an investigation, pre-arrest investigative methods are governed mostly by the Fourth and Fifth Amendments to the Constitution. The Fourth Amendment, which grants people the right "to be secure in their persons, houses, papers, and effects, against unreasonable searches and seizures," provides rules for things like when a police officer can pull your car over or search your home. The Fifth Amendment is the foundation for the famous *Miranda* warnings, which inform arrestees of their right to remain silent and to have an attorney.

The Constitution places limits on policing tactics, but police departments enjoy relatively broad discretion regarding where to focus their investigative resources. As most people who have reported the theft of personal property to the police can attest, officers are not legally obligated to pursue every lead that comes their way. Indeed, resource constraints would make it impossible for most police departments to thoroughly investigate every crime reported to them. Usually, police discretion plays out at the margins on questions like the amount of resources to dedicate to a particular investigation. Sometimes, however, police departments may decide not to enforce a particular offense at all or to turn a blind eye to certain offenders. The practice of choosing "not to enforce the narcotics laws against certain violators who inform against other 'more serious' violators," for example, is as old as drug prohibition. Joseph Goldstein, *Police Discretion Not to Invoke the Criminal Process: Low-Visibility Decisions in the Administration of Justice*, 69 Yale L. Rev. 543, 554 (1960). Police discretion can also sometimes lead to an unwarranted focus on marginalized communities or to racial profiling, which in turn can drive some of the disparities in enforcement described in Chapter 1. As a result of police enforcement discretion, the law on the books may not always perfectly match the law as it is enforced.

## 2. The Charging Decision

Just as the police have enforcement discretion, prosecutors have significant discretion over whether to charge and what charges to bring against an arrestee, whether or not to offer a plea deal, and more. (As you may recall, the concurring opinion in *Nash v. State*, presented in Chapter 1, touched on the power wielded by prosecutors.) Line prosecutors make these sorts of decisions in individual cases every day all across the country. Sometimes, prosecutor offices adopt internal policies to help guide these charging decisions, whether in the interest of conserving resources or pursuing a particular policy objective. In 2013, for example, then–Attorney General Eric Holder issued a memo to federal prosecutors with guidelines designed to limit the use of lengthy mandatory minimum penalties in federal drug cases. The memo instructed federal prosecutors not to bring charges that carried a mandatory minimum penalty against non-violent drug defendants who met certain criteria, such as having minimal criminal history. In 2017, then–Attorney General Jeff Sessions rescinded the Holder policy with a memo directing prosecutors to "charge and pursue the most serious, readily provable offense" in every case, including against non-violent drug defendants. As these two data points show, prosecutorial discretion can sometimes affect the criminal justice system as much as the law itself. Federal drug laws did not change between 2013 and 2017. But the change in prosecutorial guidelines meant that many more federal drug defendants faced mandatory minimum sentences in 2018 than in 2014.

The Holder and Sessions memoranda are examples of prosecutorial guidelines designed to further policy preferences. But the law does not require prosecutors to base their decisions on principle. Prosecutors are largely free to choose which cases to pursue for any reason or no reason at all. In one famous example, when Rudy Giuliani was the United States Attorney for the Southern District of New York in the 1980s, he implemented a charging policy dubbed "federal day." Under the "federal day" policy, "one random day a week all drug arrests [in Manhattan were] prosecuted in Federal court," where most defendants faced significantly longer sentences than they would have in state court. Stephen Labton, *Drugs and the Law: The Courts Overwhelmed*, N.Y. Times, Dec. 29, 1989, at A1. In effect, the "federal day" policy left the choice of which cases to prosecute in federal court to chance. Some federal judges criticized this approach. The Second Circuit sarcastically described the policy in an opinion by noting that, "[t]hough the case was developed by New York City police officers, concerns readily visible criminal conduct requiring no special investigatory resources or equipment, and involves a $30 transaction, the matter became the subject of a federal criminal prosecution because it occurred on 'federal day,' the day of the week when federal law enforcement authorities have decided to convert garden-variety state law drug offenses into federal offenses. Though we are urged in other contexts to tolerate missed deadlines because of the enormous burdens placed upon limited numbers of federal law enforcement personnel, on 'federal day' there are apparently enough federal prosecutors available with sufficient time to devote to $30 drug cases that have been developed solely by state law enforcement officers." *United States v. Agilar*, 779 F.2d 123, 125 (2d Cir. 1985). Despite these concerns, courts did not intervene because of the broad discretion prosecutors have in their charging decisions. As the court in *Agilar* observed after its criticism of the "federal day" policy, "the case is lawfully within the jurisdiction of the federal courts and must be decided." *Id.*

While prosecutors have a great deal of discretion, there is at least one essential constraint on prosecutorial power. There must be probable cause to believe the defendant has committed an offense to charge him with a crime, and there are modest procedural checks to help ensure probable cause actually exists. At the federal level and in some states, grand juries are responsible for deciding whether probable cause exists to support criminal charges. Other states provide for preliminary hearings — an adversarial hearing held before a judge — to make the probable cause determination. These processes are covered in detail in criminal adjudication courses. The probable cause requirement guards against prosecutions in the absence of any evidence of guilt. But once there is probable cause to believe someone may have committed a crime, the prosecutor has nearly limitless discretion over whether to bring charges for that offense or a lesser offense, or not to bring charges at all. The only other hard limits on this discretion are constitutional constraints that prohibit basing charging decisions on the defendant's race or religion, or to retaliate against the defendant for exercising certain constitutional rights.

In most jurisdictions, criminal charges are typically contained in an information or an indictment. Indictments are issued by grand juries and informations by prosecutors. In either case, the charging instrument is what marks the formal initiation of a criminal case. It notifies the defendant of the criminal statute(s) he is alleged to have violated as well as the factual basis of the allegations. Although there are exceptions, most charging instruments provide only a very brief recitation of the factual basis for the charges. Exhibit 2.1 provides an example.

## Enforcement Discretion and Racial Disparities

Although police and prosecutors have a great deal of discretion, the Constitution prohibits basing investigative and charging decisions on race. And yet, as discussed in Chapter 1, there are stark racial disparities in criminal enforcement. Standing alone, these systemic disparities are not enough to give rise to a constitutional claim in any particular case. Instead, to succeed in a discriminatory prosecution claim, a defendant must show both that the decision to prosecute "had a discriminatory effect and that it was motivated by a discriminatory purpose." *Wayte v. United States*, 470 U.S. 598 (1985).

This standard is very difficult for litigants to meet. Even when data conclusively establishes racially disparate enforcement of a particular law, the defendant must show that the disparities resulted from a discriminatory intent. As a result, selective prosecution claims are rare, and successful claims are even rarer. One sign of how just how rare they are: The Supreme Court "has not ruled in favor of a defendant raising a selective prosecution claim based on racial discrimination in over 130 years." Sherod Thaxton, *Disentangling Disparity: Exploring Racially Disparate Effect and Treatment in Capital Charging*, 45 Am. J. Crim. L. 95, 99 (2018).

**EXHIBIT 2.1**    # Example of an Information From the Federal Prosecution of Singer Lauryn Hill

[2011R01339/SLM]

UNITED STATES DISTRICT COURT
DISTRICT OF NEW JERSEY

| | | |
|---|---|---|
| UNITED STATES OF AMERICA | : | Hon. Michael A. Shipp |
| v. | : | Mag. No. 12-6081 |
| LAURYN N. HILL | : | 26 U.S.C. § 7203 |
| | : | |

**I N F O R M A T I O N**

The United States Attorney for the District of New Jersey charges:

**COUNT ONE**

(Failure to Make Tax Return - 2005)

1.    At all times relevant to this Information, defendant LAURYN N. HILL was a resident of South Orange, New Jersey, and was a singer and actress, as well as the owner and operator of four sub-chapter S corporations: (a) Obverse Creations Music, Inc.; (b) Boogie Tours, Inc.; (c) L.H. Productions 2001, Inc.; and (d) Studio 22, Inc.

2.    At all times relevant to this Information, music and movie royalties were the primary sources of income for defendant LAURYN N. HILL.

3.    During the calendar year 2005, defendant LAURYN N. HILL had and received total gross income in excess of approximately $818,000.

4.    Having received this income, defendant LAURYN N. HILL was required by law, following the close of the calendar year 2005, and on or before October 16, 2006, to make an income tax return to the United Department of Treasury, Internal Revenue Service ("IRS") stating specifically the items of her gross income and any deductions and credits to which she was entitled.

5.    On or about October 16, 2006, in Essex County, in the District of New Jersey, and elsewhere, defendant

LAURYN N. HILL,

knowing and believing the foregoing facts, did knowingly and willfully fail to make an income tax return to the IRS.

In violation of Title 26, United States Code, Section 7203.

2

**COUNT TWO**

(Failure to Make Tax Return - 2006)

1.    The allegations set forth in paragraphs 1 and 2 of Count One are realleged as if set forth in full herein.

2.    During the calendar year 2006, defendant LAURYN N. HILL had and received total gross income in excess of approximately $222,000.

3.    Having received this income, defendant LAURYN N. HILL was required by law, following the close of the calendar year 2006, and on or before October 15, 2007, to make an income tax return to the IRS stating specifically the items of her gross income and any deductions and credits to which she was entitled.

4.    On or about October 15, 2007, in Essex County, in the District of New Jersey, and elsewhere, defendant

LAURYN N. HILL,

knowing and believing the foregoing facts, did knowingly and willfully fail to make an income tax return to the Internal Revenue Service.

In violation of Title 26, United States Code, Section 7203.

**COUNT THREE**

(Failure to Make Tax Return - 2007)

1.    The allegations set forth in paragraphs 1 and 2 of Count One are realleged as if set forth in full herein.

2.    During the calendar year 2007, defendant LAURYN N. HILL had and received total gross income in excess of approximately $761,000.

3.    Having received this income, defendant LAURYN N. HILL was required by law, following the close of the calendar year 2007, and on or before October 15, 2008, to make an income tax return to the IRS stating specifically the items of her gross income and any deductions and credits to which she was entitled.

4.    On or about October 15, 2008, in Essex County, in the District of New Jersey, and elsewhere, defendant

LAURYN N. HILL,

knowing and believing the foregoing facts, did knowingly and willfully fail to make an income tax return to the IRS.

In violation of Title 26, United States Code, Section 7203.

*Paul J. Fishman*
PAUL J. FISHMAN
United States Attorney

3                                            4

# 3. Bail and Pretrial Release

Because criminal defendants are presumed innocent, the mere fact that a person has been charged with a crime should not justify detaining him for the purposes of punishment. As the Supreme Court once put it, "[i]n our society liberty is the norm, and detention prior to trial or without trial is the carefully limited exception." *United States v. Salerno*, 481 U.S. 739, 755 (1987). Notwithstanding that statement, however, many defendants today are held in jail pending trial. This is because, although the Constitution prohibits pretrial *punishment*, it allows for pretrial detention to the extent necessary to secure a defendant's appearance at trial or for defendants "who are found after an adversary hearing to pose a threat to the safety of individuals or to the community which no condition of release can dispel." *Id.*

In the United States, the primary method for securing a defendant's appearance at trial is money bail. At a bail hearing, a judge can order a defendant released on his own recognizance, set bail, or deny bail entirely. It is rare for a judge to find that a defendant poses a significant enough flight risk or threat to the community to deny bail. Instead, most defendants are given the chance to be released pending trial if they can afford to pay bail, which is set by the judge. To get out of jail before trial, a defendant must post the full amount with the court. In most jurisdictions, there is also an option to pay a percentage of the full amount to a bail bondsman who in turn posts the full amount with the court. Even if the defendant makes all of his court appearances and is ultimately acquitted, the bondsman keeps the money paid to him as a fee.

Many defendants cannot afford to pay bail or a bondsman, and must stay in jail awaiting trial as a result. The imposition of unaffordable bail is so widespread that "[t]he majority of individuals in our nation's jails are unconvicted people." Shima Baradaran Baughman, *Dividing Bail Reform*, 105 Iowa L. Rev. 947, 1024 (2020). (Note that this data point is specific to jails — jails typically house people awaiting trial and inmates who have been convicted of misdemeanors, whereas prisons typically house inmates who have been convicted of felonies.) This causes an obvious hardship for defendants who are jailed while awaiting trial solely as a result of their inability to pay bail. The system is also quite costly to taxpayers, who pay to house pretrial detainees.

## The Effect of Pretrial Detention on Case Outcomes

A defendant's ability to make bail has a significant impact on other stages of the proceedings. A number of studies have found that "offenders who are detained during pretrial proceedings are more likely to be convicted, are less likely to have their charges reduced, and are likely to have longer sentences than those who were released before trial." Thanithia Billings, *Private Interest, Public Sphere: Eliminating the Use of Commercial Bail Bondsmen in the Criminal Justice System*, 57 B.C. L. Rev. 1337, 1343 (2016).

The relationship between a defendant's ability to make bail and his leverage in plea negotiations is especially pronounced. Indeed, for some defendants who cannot afford to make bail, the quickest path to be released from jail is to plead guilty. A 2017 Human Rights Watch study of six California counties, for example, found that "70% to 80% of all misdemeanor or non-serious felony defendants plead guilty and were released before their first possible court date. This suggests that California is coercing people into giving up their right to contest their cases by giving them an ugly choice — if you assert your innocence, you stay in jail; if you plead guilty, you go home." John Raphling, *Plead Guilty, Go Home. Plead Not Guilty, Stay in Jail*, L.A. Times, May 17, 2017.

In recent years, a number of states have taken steps to reform their money bail system to try to address these concerns. In 2017, for example, New Jersey implemented a law that eliminated bail for many defendants through the use of a risk assessment tool. "Instead of the old bail system, New Jersey now has a non-monetary risk assessment approach aimed at determining who actually represents a threat to the community; it includes various reporting requirements for defendants, assuming they're considered low enough risk to be released. Whether a person can front money to cover a bail bond is no longer a factor when determining if he or she will remain in jail until trial." Scott Shackford, *Plunge in Pretrial Detention Follows Bail Reforms in New Jersey*, Reason.com Hit & Run Blog (July 28, 2017, 1:45 p.m.), http://reason.com/blog/2017/07/28/plunge-in-pretrial-jail-detention-follow. The results in New Jersey thus far "have been promising. Detention rates have plummeted, courts have almost entirely forgone financial conditions, and pretrial rearrest and appearance rates have remained steady." Sandra G. Mayson, *Detention by Any Other Name*, 69 Duke L.J. 1643, 1673 (2020). For now, New Jersey's approach is the exception and not the rule. Most jurisdictions continue to rely on the traditional money bail system.

## 4. Plea Bargaining

In law school courses, criminal trials and appellate decisions take center stage. In practice, the overwhelming majority of criminal cases never go to trial. Instead, they end in a guilty plea or dismissal. As the Supreme Court has put it, "criminal justice today is for the most part a system of pleas, not a system of trials. Ninety-seven percent of federal convictions and ninety-four percent of state convictions are the result of guilty pleas." *Lafler v. Cooper*, 566 U.S. 156, 169-70 (2012).

Plea bargaining is thus of central importance to the criminal justice system. The widespread use of plea bargaining is not without its critics, however, who argue that a system of pleas risks unjust outcomes and is inconsistent with the vision of the Founding Fathers. The Framers saw the jury trial as critical to the criminal process, "not only as a truth-seeking mechanism and a means of achieving fairness, but also as a shield against tyranny." Jed S. Rakoff, *Why Innocent People Plead Guilty*, N.Y. Rev. Books, Nov. 20, 2014. In contrast to public trials where jurors decide guilt or innocence, plea bargains are "negotiated behind closed doors and with no judicial oversight. The outcome is very largely determined by the prosecutor alone." *Id.* Proponents of plea bargaining counter that it allows the government to efficiently process cases and rewards defendants who are willing to accept blame and admit to their crime.

Whether or not plea bargaining is desirable, it is now a well-entrenched part of criminal justice system. Prosecutors will often offer a plea deal even in cases where the evidence of guilt is overwhelming. Because prosecutor offices only have the resources to take a relatively small percentage of cases to trial, avoiding trial provides a benefit to the government regardless of the strength of the case. In cases where the evidence of guilt is less strong, a prosecutor may try to account for that uncertainty by offering a more favorable plea deal. Note that this dynamic could contribute to wrongful convictions since the more favorable the plea offer, the greater the risk that it might incentivize an innocent person to plead guilty. Sometimes prosecutors may take other factors into consideration in plea negotiations, such as whether there are extenuating circumstances that make the defendant deserving (in the eyes of the prosecutor) of a lighter punishment. And, of course, prosecutors can use plea offers to incentivize the defendant's cooperation in other investigations or prosecutions.

From the defense perspective, defendants have the absolute right to a jury trial. But if a defendant is open to accepting a plea deal, it is the defense attorney's job to try to negotiate the best deal possible, and to advise the client about the risks and benefits of going to trial versus accepting the prosecutor's offer.

## 5. The Trial

Even though only a small segment of criminal cases go to trial, criminal trials and appeals remain a focal point in the criminal justice system. Plea bargaining decisions are influenced by the chances of a conviction at trial. And the odds of success at trial are influenced in part by appellate court decisions interpreting the statute the defendant has been charged with violating. Of course, substantive criminal law is only one part of the criminal trial process. The rules of evidence and criminal procedure are also essential components. Factors entirely divorced from legal doctrine, such as an attorney's ability to present a compelling narrative and to connect with the jury, also come into play.

The best way to learn about criminal trials is to go watch one. Trials are open to the public and chances are there is a courthouse not far from you. Those with an interest in practicing criminal law would be especially well served by spending a few hours watching court.

For purposes of understanding criminal law doctrine, it is not necessary to visit court or to study the trial process in detail. There are, however, two particular features of criminal trials that provide especially important context for learning about substantive criminal law: the proof beyond a reasonable doubt standard and the role of juries and jury instructions.

### *Proof Beyond a Reasonable Doubt*

To win a conviction, the prosecution must prove the defendant's guilt **beyond a reasonable doubt**. The reasonable doubt standard, which is rooted in the Constitution's Due Process Clause, is a much higher burden of proof than the preponderance of the evidence standard used in civil cases.

Although the reasonable doubt standard is a bedrock principle of criminal law, courts have some flexibility when it comes to explaining the concept to the jury. There is no single authoritative definition of the term, and the standard has not been translated into a mathematical formulation. Instead, courts have developed jury instructions that describe the standard in a way that connotes its seriousness.

Often, definitions of reasonable doubt employ the concept of moral certainty. For instance, consider this excerpt from a jury instruction that the Supreme Court held to be an acceptable definition of the standard:

> Reasonable doubt is defined as follows: It is not mere possible doubt; because everything related to human affairs, and depending on moral evidence, is open to some possible or imaginary doubt. It is that state of the case which, after the entire comparison and consideration of all the evidence, leaves the minds of the jurors in that condition that they cannot say they feel an abiding conviction, to a moral certainty, of the truth of the charge.

*Victor v. Nebraska,* 511 U.S. 1, 7 (1994).

Because every element of every crime must be proven beyond a reasonable doubt, any assessment of the merits of a criminal case must be mindful of the reasonable doubt standard. If a defendant can raise a reasonable doubt about his guilt, he is entitled to an acquittal. In some cases, the defense may home in on a single element of the crime and argue that it has not been proven. A defendant charged with arson might concede he started the fire but argue that there is insufficient proof that he did so with the intent to damage the building, for example. In other cases, the defense theory may have little to do with the individual elements of the crime, such as where the defendant argues that the police arrested the wrong person and someone else committed the crime. In everyday conversation, most people would refer to both of these examples as defenses. Technically, they are not quite defenses but rather arguments that the prosecutor has failed to meet her burden of proving guilt. In both examples, the defense position is that the prosecutor failed to prove every fact necessary to win a conviction beyond a reasonable doubt.

The lay of the land is different with respect to affirmative defenses like insanity, duress, and so forth. Many jurisdictions allocate the burden of proof to the defendant for at least some affirmative defenses, an approach that the Supreme Court has held to be constitutional. See Ben W. Studdard & Michael A. Arndt, *Georgia's Safe Harbor Ruling for Affirmative Defenses in Criminal Cases Should Be Revisited,* 68 Mercer L. Rev. 35, 46-47 (2016) (providing a comparison between states with respect to the burden of proof for affirmative defenses).

### The Jury's Role and Jury Instructions

In Criminal Law courses, students are often asked to assess the guilt or innocence of a hypothetical criminal defendant. But prosecutors and defense lawyers do not decide a defendant's guilt at trial. Nor do judges, except for in the case of bench trials, which are comparatively rare. Instead, the jury is responsible for deciding whether or not a defendant is guilty. To do this, the jury must make factual determinations based on the evidence before it and then apply the law to the facts.

Jury instructions are the vehicle for communicating the relevant legal rules that govern a case to the jurors. Typically, jurisdictions develop model (also sometimes called pattern) jury instructions based on statutes and case law. Jury instructions cover a wide range of topics, from evidentiary rules to the prohibition on jurors against searching for information about the case online until after they have rendered their verdict. Most relevant to this course, jury instructions convey the substance of the criminal law to jurors. They provide jurors with the elements of the charged offense(s) as contained in the criminal code, information about the prosecutor's burden of proof (see **Exhibit 2.2**), and more. The holdings from appellate court decisions are also sometimes translated into jury instructions. For example, if the Supreme Court of Nebraska were to issue an opinion on the meaning of the term "damage" in its arson statute, Nebraska jurors might be instructed on that interpretation in future arson trials.

Jurors take an oath to fairly consider the evidence and to follow the law. But their deliberations are held in private, without the involvement of judges or attorneys. If the jury is confused about a particular instruction, the foreperson can send

---

**EXHIBIT 2.2** **Jury Instruction on Reasonable Doubt from a 2016 California Criminal Trial**

### 220. Reasonable Doubt

---

The fact that a criminal charge has been filed against the defendant is not evidence that the charge is true. You must not be biased against the defendant just because he has been arrested, charged with a crime, or brought to trial.

A defendant in a criminal case is presumed to be innocent. This presumption requires that the People prove a defendant guilty beyond a reasonable doubt. Whenever I tell you the People must prove something, I mean they must prove it beyond a reasonable doubt.

Proof beyond a reasonable doubt is proof that leaves you with an abiding conviction that the charge is true. The evidence need not eliminate all possible doubt because everything in life is open to some possible or imaginary doubt.

In deciding whether the People have proved their case beyond a reasonable doubt, you must impartially compare and consider all the evidence that was received throughout the entire trial. Unless the evidence proves the defendant guilty beyond a reasonable doubt, he is entitled to an acquittal and you must find him not guilty.

---

Requested by Plaintiff/Defendant
Requested by Stipulation
Given/Given as Modified
Withdrawn
Refused-Reason:_____

PAULA S. ROSENSTEIN

a note to the judge asking for clarification. Otherwise, once deliberations begin, the jury is on its own. This process allows jurors to more freely debate the evidence as they deliberate. But it also means there is no guarantee that the jury will correctly apply the law. Without judicial oversight of deliberations, if the jury misunderstands an instruction there is no mechanism for identifying and correcting the problem before a verdict has been rendered. Appeals provide some checks on the jury's decision making. In a criminal case, if the jury votes to convict despite insufficient evidence of guilt, an appellate court can reverse the conviction, although the standard of review for a sufficiency of the evidence claim is difficult to satisfy. If the jury chooses to acquit someone who seems obviously guilty, the decision is unreviewable because the Fifth Amendment's Double Jeopardy Clause bars retrial after an acquittal. This is true even if after the acquittal, jurors reveal that they thought the defendant was guilty but voted to acquit because they believe the law is unjust, a phenomenon known as jury nullification. If the jury is hopelessly deadlocked and cannot agree on a verdict, the trial court will declare a hung jury, in which case the defendant can be retried without running afoul of double jeopardy principles.

## 6. Sentencing

If the defendant pleads guilty or the jury returns a guilty verdict, the court will decide on a sentence. Typically, before imposing a sentence, the court will hold a sentencing hearing at which the prosecution and defense can present arguments. Of course, in the case of a guilty plea, the court's sentencing choices might be constrained by the terms of the plea agreement.

The rules that control sentencing decisions differ significantly from one jurisdiction to the next. Unlike the law of crimes and defenses, where many of today's statutes share roots in the common law or the Model Penal Code, there is not a body of sentencing law that spans jurisdictions. Even among states with sentencing systems that are similar in broad strokes, variations in the specific factors that control a defendant's sentence and the sentencing ranges themselves mean that knowledge about one state's sentencing laws is unlikely to be transferrable to other states. A lawyer who is familiar with general criminal law principles can read the facts of a drug possession case and make an informed prediction about the likelihood that the defendant could be found guilty before reading the statute and relevant case law in the jurisdiction where the case is being prosecuted. Because sentencing schemes are so different from state to state, however, it is not possible to make an informed prediction about what sort of sentence that defendant would receive without a firm understanding of that jurisdiction's sentencing laws and practices.

Until the late 1970s, sentencing in the United States was a "highly discretionary system" in which federal and state trial judges "had nearly unfettered discretion to impose upon defendants any sentence from within the broad statutory ranges provided for criminal offenses; parole officials likewise possessed unfettered discretion to decide precisely when offenders were to be allowed to leave prison." Douglas A. Berman, *Reconceptualizing Sentencing*, 2005 U. Chi. Legal F. 1, 3. This open-ended approach to sentencing was based in large part on the idea that judges and parole boards were in the best position to tailor punishments based on the specifics of the crime and the offender.

In the 1960s and 1970s, a series of studies revealed that this discretionary system sometimes resulted in troubling sentencing disparities for similarly situated defendants based on factors like race and socioeconomic status. During the same time period, there was also a growing concern among law-and-order politicians and activists that some judges were too lenient when it came to sentencing. In combination, these two lines of thought generated bipartisan interest in proposals to make sweeping changes to criminal sentencing.

The forces interested in bringing more uniformity to criminal sentencing united around proposals that would take the kind of considerations judges had previously weighed according to their own views (the defendant's criminal history, his degree of involvement in the offense, etc.) and translate them into a set of sentencing guidelines that could be applied consistently in every case. As a result of this effort, the federal government and many states adopted sentencing guidelines systems in some form or fashion in the 1970s and 1980s. Federal sentencing is rooted in a set of comprehensive advisory guidelines. The federal sentencing guidelines look at a defendant's "offense level" and "criminal history" to set an initial sentencing range, which might then be adjusted up or down based on a variety of factors, such as whether the defendant accepted responsibility for her crime. State sentencing schemes vary as far as how much guidance and discretion they give to courts. In some states, sentencing is based on a detailed guidelines scheme similar to the federal system. Other states leave it to the judge to weigh various factors at sentencing, with relatively minimal direction. In California, for example, judges can typically choose between three different potential sentences — referred to as the lower term, middle term, and upper term — for a given offense, but they have very little discretion beyond that. Complicating matters even more, policies regarding the availability of probation or that provide an opportunity for early release — for example, parole and good-time credits — might be available in one state but not another.

## 7. Criminal Appeals

If the jury returns a guilty verdict, the defendant has the right to appeal. Many criminal appeals are based on issues that are unrelated to criminal law doctrine, such as the trial court's ruling on an evidentiary issue or its sentencing decision. The two most common types of appellate arguments that relate to criminal law doctrine are challenges to jury instructions and to the sufficiency of the evidence. Most of the cases in this book involve one or both of these types of appellate arguments.

As discussed above, jury instructions convey the legal rules that apply in a case to the jury. Where a statute is arguably ambiguous on some point, the defense and prosecution may propose alternate jury instructions to the trial court based on their interpretation of the statute. If the trial court rules in the prosecution's favor, the defendant can take his argument up on appeal. Appellate courts review these sorts of legal claims *de novo*, meaning that they do not give any deference to the trial court's interpretation. Appellate decisions on the meaning of a statutory term bind lower courts within that jurisdiction and influence how courts will instruct juries in future cases.

In an appeal based on the sufficiency of the evidence, the defendant's position is that the prosecutor's evidence was legally insufficient to support the conviction. When reviewing a sufficiency of the evidence challenge, appellate courts view the evidence in the light most favorable to the verdict. This means that the court assumes that the jury resolved any factual disputes in the evidence in the prosecution's favor. The court then asks whether a reasonable trier of fact could find guilt beyond a reasonable doubt. Appellate decisions regarding sufficiency of the evidence are helpful to lawyers in assessing the strength of future cases. If the facts of a case are similar to one where an appellate court found the evidence insufficient, the prosecution is more likely to offer the defendant a favorable plea deal in order to avoid trial and may even consider dropping the charges entirely. If the facts are nearly identical, a defense lawyer might be able to succeed in a motion to dismiss the charges before the case goes to trial. Although appeals court rulings on sufficiency of the evidence claims can help guide lawyers in plea negotiations and pretrial motions, they are typically less useful at trial. This is because evidentiary rules do not allow lawyers to present and argue court opinions to the jury. Lawyers can, however, request jury instructions based on appellate decisions regarding the sufficiency of the evidence in some cases.

## Chapter Summary

- Criminal law is statutory and legislatures are responsible for writing the statutes that define crimes. Although every jurisdiction's criminal code is unique, many criminal statutes are rooted in the common law, the Model Penal Code, or another common source such as the Uniform Controlled Substances Act.
- The days of the common law model of judge-made criminal law are gone, but courts still play an important role in interpreting criminal statutes. Appellate decisions that define the meaning of a particular statutory term guide lower courts and are often translated into jury instructions.
- Criminal offenses are made up of one or more elements, each of which the prosecutor must prove beyond a reasonable doubt in order to win a conviction. Elements typically fall into one of four categories: (1) act (*actus reus*); (2) mental state (*mens rea*); (3) causation (results elements); and (4) attendant circumstances. Nearly every crime includes at least one *actus reus* and *mens rea* element, while causal and attendant circumstances elements are only present in some offenses.
- For the act element of a crime to be satisfied, courts generally require the act to have been a voluntary one, meaning a volitional act. Similarly, omissions — meaning the failure to act — do not give rise to criminal liability except in certain limited circumstances.

- States cannot constitutionally punish people based on their status alone. As a result, while it is constitutional to criminalize illegal drug possession, a statute making it a crime to "be addicted" to an illegal drug would be unconstitutional.
- The most frequently used mental state terms are intent, purpose, knowledge, recklessness, and negligence. A statute that does not include a *mens rea* element is referred to as a strict liability statute.
- When an offense includes a causal (results) element, the government must typically prove that the defendant's actions were both the but-for and proximate cause of the prohibited result.

## Applying the Concepts

1. Recall the abridged version of Nebraska's arson statute discussed throughout Section B of this chapter, which provides: "A person commits arson in the first degree if he or she intentionally damages a building . . . by starting a fire . . . when another person is present in the building at the time and . . . the actor knows that fact[.]" Neb. Rev. Stat. § 28-502.

    On the Fourth of July, Danny invites some friends to her house for a party. During the party, Danny sets off fireworks in her backyard. The packaging for the fireworks contains the following warning: DO NOT LIGHT WITHIN 100 FEET OF A HOUSE. Danny reads the warning, but disregards it. The fireworks hit and start a fire that damages part of Danny's house.

    Can Danny be convicted of arson under Nebraska's statute?

2. Derrick's favorite football team won the Super Bowl. To celebrate, Derrick shot a gun in the air from the top of his apartment building in a densely populated area. In his excitement, it never occurred to Derrick that firing his gun into the air was dangerous. Tragically, Derrick's bullet struck Vivian, who was walking her dog a few blocks away, killing her instantly. Which of the following best describes Derrick's mental state with respect to Vivian's death?

    a. Derrick acted purposely.
    b. Derrick acted knowingly.
    c. Derrick acted recklessly.
    d. Derrick acted negligently.

3. Dominic and Vince were members of rival organized crime organizations. Dominic decided to kill Vince by wiring explosives to Vince's car. One night, Dominic went to Vince's condominium, found Vince's car, and installed the explosives. The explosives were set to detonate as soon as Vince turned the key to his ignition. Dominic knew there was a possibility that the explosion might also kill a passerby but he decided this was his best chance to kill Vince without being caught. The next morning, Vince turned on his car and was killed by Dominic's explosives. Vince's neighbor Sam, who was

getting into the car next to Victor's, was also killed. Which of the following best describes Dominic's mental state with respect to Vince's death and Sam's death?

**a.** Dominic acted purposely with respect to Vince's death and knowingly with respect to Sam's death.

**b.** Dominic acted purposely with respect to Vince's death and recklessly with respect to Sam's death.

**c.** Dominic acted purposely with respect to both Vince's and Sam's deaths.

**d.** Dominic acted knowingly with respect to both Vince's and Sam's deaths.

**4.** Denise is a convenience store worker in a state that has a strict liability statute regarding the sale of alcohol to minors. One day, Denise sells a six-pack of beer to Paul. Before selling the beer to Paul, Denise asks for Paul's state identification. Paul produces a state identification that indicates he is 22 years old. Denise scans the identification using a verification device, which appears to confirm that the identification is valid. Despite the verification device's results, Paul is actually 19 years old. His identification is a sophisticated forgery that tricked the verification device. If Denise is prosecuted for violating her state's sale-to-minors statute, will she be able to use her mistaken belief that Paul was 22 as a defense?

## Criminal Law in Practice

**1.** At the first game of the 2016 National Hockey League Stanley Cup Finals between the Pittsburgh Penguins and the Nashville Predators, a Nashville fan threw a catfish onto the ice. Predators fans have a tradition of throwing catfish onto the ice at home games for good luck. But in this case, the game was being held in Pittsburgh, and the fan threw the catfish onto the ice in the middle of the second period, requiring the game to be temporarily stopped. The fan was removed from the arena and arrested on suspicion of violating the following statutes:

> **Disorderly conduct.** A person is guilty of disorderly conduct if, with intent to cause public inconvenience, annoyance or alarm, or recklessly creating a risk thereof, he: (1) engages in fighting or threatening, or in violent or tumultuous behavior; (2) makes unreasonable noise; (3) uses obscene language, or makes an obscene gesture; or (4) creates a hazardous or physically offensive condition by any act which serves no legitimate purpose of the actor. This offense is graded as a summary offense, meaning as less serious than a misdemeanor.

> **Possessing instruments of crime.** A person commits a misdemeanor of the first degree if he possesses any instrument of crime with intent to employ it criminally.
> "Instrument of crime" means any of the following: (1) Anything specially made or specially adapted for criminal use. (2) Anything used for criminal purposes and possessed by the actor under circumstances not manifestly appropriate for lawful uses it may have.

**Disrupting meetings and processions.** A person commits a misdemeanor of the third degree if, with intent to prevent or disrupt a lawful meeting, procession or gathering, he disturbs or interrupts it.

a. You are an Assistant District Attorney in Pennsylvania. Which of these statutes, if any, do you think there is cause to believe the fan has violated?

b. Assume for purposes of this question that there is cause to believe the fan has violated one or more of the statutes. Would you use your prosecutorial discretion to file charges? Why or why not?

c. Assume for purposes of this question that your office has charged the fan with violating these statutes and that you believe the odds of obtaining a conviction at trial are very strong. The maximum penalty is a one-year term of imprisonment. Your office has left plea negotiations to your discretion, which means that you can offer the fan an agreement with a stipulated sentence of community service, decline to make any offer at all, or anything in between. What initial offer, if any, would you make to the defendant? Would you be willing to consider a sentence below your initial offer if the defendant declined it?

2. This chapter uses an abridged version of Nebraska's first-degree arson statute to illustrate the different types of elements of criminal offenses. Look up the arson statute in your state, including each of the different degrees of arson. (If you are in Nebraska, look up the arson statute in neighboring Iowa.)

a. What are the differences between how your state and Nebraska define first-degree arson, according to the abridged version of Nebraska's statute presented earlier in this chapter?

b. What factors differentiate first-degree arson in your state from the other degrees of arson?

3. Exhibit 2.2 on page 83 presents a jury instruction explaining the beyond a reasonable doubt standard from a 2016 California jury trial. Search to see if your state has a model jury instruction (called pattern or uniform jury instructions in some states) for the beyond a reasonable doubt standard. (If you are in California or if you are unable to find a model instruction for your state, look up a neighboring state's uniform jury instruction for reasonable doubt.) How does your state's model jury instruction compare to the instruction in Exhibit 2.2? Which instruction do you think does a better job at conveying the standard, and why?

# Property Offenses

The first two chapters of this book introduced the theories of punishment, the sources of criminal law, the elements of crimes, and the criminal trial process. This chapter begins our coverage of individual criminal offenses, with those that fall in the category of property crimes.

As measured by their prevalence on criminal court dockets, the category of property crimes is arguably the most important in all of criminal law. In 2018, the Federal Bureau of Investigation recorded nearly 7.5 million property offenses. Homicides, rapes, and aggravated assaults combined totaled an estimated 963,000 in the same year.

The offenses covered in this chapter are united by their connection to property; each offense exists at least in part to protect property interests. Some of the crimes covered in this chapter also implicate other concerns — robbery is a crime that involves violence; burglary and arson are concerned with protecting security inside of dwellings — but punishing interference with property interests is integral to all. This chapter starts with coverage of the following theft offenses: larceny, robbery, embezzlement, false pretenses, and extortion. The chapter concludes with two non-theft property offenses, burglary and arson.

## A. THEFT CRIMES

Theft "claims more victims and causes greater economic injury, and it may well be committed by a larger number of offenders, than any other criminal offense." Stuart P. Green, 13 Ways to Steal a Bicycle 1 (2012). At their most basic level, theft crimes are usually quite intuitive. After all, stealing "entails one of the most basic wrongs a person can do to another." *Id.* But as the material that follows will reveal, theft offenses can

## Key Concepts

- What distinguishes larceny, embezzlement, and false pretenses from each other?
- What is the difference between robbery and extortion through the use of violence?
- How and why has burglary expanded from its definition at common law?
- In what circumstances is it appropriate to use the criminal law to enforce property interests? When should disputes over property be left exclusively to civil remedies, such as breach of contract?

also sometimes involve tricky, and seemingly arbitrary, distinctions. Even in cases where it is clear that the defendant is guilty of theft, it is not always easy to determine exactly *which* theft offense he committed.

This section covers the five major theft crimes: larceny, robbery, embezzlement, false pretenses, and extortion. Although all of these offenses criminalize stealing someone else's property, each applies to a specific type of theft. We begin with larceny, which is the oldest and most common type of theft crime. The section then turns to robbery, which is in effect an aggravated larceny. Embezzlement and false pretenses — both created by the British Parliament in the 1700s to fill perceived gaps in the crime of larceny — come next. Our coverage of thefts concludes with extortion, which makes it a crime to obtain property through the use of certain kinds of wrongful threats.

## 1. Larceny

Dating back to the medieval period, larceny is the offense that applies to the typical non-violent theft of personal property. A person who hotwires a car parked on the street or who steals clothes from a department store by sneaking them into a backpack has committed larceny. The common law defined **larceny** as the trespassory taking and carrying away of the personal property of another with the intent to permanently deprive the person of possession of the property. Each of these elements is considered in turn below.

### *Trespassory*

Larceny criminalizes taking personal property by trespass. This does not mean that larceny is limited to thefts that occur when a defendant is trespassing on another person's land. Rather, trespass has a specific meaning in the context of theft crimes.

A trespassory taking is a taking possession of the property "without the property owner's consent." *People v. Williams*, 57 Cal. 4th 776, 783 (2013). In most cases, this element is straightforward. The victim's testimony will easily demonstrate that the defendant who hotwired a car or who stuffed clothes into his backpack at a department store did not have the owner's permission to take the property.

The element of taking property by trespass can become complicated in cases where a property owner is fraudulently induced to let a defendant take possession of her property. Consider, for example, the facts of the influential larceny case of *The King v. Pear*, 1 Leach 212 (1779). Pear rented a horse from a man named Finch. At the time of the rental, Pear planned to ride the horse to a different town and sell it. But, of course, Pear did not disclose this plan to Finch. Pear was caught not long after selling Finch's horse. Is this larceny? At first glance, it would seem that Pear did not commit a *trespassory* (i.e., nonconsensual) taking because Finch allowed Pear to take the horse. To get around this problem, the law provides that "a property owner who is fraudulently induced to transfer possession of the property to another does not do so with free and genuine consent." *Williams*, 57 Cal. 4th at 783. Put another way, Finch consented to giving Pear temporary physical custody of the horse as a rental. Finch never consented to giving Pear possession of the horse so that Pear could sell it. Because Pear had not obtained Finch's genuine consent, he took the horse by trespass and was guilty of larceny. This type of larceny — where the trespassory taking is accomplished by fraudulently inducing someone to turn over possession of personal property — is often called **larceny by trick**. Larceny by trick is not a separate offense. The term simply refers to a larceny where the trespassory element is accomplished by fraud.

As we will see later, distinguishing larceny by trick from the crimes of false pretenses and embezzlement is not always an easy task. For now, it is enough to know that a trespassory taking occurs when the defendant takes possession of property without the possessor's genuine consent.

## Taking and Carrying Away

The *actus reus* of larceny is taking and carrying away the property.

The taking component, also referred to as caption, is rarely contested. It requires that the defendant take "possession of, or dominion over the property, for an appreciable moment of time." *Edmonds v. State*, 70 Ala. 8, 9 (1881).

The carrying away component, also referred to as asportation, is likewise seldom at issue. It "is satisfied by any movement of the property, however slight. It is immaterial how far the property is moved — much less whether it is removed from the owner's premises — so long as it is moved in the slightest degree from the place where a defendant finds it." *State v. Spears*, 223 Or. App. 675, 698 (2008). As a result, a shoplifter has committed the *actus reus* of larceny as soon as she starts moving the property into her backpack. By holding the item in her hands, she has exercised dominion over it, and by moving it toward her backpack, she has moved it the slightest degree from the place where she found it.

## Personal Property of Another

Larceny criminalizes the theft of personal property. This means a few categories of property are excluded from the offense: real estate; labor and services; and other intangibles, like sneaking into a movie or a concert. Apart from these types of property, any item that has "a corporeal existence, that is, . . . something the physical presence, quantity, or quality of which is detectable or measurable by the senses or some mechanical contrivance" may be the subject of larceny. *People v. Ashworth*, 222 N.Y.S. 24, 28 (App. Div. 1927).

The property must also belong to someone else. In the typical larceny case, such as a defendant who shoplifts from a store, this requirement is straightforward. There are two important circumstances where determining whether property is property "of another" can be more difficult, however. They both arise from the fact that larceny criminalizes taking property that someone else has a superior claim to *possess*.

First, because larceny is concerned with possession, it is possible for a person to commit larceny by taking property she owns if someone else has lawful possession of it. For example, if Dave rents his car to Victor for one month, Victor has lawful possession of Dave's car for that month. Dave can be guilty of larceny of his own car if, during the rental period, Dave takes and carries the car away by trespass with the intent to deprive Victor of the car for the remainder of the rental period.

Second, larceny's focus on possession is key to distinguishing larceny from embezzlement. A defendant who misappropriates someone else's personal property that she already lawfully possesses is not guilty of larceny. She might be guilty of embezzlement, however. This is discussed in more detail below in connection with the coverage of embezzlement.

### Intent to Permanently Deprive

The *mens rea* element of larceny is the intent to permanently deprive the possessor of the personal property in question. Notice that a person does not need to intend to keep the property for his own benefit to be guilty of larceny. The required intent is to permanently deprive the rightful possessor of the property at the time of the taking. As a result, the *mens rea* element is satisfied whether the defendant took property with the intent to keep it, sell it, or throw it in the trash. The defendant must act with this intent at the time he takes possession of the property. Embedded in this element is the requirement that the defendant know the property he is taking belongs to someone else. After all, if the defendant takes property that he thinks is abandoned, he has not acted with the intent to deprive another of property. The same is true if a defendant takes property that he thinks is his own — if he accidentally takes a jacket that looks like his when leaving a party, for example.

The next two cases explore two features of the *mens rea* element of larceny: the extent to which a defendant's mistaken belief that property has been abandoned can constitute a defense and the meaning of permanent deprivation.

**Case Preview**

## Commonwealth v. Liebenow

To commit larceny, a defendant must intend to permanently deprive another person of property at the time of the taking. *Liebenow* addresses the question of what rule should apply when a larceny defendant claims that he mistakenly thought that the property he took was abandoned. Is a defendant's honest belief that the property was abandoned enough to defeat the *mens rea* element of larceny? Or must the defendant's belief also be objectively reasonable?

As you read the decision, consider the following questions:

1. What is the practical significance of the standard that the defendant proposes and the standard that the prosecution proposes?
2. Why does the court rule in the defendant's favor?
3. If a defendant's honest belief is enough to constitute a defense to larceny, does that mean that every defendant who testifies that she honestly thought the property she took was abandoned is entitled to an acquittal? What part of the court's opinion, if any, addresses this potential concern?

# *Commonwealth v. Liebenow*
## 470 Mass. 151 (2014)

Duffly, J.

The defendant, who was in the business of collecting and selling scrap metal, was charged with larceny . . . in connection with his removal of two lengths of steel pipe from a construction site located on private property in Pittsfield. He was convicted of that charge following a jury-waived trial in the District Court. The conviction was affirmed by the Appeals Court in a divided opinion and we granted the defendant's petition for further appellate review.

The defendant claimed . . . at trial that he lacked the requisite specific intent to steal because he honestly, albeit mistakenly, believed that the property he removed from the site was abandoned. The judge, however, erroneously viewed the . . . defense as requiring proof that the defendant's belief was objectively reasonable. This misperception appears to have arisen from the conflation of two distinct concepts that have appeared over time in our jurisprudence: the concept of good faith belief, which is subjective, and the concept of reasonable belief, which is objective. We take this opportunity to resolve the resulting confusion.

Here, the defendant adequately raised the defense of honest belief that the items he took were abandoned, and it was the Commonwealth's burden to prove beyond a reasonable doubt that the defendant's subjective belief was not honestly held but, instead, was a pretense or sham. Therefore, the conviction must be vacated and the matter remanded for a new trial.

1. *Background.* We summarize the evidence that the judge, as fact finder, could have found to support the charge of larceny. We then summarize the evidence introduced by the defendant, in the light most favorable to him, that a fact finder could have found to conclude that the defendant honestly believed that the property was abandoned.

a. *Commonwealth's evidence.* On the morning of July 27, 2010, the defendant was driving around Pittsfield in his sport utility vehicle (SUV), in search of junk metal that he could sell. He drove onto Amy Court, a privately owned cul-de-sac, which was the site of a proposed twenty-six-unit condominium complex then in the process of being constructed. Several signs stating "no trespassing" and "private property" had been posted, construction had been completed on only one unit, and the construction site contained company trucks, construction equipment, and a "job" trailer. Construction company workers had stacked leftover lengths of steel pipe and steel plates, intended for use on other projects, in an area at the bottom of the cul-de-sac where there was no construction. The items had been placed behind a pile of top soil to keep them from view, so that the area would appear attractive to prospective purchasers of the lots, and there were no trash receptacles or discarded materials in sight.

Kenneth Lufkin, an employee of the developer, observed the defendant drive down to the end of the cul-de-sac. The defendant drove behind the pile of top soil and out of Lufkin's view, but Lufkin could hear what sounded like steel banging. Lufkin stopped the defendant as he was driving from the cul-de-sac toward the public street. When Lufkin asked the defendant what he was doing, the defendant said that he was just picking up some junk steel, and drove away. Lufkin turned around to see what was in the back of the SUV and saw several steel plates and lengths of steel pipe. He wrote down the defendant's license plate number, then contacted his employer and the police.

The defendant's vehicle subsequently was located at a junkyard that purchased scrap metal. [Officer James] Parise went to the junkyard and spoke with the defendant, who admitted that he had taken the items he had in his vehicle, but said that they had not come from Amy Court. The defendant agreed to accompany Parise to Amy Court. Lufkin identified the material in the back of the defendant's vehicle as items which had been taken from the Amy Court property, and the defendant returned the items.

b. *Evidence viewed favorably to defendant.* The defendant testified that he believed the construction debris and other items he had collected had been abandoned and did not belong to anyone. The defendant knew that people dumped trash at the end of Amy Court. During the mid-morning hours of July 27, the defendant drove his vehicle to the end of the Amy Court cul-de-sac in search of discarded metal items that had been left or dumped on a dirt trail leading into the woods which began at the end of the paved cul-de-sac. This was one of several places to which he drove that morning in search of junk metal.[3] The defendant was unaware of the no trespassing signs, and did not know that Amy Court was then a private road. The defendant made no effort to conceal what he was doing. He had driven to that location previously to collect junk metal; and he conducted his search for scrap metal during daylight hours. The defendant drove from the paved road onto a dirt trail leading into the woods, and saw two lengths of steel pipe, which he picked up and placed in his SUV, along with other items.

The defendant was leaving the area when he encountered Lufkin, who had driven down the road to meet him. The defendant stopped his vehicle, and Lufkin accused him of dumping [trash onto the vacant lot area]. When the defendant replied that he was "just picking up junk steel," Lufkin said he did not have a problem with that, and the defendant drove off. Later, when he was met by [Officer] Parise at the junkyard, the defendant admitted taking the steel pipes, and said he believed they had been abandoned. He also testified, as he had told Parise, that there were steel plates in his vehicle that did not come from Amy Court. At Parise's request, the defendant voluntarily returned to Amy Court.

c. *Closing arguments.* In closing, defense counsel . . . maintained that, because the defendant "honestly thought he was entitled to have" what he believed was abandoned property, and returned it when it was claimed by the owner, the Commonwealth failed "to prove[ ] beyond a reasonable doubt that [the defendant] intended to permanently deprive [the owner] of the property."

The prosecutor argued that, even if the defendant's belief were an honest one, that belief also had to be objectively reasonable. He pointed to evidence that the construction materials had been hidden behind a pile of top soil, that signs stating the

---

[3] Officer James Parise of the Pittsfield police department testified that, at the time he encountered the defendant at the junk yard, "[t]here was all kinds of junk in the back of [the defendant's] vehicle; not only stuff that was reported missing from the property, but just scrap metal in general." It is unclear from the record when these items were placed in the defendant's sport utility vehicle (SUV), and whether they were collected before or after the defendant left Amy Court.

area was private property had been posted on trees in the vicinity of the dirt pile, and that the defendant had admitted to taking the items from that area as support for the prosecutor's claim that the defendant's belief was not reasonable.

d. *Verdict.* The judge rejected the defendant's argument. In announcing his verdict, the judge stated that "the presence of the no trespassing sign puts [the defendant] on notice that the property was not for [him] to take. [The defendant's] honest belief at that point would not be relevant."

2. *Discussion.* To convict a defendant of larceny requires that the Commonwealth prove that a defendant took the personal property of another without the right to do so, and "with the specific intent to deprive the other of the property permanently."

It has been long established that the specific intent to steal is negated by a finding that a defendant held an honest, albeit mistaken, belief that he was entitled to the property he took. See, e.g., *Commonwealth v. Brisbois*, 281 Mass. 125, 128-29, 183 N.E. 168 (1932) (jury correctly instructed that, if defendant "honestly thought" he had legal right to remove wooden building, "then there was no criminal intent to steal").

[T]he United States Supreme Court held in *Morissette v. United States*, 342 U.S. 246, 271 (1952), that an honest, though mistaken, belief that property was abandoned is a defense to larceny.[8] Noting that stealing government property was a crime of specific intent, the Court held that evidence of a defendant's honest belief should have been presented to the jury, and reversed the defendant's conviction, stating:

> "[I]t is not apparent how [the defendant] could have knowingly or intentionally converted property that he did not know could be converted, as would be the case if it was in fact abandoned or if he truly believed it to be abandoned and unwanted property."

[The trial court's conclusion in this case that the defendant's mistaken belief must be reasonable rested on *Commonwealth v. White*, 5 Mass. App. Ct. 483 (1977). In *White*,] the Appeals Court stated that the jury must acquit a defendant of larceny if they find "that the defendant honestly *and reasonably* believed that the money he took from [the victim] represented a debt actually due from [the victim] to the defendant" (emphasis supplied). *Id.* at 488.

[Although the *White* court used the phrase "reasonably believed," it also] observed that the jury should have been instructed as the defendant had requested,[10] "because it was open to the jury to find on [the defendant's] testimony that he honestly believed that he was taking his own money from [another] and that if the jury had so found, they could not have found the requisite intent to steal and would have been obliged to acquit the defendant of larceny." *Commonwealth v. White, supra* at 486.

---

[8] The facts in *Morissette v. United States*, 342 U.S. 246 (1952), are quite similar to those here: the defendant, who collected and sold junk metal, found several spent bomb casings on an Air Force bombing range that was known to be good hunting grounds and was frequented by hunters. *Id.* at 247. Several signs stating "Danger–Keep Out–Bombing Range" were placed on the range. The defendant loaded the casings into his truck in broad daylight, and testified that he believed the property was abandoned. *Id.* at 247-48.

[10] The defendant had requested an instruction that, "[i]f the defendant believed that the money he had acquired from [the victim] was actually his money, [the] defendant is not guilty of a charge of larceny." *Commonwealth v. White, supra* at 485.

Based on the foregoing, we do not think that the Appeals Court in *Commonwealth v. White* intended to depart from the long-established principle that an honest belief need not be objectively reasonable to negate the specific intent required for larceny, despite its use of the phrase "honestly and reasonably believed." The discussion of the cases and authorities in *Commonwealth v. White* reflects that court's understanding of "[t]he rather simple rule that an honest mistake of fact or law is a defense when it negates a required mental element of the crime." W.R. LaFave & A.W. Scott, Criminal Law § 47, at 357 (1972). It is of some significance that the *White* court was not asked to focus specifically on the question whether reasonableness of belief was a concept separate from good faith belief, and reasonableness of the defendant's belief was neither raised nor discussed.

Evidence of reasonableness may, however, be considered by the jury to assist in their determination whether to credit a defendant's honest belief. "Neither juries nor judges are required to divorce themselves of common sense, but rather should apply to facts which they find proven such reasonable inferences as are justified in the light of their experience as to the natural inclinations of human beings." *United States v. Tejeda*, 974 F.2d 210, 213 (1st Cir. 1992). See also *Morissette v. United States*, 342 U.S. at 276, 72 S. Ct. 240 (considering evidence of defendant's awareness that "casings were on government property, his failure to seek any permission for their removal and his self-interest as a witness," jury could disbelieve his profession of innocent intent).

A defendant may raise an honest, yet mistaken, belief as an affirmative defense.[15] A defendant's honest belief that the property he took was abandoned constitutes an affirmative defense to larceny. Abandoned property is property "to which the owner 'has relinquished all right, title, claim, and possession, but without vesting it in any other person.'"

3. *Conclusion.* The judgment of conviction is vacated and set aside, and the matter is remanded to the District Court for further proceedings consistent with this opinion.

*So ordered.*

---

**Post-Case Follow-Up**

The impact of a defendant's mistake of fact on his mental state is a recurring question in criminal law. *Liebenow* takes up this issue in the context of larceny, which requires an intent to permanently deprive another person of possession of personal property. *Liebenow* holds that a defendant's honest but mistaken belief is a defense to larceny because it negates the *mens rea* of the offense. This is true even if the defendant's mistake was unreasonable. *Liebenow* helpfully illustrates this longstanding rule.

---

[15] Although we use the term affirmative defense, in this context the Commonwealth nonetheless bears the burden of proof because the defense addresses an element of the offense of larceny, the defendant's specific intent to steal. Once a defendant meets the burden of production, the burden of proof shifts to the Commonwealth to disprove the defense.

The case also shows how a single careless remark by an intermediate appellate court can sow confusion and lead other courts astray. As *Liebenow* explains, "it has been *long established* that the specific intent to steal is negated by a finding that a defendant held an honest, albeit mistaken, belief that he was entitled to the property he took." Despite this fact, the 1977 *White* decision included the phrase "reasonably believed" in its discussion of larceny, apparently by mistake. Enterprising prosecutors seized on the *White* court's error to convince other judges, including the trial court judge in *Liebenow*, to disregard the "long established" rule. It took a decision of the Massachusetts Supreme Judicial Court to set the record straight that it continues to adhere to the widely followed rule that "[a] defendant's honest belief that the property he took was abandoned constitutes a[] . . . defense to larceny."

The intent required to convict a defendant of larceny is the intent to permanently deprive the rightful possessor of his interest in the property. This means that borrowing someone else's personal property without his permission is not larceny. A person who takes someone else's bicycle without his permission intending to return it the next day, for example, would not be guilty of larceny. See, e.g., *People v. Brown*, 105 Cal. 66 (1894) (holding that taking a bicycle with from someone else's house with the intent to return it within a reasonable time is not larceny). Of course, a jury does not need to credit a defendant's testimony that he planned to return stolen property. Indeed, even if a fact finder believes the defendant *hoped* to be able to return property, a conviction may be warranted in certain circumstances. *Marsh v. Commonwealth* considers just this kind of case.

**Case Preview**

## *Marsh v. Commonwealth*

In *Marsh*, the defendant took his girlfriend's jewelry to a pawn shop and used it as collateral for a loan. Although the defendant claimed that he intended to pay back the loan and reclaim the jewelry, there was evidence to suggest he did not have the means to get all of the jewelry back. The issue before the court was whether the evidence was sufficient to support the trial court's guilty verdict.

As you read the decision, consider the following questions:

**1.** The court's opinion highlights evidence that the defendant "did not have the substantial ability to return the property" in support of his conviction. Why was this fact so important in the court's view?
**2.** What principles does the court identify that inform the meaning of the "permanently deprive" component of larceny?

# *Marsh v. Commonwealth*
## 57 Va. App. 645 (2011)

HUMPHREYS, J.

Bernard Chesley Marsh ("Marsh") was convicted in a bench trial of grand larceny, in violation of Code § 18.2-95, and was sentenced to four years incarceration with all but sixty days suspended. On appeal, Marsh argues that the trial court erred in finding the evidence sufficient to support his conviction of grand larceny. Specifically, he contends that he never intended to permanently deprive Rhonda Gazda of her property. For the following reasons, we disagree and affirm the trial court's conviction.

"Where the issue is whether the evidence is sufficient, we view the evidence in the light most favorable to the Commonwealth, granting to it all reasonable inferences fairly deducible therefrom." So viewed, the evidence is as follows.

On October 17, 2008, Marsh went to Gazda's apartment to attend a birthday party with her. Gazda, Marsh's girlfriend of approximately two years, was getting ready when she noticed she was missing a ring from her jewelry box along with some other items. She asked Marsh if he had taken the missing items. Marsh replied he had needed some quick cash so he had pawned the items,[1] but he would get the jewelry back when he got paid the next day.[2] They then attended the birthday party together. Upon returning to her apartment after the party, Gazda told Marsh she did not want him staying with her. After Marsh left, Gazda called the police, and reported the missing items as stolen property. Gazda testified that she never allowed Marsh to take items or pawn items before even though he had done so in March 2008, with some of the same pieces and had subsequently returned them.

Detective Richard Buisch, with the Fairfax County Police Department, became involved with the case when he came in contact with Gazda on an unrelated matter. Gazda informed Detective Buisch that she had reported the stolen property, and asked what had happened with regards to the report. Detective Buisch contacted Marsh, and made arrangements with him for the return of the items. Marsh returned some of the items that he had pawned to Detective Buisch, and informed him that he was trying to save up money to purchase the other items back. After giving Marsh two to three weeks to come up with the money to retrieve the rest of the items, Detective Buisch placed a hold on them when Marsh did not obtain the rest of the items, retrieved them from Vienna Jewelry and Estate Buyers in Vienna, Virginia, and returned them to Gazda.

Suzette Marsham, the manager of Vienna Jewelry and Estate Buyers, testified that Marsh had brought in jewelry on several occasions and used it as collateral for loans. She stated that using the jewelry as collateral was different than a sales

---

[1] The pawnshop receipts contain thirty-one pieces of jewelry that Marsh used as collateral for ten different loans.
[2] Marsh testified that he had been working as a self-employed carpentry contractor on a carpentry project for which he expected to receive $2,000 in four different installments. During September and October, this was his sole source of income, and he had already received one installment of $800, none of which he used to redeem the jewelry.

transaction because using the jewelry as collateral permitted the individual to come back and retrieve the jewelry.[4] Ms. Marsham testified that on one of the occasions when Marsh brought in jewelry, a couple of the transactions had been written up as sales transactions rather than as loan transactions with the jewelry as collateral. However, upon seeing the transactions were improperly written up, Marsh insisted that the items were not to be sold, and Ms. Marsham redid the paperwork to reflect that the transactions were loan transactions and not sales transactions. The receipts indicate that Marsh received $2,975 and that payments had not been received on some of the loans. Gazda testified that she thought the approximate value of the jewelry taken was $25,000.

Marsh took the stand at trial and testified that he had taken the items and pawned them to help carry him through a job he was working on. Marsh stated that he had initially needed approximately $500. When asked why he continued to pawn more items after he received that amount, he replied "[b]y then I was in a position where I was robbing Peter to pay Paul . . . [t]hat was Ms. Gazda to pay the shop." He also stated that he had informed Gazda he would get her items back when he was paid the next day. Marsh further testified that it was always his intent "to redeem [the jewelry] and give it back to her" as soon as he received his check.

At trial, Marsh made a motion to strike the charge against him, contending that the evidence was insufficient to prove he intended to permanently deprive Gazda of the jewelry. The trial court denied the motion, and found him guilty of grand larceny. Marsh now appeals to this Court.

In a challenge to the sufficiency of the evidence, . . . [t]he reviewing court . . . does not "ask itself whether *it* believes that the evidence at the trial established guilt beyond a reasonable doubt." Instead, the reviewing court asks whether "*any* rational trier of fact could have found the essential elements of the crime beyond a reasonable doubt."

"In Virginia, larceny is a common law crime. We have defined larceny as 'the wrongful or fraudulent taking of personal goods of some intrinsic value, belonging to another, without his assent, and with the intention to deprive the owner thereof permanently.'" Code § 18.2-95 defines grand larceny and provides, in pertinent part, that "[a]ny person who . . . (ii) commits simple larceny not from the person of another of goods and chattels of the value of $200 or more . . . shall be guilty of grand larceny. . . ."

"'The defendant's intent to steal must exist at the time the seized goods are moved.'" "The element of criminal intent may, and often must, be inferred from the facts and circumstances of the case, including the actions of the defendant and any statements made by him." "'[T]he very existence of a trespassory taking permits the inference (unless other circumstances negate it) that the taker intended to steal the property.'"

---

[4] The record is silent as to what would happen if Marsh was unable to pay the loan amount, if the jewelry could be sold after certain conditions had not been met (i.e. default on the loan or passage of time), or under what conditions Marsh would be able to get the jewelry back. However, each receipt contains the following language in the "Total of Payments" box: "Amount required to redeem pawn on Maturity Date."

However, "'[o]ne who takes another's property intending at the time he takes it to use it temporarily and then to return it unconditionally within a reasonable time — and having a substantial ability to do so — lacks the intent to steal required for larceny.'" "An intent to return, however, must be unconditional. Thus it is no defense to larceny that the taker intends to return the property only if he should receive a reward for its return, or only upon some other condition which he has no right to impose."

Marsh acknowledges that there was a trespassory taking of Gazda's property, but argues that the evidence was insufficient to prove that he intended to *permanently* deprive her of that property rather than temporarily. While the fact finder could have reasonably inferred from Marsh's acknowledgment that he took the property that he intended to steal it, Marsh contends that the facts do not support this inference because they do not establish beyond a reasonable doubt that he intended to permanently deprive her of the jewelry — that there is "counterv[a]iling evidence of intention otherwise." Specifically, he argues that the evidence negates any inference that he intended to permanently deprive her of the property because the transactions were written up as loans, he had made several payments on those loans, none of the loans had gone past their maturity except the ones the police placed a hold on, and he had redeemed some of the items.

[I]n turning to the facts of this case, we hold the evidence was sufficient to support the fact finder's conclusion that Marsh did not have the substantial ability to return the property to Gazda at the time he took it because of his financial situation. Marsh testified that he took the items because he was having money troubles, and needed money in order to carry him through a job he was working on. In order to redeem the property, Marsh would need $3,272.50. However, the only job he had at that time was a contract for carpentry work in which he would receive a total of $2,000 in installments as the work was completed. In addition, he was behind on other bills, and the initial $800 installment that he received from the $2,000 went towards payment of those outstanding bills. The evidence shows that he did not have that amount at the time he pawned the items, nor was he able to get that amount when Detective Buisch gave him a few weeks to do so. Marsh had neither the present ability nor the prospective ability at the time he took the items because of his financial situation to return the property.

In addition, the trial judge, as the fact finder, was not required to believe Marsh's testimony that he intended to return the jewelry to Gazda the next day when he got paid and could retrieve the items from the pawnshop. "In its role of judging witness credibility, the fact finder is entitled to disbelieve the self-serving testimony of the accused and to conclude that the accused is lying to conceal his guilt."

For these reasons, we find the evidence supports the trial court's factual finding that Marsh intended to permanently deprive Gazda of her property. Accordingly, we hold that the trial court did not err in holding the evidence sufficient to find Marsh guilty of grand larceny in violation of Code § 18.2-95, and affirm.

*Affirmed.*

**Post-Case Follow-Up**

*Marsh* highlights a few important principles that guide courts in interpreting the permanent deprivation *mens rea* element of larceny. First, the court notes that proof of a trespassory taking alone "permits the inference (unless other circumstances negate it) that the taker intended to steal the property." Second, the court explains that while a defendant who intends to take property only temporarily is not guilty of larceny, the intent to return the property must be unconditional. A defendant who takes someone else's property with the intent to return it only if a "reward" is paid is guilty of larceny. Finally, the court holds that evidence that a defendant does not have the "substantial ability to return the property" supports a finding that he intended to permanently deprive the owner of the property.

## Liebenow *and* Marsh: *Real Life Applications*

**1.** In 1875, Davis and a companion saw a horse and carriage in front of Davis's house. Davis and his friend took the horse and carriage and drove away. The next morning, at about 10:00 A.M., the horse and carriage were found abandoned on the side of the road five miles from where they were taken. The horse, who was in an exhausted state, had not been secured and was roaming freely when he was found. Davis is charged with larceny. Assume that Davis has elected to proceed with a bench trial and that he does not testify in his own defense. You are the judge. Based on these facts, would you conclude beyond a reasonable doubt that Davis intended to permanently deprive the owner of the horse and carriage?

**2.** Jaso was shopping at a Sears department store. A security guard named Merritt observed Jaso take a blue jacket from a hanger and place it in a grey Sears shopping bag. Jaso then walked up to the checkout counter, but there were no employees there. After about 30 seconds, Jaso left the store and began walking to the parking lot.

Merritt, the security guard, followed Jaso and stopped him about 20 feet from the store's exit. Merritt asked Jaso to show him the grey shopping bag and Jaso complied. Inside the bag, Merritt found the blue jacket. Jaso told Merritt that he was planning to pay for the jacket. Jaso explained that after he reached the cash register, he realized he'd forgotten his wallet in his car. According to Jaso, he was on his way back to his car to get his wallet and pay for the garment when Merritt stopped him. Merritt did not believe Jaso, so he called the police and had Jaso arrested for larceny.

You are the prosecutor assigned to the case. You anticipate that Jaso will argue that he did not intend to permanently deprive Sears of the blue jacket and you are trying to determine the strength of that defense. As you begin preparing for trial, what additional questions would you want to ask Merritt and/or the arresting officer to help you assess the credibility of Jaso's claim that he was going to his car to retrieve his wallet?

**3.** The defendants in both *Liebenow* and *Marsh* chose to waive their right to a jury trial in favor of a bench trial. Can you think of anything about the defense position in each case that might have made a bench trial a better option from the defendant's perspective?

## 2. Robbery

The elements of robbery closely resemble those of larceny. Indeed, with good reason, courts and commentators often refer to robbery as an "aggravated larceny." *People v. Ortego*, 19 Cal. 4th 686, 694 (1998).

To be guilty of **robbery**, the defendant must take the personal property of another against his will, from his person or immediate presence by means of force or fear, with the intent to permanently deprive him of it. Three of these elements — taking, personal property of another, and the intent to permanently deprive — mirror the elements of larceny. Robbery adds two elements that make the crime more serious than larceny. "To elevate larceny to robbery, the taking must be accomplished by force or fear and the property must be taken from the victim or his presence." *People v. Gomez*, 43 Cal. 4th 249, 254 (2008).

### Force or Fear

One of the two elements that distinguish robbery from larceny is that the theft be accomplished by force or fear.

**Case Preview**

### Lear v. State

How much force or fear is necessary to transform larceny into robbery? *Lear v. State* considers this question. As the court's opinion discusses, the force inherent in grabbing an item from someone's hand is not enough. Beyond that, the bar is not especially high.

As you read the decision, consider the following questions:

**1.** Why doesn't grabbing an item from someone's hand qualify as "force" in the crime of robbery?

**2.** If grabbing an item from someone's hand is not force, what is the definition of force for purposes of robbery?

# *Lear v. State*
## 39 Ariz. 313 (1931)

Ross, J.

The appellant was convicted of robbery. He appeals and assigns as error the insufficiency of the evidence to sustain the conviction.

The prosecuting witness, George Gross, testified that around 7 o'clock on the morning of August 12, 1931, he opened the Campbell Quality Shop, located in Buckeye, Maricopa county; that just about that time appellant entered the store and inquired about purchasing some shirts and shoes; that in the meantime he had taken a box of currency and a bag of silver out of the store safe; had placed the currency in the cash register and the bag of silver on the counter; that, while he was in the act of untying or unrolling the bag of silver, and while it was on the counter, appellant grabbed it from his hands and ran out the back door; that appellant said no word at the time, exhibited no arms, and used no force other than to grab the bag as stated above. Appellant admitted taking the bag of silver and that it contained $33.

The crimes of robbery and larceny are not the same. The former is classified as a crime against the person and the latter as a crime against property. In robbery there is, in addition to a felonious taking, a violent invasion of the person. If the person is not made to surrender the possession of the personal property by means of force of fear, the dominant element of robbery is not present. The mere taking of property in possession of another, from his person or immediate presence and against his will, is not robbery. Such taking must be accomplished by force or fear to constitute robbery.

The element of fear is not in the case. Appellant made no threat or demonstration. He simply grabbed the bag of silver from the hands of the prosecuting witness and ran away with it. There was no pulling or scrambling for possession of the bag. Was the force employed by appellant the kind of force necessary to constitute robbery? We think not. As we read the cases and text-writers, "the force used must be either before, or at the time of the taking, and must be of such a nature as to shew that it was intended to overpower the party robbed, and prevent his resisting, and not merely to get possession of the property stolen." *Rex v. Gnosil* (1824) 1 Car. & P. 304.

It is said in *State v. Parsons*, 44 Wash. 299, 87 P. 349, 350: "The courts generally hold that it is not robbery to merely snatch from the hand or person of another, or to surreptitiously take from another's pocket, money or some other thing of value, as such taking lacks the element of force, or putting in fear, one or the other of which being essential to constitute the crime of burglary."

Wharton in his work on Criminal Law (11th Ed.) vol. 2, p. 1297, says: "The snatching a thing is not considered a taking by force, but if there be a struggle to keep it, or any violence, or disruption, the taking is robbery, the reason of the distinction being that, in the former case, we can infer neither fear nor the intention violently to take in face of resisting force."

In *Ramirez v. Territory*, 9 Ariz. 177, the prosecuting witness testified that he felt somebody come up behind him and run his hands in his pockets and then run off.

The conviction of the defendant was set aside; the court holding that the mere taking of money by stealth from the person of another did not constitute robbery.

The Attorney General, while expressing doubt as to whether the facts shown constitute robbery, calls our attention to the case of Brown v. State, 34 Ariz. 150 as authority that possibly robbery was committed. In that case the defendant and one Jefferson had gone to the home of the prosecuting witness, and, after she had sold them some beer, represented to her that they were prohibition officers, and that they were going to "throw her in" for violation of the prohibition law. Jefferson seized her and started towards the door. Brown intervened and suggested that, if she paid him $150, the matter could be "fixed up." The prosecuting witness went to her bedroom, obtained her purse, and dumped its contents in her lap, and while she was counting the money Brown snatched the roll of bills from her and left the premises. We held this constituted robbery. We think the *Brown* Case falls within the rule announced by many courts to the effect that threats to accuse, arrest, or prosecute, when supplemented by force, actual or constructive, will support a charge of robbery. In the *Brown* Case the defendants actually took hold of the prosecuting witness and started with her towards the door as though they would place her in jail. This demonstration of force no doubt put her in fear.

The judgment of the lower court is reversed, and the cause remanded for such further action as may seem advisable in the premises.

**Post-Case Follow-Up**

As *Lear* discusses, "it is not robbery to merely snatch" property from someone's person. As a result, pickpocketing or grabbing someone's bag on the street will not, standing alone, constitute robbery. To qualify as robbery, the defendant must use force that would be sufficient to overcome any resistance. Knocking a victim to the ground, for example, would suffice. So would more modest force, such as "pulling or scrambling for possession of the bag."

## Lear: *Real Life Applications*

1. An undercover police officer was sitting in the driver's seat of a parked car in a parking lot as part of a sting operation. A man approached the car and offered to sell the undercover officer drugs. The officer agreed and began to remove money from his wallet. As the officer was opening his wallet, a third person named Moore was passing by the car. Moore reached through the window and grabbed for the undercover officer's wallet. The officer resisted and tightened his grip on the wallet, but Moore wrestled control of it away from the officer. As a result of the struggle, the officer's arm flew backwards and hit the steering wheel. Moore ran off with the wallet. Moore was arrested a few blocks away by another officer, who had observed the entire incident in connection with the sting operation. Moore is charged with robbery.

**a.** You are the prosecutor assigned to the case. How confident would you be that the jury would conclude that Moore used "force" to take the wallet? Would you consider offering a deal for Moore to plead guilty to larceny?

**b.** Now assume that Moore's case went to trial and he was convicted of robbery. Moore has appealed, arguing that he did not use enough force to be guilty of robbery. How should the court rule on Moore's appeal?

---

*Lear* addressed the boundaries of robbery by force. Of course, robbery may also be accomplished by fear. Robbery-by-fear cases can involve an express threat to injure the victim. An express threat is not strictly required, however. A robber who pulls out a knife or a gun and demands the victim's property, for example, has clearly taken the property by fear even if he never verbally threatened to shoot the victim.

Robbery's force or fear element includes a timing component. The definition of robbery suggests that the *taking* of the property must be accomplished by force or fear. As a result, historically, most courts held that using force or fear to retain already stolen property did not constitute robbery. On this view, a shoplifter who threatens violence after being confronted by a guard would not be guilty of robbery because fear was not used in the taking of the property. The modern trend has been to interpret the force or fear element to apply to these kinds of cases. In jurisdictions that have adopted the modern interpretation of the timing component, "a robbery can be accomplished even if the property was peacefully or duplicitously acquired, if force or fear was used to carry it away." *People v. Gomez*, 43 Cal. 4th 249, 256 (2008).

## From the Victim's Person or Immediate Presence

In addition to the use of force or fear, robbery requires that property be taken from the victim's person or immediate presence.

This element of robbery is the subject of comparatively few disputes. This is because it is unusual for someone to use force or fear to take property when the property is not in the immediate presence of the victim. Occasionally, however, there will be a question as to whether the victim was sufficiently close to the property to satisfy this element. In these cases, courts ask whether the property was "so within [the victim's] reach, inspection, observation or control, that he could, if not overcome by violence or prevented by fear, retain his possession of it." *People v. Hayes*, 52 Cal. 3d 577, 626-27 (1990). Some jurisdictions interpret this requirement relatively narrowly by focusing on the physical distance between the victim and the property at the time of the taking. Others emphasize the extent to which the defendant's acts of force or fear prevented the victim from retaining possession. In *People v. Harris*, 9 Cal. 4th 407, 422 (1994), for example, the Supreme Court of California upheld a robbery conviction where the defendant was being forcibly restrained outside of the buildings from which his property was taken. The court reasoned that "but for the use of force, blindfolding, handcuffing, and the ensuing captivity, Atherton's relative proximity to his office building complex (35 to 80 feet) and home ('around the corner of the same block') 'would have allowed him to take effective physical steps to retain control of his property, and to prevent defendant and his companions from stealing it.' "

## 3. Embezzlement and False Pretenses

If the only two theft offenses were larceny and robbery, theft law would be relatively clear-cut. Theft offenses are complicated, however, by two additional crimes: embezzlement and false pretenses. Larceny, embezzlement, and false pretenses all criminalize the non-violent theft of someone else's property. What distinguishes them from each other is the manner in which the thief came into possession of the property and whether there was a transfer of ownership in addition to possession.

Although they are sometimes referred to as common law crimes, judges did not create the crimes of embezzlement and false pretenses. Instead, they were enacted by the British Parliament. In 1757, Parliament created the crime of theft by false pretenses and in 1799, it created embezzlement. See *People v. Williams*, 57 Cal. 4th 776, 784-85 (discussing the history of larceny, embezzlement, and false pretenses). To understand why Parliament felt the need to supplement larceny with two additional theft crimes, it is important to remember that felonies like larceny were punishable by death at the time. This made some courts hesitant to read larceny too broadly because they viewed death as an "excessively harsh punishment for theft crimes." *Id.* at 783. As a result, English courts held that it was "not . . . larceny — and not a crime at all — if someone in lawful possession of another's property misappropriated it for personal use (the later offense of embezzlement), or if someone acquired title to another's property by fraud (the later offense of false pretenses)." *Id.* Eventually, Parliament took action to fill these gaps by creating the non-capital statutory offenses of embezzlement and false pretenses. Both crimes were later imported to the United States.

As this brief history suggests, the distinctions between larceny, embezzlement, and false pretenses are hard to justify on policy grounds. Indeed, the differences between the offenses have been "widely criticized in this nation's legal community" as "arbitrary." *Id.* at 784. Rather than trying to make sense of embezzlement and false pretenses from a policy perspective, it is better to acknowledge them for what they are: "historical accidents." *Commonwealth v. Ryan*, 155 Mass. 523, 527 (1892) (Holmes, J.).

Because embezzlement and false pretenses were enacted to fill holes in the crime of larceny, the best way to understand the elements of both offenses is by reference to larceny. Although larceny has already been addressed in detail, for easy reference, larceny is the trespassory taking and carrying away the personal property of another with the intent to permanently deprive the person of possession of the property. Keep the elements of larceny in mind as we examine embezzlement and false pretenses.

## *Embezzlement*

Embezzlement was designed by Parliament to address a very specific gap in the crime of larceny. Hesitant to subject professionals who misappropriated property entrusted to them to the death penalty, "English courts held that only those who *took* money, not those to whom money was lawfully *entrusted*, could commit common law larceny." *United States v. Young*, 955 F.2d 99, 102 (1st Cir. 1992). This remains true today. Consider, for example, a financial manager who oversees a client's investments. The financial manager runs into money problems of her own, and she decides to convert some of her client's funds to her own use. The financial manager is not guilty of larceny because she did not commit a trespassory (nonconsensual) taking. After all, the client consented to giving his money to the financial manager. And, because the client was not fraudulently induced to give money to the manager, his consent was genuine so the larceny by trick form of larceny would not apply. The crime of embezzlement was created to solve this problem. Although not guilty of larceny, our hypothetical financial manager would be guilty of embezzlement.

**Embezzlement** is "the fraudulent conversion of the property of another by one who is already in lawful possession of it." *In re Sherman*, 603 F.3d 11, 13 (1st Cir. 2010).

The critical difference between larceny and embezzlement is how the defendant came into possession of the property. If the defendant took possession of property from the victim without her consent — either by grabbing it from her or by fraudulently inducing her to give consent — he committed a trespassory taking and is guilty of larceny (assuming all other elements are met, of course). On the other hand, if the defendant came into possession of the property with the victim's consent and then *later* misappropriated it to her own use, she is guilty of embezzlement.

Stephen Breyer, then a First Circuit judge, summarized the crime of embezzlement this way in *Young*, 955 F.2d at 102-03:

> The crime of embezzlement has long had a clear meaning. In the eighteenth century, English courts held that only those who *took* money, not those to whom money was lawfully *entrusted*, could commit common law larceny. Consequently, Parliament enacted the first embezzlement statute, designed to prohibit, say, bank tellers or guardians from converting the (lawfully *obtained*) money of others to their own use. More than one hundred years ago, the Supreme Court referred to embezzlement's "settled technical meaning," recently described as "the fraudulent conversion of the property of another by one who is already in lawful possession of it."
>
> The notion of "fraudulent conversion," at the heart of embezzlement, may sound obscure, but, in fact, it is not. It essentially refers to, say, a bank teller, trustee, or guardian using money entrusted to him by another person for his own purposes or benefit and in a way that he knows the "entruster" did not intend or authorize. Thus, one basic source says that the
>
> > word "conversion" within the meaning of embezzlement statutes is a fraudulent appropriation of a thing to one's own use and beneficial enjoyment, or an

unauthorized assumption and exercise of dominion or right of ownership over it in defiance of, or exclusion of, the owner's rights.

29A C.J.S. *Embezzlement* § 11(a), at 26 (1965) (footnotes omitted). Another says that "fraudulent conversion" is

fraudulently withholding, converting, or applying [property that is lawfully in one's possession] to or for one's own use and benefit, or to [the] use and benefit of any person other than the one to whom the money or property belongs.

*Black's Law Dictionary* 662 (6th ed. 1990). And cases offer such statements as

The gist of [embezzlement] is the appropriation to the defendant's own use of property delivered to him for a specified purpose other than his own enjoyment of it.

*People v. Parker*, 235 Cal. App. 2d 100, 44 Cal. Rptr. 909, 914 (3d Dist. 1965) (citing cases). An embezzler, like a thief or a swindler, may commit the crime in any of a myriad of different ways. But, in each instance, the embezzler will have acted for his own purposes and contrary to authorization. He will have "fraudulently converted" property entrusted to him by another.

The distinction between embezzlement and larceny is further complicated by "a highly burdensome qualification" — a person who has "custody only," rather than possession, of property commits larceny (and not embezzlement) by misappropriating it. Comment, *Possession and Custody in the Law of Larceny*, 30 Yale L. J. 613 (1921). This rule is perhaps most relevant in cases of employees who take property from their employers. In this situation, the question of whether the stolen property had been entrusted to the employee will determine whether the theft is larceny or embezzlement. For example, "a janitor . . . who takes an item left lying on a desk" is guilty of larceny, not embezzlement. *Government of Virgin Islands v. Leonard*, 548 F.2d 478, 480 (3d Cir. 1977). Although the janitor may have had authority to physically handle the item on the desk in the course of cleaning the office, he was not entrusted with it. As a result, he did not have lawful possession of the item within the meaning of the crime of embezzlement. Likewise, a warehouse worker who uses his key to open the warehouse and steal property from inside is guilty of larceny, not embezzlement, because the property was never entrusted to him. *Warren v. State*, 223 Ind. 552 (1945). By contrast, an employee who is delegated greater authority over her employer's property is considered to have possession of it, and so commits embezzlement if she takes the property. For example, an office manager who takes money from an office safe would be guilty of embezzlement, not larceny, because he was entrusted with lawful possession of the money. *Morgan v. Commw.*, 242 Ky. 713 (1932).

**Case Preview**

## State v. Lough

The element of lawful possession is what distinguishes embezzlement from larceny and false pretenses. What separates embezzlement from non-criminal conduct is the element of fraudulent conversion or misappropriation of property. Embezzlement's conversion requirement serves the same purposes as larceny's "taking and carrying away" and "intent to permanently deprive" elements. The next case addresses what it means to fraudulently convert someone else's property.

As you read the decision, consider the following questions:

1. This decision does not focus on the difference between embezzlement and larceny. But it nevertheless provides a good opportunity to review what distinguishes the two offenses from one another. Why is Lough's conduct embezzlement and not larceny?
2. The jury instructions quoted by the court define conversion. What is the definition of conversion and how does it compare to the "taking and carrying away" and "intent to permanently deprive" elements of larceny?

---

## State v. Lough
### 899 A.2d 468 (R.I. 2006)

FLAHERTY, J.

After a jury trial in May 2004, John Lough, a patrolman in the Providence Police Department, was convicted of embezzling . . . a child's minibike, valued at approximately $350. Sometime around midnight on July 14, 2003, Lough stopped to aid a fellow officer, Thomas Teft. Officer Teft had detained a juvenile, Shane, because he suspected that the young man was operating a stolen minibike. Officer Teft decided to give Shane a break because the youth insisted that he had recently purchased the bike and he claimed that he had to be at his new job early in the morning. So, rather than arresting him, Officer Teft decided to confiscate the bike and hold it at the police station until Shane could produce proof of ownership.

When Lough arrived at the scene, Officer Teft explained to him that he was unsure about the protocol for confiscating the minibike. Officer Teft's anxiety was heightened because, as a new officer, he still was on probationary status with the department. As a result, the more experienced Lough offered his assistance by volunteering to take possession of the bike and complete the necessary paperwork. Officer Teft accepted this offer and he loaded the bike into the [trunk] of Lough's police cruiser.

A short time later, as Lough and several other officers were responding to a report of a stolen vehicle, his cruiser struck the back of another officer's patrol car, apparently because of faulty brakes. Lough's supervisor instructed him and the officer driving the other vehicle to return to the police station to complete paperwork related to the accident. After finishing the paperwork, Lough left the police station intending to bring his damaged cruiser to a repair facility known as the Bucklin Street Garage.

Lough said he remembered that Shane's minibike still was in the trunk of his car while he was on his way to the garage. Lough testified at trial that because he was aggravated by the evening's events and anxious to go home, he "made a wrong decision" and decided to rid himself of the bike by leaving it behind a dumpster.

He assumed that the young man would never return to claim the bike, but this assumption proved to be wrong and Shane arrived at the police station the next morning with his mother to reclaim the confiscated bike.

Lough was indicted on one count of embezzlement . . . in violation of § 11-41-3. Following a four-day trial in May 2004, a jury returned a verdict of guilty and Lough was fined $1,000 and received a one-year suspended sentence. The defendant timely appealed.

On appeal, Lough contends that the trial justice misinterpreted § 11-41-3 and incorrectly instructed the jury that a person could violate the statute by disposing of the property of another. Lough's claim[] . . . hinge[s] on one central issue: whether a person who is lawfully entrusted with property and throws the property away can be convicted of embezzlement and fraudulent conversion pursuant to § 11-41-3 in the absence of proof that he derived a benefit from using the property.

This Court applies *de novo* review to questions of statutory construction. In so doing, "[p]enal statutes must be strictly and narrowly construed."

To determine whether a conviction for embezzlement and fraudulent conversion under § 11-41-3 requires proof that a defendant derived a benefit from his use of the property, we begin our analysis with the language of the statute itself. Section 11-41-3 provides in relevant part as follows:

> **"Embezzlement and fraudulent conversion.** — Every . . . person to whom any money or other property shall be entrusted for any specific purpose . . . who shall embezzle or fraudulently convert [the money or other property] to his or her own use . . . shall be deemed guilty of [theft]."

In [*State v.*] *Oliveira*[, 432 A.2d 664 (R.I. 1981)], this Court outlined the elements of proof required to sustain a conviction under § 11-41-3. We explained that the state must establish the following:

> "(1) that defendant was entrusted with the property for a specific use, (2) that he came into possession of the property in a lawful manner, often as a result of his employment, and (3) that defendant intended to appropriate and convert the property to his own use and permanently deprive that person of the use."

Lough concedes that he was lawfully entrusted with the minibike for the specific purpose of delivering it to the police station. Thus, there is no dispute that the state satisfied the first two elements required to sustain a conviction. He also admitted during trial that when he threw the bike away, he intended to permanently deprive the owner of its use. He maintains, however, that this is insufficient to sustain a conviction because the state also must establish that he "convert[ed] the property to his own use." According to him, this third element of proof requires evidence that he derived some personal gain from using the property.

To support this position, Lough contends that our holding in [*State v.*] *Powers*[, 644 A.2d 828 (R.I. 1994),] stands for the proposition that a person cannot be convicted under § 11-41-3 without evidence that he derived a benefit from using the property in question. In that case, the defendant, Robert Powers, was working as the director of maintenance for a school department when, using a school account, he ordered certain material valued at $1,200 and had it delivered to a private company, all in exchange for goods and services to be used by the school. After school officials learned of the transaction, Powers was charged with embezzlement and fraudulent conversion in violation of § 11-41-3. Although the barter agreement was unauthorized, there was no evidence that Powers had personally used the school department's property or derived a benefit from its use. Therefore, the Superior Court granted his motion to dismiss for lack of probable cause. The state appealed, and we affirmed. Relying on our previous holding in *Oliveira* and the plain language of § 11-41-3, we explained that "an element of the crime charged is that defendant put the property to 'his own use' or used the property for his own benefit."

Citing our language in *Powers*, Lough contends that the trial justice's instruction misstated the elements of proof required to sustain a conviction under § 11-41-3. The disputed instruction stated in part as follows:

> "The elements that the State must prove beyond a reasonable doubt in order to convict this defendant are as follows: Number one, that the defendant was entrusted with the property for a specific use or purpose; two, that he came into possession of that property in a lawful manner, and, three, that the defendant intended to appropriate and convert the property to his own use and permanently deprive that person of its use.
>
> "A conversion of property requires a serious act of interference with the owner's rights, using up the property, selling it, pledging it, giving it away, delivering it to one not entitled to it and inflicting serious damage to it, claiming it against the lawful owner, unreasonable withholding possession of it from the owner *or, otherwise, disposing of the property.* Each of these acts seriously interferes with the ownership rights and so constitutes a conversion." (Emphasis added.)

Lough argues that by instructing the jury that a person converts property to his own use by disposing of it, the trial justice permitted the jury to return a guilty verdict in the absence of evidence that he derived a benefit from his use of the minibike. This distinction is of paramount importance because Lough conceded in his testimony that he threw the minibike away. Thus, if the act of throwing the minibike away constitutes conversion, Lough's testimony was essentially an admission of guilt.

Contrary to Lough's assertion, however, *Powers* does not hold that a person must derive a personal gain from using the property to be convicted [of embezzlement]. Although we noted that the defendant in *Powers* did not derive a benefit from the bartering transaction, this observation simply underscored the fact that he did not convert the property to his own use, as required by the plain language of the statute. Therefore, under our holding in *Powers* and under the language of the statute, the relevant inquiry is not whether Lough derived a benefit from throwing the bike away, but rather, whether he put the property to " 'his own use.' "

Although we have not previously considered whether a person puts property to his own use by disposing of it, other jurisdictions have held that a person puts property to his own use when he treats it as if it were his own, even in the absence of a measurable benefit. For example, in *United States v. Santiago*, 528 F.2d 1130, 1135 (2d Cir. 1976), the Second Circuit Court of Appeals explained as follows: "[Embezzlement] does not require a showing that the misappropriation was for the personal advantage of the defendant. One's disposition of the property of another, without right, as if it were his own, is a conversion to one's own use."

In our opinion, a person puts property to his own use when he treats it as his own, and when a person discards property, he treats it as his own. When Lough decided to dispose of the minibike that had been entrusted to him, he made a decision that was properly vested in its lawful owner; in other words, by discarding the property as if it were his own, Lough converted it to "his * * * own use." Section 11-41-3. We therefore hold that the trial justice correctly instructed the jury on the elements of proof necessary to sustain a conviction under § 11-41-3.

For the reasons stated herein, we affirm the judgment of the Superior Court. The record in this case shall be remanded to the Superior Court.

---

**Post-Case Follow-Up**

In *Lough*, the court describes the standard definition of embezzlement's conversion element and holds that embezzlement does not require the conversion to be for the benefit of the defendant. A person converts property in his possession when he commits a "serious act of interference with the owner's rights," which includes acts such as "using up the property," "selling it," or "claiming it against the lawful owner." As *Lough* explains, the element of conversion is also satisfied if the defendant throws the victim's property away.

---

## Lough: *Real Life Applications*

1. Imagine if, after learning Shane had come to reclaim his minibike, Officer Lough drove to the dumpster where he had left it and was able to retrieve it. Officer Lough then delivered the bike to Shane the next day. Unfortunately for Lough, because the minibike was not at the station when Shane arrived to pick it up, Lough's superiors conducted an internal investigation and found out that Lough had left the bike behind the dumpster. When confronted by his superiors, Lough admitted that he had thrown the bike away because he thought no one would ever find out it was missing.
   a. On these facts, would Lough be guilty of embezzlement?
   b. Assume for purposes of this question that Lough's actions constitute embezzlement. You are the prosecutor assigned to Lough's case. Would the fact that Lough was able to retrieve the minibike influence your decision about whether to proceed with the charges against Lough? If so, why?

---

### False Pretenses

Distinguishing false pretenses from larceny by trick can be quite challenging. As discussed above, the concept of larceny by trick provides that a defendant who fraudulently induces another person to give him possession of property has committed a trespassory (nonconsensual) taking. The theory behind this rule is that a property owner who is fraudulently induced to transfer possession of property has not given genuine consent. Thus, the court held in the famous case of *The King v. Pear*, 1 Leach 212 (1779), that a person who rents a horse with the intent to sell it is guilty of larceny — specifically, larceny by trick — because he has taken the horse by trespass and carried it away with the intent to permanently deprive the owner of possession.

Strangely, British courts declined to extend the larceny by trick rule to "cases involving fraudulent transfer of *title*" to property, as opposed to possession. *Williams*, 57 Cal. 4th at 784 (emphasis added). The stated rationale for excluding fraudulent transfers of title to property "was that once title to property was voluntarily transferred by its owner to another, the recipient owned the property and therefore could not be said to be trespassing upon it." *Id.*

The British Parliament designed the offense of false pretenses to address this problem. **False pretenses** makes it a crime to obtain title to another's property by a false representation of a material fact with the intent to defraud the victim. The critical difference between false pretenses and larceny by trick is whether the victim was tricked into transferring mere possession of the property or *title* — meaning ownership — of the property. A person who tricks a victim into transferring mere possession has committed the crime of larceny under the larceny by trick theory. A person who tricks a victim into transferring title as well as possession has committed the crime of false pretenses.

## Case Preview

## *People v. Phebus*

The difference between larceny by trick and false pretenses — the transfer of possession versus the transfer of title — is easily stated. But the rule is not always easy to apply, particularly at the time the charging decision is made. In *People v. Phebus*, the prosecutor charged the defendant with larceny for switching price tags on merchandise he purchased at a store. The defendant moved to dismiss the charge on the ground that he was guilty, if anything, of false pretenses. The court's decision succinctly explains the distinction between larceny and false pretenses.

As you read the decision, consider the following questions:

1. Before you read *Phebus*, take a moment to review the description of *The King v. Pear*, the case of the horse thief who committed larceny by trick, on page 92. What is it that differentiates the defendant in *Phebus*, who the court finds should have been charged with false pretenses, from the horse thief?
2. Because the court's opinion focuses on the question of whether the defendant obtained possession or title to the property, it does not consider the other elements of false pretenses. If Phebus were charged with false pretenses, do you think the prosecutor would be able to prove every element of the offense based on the factual description in the case?

# *People v. Phebus*
## 116 Mich. App. 416 (1982)

ALLEN, J.

Which criminal offense, larceny or obtaining property by false pretenses, is committed when a shopper switches a price tag on merchandise he proposes to buy so that a lower price appears on the merchandise?

Defendant was charged with larceny in a building. At the preliminary examination, a store detective for Meijer's Thrifty Acres testified that she had observed defendant remove a price tag marked $1.88 from an unfinished decorator shelf and place it on a finished decorator shelf, which had been marked $6.53. The detective said that defendant walked over to his wife and spoke with her, then defendant's wife picked up the finished shelf and placed it in their shopping cart. Defendant and his wife went through the check-out area and paid the marked price of $1.88 for the finished shelf usually priced $6.53. While defendant was loading his car with the merchandise he had purchased, he was stopped by the store detectives. Defendant was arrested and charged with larceny in a building.

Defendant was bound over for trial on the charged offense. On October 27, 1980, he moved to quash the information, arguing that the evidence presented at the preliminary examination did not establish the elements of a larceny. In an order dated February 2, 1981, the Jackson County Circuit Court quashed the information, finding that the elements of false pretenses, but not those of larceny, were made out at the preliminary examination. The prosecution has appealed, raising this single issue of first impression in Michigan.

Although the elements of [larceny and false pretenses] are quite distinct, the determination of whether a certain course of action should be punished under one statute or the other is often not easily made. The [Michigan] Supreme Court noted recently in *People v. Long*, 409 Mich. 346, 350-351 (1980), quoting from *People v. Martin*, 116 Mich. 446 (1898):

> " ' "There is, to be sure, a narrow margin between a case of larceny and one where the property has been obtained by false pretenses. The distinction is a very nice one, but still very important. The character of the crime depends upon the intention of the parties, and that intention determines the nature of the offense. In the former case, where, by fraud, conspiracy, or artifice, the possession is obtained with a felonious design, and the title still remains in the owner, larceny [by trick] is established; while in the latter, where title, as well as possession is absolutely parted with, the crime is false pretenses. It will be observed that the intention of the owner to part with his property is the gist and essence of the offense of larceny, and the vital point upon which the crime hinges and is to be determined." ' "

This distinction is consistent with that made in other jurisdictions.

Based on this distinction, we conclude that here, where defendant attempted to secure both title and possession of the shelf, the applicable crime is false pretenses.

The prosecutor contends that, because the defendant switched price tags, the store clerk did not know the nature and the value of the property she was parting with and, because of this mistake of fact, title did not effectively pass to the defendant. In any crime of false pretenses, however, the victim is induced to part with title through a misrepresentation of fact. Whenever a victim relies upon the misrepresentation and passes title to a defendant, a completed crime of false pretenses is shown.

In other jurisdictions that have addressed this question, courts have held that a shopper who has switched price tags and effectively secured title should be prosecuted for false pretenses. *State v. Hauck*, 190 Neb. 534 (1973); *People v. Lorenzo*, 64 Cal. App. 3d Supp. 43 (1976). We agree.

In the case at bar, the circuit court properly recognized that the defendant should not have been prosecuted under the larceny statute. We therefore affirm the circuit court order quashing the information charging the defendant with larceny in a building.

Affirmed.

---

**Post-Case Follow-Up**

*Phebus* illustrates the central distinction between larceny by trick and false pretenses. The court holds that Phebus should have been charged with false pretenses, not larceny, because he "effectively secured title" to the shelf — not merely possession — when he purchased it. By contrast, in *The King v. Pear*, described above, the horse thief used a fraudulent representation to *rent* the horse, intending to sell it to someone else. Because the victim rented the horse to the defendant, the parties did not intend to transfer ownership of the horse to the defendant. Although determining whether a defendant has committed larceny or false pretenses is not always easy, in most cases, as in *Phebus* and *Pear*, the answer to the question of whether the parties transferred title or merely possession is reasonably clear.

---

## Phebus: *Real Life Applications*

1. Williams obtained a Visa payment card that was "re-encoded" with fraudulent credit card information. Williams used the re-encoded Visa payment card to buy $200 in gift cards at Walmart. As Williams exited the store, a security guard asked to see his receipt. Williams appeared nervous and so the security guard asked Williams to show him the Visa payment card that he had used to buy the gift cards. The security guard noticed that the last four digits on the Visa payment card did not match those on the receipt. After the security guard asked Williams about the discrepancy, Williams ran out of the store. The security guard tackled Williams about 50 yards away from the store's entrance. Williams was arrested for the theft of $200 in gift cards from Walmart. You are the prosecutor assigned to Williams's case. What theft offense — larceny, robbery, embezzlement, or false pretenses — would you charge Williams with based on these facts?

2. The distinctions between larceny, embezzlement, and false pretenses may not be intuitive but in most cases their application is relatively straightforward,

with one answer that is clearly correct. In some cases, however, courts can *still* struggle — hundreds of years after the development of the three offenses — to determine which type of theft applies. Consider the following issue, which resulted in a 19-page opinion from the California Supreme Court: "We granted review to determine what crime is committed in the following circumstances: the defendant enters a store and picks up an item of merchandise displayed for sale, intending to claim that he owns it and to 'return' it for a refund; without the defendant's knowledge his conduct has been observed by a store security agent, who instructs the clerk to give him credit for the item; the clerk gives the defendant a credit voucher, and the agent detains him as he leaves the counter with the voucher." *People v. Davis*, 19 Cal. 4th 301, 303 (1998).

The defendant in *Davis* was convicted of larceny of the merchandise. On appeal, he argued that he was guilty of no more than an attempt to commit larceny of the merchandise, and he suggested that a more appropriate charge might have been theft by false pretenses of the store credit voucher. The California Supreme Court disagreed and upheld the defendant's conviction of larceny of the merchandise. Do you agree that the elements of larceny were met? Do you think the defendant should have been charged with theft of the store credit voucher by false pretenses instead of (or in addition to) larceny of the merchandise?

## 4. Consolidated Theft Statutes

Widespread criticism of the arbitrary distinctions between larceny, embezzlement, and false pretenses has led many state legislatures to "consolidate those offenses into a single crime, usually called 'theft.'" *People v. Williams*, 57 Cal. 4th 776, 784-85 (2013). This consolidation effort was helped along in part by the Model Penal Code, which included a consolidated theft provision. Unfortunately, consolidated theft statutes have only slightly lessened the burden of these arbitrary distinctions. That is because in most states, consolidated theft statutes did *not* significantly change the elements of larceny, embezzlement, and false pretenses. Rather than redefine or completely eliminate these offenses, most consolidated theft statutes left the definitions of larceny, embezzlement, and false pretenses intact but combined them into a single offense, called theft. In practical terms, then, most consolidated theft statutes simply replaced three different crimes with a single crime (theft) that can be committed in three different ways — theft by larceny, theft by embezzlement, and theft by false pretenses. (In many states, consolidated theft statutes also include one or more other theft offenses — extortion is the most common — in addition to larceny, embezzlement, and false pretenses.)

Why did so many states make such a seemingly cosmetic reform to theft offenses? The answer lies in the requirements for pleading and proving criminal cases. Prosecutors must decide what charges to bring in advance of trial. It would be unfair to the defendant, and quite difficult for the court, if prosecutors were permitted to add new charges halfway through a trial. As a result, when larceny, embezzlement, and false pretenses were three separate crimes, prosecutors had to decide which of the three crimes to charge a defendant with before the trial. It was not uncommon for a prosecutor to charge a defendant with one theft offense (e.g., larceny), only to realize during the trial that the evidence more closely fit a different theft crime (e.g., embezzlement). Because of the rule against adding or switching charges mid-way through a trial, a prosecutor who made this mistake could not ask the jury to return an embezzlement conviction against a larceny defendant. Even if the mistake was caught earlier, it could still cause headaches for prosecutors, as the decision in *Phebus*, above—which held that the defendant should have been charged with false pretenses and not larceny—highlights.

The movement to consolidate theft offenses was designed to ameliorate this problem. Consolidated theft statutes "remove the technicalities that existed in the pleading and proof of [larceny, embezzlement, and false pretenses] at common law. Indictments and informations charging the crime of 'theft' can now simply alleged an 'unlawful taking.'" *Williams*, 57 Cal. 4th at 786. In other words, in a jurisdiction with a consolidated theft statute, a prosecutor can charge a defendant with theft and wait until later in the process to determine which type of theft—larceny, embezzlement, or false pretenses—to argue to the jury. This system still can result in overturned theft convictions based on the technical differences between larceny, embezzlement, and false pretenses. If a prosecutor requests a jury instruction on theft by embezzlement in a case where the evidence proves theft by larceny, for example, the defendant may be able to argue on appeal that the jury was improperly instructed and that there was insufficient evidence to convict him of theft by embezzlement. For that reason, the distinctions between larceny, embezzlement, and false pretenses remain important, even in states with consolidated theft statutes.

In sum, while consolidated theft statutes have made life somewhat easier for prosecutors and courts by reducing the problems caused by having to plead and prove individual theft offenses, they have been of little help to law students, who must still learn the fine distinctions between larceny, embezzlement, and false pretenses.

## Alterations to Common Law Theft Offenses

Although theft consolidation statutes did not fundamentally change the definitions of larceny, embezzlement, and false pretenses, some states have altered elements of these offenses over the years. For example, a number of jurisdictions have relaxed the requirement that the defendant intend to *permanently* deprive the owner of property. Instead, these jurisdictions require only an intent to deprive the owner of property, which includes not only permanent deprivation but also "withhold[ing] property . . . for so extended a period as to appropriate a major portion of its economic value." Model Penal Code § 223.0(1).

In addition to changes to common law theft offenses, most states have added new offenses to fill perceived gaps in the common law crimes or to target specific types of thefts for increased punishment. Often, these laws address problems that arise from new technologies or speak to the concerns of a political interest group. Beginning in the 1990s, for example, states began enacting separate statutes to criminalize identity theft. Before that, a number of states adopted so-called joyriding statutes, which make it a crime to take and drive a vehicle without the owner's permission. Other specialized theft statutes include those that single out the theft of certain types of property (like animals) or theft from certain types of victims (banks) for harsher punishment.

Finally, most modern theft statutes no longer treat all common law thefts as felonies. Typically, theft of property of a

> comparably low value — whether by larceny, embezzlement, or false pretenses — is treated as a misdemeanor. The amount that divides misdemeanor and felony theft varies from state to state, however.

# 5. Extortion

At common law, extortion was a crime targeted exclusively at "public official[s] who took 'by colour of his office' money that was not due to him for the performance of his official duties." *Evans v. United States*, 504 U.S. 255, 260 (1992). The offense is now much broader, encompassing "acts by private individuals pursuant to which property is obtained by means of force, fear, or threats." *Id.* at 261. The expansion of extortion mostly occurred during the first half of the 1900s, driven in part by the passage of a broad federal extortion statute in 1934.

Today, **extortion** is defined as "the obtaining of property from another, with his consent, induced by wrongful use of actual or threatened force, violence, or fear, or under color of official right." 18 U.S.C. § 1951(b)(2). Most state extortion statutes employ the same or a very similar definition. Because extortion criminalizes threats to obtain property, it "is a species of theft." Stuart P. Green, *Theft by Coercion: Extortion, Blackmail, and Hard Bargaining*, 55 Washburn L.J. 553, 556 (2005). But as a modern invention, extortion stands somewhat apart from larceny, robbery, embezzlement, and false pretenses. Extortion cases fall into roughly three groups: extortion by threats of violence, extortion by non-violent but "wrongful" threats, and extortion by public officials "under color of official right." In all three types of extortion, the victim must consent to giving the defendant her property.

## Extortion by Threatened Violence

Extortion by threatened or actual violence closely resembles robbery. Both involve the use of force or threatened force to obtain property. The next case considers what differentiates the two crimes.

---

**Case Preview**

## *United States v. Zhou*

In *Zhou*, the defendants called an illegal gambling parlor and told the person who answered the phone that someone would be coming by later that day to collect $10,000. True to their word, the defendants went to the gambling parlor that night. An employee of the parlor came outside to meet the defendants, who pointed guns at the employee and demanded $10,000. When the employee told the defendants that he didn't have any money, one of them hit the employee with a gun and ripped a necklace from around his neck. The defendants were convicted of extortion and conspiracy to commit extortion. On appeal, the court held that the incident was robbery, not extortion, and so reversed the convictions.

As you read the decision, consider the following questions:

1. What are the elements that distinguish robbery from extortion, and how do they apply to the facts in this case?
2. If the conduct in this case does not constitute extortion, in what kind of circumstances would obtaining property by a threat of violence qualify as extortion?

---

## United States v. Zhou
### 428 F.3d 361 (2d Cir. 2005)

MINER, J.

Defendants-appellants, Chen Xiang ("Chen") and Lin Xian Wu ("Lin"), appeal from judgments of conviction . . . following a jury trial, convicting each of the Appellants . . . of one count of conspiracy to commit extortion, in violation of 18 U.S.C. § 1951 ("Count One") [and] one count of extortion, in violation of 18 U.S.C. §§ 2 and 1951 ("Count Two")[.]*

Appellants contend that the evidence adduced at trial to prove their guilt in connection with the charged counts of extortion and of conspiracy to commit extortion was insufficient as a matter of law. We agree and, accordingly, reverse the convictions of Appellants under Counts One and Two.

### BACKGROUND

The charges in the Indictment have their genesis in a series of robberies and related incidents that occurred in Manhattan's "Chinatown" during a six-month period between the summer of 2001 and the early months of 2002. The . . . incident [that was the basis of the two extortion-related convictions] occurred in or around July 2001 at 75 Eldridge Street — an illegal gambling parlor located behind a clothing store. On or about July 23, 2001, at approximately 6:00 P.M., an unknown caller telephoned Chen Tin Hua ("Hua"), a "shareholder" in the gambling operation, and identified himself as being associated with "Vietnamese Boy" — presumably, co-defendant/cooperating witness Xiao Qin Zhou ("Xiao"). The caller stated that Vietnamese Boy would come to the gambling parlor later that day to pick up $10,000, which the caller instructed Hua to place in a red envelope. Hua told the caller that he had no money and hung up.

Later that evening, while in the parlor, Hua was summoned outside by a group of men demanding to speak with him. Awaiting Hua were Appellants — Chen and Lin — along with Xiao and co-defendant Li Wei. All four pointed guns at Hua, and Xiao demanded that he give them $10,000. Hua told the group that he had no money.

---

*In addition to the extortion-related charges, the defendants were also convicted of three counts of robbery and three counts of conspiracy to commit robbery, along with four counts of using a firearm in relation to the three robbery counts and the extortion count. The court affirmed all six robbery-related convictions and the three use-of-a-firearm convictions that were connected with the robberies. The court's discussion of the facts and legal issues related to these counts has been omitted from this edited version of the court's opinion. [Footnote by casebook author.]

Xiao struck Hua on the head, and Li Wei, using his gun, struck Hua in the stomach. Xiao then ripped a necklace from around Hua's neck, and the group fled the scene in a vehicle.

Following this foray, the gang began to terrorize the neighborhood systematically.

[A]fter a two-week trial, a jury found both Chen and Lin guilty of each of the charged offenses.

## DISCUSSION

As noted above, Appellants contend that the evidence adduced at trial was insufficient to sustain the convictions of Appellants on the extortion-related crimes. The standard under which we review a challenge to the sufficiency of the evidence in a criminal trial is familiar: [W]e will not disturb a conviction on grounds of legal insufficiency of the evidence at trial if any rational trier of fact could have found the essential elements of the crime beyond a reasonable doubt.

[Appellants were convicted of conspiracy to commit extortion and extortion. Extortion] "means the obtaining of property from another, *with his consent*, induced by wrongful use of actual or threatened force, violence, or fear." 18 U.S.C. § 1951(b)(2) (emphasis added). Extortion is frequently exemplified by "revenue-producing measures . . . utilized by organized crime to generate income" — measures "such as shakedown rackets and loan-sharking." *United States v. Nardello*, 393 U.S. 286, 295 (1969).[7] Of course, another familiar form of extortion is blackmail — where, for example, the extortioner obtains money from the victim by threatening to expose private or embarrassing conduct.

Choice on the part of the victim is a common theme in all extortion cases. As noted above, [the statute] "speaks of obtaining property from another 'with his consent.'" *United States v. Arena*, 180 F.3d 380, 394 (2d Cir. 1999). Indeed, "[t]he legislative history of the Act makes clear that its proponents understood extortion to encompass situations in which a victim is given the option of relinquishing some property immediately or risking unlawful violence resulting in other losses, and he simply *chooses* what he perceives to be the lesser harm." *Id.* at 395 (emphasis added) (citing 91 Cong. Rec. 11,904, 11,907 (discussing decision of business owner to pay tribute to extortionists rather than risk the physical destruction of his trucks: "The man pays the money to save himself and his property.")). "In order to foreclose any argument by an extortionist that the relinquishment of property in such circumstances was [truly] voluntary, [however,] the [federal statute's] definition of extortion simply prohibits the extortionist from forcing the victim to make such a choice."

At bottom, undeniably, the victim of an extortion acts from fear, whether of violence or exposure. But both the language of the statute and the relevant precedents make clear that he or she always retains some degree of choice in whether to comply with the extortionate threat, however much of a Hobson's choice that may be. Indeed, this element of consent is the razor's edge that distinguishes extortion from robbery, which, in contrast, is defined in pertinent part as "the unlawful taking or obtaining

---

[7] *See generally Nardello*, 393 U.S. at 296 n.13 ("Extortion is typically employed by organized crime to enforce usurious loans, infiltrate legitimate businesses, and obtain control of labor unions." (citing President's Commission on Law Enforcement and Administration of Justice, *Task Force Report: Organized Crime* 3-5 (1967))).

of personal property from the person or in the presence of another, *against his will*, by means of actual or threatened force, or violence, or fear of injury, immediate or future, to his person or property, or property in his custody or possession, or the person or property of a relative or member of his family or of anyone in his company at the time of the taking or obtaining." 18 U.S.C. § 1951(b)(1) (emphasis added).

Among the essential elements of the federal crime of extortion, then, are (i) the defendant's "use of actual or threatened force, violence, or fear," and (ii) the victim's consent—however forced—to the transfer of the property. 18 U.S.C. § 1951(b)(2).

Here, the Government's theory is that Appellants conspired to extort—and in fact committed extortion, and not robbery—when they "informed Hua by telephone that [Xiao] was coming to the gambling parlor to collect $10,000 from him," instructing him to leave the money for Xiao's pick-up in a red envelope, and, later, when they "summoned Hua outside the parlor and attempted to collect the money that had been demanded in the extortionate telephone call." The Government contends that "[t]his call clearly represented a request, albeit under duress, for the money, rather than a forcible taking." "After all," the Government observes, "robbers typically do not telephone in their requests to victims ahead of time." In making this distinction between robbery and extortion, however, the Government fails to identify any element of "duress," either express or implied, in the telephone call, thus calling into question whether the Government has proved each and every element of the extortion-related crimes charged in the Indictment, as required by fundamental precepts of our law.

Here, the Government sought to prove the extortion-related charges primarily through the testimony of Xiao, a co-defendant and cooperating witness, and of Hua, the victim of the gang's criminal conduct at 75 Eldridge Street. Hua, too, was cooperating with the Government—in his case, to avoid prosecution for his involvement in the gambling operation, for entering and working illegally in the United States, and for failure to report income.

Hua, the victim of the 75 Eldridge Street crime, testified as follows regarding the above-noted telephone call that he received on July 23, 2001:

Q.  Did you receive any telephone calls at the gambling parlor on July 23, 2001?
A.  Yes.
Q.  How many telephone calls did you receive that day?
A.  One call.

. . .

Q.  Did he identify himself by name?
A.  He did. He identified himself as Vietnamese [B]oy,[11] and he demanded money from me.

. . .

Q.  And what specifically did he say to you?
A.  He said Vietnamese [B]oy, he will come over to me to pick up money and I should give him $10,000.

. . .

---

[11] "Vietnamese Boy" is an alias of Xiao.

Q. What, if anything, did you say to the caller?

A. I said I have no money.

Q. Did the caller say anything back to you at that point?

A. No. I h[u]ng up the phone.

Hua further testified that four individuals came to 75 Eldridge Street at approximately 8:00 P.M. on July 23, 2001. These individuals asked another employee of the gambling parlor to summon Hua outside. When Hua went outside, four individuals were waiting, pointing guns at him. Thereafter, Xiao, aka "Vietnamese Boy," asked Hua for $10,000. When Hua said that he had no money, one of the other men poked Hua in the side with his gun, and Xiao hit Hua on his head. Xiao then ripped the necklace from Hua's neck, after which all four of the men got into a car and drove off.

[W]e are bound by the fundamental principle that "the Due Process Clause protects the accused against conviction except upon proof beyond a reasonable doubt of every fact necessary to constitute the crime with which he is charged." Here, it seems to us inescapable that this standard has not been met.

There is nothing in the Record . . . to suggest that there was an agreement to obtain the property of either Hua or the gambling operation at 75 Eldridge by consent — forced or otherwise. An inference may fairly be drawn that Appellants and others agreed to visit the 75 Eldridge Street parlor to rob it, but that is all.

[A]bsent from the Record is any indication that Appellants thought, or sought, to obtain property from Hua, or anyone else at 75 Eldridge Street, by means of a forced consent. Rather, the Record supports an agreement among, and an actual effort by, Appellants and others to get a person at that location to open a door so that Appellants and others could enter the establishment and rob it. [T]he only evidence that even arguably can be identified as indicating extortion came from Hua, who testified that he was gambling at the 75 Eldridge Street parlor when he received a phone call, either from Xiao or someone on Xiao's behalf.

Hua testified that the caller demanded $10,000. Hua refused and hung up the phone. Later, Hua was summoned to come outside the parlor, where he was confronted by Xiao, Appellants, and another gangster, all of whom were pointing guns at Hua. Xiao demanded $10,000, and Hua refused, informing the gangsters that he had no money. Xiao then hit Hua in the head, grabbing the chain from around his neck, and the gang fled. Xiao testified that the chain was later sold and that he, Appellant, and Li Wei then split the proceeds. It seems inescapable that this incident was nothing more nor less than a classic robbery.

A robbery plus a cryptic and ambiguous phone call does not equal extortion — at least, not on the facts presented to us in this case. And without some evidence in the Record to support the charges of extortion and conspiracy to extort, there was nothing to permit a rational juror to infer that what the defendants were about was anything other than a robbery and/or conspiracy to rob.

[T]here simply was no evidence of an agreement to obtain property from Hua or anyone else *with their consent* through the threat or use of force, nor of any actual effort or attempt to do so. And, as discussed above, it is this notion that the victim of extortion consents to the taking — albeit through threat or force — that separates extortion from robbery.

In light of all the foregoing, we conclude that the evidence put forward by the Government to prove the charged extortion and conspiracy to extort, even viewed in the light most favorable to the prosecution, was insufficient as a matter of law to prove the crimes charged in Counts One and Two of the Indictment. At best, the evidence proves an uncharged conspiracy to rob, and the robbery of, an individual at 75 Eldridge Street. Accordingly, we reverse the convictions of Appellants under Counts One and Two, for the crimes of conspiracy to extort and extortion, respectively.

**Post-Case Follow-Up**

The defendants in *Zhou* did not commit extortion, the court holds, because they did not obtain Hua's necklace with his consent. Instead, the evidence proved an uncharged robbery because the defendants used force to obtain the necklace against Hua's will. The facts in this case stand in sharp contrast to the typical extortion-by-threatened-violence case. In a parenthetical, citing to the legislative history of the federal extortion statute, the court cites as an example of extortion the "decision of a business owner to pay tribute to extortionists rather than risk physical destruction of his trucks: 'The man pays money to save himself and his property.'" This is also sometimes known as a protection racket: An organized crime group will approach a business owner with an implied threat, telling her that it would be a shame if some harm came to her or her business. Then the group will offer to protect the owner from the harm for a fee. This kind of situation is extortion, not robbery, because the "victim is given the option of relinquishing some property immediately or risking unlawful violence resulting in other losses, and he simply *chooses* what he perceives to be the lesser harm." Because the threatened violence is attenuated from the property transfer, extortion payments often outwardly appear to be legitimate, consensual transactions.

The *Zhou* court's observation that extortion requires taking property with the victim's consent whereas robbery requires taking property against the victim's will reflects the "traditionally accepted distinction between" the two offenses. *Commw. v. Froelich*, 458 Pa. 104, 110 (1974). This formulation can be confusing, however. After all, when robbery and extortion are accomplished by violent threats, both crimes involve the victim parting with property in order to avoid physical harm. An extortion victim who "chooses" to pays a protection fee in the face of a threat of future harm is consenting to the payment only in the most technical sense of the term. Similarly, although the victim of a gunpoint robbery is said to have property taken against his will, he also retains at least a slight "degree of choice"; he could choose to risk being shot on the spot instead of handing over his money.

With this in mind, the terms "consent" and "against his will" should not be read too literally in this area of the law. In extortion statutes, "'consent' simply signifies the taking of property under circumstances falling short of robbery." *Ocasio v. United States*, 136 S. Ct. 1423 (2016). The distinction between robbery and extortion is not so much about *whether* the victim has a choice but about the degree of choice the victim has. In a robbery by fear, the victim faces a threat of immediate harm that leaves him with no real option but to comply. Faced with this kind of imminent threat, the victim gives the robber property from his immediate presence and, in the view of the law, "against his will." In an extortion case, the victim faces a threat of future — as opposed to imminent — harm that affords him more options than the robbery victim. The extortion victim could decide to report the incident to the police, for example. After weighing his options, however, the victim chooses to give the extortionist property "with his consent." As one court explained, extortion victims are "not confronted with the threat of immediate harm; the threatened injury [is] delayed, usually for hours or days, pending the victim's failure to act upon the extortionists demands." *People v. Krist*, 97 Mich. App. 699, 676 (1980).

## Zhou: *Real Life Applications*

1. Torres was a "rent collector" in 1995 for a gang in Los Angeles. As a "rent collector," Torres collected payments from drug dealers, who in exchange were allowed to sell drugs in the gang's territory without interference from the gang. One day, Torres attempted to collect "rent" from Argueta, who was selling marijuana in the gang's territory. Argueta told Torres that he did not have the week's rent yet but that he would later that afternoon. Upset, Torres pulled out a gun and told Argueta to hand over his wallet. Argueta complied. Unknown to Torres, a police officer had observed the entire exchange from across the street. The officer arrested Torres, who was tried and convicted of robbery of Argueta. Torres appeals, arguing that he committed at most the crime of extortion. How should the court rule on Torres's appeal?

## *Extortion by Wrongful Threats (Blackmail)*

Non-violent extortion typically involves a threat to reveal embarrassing information about the victim coupled with an option for the victim to pay money in exchange for silence. An extortionist might threaten to tell the victim's spouse about an affair unless the victim agrees to pay a fee to the extortionist, for example. In this type of extortion, also called blackmail, the threat to reveal embarrassing information is used to induce fear in the victim in order to obtain her property.

Of course, to constitute extortion, the threat must also be *wrongful*. Determining exactly what should be considered wrongful continues to puzzle courts and commentators. The root of the problem is this: It is not a crime to reveal embarrassing secrets about another person. Nor is it a crime to accept a payment that is freely offered in exchange for keeping a secret. But extortion makes it a crime to threaten to reveal embarrassing information about someone to extract a payment, *if* the threat is wrongful. Why should this be the case?

Theorists continue to debate why it should be a crime to demand money in exchange for not revealing embarrassing information. This problem, often referred to as the "blackmail paradox," spills over into doctrine as courts struggle to define the concept of a wrongful threat. Courts have not yet settled on a clear definition capable of resolving every case. One important distinction that has emerged asks whether the defendant had a claim of right to the money. If the defendant's threat had a nexus to a colorable claim of right, then the threat is not considered to be wrongful for purposes of extortion law. Judge Karen Nelson Moore described the claim-of-right rule and the blackmail paradox in an extortion case that involved a threat to sell embarrassing photographs to tabloids made against the actor John Stamos:

> The law of extortion has always recognized the paradox that extortion often criminalizes the contemporaneous performance of otherwise independently lawful acts. Scholars have struggled to reconcile this paradox, both by adducing a principled explanation for the distinction between lawful bargaining and criminal extortion, and by justifying extortion's criminalization in law and economics terms. Arguably, none of these scholarly efforts has been entirely successful; the precise contours of what does and does not constitute extortion remain undefined and often riddled with inconsistency and circularity in a variety of criminal contexts.
>
> [In *United States v. Jackson*, a 1999 case in which a woman was convicted of extorting money from Bill Cosby, the Second Circuit considered] whether a . . . "wrongful" threat requirement should be read into [federal extortion law]. In *Jackson*, [the court held] that the statute criminalized . . . *wrongful* threats to reputation. [I]n adopting the wrongful-threat reading, [the court] described "the type of threat to reputation . . . [that] has no nexus to a claim of right" as one kind of "inherently wrongful" threat. The Second Circuit provided examples to illustrate the dividing line between wrongful threats and permissible threats, justified by a "claim of right." By dissecting the logic of these examples, we are convinced of the virtue of the Second Circuit's reasoning.
>
> Consider, first, the most classic extortion scenario where individual X demands money from individual Y in exchange for individual X's silence or agreement to destroy evidence of individual Y's marital infidelity. In this instance, the threat to reputation is wrongful because individual X has no claim of right against individual Y to the money demanded. This is clear because as soon as the marital infidelity is exposed individual X loses her ability to demand the money from individual Y. Individual X's only leverage or claim to the money demanded from individual Y is the threat of exposing the marital infidelity and, thus, individual X's threat has no nexus to a true claim of right. By way of contrast, consider the Second Circuit's example of a country club manager who threatens to publish a list of members delinquent in their dues if the members do not promptly pay the manager their outstanding account balances. In that instance, there is a nexus between the threat and a claim of right: The duty of the members to pay the country club the outstanding dues exists independently of the threat and will continue to exist even if the club manager publishes the list as threatened. The law recognizes the club manager's threat as a lawful and valid exercise of his enforcement rights and, therefore, does not criminalize his conduct as extortion.
>
> [The defendant asks us to limit the application of extortion to threats that are not only wrongful but unlawful. We decline to do this.] To require that a threat be unlawful would be to require that the prosecution demonstrate beyond a reasonable doubt that the threat in question was independently illegal in either the criminal or civil sense. We see no reason, nor any historical or statutory basis, for reading such a requirement into [federal extortion law].

The crime of extortion has never been defined strictly in terms of the lawfulness or unlawfulness of one of the actor's underlying supporting actions. Indeed, the hallmark of extortion, and its attendant complexities, is that it often criminalizes conduct that is otherwise lawful. Thus, to adopt the position that [the defendants] advocate would be to depart in a significant respect from the traditional understanding of extortion. Such a significant departure is unwarranted where there is no indication that this was Congress's intention, and, as the Second Circuit's analysis illustrates, the "claim of right" wrongfulness standard is readily discernible and easily understandable.

*United States v. Cross*, 677 F.3d 278, 285-87 (6th Cir. 2012).

---

## Case Preview

### *People v. Bollaert*

In addition to the question of wrongfulness, the question of whether a defendant made a threat at all is often at issue in extortion cases. There are two reasons for this. First, extortionists do not always "possess the hardihood to speak out boldly and plainly, but deal in mysterious and ambiguous phrases." *People v. Choynski*, 95 Cal. 640 (1892). Second, it is not a crime to accept a payment for keeping embarrassing information a secret if the payment is freely offered. In *People v. Bollaert*, the defendant argued on appeal that there was insufficient evidence that he threatened his extortion victims. In *Bollaert*, the defendant solicited embarrassing information (compromising photographs) to be published online on one website, while operating a second website that offered the "service" of taking the photos down for a fee. Was this a legitimate business practice? Or a business based on wrongful threats?

As you read the decision, consider the following questions:

1. What evidence demonstrates that the defendant made a threat in this case?
2. What distinguishes the defendant's conduct in this case from the conduct of Yelp in the *Levitt v. Yelp! Inc.* case discussed in *Bollaert*?

---

### *People v. Bollaert*
#### 242 Cal. App. 4th 699 (2016)

O'ROURKE, J.

A jury convicted Kevin Christopher Bollaert of extortion . . . stemming from his operation of Web sites, "UGotPosted.com," through which users posted private, intimate photographs of others along with that person's name, location and social media profile links, and "ChangeMyReputation.com," through which victims could pay to have the information removed. The trial court . . . sentenced Bollaert to a split sentence of 18 years: eight years of local confinement followed by 10 years of mandatory supervision.

Bollaert . . . contends there is insufficient evidence supporting his extortion convictions because he did not directly or implicitly threaten any of the victims to expose any secret; the alleged secrets — the photographs — were already in the public domain; and he merely engaged in a business practice whereby legally posted information could be removed.

We affirm the judgment.

In 2012, 2013 and 2014, a number of individuals discovered that photographs of themselves, including nude photographs, as well as their names, hometowns, and social media addresses, had been posted without their permission on a Web site, UGotPosted.com. Most of the pictures were taken by or for former significant others or friends. Some of the pictures the victims had taken on their own phones or placed on personal webpages for private viewing by themselves or select others. Some had been taken while the victim was drugged and in a compromised state or otherwise unaware of the photographing. Victims received harassing and vulgar messages from strangers. Many of the victims contacted the Web site administrator at UGotPosted.com to try to get their photographs and information removed, without success. The UGotPosted Web site contained a link to another Web site, ChangeMyReputation.com, where victims were told that for payment of a specified amount of money, their pictures and information would be taken down. Six of the [testifying] victims paid money to an account on ChangeMyReputation.com to have their pictures removed from the Web site.

Bollaert was the administrator and registered owner of the UGotPosted Web site. He created it with another person, Eric Chanson, who eventually declined to participate and transferred his interest to Bollaert. Bollaert was in control of the Web site, and he managed and maintained it; changed, added and deleted content; and updated software that operated the site. He designed the Web site so that he had to review the content before it was posted, and it had "required fields" by which a user who wanted to post pictures of another person had to input that other person's full name, age, location ("city, state, country") and Facebook link. Bollaert received about $800 or $900 in monthly income from advertising off on the site.

Bollaert also set up and managed the Web site ChangeMyReputation.com, to which individuals who had pictures posted on the UGotPosted.com site would be directed and told they could pay money to have the information removed. A Department of Justice forensic auditor determined that victims paid a total of $30,147.73, which eventually was forwarded to Bollaert's personal PayPal account.

At trial, victim Rebecca testified that after her manager at work had been told one of his employees "was doing suspicious activity on the Internet," she discovered that intimate photographs of herself and her ex-fiancée, as well as her full name, work location, Facebook link and age, were posted on UGotPosted.com without her consent. Rebecca felt "extremely violated" by the situation, which was very hurtful and embarrassing to her. She e-mailed the Web site and demanded the photographs be taken down, but received no response. She also e-mailed ChangeMyReputation.com, and within minutes received a response directing her to pay $249.99 via PayPal. Rebecca paid the money because she felt the images were disgusting and, though her manager and others had already seen them, she was worried the images would be exposed to more people.

Victim Brian testified he was astounded, angry and embarrassed to find his nude pictures, full name, hometown, and Facebook link posted on UGotPosted.com without his consent. He was immediately scared for his job and that his parents would find out about the situation, though they never did learn about it. He e-mailed the Web site administrator at UGotPosted.com. He also e-mailed ChangeMyReputation.com, and received a response stating: "Once you pay, they will be removed immediately. If not, you can request a refund through PayPal." Brian asked whether he could pay after he was notified the photographs were removed, and received an e-mail stating: "No, we can't remove until you pay." After he expressed concern over possibly sending money to the same operator of UGotPosted.com, he received a response telling him, "Make a payment, and we will remove the content, thanks." After Brian paid $250, the content was removed.

[Four other victims testified at trial to similar incidents.]

"Extortion is the obtaining of property from another, with his consent . . . induced by a wrongful use of force or fear. . . ." (§ 518.) Fear, for purposes of extortion "may be induced by a threat of any of the following: [¶] . . . [¶] . . . To accuse the individual threatened . . . of a crime"; or "[t]o expose, or impute to him . . . a deformity, disgrace or crime" or "expose a secret affecting him [or her]." ([Pen. Code] § 519.)

"In order to establish extortion, 'the wrongful use of force or fear must be the operating or controlling cause compelling the victim's consent to surrender the thing to the extortionist.'" "The 'secret' referred to in the statute is a matter 'unknown to the general public, or to some particular part thereof which might be interested in obtaining knowledge of the secret; the secret must concern some matter of fact, relating to things past, present or future; the secret must affect the threatened person in some way so far unfavorable to the reputation or to some other interest of the threatened person, that threatened exposure thereof would be likely to induce him through fear to pay out money or property for the purpose of avoiding the exposure.'" The threat may be implied from all of the circumstances: "'No precise or particular form of words is necessary in order to constitute a threat under the circumstances. Threats can be made by innuendo and the circumstances under which the threat is uttered and the relations between [the defendant] and the [target of the threats] may be taken into consideration in making a determination of the question involved.'"

Bollaert contends the evidence is insufficient to support his convictions for extortion. [T]he People's extortion theory [at trial was] that he threatened to injure the victims by publishing their images on his UGotPosted.com Web site and used the postings to illegally obtain money via ChangeMyReputation.com by charging to have the photos removed. Bollaert does not challenge evidence of his specific intent to extort; rather, he maintains that as an interactive computer service provider and access software provider, he was under no legal obligation to remove third party postings from his Web site even if they were negative, but instead "merely offered a service to remove the photos." According to Bollaert, he was "engaging in standard business practice," and not extortion, similar to the practices approved by the Ninth Circuit in *Levitt v. Yelp! Inc.* (9th Cir. 2014) 765 F.3d 1123. Bollaert also contends there is no evidence he directly or impliedly threatened any of the victims, and that the information, which was already publicly available and exposed on his Web site, cannot constitute a secret for purposes of extortion.

The People respond that Bollaert used the implicit threat of *continued* exposure of the victims' pictures and information to extort money from them, and because his Web site contained, and indeed required, posters to provide the victims' personal identifying information, he was obligated to remove the content.

We . . . reject Bollaert's contentions concerning the absence of evidence of any threat or secret for purposes of extortion. Whether the evidence shows Bollaert engaged in the requisite threat by referring victims who desired to remove the offensive content to ChangeMyReputation.com for the purpose of having them pay to remove it, must be analyzed in the entire factual context. We conclude the threats were inherent and implied in the very structure and content of Bollaert's Web sites, which Bollaert himself created and operated. When victims were directed via UGotPosted.com to the ChangeMyReputation.com Web site, they were informed either via the Web site or e-mail they could have their photos removed for a fee, from which victims could infer that if they did not pay, the offensive content would remain on the site in further public view. Those victims who communicated with Bollaert before they paid were told the content would only be removed upon payment, and Bollaert only removed the content when the victims paid the requested fee, which eventually was deposited in Bollaert's personal account. There is no question based on the victims' testimony that the display of their private images and information subjected them to shame, disgrace and embarrassment as to their reputation and character, and they would continue to be exposed to other people if the content was not removed. The fact Bollaert did not take affirmative action to seek out or contact the victims, but merely responded to the victims' pleas to remove their content, does not render the threat element unsupported by the evidence.

In sum, there is ample evidence from which the jury could conclude Bollaert's joint operation and connection of the two Web sites in this manner, as well as his communications to the victims, was a means to obtain their money by wrongful use of fear, namely the threat to "impute to [them] . . . disgrace" by continued display of their private nude images and further humiliation, embarrassment, and damage to their reputation, unless they paid.

We further conclude alternatively there is substantial evidence that the victims' photographs and personal identifying information constituted a secret within the meaning of the crime of extortion, notwithstanding its posting on the Internet and viewing by some individuals. We are guided by *People v. Peniston* [(1966) 242 Cal. App. 2d 719]. In *Peniston*, the victim, during her relationship with the defendant, gave the defendant partially nude photographs of herself. After the relationship ended and she married her husband, the defendant returned and asked her to give him money or he would take the pictures to her husband and parents. She paid him, but the defendant contacted her again and when she asked him to return her pictures, he asked for more money, prompting her to go to police. On appeal from his extortion and attempted extortion convictions, the defendant challenged the evidence supporting the finding that he had threatened to expose a secret, pointing to evidence that the pictures were only some of a number of modeling pictures taken of the victim that had been circulated throughout the West Coast.

The *Peniston* court pointed out that to suffice for extortion, the "'thing held secret must be unknown to the general public, *or to some particular part thereof which might be interested in obtaining knowledge of the secret'"* in addition to affecting the threatened person in some way so far unfavorable to the reputation, or to some other interest of the threatened person, that threatened exposure would be likely to induce the victim through fear to pay money so as to avoid the exposure. It held based on the evidence, a trier of fact could reasonably infer the victim feared that disclosure of the pictures to her husband and parents might lead to adverse . . . consequences . . . , making the evidence sufficient to establish a secret within the meaning of section 519.

As in *Peniston*, where dissemination of the victim's images to the general public via arcades or other means did not render the evidence insufficient to establish a secret for purposes of extortion because the victim's family had not seen them, here, the fact the victims' photographs were placed on the Internet and exposed to the public did not mean that some other "particular part [of the public]" — namely, family members, classmates, coworkers, or employers who might be interested — had seen them. The People presented direct testimony from some of the six victims concerning their fear that others would see their images if they did not pay to have them removed, as well as evidence as to all of the victims that they quickly paid for removal, from which the jury could readily infer the victims were fearful of continued exposure.

We further reject Bollaert's claim that he was engaged in a lawful or legitimate business practice and not extortionate conduct. His claim is based on . . . the Ninth Circuit's decision in *Levitt*, which he claims discussed "extortion as it relates to Internet service providers [*sic*]."

In *Levitt*, the plaintiff small businesses sued Yelp! Inc. (Yelp), an online forum for persons to express opinions about businesses, claiming it extorted or attempted to extort advertising payments from them including by manipulating or removing positive user-generated reviews about their business. They brought claims for violation of California's unfair competition law, civil extortion and attempted civil extortion, on the theory Yelp wrongfully threatened them with economic loss. Pointing out both the [federal extortion statute] and California law require the obtaining of property with consent induced by a *wrongful* use of force or fear, the Ninth Circuit held the plaintiffs failed to state a claim. It applied a "claim-of-right" defense under which a defendant cannot commit extortion by threatening economic harm to induce a person to pay for a "legitimate service." The court had previously held, for example, that a mobilehome park operator does not commit extortion by telling tenants who refused to sign leases that they would have to pay their own utility bills and be subject to future rent increases. "[T]he tenants did not allege that the park owner 'may not raise the rent of those who have not signed the lease or that it may not refuse to pay their utility bills,'" and thus they had no "pre-existing right to be free of such threats." According to the Ninth Circuit, "[a]ny less stringent standard would transform a wide variety of legally acceptable business dealings into extortion." Thus, in *Levitt*, the court held in part that the plaintiffs did not allege facts showing Yelp intended to induce payment through an implicit threat of economic harm or the exploitation of economic fears. Plaintiff "had no pre-existing right to have positive reviews appear on Yelp's website"; she did not allege a "contractual right pursuant to which Yelp must publish positive reviews, nor does any law require Yelp to publish them."

Bollaert mischaracterizes *Levitt*. The question [in *Levitt*] was whether Yelp's alleged actions were extortionate. Bollaert's conduct is nothing like the legitimate albeit "hard bargaining" business tactics discussed in *Levitt*. Bollaert, who did not merely decline to remove harmful content but solicited and developed the unlawful content, did not have a lawful right to collect a fee to remove the victims' personal information. And unlike the plaintiffs in *Levitt* who did not have a preexisting right to have positive reviews appear on Yelp's Web site, the plaintiff victims here had a preexisting right — under privacy law — to be free of Bollaert's threatened harm and not have their personal identifying information solicited and placed on UGotPosted.com without their consent.

The judgment is affirmed.

**Post-Case Follow-Up**

As explained in *Bollaert*, implied threats can serve as the basis for extortion. In this case, the court concluded that "the threats were inherent and implied in the very structure and content of Bollaert's web sites," which suggested that he would remove the private photos of his victims only if they paid him money. This amounted to a threat to continue disseminating the private photos to the public in the court's view. The court also distinguished Bollaert's threats from Yelp's business practices in *Levitt*. In *Levitt*, which involved a civil extortion claim, the plaintiffs alleged that Yelp extorted advertising payments by threatening to remove positive user reviews. The Ninth Circuit held that this was not a wrongful threat but a legitimate business practice. In *Bollaert*, the court found that the defendant did not have a lawful right to collect a fee to remove the victim's personal information, whereas Yelp did have a lawful right to solicit advertising fees.

## Bollaert: *Real Life Applications*

1. John Stamos, a well-known actor who starred in the 1990s television show *Full House*, went on a weekend trip to Florida in 2004. There, he met Allison Coss, an 18-year old, at an 18-and-over night club. Stamos invited Coss to a party at his friend's house. Coss

---

## Criminalizing Revenge Porn?

The extortion scheme in *Bollaert* depended on getting people to post nude photos of others with their identifying information to the UGotPosted.com website. This is commonly referred to as "revenge porn," and it is a problem that spread rapidly as the rise of smartphones led more and more people to share intimate photos or videos with significant others. In contrast to the old days of print photographs, recipients of these digital images retain them and can easily distribute them long after a relationship has ended.

Despite widespread concern about revenge porn, the law has had difficulty responding to it. Consider that if Bollaert had simply hosted a pornography website that relied on user-generated content, he would not have been guilty of extortion. Bollaert's crime was not hosting a revenge porn website but rather threatening to continue distributing the revenge porn unless his victim paid a fee.

In *Criminalizing Revenge Porn*, 49 Wake Forest L. Rev. 345 (2014), Danielle Keats Citron and Mary Anne Franks propose that the criminal law should be expanded to directly combat revenge porn. In discussing the facts of Kevin Bolleart's case before it had gone to trial, Professors Citron and Franks observe that "revenge porn operators who charge for the removal of images are not the only ones hosting revenge porn. There are countless other sites and blogs that host revenge porn that do not engage in extortion." *Id.* at 369. To address this gap, they argue that "[s]tates, along with the federal government, should craft narrow statutes that prohibit the publication of nonconsensual pornography." *Id.* at 390.

In recent years, more and more states have done just that, by passing laws targeting revenge porn. These laws vary significantly in their scope and application. One constant, however, is that revenge porn laws must abide by the First Amendment. As a result, they typically require a *mens rea* of knowledge that the person in the image has not consented to its distribution.

later testified that illegal drugs, including cocaine and MDMA, were used by party attendees. Coss took photographs of herself and Stamos at the party.

Four years later, Coss began dating a man named Sippola. One day, Coss showed Sippola the photographs of Stamos from her trip in 2004. Sippola suggested they try to sell the photographs to Stamos. Coss agreed and the pair created an email address under a fictitious name, Jessica Taylor. They sent an email from "Jessica" to Stamos telling Stamos that they had "bad" photographs of Stamos "partying" near illegal drugs in 2004. They offered to sell the photographs to Stamos for $650,000. The email ended with this line: "If you don't agree to the deal by Friday, we will have no choice but to sell the photographs to a tabloid. I'm sure you don't want them to become public."

Stamos forwarded the email to his lawyer who contacted the Federal Bureau of Investigation (FBI). FBI agents instructed Stamos to agree to "Jessica's" proposal and send "Jessica" the money. Using the account provided by "Jessica," the FBI tracked and arrested Coss and Sippola, who were charged with and convicted of extortion.

On appeal, Coss and Sippola argue that their offer to sell the photographs did not constitute a wrongful threat as a matter of law. In support of this argument, Coss and Sippola note that they had a lawful right to possess the photographs and a lawful right to sell them to a tabloid. As a result, they claim, it was also lawful for them to give Stamos the opportunity to purchase them.

You are a clerk for one of the appellate judges assigned to the case. Would you advise your judge to rule in favor of Coss and Sippola?

## Extortion Under Color of Official Right

The last category of extortion targets coercive thefts by public officials. Although this type of extortion has the longest lineage, it is of comparatively less consequence than other forms of extortion today because it is so narrowly focused. As the Supreme Court has explained, at common law "[e]xtortion by the public official was the rough equivalent of what we would now describe as 'taking a bribe.'" *Evans v. United States*, 504 U.S. 255, 260 (1992). This form of extortion prohibits a public official from taking money that is "not due to him for the performance of his official duties." *Id.* Put another way, "coercive extortion by a public official is the seeking or receiving of a corrupt benefit paid under an implicit or explicit threat to give the payor worse than fair treatment or to make the payor worse off than he is now. The payee is guilty of extortion; the payor is the victim of extortion." James Lindgren, *The Elusive Distinction Between Bribery and Extortion: From the*

*Common Law to the Hobbs Act*, 35 UCLA L. Rev. 815, 825 (1988). As an example, "it is extortion if a public official threatens to deny a public contract to a bidding contractor who clearly deserves to receive it unless the bidder pays off the official." *Id.* Because of its narrow focus, cases involving this type of extortion are comparatively rare.

## B. BURGLARY

Burglary is an important crime, both because of its common law pedigree and its prevalence today. In 2018, there were an estimated 1.2 million burglaries, accounting for over 16 percent of all property crimes, according to the Federal Bureau of Investigation's Uniform Crime Reporting Program.

The authoritative common law definition of burglary dates back to 1641. The common law defined **burglary** as the breaking and entering of the dwelling of another at night with the intent to commit a felony therein.

Despite its long history and continued importance, burglary is not amenable to a generic definition today. This is because "the contemporary understanding of 'burglary' has diverged a long way from its common law roots." *Taylor v. United States*, 495 U.S. 575, 593 (1990). Almost every state has altered one or more of the elements of common law burglary. But no single modern definition of the crime has emerged. Instead, "the criminal codes of the States define burglary in many different ways," depending on which elements of the common law definition of burglary they adhere to and which modern changes they have decided to adopt. *Id.* at 580. Complicating matters further, today most state laws have more than one degree of burglary.

Although no longer the law in the vast majority of states, the common law definition of burglary remains important for at least three reasons:

First, the common law definition of burglary continues to serve as "the core, or common denominator, of the contemporary usage of the term." *Id.* at 592. Very few modern statutes contain *all* of the elements of common law burglary. But every modern burglary statute includes *some* of the common law elements.

Second, "[c]ourts refer to the common law definition and rationales regularly when addressing questions about the modern statutes." Helen A. Anderson, *From the Thief in the Night to the Guest Who Stayed Too Long: The Evolution of Burglary in the Shadow of Common Law*, 45 Ind. L. Rev. 629, 666 (2012). This is true even when courts are considering elements that diverge from the common law. When there is a question about legislative intent, comparing common law burglary to the current statute can be quite helpful.

Finally, states sometimes use common law elements to differentiate degrees of burglary. For example, some states retain the common law's nighttime element for first-degree burglary, but not for lower degrees of burglary.

For these reasons, the common law definition of burglary continues to serve as the foundation for learning the elements of burglary. The discussion that follows considers the common law definition for each of the elements of burglary, along with modern variations.

## Breaking

### The Common Law Rule

Under the breaking element, a mere trespass is not enough to constitute burglary. Walking into a house through an open door or even climbing in through an open window is not considered a breaking. Instead, a breaking requires entry through the use of force. Importantly, "[u]sing even the slightest force to gain unauthorized entry satisfies the breaking element of the crime." *Davis v. State*, 770 N.E.2d 319, 322 (Ind. 2002). Under this standard, for example, "[i]f the door or window be shut" but unlocked, opening the door or window constitutes breaking. *State v. Boon*, 35 N.C. 244, 246 (1852). This is because the force used to open the unlocked door or window is enough to satisfy the slightest force rule. Similarly, while walking through an open door or window is not a breaking, in many jurisdictions "pushing a door that is slightly ajar constitutes a breaking." *Davis*, 770 N.E.2d at 322.

In addition to force, a breaking can be accomplished by fraud or threats. Cases often refer to this as a "constructive breaking." In *State v. Abdullah*, 967 A.2d 469, 477 (R.I. 2009), for example, the Supreme Court of Rhode Island ruled that the defendant had accomplished a constructive breaking when he "held up a pizza box as a ruse to trick [the victim] into opening the door." By contrast, a person who is freely invited into someone else's home has not committed a breaking.

### The Modern Approach

Only 12 jurisdictions have retained breaking as an element for at least one degree of burglary. Some states have eliminated this requirement entirely. But most have substituted a similar, albeit more lenient, requirement in its place. A majority of these states have replaced breaking with "unlawful entry." Other terms include "unauthorized," "without authority," "without consent," "trespass," and "having no right, license or privilege." While each of these terms are different, they all "generally require that the entry be unprivileged," thereby excluding cases where a person has been invited to enter a place or has entered a place that is open to the public from the crime of burglary. Wayne R. LaFave, 3 Substantive Criminal Law § 21.1(a) (3d ed. 2017).

## Entering

### The Common Law Rule

Although a breaking is almost always followed by an entry, entry is technically a separate element of burglary. It does not take much to satisfy this element. An "entry" does not require a defendant's entire body to pass the threshold of the house. Instead, "[e]ntry as an element of burglary is established by the penetration into a dwelling . . . by any part of the defendant's body." *Edelen v. United States*, 560

A.2d 527, 530 (D.C. 1989). Under this standard, sticking a hand or a foot into the house is an entry. If a would-be burglar is frightened away before part of his body has passed into the structure, however, the entry element will not be met.

### The Modern Approach

A significant minority of jurisdictions still require an entry for the crime of burglary. But in a slight majority — at least 29 — burglary can be committed by entering *or remaining* on the property. On the surface, this might seem like an odd rule. After all, since teleportation has not yet been invented, it is impossible to remain in a building without first entering it. The real significance of the expansion of the entry element to include remaining is its impact on the timing of burglary's *mens rea* element. As discussed further below, at common law, the defendant must have intended to commit a felony at the time of the entry. This is no longer always true in jurisdictions that have expanded the entry element to include remaining.

## *Dwelling of Another*

### The Common Law Rule

The dwelling element was central to the common law conception of burglary. This is because "[t]he theoretical basis of common law burglary was the ancient notion that a man's home was his castle and that he had the right to feel safe therein." *Rash v. Commw.*, 9 Va. App. 22, 25 (1989). Since "[b]urglary was, at common law, primarily an offense against the security of the habitation," the offense was limited to dwellings. *Compton v. Commw.*, 190 Va. 48, 55 (1949). A dwelling is any "place which human beings regularly use for sleeping." *Rash*, 9 Va. App. at 26. Under this definition, a structure that is used for a dual purpose — for example, a business with a bedroom in the back — can qualify as a dwelling. So long as the structure is regularly used for sleeping purposes it is a dwelling, and the fact that it might also be put to other uses is immaterial.

### The Modern Approach

Almost every state has expanded the types of structures that can be the subject of burglary beyond dwellings. In most states, burglary can be committed at any building. Some states have expanded burglary even further to include not just buildings but cars, tents, and yards. Despite this fact, the dwelling element remains an important one. In jurisdictions that divide burglary into degrees, the type of structure is often one of the factors that separate the different degrees. Indeed, almost half of the states reserve burglary in the first degree for dwellings.

## *At Night*

### The Common Law Rule

The requirement that burglary be committed at nighttime went hand in hand with its purpose of protecting the habitation. The right to security in the home was thought to be "especially true at night, when [a person] was most vulnerable because he was asleep." *Rash*, 9 Va. App. at 25. As the English judge Lord Coke, who provided the authoritative definition of common law burglary, colorfully put it in 1644, "night is the time wherein man is to rest, and wherein beasts runne about seeking their prey." Sir Edward Coke, The Third Part of the Institutes of the Laws of England 63 (W. Clarke & Sons 1817) (1644). In Lord Coke's time, night was defined as when "you cannot discern the countenance of a man" by natural daylight. *Id.* Over time, some courts discarded this definition in favor of a rule based on sunrise and sunset.

### The Modern Approach

A decisive majority of states have abandoned the nighttime element of burglary entirely. Only two states require all degrees of burglary to be committed at night. Seven more include nighttime as one of the factors that separates higher degrees of burglary from lower degrees.

## With the Intent to Commit a Felony Therein

### The Common Law Rule

There are a few components for the *mens rea* requirement of common law burglary.

First, under the common law definition, the defendant must intend to commit a *felony* inside the dwelling he is breaking and entering into. Although burglary is often associated with theft, it is not limited to people who break into a house with an intent to commit larceny or robbery. An intent to commit *any* felony will do. By contrast, a defendant who intends to commit a misdemeanor — even a misdemeanor theft — has not acted with the necessary *mens rea* at common law. Likewise, breaking and entering into someone's home without any further criminal purpose is not burglary.

Second, the *mens rea* of common law burglary incorporates a very important timing component. The intent to commit a felony must be present at the time of the entry. Consider the hypothetical case of a man who breaks and enters into a home in a remote area to get out of the cold. The man does not intend to commit a felony at the time he enters the home. But once inside, he sees a valuable piece of jewelry and decides to steal it, thereby committing larceny (a common law felony). This man is not guilty of burglary because his intent to commit larceny did not come about until *after* he had entered the dwelling. This kind of timing-based defense to burglary is rarely successful in the real world, but it is considered to be an important part of the definition of common law burglary nonetheless.

### What Purpose Does Burglary as a Distinct Offense Serve?

Because of its common law origins and continued prevalence on criminal dockets today, it is hard to imagine a criminal code without the crime of burglary. But the drafters of the Model Penal Code gave serious thought to that very idea. In fact, they "considered eliminating burglary as a distinct offense" before ultimately concluding "that '[c]enturies of history . . . are not easily discarded.'" Anderson, *supra*, at 638 (quoting Model Penal Code § 221.1 cmt. 2 at 67).

Finally, the *mens rea* element does not require the defendant to actually carry out his felonious intent. An *intent* to commit a felony inside the home is all that is required. If the defendant is caught before he has a chance to actually commit the felony, he can still be convicted of burglary so long as there is sufficient evidence of his intent.

### The Modern Approach

A significant number of states have modified the *mens rea* element of burglary in two important ways.

First, almost every state has expanded the type of crime that can be the subject of a burglarious intent beyond felonies. In a majority of states, the *mens rea* of burglary is an intent to commit *any* crime. A significant minority of states require an intent to commit any theft or felony, effectively expanding the offense to include defendants who intend to commit petty thefts.

Second, as noted briefly above in the discussion of entry, many states have done away with the timing component of burglary by expanding the entry element. Specifically, in the 29 states that "include[] 'remaining' as an alternative to entry, the criminal intent may be formed at any time while the defendant remains on the premises and need not have been formed at the time of entry." Anderson, *supra*, at 646. Most jurisdictions that have expanded the entry element in this way require proof that the defendant surreptitiously or unlawfully remained inside the building. In these states, a person who lawfully enters a store and then hides inside until after it closes would be considered to have surreptitiously or unlawfully remained in the store; if this person forms the necessary criminal intent while hiding on the premises, the *mens rea* element is satisfied. A few states have gone even further and do not require proof that the defendant unlawfully or surreptitiously remained. As the next case suggests, this can result in an offense that is considerably more expansive than common law burglary.

> To understand the argument for abolishing the crime of burglary, ask yourself what purpose the offense serves today. While there are many different versions of modern burglary, every version requires proof that the burglar intended to commit some other crime inside of a structure. Consider the classic burglary case of a person who breaks into a home in order to steal something inside. Why not just punish this person for larceny or attempted larceny? What does adding a burglary charge to a case like this achieve?
>
> Regardless of the merits of retaining burglary as a separate offense, the crime is a deeply ingrained part of our criminal law, and there are no signs to suggest any state legislature is likely to consider repealing it. Indeed, as already discussed, nearly every state has expanded the reach of the offense by modifying one or more of its elements.

**Case Preview**

## In re T.J.E.

Almost every state has altered or abandoned some elements of common law burglary. Alterations to the breaking and entering elements, which can sometimes seem like trivial requirements, have had a significant impact on the nature of the offense in some states. At the extreme, changes to these elements have the potential to "allow[] burglary to be attached to almost any crime that occurs indoors." Anderson, *supra*, at 629. The next case illustrates this point.

Here the Supreme Court of South Dakota grappled with the case of an 11-year old who was charged with burglary for eating a piece of candy at a retail store during business hours without paying for it. Although it seemed as though the plain text of South Dakota's second-degree burglary statute would apply to the child's case, a unanimous court found a way to avoid this result.

As you read the decision, consider the following questions:

1. Looking at South Dakota's second-degree burglary statute, which of burglary's common law elements have been retained and which have been eliminated or altered?
2. In most circumstances, courts find that evidence that a person stole something inside of a building is sufficient to prove that she harbored an intent to steal at the time she entered that building. The court reaches a different conclusion here. Are you persuaded by the court's reasoning?
3. Do you think the court's interpretation of South Dakota's burglary statute is faithful to the text? If not, do you think the decision is nevertheless correct?

---

## *In re T.J.E.*
### 426 N.W.2d 23 (S.D. 1988)

WUEST, J.

T.J.E., age 11, entered a retail store during business hours with her aunt. While in the store, T.J.E. took and ate a piece of candy from a display and left with her aunt without paying for the candy. T.J.E. was stopped outside of the store by the manager and ultimately admitted to him that she had eaten a piece of candy without paying for it.

State subsequently filed a petition in the circuit court alleging T.J.E. to be a delinquent child. The petition alleged second degree burglary. After an adjudicatory hearing the circuit court sustained the allegations of second degree burglary.

We find that the evidence presented by state during T.J.E.'s adjudicatory hearing was insufficient to sustain the allegations in its petition and, therefore, we deem it unnecessary to address the other issues raised by T.J.E. in her brief.

State alleged in its petition that T.J.E. committed the offense of second degree burglary in violation of SDCL 22-32-3:

> Any person who *enters* or *remains* in an occupied structure with intent to commit any crime therein under circumstances not amounting to first degree burglary, is guilty of second degree burglary. Second degree burglary is a Class 3 felony.

(emphasis added).

[The] state had the burden of proving each element of this offense beyond a reasonable doubt. It was necessary, therefore, for state to prove that T.J.E. either *entered* or *remained* in an occupied structure with the intent to commit a crime therein.

We find no proof in the record that at the time T.J.E. entered the store with her aunt she had the intent to commit a crime inside. We decline to interpret the impulsive act of this 11 year old child in taking candy after entering the store as evincing an intent *at the time of her entry* to commit theft. This clearly distinguishes this case from our affirmance of a burglary conviction in *State v. Shult*, 380 N.W.2d 352 (S.D. 1986), where the [adult] defendant took an item of merchandise from a convenience store.

The circuit court did find that T.J.E. *remained* in the store with the intent to commit theft, thereby committing second degree burglary by *remaining* in an occupied structure with the intent to commit a crime therein.

A literal reading of the word "remains" in the statute (SDCL 22-32-3) would support this finding and would end the need for further inquiry. However, where the literal meaning of a statute leads to absurd or unreasonable conclusions, ambiguity exists. To interpret the word "remains" in SDCL 22-32-3 to hold a person commits second degree burglary whenever he is present in an occupied structure with the intent to commit a crime therein would make every shoplifter a burglar. It would make the commission of any crime indoors, no matter how severe, subject to a felony burglary charge. We do not believe the legislature intended such absurd results when it amended the burglary statutes in 1976.

To read the word "remains" in the second degree burglary statute to mean that a person can commit burglary when he is lawfully present in an occupied structure not only leads to the absurdities we have discussed but also contravenes the principle observed by [courts in other states] that burglary must be committed by a person who has no right to be in the structure. However, if we were to read the word "remains" as it is qualified in the statutes of eleven other states to mean that a person can commit second degree burglary when he is *unlawfully* present or present *without authority* in an occupied structure, it would avoid the possibility for absurdity and retain the principle that burglary must be committed by a person with no right to be in the structure.

We are aware that construing the word "remains" in the second degree burglary statute to mean an *unlawful* presence in a structure may appear to be inconsistent with previous holdings of this court that an unlawful or unauthorized *entry* into a structure is not an element of . . . burglary. However, the case in which we reached this conclusion . . . [reasoned that w]here a person enters a business place open to the general public with the intent to commit a crime therein, he enters without invitation and is not one of the public invited or entitled to enter the structure. We [continue to] find this reasoning persuasive and are satisfied that it resolves any perceived inconsistency between our conclusion herein and previous holdings of this court.

We conclude, therefore, that the word "remains" in the second degree burglary statute means to *unlawfully* remain in a structure. Therefore, second degree burglary was not committed in this case where T.J.E. entered an occupied structure and *after* entry, while *lawfully* remaining in the structure, formed the intent to commit an offense therein.

We find that state failed to establish that T.J.E. either entered or *unlawfully* remained in an occupied structure with the intent to commit a crime therein. Therefore, the evidence was insufficient to sustain the allegations in state's delinquency petition. Accordingly, we reverse the circuit court's adjudication and disposition of T.J.E. as a juvenile delinquent.

**Post-Case Follow-Up**

In isolation, changes to burglary's common law elements do not fundamentally alter the crime. In the right combination, however, they can have the potential to result in an offense that is almost unrecognizable as burglary. Taken literally, South Dakota's second-degree burglary statute would appear to apply to anyone who commits any crime inside an occupied structure — including an 11-year-old girl who eats a piece of candy without paying for it. The court made two moves to prevent this outcome in *In re T.J.E.* First, the court found that "the word 'remains' in the second degree burglary statute means to 'unlawfully' remain." This limited the reach of the statute but was not alone enough to support a reversal in this case. Under the court's interpretation of the statute, if the 11-year old had intended to eat the candy at the time she entered the store, she would still be guilty of burglary. This necessitated the court's second move: concluding that the girl's theft of the candy did not support an inference that she intended to steal at the time she entered the store. This conclusion runs counter to the great weight of authority, which holds that when a person steals something inside of a house or a store, it is strong circumstantial evidence she intended to steal at the time of entry. The court's reason for reaching a different conclusion here makes some sense. There is good reason to think that an adult who breaks into a house and leaves with a television entered with an intent to steal. In this case, the theft seems much more likely to have been an impulsive act, not something planned in advance.

## T.J.E.: *Real Life Applications*

1. Bradford entered a Walmart store through an open door at around lunchtime, during regular business hours. An "asset protection associate" who thought that Bradford looked suspicious began to watch Bradford on a security monitor. After ten minutes inside of the store, Bradford picked up two DVDs from a store display. Bradford brought the two DVDs to the customer service desk. There, he told the customer service employee that a friend had given him the DVDs as a present and that he would like to return them even though he didn't have a receipt. The sales associate processed a "no-receipt" return and handed Bradford a Walmart gift card in the same amount as the value of the two DVDs. As Bradford was leaving the store, he was stopped by the asset protection associate and later arrested.
    a. If Bradford were prosecuted in a jurisdiction that adhered to the common law definition of burglary, he would not be guilty of the offense. Which elements would not be satisfied and why? Which elements, if any, would be satisfied?
    b. Assume this incident occurred in South Dakota. Could Bradford be convicted of second-degree burglary under the statute described in *In re T.J.E.*?
    c. Now, assume that this incident occurred in Illinois and that Bradford is charged with burglary under the following Illinois statute: "A person

commits burglary when without authority he or she knowingly enters or without authority remains within a building, * * * or any part thereof, with intent to commit therein a felony or theft." 720 Ill. Comp. Stat. 5/19-1(a). Could Bradford be convicted of burglary under this statute?

---

**EXHIBIT 3.1**  **Example of Jury Instructions for the Crime of Burglary From a California Trial**

### 1700. Burglary (Pen. Code, § 459)

The defendant is charged in Count 1 with burglary.

To prove that the defendant is guilty of this crime, the People must prove that:

1. The defendant entered a building;

2. When he entered a building, he intended to commit theft.

To decide whether the defendant intended to commit theft, please refer to the separate instructions that I will give you on that crime.

A burglary was committed if the defendant entered with the intent to commit theft. The defendant does not need to have actually committed theft as long as he entered with the intent to do so. The People do not have to prove that the defendant actually committed theft.

Under the law of burglary, a person *enters a building* if some part of his or her body penetrates the area inside the building's outer boundary.

A building's *outer boundary* includes the area inside a window screen.

An attached balcony designed to be entered only from inside of a private, residential apartment on the second or higher floor of a building is inside a building's *outer boundary*.

The People allege that the defendant intended to commit theft. You may not find the defendant guilty of burglary unless you all agree that he intended to commit one of those crimes at the time of the entry. You do not all have to agree on which one of those crimes he intended.

---

P~~~ ~~~~~~ ~~~~uff/Defendant
R~~~~~ ~ulation
Given ~~~~~ Modified
Withou~ ~~
Refuse~ Reason:_____

PAULA S. ROSENSTEIN

**EXHIBIT 3.1** Continued

### 1701. Burglary: Degrees (Pen. Code, § 460)

---

Burglary is divided into two degrees. If you conclude that the defendant committed a burglary, you must then decide the degree.

First degree burglary is the burglary of an inhabited house or a room within an inhabited house.

A house is *inhabited* if someone uses it as a dwelling, whether or not someone is inside at the time of the alleged entry.

All other burglaries are second degree.

The People have the burden of proving beyond a reasonable doubt that the burglary was first degree burglary. If the People have not met this burden, you must find the defendant not guilty of first degree burglary.

---

Requ~ ~~~ ~~~~ iff/Defendant
Requ~          ~iation
Given          Modified
With~d
Refu~ ~~ ~ason:_____

PAULA S. ROSENSTEIN

## C. ARSON

Like burglary, common law arson was conceived of as a crime against the habitation. Also like burglary, "the law of arson has changed dramatically from what it was at common law." John Poulos, *The Metamorphosis of the Law of Arson*, 51 Mo. L. Rev. 295, 277 (1986). At common law, arson's primary concern was not to protect the home as a piece of property; instead, the offense of arson was designed to "preserve the security of the habitation [and] to protect the dwellers within the building from injury or death by fire." *Id.* at 299-300. The contemporary crime of arson has been expanded to protect *both* "the inhabitants of dwelling houses . . . [and] property as property." *Id.* at 446. The definition of modern arson varies significantly across jurisdictions. For this reason, as with burglary, common law arson remains an important part of the criminal law canon even though most state statutes today do not employ the common law definition. Common law arson serves as a shared foundation for the many modern variations on the crime, and many of its elements are often present in modern statutes to help distinguish first-degree arson from lesser degrees of the offense.

The common law defined **arson** as the malicious burning of the dwelling house of another. Each of these elements is briefly discussed below.

## Malicious

### The Common Law Rule

The common law *mens rea* for arson, malicious, was historically "a term fraught with ambiguity." LaFave, *supra*, § 21.3. In essence, however, the term is akin to the modern mental state of criminal recklessness. Recall that to act recklessly means to consciously disregard a substantial and unjustifiable risk. A malicious "arson is committed when a person intentionally does an act . . . under circumstances in which the act creates a very high risk of burning the dwelling house of another, when the actor knew of that risk and yet did the risk-taking act despite that knowledge." Poulos, *supra*, at 321. Under this definition, failing to perceive a risk that one's actions would cause a fire would not suffice. To act maliciously, the actor must have been *subjectively aware* of a very high risk that his actions might set another's house on fire.

### The Modern Approach

There is a good deal of diversity when it comes to the *mens rea* required by today's arson statutes. Many jurisdictions continue to use the term maliciously. Others have updated the *mens rea* by using purposely, intentionally, knowingly, or recklessly. Although no single mental state prevails in the modern definition of arson, states uniformly require more than negligence with respect to the core elements of the offense.

## Burning

### The Common Law Rule

Common law arson requires the burning of the dwelling of another. This element combines both the *actus reus* and result required for the offense by targeting any act that causes a house to burn. A house has been burned within the meaning of common law arson if some part of it is at least charred by fire; discoloration or smoke damage alone is not sufficient. Burning personal property within a house was not arson at common law. Nor was damaging someone else's house by a means other than burning. But "the manner by which the arsonist caused the dwelling to burn was . . . of no importance." Poulos, *supra*, at 318. As a result, a defendant who used explosives to destroy a house would be guilty of arson *if* the explosives resulted in a fire. On the other hand, if the explosives destroyed the building without causing it to burn, it would not constitute arson.

### The Modern Approach

While fire remains an integral part of most modern arson statutes, the burning requirement has been abandoned in a decisive majority of states. Instead, most modern arson statutes have expanded this element of arson to encompass any damage to a home by the use of fire. "Under these statutes the actor must cause some physical harm to the subject matter of the crime by the use of fire, or to put it in more operational terms, the fire must cause some change (injury) to the building which lowers its value or impairs its usefulness. Thus it is arson under the damage statutes if the fire 'scorches' the paint on the building, or causes smoke damage to the building, although neither would suffice as a burning at common law." *Id.* at 358. Another group of states have gone even further by eliminating arson's results element entirely. "In these states the conduct prohibited by their arson statutes is the starting of a fire with a specified *mens rea* with respect to given property." *Id.* at 361. In jurisdictions that follow this approach to the crime, conduct that would have previously been treated as attempted arson (maliciously starting a fire without burning or damaging a building) now constitutes arson.

### Dwelling of Another

#### The Common Law Rule

Arson and burglary share the same definition of "the dwelling of another." For both crimes, a dwelling is a place that humans regularly use for sleeping. The *of another* component takes on somewhat more importance in the crime of arson than burglary, however. The idea that a person cannot burglarize her own home fits the modern conception of burglary. The same is not necessarily true of arson. Because of the *dwelling of another* requirement, it was not arson to burn one's own home in order to fraudulently collect insurance money at common law. This approach made sense in light of the purpose of the crime of arson at common law, which was "to protect the physical safety of the inhabitants of a dwelling house," and not to protect property interests in dwellings. Poulos, *supra*, at 387.

#### The Modern Approach

In most states, this element has changed significantly from the common law. First, arson has expanded to apply to all buildings, not just dwellings. Indeed, no state limits arson to dwelling houses. Second, the overwhelming majority of states have also discarded or significantly altered the requirement that the building burned belong to "another." In many states, this requirement has been removed entirely, meaning that a person can commit arson by maliciously burning his own home, regardless of his motive. Other states provide that arson covers any building, including her own, but allow for an affirmative defense if the defendant intended to destroy the building for a lawful purpose.

Changes to the *dwelling of another* element reflect the expansion of arson from a crime concerned with protecting the person and habitation to a crime that is also concerned with protecting property. This is very similar to the expansion of the crime of burglary. And, just as in burglary, the *dwelling of another* element continues to live on as a tool for grading degrees of arson. In many states, first-degree arson is limited to dwellings or to other structures that are currently occupied. The particulars vary significantly from state to state — some hew closely to the common law's *dwelling of another* formulation, others less so — but the common theme is that first-degree arson typically targets setting fire to buildings in a way that endangers people while lesser degrees of arson protect property interests only.

## Chapter Summary

- The three most significant non-violent theft offenses are larceny, embezzlement, and false pretenses. The differences between these three crimes can sometimes seem arbitrary, in part because they are accidents of history. The crimes of embezzlement and false pretenses were created by the British Parliament in the mid- to late 1700s in order to fill gaps in the law that had been left by the elements of larceny. Although most states today have enacted consolidated theft statutes, these statutes largely incorporate and retain the common law definitions of larceny, embezzlement, and false pretenses. As a result, being able to distinguish between these three types of theft offenses remains important for both criminal law students and practitioners.

- Larceny is the offense that applies to most everyday thefts. It is the trespassory taking and carrying away of the personal property of another with the intent to permanently deprive the possessor of the property. A trespassory taking means a taking without the possessor's consent. Most often, this is accomplished by taking property without ever asking for consent — for example, shoplifting, pickpocketing, or hotwiring a car. Under the larceny by trick theory, a trespassory taking also includes cases where the thief fraudulently induces a person to give over possession of her property. In the famous *The King v. Pear* case, the defendant committed larceny by trick by tricking a person into renting him a horse and then selling the horse.

- Because larceny requires the intent to permanently deprive another of her property, if the defendant genuinely believes that he has consent to take the property or that it is abandoned, then he has not committed larceny. Likewise, if he merely plans to temporarily borrow someone else's property without permission, it is not larceny.

- Embezzlement is the conversion of the property of another by one who is already in lawful possession of it. What distinguishes embezzlement from larceny is how the thief came to possess the property. Larceny requires a *trespassory* taking of the property — a taking of property without genuine consent, either by taking property without asking for consent or by tricking someone into parting with property. Embezzlement covers cases where a person comes into lawful possession of property, and then converts it to her own use. If a financial manager takes possession of her client's funds to invest and later decides to convert the funds for her own use, it is embezzlement.

- False pretenses makes it a crime to obtain title to another's property by a false representation of a material fact with the intent to defraud the victim. The difference between false pretenses and larceny by trick is not intuitive, but it is relatively straightforward in many cases. What separates the two crimes from one another is whether or not the victim transferred title (ownership) of the property to the thief. Larceny, including larceny by trick, criminalizes the trespassory taking of *mere possession* of property. A defendant who hotwires a car or who tricks someone into renting him a horse is guilty of larceny because he has gained only possession of that property. By contrast, a defendant who tricks someone into transferring ownership — for example, by purchasing an item at a store after switching the price tags — is guilty of false pretenses.

■ Robbery is the taking of the personal property of another against his will, from his person or immediate presence by means of force or fear, with the intent to permanently deprive him of it. Robbery is, in effect, an aggravated larceny. What distinguishes robbery from larceny is that robbery requires the taking of property by force or fear from the victim's person or immediate presence.

■ Extortion is "the obtaining of property from another, with his consent, induced by wrongful use of actual or threatened force, violence, or fear, or under color of official right." 18 U.S.C. § 1951(b)(2). Extortion cases tend to fall into one of three categories: extortion by threatened violence; extortion by non-violent but wrongful threats (also known as blackmail); and extortion by public officials under color of right.

■ The common law definition of burglary is the breaking and entering of the dwelling of another at night with the intent to commit a felony therein. Although almost every state has changed one or more elements of the common law offense, no single modern definition of burglary has emerged. In addition, the common law version remains important both because it is the glue that binds all modern burglary statutes and because many of the original elements are still employed as grading tools, even if they are not all required for lesser degrees of burglary. The bar exam also continues to emphasize the common law definition. As a result, the common law definition of burglary remains the foundation for learning about the offense.

## Applying the Concepts

1. Based only on memory, provide the definitions of larceny, robbery, extortion, and burglary, and briefly describe what distinguishes embezzlement and false pretenses from larceny. Then, compare what you have written to the actual definitions of the offenses. If you notice any differences between your definitions and the actual definitions, use this as an opportunity to review those aspects of the offenses that you did not remember correctly.

2. Dale takes Vern's car without Vern's consent by picking the lock to the car and driving off with it one night. Dale plans to sell Verne's car to a "chop shop," where the car will be taken apart and its parts sold. Unfortunately for Dale, the police catch him before he can sell the car, and they return the car to Vern. Has Dale committed larceny?

    **a.** Yes.

    **b.** No, because Dale did not intend to keep Vern's car for his own use.

    **c.** No, because Dale sought to obtain ownership as well as possession.

    **d.** No, because the police caught Dale before he could complete the crime.

**3.** Nancy walks into a convenience store and pulls out a gun. She points the gun at the convenience store clerk, Vicky, and tells Vicky to give her the money from the cash register. Vicky gives the money to Nancy, who takes it and leaves the store.

    Nancy is charged with robbery. The jury should find Nancy:

    **a.** Not guilty. Because Nancy did not use force, she is guilty of only larceny.

    **b.** Not guilty. Because Vicky did not resist Nancy's threat, Nancy is guilty of extortion.

    **c.** Guilty.

    **d.** Guilty, but only if the government can prove beyond a reasonable doubt that the weapon was actually loaded.

**4.** One Friday night, Victor throws a party and invites his friend Dave. At the party, Dave walks into Victor's room. Once in the room, Dave notices a rare coin. Dave puts the coin in his pocket and, at the end of the night, leaves with the coin. Two weeks later, Dave tries to sell the coin online and he is caught by the police. Assume that both larceny and false pretenses are felonies in the jurisdiction where this occurred and that the jurisdiction follows the common law definition of burglary. Dave is guilty of:

    **a.** Larceny.

    **b.** Larceny and burglary.

    **c.** False pretenses.

    **d.** False pretenses and burglary.

**5.** Dirk's girlfriend Victoria went on a two-month vacation. Victoria asked Dirk to take possession of her car while she was on vacation. Victoria did not want her car to sit unused in her driveway. Dirk parked Victoria's car in his driveway, intending to return it to Victoria when she returned from vacation. One month into her vacation, Victoria texted the following message to Dirk: "I've met someone else and I am breaking up with you."

    Depressed and jealous, Dirk decided to take Victoria's car and move to a different city. Dirk packed his belongings into Victoria's car and moved to a different city 500 miles away. When Victoria returned home, she texted Dirk asking for her car back, but Dirk never responded. Finally, Victoria called the police. Three months later, Dirk was arrested with Victoria's car.

    What crime has Dirk committed?

    **a.** Larceny.

    **b.** Embezzlement.

    **c.** False pretenses.

    **d.** No crime.

6. Evan is a waiter at a restaurant. One day, Evan learns that the restaurant uses meat broth in one of the soups that is listed as being "vegetarian" on its menu. Evan threatens to expose the restaurant's use of meat in its "vegetarian" soup to the public unless the restaurant stops using meat in its "vegetarian" soup. What crime, if any, has Evan committed?

   a. Extortion.
   b. False pretenses.
   c. Embezzlement.
   d. Evan has committed no crime.

## Criminal Law in Practice

1. As discussed in this chapter, property crimes have evolved since the common law era. Although most states have retained the definitions of larceny, embezzlement, and false pretenses, they have consolidated the offenses into a single crime, sometimes altering one or more elements of them. A number of states include other theft crimes, such as robbery, in their consolidated theft statutes. In most states, the crimes of burglary and arson have undergone even more substantial changes over the past century.

   a. Look up your state's theft statute(s). Does your state have a consolidated theft statute? If so, which offenses are included within it? How, if at all, do the definitions of the offenses differ from their common law definitions?
   b. Look up your state's burglary statute. How does it compare to the common law definition of burglary?
   c. Finally, for the offenses in your state that have changed from their common law form, which definition do you think is better and why?

2. Leanna, a 17-year old, had been living in a foster care placement for two years in California, in the same city where Leanna's grandmother lived. Leanna decided to move to Montana where her mother lived. On the weekend immediately preceding Leanna's move to Montana, Leanna's grandmother went out of town. Leanna's grandmother left the keys to her home with a neighbor named Winchell. On Friday afternoon, Leanna called Winchell and said that she needed to come to her grandmother's house to pick up some luggage for her trip to Montana. Winchell agreed to let Leanna into the house.

   In fact, Leanna did not have any luggage at her grandmother's house. Instead, that night, Leanna held a party at her grandmother's house. About 40 guests came to the party. The noise grew so loud that Winchell decided to investigate. At about 11:30 P.M., Winchell went to the house and discovered the party. Winchell told Leanna that if she did not end the party, Winchell would call the police. Leanna complied. When Leanna's grandmother came home a few days later, she discovered broken glass on the interior floor and liquid spilled on the carpet. In addition, a significant amount of Leanna's grandmother's alcohol had been consumed by the partygoers.

Leanna's grandmother called the police and Leanna was arrested.

You are the prosecutor assigned to the case. Your supervisor has instructed you to charge Leanna with all readily provable offenses. What theft offense would you charge Leanna with committing in connection with the missing alcohol? What additional evidence would you want to try to gather to prove your case? Would these facts also permit a burglary charge under either the common law definition of the offense or a modern variation?

3. Consider the following case, which involved the 1930s-era movie star Clark Gable. A British woman wrote a letter to Gable in which she claimed that Gable had fathered her child in England in 1922. The woman then demanded money from Gable. Gable had not been in England in 1922, so he knew the woman's claim was false. Assume that Gable had paid the requested money. Which theft offense has the woman committed: false pretenses or extortion?

# Drug Offenses

Arguably, no single development has had a greater impact on our criminal justice system over the past five decades than the war on drugs. In 2017, more Americans were arrested for a drug offense (1.6 million, or about 15 percent of all arrests) than for any other category of crime tracked by the FBI's Uniform Crime Report. By comparison, in that same year, the police made 1.25 million arrests for property crimes (though most property crimes that are reported to the police do not result in an arrest), and just under 1 million arrests for driving under the influence. The war on drugs has also contributed to an explosion in our prison population, with drug offenders accounting for approximately one-fifth of the 2.3 million people behind bars in the United States.

And yet, most criminal law casebooks do not include a chapter on drug offenses. The omission may be due to the fact that drug crimes did not exist at common law, and are not rooted in the Model Penal Code. Instead, drug prohibitions developed state by state, and then at the federal level, beginning in the late 1800s, with most early laws targeting opium and alcohol. Today, the basis for almost every state's drug laws is the Uniform Controlled Substances Act, promulgated in 1970 by the National Conference of Commissioners on Uniform State Laws. By design, the Uniform Controlled Substances Act largely mirrors the federal Controlled Substances Act of 1970, which remains in force more than 50 years after its passage. As a result, there is relatively little variation in the definition of drug crimes from one jurisdiction to the next. (Although controlled substances is the technical term used in these statutes, lawyers use the terms drugs and controlled substances interchangeably in the criminal law setting.)

There is a wide array of different drug offenses, including a number of somewhat unusual offenses that were adopted at the height of the war on drugs in the 1980s, such as the crime of maintaining a drug-involved premises (defined roughly as maintaining a property where

## Key Concepts

- What is the definition of possession?
- What is required to prove possession on a constructive possession theory?
- What is the willful blindness doctrine?
- What principles govern proof of intent for the crime of possession of a controlled substance with the intent to distribute?

drugs are used or sold) or the crime of using a communication facility to commit a drug felony (defined roughly as using a phone to facilitate a drug sale). Despite the abundance of anti-drug statutes, the great majority of drug prosecutions are for just two offenses: possession and possession with the intent to distribute. Section A of this chapter focuses on possession and Section B focuses on possession with the intent to distribute. (The crime of conspiracy, which is also a relatively common charge in drug cases, is covered separately in Chapter 9.)

## A. RACE, DRUG PROHIBITION, AND THE WAR ON DRUGS

Laws criminalizing the possession and distribution of mind-altering drugs are a relatively recent phenomenon in comparison to most other core criminal offenses. Early state drug prohibition laws date back to the late 1800s, but they did not become a fixture of criminal codes until the 1900s. As discussed in Chapter 1, there was a disturbing link between racism and early anti-drug laws. Many of these laws were passed expressly for the purpose of discriminating against minority populations. In an 1886 court opinion rejecting a constitutional challenge to an anti-opium law, for example, the court wrote that "it may be that this legislation proceeds more from a desire to vex and annoy the 'Heathen Chinee' [sic] . . . than to protect the people from the evil habit." *Ex parte Yung Jon*, 28 F. 308, 312 (D. Or. 1886). Overtly racist comments about African Americans and Mexican immigrants also featured prominently in the passage of many of the first criminal laws against cocaine and marijuana. In his seminal history of drug control in the United States, David Musto observed that "[t]he most passionate support for legal prohibition of narcotics has been associated with fear of a given drug's effect on a specific minority." David F. Musto, The American Disease: Origins of Narcotic Control 294 (3d ed. 1999).

For much of their history, drug laws were not as vigorously enforced as they have been during the modern war on drugs. It was not until 50 years or so ago that President Richard Nixon used the phrase "war on drugs" to describe America's drug strategy. Race was at the center of the political calculations that led to Nixon's declaration of war on drugs. In a 1994 interview, former Nixon domestic policy advisor John Ehrlichman reportedly said that Nixon used drugs as a proxy for race. "We knew we couldn't make it illegal to be either against the war or black," explained Ehrlichman. "[B]ut by getting the public to associate hippies with marijuana and blacks with heroin, and then criminalizing both heavily, we could disrupt those communities." Tom LoBianco, *Report: Aide Says Nixon's War on Drugs Targeted Blacks, Hippies*, CNN.com (Mar. 24, 2016).

Although Nixon is often cited as the architect of the modern war on drugs, it was not until the 1980s that most of the laws and criminal justice outcomes that are most closely associated with the drug war really took shape. During the first few years of Ronald Reagan's presidency, federal funding for drug treatment programs was slashed to less than one-fourth of what it had been under Nixon while the federal drug enforcement budget enjoyed a substantial increase. The increase in drug enforcement funding was accompanied by significant changes to federal drug laws. Beginning in 1984, and continuing for the rest of the decade, Congress passed a series of harsh new mandatory minimum sentences for drug offenses and developed policies to incentivize state and local law enforcement agencies to participate in the drug war. As a political issue, enthusiasm for the drug war hit its peak in the late 1980s. In 1989, a Gallup poll showed that more than six in ten Americans believed drug abuse to be the "most important" problem facing the United States. That same year, President George H.W. Bush gave an oval office speech in which he called drugs "the gravest domestic threat facing our nation," and said that the people responsible included "everyone who uses drugs" and "everyone who looks the other way."

During that period and for most of the two decades that followed, the war on drugs was enthusiastically supported by Republican and Democratic politicians alike. In part as a result, drug enforcement increased dramatically. Drug arrests tripled between 1980 and 2005. During those same years, the number of drug offenders in prisons and jails increased by 1100 percent from 41,000 in 1980 to 493,800 in 2005. See Alex Kreit, *Drug Truce*, 77 Ohio St. L.J. 1323, 1329-41 (2016).

Although the sort of overt racism that fueled early drug laws is much less prevalent in the debate about drug enforcement today, the disproportionate impact of drug enforcement on people of color is in many ways just as troubling. About 12.6 percent of the U.S. population is African-American, and Blacks use drugs at about the same rate as whites. Although we do not have much data on the racial composition of drug sellers, the evidence that does exist "suggests a racial breakdown among sellers similar to that among users." Jamie Fellner, *Race, Drugs, and Law Enforcement in the United States*, 20 Stan. L. & Pol'y Rev. 257, 268 (2009). And yet, 30.4 percent of drug arrestees in 2013 were black. The disparity grows even more when it comes to incarceration. As of 2012, 37.7 percent of state drug prisoners were black. As put succinctly in 2020 by Nora Volkow, the Director of the National Institute on Drug

**EXHIBIT 4.1** **George H.W. Bush Displays Bag of Crack in 1989 Oval Office Speech**

Abuse, "Whites and Black/African Americans use drugs at similar rates, but it is overwhelmingly the latter group who are singled out for arrest and incarceration."

Drug laws continue to be actively enforced, but the shape of the debate about them is much different than it was twenty or thirty years ago. Since 2010, political support for the drug war has faded. A number of prominent elected officials from across the political spectrum have labeled the war on drugs a failure in recent years. This has coincided with important policy reforms at the state level. Perhaps most notably, as discussed in Chapter 1, more than one-fifth of all states now have laws legalizing marijuana. Some states are going even further—as noted later in this chapter (page 164), Oregon became the first state in the nation to decriminalize the possession of all drugs in 2020. Still, in most states and at the federal level, drug laws have remained largely unchanged since the 1980s.

## B. POSSESSION

In 2017, there were 1.4 million arrests for drug possession offenses in the United States, according to the FBI's Uniform Crime Report. This number represented approximately 85 percent of all drug arrests, and about 13 percent of *all* arrests nationwide (excluding arrests for traffic infractions, which are not tracked by the FBI's report). These figures tell us drug possession as measured by its impact on the criminal justice system is undeniably one of the most important crimes in the United States today. Drug possession prosecutions make up a significant portion of the criminal docket, and almost every criminal defense attorney and prosecutor will handle hundreds if not thousands of drug possession cases during her career.

The definition of **drug possession** is deceptively simple. Drug possession statutes make it a crime "for any person knowingly or intentionally to possess a controlled substance." 21 U.S.C. § 844(a). Based on this language, it would be easy to assume that this is a fairly straightforward crime, and unlikely to raise interesting or difficult questions of law. After all, someone who is found with drugs on their person or in their car or home would seem to present a classic "open and shut" case. But while it is true that some drug possession cases are clear-cut, others can present surprisingly complicated and fascinating problems.

Conceptually, possession cases usually fall into one of two categories: actual possession or constructive possession. These categories are not separate offenses. Rather, they describe two different types of cases that implicate the crime of possession. Actual possession refers to situations in which an individual has drugs on his person. Constructive possession, by contrast,

### Possession of Other Types of Contraband

Drug possession is one of the most frequently prosecuted crimes today, but there are laws criminalizing possession of *many* other types of items in most states. These include laws against possessing firearms and other weapons, toy guns, air pistols and rifles, tear gas, body vests, burglary tools, instruments of crime, forged instruments, forgery devices, gambling devices, gambling records, usurious loan records, obscene material, fireworks, noxious materials, and undersized catfish (in Louisiana). See Markus Dirk Dubber, *Policing Possession: The War on Crime and the End of Criminal Law*, 91 J. Crim. L. & Criminology 829, 856-57 (2001). In New York state alone, there were at least 153 different possession offenses as of 2001. *Id.* at 835. The legal principles regarding drug possession covered in this chapter also apply to most statutes that criminalize possession of other types of contraband, although there are sometimes differences, particularly in the area of digital contraband.

involves circumstances where illegal drugs are found *near* a person — such as in a person's car or home.

# 1. Actual Possession

Although possession is an age-old concept in property law, courts first began to seriously grapple with the crime of possession in the criminal context during alcohol prohibition. Prohibition era possession cases employed a somewhat narrow definition of the term, in which possession required a level of control over alcohol that was almost synonymous with ownership. Courts consistently found, for example, that holding a bottle of liquor in one's hand to take a drink from it did not constitute "possession" of the liquor, at least where the person taking the drink did not own the liquor. As Judge Samford of the Alabama Court of Appeals put it, "[p]ossession of whisky within the meaning of the prohibition law contemplates a control over the whisky, whereas when the whisky is in the man the whisky controls the man." *Evans v. State*, 24 Ala. App. 196, 197 (1931).

As the case that follows shows, courts have gone on to adopt a somewhat broader understanding of what it means to possess an item. Today, in **actual possession** cases, possession requires only physical control over drugs, rather than more lasting control akin to ownership.

**Case Preview**

### State v. Fries

*Fries* involves an instance of actual possession. In this case, the court is called on to decide whether brief physical control over contraband constitutes possession.

As you read the decision, consider the following questions:

1. What does it mean to possess a drug, according to the court?
2. What role, if any, does the defendant's motive play in this case? Why do you think his motive did not provide for a defense?
3. Does this decision mean that every person who takes an item in her hand, with knowledge of what the item is, is guilty of possession? If not, under what circumstances could a person hold an item and yet not possess it?

## State v. Fries
### 344 Or. 541 (2008)

KISTLER, J.

The issue in this case is whether defendant possessed marijuana when he helped a friend move marijuana plants from one place to another. Defendant has argued that, because he was moving the plants at his friend's direction, he did not possess them. The trial court held otherwise and entered a judgment of conviction for possessing marijuana. A divided en banc Court of Appeals affirmed. We allowed defendant's petition for review to consider the issue that divided the Court of Appeals and now affirm the Court of Appeals decision and the trial court's judgment.

Because this case arises on defendant's motion for a judgment of acquittal, we state the facts in the light most favorable to the state. One evening, defendant's friend Albritton called defendant and told him that he (Albritton) was being evicted. Albritton asked defendant if he would help him move his marijuana plants to his new home. Because Albritton had a medical marijuana card, defendant understood (and we assume for purposes of review) that Albritton lawfully possessed the marijuana plants. Defendant went to Albritton's new home, picked him up, and drove Albritton to his former home to pick up the marijuana plants. Albritton's former home was in an upstairs apartment, on the top floor. Defendant and Albritton went into the back bedroom of the apartment. Albritton pointed out the plants and said, "This is what I really needed help moving." According to defendant, there were three or four marijuana plants in "one long, big-type thing," which defendant moved from Albritton's apartment to defendant's Jeep.

Defendant loaded the plants and some of Albritton's other belongings into the back of his Jeep. Albritton got in the front passenger seat of the Jeep, and defendant started driving to Albritton's new home. As they were driving, a police car began following them. Defendant pulled into a driveway. The officer drove past, circled around, and later observed defendant driving on a different street. The officer followed defendant's Jeep as defendant turned onto another street and then pulled into another driveway. Defendant and Albritton remained in the Jeep. The officer approached them and spoke with them briefly. When asked why "they were being so evasive tonight, [defendant] said, 'We didn't want to get stopped and have to answer any questions about the marijuana.'" The officer then arrested defendant and Albritton.

The state charged defendant with possessing marijuana. At the end of defendant's trial, he argued that there was no evidence from which a reasonable trier of fact could find that he had possessed the marijuana plants. Specifically, he contended that, because the evidence showed only that he moved the plants under Albritton's direction, he did not "possess" them. The trial court denied defendant's motion for a judgment of acquittal and, sitting as the trier of fact, found defendant guilty. The court found initially that defendant knew that the plants were marijuana. It then found that defendant "actually physically possessed [the marijuana plants] because he moved [them] from Point A to Point B, knowing * * * what it was." The trial court explained that, although the medical marijuana statutes permit designated caregivers to possess medical marijuana, defendant was not Albritton's designated caregiver. The court concluded:

> "Is it fair? Perhaps not. In the overall scheme of things, he was someone helping his buddy. And perhaps it's unfair that [defendant] didn't have legal permission to have that particular controlled substance. But there's actually no doubt in my mind that he knowingly possessed that controlled substance, the growing marijuana."

The court accordingly found defendant guilty of possessing marijuana and sentenced him to 18 months probation, conditioned on serving five days in jail and paying a $500 fine and costs.

As noted, a divided Court of Appeals affirmed the trial court's judgment, and we allowed defendant's petition for review to consider whether there was sufficient evidence to permit a reasonable trier of fact to find beyond a reasonable doubt that defendant possessed the marijuana plants. On that point, defendant reiterates his argument that possession of marijuana requires more than proof that he knowingly moved the marijuana plants at Albritton's direction. In his view, persons who move or hold controlled substances at another person's direction lack sufficient "sovereignty, supremacy, power or authority" over those substances to possess them.

Defendant's argument presents an issue of statutory construction, and we begin by examining the text and context of the relevant statutes. ORS 475.840(3) makes it unlawful for "any person knowingly * * * to possess a controlled substance." ORS 161.015(9) in turn provides that " '[p]ossess' means to have physical possession or otherwise to exercise dominion or control over property." As the text of that definition makes clear, a person may possess property in one of two ways. He or she may "have physical possession" of the property, which customarily is referred to as actual possession. Alternatively, even if a person does not have actual possession of the property, he or she may have constructive possession of it if the person "otherwise * * * exercise[s] dominion or control over [the] property."

Because the trial court found that defendant actually possessed the marijuana plants, we begin with the first part of the statutory definition. The legislature used the infinitive phrase "to have physical possession" to define actual possession. We note, as an initial matter, that the definition of actual possession is somewhat circular; the legislature said "possess" means to have physical "possession." That said, the definition contains some clues that aid our analysis. The dictionary defines possession as meaning,

> "1 a: the act or condition of having in or taking into one's control or holding at one's disposal . . . b: actual physical control or occupancy of property by one who holds for himself and not as a servant of another without regard to his ownership and who has legal rights to assert interests in the property against all others having no better right than himself * * *."

*Webster's Third New Int'l Dictionary* 1770 (unabridged ed. 2002).[5] The dictionary thus distinguishes possession from ownership and defines possession to mean, at its core, "control." "Physical" is an adjective that defines the type of control necessary to establish actual possession. In this context, physical means "of or relating to the body." As a general rule, "to have physical possession" of property means to have bodily or physical control of it.

The statutory definition of actual possession follows the generally understood use of that concept in the criminal law. In *State v. Oare*, 249 Or. 597, 599 (1968), for example, the court explained that a person who had a narcotic "upon his person"

---

[5] Webster's divides definitions of a word into senses and subsenses. The first sense of the word possession contains four subsenses. The first two subsenses are quoted in the text. The third subsense of possession is "copulation," and the fourth is "control of [a] playing piece (as a ball or puck) in football, basketball, ice hockey, or other game." *Webster's* at 1770. We think that, in defining "possess" as "physical possession," the legislature did not intend to refer to the third or fourth subsenses of possession.

## The Innocent Possession (Possession for Disposal) Defense

A number of jurisdictions have developed a defense to possession referred to as the innocent possession or possession for disposal defense. This doctrine generally applies where "(1) the controlled substance was attained innocently and held with no illicit or illegal purpose, and (2) the possession of the controlled substance was transitory; that is, that the defendant took adequate measures to rid himself of possession of the controlled substance as promptly as reasonably possible." *Utah v. Miller*, 2008 UT 61, ¶ 22.

In jurisdictions that recognize it, the possession for disposal doctrine is meant for cases where a person takes temporary physical control of contraband in order to turn it into the police or to throw it away — for example, a parent who finds drugs in her child's bedroom and takes temporary control of them in order to throw them away. The court-made doctrine is based on the idea that — as the court put it in *Fries* — "some physical contacts with property may be too transient or fleeting to say that a person has established physical 'control' over the property."

Not all courts that have considered the innocent possession doctrine have adopted it. Some courts have rejected it on the grounds that it is inconsistent with their understanding of the plain meaning of the word possess. In addition, among the states that recognize innocent possession, there is variation regarding the specific requirements, particularly with respect to the temporal element of the rule. In some jurisdictions, a

would actually possess it. Those authorities confirm that "to have physical possession" of property means actual physical control of property, although some physical contacts with property may be so momentary or fleeting that they are insufficient as a matter of law to establish physical control. *See* Wayne R. LaFave, 1 *Substantive Criminal Law* § 6.1(e) at 432-33 (2003) (summarizing generally understood use of possession in the criminal law).

Defendant argues that the definition of constructive possession in the second part of ORS 161.015(9) demonstrates that a person who holds property at another's direction does not actually possess it. Defendant's argument runs as follows. He notes that ORS 161.015(9) provides that "'[p]ossess' means to have physical possession or otherwise to exercise dominion or control over property." Defendant argues that, in order to prove sufficient dominion or control to establish constructive possession, the state must offer evidence of "sovereignty, supremacy, power or authority" over property. He then contends that, in using the word "otherwise," the legislature manifested its intent that actual possession requires proof of the same type of "dominion or control" that constructive possession does. From that premise, defendant concludes that a person who holds property at another's direction does not exercise sufficient sovereignty, supremacy, power, or authority over the property to constitute actual possession.

One problem with defendant's argument is that it gives too little weight to the legislature's use of the word "otherwise." "Otherwise" means "in a different way or manner." *Webster's* at 1598. As used in ORS 161.015(9), "otherwise" signals that the state may prove "possession" either by showing physical control or by showing dominion or control "in a different way or manner." To be sure, as defendant argues, actual and constructive possession share a common element — control. But the legislature's use of the word "otherwise" makes clear that actual and constructive possession contemplate different types of proof. The former requires proof of physical control. The latter contemplates proof of other attributes of dominion or control. The fact that a person holds property at another's direction does not necessarily mean that he or she does not actually possess it.

Considering the text and context of ORS 161.015(9), we conclude that the statutory phrase "to have physical possession" means what it says: to have physical control. That said, we recognize that some physical contacts with property may be too transient or fleeting to say that a person has established physical "control" over the property and that, when the duration of the physical contact is minimal, the circumstances surrounding the contact can bear on the question whether the defendant exercised sufficient physical control to find actual possession. *See* LaFave, 1 *Substantive Criminal Law* § 6.1(e) at 432 (discussing actual possession); *compare United States v. Santore*, 290 F.2d 51, 64-65 (2d Cir. 1959) (holding that no reasonable trier of fact could find a defendant who held a package of narcotics "one brief moment" before voluntarily declining to take them possessed them), *with United States v. Gregory*, 309 F.2d 536, 538 (2d Cir. 1962) (holding that a reasonable trier of fact could find that a codefendant who held narcotics briefly before throwing them away on seeing police officers approach had sufficient control to establish actual possession).

> person must dispose of the drugs almost immediately after taking temporary physical control of them in order to benefit from the defense. Other jurisdictions have adopted a more flexible approach, requiring only that disposal occur within a reasonable period of time under the circumstances.

With that background in mind, we turn to the only question that defendant's motion for judgment of acquittal presents: whether the evidence was sufficient to permit a reasonable trier of fact to find that defendant possessed the marijuana. On this record, a reasonable trier of fact could find that defendant carried Albritton's marijuana plants out of the back bedroom of Albritton's apartment, took them down the stairs, loaded the plants in the back of defendant's Jeep, and drove the Jeep for several minutes before the police stopped him. This was not a fleeting, momentary, or unintentional physical touching, or so a reasonable trier of fact could find. *Cf. Gregory*, 309 F.2d at 537 (evidence that a codefendant carried marijuana from a hotel to a car parked across the street sufficient to establish actual possession); *Commonwealth v. Harvard*, 356 Mass. 452, (1969) (evidence that a defendant who arranged a marijuana sale and passed marijuana three to four feet from seller's car to buyer's car sufficient to establish possession). Rather, defendant's acts were part of an extended effort to move the marijuana plants from one location to another location in a different part of Coos Bay—an effort that defendant and Albritton's arrest cut short.

In reaching that conclusion, we note, as the trial court did, that, for all that appears from the record, defendant was helping a friend who lawfully possessed the marijuana plants. The statutes prohibiting possession of controlled substances and authorizing the use of medical marijuana contain a number of specific exceptions. They permit, for example, designated caregivers, as well as common carriers, to possess marijuana in certain specified circumstances. Defendant does not argue that he falls within any of those exceptions, and we may not add to the exceptions that the legislature has created. Rather, the only question before us is whether a reasonable trier of fact could find that defendant knowingly possessed marijuana plants. The answer to that question is "yes." Accordingly, we affirm the trial court's judgment and the Court of Appeals decision.

The decision of the Court of Appeals and the judgment of the circuit court are affirmed.

**Post-Case Follow-Up**

The *Fries* court holds that "the statutory phrase 'to have physical possession' means what it says: to have physical control." This holding is consistent with how most courts define actual possession today. Although the *Fries* court was concerned with the definition of possession and not the *mens rea* of the crime, the outcome of the case also highlights the difference between motive and the mental states of knowledge and intent. Fries knew that the substance he possessed was marijuana. That Fries's motive for possessing the marijuana was to help his friend move and not to use it himself was no defense. This is true across criminal law. A person who shoplifts food to feed his hungry child has satisfied the *mens rea* of larceny — intent to permanently deprive — every bit as much as a pickpocket who steals someone's wallet on the subway. To be sure, a defendant's motive might impact a prosecutor's charging decision, a court's sentencing decision, or certain defenses (such as innocent possession, discussed in the sidebar at page 160). But with respect to the *mens rea* of the crime, a good motive is typically no defense.

## Fries: *Real Life Applications*

1. The facts that follow come directly from a stipulation in a prosecution for marijuana possession. *State v. Hogue*, 52 Haw. 660 (1971). This means that the prosecutor and the defense attorney in the case stipulated to the existence of these facts, and the stipulation was read verbatim to the jury:

   > That the State is able to prove by the testimony of the three arresting officers, upon the trial of Gregory Dale Hogue, that the defendant Gregory Dale Hogue on or about the 5th day of March, 1970, in the County of Kauai, State of Hawaii, did then and there at the invitation of a friend, one Charles Glagolich, who was the owner of a pipe containing marihuana in hashish form while sitted at a picnic table at Lydgate Park with Mr. Glagolich and three other friends, Stephanie Kay Stearns, Johnny Ray Griffith and Georgia Marie Shannon, did knowingly take two puffs from a pipe containing marihuana in hashish form.
   >
   > That the three officers will testify that, prior to the arrest, they observed Charles Glagolich turn over a pipe containing marihuana in hashish form to one Stephanie Kay Stearns, who after a couple of puffs turned it over to one Johnny Ray Griffith, who after a couple of puffs turned it over to defendant Gregory Dale Hogue. That defendant Gregory Dale Hogue was observed by the three arresting officers with a hashish pipe in his hands, no one else was holding it, and did take two puffs from said pipe knowing it to contain marihuana in hashish form. That after the pipe had been passed and the actions were observed by the three arresting officers, defendant together with his friends were placed under arrest for unlawful possession or control of marihuana. Defendants were properly advised of their constitutional rights.
   >
   > Defendant, if called, will testify that he took only one puff from said pipe.
   >
   > That the residue within the pipe was analyzed by Dr. Quentin Belles. Said analysis revealed an oily residue which a chemical test showed was charred marihuana.

Imagine you are Hogue's lawyer and this stipulation has been read to the jury.

   **a.** The court has asked each side for proposed jury instructions. Is there any language from the court's decision in *Fries* that you would like to ask the court to include in its jury instructions?
   **b.** Briefly formulate your closing argument to the jury. What element(s) of the crime of possession would you focus on in your argument?

**2.** For this problem, assume the same facts as in Question 1, with one difference: Gregory Dale Hogue did not take any "puffs" from the marijuana pipe. Instead, when Hogue was handed the pipe from Griffith, he said, "No thanks," and passed the pipe back to Griffith. Based on the holding in *Fries*, do you think Hogue could be found guilty of possessing marijuana on these facts?

## 2. Constructive Possession

In a typical **constructive possession** case, authorities find a controlled substance in an area that more than one person has access to, such as a shared home or a car. Imagine, for example, that the police pull over a vehicle for a traffic violation and see cocaine in plain view sitting on the console between the passenger and the driver. If one of the parties admits the cocaine belongs to him, the case might be an easy one. But what if neither of them claim the cocaine? The cocaine almost surely belongs to either the driver or the passenger (or both), and the police can place them both under arrest. See *Maryland v. Pringle*, 540 U.S. 366 (2003). Is this evidence standing alone also sufficient to prove one or both of them guilty of possession *beyond a reasonable doubt*?

The basic principle behind constructive possession is simple and intuitive: You do not have to hold an object in your hand to possess it. As one court explained, "[t]he 'constructive possession' label may confuse jurors at first — drug trial juries routinely ask to be reinstructed on the definition of possession — but the underlying idea is important and not so difficult to grasp. Courts are saying that one can possess an object while it is hidden at home in a bureau drawer, or while held by an agent, or even while it is secured in a safe deposit box at the bank and can be retrieved only when a bank official opens the vault. The problem is not so much with the idea as with deciding how far it should be carried." *United States v. Maldonado*, 23 F.3d 4, 7 (1st Cir. 1994).

The problem of how far to carry the idea of constructive possession has proved to be a difficult one. Courts have struggled to craft a constructive possession

### Portugal's Drug Decriminalization Law

The crime of drug possession has been subject to criticism from both a retributivist and utilitarian perspective, as well as from some public health and criminal justice reform advocates. Portugal's drug policy provides an example of an alternative to the criminalization of drug possession.

In 2001, Portugal removed criminal penalties for the possession of personal-use quantities of all drugs. The term "civil drug court" might be a better way to describe Portugal's policy than decriminalization, however. Instead of imposing a small fine on users — as most marijuana decriminalization laws in the United States do — people found in possession of personal-use amounts of drugs in Portugal are given a civil summons to appear before a "dissuasion panel." The panels are designed to be non-adversarial, and they are made up mostly of medical and social service professionals. If the panel members conclude that the person appearing before them does not have a substance use disorder, they provide educational information and let the person go without any sanction. In other cases, the panel has a range of options available to it, from ordering check-ins to imposing a ban on visiting certain places to requiring the person to enter a treatment program. Because drug possession is no longer a crime, however, a criminal penalty is never an option, even for those who struggle in treatment.

When Portugal first adopted its decriminalization law, the United States and the United Nations were vocal critics, claiming it would lead to drug tourism. But none of these fears have come to pass, and most observers have seen the law as a success. See, e.g., Kellen Russoniello, *The Devil (and Drugs) in the Details: Portugal's Focus on Public Health as a Model for Decriminalization of Drugs in Mexico*, 12 Yale J. Health Pol'y L. & Ethics 371, 391 (2012). In the 2020 election, Oregon voters approved a drug decriminalization ballot measure modeled after Portugal's law — the first law of its kind in the United States.

Would you favor removing criminal penalties for the possession of all drugs for personal use and adopting a system like Portugal's? Or do you think there are advantages to the U.S. approach of making simple drug possession a crime?

doctrine capable of protecting the innocent from being convicted simply for being found near someone else's drugs without making it overly difficult to convict the guilty. The result is a body of case law that can be hard to make sense of. In 1971, Judge Edward Tamm of the U.S. Court of Appeals for the District of Columbia Circuit said of constructive possession that "[t]he more cases one reads on constructive possession the deeper is he plunged into a thicket of subjectivity. Successive cases enumerate a continuing re-interpretation which can only be described as judicial whimsy. Both prosecutor and defendant's attorney present their cases with the unfortunate knowledge that the law of constructive possession is what we will say it is in our next opinion." *United States v. Holland*, 445 F.2d 701, 703-04 (D.C. Cir. 1971) (Tamm, J., concurring). Unfortunately, the law of constructive possession has not become much clearer with time.

Although constructive possession cases remain filled with conflicts and fine distinctions, almost every jurisdiction today follows at least one basic principle: Knowing proximity to contraband, standing alone, is insufficient to prove possession. This principle flows from the fact that drug possession makes it a crime to knowingly *possess* drugs, not to knowingly *be present near* drugs. As a result, courts have held that that "[p]ossession requires more than being in the presence of other persons having possession; it requires the exercise of dominion or control over the thing possessed." *Taylor v. State*, 346 Md. 452 (1997). But, if proximity to a controlled substance along with knowledge of its presence is insufficient to sustain a conviction for possession, what more is needed? On this issue, courts have continued to struggle to find a consistent set of rules or principles.

**Case Preview**

## *Rivas v. United States*

The next case, *Rivas v. United States*, applies the rule that proximity to contraband is insufficient to prove possession and discusses some of the factors that can demonstrate constructive possession.

As you read the decision, consider the following questions:

1. How does the court define constructive possession?
2. Is the ability to exercise control over contraband enough to prove possession? If not, what more is needed and why?
3. What factors can help to prove possession? Do you think all of these factors are legitimate or do any strike you as problematic?

## *Rivas v. United States*
### 783 A.2d 125 (D.C. 2001)

GLICKMAN, J.

Applying principles of constructive possession, a jury convicted appellant Baltazar Rivas and his codefendant Jose Melgar of possessing, with intent to distribute, cocaine found in plastic bags that lay between them in the console of a car in which Melgar was the driver and Rivas the front seat passenger. A division of this court affirmed both convictions in *Rivas v. United States*, 734 A.2d 655 (D.C. 1999) (*Rivas I*). We granted Rivas's petition for rehearing en banc in order to reconsider a rule followed in *Rivas I* and other recent cases that appears to ease the government's burden of proving constructive possession when drugs are found in the "close confines" of an automobile, as distinct from, say, a dwelling.

We agree with Rivas that no categorical distinction based on where drugs are found—and certainly no lessening of the government's burden of proving constructive possession on that basis—is justified. A defendant's close proximity to drugs in plain view is certainly probative in determining not only whether he knew of the drugs and had the ability to exert control over them, but also whether he had the necessary intent to control (individually or with others) their use or destiny. Nevertheless, we make clear today that there is no "automobile" exception to the settled general rule that knowledge and proximity alone are insufficient to prove constructive possession of drugs beyond a reasonable doubt. A passenger in someone else's car, who is not the driver and who does not have exclusive control over the vehicle or its contents, may not be convicted *solely* on the basis that drugs were in plain view and conveniently accessible in the passenger compartment. As in all other constructive possession cases, there must be something more in the totality of the circumstances—a word or deed, a relationship or other probative factor—that, considered in conjunction with the evidence of proximity and knowledge, proves beyond a reasonable doubt that the passenger *intended* to exercise dominion or control over the drugs, and was not a mere bystander.

Viewed in the light most favorable to the government, the evidence showed that two police officers in uniform, in a marked police cruiser, were patrolling on Hyatt Place, N.W., at around 1:00 A.M. when they saw an automobile stopped in the middle of the street. The officers pulled up behind the car, a two-door Honda occupied by the driver (Melgar, who was also the registered owner of the vehicle), a front seat passenger (Rivas), and two rear seat passengers. Seconds later the passenger-side door opened and Rivas stepped out; leaving the door open, he walked to the sidewalk where he engaged another man in conversation. Soon afterwards the Honda pulled over to the curb. The police officers activated their overhead emergency lights and moved in behind the parked car. As they did so, Rivas, who evidently saw the officers approach, left the man he was speaking with and walked a short distance around the corner onto Park Road. There he remained to talk with someone else, out of sight of the police until he was apprehended a few minutes later.

In the meantime, as the officers approached the car on foot, Officer Mitchell looked in on the passenger side and saw an open container of alcohol on the rear floorboard. The occupants were ordered out of the car, and as Mitchell reached in to retrieve the container, he saw two plastic bags containing a visible white rock substance in the console between the two front seats. Mitchell, who could see the bags because a streetlight illuminated the interior of the car, told his partner to secure the other occupants while he went looking for Rivas. He found him in the midst of conversation some twenty to thirty feet from the corner of Hyatt Place and Park Road.

The plastic bags taken from the console of the car were later determined to contain twelve and six rocks of crack cocaine, respectively, weighing in the aggregate 1,951 milligrams. This was enough, according to a police expert, to furnish 195 separate "hits" or uses of the cocaine. The expert opined, hypothetically, that if the eighteen rocks weighed the same they would sell individually for about twenty dollars on the street; in other words, that the cocaine had a total street value of a few hundred dollars. In the expert's opinion, the amount and configuration of the drugs (in small rocks) were inconsistent with possession for personal consumption.

There was no evidence to show how long Rivas had been in Melgar's car when the police arrived on the scene, or what he or anyone else in the car had been doing. No evidence was presented that Rivas's fingerprints were found on the bags of cocaine seized from the car, or that Rivas had ever handled the bags or engaged in a drug transaction. No incriminating evidence was taken from Rivas's person,[2] and he said nothing to inculpate himself.

To prove constructive possession, the prosecution was required to show that Rivas knew that the cocaine was present in the car and that he had both the ability and the intent to exercise dominion or control over it. Constructive possession may be sole or joint and may be proven by direct or circumstantial evidence.

No one disputes that the jury permissibly could find that Rivas *knew* the cocaine was in the console (given that it was in plain view), and that he had the *ability* to exercise dominion and control over it (given his proximity to it). The question before us is whether the jury rationally could find beyond a reasonable doubt that Rivas *intended* to exercise that power, in other words that he in fact "had a substantial voice vis-a-vis the drug[s]." In general, the settled rule in constructive possession cases is that "mere presence of the accused on the premises, or simply his proximity to the drug, does not itself enable . . . a deduction" beyond a reasonable doubt that he had the requisite intent. "Nor is mere association with another, standing alone, enough even when the other is known to possess the drug." Rather, there must be something

---

[2] Melgar had $236 in small denominations of bills on his person.

more in the totality of the circumstances that—together with proximity and knowledge—establishes that the accused meant to exercise dominion or control over the narcotics:

> There must be some action, some word, or some conduct that links the individual to the narcotics and indicates that he had some stake in them, some power over them. There must be something to prove that the individual was not merely an incidental bystander. It may be foolish to stand by when others are acting illegally, or to associate with those who have committed a crime. Such conduct or association, however, *without more*, does not establish the offenses here charged. *United States v. Pardo*, 636 F.2d 535, 549 (1980) (emphasis in the original).

In recent years, decisions of this court have attempted to distill at least one principle from constructive possession cases, which, when compared to one another, can sometimes seem "a thicket of subjectivity." *United States v. Holland*, 445 F.2d 701, 703 (1971) (Tamm, J., concurring). Recognizing the normal difference in size between a room in a house or other building and the interior of an automobile, our decisions have stated that "the requisite inferences [of dominion or control] may be drawn from the location of weapons [or other contraband] in plain view and substantially within a defendant's reach in the closer confines of an automobile."

Rivas criticizes these statements, contending that they amount to an unjustified relaxation of the proof requirements when persons are found near drugs in automobiles. Rivas observes that there is nothing "about the nature of a car, except its limited size, that would necessitate a different standard [of proof] in constructive possession cases." Limited size, however, is of questionable significance in this context. Rivas persuasively argues that physical proximity to drugs in the "close confines" of a car, at least one occupied jointly with other persons, may be *less* probative of possession than proximity in some larger enclosure because a passenger "is greatly restricted in her ability to distance herself from contraband in plain view. There is simply nowhere to go," especially when the car is in motion. Moreover, Rivas points out, "the relationship of a 'visitor' in a car may be far more attenuated than a visitor to a house or apartment": People offer or accept rides from colleagues or acquaintances solely because they are travelling to a common destination. We might pick someone up in bad weather, merely recognizing them as a neighbor. We arrange car pools, and drive people home from parties knowing only that we have friends in common. In all these circumstances, we find ourselves in cars with people whom we might never have occasion to invite into the privacy of our own homes. There is no reason to conclude that a "visitor" in a car, as a general rule, has any greater relationship to its contents than a visitor to a home.

We agree with these reasons why any categorical distinction between cars and other enclosed places in deciding issues of constructive possession is untenable. A special exception for automobiles does not stand up to scrutiny. Thus, to the extent that language in our decisions may have implied from the normal size of a passenger compartment that proximity to exposed drugs in a car, without more, is sufficient to prove (beyond a reasonable doubt) the requisite intention to exercise dominion or control, we disavow that language.

Lest our holding be misconstrued, we do not mean to suggest that close proximity to exposed contraband — whether in a car or in a room — has no bearing on the issue of control. It plainly does.

Acknowledging, then, the relevance of the evidence that Rivas was seen in close proximity to exposed drugs in the confined space of an automobile, we turn to the remaining issue. Was the evidence adduced in this case sufficient to prove possession by Rivas beyond a reasonable doubt? We hold that it was not.

Before discussing the sufficiency of that evidence, we think it useful to review the principles that must guide our evaluation; for this truly is a case that turns not on the absence of proof, but on the difference between the reasonable doubt standard and less stringent standards of proof.

The reasonable doubt standard of proof requires the factfinder "to reach a subjective state of near certitude of the guilt of the accused." *Jackson v. Virginia*, 443 U.S. 307, 315 (1979). This requirement, a component of due process, "'plays a vital role in the American scheme of criminal procedure,' because it operates to give 'concrete substance' to the presumption of innocence, to ensure against unjust convictions, and to reduce the risk of factual error in a criminal proceeding." *Jackson*, 443 U.S. at 315 (quoting *In re Winship*, 397 U.S. 358, 363 (1970)).

Proof beyond a reasonable doubt is not merely a guideline for the trier of fact; it also furnishes a standard for judicial review of the sufficiency of the evidence. We have an obligation to take seriously the requirement that the evidence in a criminal prosecution must be strong enough that a jury behaving rationally really could find it persuasive beyond a reasonable doubt.

Turning now to the evidence in this case, it has the quality of a snapshot — a frozen instant in time and space, crystallized but devoid of explanatory context. The police discovered two bags of cocaine, worth a few hundred dollars on the street, lying exposed to view in the front console of Melgar's vehicle. Rivas had just been seen sitting for a few moments in the front passenger seat, in the company of Melgar himself and two other passengers. But there was no evidence as to how long Rivas had been in the car, how he had come to be there, or what he had been doing. There was no evidence that the occupants of the car were actively engaged in distributing drugs or preparing them for distribution when Rivas was present. When the police arrived, Rivas made no gestures toward the drugs and did not signal in any other way an intent to hide or dispose of them. No other evidence was presented that linked Rivas to the cocaine.

There is no serious doubt that at least one of the car's occupants was in possession of the drugs, and the jury could reasonably infer that Melgar, who was the owner and driver of the automobile and who was found with $236 in cash on his person, had control over its contents. But that does not mean that any of the other occupants shared possession of the cocaine with Melgar (indeed, the government did not charge the two rear seat passengers with possession), nor that Rivas in particular had a stake in it.

The government argues that the jury could find that Rivas jointly possessed the cocaine with Melgar in light of three factors. First and foremost, the government points to Rivas's proximity to drugs lying unconcealed next to him as one factor the jury could rely on to conclude that he possessed them. Second, the government argues that the jury could infer that Rivas was Melgar's ally in distributing drugs from his car from the fact that Melgar apparently entrusted Rivas with immediate access to the drugs. And third, the government argues that Rivas's actions after the police arrived suggested a person distancing himself from drugs in his possession; for having left the car door open, Rivas evidently intended to return to the car, but he changed his mind and took evasive action when the police signaled their intent to investigate.

Could a reasonable jury find that these factors add up to proof beyond a reasonable doubt that Rivas knowingly had the ability and the intention to exercise control over the cocaine? Knowledge of the cocaine, yes; ability, yes; but intention to exercise control over the cocaine, no — not beyond a reasonable doubt. A reasonable jury perhaps could find it *more likely than not* that Rivas jointly possessed the cocaine with Melgar. But that is where we think any reasonable jury would have to draw the line. In the record before us there is no *substantial* evidence of "some action, some word, or some conduct that links [Rivas] to the narcotics and indicates that he had some stake in them, some power over them."

The first factor, Rivas's immediate proximity to unconcealed drugs in an automobile, certainly does make it more probable that he possessed the drugs. But the evidence that Rivas knowingly sat next to the cocaine in Jose Melgar's car did not by itself prove beyond a reasonable doubt that he "was not merely an incidental bystander." Perhaps, for example, Rivas accepted a ride with Melgar not knowing there were drugs present until some time after he got in the car. Or Rivas may have been aware that Melgar had cocaine in his vehicle, but rode in the car anyway, intending to do nothing more than (foolishly) ride around with a friend who was also a drug dealer.

The second factor on which the government relies is not about Rivas's state of mind; it is about Melgar's. The argument is that Melgar would not have been likely to let Rivas sit in the car next to the cocaine unless Rivas was part of his criminal operations. But whatever assumptions a jury might reasonably make about the usual operating procedures of drug dealers in general, and particularly those displaying large quantities of drugs, it is pure speculation that in this particular case Melgar — about whom we know nothing — was cautious rather than careless. Indeed, even if Melgar was cautious, he could have had many reasons to trust Rivas without Rivas having been part of his drug trafficking operation or having joint possession of his drugs. If knowing proximity to drugs is insufficient to prove guilt, being permitted to be in proximity adds virtually nothing unless the evidence also divulges *why* permission was granted. Melgar's unexplained willingness to let Rivas near his drugs in the circumstances of this case does not illuminate the intent of Rivas.

The government's third factor is Rivas's conduct after the police arrived: exiting the car when he (presumably) saw them drive up, leaving the door open behind him, and walking around the corner and out of sight when the officers approached the car on foot. We find these facts to be too equivocal to be informative on the central question of Rivas's intentions vis-a-vis the drugs. Rivas's behavior may have been evasive (though hardly stealthy or precipitous), but "in our cases, we have looked for more than 'walking away' to find manifestation of a consciousness of guilt." We have appreciated that even "leaving a scene hastily may be inspired by innocent fear, or by a legitimate desire to avoid contact with the police." "Headlong flight" may be "the consummate act of evasion: . . . not necessarily indicative of wrongdoing, but . . . certainly suggestive of such." But Rivas did not engage in headlong flight or anything close. Assuming that the jury could conclude that Rivas did mean to distance himself while the police were around, that might reinforce the implication that he knew there was cocaine in the car and did not want to be connected with it, but it does not show also that he "had some stake in" the drugs himself. The additional fact that Rivas left the car door open, while perhaps suggesting that he planned to re-enter the car and hence that he may have been more than a momentary or casual occupant, is marginally significant at best. If Rivas's guilt cannot be inferred from the fact that he was in Melgar's car for an unknown length of time, it cannot be inferred from the fact that he expected to continue to be in Melgar's car.

In short, an innocent person in Rivas's shoes might have acted exactly as he did when the police arrived. On the issue of whether he exercised control over the cocaine, Rivas's actions were insolubly ambiguous.

When the government proves the presence of contraband in an automobile, in plain view, conveniently accessible to a passenger defendant, the additional evidence necessary to prove constructive possession is comparatively minimal. As Rivas acknowledges in his brief,

> it could be a furtive gesture indicating an attempt to access, hide or dispose of the object, flight or other evidence of consciousness of guilt, evidence of participation in an ongoing criminal venture involving the contraband, an inculpatory statement, evidence of prior possession of the item, actual possession of paraphernalia relating to the use or sale of the contraband, control of the area or container in which the contraband is found, or the like.[13]

In this case, however, such additional probative evidence was lacking. The jury could only speculate about whether Rivas possessed the critical intent to exercise dominion or control over the cocaine in Melgar's car, or just happened to be present in the wrong place at the wrong time. The circumstances were suspicious, and perhaps Rivas is *probably* guilty; but on the thin record of this case, a reasonable doubt about his guilt ineluctably remains. The risk that an innocent man was convicted is therefore unacceptably large under our system of justice. Fidelity to the requirement of proof beyond a reasonable doubt in criminal cases requires that we reverse Rivas's conviction for insufficiency of the evidence.

*So ordered.*

---

[13] Needless to say, Rivas's listing of additional evidence that would, together with proximity to contraband in plain view, support a conviction for constructive possession is not exhaustive.

**Post-Case Follow-Up**

*Rivas* outlines the definition of constructive possession and applies the rule that knowing proximity to contraband alone is insufficient evidence to sustain a possession conviction. To prove possession under a constructive possession theory, the government must show the defendant "had both the ability and the intent to exercise dominion or control" over the contraband. In *Rivas*, the court found there was sufficient evidence the defendant had the ability to exercise control over the drugs but that there was insufficient evidence he had the intent to do so. This was because of "the settled rule in constructive possession cases . . . that 'mere presence of the accused on the premises, or simply his proximity to the drug, does not itself enable . . . a deduction' beyond a reasonable doubt that he had the requisite intent." Instead, there must "be something more" — something sufficient to allow the fact finder to infer that the defendant "was not merely an innocent bystander." This rule is universally followed but still presents challenges for courts, who remain divided about exactly how much more evidence beyond mere presence is necessary to sustain a conviction on a constructive possession theory.

## Rivas: *Real Life Applications*

1. Consider the following facts: Sergeant Tanner observed a vehicle traveling at a very low rate of speed while flashing its emergency lights. Tanner conducted a traffic stop to see if the driver needed assistance, and he found that the car was owned and driven by Dixon. A juvenile was sitting in the front passenger seat next to Dixon; Kier (the defendant in this case) was seated in the rear seat behind Dixon; and Kier's friend, Baker, was seated next to Kier in the back seat.

   After Tanner approached the driver's side door, Dixon rolled down his window, and Tanner noticed both the scent of marijuana coming from the vehicle and smoke inside of it. Tanner observed a hand-rolled marijuana cigarette on the rear floorboard, just behind the center console. Based on this cigarette, Tanner arrested Dixon and all three passengers for possession of marijuana.

   In a post-arrest interview with Tanner, Baker said that on the evening in question, she and Kier had gone to a local nightclub, where she encountered Dixon, who she knew from school. Baker asked Dixon if he could give Kier and her a ride home, and Dixon agreed. During that ride, Dixon and his juvenile passenger smoked a marijuana cigarette, which they disposed of when the police stopped the car. Baker, however, did not see what they did with that cigarette, because she was preoccupied with hiding her personal marijuana, obtained at the nightclub, in her underwear. Baker said that Kier did not smoke the marijuana cigarette belonging to Dixon and his juvenile passenger, that Kier was unaware that Baker had marijuana on her person, and that she never saw Kier in possession of marijuana that night.

Kier is charged with possession of marijuana.

**a.** If you were Kier's trial attorney, and the prosecutor offered to let your client plead guilty in exchange for a sentence of time served, would you advise your client to take the deal?

**b.** Assume for purposes of this question that Kier elects to go to trial and is convicted. If you were an appellate court judge, do you think there would be sufficient evidence to sustain Kier's conviction?

## 3. Proof of Knowledge and the Willful Blindness Doctrine

The *mens rea* for possession offenses is *knowing* possession. Regardless of whether the evidence suggests actual or constructive possession (or both), the prosecution must prove that the defendant both possessed the drug and did so knowingly to convict. The definition of knowledge is the same for drug possession as in other offenses where knowledge of an existing fact is required. The government must prove awareness of the stated fact or circumstance; mere suspicion that the fact or circumstance might exist is not sufficient. (Technically, most drug possession statutes criminalize knowing or intentional possession, but because it is more difficult to prove purposeful possession than knowing possession, prosecutors very rarely proceed under a theory of intentional possession.)

In drug cases, it is often easier for the government to prove knowledge than it is to prove possession. This is because it is far more common for someone to have knowledge about an item she does not possess than it is for someone to possess an item and yet not know what that item is. In *Rivas*, for example, the court found sufficient evidence that Rivas knew there were drugs in the car but overturned his conviction anyway because there was insufficient evidence he possessed the drugs.

Although it is unusual for a person to possess an item without knowing what it is, it is certainly possible. Because of the knowledge requirement, a person in that situation would not be guilty of drug possession. If, for example, a defendant had actual or constructive possession of an item that she believed was oregano but was really marijuana, the *mens rea* for possession would not be satisfied. Because knowledge is a subjective mental state, this is true even if the defendant's mistaken belief was unreasonable.

Importantly, the government is only required to prove that the defendant knew he possessed *a* controlled substance, not that the defendant knew exactly which controlled substance he possessed. This is because of the way today's controlled substances statutes are written. Both the federal Controlled Substances Act and the Uniform Controlled Substances Act (which serves as the model for almost every state's drug laws) criminalize the possession of a controlled substance, and then separately list all of the controlled substances. As a result, a defendant who knows he possesses an illegal drug but is mistaken about exactly what drug it is has still committed the crime of drug possession.

This scenario most often arises in the case of drug couriers, and it can have a huge impact on a drug defendant's sentence. This is because federal drug sentences are primarily based on the type and quantity of drug involved in an offense. In *United States v. Gomez*, 905 F.2d 1513 (11th Cir. 1990), for example, someone offered Gomez $5,000 to drive a car that they said had marijuana hidden in it from Miami to Detroit. Gomez agreed. A Georgia state trooper pulled Gomez's car over for speeding. The trooper searched the car and discovered the contraband, which turned out to be cocaine and not marijuana. The amount of cocaine found hidden inside the car—more than five kilograms—triggered a ten-year mandatory minimum prison sentence. On appeal, Gomez argued that because he thought the car contained marijuana, the "mandatory minimum penalty for cocaine could not be invoked against him." The court rejected this argument. It concluded that because "[a] defendant can be convicted of a controlled substance offense without proof that he knew the exact drug that was involved," the penalty for the drug the defendant actually possessed applies.

## Case Preview

## *United States v. Louis*

While the government is not required to prove that the defendant knew exactly which controlled substance he possessed, it must prove the defendant knew he possessed a controlled substance. Proof that a defendant thought he possessed some other kind of contraband (e.g., untaxed cigarettes) is insufficient. This requirement was put to the test in the case that follows.

As you read *Louis*, consider the following questions:

1. Although the court finds that there was insufficient evidence Louis knew he possessed a controlled substance, it says one can infer that Louis knew he was involved in something criminal. Do you agree?
2. The court distinguishes Louis's case from a previous case, *United States v. Quilca-Carpio*. What reason(s) does the court give for distinguishing *Quilca-Carpio*? Are you persuaded by the court's rationale?

## *United States v. Louis*
### 861 F.3d 1330 (11th Cir. 2017)

WILSON, J.

The burden is on the government to prove all elements of a crime beyond a reasonable doubt. When a man's liberty is at stake, we must be vigilant with this burden. The government failed to offer evidence from which a reasonable jury could find that Terry Pierre Louis had knowledge that the boxes placed in the backseat of his car contained a controlled substance. Without proof of this essential element, the government has failed to meet its burden. Therefore, we must reverse.

## I.

In September 2015, Customs and Border Protection received a tip that the *Ana Cecilia*, a coastal freighter used to export goods from the United States to Haiti, was returning from Haiti to Miami carrying narcotics. When the boat arrived Customs agents boarded the vessel and searched for narcotics for four days. None were found. At one point during the search, Louis, an employee of Ernso Borgella, the owner of the *Ana Cecilia*, brought the confined crewmembers food.[1] Following the unsuccessful search, Customs set up surveillance of the *Ana Cecilia*.

During the surveillance, an agent observed the deck watchman go inside the ship and come out carrying two large cardboard boxes. Agents later watched as a forklift picked up two boxes and drove them off the *Ana Cecilia*. Borgella was following the forklift and speaking to its driver, who placed the two boxes on the dock where an unidentified man covered them with a tarp. Later on, Borgella directed a white Nissan to park near the boxes and then reached inside the passenger rear seat and opened the door. Two unidentified men then loaded the boxes into the back seat of a white Nissan. Louis then began to slowly drive the Nissan to the front of the shipyard, while Borgella walked alongside it. Once outside the front gate of the shipyard, the Nissan was stopped by unmarked law enforcement vehicles with lights and sirens. Louis then exited the car and began to run. One of the agents pursued Louis, but lost sight of him in the shipyard. The agents found Borgella and detained him.[2] The agents searched the Nissan and found two sealed boxes in the back seat containing 111 bricks of cocaine.

Louis was charged with (1) conspiracy to possess with intent to distribute cocaine, in violation of U.S.C. §§ 841(b)(1)(A) and 846, and (2) possession with intent to distribute cocaine, in violation of 21 U.S.C. § 841(a)(1) and (b)(1)(A). During the two-day trial, the government put forth evidence including surveillance photos and videos showing that Louis was near the *Ana Cecilia*, that he drove a car containing boxes of cocaine, and that he ran when confronted by law enforcement. Following the government's case-in-chief, the defense moved for an acquittal, the motion was denied, and the defense rested. A jury found Louis guilty on both counts. Louis moved for an acquittal again after the jury verdict but his motion was denied. [Louis] was sentenced to 151 months' imprisonment.

## II.

We review de novo a district court's denial of a motion for acquittal. When considering claims regarding sufficiency of the evidence, we view the evidence in the light most favorable to the government.

---

[1] Testimony from the agent guarding the ship revealed that Louis went aboard the *Ana Cecilia* for less than five minutes to deliver the food. There was no evidence presented as to Louis's exact job duties, but the operator of the shipyard testified that he saw Louis working in an office in the shipyard and that he believed Louis performed administrative tasks for Borgella.

[2] Borgella was charged with conspiracy to possess with intent to distribute cocaine, possession with intent to distribute cocaine, conspiracy to import cocaine, and importation of cocaine. He pleaded guilty before trial and signed a plea agreement and factual proffer. He was sentenced to 108 months' imprisonment.

Eleventh Circuit precedent is clear that it is critical under § 846 and § 841 that the government must prove that the defendant had knowledge that his alleged crime involved a controlled substance. To sustain a conviction of the substantive offense of possession under § 841, the government must prove knowing possession of a controlled substance with intent to distribute it. The government must therefore prove that the defendant knew "the substance [wa]s a controlled substance."

Recently in *McFadden v. United States*, the Supreme Court reemphasized this knowledge requirement. 135 S. Ct. 2298, 2302 (2015). Justice Thomas, writing for a near unanimous court, wrote that § 841 "requires the [g]overnment to establish that the defendant knew he was dealing with 'a controlled substance.'" The Court rejected the government's proposed broader definition that the knowledge requirement would be met if the "defendant knew he was dealing with an illegal or regulated substance under *some* law."

Following the clear guidance set forth in *McFadden*, to prove that Louis "knowingly or intentionally . . . possess[ed] with intent to . . . distribute . . . a controlled substance" under § 841 the government would have to prove that Louis knew the boxes contained a controlled substance, and not just contraband illegal under *some* law.

## III.

After a careful review of the record and the parties' briefs, we conclude that no reasonable jury could find from the little evidence presented during the two-day trial that Louis is guilty of violating § 846 and § 841 beyond a reasonable doubt. Viewing the evidence in the light most favorable to the government, we can infer that Louis's presence and flight are evidence that he knew he was involved in something criminal. We cannot find, however, that the government proved beyond a reasonable doubt that Louis knew the boxes placed in his car contained a controlled substance. And because the evidence does not prove that Louis knew that the boxes contained a controlled substance, the evidence does not prove that he knew he was involved in a conspiracy to possess a controlled substance.

During a short trial, the government presented evidence that Louis was seen around the shipyard (where he worked) and was seen near Borgella (his employer). The government relied heavily on evidence that Louis fled when suddenly surrounded by law enforcement. The government's case was built upon inferences from Louis's presence and flight. However, the government presented no evidence that Louis knew that there was a controlled substance (as opposed to any other contraband) within the sealed boxes placed by others in his backseat. No one testified as to Louis's knowledge and Louis himself did not testify.

We recognize that "[e]vidence of flight is admissible to demonstrate . . . guilt," and Louis's flight might be persuasive evidence that he knew the boxes contained contraband illegal under some law. But the evidence is not enough to prove that Louis knew the boxes contained a controlled substance.

In addition to Louis's flight, the government relies on Louis's presence and interactions around the shipyard. But the government puts forth no evidence of any conversations where Louis was informed of a plan regarding a controlled substance. There is no evidence, circumstantial or otherwise, strong enough to prove beyond a reasonable doubt that Louis knew that there was a controlled substance in the boxes. The government's evidence of presence and flight was simply not enough to support a finding of knowledge beyond a reasonable doubt.

Neither are we persuaded by an entrustment theory, which attempts to imply knowledge when there is evidence of a high quantity of drugs because "a 'prudent smuggler' is not likely to entrust such valuable cargo to an innocent person without that person's knowledge." *See United States v. Quilca-Carpio*, 118 F.3d 719, 722 (11th Cir. 1997) (per curiam). We do not find *Quilca-Carpio* sufficiently analogous here, as Louis's presence with the boxes was only brief. In *Quilca-Carpio*, the defendant checked an unusually heavy roller-bag as his own luggage on an international flight from Lima, Peru to the United States. However, Louis was in the Nissan only briefly as he slowly drove with Borgella walking alongside the car. Indeed, Louis was never left completely alone with the boxes, like the defendant in *Quilca-Carpio*. This hardly supports a conclusion that Louis was sufficiently entrusted with the cocaine to establish his knowledge, and it is surely not enough to prove his knowledge beyond a reasonable doubt.

## IV.

The government is charged with proving "beyond a reasonable doubt . . . *every fact* necessary to constitute the crime with which [the defendant] is charged." We must hold the government accountable to this burden. While the circumstances presented by the government here might show that it is more likely than not that Louis knew that the boxes contained some sort of contraband, the permissible inferences do not support a holding that the government proved that Louis *knew* this was a conspiracy involving a controlled substance or that he knew he was in possession of a controlled substance. Without this requisite showing of knowledge, the government has failed to prove every fact necessary to meet its burden.

**Post-Case Follow-Up**

In *Louis*, the court applies the *mens rea* requirement for drug possession — knowledge — and holds that the evidence was insufficient to sustain the conviction. The defendant in *Louis* did not dispute that he possessed boxes that contained drugs; under the circumstances, it seems there was sufficient proof he had the power and intent to exercise control over the boxes when he began to drive the truck. But there was not enough evidence from which a reasonable jury could conclude beyond a reasonable doubt that Louis knew the boxes contained a controlled substance. The court reasoned that Louis's flight from the truck was sufficient evidence "that he knew the boxes contained contraband under some law. But the evidence was not enough to prove that Louis knew the boxes contained a controlled substance." For this reason, the court overturned Louis's convictions.

# Louis: *Real Life Applications*

**1.** In *Louis*, the court suggested there was sufficient evidence the defendant knew he possessed contraband of some kind, although not sufficient evidence that he knew he possessed a controlled substance as required by the statute. From a policy perspective, some readers might agree with this outcome on the grounds that the law should not criminalize the general possession of contraband. But others might view the outcome in *Louis* as indicative of a possible loophole in the law.

Assume for purposes of this question that you are working as an aide to a member of Congress who falls into this second camp. Your boss has been alerted by a constituent to the decision in *Louis*. She wants to introduce a bill to close the "loophole" that resulted in reversal of Louis's convictions. Please draft a short statute of no more than a paragraph that would help achieve your boss's goal. What challenges, if any, do you anticipate might arise in the interpretation and enforcement of this statute?

**2.** The court in *Louis* distinguished its decision from an earlier Eleventh Circuit case, *United States v. Quilca-Carpio*, and provided a brief summary of the facts of that case. The following is a more detailed description of the facts in *Quilca-Carpio*:

On November 26, 1995, Quilca-Carpio traveled from Lima, Peru, his native country, to the United States. After claiming the two pieces of luggage that he had checked for the flight, a blue suitcase and a black roller-bag, he proceeded through immigration and customs. He cleared immigration and a primary customs station, but was later stopped for a random check at a secondary customs station by roving inspector Dwight Sweeting. The inspector emptied the black roller-bag of its contents, which consisted of Peruvian fur rugs. He felt inside the bag and noticed an unusual thickness in its bottom. He lifted it and determined that it weighed noticeably more than this type of bag would normally weigh.

Sweeting then motioned inspector Gilberto Aguilar, an inspector with over five years of experience, for help. Aguilar later testified at trial that the bag did not look suspicious and that the weight of the bag was the only thing suspicious about it. He estimated that it weighed about eight to ten pounds, while the normal weight for that type of bag is usually about five pounds. The bag was x-rayed and revealed nothing unusual. Sweeting then obtained a probe and punctured the bottom of the roller-bag. The probe revealed a white substance hidden in the false bottom of the roller-bag. The substance field-tested as cocaine. The total weight of the cocaine was 3.94 kilograms (or about 8.5 pounds). Aguilar also testified that Quilca-Carpio's answers to his questions throughout the process were all normal and that Quilca-Carpio did not exhibit any nervousness. The prosecution rested after presenting the testimony of inspectors Aguilar and Sweeting. The defense rested without presenting any evidence.

*United States v. Quilca-Carpio*, 118 F.3d 719, 720 (11th Cir. 1997).

After reading these facts, are you persuaded by the *Louis* court's rationale for distinguishing *Quilca-Carpio*? Or do you think that the two cases are similar enough with respect to proof of knowledge that the court should have reached the same outcome in both cases?

## *Willful Blindness*

In most drug cases, the government will seek to prove that the defendant had positive knowledge that he possessed a controlled substance. But what if a person specifically avoids learning what an item in his possession is because he is concerned that it might be an illegal drug? Consider, for instance, these facts from *United States v. Jewell*, 532 F.2d 697 (9th Cir. 1976). Jewell was caught driving across the U.S.-Mexico border with 110 pounds of marijuana concealed in a secret compartment in his car. He testified that while he was on a trip in Mexico, a stranger named "Ray" approached him and asked if he wanted to buy some marijuana. Jewell declined and the stranger then asked if Jewell "wanted to drive a car back to Los Angeles for $100." After his arrest, Jewell told a Drug Enforcement Administration agent "he thought there was probably something wrong and something illegal in the vehicle" but that he did not ask the stranger any questions to confirm. At trial, Jewell acknowledged that he had briefly inspected the car and noticed "a void" where the secret compartment was located but that he decided not to investigate further. Jewell's statements, in combination with other evidence, suggested that "although [Jewell] was aware of facts making it virtually certain that the secret compartment concealed marihuana, he deliberately refrained from acquiring positive knowledge of the fact."

Courts in many jurisdictions have adopted the **willful blindness** (also called **deliberate ignorance**) doctrine to attribute knowledge to defendants in cases like *Jewell*. "Willful blindness serves as an alternate theory on which the government may prove knowledge." *United States v. Pérez-Meléndez*, 599 F.3d 31, 41 (1st Cir. 2010). The doctrine proceeds from the premise that "knowledge" is not limited to "positive knowledge" because a person can "'know' of facts of which he is less than absolutely certain." *Jewell*, 532 F.2d at 700. Courts that have adopted the willful blindness rule reason that a person who makes "the deliberate effort to avoid guilty knowledge" is as blameworthy as a person who obtains positive knowledge. *United States v. Giovannetti*, 919 F.2d 1223, 1228 (7th Cir. 1990).

The formulation for willful blindness varies slightly from one jurisdiction to the next but it typically requires proof that a defendant was (1) aware of a high probability of a fact and (2) deliberately avoided gaining positive knowledge of that fact. A number of courts also require the defendant to "have had a particular motive for remaining in ignorance: namely, to preserve a defense in the event of prosecution." Alexander F. Sachs, *Willful Ignorance, Culpability, and the Criminal Law*, 88 St. John's L. Rev. 1023, 1025 (2014).

Not everyone agrees that willful blindness is really the equivalent of knowledge. Some argue that, when given as a jury instruction, the doctrine might confuse juries and lead them to convict defendants who did not act knowingly, but instead were merely reckless. These concerns have led some courts to reject the willful blindness rule entirely. Among courts that have adopted the doctrine, most hold that juries should be given a willful blindness instruction only "in those rare circumstances where the facts point in the direction of deliberate ignorance." *Hallman v. State*, 633 So. 2d 1116, 1117 (Fla. Dist. Ct. App. 1994).

In jurisdictions that have adopted the willful blindness doctrine, it is not limited to drug cases. It can potentially apply anytime knowledge is an element of an offense. This is because willful blindness is not a distinct mental state. Rather, it is a method for proving knowledge. As a result, in any case where knowledge is an element of the offense, the prosecution can seek a willful blindness jury instruction if the evidence suggests the defendant was willfully blind to a fact. Although the willful blindness doctrine can arise in any case where knowledge is an element of the offense, the overwhelming majority of cases where it is at issue are drug prosecutions. For this reason, we cover the willful blindness doctrine in this chapter.

**Case Preview**

## United States v. Heredia

The willful blindness doctrine purports to be a method of proving knowledge, rather than a distinct mental state. But is this really the case? Or does the willful blindness rule illegitimately expand criminal liability in statutes where knowledge is required? In *United States v. Heredia*, the Ninth Circuit sitting *en banc* considered this question. In *Heredia*, the defendant argued that the court should overrule its precedent establishing the willful blindness doctrine. In the alternative, she argued that the willful blindness instruction in her case was defective because it did not include a requirement that the defendant's motive for deliberately failing to learn the truth was to avoid criminal liability. The majority upheld Heredia's conviction, but the case divided the court.

As you read *Heredia*, consider the following questions:

1. Do you agree with the majority's decision to retain the willful blindness doctrine? Or do you agree with the dissent that willful blindness is "a *mens rea* separate and distinct from knowledge," and that the doctrine is therefore inconsistent with the plain text of the statute?
2. Why does the majority conclude that willful blindness instructions do not need to include a motive prong? Why does the concurrence disagree? Which opinion do you find more persuasive on this issue?

## *United States v. Heredia*
483 F.3d 913 (9th Cir. 2007)

KOZINSKI, J.

We revisit *United States v. Jewell*, 532 F.2d 697 (9th Cir. 1976) [in which the Ninth Circuit adopted the willful blindness doctrine], and the body of caselaw applying it.

Defendant Carmen Heredia was stopped at an inland Border Patrol checkpoint while driving from Nogales to Tucson, Arizona. Heredia was at the wheel and her two children, mother and one of her aunts were passengers. The border agent at the scene noticed what he described as a "very strong perfume odor" emanating from the car. A second agent searched the trunk and found 349.2 pounds of marijuana surrounded by dryer sheets, apparently used to mask the odor. Heredia was arrested and charged with possessing a controlled substance with intent to distribute under 21 U.S.C. § 841(a)(1).

At trial, Heredia testified that on the day of her arrest she had accompanied her mother on a bus trip from Tucson to Nogales, where her mother had a dentist's appointment. After the appointment, she borrowed her Aunt Belia's car to transport her mother back to Tucson.[1] Heredia told DEA Agent Travis Birney at the time of her arrest that, while still in Nogales, she had noticed a "detergent" smell in the car as she prepared for the trip and asked Belia to explain. Belia told her that she had spilled Downey fabric softener in the car a few days earlier, but Heredia found this explanation incredible.

Heredia admitted on the stand that she suspected there might be drugs in the car, based on the fact that her mother was visibly nervous during the trip and carried a large amount of cash, even though she wasn't working at the time. However, Heredia claimed that her suspicions were not aroused until she had passed the last freeway exit before the checkpoint, by which time it was too dangerous to pull over and investigate.

The government requested a deliberate ignorance instruction, and the judge obliged, overruling Heredia's objection. The instruction read as follows:

> You may find that the defendant acted knowingly if you find beyond a reasonable doubt that the defendant was aware of a high probability that drugs were in the vehicle driven by the defendant and deliberately avoided learning the truth. You may not find such knowledge, however, if you find that the defendant actually believed that no drugs were in the vehicle driven by the defendant, or if you find that the defendant was simply careless.

On appeal, defendant asks us to overrule *Jewell* and hold that section 841(a)(1) extends liability only to individuals who act with actual knowledge. Should *Jewell* remain good law, she asks us to reverse her conviction because the instruction given to the jury was defective and because there was an insufficient factual basis for issuing the instruction in the first place.

While *Jewell* has spawned a great deal of commentary and a somewhat perplexing body of caselaw, its core holding was a rather straightforward matter of statutory

---

[1] Belia was not the aunt in the car with Heredia at the time she was stopped at the checkpoint. Belia was traveling on the same interstate at about the same time, but in a separate car.

interpretation: "'[K]nowingly' in criminal statutes is not limited to positive knowledge, but includes the state of mind of one who does not possess positive knowledge only because he consciously avoided it." In other words, when Congress made it a crime to "knowingly . . . possess with intent to manufacture, distribute, or dispense, a controlled substance," it meant to punish not only those who know they possess a controlled substance, but also those who don't know because they don't want to know.[4]

Overturning a long-standing precedent is never to be done lightly, and particularly not "in the area of statutory construction, where Congress is free to change [an] interpretation of its legislation." Even in the criminal context, where private reliance interests are less compelling, stare decisis concerns still carry great weight, particularly when a precedent is as deeply entrenched as *Jewell*. Since *Jewell* was decided in 1976, every regional circuit — with the exception of the D.C. Circuit — has adopted its central holding. Indeed, many colloquially refer to the deliberate ignorance instruction as the "*Jewell* instruction." Congress has amended section 841 many times since *Jewell* was handed down, but not in a way that would cast doubt on our ruling. Given the widespread acceptance of *Jewell* across the federal judiciary, of which Congress must surely have been aware, we construe Congress's inaction as acquiescence.[6]

That said, there are circumstances when a precedent becomes so unworkable that keeping it on the books actually undermines the values of evenhandedness and predictability that the doctrine of stare decisis aims to advance. Here, we recognize that many of our post-*Jewell* cases have created a vexing thicket of precedent that has been difficult for litigants to follow and for district courts — and ourselves — to apply with consistency. But, rather than overturn *Jewell*, we conclude that the better course is to clear away the underbrush that surrounds it.

The parties have pointed out one area where our cases have not been consistent: Whether the jury must be instructed that defendant's motive in deliberately failing to learn the truth was to give himself a defense in case he should be charged with the crime.[8] *Jewell* itself speculated that defendant's motive for failing to learn the truth in that case was to "avoid responsibility in the event of discovery." Yet the opinion did not define motive as a separate prong of the deliberate ignorance instruction.

---

[4] As our cases have recognized, deliberate ignorance, otherwise known as willful blindness, is categorically different from negligence or recklessness. A willfully blind defendant is one who took *deliberate* actions to avoid confirming suspicions of criminality. A reckless defendant is one who merely knew of a substantial and unjustifiable risk that his conduct was criminal; a negligent defendant is one who should have had similar suspicions but, in fact, did not.

[6] Our dissenting colleague seeks support for her position from the fact that Congress has, on occasion, defined the scienter requirement in some criminal statutes as "knows, or has reasonable grounds to believe." But "has reasonable grounds to believe" defines a mental state that is less than actual knowledge. By contrast, *Jewell* defines willful blindness as knowledge — and sets a much higher standard for satisfying it. Thus, under *Jewell*, the prosecution must prove that defendant was aware of a "high probability" that he is in the possession of contraband, and that he "deliberately avoided learning the truth." This standard focuses on defendant's actual beliefs and actions, whereas "has reasonable grounds to believe" is an objective standard that could be satisfied by showing what a reasonable person would believe, regardless of defendant's actual beliefs. That Congress chose to set a lower scienter requirement in some criminal statutes tells us nothing about our interpretation of "knowledge" in *Jewell*. It certainly provides an insufficient basis for rejecting an interpretation that Congress has left undisturbed for three decades and that has since been adopted by ten of our sister circuits.

[8] The motive prong usually requires the jury to find that defendant was deliberately ignorant "in order to provide himself with a defense in the event of prosecution."

And we affirmed, even though the instruction given at Jewell's trial made no mention of motive. Since then, we've upheld two-pronged instructions, similar to the one given here, in at least four other published opinions.

The first mention of the motive prong came in a dissent by then-Judge Kennedy, who also authored the dissent in *Jewell*. Judge Kennedy's chief concern was with what he viewed as the absence of *deliberate* avoidance on the part of the defendant in that case. At any rate, he was not writing for the court. Yet some of our opinions seem to have adopted the motive prong, providing little justification for doing so other than citation to Judge Kennedy's dissent. Three other federal circuits have followed suit. *See United States v. Puche*, 350 F.3d 1137, 1149 (11th Cir. 2003); *United States v. Willis*, 277 F.3d 1026, 1032 (8th Cir. 2002); *United States v. Delreal-Ordones*, 213 F.3d 1263, 1268-69 (10th Cir. 2000).

Heredia argues that the motive prong is necessary to avoid punishing individuals who fail to investigate because circumstances render it unsafe or impractical to do so. She claims that she is within this group, because her suspicions did not arise until she was driving on an open highway where it would have been too dangerous to pull over. She thus claims that she had a motive *other* than avoiding criminal culpability for failing to discover the contraband concealed in the trunk.

We believe, however, that the second prong of the instruction, the requirement that defendant have *deliberately* avoided learning the truth, provides sufficient protections for defendants in these situations. A deliberate action is one that is "[i]ntentional; premeditated; fully considered." *Black's Law Dictionary* 459 (8th ed. 2004). A decision influenced by coercion, exigent circumstances or lack of meaningful choice is, perforce, not deliberate. A defendant who fails to investigate for these reasons has not deliberately chosen to avoid learning the truth.[10]

We conclude, therefore, that the two-pronged instruction given at defendant's trial met the requirements of *Jewell* and, to the extent some of our cases have suggested more is required they are overruled. A district judge, in the exercise of his discretion, may say more to tailor the instruction to the particular facts of the case. Here, for example, the judge might have instructed the jury that it could find Heredia did not act deliberately if it believed that her failure to investigate was motivated by safety concerns. Heredia did not ask for such an instruction and the district judge had no obligation to give it sua sponte. Even when defendant asks for such a supplemental instruction, it is within the district court's broad discretion whether to comply.

Defendant also claims there was insufficient foundation to give the *Jewell* instruction.

---

[10] The concurrence would add the third prong to the *Jewell* instruction in order to protect defendants who have "innocent" motives for deliberately avoiding the truth. But the deliberate ignorance instruction defines when an individual has sufficient information so that he can be deemed to "know" something, even though he does not take the final step to confirm that knowledge. The *reason* the individual fails to take that final step has no bearing on whether he has sufficient information so he can properly be deemed to "know" the fact. An innocent motive for being deliberately ignorant no more vitiates the knowledge element of a crime than does an innocent motive vitiate any other element.

Equally misplaced is the concurrence's concern about FedEx and similar package carriers. The fact that a tiny percentage of the tens of thousands of packages FedEx transports every day may contain contraband hardly establishes a high probability that any particular package contains contraband. Of course, if a particular package leaks a white powder or gives any other particularized and unmistakable indication that it contains contraband, and the carrier fails to investigate, it may be held liable — and properly so.

In deciding whether to give a particular instruction, the district court must view the evidence in the light most favorable to the party requesting it. When knowledge is at issue in a criminal case, the court must first determine whether the evidence of defendant's mental state, if viewed in the light most favorable to the government, will support a finding of actual knowledge.[13] In deciding whether to give a willful blindness instruction, in addition to an actual knowledge instruction, the district court must determine whether the jury could rationally find willful blindness even though it has rejected the government's evidence of actual knowledge. If so, the court may also give a *Jewell* instruction.

This case well illustrates the point. Taking the evidence in the light most favorable to the government, a reasonable jury could certainly have found that Heredia actually knew about the drugs. Not only was she driving a car with several hundred pounds of marijuana in the trunk, but everyone else who might have put the drugs there — her mother, her aunt, her husband — had a close personal relationship with Heredia. Moreover, there was evidence that Heredia and her husband had sole possession of the car for about an hour prior to setting out on the trip to Tucson. Based on this evidence, a jury could easily have inferred that Heredia actually knew about the drugs in the car because she was involved in putting them there.

The analysis in the foregoing paragraph presupposes that the jury believed the government's case in its entirety, and disbelieved all of Heredia's exculpatory statements. While this would have been *a* rational course for the jury to take, it was not the only one. For example, a rational jury might have bought Heredia's basic claim that she didn't know about the drugs in the trunk, yet disbelieved other aspects of her story. The jury could, for example, have disbelieved Heredia's story about *when* she first began to suspect she was transporting drugs. The jury could have found that her suspicions were aroused when Belia gave her the unsatisfactory explanation for the "detergent" scent, or while she drove to Tucson but before the last exit preceding the checkpoint. Or, the jury might have believed Heredia that she became suspicious only after she had passed the last exit before the checkpoint but disbelieved that concerns about safety motivated her failure to stop.

All of these are scenarios the jury could rationally have drawn from the evidence presented, depending on how credible they deemed Heredia's testimony in relation to the other evidence presented. The government has no way of knowing which version of the facts the jury will believe, and it is entitled (like any other litigant) to have the jury instructed in conformity with each of these rational possibilities.

We do not share the worry that giving both an actual knowledge and a deliberate ignorance instruction is likely to confuse the jury. A jury is presumed to follow the instructions given to it and we see no reason to fear that juries will be less able to do so when trying to sort out a criminal defendant's state of mind than any other issue. Nor do we agree that the *Jewell* instruction risks lessening the state of mind that a jury must find to something akin to recklessness or negligence. The instruction requires the jury to find beyond a reasonable doubt that defendant "was aware of a high probability" of criminality and "deliberately avoided learning the truth."

---

[13] As previously noted, willful blindness is tantamount to knowledge. We use the phrase "actual knowledge" to describe the state of mind when defendant, in fact, knows of the existence of the contraband rather than being willfully blind to its existence.

Indeed, the instruction actually given in this case told the jurors to acquit if they believed defendant was "simply careless." Recklessness or negligence never comes into play, and there is little reason to suspect that juries will import these concepts, as to which they are not instructed, into their deliberations.

We decline the invitation to overrule *Jewell*, and further hold that district judges are owed the usual degree of deference in deciding when a deliberate ignorance instruction is warranted. While the particular form of the instruction can vary, it must, at a minimum, contain the two prongs of suspicion and deliberate avoidance. The instruction given at defendant's trial met these requirements, and the district judge did not abuse his discretion in issuing it.

Affirmed.

KLEINFELD, J., concurring in the result.

Suppose Heredia were a witness rather than defendant, perhaps because the government had charged her aunt who owned the car instead of her. If Heredia were asked "was there marijuana in the car," counsel would have objected for lack of foundation, and the objection would have been sustained.[1] Heredia's suspicion would not be enough to let her testify to knowledge. Yet she can be convicted under a statute that requires her to have knowledge. This is not impossible, but it is a troubling paradox for criminal knowledge to require *less* than evidentiary knowledge. To avoid injustice, the jury needs to be instructed that they must find a motivation to avoid criminal responsibility to be the reason for lack of knowledge.

In our en banc decision in *United States v. Jewell*, a man offered to sell marijuana to the defendant and his friend in a Tijuana bar, and then to pay defendant $100 to drive a car across the border. The friend refused, saying that "it didn't sound right," and he "wanted no part of driving the vehicle." But the defendant accepted the offer, even though he "thought there was probably something illegal in the vehicle." The defendant determined that there was no contraband in the glove compartment, under the front seat, or in the trunk, so he concluded that "the people at the border wouldn't find anything either." He admitted to seeing a secret compartment in the trunk (where 110 pounds of marijuana was later found), but did not attempt to open it.

We held that, in these circumstances, the knowledge element in the applicable drug statutes could be satisfied without positive, confirmed personal knowledge that the marijuana was in the trunk. We took particular note of the motive in such deliberate avoidance of knowledge cases "to avoid responsibility in the event of discovery":

> [T]he jury could conclude that . . . although appellant knew of the presence of the secret compartment and had knowledge of facts indicating that it contained marijuana, he deliberately avoided positive knowledge of the presence of the contraband *to avoid responsibility in the event of discovery.* If . . . positive knowledge is required to convict, the jury would have no choice consistent with its oath but to

---

[1] *See* F.R.E. 602 ("A witness may not testify to a matter unless evidence is introduced sufficient to support a finding that the witness has personal knowledge of the matter.").

find appellant not guilty even though he deliberately contrived his lack of positive knowledge.

We described such blindness as "wilful" and not merely negligence, foolishness or recklessness, differing from positive knowledge "only so far as necessary to encompass a calculated effort to avoid the sanctions of the statute while violating its substance."

> A court can properly find wilful blindness only where it can almost be said that the defendant actually knew. He suspected the fact; he realised its probability; but he refrained from obtaining the final confirmation because he wanted in the event to be able to deny knowledge. This, and this alone, is wilful blindness. It requires in effect a finding that the defendant intended to cheat the administration of justice. Any wider definition would make the doctrine of wilful blindness indistinguishable from the civil doctrine of negligence in not obtaining knowledge.

Then-judge Kennedy, joined by Judges Ely, Hufstedler and Wallace, vigorously dissented. They presciently warned that the majority opened the door too wide to suspicion as a substitute for scienter.

"Wilfulness" requires a "purpose of violating a known legal duty," or, at the very least, "a bad purpose." That is why wilful blindness is "equally culpable" to, and may be substituted for, positive knowledge. But to allow conviction without positive knowledge or wilful avoidance of such knowledge is to erase the scienter requirement from the statute.

The majority converts the statutory element that the possession be "knowing" into something much less—a requirement that the defendant be suspicious and deliberately avoid investigating. The imposition on people who intend no crime of a duty to investigate has no statutory basis. The majority says that its requirement is enough to protect defendants who cannot investigate because of "coercion, exigent circumstances or lack of meaningful choice." I am not sure what the latter two novelties mean (especially the term "meaningful" choice) or how a jury would be instructed to give them concrete meaning. The majority's statement that "[a]n innocent motive for being deliberately ignorant" does not bar conviction under its rule seems to contradict its proposition that coercion or exigent circumstances excuse failure to investigate. The majority seems to mean that if someone can investigate, they must. A criminal duty to investigate the wrongdoing of others to avoid wrongdoing of one's own is a novelty in the criminal law.

Shall someone who thinks his mother is carrying a stash of marijuana in her suitcase be obligated, when he helps her with it, to rummage through her things? Should Heredia have carried tools with her, so that (if her story was true) she could open the trunk for which she had no key? Shall all of us who give a ride to child's friend search her purse or his backpack?

No "coercion, exigent circumstances, or lack of meaningful choice" prevents FedEx from opening packages before accepting them, or prevents bus companies from going through the luggage of suspicious looking passengers. But these businesses are not "knowingly" transporting drugs in any particular package, even though they know that in a volume business in all likelihood they sometimes must be. They forego inspection to save time, or money, or offense to customers, not to avoid criminal responsibility. But these reasons for not inspecting are not the ones acceptable to the majority ("coercion, exigent circumstances, or lack of meaningful choice").

A *Jewell* instruction ought to require (1) a belief that drugs are present, (2) avoidance of confirmation of the belief, and (3) wilfulness in that avoidance — that is, choosing not to confirm the belief in order to "be able to deny knowledge if apprehended." The instruction should expressly exclude recklessness, negligence and mistake (the one given only excluded "simpl[e] careless[ness]" and an "actual[] belie[f]" that no drugs were in the vehicle"). Anything less supports convictions of persons whom Congress excluded from statutory coverage with the word "knowingly." People who possess drugs, but do not do so "knowingly," are what we traditionally refer to as "innocent."

The reason that I concur instead of dissenting is that defendant did not object to these deficiencies in the instruction, and the deficiencies were not "plain." To constitute plain error, "[a]n error . . . must be . . . obvious or readily apparent." Our previous cases did not make clear that the instruction had to say these things (they only made clear that the judge must decide there was some evidence of wilfulness before giving the instruction).

GRABER, J., dissenting.

[A]s a matter of statutory construction, I believe that the *Jewell* instruction is not proper because it misconstrues, and misleads the jury about, the mens rea required by 21 U.S.C. § 841(a)(1).

Under 21 U.S.C. § 841(a)(1), it is a crime to "*knowingly or intentionally* . . . manufacture, distribute, or dispense, or possess with intent to manufacture, distribute, or dispense, a controlled substance." (Emphasis added.) The plain text of the statute does not make it a crime to have a high probability of awareness of possession — knowledge or intention is required.

Instead of justifying its sleight-of-hand directly, the majority points to the fact that *Jewell* has been on the books for 30 years and that Congress has not amended the statute in a way that repudiates *Jewell* expressly. I find this reasoning unpersuasive. "[C]ongressional inaction lacks persuasive significance because several equally tenable inferences may be drawn from such inaction. . . ."

Whatever relevance congressional *inaction* holds in this case is outweighed by actual congressional *action*. Under 21 U.S.C. § 841(a)(1), a person is guilty of a crime only if the requisite act is performed "knowingly or intentionally." By contrast, both before and after *Jewell*, Congress has defined several other crimes in which the mens rea involves a high probability of awareness — but it has done so in phrases dramatically different than the one here, which lists only knowledge and intent. *See, e.g.*, 18 U.S.C. §§ 175b(b)(1) ("knows or has reasonable cause to believe"), 792 ("knows, or has reasonable grounds to believe or suspect"), 2332d(a) ("knowing or having reasonable cause to know"). Most importantly, Congress has done so in adjacent sections of the same statute, the Controlled Substances Act, and even within the same section of the same statute. "It is axiomatic that when Congress uses different text in 'adjacent' statutes it intends that the different terms carry a different meaning."

The majority recognizes that the *Jewell* instruction embodies a substantive decision that those who possess a controlled substance and "don't know because they don't want to know" are just as culpable as those who knowingly or intentionally possess a controlled substance. But Congress never made this substantive decision about levels of culpability — the *Jewell* court did. By "clear[ing] away the underbrush that surrounds" the instruction, the majority chooses to reaffirm this judge-made substantive decision. In so doing, the majority directly contravenes the principle that "[i]t is the legislature, not the Court, which is to define a crime, and ordain its punishment." *United States v. Wiltberger*, 18 U.S. (5 Wheat.) 76, 95 (1820). The majority creates a duty to investigate for drugs that appears nowhere in the text of the statute, transforming knowledge into a mens rea more closely akin to negligence or recklessness.

I agree with the *Jewell* court that "one 'knows' facts of which he is less than absolutely certain." That being so, the mens rea-reducing *Jewell* instruction not only is wrong, it also is unnecessary in the face of the kind of proof that a prosecutor is likely to produce. For example, if your husband comes home at 1:00 A.M. every Friday (after having left work at 5:00 P.M. the day before as usual), never reveals where he has been, won't look you in the eye on Fridays, and puts Thursday's shirts in the hamper bearing lipstick stains, your friends will agree that you "know" he is having an affair even if you refuse to seek confirmation. The role of a jury is to apply common sense to the facts of a given case. A sensible jury will be persuaded that a drug mule "knows" what she is carrying when confronted with evidence of how mules typically operate and how this mule acted — all without reference to a *Jewell* instruction.

Thus, I would overrule *Jewell* and interpret 21 U.S.C. § 841(a) to require exactly what its text requires — a knowing or intentional mens rea. If Congress wants to criminalize willful ignorance, it is free to amend the statute to say so and, in view of the several examples quoted above, it clearly knows how.

**Post-Case Follow-Up**

As the concurring and dissenting opinions in *Heredia* suggest, the willful blindness doctrine continues to be controversial. And, as discussed in the introduction to willful blindness above, some courts have rejected the willful blindness doctrine and others apply a more stringent version of it than the Ninth Circuit by including a motive prong. It is important to remember that the willful blindness doctrine is not meant to be a distinct mental state. It is a method for proving knowledge. Although not everyone agrees with that characterization, it is the rationale given by the courts that have adopted the willful blindness rule.

## Heredia: *Real Life Applications*

**1.** The majority in *Heredia* characterizes willful blindness as a "rather straightforward matter of statutory interpretation" of the word "knowingly." In its view, the mental state of knowledge applies "not only to those who know they possess a controlled substance, but also those who don't know because they don't want to." The majority also takes care to emphasize that willful blindness "is categorically distinct from negligence or recklessness."

Look back at the definitions of the reckless and negligence mental states in Chapter 2 at pages 68 and 69.

a. In your own words, briefly explain the difference between the willful blindness method of proving knowledge, and the mental states of recklessness and negligence.

b. Now, reread the willful blindness jury instruction that was given in *Heredia*. Do you think this instruction provided sufficient guidance to the jury? Specifically, do you think there is a risk that a jury given this instruction might convict a defendant who was merely reckless and/or negligent with respect to the presence of drugs? Or do you think the instruction adequately conveyed the statute's *mens rea* requirement that the defendant knowingly possessed drugs?

## C. POSSESSION WITH THE INTENT TO DISTRIBUTE

**Possession with the intent to distribute** is when a person knowingly possesses a controlled substance with the intent to distribute it.

To convict a defendant of possession with the intent to distribute, the government must first prove knowing possession of the substance. Recall that in *Rivas* (page 165), the court overturned the defendant's conviction for possession with the intent to distribute on the grounds that the prosecutor had presented insufficient evidence of possession. Likewise, *Heredia* (page 180) involved a prosecution for possession with the intent to distribute, although the opinion concerned the element of *knowing* possession. In both *Rivas* and *Heredia*, the defendants did not dispute the *intent to distribute* element of the offense. This section examines that element, looking at what sort of evidence is necessary to prove an intent to distribute and what conduct constitutes distribution.

As the name of the offense suggests, the difference between possession and possession with the intent to distribute is that the latter offense requires the government to prove the defendant intended to distribute the substance in her possession. Possession with the intent to distribute is the most frequently prosecuted drug trafficking crime. This is because the offense is usually easier to prove than distribution or attempted distribution. The government does not need to show that the defendant ever actually sold drugs in a possession with the intent to distribute prosecution; proof of a mere intent to distribute the drugs possessed is enough.

As is often the case, the government will not always have direct evidence of the defendant's state of mind. It is the comparatively rare case in which a defendant admits to the police that he planned to sell drugs or that the police are able to gather other direct evidence of an intent to sell, such as text messages arranging a sale. In the absence of direct evidence of intent, the government may rely on circumstantial evidence to prove intent. But circumstantial evidence can present especially difficult line drawing problems in the context of this offense. In comparison to crimes like burglary, where it may be perfectly reasonable to infer that a person who breaks into a home intends to commit a crime inside, the facts surrounding the possession of a mind-altering substance are often much more ambiguous.

Consider the following scenario: The police execute a search warrant on Denise's home and uncover a large quantity of an intoxicating substance — enough for one year of daily use by an addict, according to the government's expert witness. In addition, the police find $500 in small bills and a passport belonging to Denise in a safe. In the garage, there is a gun registered to Denise and bags that are commonly used to package the substance. Is this evidence enough to prove beyond a reasonable doubt that Denise intended to distribute the substance? If you believe that it is, what fact(s) are determinative for you? Would the quantity of the substance alone be sufficient to prove Denise intended to distribute it? Would your answer to this hypothetical change if you learned that the intoxicating substance the police found at Denise's home was alcohol? Isn't it just as likely Denise is a wine collector as it is that she is planning to sell the alcohol?

## Case Preview

## *United States v. Hunt*

Trying to determine what a person intends to do with an item in her possession can sometimes be a difficult and uncertain endeavor. In *United States v. Hunt*, the court considered whether the evidence was sufficient to sustain the defendant's conviction for possession with the intent to distribute a little less than eight grams of crack cocaine that was found in her bedroom. The decision highlights the uncertainty of the intent inquiry in this area of the law and describes some of the circumstantial evidence that can prove an intent to distribute a controlled substance.

As you read the decision, consider the following questions:

1. What role did the government's expert play in this case? If the government's expert had testified that the amount of cocaine base found in Hunt's apartment was incompatible with personal use, would the result of the case have been different?
2. What kinds of evidence does the court say can help to prove an intent to distribute?

# *United States v. Hunt*
### 129 F.3d 739 (5th Cir. 1997)

GARZA, J.

Latarsha Hunt appeals her conviction for possession of cocaine base with intent to distribute in violation of 21 U.S.C. § 841(a)(1). Finding insufficient evidence to support the verdict, we reverse, vacate the sentence, and remand for sentencing on the lesser included offense of simple possession.

A confidential informant told police that marijuana was being sold out of 832 Arthur Walk, which police identified as property leased to Hunt. Executing a search warrant on those premises, police officers discovered a brown paper bag containing marijuana on a coffee table in the living room along with loose tobacco and cigar labels on the floor. In addition, they found a loaded handgun under the couch. In Hunt's bedroom, they discovered 7.998 grams of cocaine base (or "crack") and a razor blade on a plate on the top of a dresser. The cocaine was broken into one large rock and several smaller pieces. Hunt, Dashanta Burton, who is a friend of Hunt's, and an unidentified male juvenile were present when the police entered the house. Hunt was standing near the front door when police entered, and, according to the testimony of the officers, did not appear to be expecting the police.

Detective Ruben Rodriguez testified that the cocaine was worth about $200, an amount that could be doubled depending on how it was cut, and that it was a distributable amount. Furthermore, he stated that each of the smaller rocks would be "a lot of crack for a crack head" and that the rocks are available in sizes smaller than that size. Brian Cho, a forensic drug analyst, stated that the amount of cocaine base he usually receives for testing is around 100 to 200 mg per submission, usually in the form of one small rock.

Detective Rodriguez also stated, however, that a cocaine base addict may smoke close to $500 worth in one day. He explained that although a junkie who had a rock as big as the largest one "would be in heaven," it would produce only a three-second high. When questioned about the razor blade that was found with the cocaine, he testified that a razor blade is necessary to cut the cocaine base, either for distribution or, as he conceded on cross-examination, for personal use (i.e., to fit in a smoking device).

When questioned about drug paraphernalia, Detective Rodriguez testified that crack users will smoke from homemade crack pipes, which can be made from objects such as broken car antennas, aluminum cans, and aluminum foil. The officers did not find any smoking devices, such as a smoke pipe, and, according to Detective Rodriguez, this indicated that no crack cocaine smokers were present. Furthermore, in his opinion, the tobacco and cigar wrappings they found were evidence of "blunts" being sold out of Hunt's house. He explained that blunts are made by taking the tobacco out of cigars and replacing it with marijuana and that "primos" are made by adding crack cocaine to the marijuana. He stated that in the area of town where Hunt's house was located, marijuana and crack are usually sold hand in hand, "like a little drug store." On recross, however, he stated that "primos" are one way that cocaine users smoke cocaine.

Hunt testified that she arrived at home just before the police officers and that she had not yet entered her bedroom, where the police officers found the cocaine. She admitted that she used marijuana, but claimed she did not "indulge" in crack cocaine. She said she knew the marijuana was in the house, but denied knowledge of the cocaine being there. She also denied allegations that she had ever sold drugs. She said she had given a key to the house to Burton, who was also living in the house, and that Burton had obtained the marijuana for a "get-together" they were going to have with a few friends that night. She also admitted she owned the gun, but denied owning the tobacco. Wendy Wilson, Hunt's neighbor and friend, testified that she had never seen Hunt use or deal crack cocaine.

Hunt was indicted under § 841(a)(1) for possession of cocaine base with intent to distribute. The first trial resulted in a hung jury. During the first and second trials, neither the government nor the defendant requested that the lesser included offense of possession be submitted to the jury. Moreover, neither the government nor Hunt challenged the instructions at trial or on appeal. In the second trial, the jury returned a verdict of guilty.

On appeal, Hunt contends that the evidence is insufficient to support the jury's verdict regarding the element of intent to distribute. She does not contend that the evidence was insufficient to support possession. In reviewing a challenge to the sufficiency of the evidence in a criminal case, we will affirm a conviction if a rational trier of fact could have found that the evidence established the essential elements of the offense beyond a reasonable doubt.

To establish a violation of 21 U.S.C. § 841(a)(1), the government must prove the knowing possession of a controlled substance with the intent to distribute. The elements of the offense may be proved either by direct or circumstantial evidence.

Intent to distribute may be inferred solely from the possession of an amount of controlled substance too large to be used by the possessor alone. On the other hand, a quantity that is consistent with personal use does not raise such an inference in the absence of other evidence.

Hunt contends that the 7.998 grams of crack cocaine that the police discovered in her house is insufficient as a matter of law to infer intent, and we agree. Although the government introduced testimony that this amount is a distributable amount and that the individual rocks may be larger than those that Detective Rodriguez believes are usually smoked or that Cho, the forensic analyst, usually tests, the testimony also indicated . . . that this amount was also consistent with personal use. In particular, Detective Rodriguez testified that a crack cocaine user may smoke, in one day alone, close to $500 worth, an amount that exceeds even the highest value he assigned to the cocaine found in Hunt's house. Furthermore, at oral argument, the government conceded that "the amount alone, by itself, is not sufficient" to support an inference of intent to distribute.[1]

---

[1] In considering the quantity of crack cocaine found in Hunt's house, we note that, in a few cases, other circuit courts rested their decisions that the evidence was sufficient to support an inference of intent in large part on quantities comparable to this amount. In *United States v. Lamarr*, 75 F.3d 964, 973 (4th Cir. 1996), the court quoted a letter to the editor of the Washington Post (regarding sentencing), which stated that "'five grams of crack cocaine is the equivalent of 50 street doses'" and that "'anybody holding that much crack is dealing.'" The court concluded

We must therefore examine the other evidence to determine whether it, in conjunction with the quantity of cocaine found, suffices to establish the requisite intent to distribute. *See United States v. Munoz*, 957 F.2d 171, 174 (5th Cir. 1992) (noting that even a small quantity of cocaine is sufficient to infer intent when augmented by the presence of evidence such as distribution paraphernalia or large quantities of cash). As with the quantity of drugs, however, "paraphernalia that could be consistent with personal use does not provide a sound basis for inferring intent to distribute." As evidence of intent to distribute, the government points to the razor blade, the absence of smoking pipes or other such instruments, the evidence of blunts, the gun, and Hunt's testimony. In [*United States v.*] *Skipper*, the government similarly argued that a straight-edged razor and the absence of smoking paraphernalia suggested the intent to distribute. We held that, even viewed in the light most favorable to the government, the evidence was insufficient to prove intent beyond a reasonable doubt. The same conclusion is warranted here. Detective Rodriguez testified that although a razor blade is needed to cut crack cocaine for distribution, it is also needed to cut the cocaine for personal use. Furthermore, even though Rodriguez testified that the evidence of blunts indicated drug sales, he also said that the evidence indicated use, namely, the smoking of cocaine in the form of primos. Because this evidence is also consistent with personal use, we do not believe it provides a sound basis for inferring that Hunt intended to distribute the cocaine.

The government also points to the gun found under her couch as evidence of Hunt's intent to distribute. We have often recognized that guns are tools of the trade in the drug business. In *United States v. Lucien*, 61 F.3d 366, 375 (5th Cir. 1995), the government argued that three guns that were found in the defendant's apartment were evidence that he was distributing cocaine base. In response, we noted that "although we do not discount the prevalence of guns in drug trafficking, we do not place undue weight on the presence of the guns in this case because [the defendants] could have untold reasons, nefarious and otherwise, for keeping guns in the apartment." The reasoning in *Lucien* applies with equal force to this case. Hunt's gun was found in her residence, under a couch, and not with the cocaine. Furthermore, Hunt made no move toward the gun when the police entered, and she admitted when asked that she did have a gun in the house. This evidence can be contrasted with cases in which a weapon was found in a more incriminating context. *See, e.g., United States v. Harrison*, 55 F.3d 163, 165 (5th Cir. [1995]) (noting that loaded .22 caliber pistol and ammunition were found next to 49.32 grams of cocaine base in

---

that the 5.72 grams the defendant possessed was roughly the amount a strong user would use in two months and held that, combined with testimony that the defendant was dealing, the evidence was sufficient to infer intent. *See also United States v. Haney*, 23 F.3d 1413 (8th Cir. 1994) (emphasizing the testimony of a criminologist that if an addict ingested 6.57 grams of crack in one or two days he would probably die; but also relying on confidential informant's information that defendant would be selling crack in exchange for food stamps, the $371 cash and $97 in food stamps found on defendant, and the fact that cocaine was cut into $20 pieces). Here, however, the only testimony the jury heard regarding the quantity of drugs was that a crack cocaine user can consume in one day, a value of crack greater than that found in Hunt's house and that the size of the individual rocks may be larger than those usually smoked by crack users or those tested by Brian Cho. Furthermore, we note again the government's concession at oral argument that this amount, by itself, is not sufficient to support an inference of intent. Therefore, although we recognize the import of the quantity in determining the intent to distribute controlled substances, we conclude that the quantity of cocaine base at issue here, as evaluated by the testimony presented, does not support an inference of intent to distribute.

dresser drawer). Unconnected with any such circumstances, however, the gun is no more probative of distribution of drugs than of other, non-nefarious purposes for which one may keep a gun. We therefore cannot affirm Hunt's conviction based on the presence of the gun.

The government also argues that the jury could have rejected Hunt's testimony that she had no knowledge of the cocaine and that Hunt's denial of use of cocaine necessitates a conclusion that the cocaine was kept on the premises for distribution. On appeal, however, Hunt does not challenge the jury's finding that she possessed the cocaine. Furthermore, although denial of personal consumption may be a factor in inferring intent to distribute in certain circumstances, we have stated that a defendant's "denial of guilt itself should not be permitted to become evidence of guilt." Accordingly, we reject the government's argument that Hunt's denial of use leads to the inference that she intended to distribute the crack.

When we have concluded that the evidence presented at trial was sufficient to support an inference of intent to distribute, we have pointed to evidence that is not as equally probative of possession as of distribution. *See, e.g., Lucien*, 61 F.3d at 376 (over $1200 cash, three weapons, and a plastic bag with several aluminum foil packets); *United States v. Pigrum*, 922 F.2d 249, 251 (5th Cir. 1991) (two sets of scales, coffee cup containing a test tube, cutting agent); *United States v. Onick*, 889 F.2d 1425, 1430-31 (5th Cir. 1989) (drug paraphernalia, particularly 4,063 empty gelcaps, and testimony that dealers package drugs in these gelcaps for street distribution); *United States v. Prieto-Tejas*, 779 F.2d 1098, 1101 (5th Cir. 1986) (value of cocaine between $2,200 and $9,000). We do not, however, see any evidence in this case, viewed individually or collectively, that is more probative of distribution than of possession. We therefore hold that a reasonable jury could not conclude beyond a reasonable doubt that Hunt intended to distribute the cocaine. We accordingly reverse Hunt's conviction for possession with intent to distribute.

The government asked us to remand for entry of judgment and for sentencing on the lesser included offense of simple possession if we found the evidence insufficient to support the element of intent to distribute.

In certain limited circumstances, we may exercise our power under 28 U.S.C. § 2106 and reduce a conviction to a lesser included offense.

Hunt has conceded the element of possession on appeal, challenging only the element of intent. We therefore find that reducing Hunt's conviction to possession will occasion her no undue prejudice.

For the foregoing reasons, Hunt's conviction is Reversed, the sentence is Vacated, and the cause is Remanded with instructions.

---

**Post-Case Follow-Up**

As *Hunt* explains, "[i]ntent to distribute may be inferred solely from the possession of an amount of controlled substance too large to be used by the possessor alone. On the other hand, a quantity that is consistent with personal use does not raise such an inference in the absence of other evidence." How does a jury determine whether a given quantity of drugs is clearly inconsistent with personal use? Because drug use patterns are not within the common knowledge of jurors, prosecutors and defendants must rely on expert witnesses. In this case, the government's expert testified that a crack user might smoke more than 7.998 grams "in one day alone." As a result, the quantity of crack found in the defendant's home did not prove an intent to distribute. In the absence of other indicia of sales, such as packaging materials, large amounts of cash, pay-owe sheets, or scales, the court concluded that there was insufficient evidence of an intent to distribute.

---

**Case Preview**

### *United States v. Washington*

Federal law and most states criminalize possession of a controlled substance with the intent to *distribute*, not possession with the intent to *sell*. It is clear enough from the decision in *Hunt* that a sale would constitute distribution, but what other conduct might qualify? Is sharing drugs socially with a friend distribution? In *United States v. Washington*, the court considered this question. Consistent with most jurisdictions that have addressed the issue, the Fourth Circuit held that sharing is distribution.

As you read the decision, consider the following questions:

1. Why do you think Congress decided to criminalize *distribution* rather than *sale*?
2. Does the court's interpretation of distribution risk making the vast majority of drug users traffickers in the eyes of the law? After all, as anyone who has been offered a beer at a friend's house can attest, the use of intoxicants is often a social activity, and so it is likely almost every substance user has shared with a friend at one time or another.

---

# *United States v. Washington*
### 41 F.3d 917 (4th Cir. 1994)

RUSSELL, J.

The defendant, Raymond L. Washington, was convicted of possession of cocaine with intent to distribute in violation of 21 U.S.C. § 841(a)(1). He appeals the district court's refusal to reduce his charge to simple possession of cocaine under 21 U.S.C. § 844(a). We affirm.

### I.

In March 1992, during a search incident to a lawful arrest for illegally operating a motor vehicle, Washington was found in possession of 12.1 grams of cocaine base, or "crack" cocaine. The arresting officers also found a pager and a $20 bill on Washington and a 9mm pistol in the car between the driver's seat and the transmission hump. The officers did not find any drug paraphernalia that would indicate that Washington planned to sell cocaine: the car contained no packaging materials, such as vials, plastic baggies, sandwich bags, or corners of plastic bags, and no weighing apparatus, such as a scale.

At trial, Washington testified that he was a serious drug user. He said that he had used cocaine for four years and had been hospitalized three times for drug abuse. He testified that he used about 4.5 grams of cocaine per day and that the cocaine found on his person was for his own use. Washington's girlfriend testified that Washington used drugs "a lot" and "very often." She confirmed that he had been hospitalized for drug abuse.

On cross-examination, however, Washington admitted that, although he did not have a job, he paid $450 for the cocaine. He explained that he received the money to purchase the cocaine from his friends, who gave him the money because he could purchase cocaine at a good price. He testified that he planned to return to his friends with the cocaine, which they would use together. When asked whether he intended to share the cocaine with somebody else, Washington responded in the affirmative.[1]

A grand jury indicted Washington for one count of possession with the intent to distribute in excess of five grams of cocaine base in violation of 21 U.S.C. § 841(a)(1), and one count of intentional use of a firearm in relationship to a drug trafficking crime in violation of 18 U.S.C. § 924(c)(1) and § 2. The jury returned a verdict of guilty to the possession offense and not guilty to the firearm offense. The district court sentenced Washington to 210 months imprisonment.

## II.

The record clearly demonstrates that Washington was not involved in any way in the trafficking of drugs. He did not sell drugs, and he was not a courier of drugs. He simply bought cocaine, which he planned to use himself and to share with his friends. However, Washington's intent to share the cocaine with others is sufficient for a court to find that he possessed drugs with intent to distribute.

Distribution under 21 U.S.C. § 841(a)(1) is not limited to the sale of controlled substances. "Facilitation of the sale of narcotics" was prohibited before Congress enacted § 841. 21 U.S.C. § 174 (repealed 1970). Section 841, part of the Comprehensive

---

[1] The following is an excerpt of Washington's cross-examination at trial:

Q. This amount that you were caught with, the 12.1 grams, had you bought that for someone else?
A. I bought it for all of us.
Q. All of us. And you were going to give it to some of them; is that correct, the other people?
A. We were going to get high with it.
Q. You all were going to get high, so you were going to give it to them, you were going to distribute it to them. You physically gave the drugs to somebody else?
A. I weren't physically giving it to them. We just wanted, you know, to sit around and get high.
Q. Were they your drugs or somebody else's?
A. Yes, they were mine, because I purchased them.
Q. You intended to share them with somebody else?
A. Right.

* * *

Q. Now, sir, on this particular day you were planning to take those drugs and share them with your friends, is that a fair statement?
A. Yes, sir.

Drug Abuse Prevention and Control Act of 1970 (the "1970 Act"), proscribes "distribution" of controlled substances, as opposed to "facilitation of sale." *See United States v. Hernandez*, 480 F.2d 1044, 1046 (9th Cir. 1973). The term "distribute" means "to deliver . . . a controlled substance. . . ." 21 U.S.C. § 802(11). "Deliver" means "the actual, constructive, or attempted transfer of a controlled substance . . . whether or not there exists an agency relationship." 21 U.S.C. § 802(8). Thus, in enacting the 1970 Act, Congress intended to proscribe a range of conduct broader than the mere sale of narcotics.

Sharing drugs with another constitutes "distribution" under § 841(a)(1). Washington testified at trial that he intended to share the cocaine in his possession with his friends. This admission was enough to demonstrate that he possessed the cocaine "with intent to distribute."

The Ninth Circuit considered almost the exact same factual situation in *United States v. Wright*, 593 F.2d 105 (9th Cir. 1979). In *Wright,* a friend gave the defendant $20 and asked him to purchase heroin so that the two of them could use it together; the defendant left the friend's dwelling, bought the heroin, and returned to the friend's dwelling, where they snorted the heroin together. The district court in *Wright* had refused to give the defendant's proposed jury instruction that would have directed the jury, if it found that the defendant acquired the heroin in a joint venture with the friend and used the heroin only with the friend, to conclude that there was no distribution of heroin. Instead, the district court instructed the jury simply that "distribute" meant "to transfer or deliver a substance either directly or by means of another person."

Although the defendant in *Wright* purchased the heroin alone, he argued that the purchase was part of a joint venture with the friend; thus, there was no distribution of heroin to the friend because the friend was in constructive possession of the heroin at the time he made the purchase. The Ninth Circuit, concluding that "Congress intended to prevent individuals from acquiring drugs for whatever purpose on behalf of others and then transferring the drugs to those others," rejected the defendant's joint venture theory and upheld the district court's jury instruction.

We agree with the court in *Wright* that a defendant who purchases a drug and shares it with a friend has "distributed" the drug even though the purchase was part of a joint venture to use drugs. Washington and his friends were clearly engaged in a joint venture: the friends gave Washington money to purchase cocaine, and Washington went out and purchased cocaine that all would use. The joint venture, however, does not alter the fact that Washington, from the time he purchased the cocaine until the time he was found with it, intended to distribute the cocaine to his friends. Although Washington did not intend to sell the cocaine to his friends,[3] he intended to deliver cocaine to those friends. Under § 841(a)(1),

---

[3] Although it is not crucial to our decision today, we note that Washington did, in a way, profit from the transaction. On his own, he could not have afforded to purchase cocaine in the quantities that he used it. Washington, however, knew where to purchase cocaine at a good price. In exchange for providing his services, his friends allowed him to use a portion of the cocaine purchased. Although Washington was advanced the money to purchase the cocaine and received his profits in direct drug use, he profited as much as any drug dealer who purchases drugs with his own money and profits monetarily from their sale.

Washington's intent to deliver cocaine to his friends constituted an "intent to distribute."

Washington's trial testimony that he intended to share the cocaine with his friends was, in itself, sufficient evidence for the jury to find him guilty of possession with intent to distribute. The government did not need to demonstrate an intent to distribute based upon the quantity of cocaine found on Washington and from the other circumstances of the case.

The judgment of the district court is affirmed.

*Affirmed.*

---

**Post-Case Follow-Up**

As the decision in *Washington* shows, statutes criminalizing possession with the intent to distribute encompass a much broader range of conduct than selling drugs. Sharing drugs with a friend counts as distribution. In *Washington*, this fact led the Fourth Circuit to uphold Raymond Washington's conviction, along with his prison sentence of 210 months (or 17 and a half years).

---

## Hunt *and* Washington: *Real Life Applications*

**1.** Officer Flynn pulled Devon over for a traffic violation, and asked for Devon's consent to search. Devon consented to a search of her car. Inside, the car Flynn found $227 inside a wallet, consisting of two $100 bills, a $20 bill, a $5 bill, and a $2 bill. Flynn also found torch lighters in the vehicle. Flynn then searched under the hood of the car. There, Flynn noticed that the fuse box in the upper corner of the driver's side appeared clean compared to the rest of the engine compartment. Because it was clean, Flynn thought the fuse box had recently been accessed. He looked inside and saw a cigarette box. Inside the cigarette box were a plastic baggie containing a white crystalline substance, and a glass pipe with a white residue. Laboratory tests determined that the substance in the baggie was methamphetamine. The methamphetamine weighed 11.74 grams.

After being arrested, Devon admitted the methamphetamine was hers. She said she purchased 3.5 grams about two weeks earlier and that she uses about a gram once a week. At first, she said she bought the methamphetamine for $300. She later

**Drug Sentencing**

Drug quantity is usually the single most important factor in a federal drug offender's sentence. The same is true in many states. The lengthy federal mandatory minimum sentences that apply to drug trafficking offenses, including possession with the intent to distribute, are based entirely on the type and quantity of drug involved in the offense. Drug type and quantity also play a significant role in calculating sentences under the Federal Sentencing Guidelines.

Some argue that tying sentences to drug type and quantity results in unduly harsh sentences because "[d]rug quantity is a poor proxy for culpability generally and for a defendant's role in a drug business in particular." *United States v. Dossie*, 851 F. Supp. 2d 478, 481 (E.D.N.Y. 2012).

Drug couriers and day laborers might possess large quantities of drugs even though they are often "considered by definition to be expendable" to the drug organization. *United States v. Rodriguez De Varon*, 175 F.3d 930, 957 (11th Cir. 1999) (Barkett, J., dissenting). Similarly, a lookout, driver, go-between, or girlfriend may have a small role in a drug transaction, but face a lengthy mandatory sentence if the exchange involved a large quantity of drugs. Basing drug sentences on drug type and quantity means "a defendant who does no more than help unload a truck with a ton of cocaine starts at the same sentence level as those who arranged the shipment or who negotiated the sale or purchase of the drugs." Ian Weinstein, *Fifteen Years After the Federal Sentencing Revolution: How Mandatory Minimums Have Undermined Effective and Just Narcotics Sentencing*, 40 Am. Crim. L. Rev. 87, 107 (2003).

Do you think linking drug sentences to quantity is an accurate measure of culpability? If not, why do you think lawmakers decided to place so much importance on drug quantity in sentencing?

said she bought it for $200, $150, and then back to $300 again. Devon also told the police that she sometimes gives methamphetamine to her friends in exchange for repairing her car. She called it a "bartering system."

Flynn searched Devon's cell phone with her permission. One text message from a person named "Carol" stood out to Flynn. It stated: "'Are you still at the house, if you are, can you leave me something in the center console of the couch? I just finished my job in Irvine.'"

a. Devon has been charged with possession of methamphetamine with the intent to distribute.

You are Devon's attorney, and you are preparing for trial. The prosecution plans to call Officer Blume as a drug expert. You anticipate that Officer Blume will testify that, in his opinion, the methamphetamine in Devon's car was possessed for sale. You would like to hire an expert witness to counter Blume's testimony. What kind of professional background do you think would make for the most effective witness (e.g., a former police officer, an addiction treatment specialist, etc.)?

b. Imagine you are a researcher, and you would like to find out how long 11.74 grams of methamphetamine would last a typical user. How would you go about trying to answer this question? Would you consult with police officers, or do you think other sources would produce a more reliable answer?

c. For this question, assume that Devon was convicted at trial, and that you are one of the judges hearing Devon's appeal.

In addition to the evidence already described above, prosecution witness Officer Blume testified at trial that 11.74 grams of methamphetamine is a "mid level" amount, and that half an ounce of methamphetamine (a little more than 14 grams) would sell for about $250. Blume also testified that the "typical" dose of methamphetamine is .2 grams or less, although a "heavy" user could use as much as half a gram as a single dose. Blume further testified that it was his "belief" that the text message from Carol—which asked "can you leave me something in the center console of the couch?"—was "related to narcotics sale." Finally, Blume testified that in his opinion, the evidence in this case was consistent with an intent to distribute.

Based on this evidence, do you think there is sufficient evidence to sustain Devon's conviction for possession of methamphetamine with intent to distribute?

## Chapter Summary

- Drug enforcement has a significant impact on our criminal justice system. In 2017, more Americans were arrested for a drug offense (1.6 million, or about 15 percent of all arrests) than for any other category of crime tracked by the FBI's Uniform Crime Report. The overwhelming majority of these arrests — about 85 percent — were for simple possession. This enforcement involves significant racial disparities: About 12.6 percent of the U.S. population is African-American, and Blacks and whites use drugs at about the same rate. Yet about 30 percent of drug arrestees are Black.

- The offense of possession criminalizes the knowing or intentional possession of a controlled substance. Conceptually, possession cases can be divided into two types: actual and constructive possession. These categories do not represent distinct offenses. They describe two different scenarios in which a person may be shown to have committed the crime of possession.

- In actual possession cases, most courts have defined the act of possession to mean any non-fleeting "physical control" of an item.

- To prove the act of possession on a constructive possession theory, the prosecutor must show that the defendant had both the power and intent to exercise dominion and control over the controlled substance. Under this rule, proof that a defendant was near a substance and had knowledge of its presence is insufficient to sustain a possession conviction. Instead, the prosecutor must introduce evidence that would support an inference of power and intent to exercise control. Common types of evidence include attempts to hide or dispose of the drug, evidence in participating in a criminal venture involving the drugs (e.g., of participating in a drug sales operation), and possession of drug paraphernalia.

- The *mens rea* for possession is knowing possession. Because modern drug statutes criminalize the possession of a controlled substance, and then list the drugs that qualify as a controlled substance, the prosecutor does not need to show the defendant knew exactly which substance she possessed to win a conviction. But the prosecutor still must prove the defendant knew she possessed *a controlled substance*, as opposed to some other kind of contraband.

- Typically, knowledge is proven through direct or circumstantial evidence of actual knowledge. In most, but not all, jurisdictions, the prosecutor can also prove knowledge by showing the defendant was willfully blind. Under the willful blindness doctrine, knowledge exists where the defendant was aware of a high probability of a fact and deliberately avoided gaining positive knowledge of that fact. A number of courts that have adopted the willful blindness doctrine also require proof that the defendant's motive for deliberately avoiding positive knowledge was to preserve a defense in the event of prosecution.

■ It is a crime to knowingly possess a controlled substance with the intent to distribute it. Distribution encompasses a wider range of conduct than sales and includes sharing between users. For an intent to distribute to be inferred based on drug quantity alone, the quantity must be clearly inconsistent with personal use. In addition to drug quantity, courts have held that other indicia of sales, such as packaging materials, large amounts of cash, pay-owe sheets, or scales, can help to prove drugs were possessed with the intent to distribute.

## Applying the Concepts

1. Look back at the facts of *State v. Hogue*, which are presented in Question 1 of the Fries: *Real Life Applications* on page 162. In *Hogue*, the defendant was convicted of possession. If the prosecutor had charged Hogue with distribution, do you think he could have been convicted?

2. Mikael needed to pick his friend Brad up from the airport but Mikael did not have a car. Mikael borrowed his girlfriend Jess's car. Mikael knew that Jess sometimes smoked marijuana. On the way to the airport, the police pulled Mikael's car over for speeding. The officer had a drug dog sniff the exterior of the vehicle. After the dog alerted, the officer conducted a lawful search of the vehicle and found two marijuana cigarettes in Jess's backpack in the trunk. The marijuana cigarettes were in a small pocket of the backpack that also contained one of Jess's credit cards. Mikael and Jess are both charged with marijuana possession. What is the most likely result?

3. Epps was arrested in a so-called reverse sting, in which undercover police officers pose as drug dealers, sell drugs to the purchaser, and then arrest the purchaser for possession of the drugs. This particular reverse sting involved the sale of a large amount of cocaine.

    Officer Plank conducted the sting, which took place in a parking lot near Epps's apartment complex. Epps and Officer Plank each drove separately to the parking lot. Epps was accompanied by his friend Andy. Officer Plank opened the trunk of his car to reveal two large plastic baggies of cocaine. Epps asked if Andy could sample the cocaine in order to test its purity. Officer Plank agreed. After snorting a small bump of the cocaine, Andy told Epps that it was of good quality. Epps then said, "OK, let's make the deal. I'll go get the money from my car." As soon as Epps said this, Officer Plank revealed his true identity and placed Epps under arrest.

    Epps is charged with possession of the cocaine. What is the best argument in his defense?

4. Adams is being prosecuted for possession of cocaine. At trial, Adams testifies that his friend Resek was a cocaine dealer. One day, Adams and his family were

at the park, when he saw Resek. Adams and his family had driven to the park; Resek had come on foot.

Resek asked Adams if he could borrow Adams's car keys to "store some valuables." Adams agreed and gave Resek his car keys. A few minutes later, Resek returned and said to Adams, "Thanks. I've got to go take care of a few things. I had to put some of my product in your car. I'll text you later to get it." Adams replied, "I thought you were just going to put your laptop or something in there. I don't want to be involved in your business." Resek said, "I'm sorry about this, but I've got to go and there's nowhere else to put it. I owe you one." Resek then left the park.

An hour later, Adams left the park with his family. While driving home, a police officer pulled Adams over for a traffic violation and asked to search Adams's vehicle. The officer found the cocaine and placed Adams under arrest. After his arrest, Adams told the officer, "The cocaine belongs to my friend. He put it in my car without my permission and I was going to give it back to him later today."

Is there sufficient evidence to convict Adams of possession of the cocaine?

## Criminal Law in Practice

1. There is relatively little variation in the definition of drug crimes from one jurisdiction to the next. This is because the Uniform Controlled Substances Act serves as the basis for almost every state's drug laws and mirrors the federal Controlled Substances Act. Two areas where there is some variation between jurisdictions are the innocent possession doctrine (also known as the possession for disposal doctrine, and discussed in the sidebar on page 160) and the willful blindness doctrine (also known as the deliberate ignorance doctrine).

   a. Research whether the courts in your state have considered whether to adopt the innocent possession doctrine. If so, have they adopted the doctrine, and has the issue been resolved by the highest court in your state? Research only state law; do not research federal cases. An innocent possession case from Utah was cited in the sidebar discussing this doctrine, so if you are in Utah, research the law of a neighboring state.

   b. Research whether the courts in your state have considered whether to adopt the willful blindness doctrine. If so, have they adopted the doctrine, and has the issue been resolved by the highest court in your state? Research only state law; do not research federal cases.

2. Many areas of criminal law are entirely, or almost entirely, creatures of state law. Violent crimes like homicide offenses are prosecuted almost exclusively at the state level. The same is true of many property crimes, including larceny and burglary. By contrast, although most drug prosecutions take place in state court, the federal government also plays a significant role in drug enforcement. There were over 26,000 federal drug prosecutions in 2017 — though only a fraction of the 1.6 million drug arrests that year, these prosecutions

represented about 31 percent of federal criminal cases (excluding petty misdemeanors).

The overlapping jurisdiction of state and federal law in the area of drug enforcement raises unique questions about prosecutorial discretion. This is because federal drug laws often call for lengthier sentences than analogous state drug laws. As a result, the decision about whether to bring federal or state charges against a defendant can be enormously important. Recall, for example, that although the defendant in *United States v. Washington* (page 194) was originally arrested by local police for illegally operating a motor vehicle, he was charged and convicted in federal court, where he received a sentence of 17 and a half years.

You are an intern for the United States Attorney's Office in your federal district. (Each federal district has a United States Attorney's Office, which is responsible for bringing federal criminal prosecutions in that district.) The recently appointed head of the office is thinking of adopting a new charging policy for drug cases that will guide the office in its decisions about whether to bring federal charges in a case or defer to state prosecutors. To start this process, she has asked everyone in the office to write a brief memo of no more than a paragraph, with suggestions about the factors that should guide the decision about whether to bring federal charges in a drug case. What factors would you suggest the office incorporate in its new policy and why?

3. There are stark racial disparities in drug enforcement. Although Blacks and whites use drugs at about the same rate, just over 30 percent of people arrested for drug offenses are African-American even though only 12.6 percent of the population is African-American.

You are an intern for the newly elected District Attorney, who ran on a platform of criminal justice reform that includes trying to reduce racial disparities in drug enforcement. The District Attorney has acknowledged that no single reform or set of reforms will solve this enforcement disparity, which is caused by a number of different factors. With that in mind, the District Attorney has asked everyone in the office to suggest one reform or policy that they think would be the *most* impactful in reducing racial disparities in drug enforcement. What reform would you recommend, and why? What challenges (whether political, policy, or other challenges), if any, do you think there would be in implementing your proposed reform?

# Homicide Offenses

Homicides occupy a unique place in the criminal justice system. They account for only a tiny fraction of the crimes committed in the United States every year. In 2017, there were just over 19,500 homicides, as compared to an estimated 7.7 million property crimes. Some attorneys can spend an entire career practicing criminal law and never handle a homicide case.

And yet, homicide offenses are a central area of focus in the study of criminal law. This is surely due in no small part to the seriousness of the crime. Homicides may be much less common than other crimes. But their impact on the community is far greater. Homicide offenses are also a particularly effective vehicle for learning more about important criminal law concepts, such as mental states, criminal omissions, and causation. Similarly, the law's approach to grading homicide offenses raises difficult theoretical and moral questions about punishment. For these reasons, even though few lawyers will ever try a homicide case, every law student will spend a good portion of their criminal law course learning about homicide law.

Technically, a **homicide** is any act (or omission where there is a legal duty to act) that causes death. This broad definition includes both criminal and non-criminal homicides (for example, a killing committed in self-defense). The most frequently contested issue in homicide cases — apart from guilt or innocence — is the *type* of homicide that was committed. In most states, this can make a big difference. A conviction for voluntary manslaughter instead of first-degree murder might mean a five- or ten-year sentence instead of a life sentence or the death penalty.

In this chapter, you will learn about the different degrees of homicide, as well as causation and homicides by omission.

## A. AN OVERVIEW OF DEGREES OF HOMICIDE

Even before applying to law school, you were probably familiar with the idea that there are different degrees of homicide. You may have

## Key Concepts

- What are the different forms of homicide?
- Why does the law grade homicides as it does?
- What are the legal requirements for proving each type of homicide?
- What are the requirements to prove that the defendant's act caused the victim's death?

seen a story in the news about a trial where a defendant was charged with first-degree murder but ultimately convicted of voluntary manslaughter, for example. But news reports rarely explain the legal rules that differentiate these two crimes.

The killer's mental state is most often what separates one type of homicide from another. At a general level, this makes intuitive sense. Most people would rate a reckless driver who kills a pedestrian by accident as less culpable and less in need of deterrence than a man who kills his wife for insurance money after spending weeks plotting the crime. But what about the case of a wife who comes home from work to find her husband in bed with another woman, and then kills them both? Or a parent whose young child accidentally shoots himself with a loaded gun that the parent had left lying out? How would you describe the mental state of the defendant in each of those cases? How would you rank the culpability of the betrayed spouse or the gun-owning parent in comparison to the husband who plotted his wife's murder or the reckless driver?

We will examine how the law addresses these questions in the sections that follow. Before we do, it is helpful to begin with an overview of homicide offenses. This introductory overview is meant to provide context for the more detailed examination that lies ahead, so do not worry if some of the legal definitions described in this section are difficult to follow. These concepts will all become clearer as we progress through the chapter. For now, focus on the general framework of homicide offenses as you read the rest of this section.

As with most of the criminal law, homicide statutes differ from one state to the next, sometimes radically. This chapter covers the most common forms of homicide and related doctrines. We will learn about five different homicide offenses: first-degree murder, second-degree murder, voluntary manslaughter, involuntary manslaughter (also known as reckless manslaughter), and negligent homicide.

The following is an overview of the different forms of homicide, categorized by mental state:

■ *Intent to kill*: If the killer acted with an intent to kill, the crime can be first-degree murder, second-degree murder, or voluntary manslaughter. An intentional killing will be first-degree murder if it was willful, deliberate, and premeditated. An intentional killing that was not willful, deliberate, and premeditated will be second-degree murder. If an intentional killing was done in the heat of passion, however, it will be reduced from murder to voluntary manslaughter.

■ *Intent to inflict grievous bodily injury*: If the killer acted with an intent to inflict grievous bodily injury, then the killing will be second-degree murder unless it was done in the heat of passion, in which case it will be reduced to voluntary manslaughter.

■ *Extreme recklessness (depraved heart)*: If the killer acted with an extremely reckless indifference to the value of human life, the killing will be second-degree murder. More than simple recklessness is required for this mental state. Playing Russian roulette is a frequently cited example of acting with an extremely reckless disregard for human life. A person can play Russian roulette while sincerely hoping that no one gets hurt, and so never intending to kill. But anyone who is willing to risk life in this way is acting in an extremely reckless manner — or, as the law puts it, with a depraved heart. A killing in this category can also be reduced to voluntary manslaughter if it was done in the heat of passion.

■ *Heat of passion*: As already noted, a killing that would otherwise be considered murder may be reduced from murder to voluntary manslaughter if it was done in the heat of passion. To qualify, the killer must have been acting in the heat of passion, as the result of legally adequate provocation, without having had a sufficient cooling off period.

■ *Recklessness*: If the killer acted with ordinary recklessness, the homicide will be involuntary manslaughter, also called reckless manslaughter in many jurisdictions.

■ *Negligence*: If the killer acted with criminal negligence, the homicide will be negligent homicide.

■ *Felony murder*: Felony murder is the one form of homicide that does not depend on the defendant's mental state. A person may be guilty of felony murder if he committed or attempted to commit a felony that resulted in a death. For example, if Defendant helps his friend rob a liquor store and his friend shoots and kills the store clerk, Defendant would be guilty of felony murder. This is because Defendant committed a felony (robbery) that resulted in death. A felony murder can either be first- or second-degree murder, depending on the felony that was committed. Some jurisdictions recognize a variant of this doctrine, misdemeanor-manslaughter, which holds that a killing that occurs during the course of the commission of a misdemeanor is involuntary manslaughter.

The overview above organizes homicides by the killer's mental state. This is because the most effective way to determine the type of homicide that was committed is by analyzing the killer's mental state. Although the best way to analyze a homicide case is to focus on the defendant's *mens rea*, the law organizes degrees of homicides by severity. The table below (Exhibit 5.1) outlines homicides in order of severity.

If reading the overview above felt a bit overwhelming, do not worry. This can be a difficult area of the law. It will only be possible to fully understand all of the distinctions between the different degrees of homicide offenses after examining each of them more closely, which we will be doing in the sections that follow. As you progress through the rest of the chapter, you might find it helpful to return to this section from time to time as a handy summary of how the different degrees of homicide fit together. Once you have finished this chapter, you will better appreciate all of the different concepts mentioned in the summary above. For now, if this summary left you with more questions than answers, that is okay; the answers lie ahead.

**EXHIBIT 5.1**    **Homicides by Offense**

| | |
|---|---|
| **First-degree murder** | ■ An intentional killing that is willful, deliberate, and premeditated<br>■ A felony murder, if the killing occurred during the commission or attempted commission of an enumerated felony |
| **Second-degree murder** | ■ An intentional killing that is not willful, deliberate, and premeditated<br>■ A killing committed with the intent to inflict grievous bodily injury<br>■ A killing committed with an extremely reckless indifference to the value of human life (depraved heart murder)<br>■ Any felony murder that is not a first-degree murder |
| **Voluntary manslaughter** | ■ A killing done in the heat of passion. Killings in this category would otherwise be murder because the killer either intended to kill, intended to inflict grievous bodily injury, or acted with a depraved heart. But, if the killer meets the requirements of the heat of passion doctrine, the killing is reduced from murder to manslaughter.<br>■ Imperfect self-defense (discussed in Chapter 11, which covers affirmative defenses) |
| **Involuntary (reckless) manslaughter** | ■ A killing committed with ordinary recklessness<br>■ A killing that falls under the misdemeanor-manslaughter rule, in jurisdictions that recognize this doctrine |
| **Negligent homicide** | ■ A killing that is committed with criminal negligence |

## B. INTENTIONAL KILLINGS

If the killer acted with an intent to kill the victim, the crime can either be first-degree murder, second-degree murder, or voluntary manslaughter. A killer who intends to cause grievous bodily injury to the victim — but not to kill him — can be convicted of either second-degree murder or voluntary manslaughter. This section examines the legal rules that separate first-degree murder, second-degree murder, and voluntary manslaughter in the context of intentional killings.

## 1. First-Degree Murder That Is Willful, Deliberate, and Premeditated

Although there are a number of states that do not separate murders into different degrees, among the majority of states that do, an intentional killing that is also **willful, deliberate, and premeditated** is typically classified as **murder in the first degree**. This well-established rule dates back to the late 1700s, when Pennsylvania became the first state to divide murder into two degrees. Even though the willful, deliberate, and premeditated test is more than 200 years old, courts continue to debate its meaning and often have difficulty applying it. Indeed, "the significant variations [between jurisdictions] in the time and deliberation required" to prove that a killing was willful, deliberate, and premeditated has led one scholar to describe "the doctrinal terrain [as] in a state of chaos." Kimberly Kessler Ferzan, *Plotting Premeditation's Demise*, 75 Law & Contemp. Probs. 83, 87 (2012).

The nuances of the willful, deliberate, and premeditated test have resulted in a number of jurisdictional variants. But very broadly speaking, interpretations of the willful, deliberate, and premeditated test can be divided into two different camps. In the first group of jurisdictions, courts have applied the rule so broadly that they have effectively turned nearly every intentional murder into murder in the first degree. This has been accomplished by court decisions making premeditation synonymous with intent. These jurisdictions "allow premeditation to exist instantaneously or simultaneously with the act of homicide." *Id.* at 88. In states in this group, the criminal code continues to *say* that an intentional killing is first-degree murder only if it is willful, deliberate, and premeditated. But, *in practice*, the rule is almost meaningless because the government only needs to prove the defendant intended to kill his victim to obtain a first-degree murder conviction.

In the second group of jurisdictions, the government has to prove more than just an intent to kill to satisfy the willful, deliberate, and premeditated test. Some of these states "require[] an appreciable lapse of time between the formulation of the design to kill and the actual execution of that design." *Id.* Others within this group do not require all that much time to pass between development of the intent to kill and the killing, so long as there is other evidence of reflection on the intent to kill. But, in all states in this group, the government must prove more than that the defendant intended to kill to obtain a first-degree murder conviction. What, exactly, must the government prove for a jury to find that a killing was willful, deliberate, and premeditated in these jurisdictions? In the next case, *Boatman*, the court discusses this question in some detail.

## Case Preview

## *People v. Boatman*

In the following case, the California Court of Appeal considered whether the government had introduced sufficient evidence to prove that a homicide was willful, deliberate, and premeditated.

---

## Malice Aforethought

At common law, and still in many states today, murder was defined as the killing of another human being with malice aforethought. Historically, malice aforethought had independent legal significance. But, "[o]ver time, the phrase malice aforethought became an arbitrary symbol used by common law judges to signify [the] mental states deemed sufficient to support liability for murder." *People v. Jefferson*, 748 P.2d 1223, 1226 (Colo. 1988). Today, **malice aforethought** is in effect a legal term of art that encompasses four distinct types of homicides. Malice aforethought exists if the killer acted with (1) an intent to kill; (2) an intent to inflict grievous bodily injury; (3) an extremely reckless disregard for the value of human life (this is sometimes called "depraved heart" or "abandoned and malignant heart" murder); or (4) if the killing occurred during the commission or attempted commission of a felony (this is called "felony murder"). Somewhat confusingly, notwithstanding this definition of malice aforethought, a killing in any of the first three malice aforethought categories can be reduced to voluntary manslaughter if it was done in the heat of passion.

Although the term malice aforethought continues to appear in statutes and case law in many jurisdictions, it is not especially helpful on its own. If we want to determine whether a particular homicide is murder or manslaughter, asking if the killer acted with malice aforethought will not lead us to an answer. Instead, we need to ask what the killer's state of mind was at the time of the killing and whether or not the killing falls under the felony murder rule. The answers to these questions will tell us the type of homicide that was committed, including whether or not the killer acted with malice aforethought.

As you read the decision, consider the following questions:

1. How, exactly, does the court define the willful, deliberate, and premeditated standard?
2. How easy do you think it is for attorneys to predict whether a particular case will constitute first-degree or second-degree murder using the court's test?
3. What sort of evidence is required to prove that a killing is willful, deliberate, and premeditated, and why is the evidence in this case insufficient?

## *People v. Boatman*
### 221 Cal. App. 4th 1253 (2013)

KING, J.

Defendant and appellant, Benjamin James Boatman, shot his girlfriend, Rebecca Marth, in the face, killing her. Defendant said the shooting was an accident. At trial, he argued that although he was criminally negligent, he did not commit murder. A jury convicted him of first degree murder (Pen. Code, § 187 subd. (a)) and possession of marijuana for sale (Health and Saf. Code, § 11359).

Defendant was sentenced to an indeterminate term of 25 years to life on the murder conviction[.]

Because we conclude that there is substantial evidence that defendant committed murder, but insufficient evidence to support the first degree murder elements of premeditation and deliberation, we will reduce the murder conviction to second degree murder.

### II. SUMMARY OF FACTS

At approximately 3:30 A.M. on March 18, 2010, defendant was released from jail on bail. He walked home, where he lived with his father (Jim), a sister (Hanna), an older brother (Brandon), and a younger brother (Brenton). Brandon's girlfriend, Victoria Williams, was also staying there at that time.

After talking with Brenton for awhile, defendant and Brenton drove to Marth's house, picked her up, and returned home. Defendant had been dating Marth for about one year and, he testified, was in love with her. However, defendant also had an ex-fiancée and was conflicted about whom he wanted to be with.

Around 7:05 A.M., Officer Eric Hibbard responded to a report of a shooting at defendant's house. When he arrived, he saw Brenton leaning up against the fender of a white Cadillac holding Marth in his arms. Marth had been shot in the face. Shortly after Officer Hibbard placed Marth on the ground, defendant came running out of the house with blood on his clothes and face. Defendant told Officer Gregory Hayden to "[c]all the ambulance for my girlfriend."

Officer Hibbard and two other officers conducted a safety sweep of the house. Inside, the officers found Brandon, Williams, and Hanna. Upon entering the bedroom where Marth had been shot, Officer Hibbard saw bloodstains on the bed and pillow. He also saw some marijuana and marijuana paraphernalia in the room. A trail of blood led Officer Hibbard from the bedroom to the kitchen. Officer Hibbard saw a black revolver on the kitchen floor. Both the floor and revolver appeared to be wet with water. The revolver contained five live .38-caliber rounds, as well as one fired round.

Brandon's bedroom shares a wall with the room in which Marth was shot. On the day of the shooting, Williams (who was in Brandon's room) told an investigating officer that she was awakened by a "[l]oud screaming argument between a guy and a girl for at least three minutes." She said she did not know where the yelling was coming from and that she could not tell what the "[l]oud screaming" was about. At trial, Williams did not remember characterizing the sounds she heard as "loud screaming," and said she was awoken by "loud talking." A couple of minutes after hearing the "loud talking," Williams heard a gunshot. Immediately afterward, Williams heard a commotion and screaming; "it seemed like someone was panicking, like yelling or screaming like out of fear."

Defendant was taken to the police station by a Riverside police officer. On the way to the police station, defendant asked the officer if he knew if Marth was okay. Defendant said: "I can't lose her. I would do anything for her. How is someone supposed to go on with their life when they see something like that? We were just going to watch a movie." Defendant was crying with his head down for most of the trip.

Defendant was interviewed by two homicide detectives. He gave different versions of what had happened that day and admitted at trial that he lied to the officers. In the first version, defendant claimed that Marth had accidentally shot herself. He said he was showing her a gun he had recently purchased; he did not tell her it was loaded; and as she was playing around with it, she accidentally shot herself.

In defendant's second version, he said he shot Marth, but claimed the shooting was accidental and that he did not think the gun was loaded. He explained that they were sitting on the couch; Marth pointed the gun at him, he pushed the gun away, and she pointed it at him again; he then took the gun, pointed it at her, and accidentally shot her.

In the third version, defendant said he knew the gun was loaded. He described the events this way: "She pointed it at me. I slapped it away. She pointed it at me. I slapped it away. We both knew it was loaded. And then I went like that and I cocked back the hammer just jokingly and it slipped, pow." He later added: "I pulled it back . . . [¶] . . . [¶] . . . and it slipped. [¶] . . . [¶] . . . Like I didn't get to pull it all the way back." In this version, defendant claimed that his finger was not on the trigger. At trial, this version was placed in doubt by a criminalist with an expertise in firearms who testified that, because of the multiple safeties on the gun, the gun cannot be fired by pulling the hammer back and releasing it before it is fully cocked.

Defendant testified at trial. He stated that after a few restless nights in jail, he was released on bail around 3:30 A.M. and walked home. Along the way, he sent a text message to Marth to tell her he was going to come get her. He arrived at his house around 5:00 A.M. He and Brenton picked up Marth around 5:30 that morning and returned to their house. Defendant and Marth were happy to see each other.

After the three returned to defendant's house, they planned to smoke a "blunt" — a cigarillo in which the tobacco has been removed and replaced with marijuana — and watch a movie.

Defendant and Marth were in a bedroom that had been converted from a back patio. Defendant went to his safe, which contained marijuana and money, and began weighing the marijuana and counting the money. Marth said, "[h]ey, baby." Defendant turned around and saw Marth pointing a gun at him. Marth had apparently retrieved the gun from underneath defendant's pillow. Defendant was not worried because he trusted Marth. He slapped the gun away and continued to weigh the marijuana.

At this point, a mosquito landed on Marth, causing her to "scream[ ] a little bit." She "jumped up, started waving her hands, doing a whole bunch of girly stuff. . . ." In order to tease her, defendant "grabbed the mosquito, and . . . brought it closer to her, and she got even more upset." To make up for the teasing, defendant gave Marth a hug and a kiss, then went back to weighing his marijuana.

When defendant turned around, Marth was sitting on the edge of the bed pointing the gun at him again. The bed did not have a frame and was low on the floor. Defendant, who had just finished putting the marijuana back into the safe on the floor, was squatting and about "eye to eye" with Marth. He took the gun away from Marth and pointed it at her. He knew the gun was loaded when he received it and it "had to be loaded because [he] didn't take the bullets out." He cocked the hammer back, but did not intend to threaten or shoot her. He was "[j]ust kind of being stupid[.]" Defendant then described what happened next:

"[DEFENDANT:] She slapped the gun, and as soon as she slapped the gun, the gun went off. I almost dropped it. I tried to grab hold of it. Still the gun didn't drop. As soon as I squeezed it, it went off.

"Q. Okay. Why are you squeezing it?

"A. I didn't want to drop it. I didn't want anything to happen. I guess just a reaction.

"Q. Okay.

"A. You drop something; you try not to drop it.

"Q. Did you sit there and think this through step by step or was it kind of more an instinctive reaction?

"A. It just happened so quick. It just happened. I didn't think about it at all."

Immediately after the shot, defendant told Brenton "to call the cops," which he did. Defendant tried to give Marth mouth-to-mouth resuscitation. When Marth told defendant she could not breathe, defendant and Brenton took her outside to the driveway in front of the house "to get her help."

Defendant went back into the house to get his keys. From inside the house, he heard sirens and panicked. Defendant grabbed the gun and rinsed it off in an attempt to wash off the fingerprints. He tossed the gun into the bottom of a kitchen cabinet. He then ran outside where he was met by police officers.

A recording of Brenton's 911 call was played to the jury. Brenton lied to the 911 operator, telling her his name was "Paul" and that he did not know who had shot Marth. Defendant can be heard in the background of the telephone call crying and repeatedly saying things like, "[n]oooo," "[b]aby," and "[b]aby are you alive, baby. . . ."

A forensic pathologist estimated that the gun was fired roughly 12 inches from Marth's face.

Marth's best friend, Heather Hughes, testified that she and Marth had exchanged text messages in the hours before the shooting. A text sent at 10:29 P.M. on March 17, 2010 (the night before defendant was released from jail) read: "Going to sleep soi [*sic*] can wake up when [defendant] calls." At 4:24 A.M. on March 18, 2010, Marth texted: "[Defendant']s out." Two minutes later she sent: "I alrea[d]y fuckin wish he was locked back up. . . . [O]mg [you] have no clue." At 7:02 A.M., Marth wrote: "Just were [*sic* ] fighting . . . with him right now."

## III. DISCUSSION

### A. *Sufficiency of the Evidence of First Degree Murder*

Defendant contends the evidence was insufficient to find him guilty of first degree murder. We agree. Although the evidence is sufficient for reasonable jurors to have found that defendant killed Marth with malice aforethought, there is insufficient evidence to support the finding that the killing occurred with premeditation and deliberation.

### 2. Background Principles

Murder is the unlawful killing of a human being with malice aforethought.

There are two degrees of murder. Section 189 defines first degree murder as "murder which is perpetrated by means of a destructive device or explosive, a weapon of mass destruction, knowing use of ammunition designed primarily to penetrate metal or armor, poison, lying in wait, torture, or by any other kind of willful, deliberate, and premeditated killing, or which is committed in the perpetration of, or attempt to perpetrate, arson, rape, carjacking, robbery, burglary, mayhem, kidnapping, [or] train wrecking. . . . All other kinds of murders are of the second degree."

In *People v. Thomas* (1945) 25 Cal. 2d 880, our state Supreme Court construed the meaning of " 'willful, deliberate, and premeditated' " in light of the phrase's placement among the specifically enumerated instances of a killing perpetrated, among other ways, during arson, rape, robbery, burglary, or mayhem. Applying the *ejusdem generis* rule of statutory construction, the court stated: "By conjoining the words 'willful, deliberate, and premeditated' in its definition and limitation of the character of killings falling within murder of the first degree the Legislature apparently emphasized its intention to require as an element of such crime *substantially more reflection* than may be involved in the mere formation of a specific intent to kill."

These principles underpin more recent statements of premeditation and deliberation. "The very definition of 'premeditation' encompasses the idea that a defendant thought about or considered the act beforehand." "Deliberate" means "formed or arrived at or determined upon as a result of careful thought and weighing of considerations for and against the proposed course of action." Thus, " '[a]n intentional killing is premeditated and deliberate if it occurred as the result of preexisting thought and reflection rather than unconsidered or rash impulse.' "

Courts have also emphasized that "[t]he process of premeditation and deliberation does not require any extended period of time. 'The true test is not the duration of time as much as it is the extent of the reflection.'"

Here, the only *direct* evidence of defendant's mental state at the time of the shooting is defendant's statements to investigators and his testimony at trial. Although his statements regarding the shooting were inconsistent in significant respects, there is nothing in any of his statements to indicate that he considered shooting Marth beforehand or carefully weighed considerations for and against killing her. The evidence of such premeditation and deliberation, if any, was circumstantial.

The use of circumstantial evidence in proving first degree murder was discussed in *People v. Anderson* (1968) 70 Cal. 2d 15. The court stated: "Given the presumption that an unjustified killing of a human being constitutes murder of the second, rather than of the first, degree, and the clear legislative intention to differentiate between first and second degree murder, [a reviewing court] must determine in any case of circumstantial evidence whether the proof is such as will furnish a *reasonable foundation* for an inference of premeditation and deliberation [citation] or whether it 'leaves only to *conjecture and surmise* the conclusion that defendant either arrived at or carried out the intention to kill as the result of a concurrence of deliberation and premeditation.'"

### 3. Analysis

The *Anderson* court provided guidelines "for the kind of evidence which is sufficient to sustain a finding of premeditation and deliberation." Such evidence "falls into three basic categories: (1) facts about how and what defendant did *prior* to the actual killing which show that the defendant was engaged in activity directed toward, and explicable as intended to result in, the killing — what may be characterized as 'planning' activity; (2) facts about the defendant's *prior* relationship and/or conduct with the victim from which the jury could reasonably infer a 'motive' to kill the victim, which inference of motive, together with facts of type (1) or (3), would in turn support an inference that the killing was the result of 'a pre-existing reflection' and 'careful thought and weighing of considerations' rather than 'mere unconsidered or rash impulse hastily executed'; (3) facts about the nature of the killing from which the jury could infer that the *manner* of killing was so particular and exacting that the defendant must have intentionally killed according to a 'preconceived design' to take his victim's life in a particular way for a 'reason' which the jury can reasonably infer from facts of type (1) or (2)."

To illustrate planning evidence, . . . in *People v. Young* (2005) 34 Cal. 4th 1149 . . . the defendant, after being denied entry to a house, crashed through a living room window armed with a gun before killing a resident inside the house. From such evidence, the jury could infer that the "defendant 'considered the possibility of murder in advance'[.]"

The present case lacks any planning evidence whatsoever. Defendant, along with his younger brother, picked up Marth from her house and drove back to his home, not to a remote or isolated location. The house was occupied by four other people who could identify him. There is no evidence that defendant left the room or the house to get a gun, or that he even moved from his squatting position on the floor.

Defendant's behavior following the shooting is of someone horrified and distraught about what he had done, not someone who had just fulfilled a preconceived plan. Immediately after the fatal shot, defendant tried to resuscitate Marth and directed his brother to "call the cops." Defendant could be heard crying in the background during the 911 call. He asked the first officer who arrived to call an ambulance and, when being taken to the police station, he cried and asked rhetorically how someone could "go on with their life when they see something like that." The evidence not only fails to support an inference of a plan to kill Marth, but strongly suggests *a lack* of a plan to kill. Even viewed in the light most favorable to the prosecution, there is no evidence of planning.

There is little or no relevant motive evidence here. The Attorney General points to Marth's text messages to Hughes and asserts that the jury may have inferred that "[defendant] was in a bad mood after being released from custody and he was angry with [Marth]." Other than the references to the text messages, the Attorney General does not cite to evidence defendant was in a "bad mood" or "angry" with Marth. Even if such a mood or anger can be reasonably inferred from Marth's texts and could suggest the intent to kill, it is, at most, weak evidence of a motive suggesting premeditation and deliberation. The second *Anderson* factor refers not merely to a motive to kill, but to the kind of motive that "would in turn support an inference that the killing was the result of a 'pre-existing reflection' and 'careful thought and weighing of considerations' *rather than* 'mere unconsidered or rash impulse hastily executed.'" The text messages and the evidence of a loud screaming argument, which the Attorney General relies on, do not suggest this kind of motive. To the contrary, any evidence of defendant's "bad mood" or "anger with the victim" indicates a motive to kill based on "'unconsidered or rash impulse hastily executed,'" not the sort of "'pre-existing reflection'" and "'careful thought and weighing of considerations'" required to find premeditation and deliberation.

As for the manner of killing evidence, defendant shot Marth in the face. [T]his manner of killing supports the finding of malice necessary to convict defendant of murder. To support *first degree* murder, however, the prosecution must show more than an intent to kill. It must still establish that the gunshot to the face was pursuant to a "'preconceived design' to take his victim's life[.]"

Even when manner of killing evidence is strong, cases in which findings of premeditation and deliberation are upheld typically involve planning and motive evidence as well. For example, in *People v. Cruz* (1980) 26 Cal. 3d 233, the defendant killed one of his victims, his wife, by crushing her skull with a pipe and shooting her in the face with a shotgun. The court held that the finding of premeditation and deliberation was supported by "all three types of evidence specified in *Anderson*"; the defendant resented the victims (motive), snuck out of his house to secure a pipe and load a shotgun (planning), and returned to the house to kill one of his victims by crushing her skull with the pipe followed by a shotgun blast to the face (manner of killing).

Here, as discussed above, there is no evidence of any plan to kill Marth and little or no meaningful evidence of a motive to kill her.

Cases that have found sufficient evidence of premeditation and deliberation in the absence of planning or motive evidence are those in which "[t]he manner of the killing clearly suggests an execution-style murder." (*People v. Hawkins* (1995) 10 Cal. 4th 920.) In *Hawkins*, the victim was found in a ditch in an open field with two gunshot wounds: one in the back of the neck and one in the back of the head near the base of the skull. There was also evidence that the victim was crouching or kneeling at the time. The court concluded: "In sum, although evidence of planning and motive was indeed minimal if not totally absent in the present case, we conclude that the manner-of-killing evidence was sufficiently strong to permit a trier of fact to conclude beyond a reasonable doubt that defendant committed the . . . murder with premeditation and deliberation."

Here, the Attorney General does not assert that the shooting of Marth was an "execution-style" murder. Nor is there any evidence from which jurors could reasonably infer such a manner of killing. . . . Although the gun was only 12 inches away from Marth when fired, the bullet completely missed Marth's brain; and although the gun still held five live rounds, no second shot was fired. Defendant's actions immediately afterward — directing Brenton to call 911 and attempting to resuscitate Marth and seek medical aid — are not the actions of an executioner. In short, the manner of killing Marth was not "so particular and exacting that the defendant must have intentionally killed according to a 'preconceived design'[.]"

With no evidence of planning or motive and a killing that cannot be described as "execution-style," the application of the *Anderson* factors weighs heavily in favor of concluding there was insufficient evidence for a reasonable jury to conclude that the killing was the result of premeditation and deliberation.

As the Attorney General points out, the *Anderson* factors are not exhaustive or exclusive of other considerations. . . . The question thus remains whether, in light of the whole record, there is substantial evidence from which rational jurors could have found that defendant's killing of Marth was the result of preexisting thought and the careful weighing of considerations.

[T]he Attorney General argues that defendant did not shoot Marth during the "[l]oud and screaming argument" heard by Williams, but did so only after the screaming ended. This, the Attorney General contends, "reasonably supports the inference that [defendant] had time to consider his actions before [h]e pointed his Taurus pistol at [Marth's] face and fired from close range." However, "[t]he true test [of premeditation and deliberation] is not the duration of time as much as it is the extent of the reflection[.]" Thus, the mere fact that a defendant has time to consider his actions is, without more, insufficient to support an inference that the defendant *actually* premeditated and deliberated. Indeed, if the mere passage of time was enough to infer premeditation and deliberation, then virtually any unlawful killing with malice aforethought would be first degree murder because premeditation and deliberation does not require any extended period of time. . . . Clearly, there must be some evidence that the defendant actually engaged in such reflection, and not merely had the time to do so.

Lastly, the Attorney General argues, defendant's "act of shooting [Marth] does not bear the characteristics of a rash impulse because he took the time to pull back the hammer, point the pistol at [Marth's] face, and fire the weapon." Pulling the hammer back on a loaded gun and pointing it at another is certainly evidence of an intentional act[.][4] However, the Attorney General provides no authority for the argument that these actions, without more, are sufficient to support a finding of premeditation and deliberation.

A first degree murder conviction premised upon premeditation and deliberation requires more than a showing of the intent to kill; it requires evidence from which reasonable jurors can infer that the killing is the result of the defendant's preexisting thought and reflection. Here, viewing the evidence in the entire record in the light most favorable to the prosecution, we conclude that there is ample evidence to support the jury's verdict of murder, but insufficient evidence to support the finding that defendant killed Marth with premeditation and deliberation. We will therefore reduce the conviction to second degree murder.

**Post-Case Follow-Up**

*Boatman* holds that although "premeditation and deliberation does not require any extended period of time" between formation of the intent to kill and the killing, the government must prove the killing "occurred as the result of preexisting thought and reflection rather than an unconsidered impulse." Determining whether a given case meets this test can be difficult at times. Helpfully, the court points to three categories of evidence that might show whether or not a killing was willful, deliberate, and premeditated: (1) planning activity, (2) prior relationship with the victim/motive, and (3) the manner of killing. Although this is not an exhaustive list, this formulation has been influential in the group of jurisdictions in which evidence beyond a mere intent to kill is required to prove that the defendant acted in a willful, deliberate, and premeditated manner.

## Boatman: *Real Life Applications*

**1.** Most criminal cases never go to trial. Instead, they are resolved by plea agreement. Look back at the facts in *Boatman.*
   **a.** Why do you think this case was not resolved by a plea deal?
   **b.** Imagine that you were representing Boatman. If the prosecutor had offered a deal for Boatman to plead guilty to second-degree murder, would you have advised your client to take it?
   **c.** Now imagine that you were the prosecutor and Boatman rejected your second-degree murder offer. Would you have offered to let Boatman plead guilty to voluntary manslaughter, involuntary manslaughter, or negligent homicide?

---

[4] We note that cocking, aiming, and firing a revolver essentially describes the act of shooting with a revolver. If these actions could, without more, constitute premeditation and deliberation, we would effectively add killing perpetrated by a revolver to the list of crimes specifically enumerated in section 189 and thereby substantially broaden the scope of first degree murder and eliminate the purposeful division created by the Legislature.

2. Steven was married to Joyce for about two months. The marriage was on the rocks. According to Steven's testimony, on the night of Joyce's death, the couple was at home when they got into an argument. Joyce began to taunt Steven, saying, "I never wanted to marry you and you are lousy in bed. You remind me of my dad." (Joyce's father had abused her as a child.) Joyce then told Steven she wanted a divorce. Joyce asked Steven, "What are you going to do?" With no response from Steven, Joyce continued to taunt him. Joyce then asked again, "What are you going to do?" Steven lunged at Joyce with a knife that was hidden behind a pillow and stabbed her 19 times. Steven then slit his wrists, called the police, and confessed. Steven seemed unconcerned about his own wounds when the police came. In text messages sent two days before the incident, Steven accused Joyce of having an affair with another man. After a number of messages from Joyce denying the accusation, Steven apologized and texted: "OK. I believe you. I just get jealous sometimes." Steven is charged with first-degree murder.

    **a.** You are the prosecutor preparing the case. What piece(s) of evidence would you ask the jury to focus on in its deliberations and why?

    **b.** Steven is convicted and you are representing him on appeal. Briefly outline your argument that there was insufficient evidence to support the jury's first-degree murder verdict.

---

*Boatman* represents one of the two major jurisdictional approaches to the willful, deliberate, and premeditated test. In these jurisdictions, a first-degree murder conviction requires evidence of more than merely an intent to kill. Instead, as discussed in *Boatman*, the government must prove that the defendant reflected on the intent to kill, and still went through with the act.

As noted in the introduction to this section, the second collection of jurisdictions continues to recognize the willful, deliberate, and premeditated test in name. Strangely, however, they interpret the test in a way that effectively renders all intentional killings first-degree murder. In Pennsylvania, for example, the state supreme court has held that "[p]remeditation and deliberation exist whenever the assailant possesses the consciousness of purpose to bring about death." *Commw. v. Fisher*, 564 Pa. 505, 518 (2001). Of course, a consciousness of purpose to bring about death is just another way of describing an intent to kill. Because the government only needs to prove the defendant intended to kill the victim to meet the willful, deliberate, and premeditated test in this group of jurisdictions, it is an empty test.

Why might a court interpret the willful, deliberate, and premeditated test in a way that makes it toothless? One explanation is that not everyone believes premeditation is a good measure of a killer's culpability. A killer who, while cleaning his gun, suddenly decides to take aim and shoot at his neighbor across the street simply out of boredom has not reflected on his intent to kill. But, arguably in a case like that, the crime seems especially cruel precisely because the intent to kill was so quickly and casually arrived at. On the other hand, a killer who, fighting back tears, shoots his terminally ill father so that "[h]e won't have to suffer anymore" may have planned the act in advance. *State v. Forrest*, 321 N.C. 186, 189 (1987). But "[a]lmost all would agree that someone who kills because of a desire to end a loved one's physical suffering caused by an illness which is both terminal and incurable should not be deemed in law as culpable and deserving of the same punishment as one who kills because of unmitigated spite, hatred, or ill will." *Id.* at 200 (Exum, J., dissenting). Whatever the explanation, in a significant number of jurisdictions, the willful, deliberate, and premeditated test exists in name only.

Do you think the willful, deliberate, and premeditated test is a good way of distinguishing the most culpable murders from others? If you were a legislator, would you vote in favor of a law making it the standard for dividing first- and second-degree murder? If not, is there a different standard that you would propose?

## 2. Transferred Intent

The doctrine of **transferred intent** applies to all intentional killings, regardless of whether they are classified as first- or second-degree murder. Transferred intent addresses the problem of a defendant who kills someone other than his intended victim. The basic rule here is easily stated. "The intent to kill the intended target is deemed to transfer to the unintended victim so that the defendant is guilty of murder." *People v. Bland*, 28 Cal. 4th 313, 317 (2002). This means that if DiBiase puts poison in a drink, intending to kill Virgil but Heenan drinks it instead and dies, DiBiase is guilty of murder. It is no defense that DiBiase did not intend to kill *Heenan* specifically. This is because DiBiase's intent to kill Virgil (the intended target) is "transferred" to Heenan (the unlucky, unintended victim).

The basic transferred intent rule is universally followed. Jurisdictions are split, however, on the question of whether the transferred intent doctrine allows a defendant to be convicted of *both* murder (of the unintended victim) *and* attempted murder (of the intended target). Traditionally, a defendant whose bullet struck and killed an unintended victim could be convicted of only one crime: murder of the unintended victim.

### History and Other Jurisdictional Approaches

Before Pennsylvania "revolutionized the law of homicide" in 1794, no common law jurisdiction divided murder into different degrees. Pennsylvania's decision to separate murder into two degrees based on premeditation was incredibly influential. By the middle of the twentieth century, "over three-quarters of the states used it as the dividing line between first- and second-degree murder." Today, only 26 states, the District of Columbia, and the federal government "utilize some form of the premeditation-deliberation formula" — still a majority, but only a narrow one. The shift away from dividing murder into degrees was due in part to the Model Penal Code, which does not distinguish between different degrees of murder. Michael J. Zydney Mannheimer, *Not the Crime But the Cover-Up: A Deterrence-Based Rationale for the Premeditation-Deliberation Formula*, 86 Ind. L.J. 879, 882-83 (2011).

While law school courses focus on principles of homicide law that are common to the majority of jurisdictions, each state's homicide laws are unique. Some states, like Minnesota, divide murder into *three* degrees. And, among states that follow the two-degree model, some have added to the forms of homicide that can qualify as first-degree murder. In Louisiana, for example, first-degree murder includes killings "[w]hen the offender has the specific intent to kill or to inflict great bodily harm upon a victim who is under the age of twelve or sixty-five years of age or older." La. Rev. Stat. § 14:30(5).

In recent years, some jurisdictions have expanded the transferred intent doctrine to allow for "attempted murder liability as to the *intended* target to be imposed along with transferred-intent murder as to the *unintended* (actual) victim." Nancy Ehrenreich, *Attempt, Merger, and Transferred Intent*, 82 Brook. L. Rev. 49, 51 (2016). In states that follow this approach, a defendant who kills his intended target is guilty of only one crime (murder) but a defendant who misses his intended target and kills someone else is guilty of two crimes (murder and attempted murder).

## C. MURDER WITH THE INTENT TO INFLICT GRIEVOUS BODILY INJURY

When a killer acts with the intent to inflict grievous bodily injury (also referred to as serious or great bodily injury in some jurisdictions), it is murder. Among jurisdictions that divide murder into degrees, almost all of them classify this type of killing as second-degree murder.

Because the killer did not intend to bring about the victim's death, these are technically unintentional killings. But as a practical matter, this form of murder has more in common with intentional killing cases. Imagine a case where the defendant beat someone to death. It might be difficult to prove beyond a reasonable doubt whether he intended to kill the victim or only to very seriously injure her. In this sort of case, a prosecutor can argue either theory to the jury in support of a murder conviction. "[T]he trier of fact may find the requisite intent for second-degree murder, even where the defendant did not intend to kill the victim, but did intend to inflict grievous bodily harm." *Thornton v. State*, 397 Md. 704, 732 (Ct. App. 2007).

The precise definition of grievous bodily injury varies across jurisdictions. Often the definition incorporates a requirement that the injury be severe enough that it would be likely to result in death. In other words, an injury "of a very serious character which might naturally and commonly involve loss of life[.]" *Waller v. People*, 30 Mich. 16, 20 (1874). This distinguishes an intent to inflict *grievous* bodily injury from an intent to injure. As one court put it: "Every assault involves bodily harm. But any doctrine which would hold every assailant as a murderer where death follows his act, would be barbarous and unreasonable." *Id.*

This category of killings is infrequently litigated on appeal. This is because there are rarely grounds for a person convicted of this form of murder to challenge the sufficiency of the evidence or quarrel with the jury instructions. Indeed, in a case where the prosecution is asking the jury to find the defendant guilty of first-degree murder, the defendant's attorney might be the one who argues in favor of the theory of murder with the intent to inflict grievous bodily injury. If the evidence of a premeditated plan to attack the victim is overwhelming, the defendant's best hope of avoiding a first-degree murder conviction may be to convince the jury that, although he acted with premeditation, he only intended to seriously wound the victim (which would make him guilty of murder in the second degree) rather than to kill her.

## D. HEAT OF PASSION KILLINGS: REDUCING MURDER TO VOLUNTARY MANSLAUGHTER

As we have seen, in states that divide murder into degrees, premeditation determines whether an intentional killing is first-degree murder or second-degree murder. But in some cases, an intentional killing may not even be considered murder at all. At common law, and in most states today, a killing committed in the heat of passion is not murder, but **voluntary manslaughter**. Prosecutors do not typically pursue voluntary manslaughter charges. Instead, voluntary manslaughter is more often presented to the jury by the defense, as the lesser alternative to murder. As a result, even though voluntary manslaughter is a criminal offense, courts tend to conceive of it as a partial *defense*. Specifically, it is often described as a partial defense that mitigates what would otherwise be murder to the lesser crime of voluntary manslaughter.

## 1. The Elements of Heat of Passion: Overview

In most states, any type of murder with the exception of felony murder is eligible to be reduced to voluntary manslaughter if the elements below are met. In most jurisdictions, voluntary manslaughter has three elements:

- The act was committed in a **state of passion**. First, the killer must have committed the act in a state of passion. Most often, this means rage. But other intense emotions that lead to a loss of self-control can qualify — for example, fear or jealousy.
- There was **adequate provocation**. Many killings are fueled by rage. To qualify as a heat of passion killing, the killer's passionate state must have been the result of legally adequate provocation. Historically, the law limited adequate provocation to a handful of circumstances — most notably, one spouse walking in on the other committing adultery. Only a very small number of jurisdictions continue to follow this categorical approach to adequate provocation. Most states have replaced the categories with an open-ended test that asks, in essence, whether the alleged provocation would have caused the average person to lose control.
- The killing was relatively close in time to the provocation. Specifically, there cannot have been a **cooling off period** between the killing and the provocation, defined as enough time for the reasonable person to have cooled off and regained self-control.

All three elements must be present for a voluntary manslaughter conviction. The first element — state of passion — is only infrequently litigated. After all, if the evidence conclusively shows that the killer acted in a cool and calculated manner, it would be pointless to present a voluntary manslaughter defense. As a result, there is very little case law focusing on this element, and no need to examine it individually here. By contrast, the adequate provocation and cooling off time requirements can present challenging problems. The next two subsections focus on each element in turn.

## 2. Adequate Provocation

What kind of provocation should reduce murder to manslaughter? For most of voluntary manslaughter's history, adequate provocation was limited "to categories of victim behavior considered highly offensive in Tudor-era England — namely, mutual combat, sudden injury, false arrest, and adultery." Aya Gruber, *A Provocative Defense*, 103 Cal. L. Rev. 273, 280 (2015). Today, it appears that only two states — Alabama and Illinois — have kept this so-called categorical approach to adequate provocation. *Id.* at 280, n.43.

Everywhere else, adequate provocation can be anything that would lead the reasonable or ordinary person to act from passion instead of reason. This open-ended standard often leaves the issue in the hands of the jury, with little to guide it beyond moral intuition. Even under the open-ended modern approach, there are limits to what can qualify as adequate provocation.

 **Case Preview**

### *People v. Beltran*

Nearly every jurisdiction has abandoned the categorical limits on adequate provocation in favor of a reasonable or ordinary person standard. But what sort of reaction would an ordinary person need to have to constitute adequate provocation? Is it enough that a situation would upset a reasonable person? Does the provoking event need to be so terrible that it would lead a reasonable person to *kill*? In *People v. Beltran*, the California Supreme Court examined the modern test for adequate provocation.

As you read the decision, consider the following questions:

1. The court rejects the government's argument that the provocation must be the kind that would lead the average person to kill. Why? What standard does it adopt instead?
2. Although the court disagrees with the government's proposed legal standard, it upholds the defendant's conviction. Why?

# *People v. Beltran*
## 56 Cal. 4th 935 (2013)

CORRIGAN, J.

Here we clarify what kind of provocation will suffice to constitute heat of passion and reduce a murder to manslaughter. The Attorney General argues the provocation must be of a kind that would cause an ordinary person of average disposition *to kill*. We disagree. Nearly one hundred years ago, this court explained that, when examining heat of passion in the context of manslaughter, the fundamental "inquiry is whether or not the defendant's reason was, at the time of his act, so disturbed or obscured by some passion . . . to such an extent as would render ordinary men of average disposition liable to act rashly or without due deliberation and reflection, and from this passion rather than from judgment." (*People v. Logan* (1917) 175 Cal. 45, 49.) The proper standard focuses upon whether the person of average disposition would be induced to react from passion and not from judgment.

## I. BACKGROUND

Defendant Tare Nicholas Beltran and Claire Joyce Tempongko met in November 1998 and began dating. In January 1999, defendant moved into the San Francisco apartment Tempongko shared with her nine-year-old son J.N. and her younger daughter. J.N. called defendant "dad." In several incidents, defendant physically abused Tempongko. In April 1999, he threw her to the ground and dragged her by the hair. Three weeks later, he grabbed her and tried to remove her from a friend's apartment. In November 1999, he took her into the bedroom and barricaded the door. The police were summoned and forced the door open.

At some point, defendant moved from the apartment but retained a key. Tempongko obtained a protective order requiring him to stay 100 yards away from the residence. In September 2000, defendant, who was drunk, was arrested outside of the apartment.

Tempongko's apartment building had three units. Christina Maldonado lived on the top floor. On the evening of October 22, 2000, she heard sounds of a physical altercation coming from Tempongko's apartment. There

---

## Criticism of the Adequate Provocation Standard

Should heat of passion killings really be treated differently than other intentional killings? Critics of voluntary manslaughter as a category of homicide offense have advanced a range of arguments in favor of abolishing or reforming it, including that the doctrine reinforces outdated and problematic ideas about masculinity and gender roles.

Consider the paradigmatic example of adequate provocation: infidelity. "[O]ne of the earliest cases to delineate the various forms of 'adequate provocation,' notes that adultery is the 'highest invasion of property' and thus represents the 'highest' form of provocation." Donna K. Coker, *Heat of Passion and Wife Killing: Men Who Batter/Men Who Kill*, 2 S. Cal. Rev. L. & Women's Stud. 71, 80 (1992). More recently, there have been a number of cases where heterosexual men who killed in response to a sexual advance from another man have successfully presented a voluntary manslaughter defense. These "gay panic provocation cases may be a reflection of dominant norms of masculinity that legitimize the use of physical violence in response to non-violent homosexual advances." Cynthia Lee, *The Gay Panic Defense*, 42 U.C. Davis L. Rev. 471, 478-79 (2008).

If you were drafting a homicide law from scratch, would you include a doctrine that treats "heat of passion" killings more leniently than other intentional killings?

was a muffled male voice and children screaming that they loved their mother. She did not hear an adult female voice. When Maldonado left her apartment and looked down the stairs, she saw J.N. run out of Tempongko's unit. Another neighbor caught up with J.N., who was crying. J.N. said that his "dad" stabbed his mother and ran away. The neighbors found Tempongko in her apartment bloody and unresponsive. The apartment was in disarray; the phone had been unplugged from the wall. An autopsy revealed several blunt force injuries and 17 stab wounds to Tempongko's face, upper body, arms, and hands. After running from the scene, defendant fled to Mexico where he was arrested six years later.

J.N. was 18 years old at the time of trial. He testified that, after the family got home on October 22, 2000, Tempongko received several cell phone calls. Tempongko was "frantic," arguing with someone on the phone, and telling the caller not to come to the apartment. Thirty to 45 minutes later, defendant banged loudly on the front door, then entered without being let in. He began yelling and asking Tempongko where she had been and with whom. The two argued for five or 10 minutes. Defendant then walked briskly to the kitchen, returned to the living room with a large knife, and repeatedly stabbed Tempongko. She futilely raised her arms in self-defense. Defendant continued to stab her as she slumped to the floor, then fled, taking the knife with him. Nearby, police later recovered a knife with Tempongko's blood on it.

Defendant testified that he and Tempongko had an up and down relationship. While they discussed having their own children, Tempongko was concerned that defendant would leave her as the fathers of her two other children had done. At some point, they decided Tempongko would try to become pregnant, but defendant believed she was unsuccessful. Defendant acknowledged he had grabbed Tempongko on several occasions but denied pulling her hair.

On the day of the killing, defendant and Tempongko had planned to have lunch together. However, she called him and said she was going shopping in Vallejo with a female friend. She offered to meet defendant after she returned. That evening, he went to the apartment and let himself in with a key because Tempongko was expecting him. Defendant was calm but Tempongko was upset, asking why he was late. The argument became heated. Tempongko hurled insults, calling defendant a " 'fucking illegal' " and a " 'nobody.' " She said she " 'could get better than [him].' " Defendant said he was leaving, which upset Tempongko further. She stated: " 'Fuck you. I was right. I knew you were going to walk away someday. That's why I killed your bastard. I got an abortion.' " Defendant was shocked; Tempongko had never mentioned an abortion. He remembered nothing else until he found himself standing in the living room with a bloody knife. He admitted that he discarded the knife and fled to Mexico.

Defendant was charged with murder and use of a deadly weapon. The trial court gave instructions on first and second degree murder, as well as voluntary manslaughter based upon a sudden quarrel or heat of passion. The jury found defendant guilty of second degree murder with the use enhancement.

A divided Court of Appeal concluded the voluntary manslaughter instruction was prejudicially erroneous and reversed defendant's conviction. We clarify the appropriate standard and reverse the judgment of the Court of Appeal.

## II. DISCUSSION

### A. Legal Introduction

Manslaughter is a lesser included offense of murder. A person who kills without malice does not commit murder. Heat of passion is a mental state that precludes the formation of malice and reduces an unlawful killing from murder to manslaughter. Heat of passion arises if, "'at the time of the killing, the reason of the accused was obscured or disturbed by passion to such an extent as would cause the ordinarily reasonable person of average disposition to act rashly and without deliberation and reflection, and from such passion rather than from judgment.'" Heat of passion, then, is a state of mind caused by legally sufficient provocation that causes a person to act, not out of rational thought but out of unconsidered reaction to the provocation. While some measure of thought is required to form either an intent to kill or a conscious disregard for human life, a person who acts without reflection in response to adequate provocation does not act with malice.

This case involves the nature of provocation required to give rise to the heat of passion that obscures reason and precludes the mental state of malice. The People propose a test that would require a finding not only that an ordinary person of average disposition would be liable to act rashly and without reflection, but that such a person would act rashly in a particular manner, namely, by killing. We decline to adopt that test.

### B. Trial Court Proceedings

The prosecutor argued that defendant, motivated by jealousy, went to Tempongko's apartment intending to kill her, thus acting with express malice formed after premeditation and deliberation. The sole defense theory was that defendant killed in the heat of passion. When the victim said she had aborted her pregnancy, the news was so disturbing that defendant acted not from reflection but in reaction to the provocation. The prosecutor urged the jury to reject that argument. She maintained that there was no credible evidence showing the victim had said anything about an abortion. Alternatively, even if the victim did mention an abortion, the alleged statements did not amount to adequate provocation.

The final instruction given to the jury [regarding adequate provocation] was as follows:

> "Heat of passion does not require anger, rage, or any specific emotion. It can be any violent or intense emotion that causes a person to act without due deliberation and reflection.
>
> . . .
>
> "Now, it is not enough that the defendant simply was provoked. The defendant is not allowed to set up his own standard of conduct. You must decide whether the defendant was provoked and whether the provocation was sufficient.
>
> "*In deciding whether the provocation was sufficient, consider whether a person of average disposition would have been provoked and how such a person would react in the same situation knowing the same facts.*"

During deliberations, the jury sent out the following note: "In instruction 570: 'In deciding whether the provocation was sufficient, consider whether a person of average disposition would have been provoked and how such a person would react in the same situation knowing the same facts.' Does this mean to commit the same crime (homicide) or can it be other, less severe, rash acts[?]" After consulting counsel, the trial court responded: "The provocation involved must be such as to cause a person of average disposition in the same situation and knowing the same facts to do an act rashly and under the influence of such intense emotion that his judgment or reasoning process was obscured. This is an objective test and not a subjective test." As noted, the jury convicted defendant of second degree murder.

### C. Court of Appeal Opinion

On appeal, defendant argued the instruction given was misleading. Defendant claimed that telling jurors to consider how "a person would *react*" in the face of the provocation led them to question whether an average person would react *physically* and kill, as opposed to reacting *mentally*, experiencing obscured reason precluding the formation of malice.

The Court of Appeal agreed with defendant that the given instruction was ambiguous and rejected the Attorney General's argument that the relevant standard was whether an ordinary person of average disposition would kill under the same circumstances. A majority of the Court of Appeal concluded the ambiguity in the instruction prejudiced defendant and reversed his murder conviction.

### D. The Proper Standard for Provocation

The People argue the proper standard for assessing the adequacy of provocation is whether an ordinary person of average disposition would be moved to kill. They urge that juries should be expressly told to consider whether an ordinary person would kill under the circumstances at issue.

The People assert their view is supported by the common law. However, a review of the common law, from which our manslaughter statute originally derived, undermines their argument. Originally at common law, voluntary manslaughter did not refer to a person of average disposition. Rather, the early cases simply defined voluntary manslaughter as occurring under specified circumstances. Those circumstances did not justify the killing but, nevertheless, rendered it less blameworthy than murder because of adequate provocation. In the seminal case of *Regina v. Mawgridge* (1707) 84 Eng. Rep. 1107, Lord Holt explained at length what particular circumstances would and would not constitute voluntary manslaughter at common law. "[P]rovocations which may under the circumstances be adequate were said to be (1) angry and sudden assaults upon one; (2) similar assaults upon one's friend who is with one at the time; (3) seeing any person abused by force and going to his rescue; (4) unlawful arrest; and (5) seeing one's wife in an act of adultery." ([S]ee also *Manning's Case* (1670) 83 Eng. Rep. 112 [concluding the defendant's killing of a man "committing adultery with his wife in the very act" constituted "but manslaughter" and ordering the defendant's hand be burned as punishment but directing "the executioner to burn him gently, because there could not be greater provocation than this"].)

At some point, cases introduced the concept of the ordinary person of average disposition to the analysis, not only to generalize the circumstances that would mitigate murder to manslaughter, but also to allow the jury to determine what circumstances would constitute adequate provocation. One of the earliest cases recognizing the role of the person of average disposition in voluntary manslaughter jurisprudence was *Maher v. People* (Mich. 1862) 10 Mich. 212 (*Maher*). *Maher* examined what level of provocation was necessary, noting that "[i]t will not do to hold that reason should be entirely dethroned, or overpowered by passion so as to destroy intelligent volition" since "[s]uch a degree of mental disturbance would be equivalent to utter insanity, and, if the result of adequate provocation, would render the perpetrator morally innocent." However, because manslaughter remains a felony, *Maher* recognized that a killing in response to adequate provocation is a less serious crime than murder. Thus, as *Maher* reasoned, adequate provocation must "never [be] beyond that degree within which ordinary men have the power, and are, therefore, morally as well as legally bound to restrain their passions. It is only on the idea of a violation of this clear duty, that the act can be held criminal." *Maher* concluded adequate provocation means "that *reason* should, at the time of the act, be disturbed or obscured by passion to an extent which might render ordinary men, of fair average disposition, *liable to act rashly or without due deliberation or reflection, and from passion, rather than judgment.*"

The development of the law in California tracks this move away from specified categories of provocation to a more generalized standard based on the concept of an ordinary person of average disposition, leaving for the jury whether the given facts show adequate provocation.

[In the 1917 case, *Logan, supra,*] we cited *Maher*, essentially quoting verbatim the standard articulated there, that the fundamental "inquiry is whether or not the defendant's reason was, at the time of his act, so disturbed or obscured by some passion — not necessarily fear and never, of course, the passion for revenge — to such an extent as would render ordinary men of average disposition liable to act rashly or without due deliberation and reflection, and from this passion rather than from judgment."

The Attorney General's position, that adequate provocation for voluntary manslaughter requires a finding that an ordinary person of average disposition would *kill*, is inconsistent with the *Logan* standard. It is also inconsistent with the conceptual underpinnings of heat of passion as a circumstance which *mitigates* culpability for a killing but does not *justify* it. As *Maher* suggested, society expects the average person not to kill, even when provoked. As Professor Dressler stated, we punish a person who kills in the heat of passion or upon provocation because "[h]e did not control himself as much as he *should* have, or as much as common experience tells us he *could* have, nor as much as the ordinarily law-abiding person *would* have." (Dressler, *Rethinking Heat of Passion: A Defense in Search of a Rationale* (1982), 73 J. Crim. L. & Criminology 421, 467, original italics.) However, if one *does* kill in this state, his punishment is mitigated. Such a killing is not justified but *understandable* in light of "the frailty of human nature." (*Maher, supra,* 10 Mich. at p. 219.)

The killing reaction therefore is the *extraordinary* reaction, the unusual exception to the general expectation that the ordinary person will not kill even when provoked.

Adopting a standard requiring such provocation that the ordinary person of average disposition would be moved to *kill* focuses on the wrong thing. The proper focus is placed on the defendant's state of mind, not on his particular act. To be adequate, the provocation must be one that would cause an emotion so intense that an ordinary person would simply *react*, without reflection. To satisfy *Logan*, the anger or other passion must be so strong that the defendant's reaction bypassed his thought process to such an extent that judgment could not and did not intervene. Framed another way, provocation is not evaluated by whether the average person would *act* in a certain way: to kill. Instead, the question is whether the average person would *react* in a certain way: with his reason and judgment obscured.

The Attorney General argues that if provocation is adequate without reference to whether an ordinary person of average disposition would be moved to kill, then the standard would be too low. She asserts that "'acting rashly' means nothing more than acting hastily or imprudently, without consideration" and "[t]here are countless experiences in everyday life which would cause an ordinary person to act 'rashly,' such as being cut off on the road by an inattentive driver, having coffee spilled on him by a careless waiter, receiving a negative evaluation from a supervisor, or observing an umpire's bad call at his child's little league game." The argument misconstrues the standard.

The Attorney General's concern that the proper standard is too low is unfounded for two reasons. First, case law and the relevant jury instructions make clear the extreme intensity of the heat of passion required to reduce a murder to manslaughter. This passion must be a "[v]iolent, intense, high-wrought or enthusiastic emotion." The emotional response required goes far beyond the type of irritation a person of ordinary disposition would be prompted to feel by the mundane annoyances described above.

Second, *Logan* emphasized that the relevant standard is an objective one. *Logan* recognized that "no defendant may set up his own standard of conduct and justify or excuse himself because in fact his passions were aroused, unless further the jury believe that the facts and circumstances were sufficient to arouse the passions of the ordinarily reasonable man. Thus, no man of extremely violent passion could so justify or excuse himself if the exciting cause be not adequate, nor could an excessively cowardly man justify himself unless the circumstances were such as to arouse the fears of the ordinarily courageous man. Still further, while the conduct of the defendant is to be measured by that of the ordinarily reasonable man placed in identical circumstances, the jury is properly to be told that the exciting cause must be such as would naturally tend to arouse the passion of the ordinarily reasonable man. But as to the nature of the passion itself, our law leaves that to the jury, under these proper admonitions from the court." (*Logan, supra*, 175 Cal. at p. 49.)

### E. Instructional Error

As noted, the version of CALCRIM No. 570 given by the trial court stated in relevant part: "In deciding whether the provocation was sufficient, consider whether a person of average disposition would have been provoked and how such a person would react in the same situation knowing the same facts." The Court of Appeal properly rejected the Attorney General's claim that this instruction did not go far enough by failing to expressly tell the jury to consider the conduct the provocation might cause in an ordinary person of average disposition and whether such a person would kill in the face of the same provocation. However, the Court of Appeal reasoned the given instruction was potentially ambiguous because it "did not expressly limit the jurors' focus to whether the provocation would have caused an average person to act out of passion rather than judgment" and "allowed, and perhaps even encouraged, jurors to consider whether the provocation would cause an average person to do what the defendant did; i.e., commit a homicide."

We disagree that the instruction is ambiguous as written. As noted, the court instructed that the heat of passion principle came into play if defendant acted under the influence of intense emotion that obscured his reasoning or judgment. Telling the jury to consider how a person of average disposition "would react" properly draws the jury's attention to the objective nature of the standard and the effect the provocation would have on such a person's state of mind.

Defendant argues the trial court's response to the jury's question did not resolve the ambiguity because the trial court directed the jury to consider whether the provocation would cause a person of average disposition "to do an act rashly" rather than "to act rashly." Defendant suggests the former formulation continued to improperly focus the jury on the "act" performed, i.e., the act of killing, and whether an ordinary person would commit the act of killing in response to provocation. The trial court's response, taken as a whole, cannot support such a strained interpretation. As discussed, the trial court told the jury to consider whether a person of average disposition would "do an act rashly and under the influence of such intense emotion that his judgment or reasoning process was obscured." This instruction properly focused upon the *rashness* of the act, not on the act alone.

## III. CONCLUSION

We reaffirm today the standard for determining heat of passion that we adopted nearly a century ago. Provocation is adequate only when it would render an ordinary person of average disposition "liable to act rashly or without due deliberation and reflection, and from this passion rather than from judgment." (*Logan, supra,* 175 Cal. at p. 49.) We decline the Attorney General's invitation to deviate from this venerable understanding that has been faithfully applied by juries for decades.

[Nevertheless, because we find the trial court's instructions] properly conveyed the *Logan* test, [we reverse the Court of Appeal's decision in favor of defendant.]

The judgment is reversed and the matter remanded to the Court of Appeal for further proceedings consistent with the views expressed herein.

**Post-Case Follow-Up**

*Beltran* holds that the standard for adequate provocation is not whether an ordinary person of average disposition would be moved to kill. Instead, quoting the 1862 *Maher* case, the court describes the standard as focused on whether the ordinary person would act from passion and not judgment. This is an open-ended test. Although, as *Beltran* explains, "[t]he emotional response required goes far beyond the type of irritation" that would be caused by "mundane annoyances" like spilled coffee, the decision does not provide much guidance about what sorts of events would suffice. Ultimately, "as to the nature of the passion itself, our law leaves that to the jury, under these proper admonitions from the court."

Mere words continue to be treated differently from other types of provocation. In a few jurisdictions, words alone can *never* qualify as adequate provocation. Most courts today allow some cases that involve only provoking words to go to a jury. But even in these jurisdictions, there are still many circumstances where words alone are held to be insufficient to qualify as provocation as a matter of law.

**Case Preview**

## People v. Pouncey

In *People v. Pouncey*, the court considers whether a murder defendant who killed following a heated verbal exchange should have been entitled to a jury instruction on voluntary manslaughter. Although the court concludes that the provoking words in this case did not warrant a voluntary manslaughter jury instruction, it declines to hold that words alone can never constitute adequate provocation.

As you read the decision, consider the following questions:

1. What kinds of provoking words do you think would allow for a jury instruction on adequate provocation?
2. The opinion distinguishes "insulting words" from "informative words," saying that the insults are less likely to qualify as adequate provocation. Why do you think this is?

## People v. Pouncey
### 437 Mich. 384 (1991)

MALLETT, J.

The defendant-appellee, Ollie Pouncey, was convicted of one count of second-degree murder and one count of possessing a firearm at the time of commission or attempted commission of a felony.

The conviction arose out of an altercation that occurred on May 4, 1987. The defendant and his two friends, Mr. White and Mr. Johnston, were at Mr. White's home. They left Mr. White's house, drove around the corner to the home of Mr. Bland and accused him of stealing Mr. White's car. When Mr. Bland denied stealing the car, the defendant and his friends returned to Mr. White's home. As they pulled into the driveway of Mr. White's home, Mr. Bland, accompanied by his older brother and the victim, Steven Powers, approached.

Mr. Bland repeatedly denied knowing anything about the theft. At this point, Mr. White went into his house and did not come back outside until after the shooting. The defendant, as well as Mr. Johnston, the two Bland brothers, and Mr. Powers, remained outside.

As the argument continued, Mr. Powers threatened to put the defendant "on his head" and called the defendant names. The decedent walked towards the defendant, but Mr. Bland held the decedent back. The defendant said "don't walk up on me." There were no blows struck; indeed, there was no physical contact of any kind between the decedent, the defendant or anyone else. The defendant testified that the decedent was not armed.

After this verbal exchange, the defendant walked into the house. He went to the back of the house and retrieved a gun from a closet. He then came back outside, approximately thirty seconds later, carrying a shotgun. As he was coming out, he instructed Mr. Johnston to hit Mr. Powers with a monkey wrench. Mr. Johnston swung the wrench, but the decedent ducked out of the way. At that point, the defendant fired one shot, hitting Mr. Powers in the abdomen. Mr. Johnston ran home, as did the two Bland brothers, who called the police. The defendant and Mr. White drove off in the defendant's car.

The defendant was charged with first-degree murder and possession of a firearm during the commission of a felony. On the murder charge, the judge instructed the jury on first-degree murder, second-degree murder, involuntary manslaughter, and careless and reckless use of a firearm resulting in death. The judge refused the defendant's request for an instruction on voluntary manslaughter, finding that the evidence offered at trial did not support this offense. On September 22, 1987, the jury found the defendant guilty of second-degree murder and felony-firearm [possession]. He was sentenced to a term of ten to fifteen years for the murder conviction and a mandatory term of two years for the felony-firearm conviction.

The Court of Appeals reversed the decision of the trial court and remanded for a new trial. The panel believed there was sufficient evidence of provocation and passion in the record to support an instruction on voluntary manslaughter. The panel based its finding on various witnesses' testimony regarding the argument between the defendant and the decedent.

This Court granted leave to appeal by order dated July 18, 1990, to consider whether the trial judge erred in not instructing on voluntary manslaughter.

## I

It is the duty of the court to "instruct the jury as to the law applicable to the case. . . ."

The court's duty to instruct on the law applicable to the case depends on the evidence presented at trial. This case deals with a cognate lesser included offense. The test to determine whether an instruction on a cognate lesser included offense must be given is as follows: The record must be examined, and if there is evidence which would support a conviction of the cognate lesser offense, then the trial judge, if requested, must instruct on it. If the evidence presented could not support a conviction of the lesser offense, then the judge should not give the requested instruction.

## II

### A

Murder and manslaughter are both homicides and share the element of being intentional killings. However, the element of provocation which characterizes the offense of manslaughter separates it from murder. Murder and manslaughter are separate offenses, but, as noted above, voluntary manslaughter is a cognate lesser included offense of murder.

The . . . definition of voluntary manslaughter encompasses several components which comprise the test for voluntary manslaughter: First, the defendant must kill in the heat of passion. Second, the passion must be caused by an adequate provocation. Finally, there cannot be a lapse of time during which a reasonable person could control his passions.

### B

The provocation necessary to mitigate a homicide from murder to manslaughter is that which causes the defendant to act out of passion rather than reason. One commentator interprets the law as requiring that the defendant's emotions be so intense that they distort the defendant's practical reasoning:

> "The law does not excuse actors whose behavior is caused by just any . . . emotional disturbance. . . . Rather, the law asks whether the victim's provoking act aroused the defendant's emotions to such a degree that the choice to refrain from crime became difficult for the defendant. The legal doctrine reflects the philosophical distinction between emotions that only cause choice and emotions so intense that they distort the very process of choosing."

In addition, the provocation must be adequate, namely, that which would cause the reasonable person to lose control. Not every hot-tempered individual who flies into a rage at the slightest insult can claim manslaughter.[7] The law cannot countenance the loss of self-control; rather, it must encourage people to control their passions.

The determination of what is reasonable provocation is a question of fact for the factfinder. However, the judge does play a substantial role. The judge furnishes the standard of what constitutes adequate provocation, i.e., that provocation which would cause a reasonable person to act out of passion rather than reason. When, as a matter of law, no reasonable jury could find that the provocation was adequate, the judge may exclude evidence of the provocation.

---

[7] "If reasonableness were not required, a man who flew into a rage and killed a woman for refusing to have sex with him would be guilty of nothing more than manslaughter. Furthermore, when the law rewards irrational behavior, it encourages people to feign irrationality. Thus, if the man in the above hypothetical had coolly decided to kill the woman as punishment for her refusal, he would be encouraged to feign rage in order to mitigate his crime." Loewy, *Culpability, dangerousness, and harm: Balancing the factors on which our criminal law is predicated*, 66 NCLR 283, 302-303 (1988).

## III

[T]he claimed provocation in this case consists only of words, which other courts generally have held do not constitute adequate provocation[.] However, words of an informative nature, rather than mere insults, have been considered adequate provocation. But this is not such a case, for this case involves insulting words, not words of an informational character. Nonetheless, we decline to issue a rule that insulting words per se are never adequate provocation. Instead, we reiterate that what constitutes adequate provocation is a factual question, and on these facts, the provocation was not adequate.

The evidence offered at trial painted a picture of a verbal fracas between six young men. The decedent insulted the defendant, but there were no punches thrown. There was no physical contact of any kind between the defendant, the decedent, or any of the six. The judge was absolutely correct in ruling that as a matter of law there was insufficient evidence to establish an adequate provocation.

The evidence adduced at trial would not support finding the defendant guilty of voluntary manslaughter. This is the finding that the trial judge made in deciding not to give the requested instruction on voluntary manslaughter. Because of this, the trial judge was correct in refusing the requested instruction on voluntary manslaughter. To instruct the jury on an offense not supported by the evidence would confuse the jury, and be "a distortion of the factfinding process."

## CONCLUSION

The law of voluntary manslaughter developed as a means of taking into consideration the weaknesses of human beings. Key to any finding of voluntary manslaughter is evidence of adequate provocation that a reasonable factfinder could conclude that the defendant, overcome by emotion, could not choose to refrain from the crime. Adequate provocation does not excuse or justify murder, but rather designates one guilty of manslaughter less culpable than one guilty of murder.

We reverse the decision of the Court of Appeals.

**Post-Case Follow-Up**

*Pouncey* is a fairly representative example of how most courts apply the adequate provocation requirement to mere words. Within the category of mere words, informational words (words that alert to the defendant of a provoking event like an affair) are treated much differently than insulting words (mere name calling). In most jurisdictions, insulting words alone are rarely, if ever, sufficient to instruct the jury on adequate provocation. Informational words, by contrast, are usually treated more like provoking acts. Even within the informational words category, however, courts are more likely to find provocation inadequate as a matter of law than in the case of actions. Still, words that convey especially provoking information are enough to support an adequate provocation jury instruction in most jurisdictions.

## Beltran *and* Pouncey: *Real Life Applications*

1. The jury in *Beltran* was instructed on voluntary manslaughter, even though the alleged provocation was only words. Look back at the facts of *Beltran* and notice that the case involved both informational and insulting words. Assume that you believe the defendant's version of the events. Which of the victim's words strike you as more provocative: her insults calling the defendant a "fucking illegal" or the informational words that she had gotten an abortion? If you were the defendant's lawyer in *Beltran*, which words would you focus on in your arguments to the jury?

2. Let's revisit the hypothetical from the *Real Life Applications* following *Boatman*: Steven was married to Joyce for about two months. The marriage was on the rocks. According to Steven's testimony, on the night of Joyce's death, the couple was at home when they got into an argument. Joyce began to taunt Steven, saying, "I never wanted to marry you and you are lousy in bed. You remind me of my dad." (Joyce's father had abused her as a child.) Joyce then told Steven she wanted a divorce. Joyce asked Steven, "What are you going to do?" With no response from Steven, Joyce continued to taunt him. Joyce then asked again, "What are you going to do?" Steven lunged at Joyce with a knife that was hidden behind a pillow and stabbed her 19 times. Steven then slit his wrists, called the police, and confessed. Steven seemed unconcerned about his own wounds when the police came. In text messages sent two days before the incident, Steven accused Joyce of having an affair with another man. After a number of messages from Joyce denying the accusation, Steven apologized and texted: "OK. I believe you. I just get jealous sometimes." Steven is charged with first-degree murder.

   a. Should the court instruct the jury on voluntary manslaughter in this case? Do you think the courts in *Pouncey* and *Beltran* would reach the same conclusion on this question?

   b. Assume that the trial court instructs the jury on voluntary manslaughter. Imagine you are Steven's lawyer. What would you argue to the jury to support a finding of adequate provocation? How do you think the jury would be likely to resolve the issue?

---

## 3. Cooling Off Time

While most disputes in voluntary manslaughter cases involve the **adequate provocation** element, the no cooling off period requirement can also present challenges. Sometimes rage can build up slowly over time. But voluntary manslaughter generally requires a rapid onset of emotion under the cooling off time element. If a reasonable person would have "cooled off" during the time between the provocation and the killing, this requirement will not be met.

Like adequate provocation, the question of cooling off time is often given to the jury with an open-ended instruction. In Maryland, for example, the model jury instruction for voluntary manslaughter provides that juries must find "there was not enough time between the provocation and the killing for a reasonable person's rage to cool." *Md. Pattern Jury Instr.-Crim.* 4:17.4. Similarly, in California, juries are instructed: "If enough time passed between the provocation and the killing for a person of average disposition to 'cool off' and regain his or her clear reasoning and judgment, then the killing is not reduced to voluntary manslaughter[.]" *Cal. Crim. Jury Instr.* 570.

Although often left to the jury, trial courts do sometimes find that this element has not been satisfied as a matter of law (and, of course, then refuse to let the jury consider voluntary manslaughter as a result). At some point, all would agree that a reasonable person would have cooled off — for example, if a defendant walks in on her spouse in bed with someone else and three weeks later kills them both. But there is no bright-line rule governing how much time is too long.

Two legal questions are worth highlighting with respect to this element. First, to what extent should the nature of the provocation impact the cooling off period? And, second, can an event rekindle passion that was provoked earlier? On the first question, courts will often expand or contract the cooling off window based on the provoking act involved in the case. More serious provocations will allow for longer cooling off periods. As the Supreme Court of Nevada has explained: "Whether the interval between the provocation and the killing is sufficient for the passions of a reasonable person to cool is not measured exclusively by any precise time. What constitutes a sufficient cooling-off period also depends upon the magnitude of the provocation and the degree to which passions are aroused." *Allen v. State*, 98 Nev. 354, 356 (1982).

The **rekindling** question arises relatively infrequently, but courts have split on how to answer it. In rekindling cases, a provoking event is followed later by some other non-provoking event that reminds the killer of the first event and triggers the killing. In *Dandova v. State*, 72 P.3d 325 (Alaska Ct. App. 2003), for example, the defendant (Dandova) had discovered information that led her to think the victim had molested her child. Sometime after this discovery, Dandova saw the victim, became enraged, and killed him. "[W]hen Dandova observed physical evidence suggesting that [the victim] had sexually abused [her child], this might have constituted provocation adequate to mitigate an ensuing homicidal assault," the court noted. But could an event that merely reminded Dandova of the earlier provocation re-start the clock for purposes of the cooling off period? The court in *Dandova* surveyed the law on this issue:

> As noted in [the legal treatise written by] LaFave & Scott, "[n]ot infrequently, there is a considerable time interval between the victim's act of provocation and the defendant's fatal conduct — time enough for passion to subside. [Then,] some event occurs which rekindles the defendant's passion." According to LaFave & Scott, "if this new occurrence is enough to trigger the passion of a reasonable man, the cooling-off period should start with the new occurrence."
>
> [In the] typical heat-of-passion manslaughter case[,] one specific event (of one of the kinds previously discussed) immediately produces a rage in the defendant. This may account for the fact that modern codes usually state that [the] defendant's passion must be "sudden." However, a more realistic appraisal of how human

emotions work compels the conclusion — which some courts have reached — that a reasonable provocation can be produced by a series of events occurring over a considerable span of time. When that is the case, then . . . the measurement of the cooling time should commence with . . . the last provocative event.

[The legal treatise written by] Perkins & Boyce agrees that a later event can rekindle passion — "that passion may be suddenly revived by circumstances that bring the provocation vividly to mind." However, LaFave & Scott concedes that the court decisions on this topic "have not always recognized" the idea that the cooling-off period should recommence with the most recent provocative act.

The court in *Dandova* ultimately found it unnecessary to take sides on the rekindling question by resolving the case on other grounds. As *Dandova* indicates, however, the weight of authority favors allowing for rekindling arguments in at least some cases, although not all courts agree.

## E.  ACCIDENTAL KILLINGS

Not all accidental deaths give rise to criminal liability. If a driver swerves into another lane to avoid a falling tree and causes a deadly crash, she has committed no crime. Although swerving into another lane is very risky, the risk is justifiable if it is done to avoid a tree falling in the road. By contrast, when accidental death is the result of *unjustified* risk taking — if a driver swerves into another lane while joy riding, for example — it may lead to homicide charges.

In most jurisdictions, there are three different homicide offenses that target accidental killings: second-degree murder, involuntary (or reckless) manslaughter, and negligent homicide. Broadly speaking, the difference between these three offenses is a function of the degree of risk taking involved and the defendant's awareness of the risk. This section presents each of these offenses in turn. (Related to accidental killings, felony murder provides for homicide liability without regard to the defendant's intent. Felony murder is covered in Section F of this chapter.)

Before continuing further, a word about terminology is in order. The vocabulary in this area of homicide law is complicated by the fact that the common law treated both reckless and criminally negligent killings as involuntary manslaughter. Some jurisdictions continue to follow this approach and define involuntary manslaughter as either a reckless *or* a criminally negligent killing. For the practicing lawyer applying the law in a single jurisdiction, this state of affairs is not at all problematic. But for the law student who is tasked with learning the general principles of criminal law, it can be frustrating and cause needless confusion. This is largely a matter of semantics, however. Regardless of the terminology a state uses to describe its homicide offenses, the legal principles that separate extreme recklessness, ordinary recklessness, and criminal negligence from one another tend to be the same across jurisdictions. For the sake of simplicity, then, this book uses the terms involuntary (or reckless) manslaughter to refer to reckless killings and the term negligent homicide to refer to criminally negligent killings.

# 1. Depraved Heart Murder

The notion that some accidental killings constitute murder can initially strike some people as confusing, especially in light of the fact that intentional killings are sometimes punished as manslaughter. For better or worse, however, most jurisdictions include a relatively narrow category of accidental killings in their definition of murder: those where the perpetrator acted with an extremely reckless indifference to the value of human life. Killings in this category are graded as second-degree murder in most jurisdictions. This variety of second-degree murder is often referred to by shorthand as **depraved heart murder** or extreme recklessness murder.

At common law and still in some homicide statutes today, depraved heart murder was defined in somewhat unhelpful terms. California, for example, defines this form of homicide as occurring "when the circumstances attending the killing show an abandoned and malignant heart." Cal. Penal Code § 188. Over the years, courts and legislatures have translated "amorphous" phrases like this into "a tangible standard that a jury can apply" by relying on modern *mens rea* terminology. *People v. Protopappas*, 201 Cal. App. 3d 152, 163 (1988). Although the precise definition can vary from one jurisdiction to the next, most define the mental state for depraved heart murder as extreme recklessness — that is, recklessness that involves "an extreme indifference to human life." *King v. State*, 505 So. 2d 403, 404 (Ala. Crim. App. 1987).

Recall that recklessness is typically defined as acting with a conscious disregard of a substantial and unjustifiable risk that a given harm (in this case death) will result. What distinguishes extreme recklessness from recklessness? Courts and commentators often point to two considerations: the degree of the risk and the social utility of the act. The paradigmatic examples of depraved heart murder — shooting into an occupied building, for instance — all involve acts with a very low social utility and a very high risk of death. In the language of recklessness, the risk taking required for depraved heart murder is generally both more substantial and more unjustifiable than the risk taking that constitutes involuntary manslaughter.

## Case Preview

### *People v. Roe*

In *People v. Roe*, the Court of Appeals of New York — the state's highest court — considered whether there was sufficient evidence to sustain the murder conviction of a 15-year-old defendant who shot his friend while playing Russian roulette. The court upheld the defendant's conviction, noting that Russian roulette is often cited as a classic example of depraved heart murder. Nevertheless, one judge issued a forceful dissent.

As you read the case, consider the following questions:

1. The court cites a number of "[e]xamples of conduct which have been held sufficient to justify a jury's finding of depraved indifference." What qualities do you think these examples have in common to separate them from ordinary recklessness?
2. How does the majority define depraved indifference murder? Which do you find more helpful to understanding the distinction between depraved heart murder and ordinary recklessness — the court's definition or the examples it provides?
3. The majority opinion in *Roe* is representative of how the vast majority of courts would resolve this case. But the dissenting opinion is still noteworthy. In upholding the defendant's conviction, the majority focuses on the gravity of the risk posed by the defendant's conduct. Does the dissent dispute that the defendant's acts presented a grave risk? If not, what considerations lead the dissent to conclude there was insufficient evidence to sustain the conviction?

---

## *People v. Roe*
### 74 N.Y.2d 20 (1989)

HANCOCK, J.

In defendant's appeal from his conviction for depraved indifference murder (Penal Law § 125.25[2])[1] for the shooting death of a 13-year-old boy, the sole question we address is the legal sufficiency of the evidence. Defendant, a 15 ½-year-old high school student, deliberately loaded a mix of "live" and "dummy" shells at random into the magazine of a 12-gauge shotgun. He pumped a shell into the firing chamber not knowing whether it was a "dummy" or a "live" round. He raised the gun to his shoulder and pointed it directly at the victim, Darrin Seifert, who was standing approximately 10 feet away. As he did so, he exclaimed "Let's play Polish roulette" and asked "Who is first?" When he pulled the trigger, the gun discharged sending a "live" round into Darrin's chest. Darrin died as a result of the massive injuries.

Defendant was convicted after a bench trial and the Appellate Division unanimously affirmed, holding that the evidence was legally sufficient to establish defendant's guilt. In defendant's appeal, . . . we address only the central legal issue presented: sufficiency of the proof — i.e., "whether 'after viewing the evidence in the light most favorable to the prosecution, *any* rational trier of fact could have found

---

[1] Penal Law "§ 125.25 *Murder in the second degree.*

"A person is guilty of murder in the second degree when:

"2. Under circumstances evincing a depraved indifference to human life, he recklessly engages in conduct which creates a grave risk of death to another person, and thereby causes the death of another person."

the essential elements of the crime beyond a reasonable doubt.'" On our review of the record, we conclude, as did the Appellate Division, that the proof is legally sufficient. Accordingly, there should be an affirmance.

Preliminarily, it must be made clear that defendant does not challenge . . . the soundness of the policy underlying the legislative judgment in making persons 13, 14, or 15 years of age criminally responsible as adults for murder in the second degree under Penal Law § 125.25(1) and (2). Nevertheless, the dissenter expresses evident dissatisfaction with these legislative measures which, as interpreted, permit the "enormous penological regression" of charging, convicting and sentencing a 15 ½-year-old defendant, as an adult, for murder in the second degree. But whether . . . it is proper that a person under the age of 16 be held accountable as an adult for this specific crime . . . do[es] not pertain to the legal issue actually presented to us: is the evidence in this record sufficient to support the verdict under the legislative enactments applicable to the crime in question?

Before analyzing the evidence and its legal sufficiency, a brief examination of the crime of depraved indifference murder and its elements is instructive. Depraved indifference murder, like reckless manslaughter[,] is a *nonintentional* homicide. It differs from manslaughter, however, in that it must be shown that the actor's reckless conduct is imminently dangerous and presents a grave risk of death; in manslaughter, the conduct need only present the lesser "substantial risk" of death. Whether the lesser risk sufficient for manslaughter is elevated into the very substantial risk present in murder (*see*, LaFave & Scott, Criminal Law § 70, at 542) depends upon the wantonness of defendant's acts — i.e., whether they were committed "[u]nder circumstances evincing a depraved indifference to human life."

Generally, the assessment of the objective circumstances evincing the actor's "depraved indifference to human life" — i.e., those which elevate the risk to the gravity required for a murder conviction — is a qualitative judgment to be made by the trier of the facts. If there is evidence which supports the jury's determination, it is this court's obligation to uphold the verdict. Examples of conduct which have been held sufficient to justify a jury's finding of depraved indifference include: driving an automobile on a city sidewalk at excessive speeds and striking a pedestrian without applying the brakes; firing several bullets into a house; . . . and playing "Russian roulette" with one "live" shell in a six-cylinder gun.

With this background, we turn to the issue before us, now more fully stated: whether, viewing the evidence in the light most favorable to the People, any rational trier of the fact could have concluded that the objective circumstances surrounding defendant's reckless conduct so elevated the gravity of the risk created as to evince the depraved indifference to human life necessary to sustain the murder conviction. A brief summary of the evidence is necessary.

On the afternoon of August 14, 1984, the day of the shooting, defendant was at his home in the Village of Buchanan, Westchester County. There is uncontr[o]verted proof that defendant, who had completed his first year in high school, had an intense interest in and detailed knowledge of weapons, including firearms of various kinds.[5] He was familiar with his father's 12-gauge shotgun and, indeed, had cleaned it approximately 50 times. The cleaning process involved oiling the firing pin and pulling the trigger, using a "dummy" shell to avoid "dry firing" the weapon.[6]

At approximately 3:00 P.M., Darrin and his friend, Dennis Bleakley, also a 13-year old, stopped by to await the arrival of Darrin's older brother who was expected shortly. Defendant entertained the two boys by showing them his sawed-off shotgun, gravity knife, and Chuka sticks which he kept in a bag under his bed; he demonstrated how he assembled and disassembled the sawed-off shotgun.

Defendant then escorted Darrin and Dennis to his parents' room where he took out his father's 12-gauge shotgun. He asked Darrin to go back to his bedroom to get the five shotgun shells which were on the shelf. Defendant knew that three of these shells were "live" and two were "dummies." He randomly loaded four of the five shells into the magazine and pumped the shotgun, thereby placing one shell in the firing chamber. Because he loaded the magazine without any regard to the order in which the shells were inserted, he did not know if he had chambered a "live" or "dummy" round.

It was at this point, according to Dennis's testimony, that defendant raised the shotgun, pointed it directly at Darrin, and said "Let's play Polish roulette. Who is first?" He pulled the trigger discharging a "live" round which struck the 82-pound Darrin at close range. The shot created a gaping wound in Darrin's upper right chest, destroyed most of his shoulder, produced extensive damage to his lung, and eventually caused his death.

Defendant disputed this version of the incident. He testified that he had one foot on his parents' bed and was resting the butt of the gun on his inner thigh with the barrel pointing up and away from the victim. While he was demonstrating how the gun worked, he claimed, his foot slipped and the shotgun became airborne momentarily. Defendant testified that when he attempted to catch the gun, the butt kicked up under his armpit and he accidentally hit the trigger and discharged the gun.

The evidence . . . surrounding defendant's point-blank discharge of the shotgun is, in our view, sufficient to support a finding of the very serious risk of death required for depraved indifference murder. [W]ithout relevance are the dissent's references to defendant's claimed ignorance concerning the order in which cartridges, once loaded in the magazine, would enter the firing chamber. Such lack of knowledge can make no difference when, as is concededly the case here, the shooter knowingly loaded the mix of "live" and "dummy" cartridges with no regard to the order of their insertion into the magazine.

---

[5] In addition to proof that defendant had handled and used his sawed-off shotgun and his father's shotgun, the People introduced evidence that defendant had previously used a .22-caliber rifle, an air rifle, a .22-caliber air pistol, and a BB gun. Defendant had read magazine articles and books concerning guns, given several speeches in school about weapons, and drawn pictures of various guns. This evidence was admissible to prove recklessness — i.e., that defendant was aware of the risks involved — by showing that he was familiar with weapons in general and with this gun in particular.

[6] According to defendant, "dry firing" is releasing the firing pin when there is no cartridge in the chamber and nothing for the pin to strike against. To avoid the damage to the pin which "dry firing" can cause, "dummy" cartridges are used.

The comparable case here is not that of a person, uneducated in use of weapons, who, while playing with a gun that he does not know is loaded, accidentally discharges it; rather, the apt analogy is a macabre game of chance where the victim's fate — life or death — may be decreed by the flip of a coin or a roll of a die. It is no different where the odds are even that the shell pumped into the firing chamber of a 12-gauge shotgun is a "live" round, the gun is aimed at the victim standing close by, and the trigger is pulled (*see*, 2 LaFave & Scott, Substantive Criminal Law § 7.4, at 202 ["Russian roulette" with one "live" shell in a six-chamber gun is a classic example of depraved indifference murder]).

The sheer enormity of the act — putting another's life at such grave peril in this fashion — is not diminished because the sponsor of the game is a youth of 15. As in [*People v.*] *Register*, where bullets which might kill or seriously injure someone, or hit no one at all, were fired at random into a crowded bar, the imminent risk of death was present here. That in one case the gamble is that a bullet might not hit anyone and in the other that the gun might not fire is of no moment. In each case, the fact finder could properly conclude that the conduct was so wanton as to amount to depraved indifference to human life.

It is conceivable that another trier of fact hearing this evidence could have been persuaded to arrive at a different verdict. Our proper function on appeal, however, is vastly different from that of the prosecutor in determining which crimes to charge, [or] that of the Judge or jury in hearing the evidence and making factual conclusions[.] We do not find facts or exercise such discretion. Our sole authority is to review legal questions such as the one considered here: whether the evidence was legally insufficient. As to this question, we have little difficulty in concluding that the unanimous Appellate Division correctly held that the evidence was sufficient to support the verdict.

Accordingly, the order of the Appellate Division should be affirmed.

BELLACOSA, J. (dissenting).

I vote to reverse this conviction of a 15-year-old person for . . . depraved indifference murder. [U]ntil recently, persons under 16 years of age in this State were legal infants incapable of being convicted of *any* crime as an adult, no less of the prime, most heinous crime punishable under our law — murder.

One of the three definitions of murder in this State is recklessly engaging in conduct which creates a grave risk of death and causing the death of another under circumstances evincing a depraved indifference to human life. That is the one at issue in this case. Manslaughter, second degree, is defined as recklessly causing the death of another person.

While the tangible content of "depraved indifference to human life" is . . . elusive, the wantonness of the conduct augmenting the reckless culpable mental state must also manifest a level of callousness and extreme cruelty as to be "equal in blameworthiness to intentional murder."

## Prosecuting Juveniles as Adults

The defendant in *Roe* was 15, but he was prosecuted as an adult. The practice of prosecuting juveniles in adult court, and exposing them to adult penalties, has been the subject of criticism. From the establishment of juvenile courts until the 1970s, the prosecution of minors in adult court was quite rare. Between 1970 and the 2000s, however, laws providing for "automatic and prosecutor-controlled transfer [of juveniles to adult court] proliferated steadily." Office of Juvenile Justice and

Delinquency Prevention, U.S. Dep't of Justice, *Trying Juveniles as Adults: An Analysis of State Transfer and Reporting* 8 (2011).

Critics of the transfer of juveniles to adult court point to "widespread agreement among developmental psychologists" that adolescents "are more impulsive and less risk-averse" than adults, "more susceptible to the influence of peers," and "less able to represent the interests of others adequately." David O. Brink, *Immaturity, Normative Competence and Juvenile Transfer: How (Not) to Punish Minors for Major Crimes*, 82 Tex. L. Rev. 1555, 1571 (2004). Based in part on these concerns, the United States Supreme Court has held that imposing the death penalty or mandatory life without parole on juveniles constitutes cruel and unusual punishment in violation of the Eighth Amendment. See *Roper v. Simmons*, 543 U.S. 551 (2005); *Miller v. Alabama*, 567 U.S. 460 (2012). Apart from these limitations, states are mostly free to decide whether and when to subject juveniles to the same punishment as adults. When, if ever, do you think juveniles should be prosecuted as adults? Who do you think should make the decision about whether to charge a juvenile as an adult — a prosecutor, a court, the legislature, or some combination of the three?

The depraved indifference category of murder reflects the Legislature's policy refinement that there is a type of reckless homicide that is so horrendous as to qualify, in a legal fiction way, for blameworthiness in the same degree as the taking of another's life intentionally. Early cases reveal that the concept of "depraved mind" murder as an escalating factor emerged from this common-law notion and was applied in cases where, despite evidence that a defendant had no desire to kill, the conduct nonetheless demonstrated a substitutive aggravating "malice in the sense of a wicked disposition" (*see*, Gegan, *A Case of Depraved Mind Murder*, 49 St. John's L. Rev. 417, 423-27). Modern statutes have borrowed and recast the concept "of a wicked disposition" to speak in terms of "extreme indifference to the value of human life."

In this case, a 15-year-old person stands convicted of the tragic and senseless killing of the 13-year-old brother of his best friend. The shooting occurred around three o'clock in defendant's home on a summer afternoon. Thirteen-year-old Darrin Seifert and another youngster, Dennis Bleakley, went to defendant's home where they were invited to defendant's upstairs bedroom. They examined defendant's weapons collection, which included a sawed-off shotgun. After the weapons were returned to their storage places, defendant and his two companions walked down the hallway to defendant's parents' room where defendant removed a 12-gauge shotgun from a gun case. Defendant asked Darrin to retrieve some shotgun shells located on a shelf in defendant's room. Darrin and Dennis went to defendant's room and took five shells. Three were live ammunition and two were "dummies." Returning to the master bedroom, Darrin handed the shells to defendant, who proceeded to load the shotgun with four shells. Testimony established that defendant knew two of the shells he loaded into the gun were "live" and two

were "dummies." There was also conflicting testimony as to whether the defendant understood that the gun worked in such a manner that the first shell inserted into the gun would be the last fired from the gun or vice versa. The two police investigators testified that, shortly after the incident, defendant indicated he thought he had chambered a "dummy" shell and appeared stunned when he learned the gun operated on a "first in — last out" order of fire. Defendant contradicted this testimony when he testified he had not paid attention to the order in which he loaded the shells into the gun. Both theories, in any event, suggest only recklessness, not depravity.

Moreover, after loading the gun and while standing 10 feet away from the other two boys, defendant exclaimed, "Let's play Polish roulette. Who's first?" Defendant raised the shotgun, pointed it at his two companions and pulled the trigger. The gun fired a live shell which hit Darrin's right chest and shoulder area, knocking him to the floor. Defendant dropped the shotgun and ran over to Darrin, screaming, "Don't die. I killed my best friend's brother." He quickly directed Dennis to go downstairs to call an ambulance, which was done. A neighbor, hearing the shot, entered the house and ran upstairs. She observed defendant straddled over Darrin's body and heard him say, "Is he alright? Is he alright? Tell me." When the police arrived shortly thereafter, they observed the defendant pounding his fists against the wall, crying, "I can't believe I shot him. I can't believe I shot my best friend. Help, please, oh my God, help." The ambulance arrived and Darrin was taken to the hospital where he was pronounced dead on arrival.

The question is whether defendant's conduct "was of such gravity that it placed the crime upon the same level as the taking of life by premeditated design * * * [and whether] defendant's conduct, though reckless, was equal in blameworthiness to intentional murder."

I disagree that defendant's conduct qualifies for this lofty homicidal standard. He acted recklessly, of that there can be no doubt. He could also have been punished proportionately as an adult criminal, of that, too, there should not be any doubt. But the accusation and the conviction at the highest homicidal level, predicated on callous depravity and complete indifference to human life, are not supportable against this 15-year old on a sufficiency review and are starkly contradicted by the whole of the evidence adduced.

The testimony of the only other eyewitness, Dennis Bleakley, established that defendant was shaken and distraught immediately upon realizing that he had shot their companion. Defendant also immediately ran to his victim and instructed Dennis to call an ambulance; the neighbor testified that when she arrived on the scene, seconds after hearing the shot, defendant was kneeling over his friend's body and crying. Similarly, the police officer who arrived on the scene testified that defendant was extremely distraught and overcome with grief. This is not evidence beyond a reasonable doubt of that hardness of heart or that malignancy of attitude qualifying as "depraved indifference." Frankly, the evidence proves the opposite.

[U]nder the particular facts of this case, the conviction of this 15-year-old defendant for depraved indifference murder becomes even more unsettling because, prior to 1978, persons under the age of 16 were infants, legally presumed to be without capacity to commit any crime as an adult. Children under the age of 16, proven to have committed an act which if committed by an adult would be a crime, were up to then adjudicated juvenile delinquents in Family Court. In 1978, the Governor and Legislature, reacting to a particularly heinous criminal act by someone who would qualify only as a juvenile delinquent, carved out some narrow high level adult prosecution exceptions to the traditional infancy defense. After that date, persons aged 13 through 15 could be criminally responsible as adults for intentional and depraved indifference murder.

The majority avoids these objective realities and the inextricably intertwined statute, which could not be more self-evidently relevant to this adolescent defendant, even in the title of this criminal proceeding, by attributing to me a *sua sponte* injection of the issue into the case. They even imply that I question the wisdom of the Legislature's policy choice in enacting the juvenile offender law, which I surely do not. I question the injustice against this defendant in the application of that exceptional authorization for this depraved indifference case, within the framework of this court's traditional review role. The notion that our review power should be so "scientific" and "mechanical" should be repulsed.

**Post-Case Follow-Up**

*Roe* involves a paradigmatic example of depraved heart murder. The majority defines depraved heart murder as reckless conduct that "presents a grave risk of death," in contrast to reckless manslaughter, which only involves a "substantial risk of death." In addition to this description, the court defines depraved heart murder by analogy, citing as examples intentionally driving a car onto a city sidewalk at an excessive speed, firing several bullets into a house, and, finally, playing Russian roulette. All of this is representative of how most jurisdictions approach depraved heart murder. Complications arise, however, when facts fall outside of these classic examples. How much leeway should juries have to determine the difference between "grave" and "substantial" risks on a case-by-case basis? On this point, there is much more diversity from state to state.

## Roe: *Real Life Applications*

1. You are the law clerk, working for a judge who presides over your state's commission on uniform jury instructions. The commission is in the process of revising your state's jury instruction on depraved heart murder. How would you define depraved heart murder in a jury instruction? Do you think it would be helpful to juries if examples like the ones the court provided in *Roe* were part of the jury instruction?

2. In cases like *Roe*, where the facts could plausibly fit more than one offense, a prosecutor's charging decision is especially important. If you were the prosecutor in *Roe*, would you have charged the defendant with murder? Or would you have exercised your discretion to charge the defendant with reckless manslaughter instead? What considerations would you have taken into account to guide your decision?

## 2. Involuntary (Reckless) Manslaughter

Not all reckless killings rise to the level of murder. Reckless killings that are not murder are usually referred to as **reckless manslaughter** or **involuntary manslaughter**.

Both involuntary manslaughter and depraved heart murder (presented in the subsection immediately above) involve unintentional killings where the perpetrator disregards a known risk. So what separates the two offenses? According to *People v. Roe*, 74 N.Y.2d 20 (1989), the difference lies in "the wantonness of defendant's acts — i.e., whether they were committed '[u]nder circumstances evincing a depraved indifference to human life.'" But the "wantonness" of a defendant's acts — the social utility of a defendant's acts and the severity of the risk of death they present — is a matter of degree. At one end of the spectrum are noncriminal accidents where an act that is not especially risky tragically causes death — a line drive baseball that strikes another player in the head, killing him, for example. At the other end of the spectrum are acts that pose a grave risk of death, such as the defendant's acts in *Roe*. Involuntary manslaughter punishes unintentional killings that involve ordinary recklessness, which falls somewhere in between these two extremes.

Recall that the Model Penal Code provides the following definition of recklessness:

> A person acts recklessly with respect to a material element of an offense when he consciously disregards a substantial and unjustifiable risk that the material element exists or will result from his conduct. The risk must be of such a nature and degree that, considering the nature and purpose of the actor's conduct and the circumstances known to him, its disregard involves a gross deviation from the standard of conduct that a law-abiding person would observe in the actor's situation.

Model Penal Code § 2.02(2)(c). Most jurisdictions follow this definition of recklessness or use one that is very similar.

## Case Preview

### State v. Janklow

A recurring issue in involuntary manslaughter cases is the degree of risk necessary to constitute recklessness. Riskiness is one of the key factors that differentiates depraved heart murder from reckless manslaughter, and reckless manslaughter from non-criminal accidental death. In *State v. Janklow*, the Supreme Court of South Dakota considered a defendant's sufficiency of the evidence challenge to his conviction for involuntary manslaughter. The defendant, who was a congressman and former governor, ran through a stop sign at a high rate of speed and struck a motorcyclist, killing him. On appeal, Janklow argued that "the State only established that he ran a stop sign" and that this did not present a significant enough risk to constitute recklessness. In addition, Janklow claimed there was insufficient evidence that he consciously disregarded the risk (at trial, he testified he did not intentionally run the stop sign).

As you read the case, consider the following questions:

1. Recklessness requires a person to consciously disregard a substantial and unjustifiable risk. As you read the opinion, consider each of these

components — substantial risk, unjustifiable risk, and conscious disregard — separately. Does the court's opinion do a good job at separating one from another in its analysis?

2. Every year, tens of thousands of people die in car crashes in the United States (36,560 in 2018). Based on the court's decision, how would you define the point at which a traffic violation is sufficiently risky to constitute recklessness?

3. The court notes in its opinion that the standard of review on appeal "is not whether we would have reached the same verdict, but whether the 'evidence was sufficient to sustain the convictions.'" If you were a juror, based on the court's recitation of the facts, would you have voted to convict?

---

## *State v. Janklow*
### 2005 SD 25

Severson, J.

William J. Janklow (Janklow) appeals from a jury verdict finding him guilty of . . . [involuntary] manslaughter for a[] . . . collision which killed Randolph Scott (Scott). We affirm.

On August 16, 2003, Janklow was driving a white Cadillac south on Moody County Highway 13. He was traveling from Aberdeen, South Dakota to his home in Brandon, South Dakota after giving a speech at a county fair.[1] Janklow's chief of staff, Chris Braendlin (Braendlin) was a passenger in the vehicle. Meanwhile, fifty-five year old Scott and his friend, Terry Johnson (Johnson), were riding their motorcycles westbound on Moody County Highway 14.

Highways 13 and 14 intersect ten miles south of Flandreau, South Dakota. The intersection is controlled by stop signs for north- and southbound traffic on Highway 13. The east- and westbound traffic on Highway 14 does not have a stop sign at that intersection. The speed limit on both highways is 55 miles per hour. A corn field located northeast of the intersection blocked the view for southbound and westbound motorists approaching the intersection.

Approximately three or four miles north of the intersection, Janklow passed another vehicle traveling south on Highway 13. The driver of that vehicle testified that she was traveling approximately 55 to 60 miles per hour when she was passed by Janklow. She testified that, "he passed me as if I was standing still. I felt like I was parked on the side of the road and the car just went past real fast." At approximately 4:40 P.M., Janklow's southbound vehicle and the westbound motorcycles ridden by Scott and Johnson converged at the intersection. Johnson safely passed through the intersection approximately 50 yards ahead of Scott. Scott's motorcycle hit the side of Janklow's vehicle. Scott was thrown from his motorcycle and was pronounced dead at the scene. Janklow's vehicle came to a stop in the soybean field approximately

---

[1] Janklow was a United States Congressman at the time of the collision. Prior to being elected to the United States House of Representatives, Janklow was the Governor of South Dakota for four terms from 1979 to 1987 and 1995 to 2003.

285 feet south of the intersection. There was extensive damage to the side and rear portion of Janklow's vehicle.

Janklow was charged in Moody County with . . . manslaughter. A jury trial commenced on December 1, 2003, in Flandreau. Janklow did not dispute that he failed to stop at the stop sign, nor did he dispute that he was driving in excess of the speed limit. However, there was conflicting testimony at trial as to his actual speed at the point of impact. The State's expert estimated that Janklow was traveling 71 miles per hour and Scott was traveling 59 miles per hour at the point of impact. Janklow's expert calculated Janklow's speed at 63 to 64 miles per hour at the point of impact.

In his defense, Janklow asserted that he was suffering from hypoglycemia at the time of the collision and did not consciously run the stop sign.

Several witnesses testified that immediately after the collision Janklow said that he went through the intersection because he was trying to avoid hitting a white car. Because the accident involved a fatality, law enforcement asked Janklow for a blood sample to determine his blood alcohol level.[2] South Dakota Highway Trooper Jeff Lanning (Trooper Lanning) transported Janklow to the Flandreau hospital for the blood draw. The video camera in Trooper Lanning's patrol car recorded, with Janklow's knowledge, their conversation during the drive. The video was played for the jury at trial. On the tape, Janklow described approaching the intersection and slowing down for the stop sign when a white car came toward him from the east. Janklow told Trooper Lanning that he "gunned it" to avoid being hit by the white car and that he initially thought he had been hit by the white car. Eyewitnesses reported that the white car Janklow described was not in the intersection at the time of the collision.

On December 8, 2003, the jury returned [a] guilty verdict[]. Pursuant to SDCL 23A-27-13, the trial court granted a suspended imposition of sentence on the second degree manslaughter charge.*

Janklow argues that the trial court erred in denying his motion for judgment of acquittal because the State failed to present sufficient evidence to establish beyond a reasonable doubt that he was guilty of [involuntary] manslaughter.

The standard of review for denial of a motion for judgment of acquittal is whether the "evidence was sufficient to sustain the convictions." "A guilty verdict will not be set aside if the state's evidence and all favorable inferences that can be drawn therefrom support a rational theory of guilt."

Janklow was charged with [involuntary] manslaughter in violation of SDCL 22-16-20. That statute provides:

Any reckless killing of one human being, including an unborn child, by the act or procurement of another which, under the provisions of this chapter, is neither murder nor manslaughter in the first degree, nor excusable nor justifiable homicide, is manslaughter in the second degree. Manslaughter in the second degree is a Class 4 felony.

---

[2] Testing indicated that there was no alcohol present in Janklow's blood.

* Janklow was sentenced to three years of probation and 100 days in county jail. The grant of a suspended imposition meant that after successfully completing his term of probation, Janklow's record of conviction would be sealed. See P.J. Huffstutter, 'Remorseful' Janklow Gets 100 Days in Jail, L.A. Times, Jan. 23, 2004. [Footnote by casebook author.]

The State had the burden of proving that Janklow recklessly killed Randolph Scott. SDCL 22-1-2(1)(d) defines "reckless" as:

(1) If applied to the intent with which an act is done or omitted:

(d) The words "reckless, recklessly" and all derivatives thereof, import a conscious and unjustifiable disregard of a substantial risk that the offender's conduct may cause a certain result or may be of a certain nature. A person is reckless with respect to circumstances when he consciously and unjustifiably disregards a substantial risk that such circumstances may exist[.]

"[F]or someone's conduct to be deemed reckless, they must consciously disregard a substantial risk." "Recklessness requires more than ordinary negligent conduct." "The difference between reckless behavior and negligent behavior is primarily measured by the state of mind of the individual." "The reckless actor is *aware* of the risk and disregards it; the negligent actor is *not aware* of the risk but should have been aware of it."

Janklow argues that the State only established that he ran a stop sign. "However, the operation of a motor vehicle in violation of the law is not in and of itself sufficient to constitute reckless conduct, even if a person is killed as a result thereof." "Criminal responsibility for death resulting from the operation of a motor vehicle in violation of the law will result only if the violation is done in such a manner as to evidence a reckless disregard for the safety of others." "Mere carelessness or inadvertence or thoughtless omission is insufficient."

The State argues that the risk that Janklow disregarded was the potential harm arising out of his speeding through a blind intersection without stopping. "Although it is not always possible for the State to directly establish that a defendant was aware of a risk, it can be done indirectly through the defendant's conduct." The State maintains that Janklow's disregard for the safety of others and his indifference to the consequences of his actions were demonstrated by his conduct of speeding through a stop sign at a blind intersection of two highways without stopping or looking for oncoming traffic.

[T]his Court cannot say as a matter of law that Janklow's conduct did not constitute recklessness. Reasonable minds could differ as to this issue. In reviewing the denial of a motion for judgment of acquittal, this Court accepts "the evidence and the most favorable inferences that the jury might have fairly drawn from the evidence to support the verdict." The State presented evidence that Janklow was speeding prior to the collision and passed a vehicle before the intersection at a high rate of speed. Although they disagreed as to the precise speed, both the State's expert and Janklow's expert calculated that Janklow was exceeding the 55 mph speed limit for the highway. The intersection where the collision occurred was a blind intersection due to a corn field blocking Janklow's vision to the east. The State presented evidence that Janklow was familiar with this intersection and was aware of the stop sign. There was a "stop ahead" sign warning of the stop sign at the intersection. Evidence was also presented that Janklow indicated immediately after the accident that he was slowing down for the stop sign, but went through the stop sign because of a white car in his lane. However, eyewitnesses refuted Janklow's statements regarding a white car. Janklow's passenger, Braendlin, testified that he recalled Janklow yelling a warning just before the collision. "[I]t is the function of the jury in resolving factual conflicts, to weigh the credibility of those who testify, and ascertain the truth." Our standard of review is not whether we would have reached the same verdict, but whether the "evidence was sufficient to sustain the convictions." There was sufficient evidence from which the jury could conclude that Janklow was aware of, yet disregarded, the risk of an accident occurring as a result of his conduct. Therefore, the trial court did not err in denying Janklow's motion for judgment of acquittal.

Affirmed.

**EXHIBIT 5.2** William Janklow (Center) Leaving the Courthouse After the Jury's Guilty Verdict

**Post-Case Follow-Up**

*Janklow* concerns the all-too-common scenario of a car crash that resulted in death. The court's statement that "operating a motor vehicle in violation of the law is not in and of itself sufficient to constitute reckless conduct" is in line with how most jurisdictions approach this issue. In this case, there was evidence of much more than a common traffic violation — the defendant sped through a stop sign at a blind intersection on a highway. Most courts would find this evidence sufficient to sustain a conviction. But, of course, this does not mean all juries would convict on these facts. When it comes to evaluating whether a defendant's actions are sufficiently dangerous to constitute a substantial risk, the law can only provide so much guidance. The definition of recklessness necessarily calls for jurors to use their judgment on the question of which risks are substantial and which are not.

### Brasse v. State

In *Janklow*, in addition to challenging the severity of the risk, the defendant argued that there was insufficient evidence he was *aware* of the risk. The court rejected this argument, citing evidence that Janklow said he had driven through the stop sign because a white car was in his lane but eyewitnesses said there was no white car. The next case, *Brasse*, also addresses whether there was sufficient evidence of a defendant's awareness of a risk. But in this case, the defendant prevails.

As you read the opinion, consider the following questions:

1. The court finds that there was insufficient evidence the defendant was aware of a substantial risk of death. What sort of evidence, if any, do you think would have been sufficient in this case to prove the defendant was aware of, but consciously disregarded, a substantial risk?

2. In addition to challenging the sufficiency of the evidence that he was aware of the risk, the defendant argued there was insufficient evidence that his conduct was not a gross deviation from the standard of care that an ordinary person would exercise under all the circumstances. Because the court found there was insufficient evidence the defendant was aware of the risk, it did not need to reach his "gross deviation" argument. As you read the facts, ask whether you think there was sufficient evidence that his conduct was a gross deviation from the standard of care an ordinary person would have exercised. What factors would play into your analysis of that issue?

---

## Brasse v. State
### 392 S.W.3d 239 (Tex. App. 2012)

SIMMONS, J.

Eight-year-old Sarah Brasse reported to the school nurse complaining of a stomach ache. After sending Sarah back to class twice, the school nurse called Sarah's father, David Brasse, and Sarah's stepmother, Samantha Amity Britain. Britain picked Sarah up from school and took her home. Sarah began vomiting that evening and her brother testified he heard her vomit three times. Brasse left for work very early the next morning. Sarah stayed home from school with Britain. Sarah continued to vomit during the day and although she drank fluids she did not eat. Sarah's brother checked on her when he arrived home from school and covered her with a blanket. She died shortly thereafter from complications arising from appendicitis. Because the chronology of events is important in determining the sufficiency of the evidence, a table referencing the evidence is provided below.

| Date | Time | Event |
|------|------|-------|
| 2/4/08 | Approximately 8:15 A.M. | Sarah goes to her school nurse with a "tummy ache." Nurse sends Sarah back to class. |
| 2/4/08 | Approximately 9:15 A.M. | Sarah, still not feeling well, returns to nurse's office. Nurse sends Sarah back to class. |
| 2/4/08 | Approximately 10:50 A.M. | Sarah, tearful, returns to the nurse's office saying that her tummy hurts and she is not feeling well. The nurse checks her temperature, listens to her bowel sounds, palpates her abdomen, and checks her vital signs. The examination is normal. Because it is Sarah's third visit and she is crying, the nurse calls Britain and Brasse to pick Sarah up from school. |
| 2/4/08 | Approximately 12:00 P.M. | Britain picks Sarah up from school. Sarah is feeling better and runs to hug Britain. |
| 2/4/08 | Evening hours | Sarah vomits for the first time. Brasse is unsure whether Sarah ate her dinner. |
| 2/4/08 | Throughout the night | Sarah's brother hears her vomit three times during the night. |
| 2/5/08 | 4:30 A.M. | Brasse departs for work, leaving Sarah in Britain's care. |
| 2/5/08 | 7:05 A.M. | Sarah is still not feeling well so Britain keeps her home from school. |
| 2/5/08 | Throughout the day | Sarah vomits four to five times, develops diarrhea, and is unable to eat. |
| 2/5/08 | Approximately 4:00 P.M. | Sarah's brother checks on her when he returns home from school. |
| 2/5/08 | Approximately 5:00 P.M. | Sarah's brother takes her water. Sarah says she is cold so he covers her with a blanket. |
| 2/5/08 | Approximately 6:00 P.M. | Britain checks on Sarah; Sarah is dead. |
| 2/5/08 | Between 7:00 P.M. and 8:00 P.M. | Brasse tells Michelle Garcia, his co-worker, that he believed Sarah was sick with a stomach virus that he and Britain had the week before and he could not understand how she died. |

In his first point of error, Brasse challenges the legal sufficiency of the evidence supporting his conviction for [involuntary] manslaughter because (1) he was not aware of a substantial and unjustifiable risk that Sarah would be seriously injured or would die, and (2) his failure to seek medical treatment was not a gross deviation from the standard of care that an ordinary person would exercise under all of the circumstances as viewed from his standpoint.

In reviewing the legal sufficiency of the evidence, we must view "the evidence in the light most favorable to the prosecution" and determine whether "any rational trier of fact could have found the essential elements of the crime beyond a reasonable doubt."

A person commits the offense of [involuntary] manslaughter "if he recklessly causes the death of an individual." Tex. Penal Code Ann. § 19.04 (West 2011). Manslaughter is a result-oriented offense — the defendant's culpable mental state must relate to the result of his or her conduct.

"A person acts recklessly . . . when he is aware of but consciously disregards a substantial and unjustifiable risk that the circumstances exist or the result will occur." The risk created "must be of such a nature and degree that its disregard constitutes a gross deviation from the standard of care that an ordinary person would exercise under all the circumstances as viewed from the actor's standpoint." "[D]etermining whether an act or omission involves a substantial and unjustifiable risk 'requires an examination of the events and circumstances from the viewpoint of the defendant at the time the events occurred, without viewing the matter in hindsight.'" "'[M]ere lack of foresight, stupidity, irresponsibility, thoughtlessness, ordinary carelessness, however serious the consequences may happen to be,'" does not rise to the level of criminal recklessness.

Because the requisite mental state for manslaughter is criminal recklessness, we review the record for evidence that Brasse was subjectively aware of a substantial and unjustifiable risk that Sarah would die without medical treatment. The State argues Brasse should have known his failure to seek medical treatment for Sarah would create a substantial and unjustifiable risk of her death. This confuses the requisite mental states of criminal recklessness and criminal negligence. Criminal recklessness, the mens rea for the offense of [involuntary] manslaughter requires that the defendant possess a subjective and actual awareness of a substantial and unjustifiable risk. Compared to criminal recklessness, criminal negligence requires a less culpable mental state — the defendant should have known or "ought to be aware" of such risk. In our review, we consider the evidence "in the light most favorable to the prosecution" and determine whether any rational trier of fact could have found that Brasse was actually and subjectively aware that his failure to seek medical attention for Sarah created a substantial risk that she would die.

The record indicates that when Brasse left work at 4:30 A.M. on February 5th, he was aware that Sarah visited the school nurse three times the previous day complaining of a stomach ache and was sent home from school, and that she vomited before she went to bed. Brasse was unsure whether Sarah ate dinner that evening. No evidence indicates he knew Sarah vomited several times during the night of February 4th or that he was apprised of any additional information about her condition at any point after he left for work at 4:30 A.M. but before her death on February 5th. The State asks us to infer that Brasse knew Sarah vomited several times throughout the night because her brother heard her. However, there is nothing in the record that permits the jury to draw this inference. The State fails to offer any argument as to how a rational jury could have appropriately concluded that

Brasse was aware of the substantial risk of death based on the evidence presented. Although the jury is permitted to draw appropriate conclusions and inferences from the evidence, it was not rational for the jury to conclude the requisite knowledge based on the record before us.

Reviewing the evidence in the light most favorable to the jury's verdict, we nevertheless conclude that the evidence is legally insufficient for the jury to have found that Brasse was subjectively aware of and consciously disregarded a substantial and unjustifiable risk that Sarah would die if she did not receive medical treatment.

Because we conclude the evidence is legally insufficient on an essential element of manslaughter, Brasse's additional points of error are rendered moot and we need not address them.

We reverse the trial court's judgment of conviction for manslaughter and render a judgment of acquittal.

**Post-Case Follow-Up**

*Brasse* highlights the critical element that distinguishes recklessness from criminal negligence: awareness of the risk. As the court explains, recklessness "requires that the defendant possess a subjective and actual awareness of a substantial and unjustifiable risk" whereas negligence requires only that the defendant "should have known or 'ought to be aware' of such risk." In what may have been a sign of the weakness of the prosecution's case, the State appears to have tried to muddy the waters between the two standards in its appellate briefing by arguing that "Brasse should have known his failure to seek medical treatment for Sarah would create a substantial and unjustifiable risk of her death." The court rightly rejected the government's position on the law. With respect to the facts, the court convincingly pointed out that there was no evidence that Brasse knew anything about his daughter's condition during the night of February 4 and the day of February 5. Even if Brasse had known more about his daughter's condition during that period of time — if Brasse had known that she had vomited three times during the night and five times throughout the day — do you think that would have been sufficient evidence to sustain a conviction?

## Janklow *and* Brasse: *Real Life Applications*

1. One morning, Darrell was driving in rural Utah when he saw a 42-inch long rattlesnake by the side of the road. Darrell stopped his car and used a tire iron to put the snake into a bag. Darrell put the bag in his car and drove back home, where he lived with his girlfriend, Jeri Ann, and her 2-year-old daughter Stevie. After exiting the car, Darrell put the snake around his neck and went inside the house. Once inside, Darrell was confronted by Jeri Ann, who told Darrell to leave immediately. Instead, Darrell kissed the snake's head and then teased Jeri Ann with the snake in an attempt to get her to touch it. In response, Jeri Ann

warned Darrell that the snake was dangerous and demanded that he take the snake outside. Darrell told Jeri Ann she was overacting. He kissed the snake's head and went to the other room where Stevie was playing with her cat. Darrell snuck up behind Stevie and draped the snake's tail over Stevie's shoulder. At this point, Darrell was holding the snake four or five inches below its head. Stevie screamed. Darrell tried to remove the snake from Stevie's shoulder. In the process, he lost his grip on the snake's head and the snake bit Stevie on her neck. Darrell flung the snake across the room and began trying to suck the venom out of the wound on Stevie's neck. Jeri Ann came into the room and called 911. Stevie died a few hours later at the hospital.

a. You are the prosecutor assigned to the case. Would you charge Darrell with depraved heart murder, involuntary manslaughter, or negligent homicide?

b. Staying in the role of the prosecutor, assume for purposes of this question that you decided to charge Darrell with involuntary manslaughter. At trial, the only contested issue in the case is whether or not Darrell was aware of the risk posed by his actions. You are preparing for closing arguments. What facts would you direct the jury's attention to in order to try to demonstrate Darrell's awareness of the risk?

c. Now, imagine you are Darrell's attorney. You are preparing for closing arguments. What facts would you direct the jury's attention to in order to try to raise a reasonable doubt as to whether Darrell was aware of the risk posed by his actions?

## 3. Negligent Homicide

The crime of negligent homicide punishes killings in cases where the perpetrator was criminally negligent. Recall that the Model Panel Code provides this definition for negligence:

> A person acts negligently with respect to a material element of an offense when he should be aware of a substantial and unjustifiable risk that the material element exists or will result from his conduct. The risk must be of such a nature and degree that the actor's failure to perceive it, considering the nature and purpose of his conduct and the circumstances known to him, involves a gross deviation from the standard of care that a reasonable person would observe in the actor's situation.

Model Penal Code § 2.02(2)(d).

As we have already seen, recklessness and criminal negligence are very similar mental states. But there is one significant difference between the two: the defendant's awareness of the risk. A defendant who is truly unaware of a risk has not acted recklessly, no matter how grave the risk. This fact distinguishes negligent homicide from *both* depraved heart murder and involuntary manslaughter. In theory, a defendant who kills another person while playing Russian roulette and is *genuinely unaware* that playing Russian roulette is risky would be guilty of only negligent homicide. Of course, in practice, people are exceedingly unlikely to be blind to the risks posed by something as dangerous as playing Russian roulette. In cases that involve less risky conduct, by contrast, naivety, wishful thinking, or some other factor can often leave a person genuinely unaware of the risks.

## Case Preview

## *People v. Cabrera*

An actor's awareness of a substantial risk separates reckless-ness from criminal negligence. But what distinguishes crimi-nal negligence from civil negligence? *People v. Cabrera* raises this question in the context of a car crash that resulted from a 17-year-old driver speeding toward a curve.

As you read the opinion, consider the following questions:

1. According to the court, what differentiates civil negligence from criminal negligence?
2. What do you think the court means by "seriously blameworthy" carelessness? How is the concept of blameworthy carelessness different from the conscious disregard of a risk that gives rise to recklessness?
3. What role, if any, do you think the defendant's age and inexperience as a driver played in the court's decision?

## *People v. Cabrera*
### 10 N.Y.3d 370 (2008)

READ, J.

Late in the afternoon on a bright, summery June day in 2004, a group of Sullivan County youths set out for a local lake to go swimming. They piled into two vehicles to make the trip. One was operated by 19-year-old Monica Mendoza, with her younger sister as a passenger; the other, by defendant Brett Cabrera, a 17 year old with a junior "class DJ" license. Cabrera was driving his parents' 2004 Mercury Mountaineer, a midsized SUV; the Mountaineer had no mechanical defects and nearly new tires. Cabrera was transporting four teenage passengers; none were fam-ily members.

Cabrera's junior license imposed several restrictions: as relevant here, the holder of a class DJ license, which "shall *automatically* become a [normal, unre-stricted noncommercial] license when the holder becomes eighteen years of age," may not operate a vehicle with more than two passengers under 21 years of age who are not members of the junior licensee's immediate family, and must ensure that all passengers have buckled their seat belts. But on this trip to the lake, none of Cabrera's four passengers — a 14 year old, a 15 year old, a 17 year old and an 18 year old — wore a seat belt. Cabrera himself did.

Because she did not know the way to the lake, Monica followed Cabrera. They were driving "at the same speed" and it was, in Monica's estimation, "a reasonable speed," perhaps 40 miles per hour. She also, however, stated that her mind was so "blurry" that she "really never knew how fast [they] were going."

Cabrera and Monica eventually turned onto Sackett Lake Road, where the posted speed limit was 55 miles per hour. At a point where the roadway curved to the right, Monica "slowed down" her car because she was "not always used to driving" that type of hilly, winding road. When she reduced her speed, Cabrera "just kept on the same speed[,] so he pulled away . . . from [her] a little . . . [b]ecause [she] slowed down." But "by the time [Monica] was getting into" a second curve (presumably the curve to the left before the accident scene), she "just saw the back of the car [Cabrera was driving] . . . and then [she] lost" sight of it "for . . . a second or two and then when [she] saw the car again[,] it was just . . . losing control . . . going to the side of the road" before crashing. Three of the passengers in the Cabrera vehicle died in this accident, and one was critically injured. Cabrera suffered noncritical injuries. He tested free of drugs and alcohol.

Santiago Mendoza, the only surviving passenger in Cabrera's vehicle, testified at trial about "[w]hat was going on in [Cabrera's] car" leading up to the accident. The passengers were talking amongst themselves and listening to rap music; they were not interacting with Cabrera. When asked what Cabrera was doing, Santiago answered simply: "Driving." Asked by the prosecutor if "there [was] any conversation in the car about how fast or speed . . . or anything about that," he answered "No." Indeed, the first time Santiago noticed anything distinctive about Cabrera's driving was when he "felt the car lose control" and "felt the back end slide . . . [and] hit the dirt on the opposite side of the road."

According to Deputy Sheriff Amanda Cox, the first quarter of a mile or so on the stretch of Sackett Lake Road leading to the accident scene is flat or uphill; the road crests and goes down along a straightaway past a turnoff. The road then goes up slightly before bending to the left and sloping downhill. At the bottom of this descent is a dip in the road before it starts back uphill and slants to the right; the accident occurred "right at the dip."

There is a "40 mph curve" sign near the point at which Sackett Lake Road veers left into the downhill slope. When Cabrera's vehicle went off the left-hand side of the road, it slid down a 25-to-30-foot embankment. Deputy Cox knew of other accidents at this location. Similarly, Detective Don Starner had "investigated several accidents . . . most of them caused by either speed and or alcohol" on Sackett Lake Road near the crash site.

Trooper Shane Conklin, a collision reconstructionist for the New York State Police . . . [determined that] tire marks from the Cabrera vehicle were made by "critical speed yaw." This occurs when a vehicle begins spinning on its central axis and the tires are "side slipping" while rotating; in other words, the tire marks were caused by the vehicle as it spun out of control, not by skidding upon braking.

Trooper Conklin ultimately concluded that Cabrera's "vehicle was attempting to negotiate the curve at a speed that was too great to be negotiated . . . [a]nd the speed was between 70 and 72 miles an hour," causing the SUV to enter into critical speed yaw. He observed that once a critical speed yaw is entered, "it is very difficult to bring the car back under control."

Cabrera was charged with three counts of criminally negligent homicide.

The jury convicted Cabrera on all counts and the trial judge sentenced him to the maximum term allowed by statute — an aggregate term of 1⅓ to 4 years in prison — and fined him $800. Cabrera was then remanded to the custody of the New York State Department of Correctional Services, and served out his sentence in a maximum security prison.

The Appellate Division, three-two, affirmed the conviction, with one of the two dissenting justices granting Cabrera leave to appeal to us. Cabrera . . . [argues] that the evidence adduced at trial was insufficient as a matter of law to sustain his convictions for criminally negligent homicide.

"A person is guilty of criminally negligent homicide when, with criminal negligence, he causes the death of another person" (Penal Law § 125.10). Since . . . Cabrera "cause[d] the death of" three of his passengers insofar as he may have been criminally negligent, the parties contest only whether he acted with the requisite mens rea. Under section 15.05 (4) of the Penal Law,

"[a] person acts with criminal negligence with respect to a result . . . when he fails to perceive a substantial and unjustifiable risk that such result will occur or that such circumstance exists. The risk must be of such nature and degree that the failure to perceive it constitutes a gross deviation from the standard of care that a reasonable person would observe in the situation."

We have examined section 15.05 (4) in detail on numerous occasions, most recently in *People v Conway* (6 NY3d 869 [2006]). There, we explained that "the carelessness required for criminal negligence is appreciably more serious than that for ordinary civil negligence, and that the carelessness must be such that its *seriousness would be apparent to anyone who shares the community's general sense of right and wrong*."

In 1990, . . . we decided two companion cases involving criminally negligent homicide arising out of automobile accidents: *People v Boutin* (75 NY2d 692 [1990]) and *People v Paul V.S.* (75 NY2d 944 [1990]). In *Boutin*, we reversed a conviction for criminally negligent homicide where the defendant — traveling near, and possibly under, the speed limit — struck a marked police car stopped in the right-hand travel lane of Interstate 87 on a rainy, foggy night. In *Paul V.S.*, decided in a memorandum the same day as *Boutin*, we affirmed a conviction for criminally negligent homicide where the defendant was traveling 90 miles per hour in a 55 miles per hour "radar zone," accelerated after being warned by his passenger to slow down, continued past a line of cars that had been stopped by police, and ultimately struck and killed a state trooper attempting to direct him off the highway.

When discussing our precedents in *Boutin*, we observed that the common thread was the "creation," rather than the "nonperception," of risk. *Boutin* implicated noncriminal "risk nonperception" because the defendant had simply "fail[ed] to see the vehicle stopped in the lane ahead of him[,] result[ing] in the fatal accident." This was to be distinguished from cases where there was "criminally culpable risk-creating conduct — e.g., *dangerous* speeding, racing, failure to obey traffic signals, *or* any other misconduct that created or contributed to a 'substantial and unjustifiable' risk of death."

In short, it takes some additional affirmative act by the defendant to transform "speeding" into "dangerous speeding"; conduct by which the defendant exhibits the kind of "serious[ly] blameworth[y]" carelessness whose "seriousness would be apparent to anyone who shares the community's general sense of right and wrong." Thus, in the cases where we have considered the evidence sufficient to establish criminally negligent homicide, the defendant has engaged in some other "risk-creating" behavior in addition to driving faster than the posted speed limit (*compare People v Haney*, 30 NY2d 328 [1972] [defendant was speeding on city street and failed to stop at red light before killing pedestrian crossing street with green light in her favor] *with People v Perry*, 123 AD2d 492, 493 [4th Dept 1986] [no criminal negligence present where defendant was driving approximately 80 miles per hour in a 55 miles per hour zone "on a rural road, on a dark night," struck a utility pole, and killed two passengers; defendant's "conduct . . . d(id) not constitute a gross deviation from the ordinary standard of care held by those who share the community's general sense of right and wrong"]).

[In this case, t]here was testimony and forensic evidence that Cabrera, a young and inexperienced but sober driver, entered a tricky downhill curve, the site of other accidents, at a rate of speed well in excess of the posted warning sign. This behavior is certainly negligent, and unquestionably "blameworthy." But our decisions have uniformly looked for some kind of morally blameworthy component to excessive speed in determining criminal negligence; for example, consciously accelerating in the presence of an obvious risk. No such morally blameworthy behavior could be inferred from the testimony in this case. For a 17 year old to badly misgauge his ability to handle road conditions is not the kind of seriously condemnatory behavior that the Legislature envisioned when it defined "criminal negligence," even though the consequences here were fatal. This crash resulted from noncriminal failure to perceive risk; it was not the result of criminal risk creation.

Next, at the time of the accident, Cabrera was transporting more than two teenagers who were nonfamily members, and his passengers were not wearing seat belts. The Legislature adopted a graduated licensing scheme to reduce the level of teen automobile crashes — the leading cause of death among teenagers — by making full driver's licensing privileges contingent upon a period of safe driving during which various restrictions apply, including those limiting the number of minor passengers who are nonfamily members and requiring the wearing of seat belts. Yet even if . . . New York's graduated licensing scheme was meant to reduce the likelihood of "risky driving behavior to impress peers," Santiago Mendoza's trial testimony does not support the inference that Cabrera was showing off or was distracted by conversation with his passengers in the moments prior to the accident.

In sum, even when viewed in the light most favorable to the People, the evidence adduced at Cabrera's trial was insufficient as a matter of law to sustain his convictions for criminally negligent homicide.

GRAFFEO, J. (dissenting).

Not surprisingly, a number of our precedents addressing the legal sufficiency of convictions predicated on criminal negligence involve automobile accidents. As recounted by the majority, we have repeatedly determined that excessive speed, when coupled with some other culpable conduct — such as drag racing, driving the wrong way or running a red light — constitutes legally sufficient evidence. In this regard, we have indicated that sufficiently criminal, culpable risk-creating conduct may include "dangerous speeding, racing, failure to obey traffic signals, or any other misconduct that created or contributed to a 'substantial and unjustifiable' risk of death."

The issue in this case is whether defendant possessed the requisite mens rea of criminal negligence at the time he lost control of his vehicle.

It is well established that, in cases where criminal negligence is at issue, the jury "must evaluate the actor's failure of perception and determine whether, under *all* the circumstances, it was serious enough to be condemned." In other words, a determination of what amounts to criminal negligence depends "entirely on the circumstances of the particular conduct." Relatedly, we have recognized that criminally negligent homicide "serves to provide an offense applicable to conduct which is obviously socially undesirable. It proscribes conduct which is inadvertent as to risk only because the actor is insensitive to the interests and claims of other persons in society."

Here, even excluding consideration of the evidence relating to defendant's junior license violations, I believe that this case falls within the ambit of our precedents sustaining convictions for criminally negligent homicide. Viewing the evidence in a light most favorable to the People, this case involved much more than excessive speed. Defendant was familiar with Sackett Lake Road, a two-lane country byway divided by a double yellow line with a posted speed limit of 55 miles per hour. A warning sign with a recommended speed limit of 40 miles per hour preceded the left-hand curve where the accident occurred. The evidence demonstrated that defendant did not apply his brakes as he approached the curve or even when he attempted to negotiate it. Rather, he drove 70 to 72 miles per hour into the curve, at which point his SUV entered "critical speed yaw," rotated and slid off the road, crashing into and severing a utility pole.

Giving the People all the favorable inferences from the proof presented, as we must, there was ample evidence for the jury to find that defendant was attempting to achieve a racing car-type stunt as he drove into the curve.

**Post-Case Follow-Up**

*Cabrera* describes the line between civil negligence and criminal negligence and illustrates how difficult it can be to separate the two. As the court puts it, "the carelessness required for criminal negligence is appreciably more serious than that for ordinary civil negligence, . . . the carelessness must be such that its *seriousness would be apparent to anyone who shares the community's general sense of right and wrong.*" This concept implicates the requirement that criminal negligence involves a *substantial* risk and that the failure to perceive the risk is a *gross* deviation from a reasonable standard of care. There is no bright line between substantial risks and moderate risks or between gross deviations and regular deviations. In this case, the majority and dissent differed both on where to try to draw the line and on how much deference to give to jury determinations on these questions.

## Cabrera: *Real Life Applications*

**1.** Review the facts in *Janklow*, above. Both *Janklow* and *Cabrera* involved car crashes where there was evidence that the defendant was driving in a risky manner. In *Janklow*, the defendant's conviction for involuntary manslaughter (which requires a *mens rea* of recklessness) was upheld but in *Cabrera*, the defendant's conviction for the lesser crime of negligent homicide was reversed. Thinking about each of the main components of recklessness and negligence — awareness of the risk, substantial risk, unjustifiable risk, gross deviation — what facts do you think account for different outcomes?

**2.** After trial, Cabrera was sentenced to one and a third to four years in prison, "the maximum term allowed by statute." Imagine you were Cabrera's trial attorney. The prosecutor offers your client a deal to plead guilty to one count of criminally negligent homicide with a recommended sentence of six months in jail. Assume also that your client has been unable to make bail and, as a result, he is in jail awaiting trial. What advice would you give to your client about the prosecutor's plea offer? To help inform your advice, what questions, if any, might you want to ask your client about his priorities with respect to the outcome of the case?

## F. FELONY MURDER

The bulk of homicide law ties culpability to fine-grained distinctions about a killer's mental state. For example, to determine whether an intentional killing is first- or second-degree murder, we ask whether it was willful, deliberate, and premeditated. A reckless killing is graded as manslaughter but an extremely reckless killing can constitute murder.

The felony murder rule throws out all of these *mens rea* distinctions in a narrow category of cases. Under the **felony murder** doctrine, a person who commits or attempts to commit a felony can also be convicted of murder if someone dies during the commission or attempted commission of the felony. No *mens rea* with respect to the death is required.

Taken to its extreme, the felony murder doctrine can impose strict liability for *any* death that results from the commission or attempted commission of any felony. In *Malaske v. State*, 89 P.3d 1116 (Okla. Crim. App. 2004), for example, the defendant was convicted of murdering his sister's underage friend, who died of alcohol poisoning after drinking some vodka that the defendant had given to his sister (who was also underage). Based on the homicide principles we have covered so far, it would be a stretch to imagine a person being convicted of even negligent homicide as a result of buying vodka for his underage sister. But, because Oklahoma made it a felony to furnish alcohol to a minor, John William Malaske was convicted of murder under the felony murder rule, and sentenced to ten years imprisonment for the death of his sister's friend.

When applied broadly, the felony murder rule can also result in sweeping liability based on an accomplice's actions. Ryan Holle lent his car to a friend who used the car to drive to and from a burglary. One of the burglars spontaneously killed someone during the crime. Holle was a mile and a half from the scene of the crime. His only role in the burglary was letting the perpetrators use his car. But that was enough to make Holle guilty of burglary as an accomplice (we will see why this is so in Chapter 8, which examines accomplice liability). As a result, Holle was also convicted of first-degree murder and sentenced to life without the possibility of parole under the felony murder rule. Adam Liptak, *Serving Life for Providing Car to Killers*, N.Y. Times, Dec. 4, 2007.

The felony murder rule has its roots in the common law. As noted at the beginning of this chapter on page 207, today, malice aforethought is effectively a legal term of art that simply refers to the four types of homicides that are typically classified as murder (intent to kill; intent to inflict grievous bodily injury; extremely reckless disregard for the value of human life; and felony murder). At the time the felony murder rule was established, however, malice had independent legal meaning. The felony murder rule "was developed to elevate to murder a homicide committed during the course of a felony *by imputing malice to the killing*. The justification for imputing malice was the theory that the increased risk of death or serious harm occasioned by the commission of a felony demonstrated the felon's lack of concern for human life." *King v. Commw.* 6 Va. App. 351, 354 (1988) (emphasis added). In other words, the theory went, "[p]roof of the criminal's intent to commit the underlying felony establishes the 'malice' required for a murder conviction." Kevin Cole, *Killings During Crime: Toward a Discriminating Theory of Strict Liability*, 28 Am. Crim. L. Rev. 73, 74 (1990). This is a "highly artificial concept," and it can sometimes lead to counterintuitive results. *People v. Phillips*, 64 Cal. 2d 574, 582 (1966).

As a matter of doctrine, the basic felony murder rule is fairly straightforward: If death results from the commission or attempted commission of a felony, the perpetrator(s) can also be convicted of murder. As discussed in the material that follows, additional rules place important constraints on the application of felony murder in most jurisdictions. Before turning to limitations on felony murder liability, it is worth briefly examining the debate over whether felony murder should exist at all.

The felony murder doctrine has been "one of the most widely criticized features of American law." Guyora Binder, *Making the Best of Felony Murder*, 91 B.U. L. Rev. 403, 404 (2011). The country that pioneered the felony murder rule, England, abolished in it in 1957. Nevertheless, it remains "a part of the law of almost every American jurisdiction." *Id.* Critics of the felony murder doctrine argue that classifying unintended deaths that occur during the commission of a

---

### Limiting Felony Murder for Accomplices in California

In 2018, California legislators passed Senate Bill 1437, which narrows application of the felony murder doctrine in the state. The purpose of the bill, which took effect January 1, 2019, was to prevent application of the felony murder doctrine to accomplices who are "not a major participant in the underlying felony." *People v. Solis*, 46 Cal. App. 5th 762, 775 (2020). To accomplish this goal, the law provides: "A participant in the perpetration or attempted perpetration of a felony . . . in which a death occurs is liable for murder only if one of the following is proven: (1) The person was the actual killer. (2) The person was not the actual killer, but, with the intent to kill, aided, abetted, counseled, commanded, induced, solicited, requested, or assisted the actual killer in the commission of murder in the first degree. (3) The person was a major participant in the underlying felony and acted with reckless indifference to human life, as described in subdivision (d) of Section 190.2." *Id.* (quoting Cal. Penal Code § 189). The law applies retroactively, allowing people with murder convictions that would not constitute felony murder under the new law to petition to have their convictions vacated.

Under a law like California's Senate Bill 1437, it is very unlikely that Ryan Holle — whose case is described earlier in this section — could have been convicted of felony murder. This is because Holle's only involvement in the felony during which the killing occurred was to let the perpetrators use his car. (Holle was prosecuted in Florida, so his case is unaffected by California's law.) It remains to be seen whether California's law will spark interest in felony murder reform for accomplices in other states.

felony as murder is at odds with the rest of criminal law in general and homicide law in particular. Homicide law aims to carefully calibrate criminal liability based on blameworthiness. The felony murder doctrine, critics claim, "erodes the relation between criminal liability and moral culpability." *People v. Washington*, 62 Cal. 2d 777, 783 (1965).

To be sure, felony murder has its defenders. Most state legislatures have resisted calls to repeal the felony murder rule. This suggests politicians believe felony murder is popular with voters, or at least that repealing felony murder would be unpopular with voters. Among scholars who support the felony murder rule, most cite deterrence in its defense. The threat of liability for murder in the event of accidental death could lead would-be felons to "shy way from the entire felonious enterprise" or to take "greater care in the performance of felonious acts," the argument goes. James J. Tomkovicz, *The Endurance of the Felony-Murder Rule: A Study of the Forces That Shape Our Criminal Law*, 51 Wash. & Lee L. Rev. 1429, 1449 (1994). Critics respond that there is little or no empirical evidence of felony murder's value as a deterrent. *Id.* at 1457 (arguing that "[a]ssertions that the doctrine exists to prevent killings that occur in the course of felonies *and* that it actually achieves its goal are rooted in blind faith or self-delusion").

Whatever one thinks about felony murder, it remains an important part of homicide law in the United States. The remainder of this section is devoted to the doctrinal nuances and limitations on felony murder liability.

## 1. In the Perpetration of a Felony (*Res Gestae*)

The felony murder rule applies to killings that occur during the commission or attempted commission of a felony. In many cases, this requirement is straightforward. In others, it can raise challenging questions about the outer limits of felony murder.

Consider this hypothetical. A bank robber hands a note to a teller asking for money and the teller quietly complies. The robber walks out of the bank, hops into a waiting getaway car, and speeds away. None of the bank's customers are even aware a robbery has taken place. Nevertheless, two deaths occur close in time to the robbery. First, as the robbery is in progress, a customer slips and hits her head in the bank's bathroom, dying of the injury. Second, three blocks from the bank, the getaway driver hits and kills a pedestrian while going 20 miles over the speed limit. Can the robber be convicted of felony murder for either or both of these deaths? In a sense, one could say the customer died "during the commission of" the robbery — she fell and hit her head inside the bank while the robbery was taking place. But the robbery did nothing to cause the accident. There is a much stronger causal connection between the robbery and the pedestrian's death, which resulted from the getaway car speeding away from the bank to avoid being caught by the police. But the car crash happened after the robbers had already left the bank.

To address these kinds of problems, courts ask whether the death is within the ***res gestae*** (Latin for "things done") of the felony or attempted felony. A "homicide is within the res gestae of the initial felony and is an emanation thereof, [if] it is committed in the perpetration of that felony. Thus, the felony-murder statute applies where the initial felony and the homicide were parts of one continuous transaction, and were closely related in point of time, place, and causal connection, as where the killing was done in flight from the scene of the crime to prevent detection or promote escape." *Haskell v. Commw.*, 218 Va. 1033, 1041 (1978).

## Case Preview

### *People v. Wilkins*

Flight from the scene of a felony is considered to be within the *res gestae* of the crime. But when does flight end? If a defendant steals something a hundred miles from his home, does the crime continue for purposes of felony murder until he steps through his doorway? In *People v. Wilkins*, the California Supreme Court considered the rule for determining when a crime ends for purposes of the felony murder rule.

As you read the opinion, consider the following questions:

1. What is the rule for determining when a fleeing felon who causes an accidental death is no longer subject to the felony murder rule?
2. Do you agree with the "escape rule" articulated by the court? If you were in charge of defining the temporal limits of felony murder, to what extent would you apply the felony murder rule to deaths that occur while the perpetrator is leaving the scene of a felony?
3. The government argues that a ruling in favor of the defendant would result in "treating cases differently depending on whether the killing occurred before or after the defendant reached a place of safety even though the defendant's conduct may have been equally culpable." How does the court respond to this objection?

# *People v. Wilkins*
## 56 Cal. 4th 333 (2013)

CANTIL-SAKAUYE, C.J.

Defendant Cole Allen Wilkins was convicted of first degree murder under a felony-murder theory that the victim was killed during the commission of a burglary. The evidence at trial established that defendant burglarized a house under construction and loaded some large household appliances onto the back of a pickup truck. Sometime later, as he was driving on a freeway, an unsecured stove stolen in the burglary fell off his truck. Another driver swerved to avoid the stove, crashed into a large truck, and was killed. The trial court instructed the jury that in order for the felony-murder rule to apply, the burglary and the act causing the death must be part of one "continuous transaction." It refused defendant's request that the jury be instructed that, for purposes of felony murder, the felony continues only until the perpetrator has reached a place of temporary safety. The Court of Appeal found no error in the trial court's refusal to instruct the jury on the so-called "escape rule" and affirmed.

We conclude that it was error to refuse the instruction on the escape rule and that the error requires reversal of defendant's conviction.

## FACTS

In 2005, defendant entered into an arrangement with a former girlfriend, Kathleen Trivich, under which she purchased a piece of property in Palm Springs and defendant, as co-owner, was to oversee the construction of a house on that property. Trivich also purchased a truck for defendant's use, but the title remained in her name. Defendant lived in Long Beach with his girlfriend Nancy Blake.

In 2006, Dennis Kane was building a home in Menifee, a city in Riverside County located roughly between Long Beach and Palm Springs. Kane had purchased a large number of appliances and other items for the house, including a stove, refrigerator, dishwasher, microwave, light fixtures, ceiling fans, door locks, and a sink. These items were last seen in the house about 8:00 P.M. on the evening of Thursday, July 6, 2006, when Kane's brother-in-law locked up the house.

Trivich testified at trial that on Friday, July 7, 2006, she twice spoke to defendant on the phone. The first time, at 12:45 A.M., he told her that he "got some big items for the kitchen." He did not tell her exactly what the items were. The second time, at 1:12 A.M., he told her that he was on his way to Palm Springs.

Shortly before 5:00 A.M. on Friday, July 7, 2006, defendant was driving Trivich's pickup truck westbound on "the 91 freeway" just east of the Kraemer Boulevard exit in Anaheim. He was travelling about 60 to 65 miles per hour, heading in the direction of his home in Long Beach. He was about 62 miles northwest of the Kane home in Menifee. The bed and cab of the pickup truck were loaded with appliances that had been stolen from the Kane home. The tailgate of defendant's truck was down and none of the items in the bed of the truck were tied down.

A stove fell off defendant's truck onto the 91 freeway. A driver behind defendant's truck, Danny Lay, struck the stove with his car. Lay attempted to get defendant to pull over by flashing his lights and honking his horn. Defendant slowed down and pulled over, but then accelerated again. Lay pulled up next to defendant's truck, rolled down the window, and told defendant to get off the freeway. Defendant pulled over at the next exit and stopped. He got out of the truck and threatened Lay, but when Lay told him that something had fallen off his truck, defendant exclaimed, "Oh my God, it's a thousand-dollar stove."

Defendant falsely told Lay that his name was Michael Wilkins. He gave Lay the name of the registered owner of the truck, Kathleen Trivich, but gave him several false telephone numbers. Defendant then continued on to his home in Long Beach. In the meantime, the stove was still on the four-lane 91 freeway, in either the fast lane or the lane just to the right of it. At 5:00 A.M., David Piquette, driving his car in the fast lane, suddenly swerved to the right, apparently to avoid hitting the stove. His car crossed the middle lanes and struck a big rig truck that was travelling in the far right lane. Piquette died.

When defendant arrived home in Long Beach about 5:30 or 6:00 A.M. on Friday, July 7, 2006, he and his girlfriend, Nancy Blake, moved some of the stolen items into Blake's trailer.

That same Friday morning, between 7:00 and 7:30 A.M., Kane received a telephone call advising him that the appliances were missing from his house in Menifee, and reported the matter to the police. The police subsequently recovered the items from Nancy Blake's trailer and . . . arrested defendant.

To trace defendant's whereabouts, cell phone records were used.

There was, however, no direct evidence of when the burglary took place. The prosecution's theory [based on the cell phone records] was that [defendant stole the appliances and drove away from the scene of the burglary a little before 4:00 A.M.].

Defendant testified in his own defense. He denied the burglary and testified that he did not take the appliances from the Kane home but that he bought them from an acquaintance named "Rick" at a Home Depot parking lot off the 91 freeway.

## DISCUSSION

Defendant was convicted of first degree murder under the felony-murder theory that the killing of David Piquette occurred in the commission of a burglary. The felony-murder rule provides that "[a]ll murder . . . which is *committed in the perpetration of*, or attempt to perpetrate, arson, rape, carjacking, robbery, burglary, mayhem, [or] train wrecking . . . is murder of the first degree." (Pen. Code, § 189, italics added.) "Under the felony-murder rule, a strict causal or temporal relationship between the felony and the murder is not required; . . . [a] killing committed by a robber during his or her flight from the scene of the crime, and before reaching a place of temporary safety, comes within section 189."

At trial, defense counsel requested that the jury be instructed on the escape rule, as set out in [model jury instruction] CALCRIM No. 3261. That instruction . . . reads: "The crime of burglary continues until the perpetrator has actually reached a temporary place of safety. The perpetrator has reached a temporary place of safety if he has successfully escaped from the scene, is no longer being chased[, and has unchallenged possession of the property]." The trial court refused defendant's request for this instruction [and the jury convicted him of first-degree murder].

The Court of Appeal reached the conclusion that "for purposes of the felony-murder rule, a robbery or burglary continues, *at a minimum*, until the perpetrator reaches a place of temporary safety. . . . But reaching a place of temporary safety does not, in and of itself, terminate felony-murder liability so long as the felony and the killing are part of one continuous transaction."

That statement may be accurate in some circumstances[, for example if] one perpetrator had escaped to a place of safety while another remained at the scene of the felony and the killing. However, in cases like the present one, involving a single perpetrator, we have never suggested that if the perpetrator flees the scene of the crime and reaches a place of temporary safety before the killing, the killing and the felony could still be considered part of one continuous transaction. Respondent cites no case that so suggests.

Rather, when the killing occurs during the flight from a felony, this court [has] . . . consistently applied the escape rule to test the sufficiency of the evidence that a killing occurred in the commission of the felony.

"Felony-murder liability continues throughout the flight of a perpetrator from the scene of a robbery until the perpetrator reaches a place of temporary safety because the robbery and the accidental death, in such a case, are parts of a 'continuous transaction.'" When the killing occurs during flight, . . . the escape rule establishes the "outer limits of the 'continuous-transaction' theory." "Flight following a felony is considered part of the same transaction *as long as the felon has not reached a 'place of temporary safety.'* "

[The People] argue[] that . . . the escape rule . . . result[s] in treating cases differently depending on whether the killing occurred before or after the defendant reached a place of safety even though the defendant's conduct may have been equally culpable. The felony-murder rule, however, does not take into account the relative culpability of the defendant's actions or state of mind. Its application depends only on whether the murder was "committed *in the perpetration of*" the felony. (Pen. Code, § 189, italics added.) As we have noted [in a prior case], the "Legislature has said in effect that [the] deterrent purpose [of the felony-murder rule] outweighs the normal legislative policy of examining the individual state of mind of each person causing an unlawful killing. . . . Once a person perpetrates or attempts to perpetrate one of the enumerated felonies, then in the judgment of the Legislature, he is no longer entitled to such fine judicial calibration, but will be deemed guilty of first degree murder for any homicide committed in the course thereof."

[The People] finally argue[] that there need be only a "causal nexus" between the burglary and the homicide. In the present case, [the People] argue[], there is a sufficient nexus between the burglary and the homicide because the homicide was caused by defendant's act of driving away from the scene of the crime with his truck loaded with stolen items that were not secured. Our opinion in [a prior case] made clear, however, that "the felony-murder rule requires both a *causal* relationship and a *temporal* relationship between the underlying felony and the act resulting in death." The causal relationship is established by a "logical nexus" between the felony and the homicidal act, and "[t]he temporal relationship is established by proof the felony and the homicidal act were part of one continuous transaction."

When a legally correct instruction is requested . . . it should be given "if it is supported by substantial evidence, that is, evidence sufficient to deserve jury consideration." In the present case, defendant requested an instruction on the escape rule, and there was substantial evidence supporting the instruction.

Even under the prosecution's theory of events, defendant was 62 miles away from the scene of the burglary when the stove fell off his truck and he had been driving on the freeway at normal speeds for about an hour. There was no evidence that anyone was following him or that anyone was even aware of the burglary. A jury could have concluded that the fatal act occurred when the stove fell off the truck and that defendant had reached a place of temporary safety before the fatal act occurred.

There is more than an abstract possibility that the instructional error affected the verdict in this case.

## DISPOSITION

The judgment of the Court of Appeal upholding defendant's conviction for first degree murder is reversed, and the matter is remanded for further proceedings consistent with this opinion.

**Post-Case Follow-Up**

When it comes to felony murder, a crime does not end when the perpetrator leaves the scene. It continues while the defendant is fleeing until he reaches "a temporary place of safety." This rule places a temporal limit on felony murder. Notice, however, that this "limit" is still much broader than how some lay people would describe the conclusion of a crime in everyday conversation; some would say that a robbery or a burglary ends as soon as the perpetrator leaves the scene. Although defense attorneys have attempted to persuade courts to limit felony murder to deaths that occur at the scene of the crime, most jurisdictions follow the approach outlined in *Wilkins*.

**Case Preview**

## *King v. Commonwealth*

In addition to the temporal relationship between the felony and the death, to be within the *res gestae* of the felony, there must be a causal relationship as well. The causal relationship requirement prevents the felony murder rule from applying to deaths that are connected to a crime only by place and time, such as the hypothetical bank customer from the introduction to this section who slipped and fell in the bathroom "during" a robbery she didn't even know was happening. The next case, *King v. Commonwealth*, addresses felony murder's causal relationship requirement.

As you read the opinion, consider the following questions:

1. The court acknowledges that the felony is a "but for" cause of the death. Why, then, does the court find that there is an insufficient causal relationship between the felony and the death? What more is required?
2. If you were tasked with drafting a brief jury instruction that explains the court's causal relationship rule, what would you write?

---

## King v. Commonwealth
### 6 Va. App. 351 (1988)

COLEMAN, J.

We consider whether the facts in this case constitute a violation of the felony-murder statute, Code § 18.2-33.

On October 17, 1984, King and his copilot, Mark Lee Bailey, were flying a Beechcraft Bonanza airplane carrying over five hundred pounds of marijuana to the New River Valley airport in Dublin, Virginia. They were flying for Wallace Thrasher, who owned the airplane and ran the drug smuggling operation. King was a licensed pilot; Bailey was not. The two encountered heavy cloud cover and fog near Mt. Airy, North Carolina and apparently became lost. In an effort to navigate through the cloud cover and fog, they flew the plane to a lower altitude in order to follow U.S. Route 52. Bailey was piloting the plane at this time. As Bailey flew, King was examining navigation maps in an attempt to determine the plane's whereabouts. The airplane crashed into Fancy Gap Mountain killing Bailey almost instantly. King was thrown from the plane and survived. King was charged with felony homicide under Code § 18.2-33 for Bailey's death. A jury convicted King of second degree murder under the statute and recommended a six-year penitentiary sentence.

Code § 18.2-33 defines second degree felony homicide: "The killing of one . . . while in the prosecution of some felonious act other than those specified in §§ 18.2-31 and 18.2-32, is murder of the second degree and is punishable as a Class 3 felony." This statute and its companion, § 18.2-32, defining first degree felony-murder, codify the common law doctrine of felony-murder. The doctrine was developed to elevate to murder a homicide committed during the course of a felony by imputing malice to the killing. The justification for imputing malice was the theory that the increased risk of death or serious harm occasioned by the commission of a felony demonstrated the felon's lack of concern for human life.

Criminal statutes are to be "strictly construed against the Commonwealth and in favor of [a] citizen's liberty." Strict construction, however, does not justify nullification of the evident purpose and meaning of a statute. A penal statute must be construed so as to proscribe only conduct which the legislature clearly intended to be within the statute's ambit.

The second degree felony-murder statute in Virginia contemplates a killing with malice. Indeed, "the commission of *any* felonious act . . . supplies the malice which raises the incidental homicide to the level of second-degree murder."

It does not follow, however, that any death of any person which occurs during the period in which a felony is being committed will subject the felon to criminal liability under the felony-murder rule. To construe our statute to encompass every accidental death occurring during the commission of a felony, regardless of whether it causally relates to or results from the commission of the felony, is to make felons absolutely liable for the accidental death of another even though such death is fortuitous and the product of causes wholly unrelated to the commission of the felony. Recognizing the potentially harsh and far reaching effects of such a construction of the felony-murder doctrine, the Virginia courts, as well as others, have limited its application.

In Virginia, it is clear when the homicide is within the *res gestae* of the initial felony and emanates therefrom, it is committed in the perpetration of that felony. The [Supreme] Court [of Virginia] explained that "the felony-murder statute applies where the killing is so closely related to the felony in time, place, and causal connection as to make it a part of the same criminal enterprise." Thus, the court in *Haskell* [*v. Commonwealth*] affirmed first degree murder convictions when the murder of a robbery victim was within five feet of the site of the robbery, within moments of the robbery, and was to facilitate the robbers' escape without being identified. Under these circumstances, the killing was obviously causally related to the robbery and was part of the same enterprise. The Court did not elaborate on the degree of causal connection required under the statute.

In a leading case involving the felony-murder doctrine, which the Virginia Supreme Court has cited with approval, the Pennsylvania Supreme Court addressed the causation problem at length. [In *Commonwealth v. Redline*], the court stated: "The mere coincidence of homicide and felony is not enough to satisfy the requirements of the felony-murder doctrine. . . . "Death must be a consequence of the felony . . . and not merely coincidence." *Commonwealth v. Redline*, 391 Pa. 486, 495 (1958).

In the present case, King and Bailey were in the airplane to further the felony of possession of marijuana with the intent to distribute. They were flying over the mountains while committing the felony. The time and the place of the death were closely connected with the felony. However, no causal connection exists between the felony of drug distribution and the killing by a plane crash. Thus, no basis exists to find that the accidental death was part or a result of the criminal enterprise. The felony-murder rule does not exist to enable courts to impute "the act of killing" where an accidental death results from fortuitous circumstances and the only connection with the felony is temporal.

The cause of Bailey's death was Bailey's piloting and adverse weather conditions. The accident stemmed not from the possession or distribution of drugs, but from fog, low cloud cover, pilot error, and inexperience. Had Bailey and King been transporting drugs in an automobile when they encountered heavy fog and Bailey, not seeing a curve, had driven off the mountain, the legal consequences would be the same. The commission of the felony merely accounted for their presence at the location of the accident, and nothing directly related to the commission of the felony caused the accident. Thus, flying into the mountain was not a direct consequence of the felony. Had the plane been flying low or recklessly to avoid detection, for example, the crash would be a consequence or action which was directly intended to further the felony and a different result might obtain. *See People v. Ulsh*, 27 Cal. Rptr. 408, 416-17 (1962) (death in automobile accident a consequence of high speed chase during attempted escape after felony).

If King and Bailey had been transporting legal cargo that day, the crash would still have occurred. It is true, of course, that but for the felony, King and Bailey probably would not have been in the plane. However, criminal liability for felony-murder requires more than a finding that "but for" the felony the parties would not have been present at the time and location of the accidental death.

Reversed and dismissed.

---

**Post-Case Follow-Up**

As the *King* court explained, the felony murder rule does not apply "where an accidental death results from fortuitous circumstances and the only connection with the felony is temporal." This limitation makes sense. Without it, a felon could theoretically be convicted of murder for any nearby death that occurred during the time she was committing the crime (as in the bank customer hypothetical described above, for example). The case for a causal relationship in *King* was stronger than in the bank customer hypothetical, however. In contrast to the bank customer hypothetical, the felony in *King* was a but-for cause of the death: "but for the felony, King and Bailey probably would not have been in the plane." Still, the court found the evidence insufficient because "[t]he commission of the felony merely accounted for their presence at the location of the accident, and nothing directly related to the commission of the felony caused the accident."

---

## King *and* Wilkins: *Real Life Applications*

1. It is 2014 and you are an Assistant District Attorney in Orange County. Your supervisor has asked for your opinion about whether or not to retry Cole Allen Wilkins following the California Supreme Court's reversal of his conviction in the decision presented above. Assume that your supervisor has already decided that if she does not retry Wilkins for felony murder, she will try him on a charge of negligent homicide. In light of the California Supreme Court's holding, what recommendation would you make to your supervisor? What role, if any, would the potential impact of the charging decision on plea negotiations play in your recommendation?

2. Now assume that Cole Allen Wilkins was retried following the California Supreme Court's decision, and that he was once again convicted of felony murder. You are an appellate attorney in the California Attorney General's office. You have been assigned to work on the brief to the Court of Appeal in *Wilkins*. In his opening brief before the Court of Appeal, Wilkins argues there was insufficient evidence of a causal relationship between his felony and

the death. Citing *King*, he claims that although his burglary may have been a "but for cause" of the death, "nothing directly related to the commission of the felony caused the accident." Your supervisor has asked you to write a very brief paragraph outlining your thoughts on how to respond to the defendant's causal relationship argument. Be sure to carefully review the facts of *Wilkins* to inform your answer.

---

## Liability for Killings by Non-Felons

Some jurisdictions interpret the *res gestae* rule to include one additional limitation on felony murder liability: that it does not apply to killings by non-felons that occur during the felony. Imagine that Felon walks into a convenience store, pulls out a gun, and instructs Employee to open the register and hand over all the money. Instead of complying, Employee grabs a gun from behind the register and shoots at Felon. The shot misses Felon but strikes and kills Customer, an innocent bystander who was in the store when Felon walked in. Can Felon be convicted of murder in the death of Customer under the felony murder rule?

The majority rule, sometimes called the **agency rule**, provides that Felon is not guilty of murder in this circumstance. From a culpability standpoint, this can seem like a strange rule. After all, felony murder liability usually extends to accidental deaths. If Customer had died of a heart attack brought on by panic during the robbery, Felon would be guilty of murder. Why should the outcome be different when a failed attempt to defend against the felony results in death? The primary rationale for the agency rule is that a killing that results from an effort to stop the commission of a felony cannot be said to have occurred *in perpetration* of that felony. In other words, a felon should not be held responsible for an act "committed by a person who is . . . [the] direct and immediate adversary" of the felon, "and who is, at the moment, when the alleged criminal act is done, actually engaged in opposing and resisting" the felon. *Commw. v. Campbell*, 7 Allen 541, 545 (Mass. 1863). The agency rule name is meant to distinguish killings by third parties who are trying to stop the felony from killings by co-felons. In jurisdictions that apply the agency rule, a felon is liable for deaths that are attributable to his actions or those of his co-felons (his "agents"), but not for killings committed by third parties acting in opposition to the felony.

A healthy minority of jurisdictions reject the agency rule in favor of what is often called the **proximate cause rule**. Under this rule, a felon can "be held liable even when the shot is fired by a victim, police officer, or bystander," so long as the felony proximately caused the third party's actions. Michelle S. Simon, *Whose Crime Is It Anyway?: Liability for the Lethal Acts of Nonparticipants in the Felony*, 71 U. Det. Mercy L. Rev. 223, 245 (1994). Courts that have adopted the proximate cause rule reason that "when a felon's attempt to commit a . . . felony sets in motion a chain of events which" result in a death, the death should fall within the scope of the felony murder rule. *People v. Lowery*, 178 Ill. 2d 462, 467 (1997). In proximate cause rule jurisdictions, because "[i]t reasonably might be anticipated that an attempted robbery would be met with resistance, during which the victim might be shot either by himself or someone else in attempting to prevent the robbery . . . those attempting to perpetrate the robbery would be guilty of murder." *People v. Payne*, 359 Ill. 246 (1935). As a result, in a proximate cause rule jurisdiction, the felony murder doctrine would make Felon guilty of murder in the death of Customer in the convenience store robbery hypothetical above.

## 2. Grading Felony Murder, Enumerated Felonies, and the Inherently Dangerous Felony Limitation

There is a good deal of diversity when it comes to grading felony murder. In some jurisdictions, the felony murder rule can result in a conviction for either first- or second-degree murder. This section describes what typically differentiates first- and second-degree felony murder in the jurisdictions that recognize first-degree felony murder, along with an important limitation that many states apply to the felony murder rule.

Before taking a look at the current state of the law, a bit of historical background is helpful here. The felony murder rule was first established in the early 1700s in England, at a time when the common law recognized only a very small number of crimes as felonies — namely, "murder, manslaughter, rape, burglary, arson, robbery, theft, and mayhem." Guyora Binder, *The Origins of American Felony Murder Rules*, 57 Stan. L. Rev. 59, 91 (2004). Part of the justification for felony murder liability was the belief that the commission of a felony inherently endangered the lives of others, a claim that arguably made sense in the early 1700s because of the limited number of crimes that were classified as felonies. As Guyora Binder notes in his authoritative history of felony murder, "[o]f the traditional common law felonies, all but burglary and theft involve a direct threat to the person." *Id.* Moreover, common law burglary, which "involved breaking into a dwelling at night to commit another felony," and common law larceny, which "was seen as a breach of the peace that challenged the victim or the sheriff to use deadly force to stop the thief," could very plausibly have been considered "necessarily dangerous to life." *Id.* at 91-92.

When felony murder took hold in the United States, many states limited its application to deaths that occurred during "enumerated particular predicate felonies." Binder, *Making the Best of Felony Murder*, *supra*, at 415. In most states, the list of enumerated felonies closely tracked the traditional common law felonies. For example, Pennsylvania's influential 1794 murder statute listed as predicate felonies "robbery, rape, arson, [and] burglary." *Id.* To explain why some felonies, but not others, could give rise to felony murder liability, some "courts emphasized the dangerousness of certain felonies." *Id.* at 416. Not all states followed this approach, however. Some passed laws defining killings in the course of "*all* felonies as murder." *Id.* at 415 (emphasis added). A third group "combined a felony murder provision with a grading provision predicating first degree murder on enumerated felonies." *Id.* In these states, a killing during an enumerated felony was first-degree murder while a killing during any other felony was second-degree murder. Regardless of the approach a state followed, "[o]ver the course of the [1800s] courts increasingly relied on the dangerousness of the felony in explaining felony murder." *Id.* at 418.

Fast forward to today. Hundreds, perhaps thousands, of crimes may be classified as felonies in any given state. (The most common definition of a felony is an offense with a punishment of more than one year, although not all states use this definition.) In some states, literally any felony can give rise to felony murder liability. For example, in *Malaske v. State*, the case discussed at the beginning of our coverage of felony murder, John William Malaske's felony murder conviction was predicated on the felony of furnishing alcohol to a minor. In most states, felony murder does not apply quite so broadly. This is because, in most jurisdictions, the related concepts of enumerated felonies and inherently dangerous felonies limit the reach of felony murder statutes. Jurisdictions have incorporated these limits into their felony murder regimes in a range of different ways. One approach followed in a number of states is to classify a death that occurs during the commission of an enumerated felony as first-degree murder. A death that occurs during the commission of any other felony will constitute second-degree murder, but only if there is a determination that the felony was inherently dangerous. The remainder of this section describes this approach to grading felony murder in more detail.

## First-Degree Felony Murder and Enumerated Felonies

To determine whether a felony murder conviction will be classified as first- or second-degree murder, the predicate felony controls. States that recognize first-degree felony murder set out a list of enumerated felonies that can establish first-degree murder. In these states, if death occurs during the commission or attempted commission of any of these enumerated felonies, then it is considered to be first-degree murder.

This framework is relatively straightforward. Finding out whether a particular case qualifies as first- or second-degree murder is as simple as looking up the statute that contains the list of **enumerated felonies**. That list is different from state to state but almost all states that follow this approach include arson, burglary, rape, robbery, and kidnapping as enumerated felonies. In *People v. Wilkins*, presented on page 262, for example, the defendant was convicted of first-degree murder because the predicate felony was burglary, and California's felony murder statute lists burglary as an enumerated felony.

Using enumerated felonies to separate first- and second-degree felony murder has the advantage of simplicity. But it can sometimes seem arbitrary. Why should a death that occurs during a burglary constitute first-degree murder, but a death that occurs during, say, felony elder abuse is second-degree murder? Partly, the answer is that today's enumerated felonies may be something of a relic from the era of the traditional common law felonies. Without a compelling reason to tinker with the list of enumerated felonies, legislatures in many states have been content to leave them largely unchanged over the years. But there is also a policy rationale for enumerated felonies. Legislators decided (at some point in the past) that these enumerated felonies pose a greater risk to human life than other felonies, and so should be graded more seriously for purposes of felony murder. To be sure, many critics argue that this is not an especially convincing justification for treating deaths that occur during enumerated felonies more harshly than those that occur during other felonies. But it does at least provide an explanation for the practice.

### Second-Degree Felony Murder and the Inherently Dangerous Felony Rule

In states that separate felony murders into degrees, a death that results from the commission or attempted commission of an unenumerated felony can constitute second-degree felony murder. In some jurisdictions, second-degree felony murder liability attaches to a death that results from *any* unenumerated felony. But most jurisdictions impose an additional limitation on second-degree felony murder: The felony must be inherently dangerous to life. This is often referred to as the **inherently dangerous felony limitation**.

What does it mean for a felony to be inherently dangerous? There are two different approaches to the inherently dangerous felony rule.

The majority of jurisdictions require the felony to have been **inherently dangerous as committed**. In these jurisdictions "the trier of fact . . . consider[s] the facts and circumstances of the particular case to determine if [the] felony was inherently dangerous in the manner and the circumstances in which it was committed[.]" *State v. Stewart*, 663 A.2d 912, 919 (R.I. 1995). Here, dangerousness hinges on the degree to which the felony, as it was committed, created a foreseeable risk of death. Because this issue is treated as a factual question, appellate courts often defer to the jury's finding. Indeed, it can sometimes seem as if appellate courts are willing to uphold a jury's finding of inherent dangerousness "whenever a fatality occurs, however improbably." Binder, *Making the Best of Felony Murder*, *supra*, at 472. In some cases, however, courts have been willing to overturn convictions on the grounds that a felony was not committed in a dangerous way. In *Ford v. State*, 262 Ga. 602 (1992), for example, the Supreme Court of Georgia overturned a felony murder conviction based on the predicate felony of possession of a firearm by a convicted felon. In *Ford*, the defendant was trying to unload a pistol at his girlfriend's apartment when it accidentally fired, "sending a bullet through the floor" and into a basement apartment below, killing the victim. *Id.* "There was no evidence that at the time of the shooting [the defendant] was aware of the existence of the [basement] apartment." *Id.* The court held that although "circumstances may

> ## Revisiting Criticisms of the Felony Murder Doctrine
>
> Critics of felony murder charge that the doctrine divorces criminal liability from blameworthiness. In cases like Ryan Holle's — the 20-year old who was convicted of felony murder for lending his car to a friend to use in a burglary — the culpability argument against felony murder is a strong one. But are cases like Holle's truly representative of the felony murder rule?
>
> As we have seen, most states limit the application of felony

well exist under which" possession of a firearm could be committed in an inherently dangerous way, "such circumstances are undeniably absent from this case." *Id.* at 603.

The minority rule considers whether the predicate felony is **inherently dangerous in the abstract**. Under this jurisdictional variant, to "determin[e] whether a felony is inherently dangerous, the court looks to the elements of the felony in the abstract, not the particular facts of the case, i.e., not to the defendant's specific conduct." *People v. James*, 62 Cal. App. 4th 244, 258 (1998). A felony is inherently dangerous in the abstract if, "by its very nature, it cannot be committed without creating a substantial risk that someone will be killed[.]" *People v. Burroughs*, 35 Cal. 3d 824, 833 (1984). In contrast to the as-committed approach, this rule can place very serious limits on the application of felony murder. In one well-known case, the California Supreme Court overturned the felony murder conviction of a doctor who had falsely told the parents of an 8-year-old girl suffering from eye cancer that he could cure the disease without surgery. *People v. Phillips*, 64 Cal. 2d 574 (1966). The doctor charged $700 for treatments that did nothing to help the girl, who died a few months later. The doctor was convicted of felony grand theft and felony murder. In overturning the felony murder conviction, the court reasoned that grand theft — which "requires proof that the victim relied on defendant's representations and that he actually parted with value" — can be (and often is) committed without endangering life and so the felony was "not inherently dangerous to life" in the abstract. *Id.* at 582-83. (If *Phillips* had arisen in an as-committed jurisdiction, the conviction would surely have been upheld since the manner in which the crime was committed clearly endangered the little girl's life.) Although it is rare for a felony to satisfy the inherently dangerous in the abstract test, there are some offenses that meet it. For example, the crime of arson of a motor vehicle (a distinct offense from arson) has been held to be inherently dangerous in the abstract; setting fire to a car could cause it to explode, and so the offense cannot be committed without a substantial risk that someone will be killed. *People v. Nichols*, 3 Cal. 3d 150 (1970).

murder in significant ways through the use of enumerated felonies and the inherently dangerous felony doctrine. With this in mind, some claim that "many arguments against the felony-murder rule begin with an unrealistically broad definition of the rule." David Crump, *Should We Have Different Views of Felony Murder, Depending on the Governing Statute?*, 47 Tex. Tech L. Rev. 113, 114 (2014). Similarly, Guyora Binder's study of felony murder has led him to conclude that cases like Holle's (or Malaske's, the Oklahoma man convicted of felony murder for buying a bottle of vodka for his underage sister) "are anomalous rather than paradigmatic — misapplications of a rational doctrine rather than illustrations of an irrational one." Binder, *Making the Best of Felony Murder*, supra, at 407. If cases like Holle's and Malaske's are indeed anomalous, however, this fact may be due to prosecutorial discretion, rather than doctrinal constraints on felony murder. After all, Holle was convicted of burglary, an enumerated felony in almost every state.

Assuming felony murder could be reformed to exclude its application in cases like Holle's and Malaske's, do you believe it would be consistent with the purposes of criminal punishment? Imagine, for example, a defendant who enters a convenience store with a gun and demands money. As the defendant reaches across the counter to get money from the cash register, his gun accidentally discharges. Do you believe murder, under the felony murder rule, is an appropriate punishment? Or do you agree with those who argue that the doctrine should be abandoned in its entirety?

## 3. Independent Felony Rule

The **independent felony rule**, also sometimes called the **merger rule**, provides one last constraint on felony murder. The independent felony rule states, in essence, that the predicate felony must be independent of and collateral to the homicide.

The necessity for this rule becomes clear when one reflects on the fact that manslaughter is a felony. Without the independent felony rule, manslaughter would cease to exist. Because manslaughter is a felony, in every manslaughter case the victim will have necessarily died during the commission of a felony — namely, manslaughter. As a result, the merger rule is necessary "to ensure that varying degrees of murder, manslaughter, and other homicides remain distinct categories"; without it, "all felonious assaults that resulted in death would be bootstrapped up to" murder. *Lewis v. State*, 34 So. 3d 183, 184-85 (Fla. Dist. Ct. App. 2010).

In *State v. Shock*, 68 Mo. 552, 557 (1878), for example, the defendant was convicted of felony murder for beating a 6-year-old boy "with a piece of sycamore fishing-pole" and causing his death. The prosecutor's theory was that because Shock had committed a felony by beating the child, he could also be convicted under the felony murder rule for the child's death. The Supreme Court of Missouri rejected this theory, holding that the felony murder rule applies only to "collateral felon[ies], and not to those acts of personal violence to the deceased which are necessary and constituent elements of the homicide itself, and are, therefore, merged in it, and which do not, when consummated, constitute an offense distinct from homicide." *Id.* at 561-62.

Nearly every jurisdiction agrees that the independent felony limitation applies to all homicide offenses and all assault-based felonies. This means that a homicide or a felony assault can *never* serve as the predicate felony in a felony murder prosecution. There must be some other felony — a collateral felony like arson, burglary, robbery, etc. — to allow for a felony murder prosecution.

## 4. Misdemeanor Manslaughter

Before completing our coverage of felony murder, a brief word about the related doctrine of misdemeanor manslaughter is in order. In a number of states, a defendant can be convicted of manslaughter if a death occurs during the commission or attempted commission of a misdemeanor. This is referred to as **misdemeanor manslaughter** or unlawful act manslaughter.

In its broadest form, misdemeanor manslaughter operates exactly like felony murder, with the only difference being the severity of the predicate offense. Not surprisingly, the misdemeanor manslaughter rule has been subject to the same criticisms as felony murder. But in contrast to felony murder, "legislatures have been somewhat more receptive to arguments for abolition of misdemeanor-manslaughter." Kevin Cole, *Killings During Crime: Toward a Discriminating Theory of Strict Liability*, 28 Am. Crim. L. Rev. 73, 73-74 (1990). As a result, the doctrine no longer exists in many states.

In jurisdictions that retain misdemeanor manslaughter, it is usually subject to a number of significant limits beyond those that apply to felony murder. Most notably, in most states that retain the misdemeanor manslaughter doctrine, "a homicide that occurs in the course of a misdemeanor is involuntary manslaughter only if the offense is *malum in se* rather than *malum prohibitum*." Fred T. Harring, *The Misdemeanor-Manslaughter Rule: Dangerously Alive in Michigan*, 42 Wayne L. Rev. 2149, 2169 (1996). This constraint can greatly limit the reach of misdemeanor manslaughter liability. Partly as a result, the doctrine appears to be very rarely (if ever) used in the jurisdictions in which it exists. Although misdemeanor manslaughter has little practical relevance in most jurisdictions, it is still bar-tested and so it is worth being aware of, if only for that reason.

## G. CAUSATION

As discussed in the introduction to causation in Chapter 2, if an offense includes a results element, the prosecution will need to prove that the defendant caused that result to win a conviction. Many crimes do not include a results element. Among those that do, causation is rarely contested. Because disputes about causation arise most often in homicide prosecutions, we return to the subject of causation here. To be convicted of a homicide — whether murder or manslaughter — the government must prove the defendant caused the victim's death. The one exception is felony murder, where the relevant causal relationship is between the *felony* and the death, not the defendant's acts and the death. Specifically, as discussed above, the death must be within the *res gestae* of the felony for the felony murder rule to apply. For all other homicide offenses, the causation principles discussed in this section govern.

How do we determine if an act legally caused a result? Philosophers and legal theorists have made careers debating this question. Although the material that follows will touch on a few of these theoretical questions, it focuses primarily on doctrine. To prove that a defendant legally caused another's death, the prosecutor must show that the defendant's acts were both a but-for cause and a proximate cause of the death. Each requirement is addressed in turn below.

## 1. But-For Causation

The first step to determining whether a defendant's acts caused death is the but-for causation requirement. **But-for causation**, also referred to as **actual causation**, limits the universe of acts and events to the conditions that were necessary to achieve a result. It requires the prosecutor to prove that, but for the defendant's acts, the harm would not have occurred when it did.

But-for causation is easily met in almost every case. If Denise sells Vance heroin, and Vance ingests the heroin and dies of a heroin overdose, Denise's drug sale is a but-for cause of Vance's death. But-for causation is almost always as simple as that.

In practice, when disputes about but-for causation arise, they tend to center around conflicting expert testimony. For example, imagine if in the hypothetical just described that Vance had ingested large amounts of alcohol in addition to the heroin he bought from Denise. At Denise's trial, a toxicologist testifies for the prosecution that the heroin caused Vance's death. Then, a different toxicologist testifies for the defense that Vance died of alcohol poisoning. If the defense witness's assessment is correct, then the heroin was not a but-for cause of death; Vance would have died of alcohol poisoning even if he had not taken the heroin. In a case like this, although the facts are in dispute, the legal standard for but-for causation remains straightforward: But for Denise's acts, would the harm have occurred when it did? The answer will depend on whether or not the jury believes the prosecution's expert witness regarding the cause of death.

Legal complications around but-for causation tend to arise only in unusual cases. Two scenarios that are often discussed in the literature, but that seldom occur in real life, are referred to by shorthand as accelerating the result and multiple sufficient causes.

The **accelerating the result** scenario refers to cases where a defendant does something to hasten the death of a victim who has already been fatally injured. Suppose, for example, that Dan shoots and kills Vick. Unknown to Dan, moments before he fired his gun, Vick had suffered a heart attack that would have proved fatal. Is Dan a but-for cause of Vick's death even though Vick would have died from the heart attack anyway? The answer is yes, under the "well settled" principle that "conduct which hastens . . . a person's death is a cause of death." *Jefferson v. State*, 372 Ark. 307, 313 (2008). Because Dan's shot accelerated Vick's death "even by a moment or instant of time," the shot is considered a but-for cause of the death. *State v. Hanahan*, 96 S.E. 667, 671 (S.C. 1918). This rule makes intuitive sense because "[i]f the but-for test were applied without a temporal component, then no homicide defendant would ever qualify as a cause of the victim's death, since every victim is bound to die sooner or later." Eric A. Johnson, *Cause-in-Fact After* Burrage v. United States, 68 Fla. L. Rev. 1727, 1149 (2016).

The **multiple sufficient causes** question involves an even stranger scenario. Imagine that Dan and Dave each independently and simultaneously shoot Vick. Either shot alone would have killed Vick instantly. The but-for causation rule would appear to exonerate *both* Dan and Dave because neither of their acts accelerated Vick's death. The multiple sufficient causes rule solves this problem by providing that "when multiple sufficient causes independently, but concurrently, produce a result," each of them satisfies the but-for causation test. *Burrage v. United* States, 571 U.S. 204, 214 (2014).

## 2. Proximate Causation

The but-for causation requirement narrows the world of potential culpable causes of a result. But-for causation can still include a large number of acts and events that most would consider unworthy of punishment, however. Proximate cause addresses this problem.

**Proximate cause**, also called legal cause, is a way of identifying a but-for cause "that we're particularly interested in, often because we want to eliminate it. We want to eliminate arson, but we don't want to eliminate oxygen, so we call arson the cause of a fire set for an improper purpose rather than calling the presence of oxygen in the atmosphere the cause, though it is a but-for cause just as the arsonist's setting the fire is." *United States v. Hatfield*, 591 F.3d 945 (7th Cir. 2010).

Proximate cause is in dispute in a greater number of cases than but-for causation. But it is still a relatively rarely contested issue. In most cases, it is perfectly clear that the defendant's act is exactly the type of cause that, in the words of *Hatfield*, "we're particularly interested in." One does not need to have studied criminal law to safely conclude that if the defendant shoots the victim and the victim dies from the bullet wound, the defendant has legally caused the victim's death. Proximate cause exists to address the more difficult cases, where death may not have been foreseeable or where there was an independent intervening act between the defendant's act and the death.

The foreseeability principle provides that to establish proximate cause, death must have been **reasonably foreseeable**. This requirement is almost always easily met in homicide prosecutions because the *mens rea* for all of the major homicide offenses usually makes foreseeability a moot point. After all, if the prosecutor can establish that the defendant acted with a culpable mental state with respect to the victim's death, then she will necessarily have established that the victim's death was foreseeable in most cases.

Foreseeability is most often at issue in cases where the defendant acted with a culpable mental state with respect to the victim's death, but the death occurred in an unexpected way. In these cases, defendants sometimes argue that death was not reasonably foreseeable. In *People v. Armitage*, 194 Cal. App. 3d 405 (1987), for example, the defendant was drunkenly driving a boat with his friend when the boat flipped over as a result of the defendant's reckless driving. The defendant held onto the overturned boat and urged his friend to do the same. His friend disregarded the advice, tried to

## Drug-Induced Homicide Statutes

Over the years, many states have added new crimes to the traditional list of homicide offenses. Drug-induced homicide has been one of the most widely adopted add-on homicide offenses. More than 20 states and the federal government have a drug-induced homicide statute. Under these laws, "the illegal manufacture, sale, distribution, or delivery of a controlled substance that causes death results in a [homicide] charge, usually manslaughter or murder." Drug Policy Alliance, An Overdose Death Is Not Murder: Why Drug-Induced Homicide Laws Are Counterproductive and Inhumane 9 (2017). Many of these laws do not include a *mens rea* requirement, making defendants strictly liable when death results from drug distribution.

Drug-induced homicide laws can sometimes present difficult causation problems. Most drug users make a free, deliberated, and informed choice to purchase and use drugs. Indeed, drug buyers usually seek out sellers to make a purchase, not vice-versa. As a result, some courts have held that the intervening cause rule does not apply to drug-induced death statutes, on the theory that applying the rule would be at odds with the purpose of the law. Whether the foreseeability requirement applies to drug-induced death statutes presents a closer question. Federal courts have split on the issue and the United States Supreme Court has yet to address it.

Drug-induced homicide prosecutions have risen dramatically in the past few years, in response to the opioid crisis. But the laws also have come under heavy criticism. Some argue that these prosecutions actually "amplif[y] the risk of fatal overdoses and diseases by increasing stigma and marginalization and driving people away from needed medical care, treatment, and harm reduction services." Drug Policy Alliance, *supra*, at 4.

swim for help, and drowned. On appeal, the defendant argued there was insufficient proof he had proximately caused his friend's death "because the victim, against his warning, turned loose of the overturned boat and drowned while foolhardily attempting to swim ashore." *Id.* at 410. The court explained that to be unforeseeable, the result must be "an extraordinary and abnormal occurrence." *Id.* at 420. Applying this standard, the court held that the victim's actions were sufficiently foreseeable to satisfy proximate causation, reasoning that "[t]he fact that the panic-stricken victim recklessly abandoned the boat and tried to swim ashore was not a wholly abnormal reaction to the perceived peril of drowning." *Id.* at 421.

Foreseeability is one of two prominent proximate cause doctrines in criminal law. The other holds that an independent **intervening act** between the defendant's conduct and the result can break the causal chain and defeat proximate cause. A leading treatise on causation explained the idea this way: "The free, deliberate, and informed intervention of a second person, who intends to exploit the situation created by the first, but is not acting in concert with him, is normally held to relieve the first actor of criminal responsibility." H.L.A. Hart & Tony Honoré, Causation and the Law 326 (2d ed. 1985). This is often true even if the intervening act was foreseeable. The critical requirement is that the intervening act be sufficiently free, deliberate, and informed to be considered independent of the defendant's conduct.

## Case Preview

### Lewis v. State

In *Lewis v. State*, the court applied the intervening act rule to overturn the defendant's negligent homicide conviction.

As you read the opinion, consider the following questions:

1. Why does the court hold there was insufficient evidence of proximate causation?
2. Can this case be reconciled with the outcome in *People v. Armitage* (described immediately above in the introduction to this section)? If the deceased's act of "free will" broke the causal chain in this case, why didn't the deceased's decision to try to swim to safety break the causal chain in *Armitage*?

## *Lewis v. State*
### 474 So. 2d 766 (Ala. Crim. App. 1985)

TYSON, J.

Alvin Ronald Lewis was indicted for murder in violation of § 13A-6-2, Code of Alabama 1975. At the conclusion of the State's evidence, the trial judge granted the appellant's motion for judgment of acquittal as to the offenses of murder and manslaughter. The case was then submitted to the jury on the charge of criminally negligent homicide. The jury found the appellant "guilty" and he was sentenced to twelve months' imprisonment in the county jail.

The appellant urges this court to reverse his conviction on the ground that . . . his acts were not the proximate cause of the victim's death.

The appellant was convicted of the offense of criminally negligent homicide. "A person commits the crime of criminally negligent homicide if he causes the death of another person by criminal negligence." Ala. Code, § 13A-6-4(a) (1975).

The relevant evidence to this problem can be stated briefly. The victim had been present when the appellant and his brother played Russian Roulette with a loaded gun some time during the week prior to the victim's death. The appellant and the victim had played Russian Roulette on the day of the victim's death. It is unclear whether the gun was loaded or not during this time but there was some evidence that it was not. After the two finished playing the game, the appellant put the gun away. Later, the victim was seen alone holding a gun and spinning the chamber. A few minutes later, a noise which sounded like a gunshot was heard. At approximately the same time, the appellant ended a phone conversation because "something's happened." The coroner testified that the victim's wound was typical of a self-inflicted gunshot wound.

The evidence is clear that the deceased either committed suicide or fell victim to an unfortunate misadventure. Therefore, this Court is faced with a different question. "When may one human being be held criminally liable for the self-destruction of another?" Brenner, *Undue Influence in the Criminal Law: A Proposed Analysis of the Criminal Offense of "Causing Suicide"* 47 Albany L. Rev. 62, 63 (1982). "The problem lies, of course, in determining when, and if, an accused did in fact cause his alleged victim to commit suicide. This difficult determination requires proof that the suicide was caused by the accused's actions and was not the result of the victim's own free will." Brenner, supra at 63.

Clearly, the problem encountered in this case is causation. The State contends that the appellant's acts were the proximate cause and the cause in fact of the victim's death. The basis of the State's contention is that the victim would not have killed himself playing Russian Roulette if the appellant had not "directed, instructed and influenced" him to play the game and that the appellant should have been aware of the risk that the victim might be killed playing Russian

Roulette by himself when he directed, instructed and influenced the victim to play the game.

If the victim had shot himself while he and the appellant were playing Russian Roulette, or if the appellant was present when the victim was playing the game by himself, the appellant's conduct of influencing the victim to play would have been the cause-in-fact and the proximate cause of the victim's death. However, the evidence in the case at bar indicates the appellant was not present when the victim shot himself . . . [and] that the appellant had put the gun away after they finished playing the "game."

A determination as to whether the conduct of a person caused the suicide of another must necessarily include an examination of the victim's free will. Cases have consistently held that the "free will of the victim is seen as an intervening cause which . . . breaks the chain of causation." Brenner, supra at 83. Therefore, the crux of this issue is whether the victim exercised his own free will when he got the gun, loaded it and shot himself. We hold that the victim's conduct was a supervening, intervening cause sufficient to break the chain of causation.

Even though the victim might never have shot himself in this manner if the appellant had not taught him to play Russian Roulette, . . . the causal link between the appellant's conduct and the victim's death was severed when the victim exercised his own free will.

Therefore, for the reasons shown this case must be reversed and this cause rendered.

Reversed and Rendered.

---

**Post-Case Follow-Up**

As *Lewis* illustrates, an independent act of free will is considered an "intervening cause sufficient to break the chain of causation." Although this rule is easily stated, it can sometimes be difficult to apply. This is because "free will" has a somewhat narrower meaning in this context than it might in other settings. After all, some would say that the decedent in *Lewis* was also exercising free will *while* playing Russian roulette with the defendant. But the court found that "[i]f the victim had shot himself while he and the appellant were playing Russian roulette," the proximate cause requirement would have been satisfied. Why did the fact that "appellant was not present when the victim shot himself" lead to a different result? The "free, deliberate, and informed" formulation helps to provide an answer. To be considered an intervening cause, an act of free will must be sufficiently independent of the defendant's influence. If the decedent had shot himself while he was playing Russian roulette *with* the defendant, the decedent's involvement in the game would not have been sufficiently independent of the defendant's act to break the causal chain. Not everyone will find this reasoning to be convincing from the perspective of assessing blameworthiness. But it is how most jurisdictions approach the issue.

---

# Lewis: *Real Life Applications*

1. Consider the following cases in light of the principles discussed in *Lewis* and *Armitage* (described in the introduction to this section). Do you think proximate cause is satisfied in each case? Why or why not?

    **a.** Defendant St. James was the owner of a business called Party Bus of Santa Cruz. St. James's business consisted of renting out a bus (with driver) to customers for bachelor parties and other similar events. The driver would shuttle passengers around Santa Cruz, California, often from bar to bar. Passengers were permitted to drink alcohol on the party buses. In late 2011, St. James became aware of a problem with one of his buses. The passenger door to the bus was broken and would no longer fully close. In the closed position, there was a three-inch gap between the door and the body of the bus. On one occasion, in early 2012, the bus door slid all the way open while a driver was on the freeway. The driver reported the problem to St. James who replied, "That's broken. It's just the way it is."

    On July 27, 2012, Carol rented a bus from St. James to celebrate a friend's birthday with a group trip to a concert in Mountain View, 40 minutes from Santa Cruz. During the drive back, an altercation ensued between two women on the bus. The two women, who were both intoxicated, grabbed one another and fell directly onto the passenger door. The door opened and the women fell out. They both died instantly.

    St. James was convicted of criminally negligent homicide. On appeal, he argued that there was insufficient evidence his negligence caused the deaths. Specifically, he argued that there were two independent intervening causes: the intoxicated passengers' behavior and the bus driver's failure to stop the passengers from fighting.

    **b.** Cervantes and his friends, all in their late teens, got into an argument with Linares and his friends at a house party. When the argument became physical, Cervantes pulled a gun and shot Linares in the arm. Cervantes then said to Linares's friends, "That's what you get for messing with us. If you want to do something about it, you know where to find us."

    Cervantes and his friends then left the party and returned to Cervantes's house. A few hours later, Linares's friends committed a "drive by" shooting at Cervantes's house. A bullet struck and killed one of Cervantes's friends who was inside the house, killing him.

    Cervantes was convicted of criminally negligent homicide in connection with his friend's death. On appeal, he argued that the government had failed to prove proximate causation because the "drive by" shooting broke the causal chain.

    **c.** Rex sold a heroin to Everly at a bar. Everly went to the bar bathroom to use the heroin. While in the bathroom, the ceiling collapsed, killing Everly. Rex was prosecuted and convicted under a statute that makes it a homicide offense to distribute a controlled substance "if death or serious bodily results from the use of such substance." On appeal, Rex argues that there was insufficient evidence of causation.

## H. HOMICIDE BY OMISSION

Unlike many other crimes, homicide does not have a specific *actus reus* element. Larceny requires the defendant to take property. Distribution of a controlled substance requires the defendant to convey an illegal drug to someone else. For homicide offenses, the *actus reus* is defined entirely by reference to the result. A homicide prosecution can rest on literally *any* voluntary act that causes death. Whether the defendant fired a bullet or struck the victim with a car, if the defendant's voluntary act caused the victim's death, then the *actus reus* element of homicide has been satisfied.

Most homicide prosecutions are based on an affirmative act taken by the defendant. But in certain circumstances, the failure to act (an omission) can serve as the basis for a homicide prosecution. We have already encountered one homicide-by-omission case in this chapter, *Brasse v. State*, where the defendant was convicted of involuntary manslaughter for his failure to seek medical treatment for his daughter. As you will recall, Brasse's conviction was overturned because there was insufficient evidence of his *mens rea*. But what about the *actus reus* and causation elements? Where a homicide prosecution is predicated on a defendant's failure to act, under what circumstances can the omission give rise to criminal liability?

The subject of omissions was introduced in Chapter 2. There, we learned that the default position is that criminal statutes do not create a general legal duty to act and therefore do not punish omissions. There are good reasons for this rule. Punishing omissions could result in sweeping criminal liability. Imagine an intruder breaks into a woman's apartment at 2 A.M. and she screams for help. No one calls 911, and the intruder kills the woman. If the failure to act were treated the same as a voluntary act, every one of the neighbors who heard the woman's screams but failed to call 911 could potentially be prosecuted for negligent homicide. Assigning criminal blameworthiness to the neighbors in this way would arguably be at odds with what we know about how people tend to behave in groups. Most likely, the neighbors who heard the woman and did not phone 911 assumed that someone else had already made the call. In fact, studies show that "the more people who witness an emergency, the less likely any of them will intervene to help. Being part of a passively observing group means that each individual assumes that others are available who could or will help, so there is less pressure to initiate action than there is when people are alone or with only one observer." Phillip Zimbardo, The Lucifer Effect 315 (2007).

Although the criminal law does not usually punish omissions, there are exceptions to this rule. In some cases, lawmakers criminalize the failure to perform a specific legal duty—the failure to file an income tax return, for example. Because homicide statutes define the *actus reus* as any act that causes the death of another human being, homicide-by-omission cases present a trickier problem. This definition clearly encompasses voluntary acts that cause another person's death. But there are a handful of circumstances where the law treats the failure to take action to prevent death as equivalent to an act causing death.

For inaction to give rise to homicide liability, the defendant must have been under a **legal duty to act**. Most jurisdictions recognize a legal duty to act in the following circumstances:

- *Special relationships*: The criminal law does not impose a duty to help our neighbors or even our close friends. But our relationships can occasionally create a legal duty to act. Two types of relationships, in particular, fall into this category. Parents (or legal guardians) have a legal duty to prevent harm to their minor children and spouses have a legal duty to prevent harm to each other. This kind of duty was the foundation for the prosecution in *Brasse*. The defendant's failure to seek medical care for the decedent in *Brasse* could be treated as a voluntary act causing death because the defendant was the decedent's father. Of course, the court reversed Brasse's conviction due to insufficient evidence of his *mens rea*. But when a parent's failure to seek care for a child is accompanied by the necessary culpable mental state, that omission can result in criminal liability.

- *Contractual obligations*: Some jobs come with an express or implied duty to care for another person's safety. The most prominent examples of jobs in this category are physicians, nursing home staff, lifeguards, and childcare providers. If a person hears her neighbor scream for help and fails to take action, she cannot be prosecuted for her omission. By contrast, if an employee at an assisted-living community hears a resident scream for help, her failure to act could result in criminal liability. The critical difference is that the assisted-living employee has a duty to act by virtue of her job. Because this kind of duty is linked to employment, it only exists when a person is on the job. A lifeguard who is relaxing at the beach on her day off would have no duty to care for the safety of other swimmers, for example.

- *Assumption of care*: In limited circumstances, a person who begins to provide aid to someone can be prosecuted if she stops mid-way through. This type of duty applies only if a person takes on sole or primary responsibility for helping someone at risk. In *West v. Commw.*, 935 S.W.2d 315 (Ky. Ct. App. 1996), for example, Russell West was convicted of a homicide offense based on his failure to sufficiently care for his 54-year-old disabled sister. West's sister, who had been born with Down Syndrome and a heart condition, lived with her mother until her mother passed away in 1983. At that time, West let his sister move in with him and took on responsibility for her care. Although adult siblings do not have a duty to care for one another by virtue of their relationship, the court upheld West's conviction on the grounds that he had "voluntarily assumed the care of another and so secluded the helpless person as to prevent others from rendering aid." *Id.* at 317 (quoting *Jones v. United States*, 308 F.2d 307, 310 (D.C. Cir. 1962).

- *Failing to assist after creating the risk*: Finally, a defendant who puts someone in harm's way may have a duty of care for that person. This concept can sometimes cause confusion. After all, if a defendant's act caused another's death, why would we need to resort to the concept of omissions? To understand when this duty can arise, consider the hypothetical case of Vernon, who drowns after being pushed into a swimming pool by Daria. If Daria knew that Vernon couldn't swim and pushed him into the pool intending to kill him, then Daria would be guilty of a homicide offense based on her act. If Daria mistakenly believed that Vernon could swim and pushed him into the pool as a prank, however, Daria would not have acted with the *mens rea* necessary to be convicted of even negligent homicide. Nevertheless, if Daria failed to help Vernon once she realized that Vernon could not swim, Daria could be prosecuted for her failure to act. Daria would have a legal duty to help Vernon in this circumstance because she created the risk when she pushed him into the pool.

Where a defendant has a duty to act and fails to do so, that omission can be considered an act causing death for purposes of homicide liability. Note that these categories can often leave morally reprehensible failures to act outside the bounds of criminal punishment. Imagine that Vincent, who cannot swim, falls into a pool and begins to flail around and scream for help. Doug, a world class swimmer, walks by and hears Vincent's call for help. Doug, who is late for an appointment, continues on his way instead of coming to Vincent's rescue. Vincent drowns and dies. In this (often used) hypothetical example, Doug cannot be convicted of a homicide offense because he had no legal duty under the criminal law to help Vincent.

The existence of a legal duty to act is a prerequisite to a homicide-by-omission prosecution. But in order for a homicide-by-omission prosecution to result in a conviction, the government will also have to prove that the defendant failed to satisfy his duty. What does the duty to act require? If a person is under a duty to act and does nothing at all, that is clearly insufficient. Beyond that, the issue can become more difficult. If a child is dangling from a 20-foot-high tree branch, does a parent need to climb up to try to rescue the child personally to fulfill her duty of care, or will a call to 911 suffice? Whether due to the exercise of prosecutorial discretion or some other factor, there is very little case law on this question. The published decisions suggest that the duty to act is not satisfied by just *any* action, but that heroic measures are not required. As one court has put it, "acts which are so feeble as to be ineffectual" are insufficient. *Commw. v. Cardwell*, 357 Pa. Super. 38, 46 (1986). Instead, "the person charged with the duty of care is required to take steps that are reasonably calculated to achieve success." *Id.*

## Chapter Summary

- Although every state's homicide statute is unique, the most common approach to grading homicides divides them into five different categories. First-degree murder punishes (a) killings that are willful, deliberate, and premeditated and (b) some felony murders. Second-degree murder punishes (a) intentional killings that are not willful, deliberate, and premeditated, (b) killings committed with the intent to inflict grievous bodily injury, (c) depraved heart murder, and (d) some felony murders. Voluntary manslaughter punishes killings that would otherwise constitute murder but that were done in the heat of passion. Involuntary/reckless manslaughter punishes killings where the perpetrator acted with ordinary recklessness. Negligent homicide punishes killings where the perpetrator acted with criminal negligence.

- The willful, deliberate, and premeditated test determines whether an intentional killing constitutes first- or second-degree murder. Jurisdictions are split on the question of how this test applies. One camp holds that premeditation can be formed in an instant, meaning that evidence that a person acted with the intent to kill is also sufficient to prove that the killing was willful, deliberate, and premeditated. In these jurisdictions, from the perspective of how appellate courts apply the law, there is effectively no distinction between first- and second-degree murder. The other camp holds that for a killing to be willful, deliberate, and premeditated, there must be proof that it resulted from pre-existing thought and reflection, which can be proven by evidence of planning activity, motive and prior relationship with the victim, and the manner of the killing.

- A crime that would otherwise constitute murder is graded as voluntary manslaughter if three requirements are met. First, the killer must have committed the crime in a state of passion. Second, the killer's passionate state must have been due to legally adequate provocation. Finally, under the cooling off period requirement, the killing must be relatively close in time to the provocation.

- An accidental killing constitutes murder if the killer acted with extreme recklessness. This type of homicide is sometimes referred to as depraved heart murder. What sets depraved heart murder apart from reckless manslaughter is the degree of risk and the social utility of the act. The kinds of acts that constitute depraved heart murder are those that carry a grave risk of death and have very little social utility. By committing an act like this, the defendant has demonstrated an extreme indifference to the value of human life.

- A person who kills recklessly is guilty of involuntary manslaughter (also referred to in some jurisdictions as reckless manslaughter). A person acts recklessly when he consciously disregards a substantial and unjustifiable risk that death will result from his conduct. The risk must be of such a nature that its disregard involves a gross deviation from the standard of care a law-abiding person would take.

- Negligent homicide punishes criminally negligent killings. The key factor that separates negligent killings from reckless killings is the defendant's awareness of the risk. A person who consciously disregards a substantial and unjustifiable risk acts recklessly, while a person who is not aware of a substantial and unjustifiable risk but should have been acts negligently. (Confusingly, some jurisdictions refer to both reckless and criminally negligent homicides as "involuntary manslaughter." This book avoids this semantic quirk by reserving the term involuntary manslaughter for reckless killings.)

- The felony murder rule provides that a death that results from the commission or attempted commission of a felony is murder. For the felony murder rule to apply, the death must have been within the *res gestae* of the felony. The *res gestae* requirement imposes both a temporal and a causal limit. First, the death must occur while the felony was being committed, a period that extends until a fleeing suspect has reached a place of temporary safety. Second, there must be a sufficient causal connection between the felony and the death.

■ The defendant's *mens rea* is typically what distinguishes the degrees of homicide offenses. The *actus reus* for all homicide offenses is any voluntary act that causes death (with the exception of felony murder, where the relevant causal connection is between the felony and the death). Causation is infrequently contested but must be proven in every homicide case. It requires a showing of but-for and proximate causation. In rare cases, where the defendant has a legal duty to help someone but fails to do so, an omission can substitute for the *actus reus* and causation requirements.

## Applying the Concepts

1. What do you think of how the law grades homicide offenses? If you were a legislator writing a homicide statute from scratch, would you follow the current approach? If not, how would your rules for categorizing homicides differ from the law today?

2. Derrick's favorite football team won the Super Bowl. To celebrate, Derrick shot a gun in the air from the top of his apartment building in a densely populated area. In his excitement, it never occurred to Derrick that firing his gun into the air was dangerous. Tragically, Derrick's bullet struck Vivian, who was walking her dog a few blocks away, killing her instantly. Assuming the jury believes Derrick's testimony that he did not know that firing his gun into the air was dangerous, what homicide offense should it convict Derrick of?

   a. Reckless manslaughter.
   b. Negligent homicide.
   c. Murder in the second degree.
   d. Murder in the first degree.

3. Dad owns a firearm. One day, Dad is cleaning his gun and grows tired. Dad decides to go to sleep without putting the gun away in its safe. Dad leaves the gun on the kitchen table. Son, who is 8 years old, wakes up in the middle of the night to get a snack. Son sees the gun and starts to play with it. While Son is playing with the gun, it fires and the bullet strikes Son in the head, killing him. Can Dad be convicted of a homicide offense in this case?

   a. Yes, because Dad owed a duty to Son, his failure to put the gun away is a criminally blameworthy omission.
   b. Yes, because Dad's voluntary act of leaving the gun out caused Son's death.
   c. No, because Son's act of playing with the gun was an intervening cause.
   d. No, because no jury could find that Dad acted with a sufficiently culpable *mens rea*.

4. Deborah, an African-American woman in her mid-20s, is at a bar one night. Deborah has a few drinks but is sober enough that she can form culpable mental states. An older white man named Vlad, who is severely intoxicated, walks up to Deborah and begins to call her names, using racial epithets. Deborah ignores Vlad at first but Vlad continues his racist rant. Deborah politely asks Vlad to stop. Vlad again refuses and says to Deborah: "If you're so upset, why don't you make me stop?" Vlad then emphasizes his point by calling Deborah racial and gender-based slurs. Deborah suddenly snaps. She sees a sharp knife a few steps away at the edge of the bar. Deborah decides right then to stab Vlad. Deborah walks over to the knife, grabs it, and lunges toward Vlad's heart. The knife strikes Vlad right in the middle of his chest and he dies a few minutes later. What homicide offense, if any, can Deborah be convicted of?

5. Depraved heart murder, reckless manslaughter, and negligent homicide all punish accidental killings. In your own words, briefly describe what differentiates these types of homicides from one another. Then, as best as you are able to do from memory alone, briefly describe the facts and holdings of the cases you read that addressed these offenses. Finally, look back at the cases and material and see how well your memory matched up to what was assigned.

6. Vincent, Jules, and Marvin decide to rob a convenience store together. Jules drives the group to the store and waits in the car while Vincent and Marvin go inside. Vincent pulls a gun from his waistband and demands money. The cashier hands all of the money from the register over to Marvin. Vincent and Marvin run back out to the car and Jules drives off. Three blocks from the convenience store, Vincent, who is in the front passenger seat, turns around and starts talking with Marvin, who is seated in the back. Vincent still has the gun in his hand. Because Vincent rests his hand near the top of the passenger's seat during his conversation with Marvin, the gun is pointed in Marvin's direction. Seven blocks from the convenience store, the car hits a big bump in the road, causing Vincent to accidentally pull the trigger on the gun. The bullet strikes Marvin, killing him instantly. What homicide offense, if any, can Vincent be convicted of? What homicide offense, if any, can Jules be convicted of? Assume for purposes of this question that Vincent and Jules are both guilty of robbery, a felony.

## Criminal Law in Practice

1. This chapter describes the predominant approach to grading homicide offenses. As with most of the criminal law, however, homicide statutes differ from one state to the next. Look up the statutory provisions in your state that grade homicide offenses. (In some states, this might be contained in a single part of the penal code, while other states use multiple code sections.) Are there any differences between the predominant method of grading homicide offenses covered in this chapter and your state's homicide statute? If so, what are they? Which approach do you think is a better one?

2. Search to see if your state has a model jury instruction for first-degree murder that addresses the requirement of premeditation. If you are unable to find a model instruction for your state — either because your state does not follow the premeditation rule or because model instructions are not readily available online — look up Florida's standard jury instruction for first-degree murder. How does your state's jury instruction define the premeditation rule? How does that definition compare to the two main approaches to premeditation discussed in this chapter?

3. You are a public defender representing Michelle, who is 20 years old and charged with involuntary manslaughter. Michelle's boyfriend, Conrad, who was 18, texted her that he was thinking of committing suicide by using car exhaust fumes. Conrad had been depressed for some time and had spoken like this to Michelle before. This time, Michelle replied to Conrad that he should go through with it. Conrad then got into his car and began the process of filling it with carbon monoxide. All the while, Conrad continued to exchange text messages with Michelle. Suddenly, Conrad had second thoughts and exited the vehicle. When Conrad texted Michelle to let her know, Michelle responded with a text encouraging him to "get back in" the car. "The time is right and you are ready . . . just do it babe. You said you were gonna do it. Like, I don't get why you aren't," Michelle texted. After receiving the texts, Conrad got back into the car and died from carbon monoxide poisoning.

   a. You are preparing for the trial. You plan to argue to the jury that there is insufficient evidence of causation because Conrad's acts were an intervening cause. Draft a summary of how you would frame this argument to the jury.

   b. Two days before trial, the prosecutor offers your client a plea deal. Under the deal, Michelle would plead guilty to the crime of negligent endangerment, a misdemeanor, with a recommended sentence of six months of probation. Would you advise Michelle to accept this plea offer? Or do you think Michelle has a sufficiently strong chance of success at trial that you would advise her to reject this plea offer?

4. Imagine you are the prosecutor in a case with the same facts described in Question 3 from the *Applying the Concepts* section immediately above. As a matter of your exercise of prosecutorial discretion, would you bring homicide charges against Dad? If so, what homicide offense would you charge him with, and why? If you could charge Dad with a lesser offense, such as child neglect, would that impact your charging decision with respect to the homicide offense?

# Sex Offenses

Sex offenses are considered to be a particularly serious category of crime. The average time served in prison by people convicted of rape or sexual assault (6.2 years) is second only to that of people convicted of murder or voluntary manslaughter (15 years) and greater than that of people convicted of negligent homicide (5.2 years). Danielle Kaeble, Bureau of Justice Statistics, U.S. Dep't of Justice, NCJ 252205, *Time Served in State Prison, 2016*, at 2 tbl. 1 (Nov. 2018). (Note that because these figures do not include time served while in jail awaiting trial, the average time of total incarceration is longer for each of these offenses.) In addition to rape, there are myriad other sex offenses, including statutory rape, child molestation, and crimes related to child pornography. For many sex offenses, a conviction also requires the defendant to register as a sex offender after release from custody. Notably, in many states, sex offender registration requirements are not reserved for offenses like rape and child molestation but can also apply to less serious sex offenses, such as indecent exposure.

In this chapter, we focus on three areas: rape, statutory rape, and laws against child pornography. As we will see, with respect to legal doctrine, there is an especially high degree of jurisdictional variation when it comes to these offenses. The crime of rape has changed significantly from its common law form, largely as a result of feminist critiques of rape law in the 1970s and 1980s. The extent to which the law has changed varies from state to state, however. States also take different approaches to statutory rape when it comes to the *mens rea* required (if any) regarding the age of the victim. Other significant sex offenses, like child pornography–related crimes, came into existence relatively recently and a uniform approach has yet to emerge.

## Key Concepts

- What are the major jurisdictional approaches to the elements of the crime of rape?
- How do the force and *mens rea* elements of rape relate to one another?
- What *mens rea*, if any, is required for the crime of statutory rape?
- What are the different approaches states have taken with respect to the application of child pornography statutes to a teenager who sends a pornographic image of him- or herself to someone else?

# A. RAPE

In nearly every jurisdiction today, the core elements of the crime of **rape** include (1) sexual intercourse (2) without consent. A majority of jurisdictions include a third element: force, or a threat of force. Closely related to the element of force, a minority of jurisdictions also require resistance on the part of the victim. As we will see, jurisdictions are split in how they define the force element and the resistance requirement. Jurisdictions are also split on the *mens rea* required for the offense — specifically, with respect to the victim's lack of consent.

Before examining the modern elements of rape further, it is helpful to have some background about the history of the offense and the practical significance of the issues on which jurisdictions are split today.

Rape law has a troubling history. As Susan Estrich put it in her influential article, *Rape*, 95 Yale L.J. 1087, 1089 (1986): "The history of rape, as the law has been enforced in this country, is a history of both racism and sexism." When the common law offense of rape developed in medieval England, it "appears to have been seen more as an offense against the honor and property of the victim's family than as a crime against her sexual autonomy." Guyora Binder & Robert Weisberg, *What Is Criminal Law About?*, 114 Mich. L. Rev. 1173, 1184 (2016). Put more directly: "Rape became a crime solely because of male interests in their current or prospective spouses." Corey Rayburn Yung, *Rape Law Fundamentals*, 27 Yale J.L. & Feminism 1, 15 (2015). This was, of course, consistent with the common law's subjugation of woman more broadly, including the doctrine of coverture, under which a wife had no legal identity separate from her husband. As might be expected, rape law's misogynistic roots shaped the common law definition of the crime. Under the common law definition, the offense was limited to sexual intercourse between a man and a woman who was not his spouse. This meant that a man could not commit rape against his wife. This definition also "rendered the 'rape' of a man as 'not rape.'" Bennett Capers, *Real Rape, Too*, 99 Cal. L. Rev. 1259, 1290 (2011). In addition, although not a product of criminal law doctrine per se, "[d]uring slavery, the rape of a black woman by any man, white or black, was simply not a crime." Angela P. Harris, *Race and Essentialism in Feminist Legal Theory*, 42 Stan. L. Rev. 581, 599 (1990).

The common law elements of the crime of rape included a very strict requirement of force or the threat of force overcoming physical resistance. The physical resistance element, in particular, resulted in an offense that applied in only a very narrow set of circumstances. Under this element, a conviction for rape required the victim to have engaged in the "utmost resistance"; "[m]ere verbal unwillingness," or even active physical resistance by the victim, was not sufficient. *State v. Cowing*, 99 Minn. 123, 126 (1906). One representative decision described the utmost resistance requirement in this way: "Not only must there be an entire absence of mental consent or assent, but there must be the most vehement exercise of every physical means or faculty within the woman's power to resist the penetration of her person, and this must be shown to persist until the offense is consummated." *Brown v. State*, 127 Wis. 193, 199 (1906). Under that requirement, "[c]ourts held that, even in the face of specific violent threats, consent could be given through 'voluntary' submission to the rapist." Yung, *supra*, at 15. As a result, published court decisions from this era frequently overturned convictions involving violent attacks on the ground that the victim "eventually gave up resisting" the rape. *Id.* The strict force and resistance requirements also effectively rendered the perpetrator's mental state a non-issue because the conduct required for a conviction itself "was manifestly incriminating." Binder & Weisberg, *supra*, at 1185.

Even as the legal status of women began to shift in the 1800s and 1900s, the common law definition of rape remained largely unchanged in the United States. During this period, "American rape law was part of the larger state effort to police sexuality in general, entrench male domination over women through chastity and ownership paradigms, and enforce white racial supremacy." Aya Gruber, *Rape, Feminism, and the War on Crime*, 84 Wash. L. Rev. 581, 587 (2009). Race figured prominently in the conception of rape law of the 1800s and early 1900s: "During this era, the law of rape incorporated the paradigm of a pathological stranger, prototypically a black man, lurking in the shadows, ready to violently assault the presumed-chaste (white) woman. White men, by contrast, had a virtual license to rape, as the law required 'true' victims to be ultimately innocent ladies who would rather fight to the death than give up their virginity. Owing to these paradigms, black men became primary targets of rape prosecutions (officially), and lynchings (less officially). For this reason, some of the earliest progressive objections to rape law were that they were overenforced, not underenforced." *Id.* at 587-88.

Rape law began to undergo a dramatic shift in the latter half of the twentieth century. The utmost resistance requirement, in particular, became a focal point of criticism during this period. "The intensely chauvinistic parameters of rape law were not lost on feminists, and in the 1970s and 1980s, 'second-wave' feminist activists engaged in concerted efforts to reform rape law and educate the public about sexual assault stereotypes." *Id.* at 591-92. Scholars and advocates including Susan Brownmiller, Catharine MacKinnon, and Susan Estrich helped to lead an effort to reform rape law. Their work resulted in a number of significant changes. Some of their proposals, such as expanding the offense to include marital rape and eliminating the utmost resistance requirement, were universally or nearly universally adopted. Other proposals, like eliminating the force requirement, have been adopted in some states and not others. Most states have also expanded rape to cover not only vaginal intercourse but additional penetrative sex acts as well.

This short historical background will be helpful to better understanding the modern rape doctrine and jurisdictional variants covered in the rest of this section. As we will see, in states that have retained the element of force or threat of force, courts have struggled over how to define it. Similarly, courts continue to face difficult cases regarding *mens rea* — an issue that has become more relevant in large part because of the rejection of the utmost resistance requirement and reforms to the force/threat of force element.

Before proceeding, it is worth highlighting one point about the limited practical significance, in many cases, of the jurisdictional variations regarding the elements of the crime of rape. In many rape trials, the acts alleged by the prosecution and testified to by the victim would constitute rape under any modern statute. Instead of a dispute about the law, the verdict often depends entirely on whether the jury credits

## Underenforcement of Rape Laws

Although rape is classified as an especially serious offense, there is evidence to suggest that it is also seriously underenforced. An analysis of federal data by the advocacy group RAINN (the Rape, Abuse and Incest National Network) concluded that just 31 percent of rapes are reported to the police, and that only 0.7 percent of rapes result in a felony conviction. See Andrew Van Dam, *Less Than 1% of Rapes Lead to Felony Convictions*, Wash. Post, Oct. 6, 2018 (reporting on RAINN's findings). Reasons for underreporting by victims include "shame, denial, fear of retaliation, and doubts that they would be believed or that any appropriate response would be forthcoming." Deborah L. Rhode, *#metoo: Why Now? What Next?*, 69 Duke L.J. 377, 409 (2019). There are many factors that contribute to the low felony conviction rate for reported rapes. A major one is that " '[a]cquaintance rape' cases, . . . which occur when the defendant knows the victim, are the most common type of rape in the United States. Yet they are also the cases that police are least likely to investigate and that prosecutors are least likely to pursue, and, ultimately, those in which juries are least likely to convict." Margo Kaplan, *Rape Beyond Crime*, 66 Duke L.J. 1045, 1059-60 (2017).

the victim's testimony or the defendant's testimony. As former Congresswoman Susan Molinari put it when arguing in support of an amendment to the Federal Rules of Evidence for rape cases, "adult-victim sexual assault cases are distinctive, and often turn on difficult credibility determinations. Alleged consent by the victim is rarely an issue in prosecutions for other violent crimes — the accused mugger does not claim that the victim freely handed over his wallet as a gift — but the defendant in a rape case often contends that the victim engaged in consensual sex and then falsely accused him." *Floor Statement of the Principal House Sponsor, Representative Susan Molinari, Concerning the Prior Crimes Evidence Rules for Sexual Assault and Child Molestation Cases*, 140 Cong. Rec. H8991-92 (daily ed. Aug. 21, 1994). This dynamic is aggravated by the fact that, in comparison to many other offenses, rape cases are more likely to be committed in a private setting, and so are less likely to have a non-victim witness. As a result, many rape prosecutions involve so-called swearing matches, in which the victim testifies that the defendant engaged in conduct that would constitute rape under any modern definition of the crime, while the defendant testifies that the victim affirmatively consented to sex and is now falsely accusing him. Criminal law doctrine can occasionally play an important role in these kinds of cases, but not often. This is because if the defendant's position at trial is that the victim affirmatively consented to sex and is now testifying falsely, the verdict will almost always depend entirely on whether the jury credits the victim's testimony.

Of course, in a criminal law course, our focus is on learning about the elements of the crime of rape, including important jurisdictional variations. In some cases, these jurisdictional differences can be outcome determinative. But it is worth keeping in mind that in so-called swearing match cases, differences in jurisdictional variations regarding the elements of the crime are unlikely to have much practical significance.

## 1. Force, Threat of Force, and Resistance

As discussed above, two of the most significant changes to rape law that emerged in the 1970s and 1980s involved the force and resistance elements. These two elements are very closely related, and we examine them together in this section.

## **Case Preview**

### *State v. Jones*

In the case that follows, the court considered and applied the force and resistance elements in a case that involved two rape convictions. The court upheld one of the two convictions and overturned the other.

As you read the decision, consider the following questions:

1. How many jurisdictions continue to maintain a resistance element in the crime of rape?
2. What sort of evidence is sufficient to prove resistance under the approach adopted by the court?
3. What is the difference between the extrinsic force standard and intrinsic force standard?
4. Which force standard does the court adopt, and what sort of evidence is sufficient to satisfy the force element under that standard?

---

## *State v. Jones*
### 2011 WL 4011738 (Idaho Ct. App. Sept. 12, 2011)

GUTIERREZ, J.

Russell G. Jones appeals from the judgments of conviction entered upon jury verdicts finding him guilty of two counts of rape. For the reasons set forth below, we affirm in part and reverse in part. More specifically, we uphold the conviction in regard to Count I and vacate the conviction in regard to Count II.

Jones, A.S., and Craig Carpenter had been friends for approximately fifteen years in the spring of 2008. A.S. and Carpenter were engaged and had children together. However, unbeknownst to Carpenter, Jones and A.S. had been having a sexual relationship for approximately four years. On May 22, 2008, after spending the night alone together in Jackpot, Nevada, Jones and A.S. returned to A.S.'s apartment—deciding on the drive back to Idaho they should end their affair. However, the next morning they engaged in consensual sex. Afterwards, A.S. went to the bathroom and when she returned to the bedroom Jones was on the computer looking at pornographic material. He sat down on the bed next to her and began to touch her. A.S. reacted by telling Jones, "[I] thought we had decided that the time before that was the last time and it wasn't going to happen anymore." Jones stopped touching her, got up, and walked around behind her. A.S. got up on her elbows and saw that Jones was unfastening his pants. She protested that she did not want to engage in intercourse, but he "leaned forward" and A.S. was "pushed down . . . to where [she] couldn't get up" and her arms were pinned beneath her body. Jones then moved A.S.'s underwear aside and had intercourse with her. Afterward, Jones apologized to A.S., asked her if she was alright, and told her that she could "press charges" if she wanted to because he was "out of line" and had "lost control." After Jones left the residence, A.S. called the Women's Center at Boise State University and spoke to a counselor. After telling the counselor that she had been raped, she was advised to call the police, which she did not do. She continued to be in contact with Jones, including going with him again to Jackpot.

Several days later on May 27, Jones came to watch movies at A.S.'s residence. Jones spent the night on A.S.'s couch and remained in the apartment after Carpenter left for work and A.S.'s children left for school. A.S. testified that during this time she was taking a prescribed anti-anxiety medication which caused her to experience marked drowsiness and had taken an over-the-counter antihistamine to treat a bee sting, which also caused her to feel drowsy. Due to her drowsiness, A.S. lay down on the couch in the living room, while Jones used the computer in her bedroom. Jones entered the living room, sat next to her, and began to stroke her hair. A.S. testified that Jones pulled her hair, but A.S. did not respond and pretended to be asleep. Jones then grabbed at A.S.'s breasts, forcefully touched her private area, and proceeded to engage in intercourse with her while she was lying on the couch and not moving. A.S. testified that she was "paralyzed by fear" and neither physically resisted Jones nor made any verbal protest. A.S. testified that she had hoped Jones would cease if she did not respond to him physically.

After the encounter, the two went to the bedroom and shared a cigarette. Jones assisted A.S. in getting into bed and again began to have sexual intercourse with her. There was no testimony by A.S. that she protested or asked Jones to stop during this second encounter, and he stopped on his own accord, stating "Baby, I do have a problem." He asked if they could resume having sex, which she refused. Jones eventually left the residence.

A.S. drove to Carpenter's brother's house and told him and his girlfriend that Jones had raped her. They took A.S. to the hospital, where she told staff that she had been sexually assaulted, but did not want to press any legal charges. However, law enforcement officers were contacted and A.S. provided a statement to the police while at the hospital.

On May 29, A.S. met with a detective who arranged a recorded confrontation call. On the tape, Jones is heard apologizing for both incidents, admitting to A.S. that he "continued" with the sexual acts despite her telling him no in the first instance and her not responding in the second instance, and agreeing that, after the first instance, he sent her text messages "promising [her] it wouldn't happen again."

Jones was charged with two counts of forcible rape, Idaho Code § 18-6101(3), based on the May 22 incident in the bedroom (Count I) and the May 27 incident on the couch (Count II). At trial, A.S. testified as to her version of the events regarding the two counts of rape and admitted that she had never informed police that she and Jones had been involved in a consensual sexual relationship for four years at the time of the incidents. She also admitted that she had given police an incomplete account of the facts when providing them with her statements — specifically, she did not tell them that she had engaged in consensual sex with Jones earlier in the day on May 22, and while she had shown officers text messages from Jones that she thought were incriminating, she did not reveal to the officers other text messages that she had sent to Jones indicating that she loved him and that would have revealed their past relationship. Additionally, A.S. admitted that as of the time of trial she was still concealing her past sexual relationship with Jones from Carpenter.

Defense counsel cross-examined A.S. at length about a letter she had written in which she recanted her allegations of rape—which had been notarized and given to the prosecution prior to trial. In the letter, A.S. characterized the events forming the basis of her allegations of rape as a misunderstanding between her and Jones and asserted that Jones was being wrongfully charged. A.S. later sent the prosecutor another letter retracting her retraction and indicating her desire to go forward with the rape charges—a change of heart which she indicated was due to having undergone counseling.

The State presented the testimony of the registered nurse who performed the examination of A.S. on May 28. The nurse indicated that A.S. appeared frightened, was crying, spoke in a soft tone of voice, did not make eye contact, and curled up in the fetal position after the examination. The nurse also testified that she found no physical findings of trauma consistent with rape during the examination, specifically that there was no evidence of bruising, scraping, or scratches anywhere on A.S.'s body.

At the close of evidence, Jones moved for a directed verdict based on the failure of the State to prove that A.S. resisted sexual intercourse and that her resistance was overcome by force. The district court denied the motion. The jury convicted Jones of both counts of rape and Jones was sentenced to concurrent twenty-five year sentences, with five years determinate for each count. Jones now appeals.

## ANALYSIS

Jones contends that there was insufficient evidence to support the jury's verdicts on both counts because the State failed to prove, beyond a reasonable doubt, both that A.S. physically resisted Jones and that her resistance was overcome by force or violence, elements that are required by the statute.

Appellate review of the sufficiency of the evidence is limited in scope. A judgment of conviction, entered upon a jury verdict, will not be overturned on appeal where there is substantial evidence upon which a reasonable trier of fact could have found that the prosecution sustained its burden of proving the essential elements of a crime beyond a reasonable doubt. We will not substitute our view for that of the jury as to the credibility of the witnesses, the weight to be given to the testimony, and the reasonable inferences to be drawn from the evidence.

Jones was charged solely under I.C. § 18-6101(3) in both counts. At the time of the charged offenses, the statute provided that:

Rape is defined as the penetration, however slight, of the oral, anal or vaginal opening with the perpetrator's penis accomplished with a female under any one (1) of the following circumstances:

. . .

(3) Where she resists but her resistance is overcome by force or violence.

As stated in the comment to Idaho Criminal Jury Instruction 904, entitled "Resistance to Rape," which was given to the jury in this case:

In Idaho, a rape victim is not required to resist to the utmost of the victim's ability. The importance of resistance by the victim is simply to show two elements of the crime — the assailant's intent to use force in order to have sexual intercourse and the victim's non-consent.

### 1. Count I

Jones contends that in regard to Count I, there was insufficient evidence to support the charge because there were no facts establishing "either physical force on the part of Mr. Jones, nor any physical resistance in any fashion on the part of [A.S.]."

### a. Resistance

Jones contends that while A.S. testified that during the May 22 encounter she told Jones several times that she did not want to have sex with him, this evidence goes to a lack of consent, but does not, in itself, "show any proof of physical resistance on her part, nor the use of force or violence on the part of Mr. Jones." He cites to *State v. Roles*, 122 Idaho 138 (Ct. App. 1992) for the proposition that Idaho case law has "implicitly recognized the distinction between force and lack of consent in forcible rape." Jones contends that under Idaho case law, "while lack of consent is an implied element of rape, proof of mere lack of consent cannot substitute for actual evidence of force and resistance where the state charges a defendant with forcible rape pursuant to I.C. § 18-6101(3)."

Thus, we first examine whether there was sufficient evidence presented that A.S. "resisted" Jones as to Count I. Because it is undisputed that the only possible resistance that A.S. engaged in was verbal, the question is specifically whether Jones is correct in his assertion that the statute requires physical resistance or whether verbal resistance alone satisfies the element.

The term "resistance" is not defined in the statute, nor is there any attendant legislative history. We note that at common law a state had to prove beyond a reasonable doubt that the woman resisted her assailant to the utmost of her physical capacity to prove that an act of sexual intercourse was rape — known as the "utmost resistance" standard. Michelle J. Anderson, *Reviving Resistance in Rape Law*, U. Ill. L. Rev. 953, 962 (1998). Thus, legal decision-makers have historically ignored evidence of a woman's verbal resistance; under the law, verbal resistance was simply inadequate to prove anything.

When it became apparent that the "utmost" resistance standard made rape nearly impossible to prove, many states began to abandon the requirement. In its place, some states required that women exert only "earnest" resistance to establish that an act of sexual intercourse was without consent and by force — a standard which remains codified in two states. Rejecting the "utmost" and "earnest" resistance requirements, other jurisdictions have moved to require only "reasonable" resistance on the part of the rape victim. This standard, still codified by six states, requires that a woman offer resistance which is "reasonable under the circumstances," and she is not required to actively resist if she reasonably believes that resistance would be useless and would result in serious bodily injury.

[A]pproximately thirty-two states, . . . the District of Columbia Code, and the Uniform Code of Military Justice eliminated the formal resistance requirement altogether by not mentioning resistance in the statutory language describing rape, allowing prosecutors to establish that a rape occurred even in the absence of any resistance by the woman. Six more states explicitly note in their criminal codes that physical resistance is not required to substantiate a rape charge. Thus, Idaho remains one of few states that still statutorily require resistance to prove forcible rape and one of even fewer whose statute does not specify the requisite amount of resistance that will suffice.

While not explicitly addressing the issue, early twentieth-century Idaho cases provide insight into the nature of the statute's resistance requirement. In *State v. Neil*, 13 Idaho 539, 547 (1907), the Idaho Supreme Court held that a victim need not resist to the utmost of her ability, thus deviating from the common-law requirement of utmost resistance. The Court further explored the resistance requirement stating: "[t]he importance of resistance by the woman is simply to show two elements of the crime — the assailant's intent to use force in order to have carnal knowledge, and the woman's non-consent." We interpret [*Neil*] as pointing toward a less restrictive interpretation of the resistance requirement than is argued by Jones.

Given Idaho's statutory and case law history, we . . . ascertain that "resist" as it is used in Idaho's forcible rape statute does not require that the victim have *physically* resisted. First and foremost, the plain language of the statute does not indicate that resistance must be physical. In addition, it has also been established that a victim need not resist to the utmost of her ability and that the importance of resistance by the victim is simply to show two elements of the crime — the assailant's intent to use force in order to have sexual intercourse and the victim's non-consent. To interpret the statute rigidly as requiring physical resistance is contrary to the general tenor of these decisions. Accordingly, we hold that whether the evidence establishes the element of resistance is a fact-sensitive determination based on the totality of the circumstances, *including the victim's words* and conduct.

We note that this standard is not a "reasonable" resistance standard which determines the reasonableness of a victim's resistance against an objective standard of reasonableness. Such an approach is problematic because it defeats the very rationale that brought about its existence (in a progression from the utmost resistance standard), which is the fact that not every victim reacts similarly to rape. It is very difficult, if not impossible, to quantify how a rape victim would react under "same or similar circumstances." Rather, the standard we apply includes consideration of the victim's individual characteristics in determining whether she exhibited legally recognizable resistance.

Turning to the facts of the instant case [for Count I], we conclude that there was substantial evidence that the jury could find that A.S. resisted Jones's advances. A.S. testified that she "kept yelling at [Jones] and pleading for him to stop and please quit" and was unable to physically resist because he was on top of her, pinning her arms beneath her body. Jones's statements to her afterwards indicate that he knew she did not want to engage in the act — including telling her that he had "lost control." This evidence unequivocally shows that A.S. explicitly communicated to Jones her non-consent to sexual intercourse. Accordingly, we conclude that there was substantial evidence for a reasonable trier of fact to conclude that A.S. "resisted" as required by the statute.

## b. Force or Violence

Jones also contends there was insufficient evidence to prove that he used force or violence to overcome A.S.'s resistance. Specifically, he notes that there was no evidence presented that he was violent towards A.S., nor that he applied any physical force beyond that required to accomplish the actual penetration. The State counters, contending evidence that Jones pushed A.S. down, pinned her arms under her, adjusted her underwear, and proceeded to engage her sexually was sufficient evidence of force or violence.

While Idaho's forcible rape statute identifies the necessary *effect* of the force (that it overcome the victim's resistance), it does not otherwise indicate the *quantum* of force required. The amount of force required by the forcible rape statute — specifically, whether the force exerted must be more than is inherent in the sexual act — is an issue of first impression in Idaho.

[B]ecause the statutes defining the crime of rape typically do not establish an amount of physical coercion sufficient to demonstrate that sexual activity was accomplished "by force," the requisite degree of force mandated by the courts has been subject to considerable dispute and variation. For the most part, however, the treatment by the courts of this issue reflects one of two standards — which represent different approaches to the force element and to the degree and mechanisms of force that the prosecution must show in order to obtain a rape conviction — the intrinsic force standard and the extrinsic force standard. The latter approach reflects the more traditional view, which is that the force requirement ordinarily requires proof of use of force or threat of force *above and beyond* that inherent in the act of nonconsensual intercourse, while the intrinsic force standard is the opposite, that force inherent in the act itself suffices.

An over one-hundred-year-old United States Supreme Court case, *Mills v. United States*, 164 U.S. 644 (1897), set the precedent that in certain instances, the defendant must have demonstrated force beyond the act of raping the victim in order for a rape conviction to be sustained. This extrinsic force standard is still the most commonly adopted. In *Commonwealth v. Berkowitz*, 537 Pa. 143 (1994), the Pennsylvania Supreme Court applied the standard, holding that the defendant had not committed rape because the victim failed to show that the defendant had used the requisite force or threat of force to compel her to have intercourse. The victim in the case had entered the defendant's dorm room in search of the defendant's roommate. After locking the door, the defendant sat beside the victim, lifted up her shirt, and fondled her breasts. The victim offered no physical resistance as he proceeded to engage in sexual intercourse with her, but testified that she had repeatedly stated "no" during the encounter. Noting that the issue of force is "relative and depends on the facts of the case," the court determined that the prosecution had not demonstrated the forcible compulsion element, focusing primarily on the actual degree of physical force exerted by the defendant — specifically the precise degree of the shove by which the defendant had put the victim on the bed and whether the untying of her sweatpants was the only physical contact made with the defendant. The court also noted the victim had agreed that the defendant had not verbally threatened her, the defendant's hands were not restraining her in any manner during the actual penetration, and that the weight of his body on top of her was the only force applied.[7] *Cf. Commonwealth v. Garaffa*, 440 Pa. Super. 484 (1995) (distinguishing *Berkowitz* where the defendant had *pushed* the victim down on the bed and the victim had fought the defendant's advances and pushed him away).

On the other hand, the adoption of the intrinsic force standard is indicative of a modern trend toward the eradication of the element of force and is most clearly observed in recent court opinions that narrowly construe sexual assault provisions in favor of the victim. In New Jersey, for example, forcible sexual assault is defined as "sexual penetration with another person" with the use of "physical force or coercion." N.J. Stat. Ann. § 2C:14-2c(1) (West 2011). [In *In re M.T.S.*, 129 N.J. 422 (1992), t]he New Jersey Supreme Court . . . adopt[ed] the intrinsic force standard which effectively eliminates the need for the prosecution to demonstrate any extra force beyond the actual intercourse with the victim. In *M.T.S.*, the victim testified that she fell asleep on her bed and awoke to find that her shorts and underwear were removed and the defendant was lying on top of her in the act of penetration. The court first concluded that, as evidenced by disagreements among lower courts and the parties, as well as the variety of possible usages as defined in the dictionary, the statutory words "physical force" did not evoke a single meaning that was obvious and plain, and thus the court had to engage in statutory construction. The court then traced the history of rape law and its now seemingly arcane requirements which essentially put the victim "on trial" and then, in this context, recognized that the current rape statute had been conceived of as a reform measure which would result in the treatment of rape victims just like those of other violent crimes — an important consideration in understanding the legislative intent and determining the objectives of the law.

While generally considered progress in the area of rape law reform, the intrinsic force standard essentially renders the issue of force moot, instead shifting the analysis to the issue of consent. It removes rape from the special category of violent crimes where most courts have pigeonholed it, placing it in the group of assaultive crimes where contact is measured by its unlawfulness and not by the degree of forcefulness. In this sense, it is incompatible with Idaho's statutory scheme, which places significant emphasis on the element of force — prescribing that it must be sufficient to "overcome" a victim's resistance and which has not been subject to the rape law reforms seen in much of the country. In the case at issue here, the nonconsent of the victim was certainly at issue — in the form of whether she resisted — especially where the two were adults that had engaged in a prolonged consensual sexual relationship and had engaged in consensual sex, in regard to Count I, mere minutes before.

Most courts with similar language to that found in Idaho's rape statute, requiring that the force or violence "overcome" resistance, have interpreted their statutes to require extrinsic force. Quite simply, this terminology implies that force other than that inherent in the proscribed sexual act be used to overcome a

---

[7] Following the *Berkowitz* decision, the Pennsylvania legislature responded by enacting a statute intended to fill the loophole left by the rape and involuntary deviate sexual intercourse statutes by criminalizing nonconsensual sex where the perpetrator employs little or no force, 18 Pa. C.S.A. § 3124.1 (West 2011), and by defining "forcible compulsion" as "[c]ompulsion by use of physical, intellectual, moral, emotional or psychological force, either express or implied." 18 Pa. C.S.A. § 3101 (West 2011).

victim's resistance — implying that the force must occur before penetration. *See, e.g., Commonwealth v. Wallace*, 76 Mass. App. Ct. 411 (2010) (interpreting rape statute to mean the Commonwealth must prove that the defendant *compelled* the victim to submit by force and against his will). The Idaho Legislature has not undertaken the rape law reform that characterizes those states which have departed from the traditional extrinsic force standard. Thus, we conclude that the extrinsic force standard is applicable in regard to Idaho's forcible rape statute.

In the conduct charged as Count I here, it is undisputed that the extent of Jones's physical contact with A.S. during the incident, aside from penetration, was coming up from behind her, laying on top of her, pushing her down from being propped up on her elbows, thus causing her arms to be pinned beneath her by his body weight, and moving her underwear aside. Accordingly, we must determine whether Jones exerted the requisite force beyond penetration to overcome A.S.'s resistance.

One criticism of the extrinsic force standard is that it is inherently more ambiguous than the intrinsic force standard because it requires more evidence and naturally gives rise to the question of just how much more will suffice. Another commentator has noted that because the "distinction between the 'force' incidental to the act of intercourse and the 'force' required to convict a man of rape is one commonly drawn by courts," it "would seem to require the courts to define what additional acts are needed to constitute prohibited rather than incidental force." As a result, the outcomes are generally all over the map, with the degree of force required varying from state to state and generally being a function of the facts and circumstances of each case.

For example, on one end of the spectrum is the holding in *Berkowitz*, 641 A.2d at 1164, where the Pennsylvania Supreme Court held that the requisite force had not been shown where the defendant had not verbally threatened the victim, the defendant's hands were not restraining her in any manner during the actual penetration, and the weight of his body on top of her was the only force applied. On the other hand, numerous jurisdictions have found the requisite force under circumstances similar to those in *Berkowitz*. In [*State v. Jacques*, 536 A.2d 535 (R.I. 1988)], after adopting the extrinsic force standard . . . , the Rhode Island Supreme Court applied the standard to the facts of the case. There, the defendant who was allegedly performing a photo shoot, instructed the victim to walk to a wing-back chair, which was against the wall opposite the desk. As she proceeded toward the chair, the defendant told her that he was getting excited by her body. The victim testified that at this point she became very frightened. As she arrived at the chair, she felt the pressure of the defendant's chest pushing against her back. This pressure caused her to fall into a kneeling position onto the chair facing the wall, after which he sexually assaulted her. On appeal, the defendant contended that he had not exerted the requisite force to be convicted of first degree sexual assault. The Supreme Court disagreed, noting that "the force of [the defendant's] chest pushing against her caused her to kneel in the chair" such that "[a]s a result of [the defendant's] approach from the rear, [the victim] was forced into a position of helplessness" and that "[o]nce [the victim] was in this position, [the defendant] moved to the attack."

While we are not bound by the [decision in *Jacques* and similar decisions in other jurisdictions], we find their holdings . . . to be [more] persuasive [than the holding in

*Berkowitz*].[10] As a whole, we conclude that these jurisdictions have not interpreted the extrinsic force standard to require significant impositions of force above, for example, the pushing of a victim into a prone position or down on her knees, the removal of the victim's clothes and/or underwear, or the weight of a defendant's body on top of the victim, where they were taken over the victim's verbal and/or physical resistance and lead to subsequent sexual acts. This leads us to conclude that in this case, reasonable minds could have determined that Jones utilized more force in addition to that inherent in the sexual act and thus satisfied the force element. Jones's use of his body weight on top of A.S. to push her down from having been propped up on her arms and to pin her arms beneath her, rendered her unable to physically resist or escape his grasp and overcame her verbal resistance. Like in *Jacques*, A.S. was "forced into a position of helplessness" by Jones, after which he initiated the sexual act — to which A.S. had clearly communicated her resistance and non-consent. We conclude that there was sufficient evidence to satisfy the resistance and force elements of Count I.

### 2. Count II

Jones also contends that the evidence presented was insufficient to support a conviction for forcible rape on Count II. Specifically, he contends that there was no evidence of resistance because A.S. never even verbally communicated to him that she did not want to engage in sexual activity, nor was there evidence that he used force or violence to overcome any resistance. Because we conclude that the resistance element is dispositive, we do not reach the issue of force in regard to this count.

Even applying Idaho's resistance standard, which credits verbal resistance as well as physical resistance, there was simply no evidence presented at trial that A.S. resisted in any manner. A.S. testified she had pretended to be asleep and had not said anything to Jones during the entirety of the incident and explained that she believed that if she lay still, he would leave her alone. After he was finished, she testified that Jones had "woken her up" and tried to get her to go into the bathroom — thus also implying that she had not expressed anything during the incident since he believed she was asleep. She also stated that she had not fought Jones because she was scared and because "the first time I kept begging and pleading, and he just wouldn't quit." While we certainly recognize that A.S. testified that Jones's sexual advances were unwanted, we are constrained to apply the statute under which he was charged — which specifically includes a resistance requirement. As such, we conclude that there was insufficient evidence to support a conviction for Count II.

## CONCLUSION

We conclude there was sufficient evidence to convict Jones of Count I because there was evidence by which a reasonable trier of fact could find that A.S. offered "resistance" and that Jones overcame this resistance by "force or violence." However, there was insufficient evidence to find that A.S. resisted in regard to Count II and we vacate this conviction.

---

[10] *Berkowitz* has been subject to considerable criticism, and as noted above, the Pennsylvania legislature responded to the case by criminalizing the act that the court had concluded was not covered by the forcible rape statute.

**Post-Case Follow-Up**

In *Jones*, the court interpreted and applied the resistance and force elements of Idaho's rape statute, and discussed how other jurisdictions have approached these elements. With respect to resistance, the common law's "utmost" resistance requirement has been universally rejected. Thirty-eight states have eliminated the resistance requirement entirely. Among the states that retain a resistance requirement, none require physical resistance on the part of the victim, although there is variation with respect to how they define resistance. With respect to force, the majority of states continue to include force as an element in their rape statutes. There is a jurisdictional split on the definition of force in this context, however. Under the so-called intrinsic force standard, "the force inherent in the [sex] act itself suffices." Under the so-called extrinsic force standard, there must "proof of use of force or threat of force *above and beyond* that inherent in the act of nonconsensual intercourse."

## Jones: *Real Life Applications*

1. In a portion of the *Jones* opinion that was not included in the excerpt above, the court described the facts of *State v. McKnight*, 54 Wash. App. 521 (1989):

   [T]he victim, a fourteen-year-old girl, had invited a casual acquaintance, a seventeen-year-old boy, into her home because she was "bored and lonely." The two started kissing, but the victim testified that when she told the defendant to stop he started to slowly push her down on the couch and take off her clothes. She continued to tell him to stop and testified that at this point she was "scared." The defendant then lay on top of her and had sexual intercourse with her. It was undisputed that the victim had not physically resisted the defendant.

   The defendant was charged with rape.
   a. In a jurisdiction whose rape statute includes a resistance element and that applies a standard like the one adopted in *Jones*, would the resistance element be satisfied?
   b. In a jurisdiction whose rape statute includes a force element and that applies the intrinsic force standard, would the force element be satisfied?
   c. In a jurisdiction whose rape statute includes a force element and that applies the extrinsic force standard, would the force element be satisfied?

## The Force Requirement and Incapacity to Consent

A majority of states continue to include force or a threat of force as an element in their rape statutes. This does not mean that force (or a threat of force) is required to prove rape in *all* cases in these states, however. This is because rape statutes — including in states that have retained the force requirement — have separate **incapacity provisions** that cover circumstances where the victim is incapable of giving consent. There is some variation among states regarding these incapacity provisions. Some state statutes list specific incapacitating conditions; others "use more general language, just referencing 'mental incapacity' or 'unsoundness of mind.'" Alexander A. Boni-Sanez, *Sexuality and Incapacity*, 76 Ohio St. L.J. 1201, 1216 (2015). Under either approach, nearly every state's rape statute applies where the victim is incapacitated due to sleep, intoxication, or developmental disability. If one of these conditions is met, the victim's incapacity effectively negates the elements of consent and force. As a result, when incapacity is shown, it is not necessary to prove force, even in states that have retained the force element in the case of victims who are not incapacitated. The same is true of resistance in the minority of jurisdictions that have retained it as an element of rape.

Note that in *State v. Jones*, presented immediately above, the court overturned the defendant's conviction for Count II because the victim did not resist and instead pretended to be asleep. Why wasn't Jones's conviction for Count II upheld under Idaho's incapacity provision, which criminalizes intercourse "accomplished . . . [w]here the victim . . . [w]as unconscious or asleep"? Idaho Code § 18-6101(7)(a). Two reasons. First, Jones was charged and convicted "solely under" the provision of Idaho's rape statute that applies where "resistance is overcome by force or violence," and *not* under Idaho's incapacity provision. As the court wrote, "we are constrained to apply the statute under which [Jones] was charged—which specifically includes a resistance requirement." Second, the victim was not actually incapacitated; she "*pretended* to be asleep." Because there was no actual incapacitation, Jones could not have been convicted of rape under Idaho's incapacity provision. This does not mean the conduct charged in Count II could not give rise to criminal liability. Under these circumstances, it is quite likely that Jones could have been convicted of *attempted* rape under Idaho's incapacity provision, but he was not charged with that offense. (The law of attempts is covered in Chapter 7.)

## 2. *Mens Rea* and Consent

Until the 1970s, courts rarely, if ever, had reason to consider the question of the defendant's *mens rea* in rape

---

### Rape by Fraud

If a person's consent to have sex is induced by fraud, can this constitute rape? Yes, but only in very limited circumstances. Although there are relatively few published court decisions addressing this issue and some variation in state statutes, there appears to be widespread agreement that two types of fraud constitute rape. The first type is where there is fraud about the nature of the act — for example, "if the doctor pretends to perform a routine pelvic exam and instead has sexual intercourse with the woman, then it is rape because this is fraud in the factum which vitiates her consent. The woman never consented to sexual intercourse because she was deceived about the act itself." Patricia J. Falk, *Rape by Fraud and Rape by Coercion*, 64 Brook. L. Rev. 39, 158 (1998). The second type is where consent is fraudulently induced because the victim believes that the perpetrator is her spouse or, in some jurisdictions, her significant other. "The archetypical fact pattern for such category is a defendant impersonating a woman's husband by getting into bed with her and engaging in sexual intercourse before the woman becomes aware of his real identity." *Id.* at 65.

Some courts and commentators refer to these categories of fraud as "fraud in the factum," meaning fraud where there was "deceit about the nature of the act itself . . . or [where the defendant] literally claimed to be someone else." Irina D. Manta, *Tinder Lies*, 54 Wake Forest L. Rev. 207, 216 (2019). In some jurisdictions, rape-by-fraud can also be committed in other circumstances, such as when there is fraud involving the misuse of medical status — for example, where consent to sex is obtained "under the guise of providing professional diagnosis, counseling or treatment." Del. Code Ann. tit. 11, § 761.

States have been resistant to extend rape-by-fraud beyond these narrow categories, however. As a result, rape statutes generally do not apply where consent is induced by fraud about a person's attributes, such as one's age, income level, or marital status. Likewise, "[f]raud as to the degree of the perpetrator's affection for, or romantic commitment to, the victim is commonly not treated as rape." Russell L. Christopher & Kathryn H. Christopher, *Adult Impersonation: Rape by Fraud as a Defense to Statutory Rape*, 101 Nw. U. L. Rev. 75, 89 (2007). Some courts and commentators refer to these kinds of falsehoods as "fraud in the inducement," to distinguish them from the fraud in the factum category of cases.

prosecutions. Given the importance of *mens rea* to the offenses covered in previous chapters, this fact may be somewhat surprising. But when one considers the history of the crime of rape, it is easy to see why disputes about the mental state of defendants were so rare in pre-1970s rape cases.

Recall that before the 1970s, in almost every jurisdiction the crime of rape required proof that the victim resisted to the *utmost* and that the defendant used physical force or the threat of force to overcome that resistance. This rendered the defendant's mental state with respect to the victim's nonconsent effectively irrelevant. After all, "[a] man who uses a gun or a knife against his victim is not likely to be in serious doubt as to her lack of consent, and the more narrowly force is defined, the more implausible the claim that he was unaware of nonconsent." Susan Estrich, *Rape*, 95 Yale L.J. 1087, 1099 (1986).

To the extent that the issue of *mens rea* arose in pre-1970s rape cases, the prevailing view was that "[t]here was no requirement to prove knowledge of nonconsent." Guyora Binder & Robert Weisberg, *What Is Criminal Law About?*, 114 Mich. L. Rev. 1173, 1185 (2016). At first blush, this might appear to have been a prosecution-friendly standard — in effect, making rape a strict liability crime. But as Susan Estrich has persuasively argued, the common law's avoidance of *mens rea* was facilitated by "a definition of the crime of rape that is so limited that it leaves little room for men to be mistaken, reasonably or unreasonably, as to consent." Estrich, *supra*, at 1096. Professor Estrich, writing in 1986, continued by observing that "[t]o refuse to inquire into *mens rea* leaves two possibilities: turning rape into a strict liability offense where, in the absence of consent, the man is guilty of rape regardless of whether he (or anyone) would have recognized nonconsent in the circumstances; or defining the crime of rape in a fashion that is so limited that it would be virtually impossible for any man to be convicted where he was truly unaware or mistaken as to nonconsent. In fact, it is the latter approach which has characterized all of the older, and many of the newer, American cases." *Id.* at 1098. And so, although *mens rea* was technically absent from common law rape doctrine, the common law's demanding force and resistance requirements functioned as "substitute[s] for *mens rea* to ensure that the man has notice of the woman's nonconsent." *Id.* at 1099.

In the years since Professor Estrich published her article in 1986, more states have reformed their rape statutes. As states have abolished or redefined the force and resistance requirements, the question of *mens rea* in rape law has become more salient. Under the common law's definition of force, it was "difficult to imagine an accidental or mistaken use of force." *Id.* at 1096. By contrast, under some modern approaches to force and resistance, arguably "it is not at all difficult to imagine cases in which a man might claim that he did not realize a woman was not consenting to sex." *Id.* As a result, the possibility of a genuine misunderstanding regarding consent is now much more legally significant than it was in the pre-reform era — particularly in jurisdictions that eliminated the force and resistance elements entirely.

Today, jurisdictions are split on the *mens rea* element for rape, as the court's discussion in the next case, *Commonwealth v. Lopez*, reveals.

**Case Preview**

## Commonwealth v. Lopez

Does the crime of rape require the government to prove that the defendant acted with a culpable mental state (e.g., knowledge, recklessness, or negligence) with respect to the victim's nonconsent? In the case that follows, the Massachusetts Supreme Judicial Court addresses this question.

As you read the decision, consider the following questions:

1. How would you categorize the jurisdictional approaches to *mens rea* for the crime of rape?
2. Is there a relationship between the jurisdictional split on the issues of force and resistance, and the jurisdictional split on the issue of *mens rea*?
3. Why does the court hold that "[a]ny perception (reasonable, honest, or otherwise) of the defendant as to the victim's consent is . . . not relevant to a rape prosecution"?

## Commonwealth v. Lopez
### 433 Mass. 722 (2001)

SPINA, J.

The defendant, Kenny Lopez, was convicted on two indictments charging rape and one indictment charging indecent assault and battery on a person over the age of fourteen years. We granted his application for direct appellate review. The defendant claims error in the judge's refusal to give a mistake of fact instruction to the jury. He asks us to recognize a defendant's honest and reasonable belief as to a complainant's consent as a defense to the crime of rape, and to reverse his convictions and grant him a new trial. Based on the record presented, we decline to do so, and affirm the convictions.

1. *Background.* We summarize facts that the jury could have found. On May 8, 1998, the victim, a seventeen year old girl, was living in a foster home in Springfield. At approximately 3 P.M., she started walking to a restaurant where she had planned to meet her biological mother. On the way, she encountered the defendant. He introduced himself, asked where she was going, and offered to walk with her. The victim met her mother and introduced the defendant as her friend. The defendant said that he lived in the same

foster home as the victim and that "they knew each other from school." Sometime later, the defendant left to make a telephone call. When the victim left the restaurant, the defendant was waiting outside and offered to walk her home. She agreed.

The two walked to a park across the street from the victim's foster home and talked for approximately twenty to thirty minutes. The victim's foster sisters were within earshot, and the victim feared that she would be caught violating her foster mother's rules against bringing "a guy near the house." The defendant suggested that they take a walk in the woods nearby. At one point, deep in the woods, the victim said that she wanted to go home. The defendant said, "trust me," and assured her that nothing would happen and that he would not hurt her. The defendant led the victim down a path to a secluded area.

The defendant asked the victim why she was so distant and said that he wanted to start a relationship with her. She said that she did not want to "get into any relationship." The defendant began making sexual innuendos to which the victim did not respond. He grabbed her by her wrist and began kissing her on the lips. She pulled away and said, "No, I don't want to do this." The defendant then told the victim that if she "had sex with him, [she] would love him more." She repeated, "No, I don't want to. I don't want to do this." He raised her shirt and touched her breasts. She immediately pulled her shirt down and pushed him away.

The defendant then pushed the victim against a slate slab, unbuttoned her pants, and pulled them down. Using his legs to pin down her legs, he produced a condom and asked her to put it on him. The victim said, "No." The defendant put the condom on and told the victim that he wanted her to put his penis inside her. She said, "No." He then raped her, and she began to cry. A few minutes later, the victim made a "jerking move" to her left. The defendant became angry, turned her around, pushed her face into the slate, and raped her again. The treating physician described the bruising to the victim's knees as "significant." The physician opined that there had been "excessive force and trauma to the [vaginal] area" . . . [and] noted that in his experience it was "fairly rare" to see that much swelling and trauma.

The defendant told the victim that she "would get in a lot of trouble" if she said anything. He then grabbed her by the arm, kissed her, and said, "I'll see you later." The victim went home and showered. She told her foster mother, who immediately dialed 911. The victim cried hysterically as she spoke to the 911 operator.

The defendant's version of the encounter was diametrically opposed to that of the victim. He testified that the victim had been a willing and active partner in consensual sexual intercourse. Specifically, the defendant claimed that the victim initiated intimate activity, and never once told him to stop. Additionally, the defendant testified that the victim invited him to a party that evening so that he could meet her friends. The defendant further claimed that when he told her that he would be unable to attend, the victim appeared "mildly upset."

Before the jury retired, defense counsel requested a mistake of fact instruction as to consent.[1] The judge declined to give the instruction, saying that, based "both on

---

[1] The defendant proposed the following instruction: "If the Commonwealth has not proved beyond a reasonable doubt that the defendant was not motivated by a reasonable and honest belief that the complaining witness consented to sexual intercourse, you must find the defendant not guilty."

the law, as well as on the facts, that instruction is not warranted." Because the defendant's theory at trial was that the victim actually consented and not that the defendant was "confused, misled, or mistaken" as to the victim's willingness to engage in sexual intercourse, the judge concluded that the ultimate question for the jury was simply whether they believed the victim's or the defendant's version of the encounter. The decision not to give the instruction provides the basis for this appeal.

2. *Mistake of fact instruction.* The defendant claims that the judge erred in failing to give his proposed mistake of fact instruction. The defendant, however, was not entitled to this instruction. In *Commonwealth v. Ascolillo*, 405 Mass. 456 (1989), we held that the defendant was not entitled to a mistake of fact instruction, and declined to adopt a rule that "in order to establish the crime of rape the Commonwealth must prove *in every case* not only that the defendant intended intercourse but also that he did not act pursuant to an honest and reasonable belief that the victim consented" (emphasis added). Neither the plain language of our rape statute nor this court's decisions prior to the *Ascolillo* decision warrant a different result.

A fundamental tenet of criminal law is that culpability requires a showing that the prohibited conduct (actus reus) was committed with the concomitant mental state (mens rea) prescribed for the offense. The mistake of fact "defense" is available where the mistake negates the existence of a mental state essential to a material element of the offense.[3] In determining whether the defendant's honest and reasonable belief as to the victim's consent would relieve him of culpability, it is necessary to review the required elements of the crime of rape.

At common law, rape was defined as "the carnal knowledge of a woman forcibly and against her will." 4 W. Blackstone, Commentaries 210. Since 1642, rape has been proscribed by statute in this Commonwealth. While there have been several revisions to this statute, the definition and the required elements of the crime have remained essentially unchanged since its original enactment. The current rape statute, G.L. c. 265, § 22(b), provides in pertinent part:

> "Whoever has sexual intercourse or unnatural sexual intercourse with a person and compels such person to submit by force and against his will, or compels such person to submit by threat of bodily injury, shall be punished by imprisonment in the state prison for not more than twenty years."

This statute . . . requires the Commonwealth to prove beyond a reasonable doubt that the defendant committed (1) sexual intercourse (2) by force or threat of force and against the will of the victim.

As to the first element, there has been very little disagreement. Sexual intercourse is defined as penetration of the victim, regardless of degree. The second element has proven to be more complicated. We have construed the element, "by force and against his will," as truly encompassing two separate elements each of which

---

[3] Thus understood, a mistake of fact is not truly a defense, but rather a means of demonstrating that the prosecution has failed to prove beyond a reasonable doubt the essential elements of the crime. See Keedy, *Ignorance and Mistake in the Criminal Law*, 22 Harv. L. Rev. 75, 86 n.4 (1908) ("Such defenses as mistake and alibi, each of which denies one of the elements of guilt, must not in this connection be confounded with defenses of an affirmative character under which the defendant admits the commission of the crime but claims exemption from punishment because of some excusing fact, such as self-defense").

must independently be satisfied. Therefore, the Commonwealth must demonstrate beyond a reasonable doubt that the defendant committed sexual intercourse (1) by means of physical force; nonphysical, constructive force; or threats of bodily harm, either explicit or implicit; and (2) at the time of penetration, there was no consent.

Although the Commonwealth must prove lack of consent, the "elements necessary for rape do not require that the defendant intend the intercourse be without consent." *Commonwealth v. Grant*, 391 Mass. 645, 650 (1984). See *Commonwealth v. Cordeiro*, 401 Mass. 843, 851 n.11 (1988) ("The Commonwealth is not required to prove either that the defendant intended the sexual intercourse be without consent or that he had actual knowledge of the victim's lack of consent"). Historically, the relevant inquiry has been limited to consent in fact, and no mens rea or knowledge as to the lack of consent has ever been required.

A mistake of fact as to consent, therefore, has very little application to our rape statute. Because G.L. c. 265, § 22, does not require proof of a defendant's knowledge of the victim's lack of consent or intent to engage in nonconsensual intercourse as a material element of the offense, a mistake as to that consent cannot, therefore, negate a mental state required for commission of the prohibited conduct. Any perception (reasonable, honest, or otherwise) of the defendant as to the victim's consent is consequently not relevant to a rape prosecution.

This is not to say, contrary to the defendant's suggestion, that the absence of any mens rea as to the consent element transforms rape into a strict liability crime. It does not. Rape, at common law and pursuant to G.L. c. 265, § 22, is a general intent crime, and proof that a defendant intended sexual intercourse by force coupled with proof that the victim did not in fact consent is sufficient to maintain a conviction. See Bryden, *Redefining Rape*, 3 Buff. Crim. L. Rev. 317, 325 (2000) ("At common law, rape was a 'general intent' crime: The requisite intention was merely to perform the sexual act, rather than have nonconsensual intercourse").

Other jurisdictions have held that a mistake of fact instruction is necessary to prevent injustice. New Jersey, for instance, does not require the force necessary for rape to be anything more than what is needed to accomplish penetration. See *In re M.T.S.*, 129 N.J. 422, 444 (1992) ("physical force in excess of that inherent in the act of sexual penetration is not required for such penetration to be unlawful"). Thus, an instruction as to a defendant's honest and reasonable belief as to consent is available in New Jersey to mitigate the undesirable and unforeseen consequences that may flow from this construction. By contrast, in this Commonwealth, unless the putative victim has been rendered incapable of consent, the prosecution must prove that the defendant compelled the victim's submission by use of physical force; nonphysical, constructive force; or threat of force. Proof of the element of force, therefore, should negate any possible mistake as to consent. See also Estrich, *Rape*, 95 Yale L.J. 1087, 1098-99 (1986) ("The requirement that sexual intercourse be accompanied by force or threat of force to constitute rape provides a [defendant] with some protection against mistakes as to consent").

We are cognizant that our interpretation is not shared by the majority of other jurisdictions. States that recognize a mistake of fact as to consent generally have done so by legislation. Some State statutes expressly require a showing of a defendant's intent as to nonconsent. Alaska, for example, requires proof of a culpable state of mind. "Lack of consent is a 'surrounding circumstance' which under the Revised Code, requires a complementary mental state as well as conduct to constitute a crime." *Reynolds v. State*, 664 P.2d 621, 625 (Alaska App. 1983). Because no specific mental state is mentioned in Alaska's statute governing sexual assault in the first degree, the State "must prove that the defendant acted 'recklessly' regarding his putative victim's lack of consent." So understood, an honest and reasonable mistake as to consent would negate the culpability requirement attached to the element of consent. See Colo. Rev. Stat. § 18-3-402(1) (1999) ("Any actor who knowingly inflicts sexual intrusion or sexual penetration on a victim commits sexual assault . . ."); Or. Rev. Stat. §§ 161.115(2) (1999) ("Except as provided in [Or. Rev. Stat. §] 161.105, if a statute defining an offense does not prescribe a culpable mental state, culpability is nonetheless required and is established only if a person acts intentionally, knowingly, recklessly or with criminal negligence"); Tex. Penal Code § 22.021(a)(1)(A)(i) (West Supp. 2001) ("A person commits an offense if the person . . . intentionally or knowingly . . . causes the penetration of the anus or female sexual organ of another person by any means, without that person's consent").

The New Jersey statute defines sexual assault (rape) as "any act of sexual penetration engaged in by the defendant without the affirmative and freely-given permission of the victim to the specific act of penetration." *In re M.T.S., supra* at 444, 609 A.2d 1266. A defendant, by claiming that he had permission to engage in sexual intercourse, places his state of mind directly in issue. The jury must then determine "whether the defendant's belief that the alleged victim had freely given affirmative permission was reasonable."

The mistake of fact "defense" has been recognized by judicial decision in some States. In 1975, the Supreme Court of California became the first State court to recognize a mistake of fact defense in rape cases. See *People v. Mayberry*, 15 Cal. 3d 143 (1975) (en banc). Although the court did not make a specific determination that intent was required as to the element of consent, it did conclude that, "[i]f a defendant entertains a reasonable and bona fide belief that a prosecutrix [*sic*] voluntarily consented . . . to engage in sexual intercourse, it is apparent he does not possess the wrongful intent that is a prerequisite under Penal Code section 20 to a conviction of . . . rape by means of force or threat." Thus, the intent required is an intent to engage in nonconsensual sexual intercourse, and the State must prove that a defendant intentionally engaged in intercourse and was at least negligent regarding consent.

Other State courts have employed a variety of different constructions in adopting the mistake of fact defense. See *State v. Smith*, 210 Conn. 132, 142 (1989) ("We arrive at that result, however, not on the basis of our penal code provision relating to a mistake of fact . . . but on the ground that whether a complainant should be found to have consented depends upon how her behavior would have been viewed by a reasonable person under the surrounding circumstances"); *State v. Koonce*, 731 S.W.2d 431, 437 n.2 (Mo. Ct. App. 1987) (construing rape statute to require defendant acted at least recklessly as to consent).

However, the minority of States sharing our view is significant. See *People v. Witte*, 115 Ill. App. 3d 20, 26 n.2 (1983) ("whether the defendant intended to commit the offense[s] without the victim's consent is not relevant, the critical question being whether the victim did, in fact, consent. This involves her mental state, not the defendant's"); *State v. Reed*, 479 A.2d 1291, 1296 (Me. 1984) ("The legislature, by carefully defining the sex offenses in the criminal code, and by making no reference to a culpable state of mind for rape, clearly indicated that rape compelled by force or threat requires no culpable state of mind"); *Commonwealth v. Williams*, 294 Pa. Super. 93, 100 (1982) ("The crux of the offense of rape is force and lack of [the] victim's consent. . . . When one individual uses force or the threat thereof to have sexual relations with a person . . . and without the person's consent he has committed the crime of rape").

This case does not persuade us that we should recognize a mistake of fact as to consent as a defense to rape in *all* cases. Whether such a defense might, in some circumstances, be appropriate is a difficult question that we may consider on a future case where a defendant's claim of reasonable mistake of fact is at least arguably supported by the evidence. This is not such a case.

*Judgments affirmed.*

---

**Post-Case Follow-Up**

*Lopez* described the different approaches to *mens rea* for the crime of rape. The majority of jurisdictions require proof that the defendant acted with a culpable mental state with respect to the victim's nonconsent. In these jurisdictions, a defendant's mistaken belief that the victim consented to sex *may* be enough to raise a reasonable doubt as to guilt. But these jurisdictions are further split on the question of exactly what mental state is required. Some states require the government to prove that the defendant *knew* the victim was not consenting. In others, proof that the defendant was reckless or negligent with respect to the victim's nonconsent will suffice.

Although the majority of jurisdictions require some *mens rea* with respect to the victim's nonconsent, a "significant" minority of states do not. Under the minority approach, which the court in *Lopez* followed, "[a]ny perception (reasonable, honest, or otherwise) of the defendant as to the victim's consent is . . . not relevant to a rape prosecution."

As the opinion in *Lopez* suggests, there is often a relationship between a state's approach to the force and resistance elements and its approach to *mens rea*. The *Lopez* court cited Massachusetts's adherence to the requirement of extrinsic force to explain the absence of a *mens rea* requirement with respect to the victim's nonconsent. "Proof of the element of force . . . should negate any possible mistake as to consent," the court explained. By contrast, the court reasoned that in states that have eliminated or significantly reformed the force element, a *mens rea* requirement may be "necessary to prevent injustice."

---

As discussed in the *Lopez* decision, states are split on the question of what *mens rea* with respect to the victim's nonconsent, if any, is required for a rape conviction. The case that follows, issued by the Supreme Judicial Court of Maine in 2020, reveals that the issue is still unresolved in some states.

**Case Preview**

## *State v. Asaad*

The defendant in *Asaad* argued on appeal that Maine's rape statute should be read to require proof of knowledge of the victim's nonconsent. The decision provides an example of a court applying the knowledge standard for consent, and highlights the lingering uncertainty in this area of the law.

As you read the decision, consider the following questions:

1. What evidence leads the court to conclude that there was sufficient evidence the defendant knew the victim was not consenting?
2. Why does the court hold that some culpable mental state with respect to nonconsent is required?
3. Why does the court decline to reach the issue of *which* culpable mental state with respect to nonconsent is required?

## *State v. Asaad*
### 224 A.3d 596 (Me. 2020)

GORMAN, J.

Ahmed M. Asaad appeals from a judgment of conviction of gross sexual assault, 17-A M.R.S. § 253(2)(M) (2018), entered by the court (Sagadahoc County, Billings, J.) after a jury-waived trial. Asaad argues that the evidence was insufficient to support the trial court's finding that he possessed the requisite *mens rea*. We affirm the judgment.

### I. BACKGROUND

The trial court made the following findings of fact, which are supported by competent record evidence.

Asaad and the victim met through an online dating site. On November 29, 2017, Asaad went to the victim's house and eventually they began to engage in consensual sexual activity. When Asaad "inserted his penis inside of [the victim]," she asked him to stop; despite the victim "saying no and stop on several occasions," Asaad "continued to penetrate her until he ejaculated."

On April 11, 2018, Asaad was indicted on one count of gross sexual assault. He pleaded not guilty and waived his right to a jury trial.

After a two-day jury-waived trial, the court found Asaad guilty. On May 9, 2019, the court entered a judgment of conviction and sentenced Asaad to three years in prison, with all but nine months suspended. Asaad timely appealed.

### II. DISCUSSION

Asaad's argument boils down to two assertions: first, that despite the lack of any expressed *mens rea*, 17-A M.R.S. § 253(2)(M) must be read to require proof that

## Affirmative Consent

Although states are split on the *mens rea* (if any) required with respect to the victim's nonconsent, nonconsent is one of the elements of the offense in nearly every state. Some argue the nonconsent standard should be abandoned in favor of an affirmative consent standard. The affirmative consent standard has started to become the norm in university disciplinary codes — as of 2016, "[a]n estimated 1,400 institutions of higher education ha[d] adopted disciplinary standards that codify an affirmative definition of sexual consent." Deborah Tuerkheimer, *Affirmative Consent*, 13 Ohio St. J. Crim. L. 441, 442 (2016). Only a few states have incorporated an affirmative consent standard into their rape statutes, however; Professor Tuerkheimer classifies just three states — Wisconsin, Vermont, and New Jersey — as "pure consent jurisdictions." *Id.* at 451.

As Aya Gruber has observed in *Consent Confusion*, 38 Cardozo L. Rev. 415, 430 (2016), there "is a spectrum of affirmative consent formulations." A review of various potential affirmative consent standards proposed by advocates shows that "[t]he meaning of 'affirmative consent' . . . can range from narrow communicative prescriptions (contract, verbal yes) to any behavior that conveys internal agreement (foreplay, acquiescence)." *Id.* Although there are different possible affirmative consent standards, at a minimum it would require some positive indication of consent. Under this approach to affirmative consent, a prosecutor would have to "demonstrate that the defendant engaged in intercourse without

the charged individual *knew* that the person with whom he was engaging in a sexual act "ha[d] not expressly or impliedly acquiesced to the sexual act"; and, second, that the evidence presented at trial was insufficient to support a finding that he knew that the victim had not "expressly or impliedly acquiesced" to the sexual activity. 17-A M.R.S. § 253(2)(M). We address those assertions in reverse order.

### A. Sufficiency of the Evidence

For purposes of this appeal only, while recognizing that section 253(2)(M) does not expressly provide a *mens rea*, we will assume that knowledge is the required *mens rea* and directly address Asaad's argument that the evidence was insufficient to support a finding that he acted knowingly.

"When a defendant challenges the sufficiency of the evidence supporting a conviction, we determine, viewing the evidence in the light most favorable to the State, whether a trier of fact rationally could find beyond a reasonable doubt every element of the offense charged."

"A person acts knowingly with respect to attendant circumstances when the person is aware that such circumstances exist." 17-A M.R.S. § 35(2)(B) (2018). Here, there was ample evidence to support a finding, beyond a reasonable doubt, that Asaad was "aware" that the victim had not "expressly or impliedly acquiesced" to unprotected vaginal intercourse. The victim, whom the trial court found credible, testified that over the weeks preceding their date, she had repeatedly told Asaad that if they had sex, they "had to use condoms." She also testified that on the night of the assault, as she and Asaad were beginning to engage in sexual activity, she asked if he had brought a condom; the victim stated that, in response to her question, Asaad "did the thing like people do when they go out to dinner and they intentionally leave behind their wallet," saying that he had forgotten to bring condoms and acting disappointed. The victim testified that after learning that Asaad had not brought a condom, she "rolled over and looked at [her] phone."

It would be reasonable to infer from this testimony alone that, even before he arrived at the victim's home, Asaad was "aware" that the victim was not willing to engage in unprotected vaginal intercourse. In fact, we are hard-pressed to imagine a way in which the victim could have made it clearer to Asaad that she was not willing to engage in vaginal intercourse without a condom. Unprotected sex may carry risks for all participants, and it hardly need be said that the consequences of unprotected vaginal intercourse can be vastly different for a woman than for a man.

Even without that testimony, however, the court's determination that Asaad engaged in unprotected vaginal intercourse with the victim after she said "stop" was fully supported by the evidence. The victim testified that as she was lying on her stomach looking at her phone after Asaad acknowledged that he did not have a condom, Asaad "turned [the victim] over" — quickly enough that she "dropped [her] phone" — got on top of her, and "inserted his penis inside of [her]." The victim, who is considerably smaller than Asaad, began hitting and slapping Asaad's back, repeatedly saying "no" and "stop," but he continued to "thrust" for at least a few minutes until he ejaculated. Although Asaad claimed that he stopped when the victim told him to stop, the trial court explicitly rejected Asaad's testimony on this point.

In sum, the evidence was more than sufficient to support a finding that Asaad engaged in a sexual act that he knew the victim had not "expressly or impliedly acquiesced" to. We therefore affirm the conviction.

### B. Mens Rea *for 17-A M.R.S. § 253(2)(M)*

Because we conclude that the evidence was sufficient to support a verdict to the *mens rea* standard for which Asaad argues, we do not answer the question of precisely what state of mind section 253(2)(M) requires: criminal negligence, recklessness, or knowledge. We do, however, reject the State's contention that section 253(2)(M) is a strict liability statute; the statute's plain language precludes such an interpretation. A conviction pursuant to section 253(2)(M) requires that the victim "has not expressly or impliedly acquiesced" to the sexual act, which means that the lack of acquiescence must be communicated in some fashion, verbally or otherwise. *See Acquiesce*, Black's Law Dictionary (11th ed. 2019) ("to give implied consent to [an act]"). After all, expression and implication both involve a "target" — another person who heard, saw, or felt the expression or implication. The State's strict liability interpretation, which would foreclose any inquiry into whether the defendant actually received (let alone understood) the victim's communication, ignores the plain language of the statute.

Nevertheless, we do not here resolve the question of whether a defendant is liable pursuant to section 253(2)(M) only if he *actually* understands the victim's communication (that is, to the standard of "knowingly") or if, instead, he misunderstands the victim's communication but his misunderstanding is reckless or criminally negligent.

---

the alleged victim's consent, which must be manifested in an affirmative manner" in order to convict. Tuerkheimer, *supra*, at 449. By contrast, the "without consent" standard arguably "require[s] a demonstration of unwillingness to engage in sexual conduct, or what might be conceived as verbal resistance." *Id*. at 448.

Moving to an affirmative consent standard would affect the *mens rea* required for the offense. Although "affirmative consent laws and policies do not eliminate *mens rea* . . . , under a yes-means-yes standard, if 'yes' is absent, defendants cannot argue that they reasonably believed the complainant wanted sex[.]" Gruber, *supra*, at 450.

Do you think states should amend their rape statutes to adopt an affirmative consent standard? If so, what type of affirmative consent requirement would you support — would any affirmative manifestation of consent suffice or should a higher standard (such as a verbal yes) be required?

In this complicated and nuanced area of human behavior in which norms — and, nationally, legal standards — are varied and rapidly changing, courts must look to the Legislature for broad-based policy judgments. *See, e.g.,* Aya Gruber, *Consent Confusion*, 38 Cardozo L. Rev. 415, 419, 425-30 (2016).

Thus, we emphasize that, because we recognize that this issue should be addressed by the Legislature, we are not here determining the *mens rea* requirement for 17-A M.R.S. § 253(2)(M). There is a substantial difference between imposing felony liability when a defendant knowingly violates a victim's desire not to have sex and imposing that liability when a defendant recklessly or criminally negligently misunderstands that a victim does not consent. Given the significance of this distinction, in this important and unsettled area of law the standard of behavior should be determined by the people's elected representatives.

The entry is:

Judgment affirmed.

---

**Post-Case Follow-Up**

The court found that there was "ample evidence to support a finding, beyond a reasonable doubt, that Asaad was 'aware' that the victim had not 'expressly or impliedly acquiesced' to unprotected vaginal intercourse." Because the court held that there was sufficient evidence Asaad knew of the victim's nonconsent, it found it unnecessary to "answer the question of precisely what state of mind section 253(2)(M) requires: criminal negligence, recklessness, or knowledge." The court did hold that *some* culpable mental state with respect to nonconsent is required. As to which mental state, the court concluded that the "issue should be addressed by the Legislature."

---

## Lopez *and* Asaad: *Real Life Applications*

1. You are a criminal defense attorney in Maine. Your client has been charged with rape and is going to trial. The prosecutor has proposed the following jury instruction with respect to the *mens rea* required for the offense:

   In order to find Defendant guilty of rape, you must find the following:

   1. Defendant;
   2. Intentionally or knowingly;
   3. Had sexual intercourse with Victim;
   4. That said act of intercourse was without the consent of Victim

   Keeping the decision in *Asaad* in mind, would you object to this instruction? If so, what change(s) or addition(s) would you request? Would you request any supplemental instruction with respect to your client's mental state?

2. You are a judge in Massachusetts overseeing a rape trial. The prosecutor has requested a jury instruction identical to the one described in Question 1.

Defense counsel objects on the ground that the proposed instruction does not accurately reflect the *mens rea* for rape in Massachusetts. Based on the decision in *Commonwealth v. Lopez*, how would you rule?

3. In *Asaad*, the Supreme Judicial Court of Maine declined to "resolve the question of whether a defendant is liable pursuant to [the state's rape statute] only if he *actually* understands victim's communication (that is, to the standard of 'knowingly') or if, instead, he misunderstands the victim's communication but his misunderstanding is reckless or criminally negligent." The court reasoned that, "[g]iven the significance of this distinction, in this important and unsettled area of law the standard of behavior should be determined by the people's elected representatives."

   a. Imagine that you are a state legislator in Maine. A staff member brings the court's decision in *Asaad* to your attention and suggests that you consider introducing a bill to address the *mens rea* requirement in Maine's rape statute. What *mens rea*, if any, would you propose and why? Would you consider making any other changes to the statute as part of your proposal?

   b. The *Asaad* court was only in a position to leave the *mens rea* issue to the legislature because of the facts and procedural background of the case. Because Asaad was convicted in a bench trial and there was sufficient evidence that he had acted with knowledge of the victim's nonconsent, the court did not need to resolve whether knowledge was required to uphold his conviction.

      If the evidence against Asaad had been weaker — if, for example, there had been sufficient evidence to show that Asaad was criminally negligent but insufficient evidence he had acted with knowledge — the court would have been forced to resolve the question of whether knowledge is required. Similarly, if Asaad had been tried before a jury, rather than in a bench trial, his lawyer presumably would have requested a jury instruction on the issue of knowledge. If that request had been rejected, the Supreme Judicial Court might have been forced to reach the question of whether knowledge — or some other mental state — is required under its statute.

      Imagine that you are a clerk for Justice Gorman, the author of the court's opinion in *Asaad*. It has been over one year since the *Asaad* decision was issued, but Maine's legislature has not amended its statute. The court is considering another appeal from a conviction under the same statute that was at issue in *Asaad*. In this case, the defendant was tried before a jury. At trial, the defendant requested that the jury be instructed there must be proof that he acted with knowledge of the victim's nonconsent, but his request was denied. As a result, the court will be forced to reach the issue it left unresolved in *Asaad*; deferring to the legislature is not an option.

      Justice Gorman has asked you to write her a bench memo recommending which *mens rea* standard to adopt — knowledge, recklessness, or negligence. What would you recommend, and why?

## B. STATUTORY RAPE

Statutory rape criminalizes sex with a minor. The definition of minor in this context varies from state to state — 33 jurisdictions set the age of consent at 16 years old, with the remaining jurisdictions split between 17 and 18 years old. Paul H. Robinson & Tyler Scot Williams, Mapping American Criminal Law: Variations Across the 50 States 207-09 (2018). Those under the age of consent are deemed to be legally incapable of consenting to sexual activity. As a result, even if the evidence "demonstrate[s] that the victim engaged in the sexual activity voluntarily, the victim is presumed to lack the capacity to consent because of the victim's age." Catherine L. Carpenter, *On Statutory Rape, Strict Liability, and the Public Welfare Offense Model*, 53 Am. U. L. Rev. 313, 335 (2003).

About two-thirds of all jurisdictions "recognize an exception to the statutory rape offense for persons who are close in age to the underage partner." Robinson & Williams, *supra*, at 209. There is a good deal of variation when it comes to the specifics of these exceptions, however. In some states, the exception is based on relative age (e.g., within two years) and in others it is based on absolute age (e.g., where the actor is 21 years old or younger). About one-third of states do not have a close-in-age exception. In a jurisdiction without a close-in-age exception and where the age of consent is 18, an 18-year old could be convicted of statutory rape for having consensual sex with her 17-year-old partner.

One aspect of statutory rape that has generated a great deal of debate is the *mens rea* — or lack thereof — required for the offense. At common law, statutory rape was a strict liability offense. This meant that a defendant's mistaken belief about the victim's age was not a defense; even a defendant who reasonably believed the victim was above the age of consent could be convicted. Until the 1960s, "strict liability as to the victim's age was uniformly followed in America." Russell L. Christopher & Kathryn H. Christopher, *The Paradox of Statutory Rape*, 87 Ind. L.J. 505, 517 (2012). This began to change when the California Supreme Court recognized a "mistake of age" defense to the crime in a 1964 decision. Today, states are very closely split on the question of whether statutory rape requires the defendant to have acted with a culpable mental state with respect to the victim's age. Statutory rape remains a strict liability crime in slightly more than half of all jurisdictions, but a sizeable minority have adopted a *mens rea* requirement of some kind with respect to age. The issue is complicated by the fact that, because not all legislatures have directly addressed the issue, "[m]any state statutory rape laws remain ambiguous as to the availability of a 'mistake of age' defense." Kathleen Houck, *"Mistake of Age" as a Defense?: Looking to Legislative Evidence for the Answer*, 55 Am. Crim. L. Rev. 813, 816 (2018).

**Case Preview**

### Garnett v. State

Should statutory rape be a strict liability crime? In the case that follows, the Court of Appeals of Maryland considered whether the state's statutory rape law required proof that the defendant acted with a culpable mental state with respect to the victim's age. The outcome of the case turned on specific attributes of Maryland's statute. But the majority and the dissenting opinions provide insight into the history of the offense and the debate about whether it should be a strict liability crime. (Note that the decision, which was issued in 1993, contains an outdated and offensive term to describe the defendant's intellectual disability.)

As you read the decision, consider the following questions:

1. What are the policy arguments in favor of the traditional view of statutory rape as a strict liability crime?
2. What are the policy arguments against imposing strict liability for the crime of statutory rape?
3. What leads the majority to interpret Maryland's statutory rape law to impose strict liability?

---

## Garnett v. State
### 332 Md. 571 (1993)

MURPHY, J.

Maryland's "statutory rape" law prohibiting sexual intercourse with an underage person is codified in Maryland Code Art. 27, § 463, which reads in full:

"Second degree rape.

(a) *What constitutes.* — A person is guilty of rape in the second degree if the person engages in vaginal intercourse with another person:

. . .

(2) Who is mentally defective, mentally incapacitated, or physically helpless, and the person performing the act knows or should reasonably know the other person is mentally defective, mentally incapacitated, or physically helpless; or

(3) Who is under 14 years of age and the person performing the act is at least four years older than the victim.

(b) *Penalty.* — Any person violating the provisions of this section is guilty of a felony and upon conviction is subject to imprisonment for a period of not more than 20 years."

Subsection (a)(3) represents the current version of a statutory provision dating back to the first comprehensive codification of the criminal law by the Legislature in 1809.[1] Now we consider whether under the present statute, the State must prove that a defendant knew the complaining witness was younger than 14 and, in a related question, whether it was error at trial to exclude evidence that he had been told, and believed, that she was 16 years old.

---

[1] "If any person shall carnally know and abuse any woman-child under the age of ten years, every such carnal knowledge shall be deemed felony, and the offender, being convicted thereof, shall, at the discretion of the court, suffer death by hanging . . . or undergo a confinement in the penitentiary for a period not less than one year nor more than twenty-one years." Ch. 138, Sec. 4, 7th. (1809) compiled in 1 Dorsey's *General Public Statutory Law and Public Local Law of the State of Maryland* 575 (1840). The minimum age of the child was raised from 10 years to 14 years in Chapter 410 of the Acts of 1890.

I

Raymond Lennard Garnett is a young retarded man. At the time of the incident in question he was 20 years old. He has an I.Q. of 52. His guidance counselor from the Montgomery County public school system, Cynthia Parker, described him as a mildly retarded person who read on the third-grade level, did arithmetic on the 5th-grade level, and interacted with others socially at school at the level of someone 11 or 12 years of age. As Raymond was unable to pass any of the State's functional tests required for graduation, he received only a certificate of attendance rather than a high-school diploma.

In November or December 1990, a friend introduced Raymond to Erica Frazier, then aged 13; the two subsequently talked occasionally by telephone. On February 28, 1991, Raymond, apparently wishing to call for a ride home, approached the girl's house at about nine o'clock in the evening. Erica opened her bedroom window, through which Raymond entered; he testified that "she just told me to get a ladder and climb up her window." The two talked, and later engaged in sexual intercourse. Raymond left at about 4:30 A.M. the following morning. On November 19, 1991, Erica gave birth to a baby, of which Raymond is the biological father.

Raymond was tried before the Circuit Court for Montgomery County (Miller, J.) on one count of second degree rape under § 463(a)(3) proscribing sexual intercourse between a person under 14 and another at least four years older than the complainant. At trial, the defense twice proffered evidence to the effect that Erica herself and her friends had previously told Raymond that she was 16 years old, and that he had acted with that belief. The trial court excluded such evidence as immaterial, explaining:

> "Under 463, the only two requirements as relate to this case are that there was vaginal intercourse, [and] that . . . Ms. Frazier was under 14 years of age and that . . . Mr. Garnett was at least four years older than she.
>
> "In the Court's opinion, consent is no defense to this charge. The victim's representation as to her age and the defendant's belief, if it existed, that she was not under age . . . is in fact no defense to what amount[s] to statutory rape.
>
> "It is in the Court's opinion a strict liability offense."

The court found Raymond guilty. It sentenced him to a term of five years in prison, suspended the sentence and imposed five years of probation, and ordered that he pay restitution to Erica and the Frazier family.

II

In 1975 the Legislative Council of the General Assembly established the Special Committee on Rape and Related Offenses, which proposed a complete revision of Maryland law pertaining to rape and other sex crimes. Based on the Committee's work, Senate Bill 358 was introduced, amended, and enacted on May 17, 1976. In part, it repealed the common law crime of rape, the former statutory prohibition of carnal knowledge of underage girls, and other related crimes and replaced them with the current array of criminal laws delineating two degrees of rape and four degrees of sexual offenses.

The new legislation reformulated the former statutory rape law by introducing the element of a four-year age difference between the accused and the underage complainant.

Section 463(a)(3) does not expressly set forth a requirement that the accused have acted with a criminal state of mind, or *mens rea*. The State insists that the statute, by design, defines a strict liability offense, and that its essential elements were met in the instant case when Raymond, age 20, engaged in vaginal intercourse with Erica, a girl under 14 and more than 4 years his junior. Raymond replies that the criminal law exists to assess and punish morally culpable behavior. He says such culpability was absent here. He asks us either to engraft onto subsection (a)(3) an implicit *mens rea* requirement, or to recognize an affirmative defense of reasonable mistake as to the complainant's age. Raymond argues that it is unjust, under the circumstances of this case which led him to think his conduct lawful, to brand him a felon and rapist.

## III

Raymond asserts that the events of this case were inconsistent with the criminal sexual exploitation of a minor by an adult. As earlier observed, Raymond entered Erica's bedroom at the girl's invitation; she directed him to use a ladder to reach her window. They engaged voluntarily in sexual intercourse. They remained together in the room for more than seven hours before Raymond departed at dawn. With an I.Q. of 52, Raymond functioned at approximately the same level as the 13-year-old Erica; he was mentally an adolescent in an adult's body.

[I]t is well understood that generally there are two components of every crime, the *actus reus* or guilty act and the *mens rea* or the guilty mind or mental state accompanying a forbidden act. The requirement that an accused have acted with a culpable mental state is an axiom of criminal jurisprudence.

To be sure, legislative bodies since the mid-19th century have created strict liability criminal offenses requiring no *mens rea*. Almost all such statutes responded to the demands of public health and welfare arising from the complexities of society after the Industrial Revolution. Typically misdemeanors involving only fines or other light penalties, these strict liability laws regulated food, milk, liquor, medicines and drugs, securities, motor vehicles and traffic, the labeling of goods for sale, and the like.

Modern scholars generally reject the concept of strict criminal liability. Professors LaFave and Scott summarize the consensus that punishing conduct without reference to the actor's state of mind fails to reach the desired end and is unjust:

> "'It is inefficacious because conduct unaccompanied by an awareness of the factors making it criminal does not mark the actor as one who needs to be subjected to punishment in order to deter him or others from behaving similarly in the future. It is unjust because the actor is subjected to the stigma of a criminal conviction without being morally blameworthy. Consequently, on either a preventive or retributive theory of criminal punishment, the criminal sanction is inappropriate in the absence of *mens rea*.'"

Conscious of the disfavor in which strict criminal liability resides, the Model Penal Code states generally as a minimum requirement of culpability that a person is not guilty of a criminal offense unless he acts purposely, knowingly, recklessly, or negligently, *i.e.*, with some degree of *mens rea*. Model Penal Code § 2.02 (Official Draft and Revised Comments 1980). The Code allows generally for a defense of ignorance or mistake of fact negating *mens rea*. The Model Penal Code generally recognizes strict liability for offenses deemed "violations," defined as wrongs subject only to a fine, forfeiture, or other civil penalty upon conviction, and not giving rise to any legal disability. *Id.* at §§ 1.04, 2.05.[2]

Two sub-parts of the rationale underlying strict criminal liability require further analysis at this point. Statutory rape laws are often justified on the "lesser legal wrong" theory or the "moral wrong" theory; by such reasoning, the defendant acting without *mens rea* nonetheless deserves punishment for having committed a lesser crime, fornication, or for having violated moral teachings that prohibit sex outside of marriage. Maryland has no law against fornication. It is not a crime in this state. Moreover, the criminalization of an act, performed without a guilty mind, deemed immoral by some members of the community rests uneasily on subjective and shifting norms. We acknowledge here that it is uncertain to what extent Raymond's intellectual and social retardation may have impaired his ability to comprehend imperatives of sexual morality in any case.

## IV

The legislatures of 17 states have enacted laws permitting a mistake of age defense in some form in cases of sexual offenses with underage persons. In Kentucky, the accused may prove in exculpation that he did not know the facts or conditions relevant to the complainant's age. In Washington, the defendant may assert that he reasonably believed the complainant to be of a certain age based on the alleged victim's own declarations. In some states, the defense is available in instances where the complainant's age rises above a statutorily prescribed level, but is not available when the complainant falls below the defining age. *E.g.* Pa. Cons. Stat. Ann. tit. 18, § 3102 (1983) (defining critical age at 14); W. Va. Code Ann. § 61-8B-12 (1992 Repl. Vol.) (defining critical age at 11, defense subject to a recklessness standard); Or. Rev. Stat. Ann. § 163.325 (1990 Repl. Vol.) (defining critical age at 16).

In addition, the highest appellate courts of four states have determined that statutory rape laws by implication required an element of *mens rea* as to the complainant's age. In the landmark case of *People v. Hernandez*, 61 Cal. 2d 529 (1964), the California Supreme Court . . . reversed the trial court's refusal to permit the defendant to present evidence of his good faith, reasonable belief that the complaining witness had reached the age of consent. The court . . . rejected the traditional view that those who engage in sex with young persons do so at their peril, assuming the risk that their partners are underage:

---

[2] With respect to the law of statutory rape, the Model Penal Code strikes a compromise with its general policy against strict liability crimes. The Code prohibits the defense of ignorance or a reasonable mistake of age when the victim is below the age of ten, but allows it when the critical age stipulated in the offense is higher than ten. Model Penal Code, *supra*, at §§ 213.1, 213.6(1). The drafters of the Code implicitly concede that sexual conduct with a child of such extreme youth would, at the very least, spring from a criminally negligent state of mind. The available defense of reasonable mistake of age for complainants older than ten requires that the defendant not have acted out of criminal negligence.

"[I]f [the perpetrator] participates in a mutual act of sexual intercourse, believing his partner to be beyond the age of consent, with reasonable grounds for such belief, where is his criminal intent? If it occurs that he has been mislead, we cannot realistically conclude for such reason alone the intent with which he undertook the act suddenly becomes more heinous. . . . [T]he courts have uniformly failed to satisfactorily explain the nature of the criminal intent present in the mind of one who in good faith believes he has obtained a lawful consent before engaging in the prohibited act."

**V**

We think it sufficiently clear, however, that Maryland's second degree rape statute defines a strict liability offense that does not require the State to prove *mens rea*; it makes no allowance for a mistake-of-age defense. The plain language of § 463, viewed in its entirety, and the legislative history of its creation lead to this conclusion.

Section 463(a)(3) prohibiting sexual intercourse with underage persons makes no reference to the actor's knowledge, belief, or other state of mind. As we see it, this silence as to *mens rea* results from legislative design. First, subsection (a)(3) stands in stark contrast to the provision immediately before it, subsection (a)(2) prohibiting vaginal intercourse with incapacitated or helpless persons. In subsection (a)(2), the Legislature expressly provided as an element of the offense that "the person performing the act *knows or should reasonably know* the other person is mentally defective, mentally incapacitated, or physically helpless." Code, § 463(a)(2) (emphasis added). In drafting this subsection, the Legislature showed itself perfectly capable of recognizing and allowing for a defense that obviates criminal intent; if the defendant objectively did not understand that the sex partner was impaired, there is no crime. That it chose not to include similar language in subsection (a)(3) indicates that the Legislature aimed to make statutory rape with underage persons a more severe prohibition based on strict criminal liability.

Second, an examination of the drafting history of § 463 during the 1976 revision of Maryland's sexual offense laws reveals that the statute was viewed as one of strict liability from its inception and throughout the amendment process. As originally proposed, Senate Bill 358 defined as a sexual offense in the first degree a sex act committed with a person less than 14 years old by an actor four or more years older. The Senate Judicial Proceedings Committee then offered a series of amendments to the bill. Among them, . . . Amendment # 16 . . . added a provision defining a sexual offense in the second degree as a sex act with another "under 14 years of age, which age the person performing the sexual act knows or should know."

Senate Bill 358 in its amended form was passed by the Senate on March 11, 1976. The House of Delegates' Judiciary Committee, however, then proposed changes of its own. It rejected the Senate amendments, and defined an offense of rape, without a *mens rea* requirement, for sexual acts performed with someone under the age of 14. The Senate concurred in the House amendments and S.B. 358 became law. Thus the Legislature explicitly raised, considered, and then explicitly jettisoned any notion of a *mens rea* element with respect to the complainant's age in enacting the law that formed the basis of current § 463(a)(3). In the light of such legislative action, we must inevitably conclude that the current law imposes strict liability on its violators.

This interpretation is consistent with the traditional view of statutory rape as a strict liability crime designed to protect young persons from the dangers of sexual exploitation by adults, loss of chastity, physical injury, and, in the case of girls, pregnancy. The majority of states retain statutes which impose strict liability for sexual acts with underage complainants. We observe again, as earlier, that even among those states providing for a mistake-of-age defense in some instances, the defense often is not available where the sex partner is 14 years old or less; the complaining witness in the instant case was only 13.

### VI

Maryland's second degree rape statute is by nature a creature of legislation. Any new provision introducing an element of *mens rea*, or permitting a defense of reasonable mistake of age, with respect to the offense of sexual intercourse with a person less than 14, should properly result from an act of the Legislature itself, rather than judicial fiat. Until then, defendants in extraordinary cases, like Raymond, will rely upon the tempering discretion of the trial court at sentencing.

*Judgment affirmed, with costs.*

BELL, J., dissenting.

I do not dispute that the legislative history of Maryland Code Art. 27, section 463 may be read to support the majority's interpretation that subsection (a)(3) was intended to be a strict liability statute. I do not believe, however, that the General Assembly, in every case, whatever the nature of the crime and no matter how harsh the potential penalty, can subject a defendant to strict criminal liability.

In the case *sub judice*, according to the defendant, he intended to have sex with a 16, not a 13, year old girl. This mistake of fact was prompted, he said, by the prosecutrix herself; she and her friends told him that she was 16 years old. I would hold that the State is not relieved of its burden to prove the defendant's intent or knowledge in a statutory rape case and, therefore, that the defendant may defend on the basis that he was mistaken as to the age of the prosecutrix.

### I. *MENS REA* GENERALLY

Generally, a culpable mental state, often referred to as *mens rea* . . . is, and long has been, an essential element of a criminal offense. A crime ordinarily consists of prohibited conduct *and* a culpable mental state; a wrongful act and a wrongful intent must concur to constitute what the law deems a crime, the purpose being to avoid criminal liability for innocent or inadvertent conduct. Historically, therefore, unless the actor also harbored an evil, or otherwise culpable, mind, he or she was not guilty of any crime.

### II. STRICT LIABILITY CRIMES

Strict liability crimes are recognized exceptions to the "guilty mind" rule in that they do not require the actor to possess a guilty mind, or the *mens rea*, to commit a crime. His or her state of mind being irrelevant, the actor is guilty of the crime at the moment that he or she does the prohibited act.

In the evolution of the statutory criminal law, two classes of strict liability crimes have emerged. One of them consists of "public welfare" offenses. Typical of this class are statutes involving, for example, the sale of food, drugs, liquor, and traffic offenses, designed to protect the health, safety, and welfare of the community at large; violation of such statutes "depend on no mental element but consist[s] only of forbidden acts or omissions." In the case of public welfare offenses, strict liability is justified on several bases, including: (1) only strict liability can deter profit-driven manufacturers from ignoring the well-being of the consuming public; (2) an inquiry into *mens rea* would exhaust the resources of the courts; (3) imposition of strict liability is not inconsistent with the moral underpinnings of the criminal law because the penalties are small and carry no stigma; and (4) the legislature is constitutionally empowered to create strict liability crimes for public welfare offenses.

Obviously, . . . "statutory rape" is not merely a public welfare offense; it simply does not "fit" the characteristics of such an offense: it is a felony, not a misdemeanor. In striking contrast to "other strict liability regulatory offenses and their light penalties," the potential penalty of 20 years imprisonment is not a light penalty; unlike the "garden variety" strict liability penalty, the penalty under section 463(a)(3), is neither so insignificant that it can be ignored as a criminal sanction; and section 463's primary purpose is to penalize the "rapist," not to correct his or her behavior.

The second class of strict liability offenses, having a different justification than public welfare offenses, consists of . . . bigamy, adultery, and statutory rape crimes. State legislatures have historically used two theories to justify imposing strict liability in this class of offense: "lesser legal wrong" and "moral wrong."

The lesser legal wrong theory posits that a defendant who actually intended to do some legal or moral wrong is guilty not only of the crime intended but of a greater crime of which he or she may not have the requisite mental state. The elimination of a *mens rea* element for statutory rape is rationalized by focusing on the defendant's intent to commit a related crime. In other words, if fornication,[8] engaging in sexual intercourse out of wedlock, is a crime, a defendant intending to engage in sex out of wedlock is made to suffer all of the legal consequences of that act. Statutory rape is such a legal consequence when the other participant is below the age of consent. The theory is premised, in short, upon the proposition that, as to certain crimes, "a 'guilty mind' in a very general sense, should suffice for the imposition of penal sanctions even when the defendant did not intentionally or knowingly engage in the acts proscribed in the statute."

The seminal case in this area is *Regina v. Prince*, L.R. 2 Cr. Cas. Res. 154 (1875). There, the defendant was charged with unlawfully taking a girl under the age of 16 out of the possession of the father against his will. The defendant claimed that he acted on the reasonable belief that the girl was 18. The court held that it was no defense that he thought he was committing a different kind of wrong from that which he, in fact, was committing, it being wrong to remove a daughter, even one over 16, from her father's household.

---

[8] American penal statutes against fornication are generally unenforced, which may be reflective of the view that such a use of the penal law is improper.

The lesser legal wrong theory does not provide a viable rationale for holding a defendant strictly liable for statutory rape where premarital sex is not criminal. Fornication is not a crime in Maryland. Accordingly, in Maryland, there is no underlying offense from which to transfer intent.

In utilizing the moral wrong theory, State legislatures seek to justify strict criminal liability for statutory rape when non-marital sexual intercourse is not a crime on the basis of society's characterization of it as immoral or wrong, *i.e., malum in se.*[12] The intent to commit such immoral acts supplies the *mens rea* for the related, but unintended crime; the outrage upon public decency or good morals, not conduct that is wrong only because it is prohibited by legislation, *i.e., malum prohibitum*, is the predicate.

There are significant problems with the moral wrong theory. First, it is questionable whether morality should be the basis for legislation or interpretation of the law. Immorality is not synonymous with illegality; intent to do an immoral act does not equate to intent to do a criminal act. In addition, the values and morals of society are ever evolving.

Second, classifying an act as immoral, in and of itself, divorced from any consideration of the actor's intention, is contrary to the general consensus of what makes an act moral or immoral. Ordinarily, an act is either moral or immoral depending on the intention of the actor.

Therefore, although in the case *sub judice*, the defendant engaged in sexual relations with a girl 13 years old, a minor below the age of consent, his conduct is not *malum in se*, and, so, strict liability is not justified.

## III.   MISTAKE OF FACT

Generally, a mistake of fact negates the mental state required to establish a material element of the crime. A person who engages in proscribed conduct is relieved of criminal liability if, because of ignorance or mistake of fact, he or she did not entertain the culpable mental state required for the commission of the offense.

Statutory rape is defined as sexual intercourse, by a person four or more years older, with a person under the age of 14. Maryland Code Art. 27, § 463(a)(3). That statute conclusively presumes that a person under that age is incapable of legally consenting to sexual intercourse.[15] Consequently, a person engaging in intercourse with a female, whom he knows to be under 14 may not set up her consent as a defense. This does not mean, however, that one who does not know that the female is under 14 should not be able to set up his mistake of fact as a defense.

---

[12] An offense *malum in se* is properly defined as one which is naturally evil as adjudged by the sense of a civilized community. Acts *mala in se* have, as a general rule, become criminal offenses by the course and development of common law. In comparison, an act *malum prohibitum* is wrong only because made so by statute. *Malum in se* crimes usually include all felonies, injuries to property, adultery, bigamy, indecent acts committed upon underage children, and conduct contributing to the delinquency of a minor.

[15] [P]ursuant to section 463(a)(3) sexual intercourse with a person under 14 years of age, if the actor is at least four years older than the victim, is a second degree rape offense punishable by a possible twenty years imprisonment. Under section 464C, defining a fourth degree sexual offense, the same conduct if committed with a child 14 or 15 is punishable by a possible 1 year sentence. Thus, the law creates a potential disparity of up to 19 years for a difference of as little as one day in the victim's age.

# IV. CONSTITUTIONAL LIMITATIONS ON STRICT CRIMINAL LIABILITY

A State Legislature *does* have the power to define the elements of the criminal offenses recognized within its jurisdiction.

To recognize that a State legislature may, in defining criminal offenses, exclude *mens rea*, is not to suggest that it may do so with absolute impunity, without any limitation whatsoever.

Due process, whether pursuant to that clause of the Fourteenth Amendment[21] or the corresponding clause in a state constitution, protects an accused from being convicted of a crime except upon proof beyond a reasonable doubt of every element necessary to constitute the crime with which the accused is charged.

[T]here is precedent that a felony statute which prescribes substantial penalties and conviction of which will subject the defendant to significant social stigma, violates due process unless it requires the State to prove intent or knowledge.

[For example,] the Supreme Court of Alaska [relied on this principle to hold that] a reasonable mistake of age defense was permitted [for the charge of statutory rape], the court submitted:

> [W]here a particular statute is not a public welfare type of offense, either a requirement of criminal intent must be read into the statute or it must be found unconstitutional. . . . Since statutes should be construed where possible to avoid unconstitutionality, it is necessary here to infer a requirement of criminal intent.

*State v. Guest*, 583 P.2d 836, 839 (Alaska 1978).

Similarly, the prosecution of statutory rape in Maryland necessarily brings into conflict the State's interests in protecting minors and defendants' due process rights because section 463(a)(3) operates "'to exclude elements of knowledge and diligence from its definition,'" and, thus, removes reasonable ignorance of the girl's age and consequent lack of criminal intent as a defense. The failure of section 463(a)(3) to require proof of a culpable mental state conflicts both with the substantive due process ideal requiring that defendants possess some level of fault for a criminal conviction of statutory rape and the procedural due process ideal requiring that the prosecution overcome the presumption of innocence by proof of the defendant's guilt beyond a reasonable doubt. Where there is no issue as to sexual contact, which is more likely than not to be the case in statutory rape prosecutions, proof of the prosecutrix's age is not only proof of the defendant's guilt, it is absolutely dispositive of it and, at the same time, it is fatal to the only defense the defendant would otherwise have. So interpreted, section 463(a)(3) not only destroys absolutely the concept of fault, but it renders meaningless, in the statutory rape context, the presumption of innocence and the right to due process.

I respectfully dissent.

---

[21] The due process clause of the Fourteenth Amendment of the United States Constitution guarantees that no State shall "deprive any person of life, liberty or property without due process of law." This clause has been interpreted as "a restraint on the legislative as well as on the executive and judicial powers of the government and [it] cannot be . . . construed as to leave Congress free to make any process 'due process' of law by its mere will." *Murray's Lessee v. Hoboken Land & Improvement Co.*, 59 U.S. (18 How.) 272, 276 (1855).

**Post-Case Follow-Up**

*Garnett* provides an example of how courts have weighed the question of whether statutory rape is a strict liability crime. Those who support imposing strict liability for statutory rape typically point to one or two policy justifications: the lesser legal wrong theory and the moral legal wrong theory. The lesser legal wrong theory proceeds from the idea that a defendant who acted with *mens rea* with respect to a lesser crime (e.g., fornication) can be held strictly liable for a greater crime (e.g., statutory rape). In the context of statutory rape, the moral wrong theory holds that because statutory rape defendants have engaged in sex outside of marriage and because sex outside of marriage is morally wrong, it is acceptable to impose strict liability for the crime of statutory rape. The majority did not appear to be persuaded by either theory, noting that "Maryland has no law against fornication" and that what is "deemed immoral by some members of the community rests uneasily on subjective and shifting norms." The majority also observed that, as of 1993, 21 states no longer treated statutory rape as a strict liability crime. Nevertheless, the majority concluded that Maryland's legislature intended for the law to "make[] no allowance for a mistake-of-age defense." Jurisdictions remain split on this issue — in a majority, statutory rape remains a strict liability offense; a sizeable minority have adopted a *mens rea* requirement of some kind with respect to age. Among jurisdictions in the latter group, the most common approach appears to be a negligence standard under which the defendant's mistake as to the victim's age must be reasonable.

## Garnett: *Real Life Applications*

1. In *Garnett*, the majority concluded by stating that, unless and until the legislature amends Maryland's statutory rape law to require *mens rea*, "defendants in extraordinary cases . . . will rely upon the tempering discretion of the trial court at sentencing." Courts are not the only actors in the criminal justice system with discretion and power, however. Prosecutors have the discretion to decide whether or not to bring charges against a defendant and typically have significant negotiating power in plea bargaining.

   Imagine that you were the prosecutor in the *Garnett* case. Assume that your office's interview with the victim confirmed that she and her friends told Raymond Garnett that she was 16. Assume further that your office hired an expert on intellectual disabilities and that this expert confirmed that Garnett had the social and interpersonal skills of an 11-year old.

   a. Would you have chosen to charge Garnett with statutory rape under these circumstances?

   b. Garnett's statutory rape conviction carried a maximum penalty of 20 years. Footnote 15 of the dissenting opinion notes that at the time of the *Garnett* case, Maryland had a separate statute (§ 464C) that made sex with a 14- or 15-year-old minor a fourth-degree sexual offense, punishable by up to one year in prison. Would you have considered offering to let Garnett plead guilty to the lesser § 464C offense? If so, do you think there might be any impediment to having the trial court accept a guilty plea by Garnett to violating § 464C?

2. You are a member of the Maryland General Assembly. A constituent who is opposed to strict liability offenses comes to you and asks that you propose a bill to amend Maryland's statutory rape law. Would you do so? If so, what standard would you propose adopting with respect to the defendant's mental state and the age of the victim?

## C. CHILD PORNOGRAPHY

Laws criminalizing the production, distribution, and possession of child pornography have existed since the mid-1970s, and laws against obscenity go back even further. For much of that time, the distribution of child pornography was a relatively rare occurrence. The landscape has changed dramatically over the past two to three decades, however. The rise of digital photography and access to the Internet in the late 1990s and early 2000s made it easier and less expensive for people to produce and share photographs than ever before. In the mid- to late 2000s, cell phone cameras and texting rapidly became part of everyday life. As a result of these technological advances, people today take and share photographs and videos on a scale that would have been unimaginable at the turn of the century. These same advances have also led to an increase in the production and distribution of child pornography.

Legislatures have reacted to these developments in part by increasing penalties for child pornography offenses. At the federal level, "[t]he punishment for the possession of child pornography now equals or exceeds the penalties for many other serious crimes. For example, a federal defendant found guilty of possessing twenty images of child pornography will receive a longer prison sentence than federal defendants who committed arson, burglary, robbery, or sexual abuse of a minor." Carissa Byrne Hessick, *The Limits of Child Pornography*, 89 Ind. L.J. 1437, 1438 (2014). Many states have similarly "increased criminal sentences for possession of child pornography; those increases have sometimes resulted in the imposition of sentences that are longer than those imposed on defendants who sexually assaulted children." *Id.* at 1438-39.

Legislatures and courts have also had to grapple with the phenomenon of minors taking and sharing sexually explicit photographs with one another. The next case addresses that issue.

**Case Preview**

### In re S.K.

"[C]an a minor legally engaged in consensual sexual activity be his or her own pornographer through the act of sexting?" That question, presented in the next case, is one that courts and legislatures across the country have wrestled with since the mid- to late 2000s. As discussed in the opinion that follows, jurisdictions have taken a number of different approaches to this issue.

As you read the decision, consider the following questions:

1. What are some of the different types of legislation states have adopted to address the issue of minors sharing pornographic images of themselves with one another?
2. What are the policy rationale(s) for criminalizing the possession and distribution of child pornography and which of those rationale(s), if any, apply in the case of minors who share images of themselves with other minors?
3. Why does the court hold that Maryland's child pornography statute applies to S.K.'s conduct?

---

## *In re S.K.*
### 466 Md. 31 (2019)

GETTY, J.

As a matter of first impression, the main issue before this Court is whether a minor may be adjudicated delinquent under the current statutory scheme as the "person" who is a distributor of child pornography and a displayer of obscene matter when she is also the minor participant in the sex act. Put more dramatically, can a minor legally engaged in consensual sexual activity be his or her own pornographer through the act of sexting?

### BACKGROUND

During the 2016-17 school year, two sixteen-year-old females, A.T. and S.K., and a seventeen-year-old male, K.S., were best friends attending Maurice J. McDonough High School in Charles County, Maryland. S.K. and A.T. had been friends since elementary school. The trio had a group chat on their cellphones in which they would communicate with one another by text message. A.T. stated the group chat was used, among other things, to send silly photos and videos to "one-up" each other. The trio frequently hung out together and trusted one another to keep their group text messages private.

In October, A.T. and K.S. received a text message containing a video recording from S.K.'s cellphone number. The video was approximately one minute in length and showed S.K. performing fellatio on a male. The male's identity and age were not established in the testimony at the adjudication. In the video, S.K. is nude and her upper torso, including an exposed breast, is visible throughout most of the video. The nude male's mid-torso and erect penis are shown during the majority of the video although an unfocused view of his face is visible momentarily at the video's conclusion. The male appears to be the one filming the video through an extended reach of his arm similar to taking a selfie.[1]

---

[1] A "selfie" is defined as "an image that includes oneself (often with another person or as part of a group) and is taken by oneself using a digital camera especially for posting on social networks." Selfie, Merriam-Webster, http://www.merriam-webster.com/dictionary/selfie.

In December, S.K. and K.S. had a falling out. K.S. began urging A.T. to go with him to the school resource officer to report the video of S.K. Eventually, A.T. relented. K.S. testified he was worried about S.K. and wanted her to receive help. However, A.T. testified that the motives of K.S. were not so pure. A.T. testified that K.S. was bragging around school about S.K. going to jail if he were to report the text message to the school resource officer. She stated, "he has a strong hate towards her. And he kinda [sic] just pulled me along with him because he knew I would be on his side."

A.T. and K.S. went to the school resource officer, Officer Eugene Caballero of the Charles County Sheriff's Office. At the meeting, A.T. and K.S. told Officer Caballero about the video. At that point, K.S. possessed the video as an email attachment. He displayed the email and video on Officer Caballero's computer. Officer Caballero then instructed K.S. to delete the video from his email account.

After receiving a copy of the video from K.S., Officer Caballero met with S.K. at the Robert D. Stethem Educational Center in Charles County. S.K. was read her *Miranda* rights and agreed to speak with Officer Caballero. In his police report, Officer Caballero stated S.K. cried during their meeting and was upset that the video was going around the school.[3] S.K. was under the impression that Officer Caballero met with her to stop the video from further distribution to other students. At no point during this meeting did Officer Caballero inform S.K. that she was considered a suspect for criminal activity. S.K. provided Officer Caballero with a written statement admitting that she was in the video and had only sent it to her two friends.

The police report was referred to the State's Attorney for Charles County who had discretion as to whether to file the criminal charges. After review, the State charged S.K., as a juvenile, with three counts as follows: Count 1: filming a minor engaging in sexual conduct in violation of Maryland Code, Criminal Law ("CR") § 11-207(a)(2); Count 2: distributing child pornography in violation of CR § 11-207(a)(4); and Count 3: displaying an obscene item to a minor in violation of CR § 11-203(b)(1)(ii).

The adjudicatory hearing was held on April 27, 2017 before the Circuit Court of Charles County sitting as a juvenile court. At the conclusion of the hearing, Count 1, filming a minor engaging in sexual conduct, was dismissed because there was no evidence presented that S.K. was filming the video. At the end of closing argument, the juvenile court found S.K. involved as to Counts 2 and 3.[4]

At a subsequent disposition hearing on May 18, 2017, S.K. was placed on electronic monitoring until June 9, 2017 and supervised probation administered by the Department of Juvenile Services. S.K. was not ordered to register as a sex offender. On September 27, 2018, after fulfilling her probation requirements, this case was ordered closed and sealed.

S.K. appealed the delinquency finding and subsequent disposition to the Court of Special Appeals[, which affirmed the delinquency adjudication as to the child pornography finding but reversed as to the obscenity finding.] In a reported opinion,

---

[3] A.T. testified that K.S. was the one who distributed the video throughout the school. K.S. testified he never showed anyone else the video, but stated he discussed the contents of the video with others. At the time of the adjudicatory hearing, neither K.S. nor A.T. was charged for the possession or distribution of the video.

[4] Meaning she was involved in a delinquent act "which would be a crime if committed by an adult." Md. Code (2006, 2013 Repl. Vol.), Cts. & Jud. Proc. § 3-8A-01(l).

the Court of Special Appeals held, relevant to the issue before us, that a minor legally engaged in consensual sexual activity is not exempted from CR § 11-207(a)(4) and thus is in violation of the child pornography statute. As to the [obscenity finding], the Court of Special Appeals held that the digital file S.K. sent by text message was not an "item" covered within the [obscenity] statute.

S.K. filed a petition for writ of certiorari with this Court [and] the State filed a conditional cross-petition for writ of certiorari, [both of] which [were] granted.

## DISCUSSION

For the first time, this Court is confronted with the complexities of the socio-cultural phenomenon of sexting by minors in the context of Maryland's criminal statutes as applied in a juvenile proceeding. We are asked to determine whether it is a violation of the child pornography statute for a sixteen-year-old minor female to distribute a one-minute video via text message to her best friends in which she is engaging in sexual conduct that is not criminal. Further, we are asked whether the distribution of the text message video qualifies as an "item" codified in the obscenity statute criminalizing the display of obscene matter to a minor.

Central to this issue is the dominant role cellphones play in our society. In *Riley v. California*, Chief Justice John Roberts observed that "modern cellphones . . . are now such a pervasive and insistent part of daily life that the proverbial visitor from Mars might conclude they were an important feature of human anatomy." Undoubtedly, smartphone use has become ubiquitous across all generations. However, Generation Z, loosely comprising of those born after 1997, has a distinctive relationship with this technology. Unlike the Silent Generation, Baby Boomers, Generation X, or Millennials, Generation Z has never known life without access to a smartphone.

Today, ninety-five percent of teens have access to smartphones and ninety-seven percent of teens use at least one of the seven major online platforms. Forty-five percent of teenagers report to be online on a virtually constant basis. In a 2010 study, one in three teenagers sends more than one hundred text messages a day, or three-thousand text messages a month.

Sexting is a sociocultural phenomenon that has evolved from the use of smartphones. Black's Law Dictionary identifies the origin of the word "sexting" in the year 2005 and defines it as "the sending of sexually explicit messages or images by cellphone." Consistent with the rise in smartphone usage, at least 18.5% of middle and high schoolers report having received sexually explicit images or videos on their phones or computers.

As sexting has grown in popularity, so has the attention given to the issue. As early as 2007, the legal community began to debate what was coined "self-produced child pornography." *Compare* Mary Graw Leary, *Self-Produced Child Pornography: The Appropriate Societal Response to Juvenile Self-Sexual Exploitation*, 15 Va. J. Soc. Pol'y & L. 1 (2007) with Stephen F. Smith, *Jail for Juvenile Child Pornographers?: A Reply to Professor Leary*, 15 Va. J. Soc. Pol'y & L. 505 (2008). In 2009, in response to the national attention focused on teenage sexting, additional legal scholars began to address the issue by distinguishing this activity from child pornography and discussing appropriate sanctions.

In addition to the attention many legal scholars gave the issue, other states responded with specific legislation addressing teenage sexting.[14] States have addressed this issue by including provisions such as separate offenses applied to minors, affirmative defenses for minors, and lower penalties if the minor is found delinquent. The lower "penalties" include services like classes specifically addressing sexting and phone usage, community service, and counseling. Although the majority of states have passed legislation to amend their child pornography statute relative to sexting, Maryland is one of twenty-one states that have not passed any such legislation and thus permit teenagers to be charged under the child pornography statute.

Occasionally, other state courts have considered the breadth of their child pornography statute vis-à-vis sexting. In *State v. Gray*, the Washington Supreme Court addressed whether a seventeen-year-old boy's act of "electronically sending an unsolicited picture of his erect penis to an adult woman" violated the language of Wash. Rev. Code § 9.68A.050(2)(a) that "[a] person commits the crime of dealing in depictions of a minor engaging in sexually explicit conduct in the second degree when he or she . . . [k]nowingly . . . disseminates . . . any visual or printed matter that depicts a minor engaged in an act of sexually explicit conduct." 189 Wash. 2d 334, 337 (2017). The majority upheld the conviction, holding that the statute was unambiguous, thus the minor's conduct violated the statute.[16]

In a recent Colorado case, a male teenager was romantically involved with two female teenagers during the 2012-2013 school year. *People in Interest of T.B.*, 445 P.3d 1049 (Colo. 2019). He exchanged nude selfies by text message with the females. The male kept the photos on his cellphone, and, when he was arrested in 2013 on an unrelated sexual assault charge, police discovered the photographs of the nude females on his cellphone. He was charged and adjudicated delinquent for sexual exploitation of a child under section 18-6-403(3), C.R.S. (2018). The majority upheld the conviction.[17] The majority determined the statute was not ambiguous and refused to read into the statute an exemption for minors.

While sexting, specifically when engaged in by teenagers, has been addressed extensively in the literature, the media, and by state legislatures in other jurisdictions,

---

[14] *See* Arkansas Rev. State. Ann. § 5-27-609 (possession of sexually explicit digital material) (creating a separate offense, disposition, and affirmative defenses for minors); Conn. Gen. Stat. § 53a-196h (possessing or transmitting child pornography by minor: Class A misdemeanor); Fla. Stat. § 847.0141(3) (sexting; prohibited acts; penalties) (applying to minors); N.Y. Penal Laws § 60.37 (directing that those who sext may be eligible to participate in an education program in lieu of adjudication); R.I. Gen. Laws. Ann. § 11-9-1.4 (minor electronically disseminating indecent material to another person — "Sexting"); S.D. Codified Laws § 26-10-33 (juvenile sexting prohibited — violation as misdemeanor).

[16] We note that the Washington State Legislature acted to amend its statute partially in response to this case.

[17] The General Assembly in Colorado recently enacted H.B. 17-1302 in response to the concern over teen sexting. Although the new statute did not apply to the earlier conduct of T.B., the court explained the revised statute:

> created, among other lower-level offenses, the civil infraction of "exchange of a private image" by a juvenile. Under this new offense, a juvenile who knowingly possesses a sexually explicit image of another person who is at least fourteen years old or less than four years younger than the juvenile, and who reasonably believes the depicted person transmitted the image or otherwise agreed to its transmittal, commits a civil infraction punishable by a fine of up to $50 or participation in a program addressing the risks and consequences of such behavior.

*People in Interest of T.B.*, 445 P.3d at 1052. There, since the juvenile's actions predated the statutory change, he was subject to registration as a sex offender rather than a civil penalty.

the General Assembly has not updated Maryland's statutes to address this contemporary issue. The present case turns on whether a minor who privately distributes a video to her friends in which she is depicted engaging in an act that in itself is not illegal may be deemed delinquent under CR § 11-207(a)(4) or CR § 11-203(b)(1)(ii). We will review each statute in turn.

### A. The Plain Language of CR § 11-207(a)(4) Subsumes Situations Where a Minor Produces and Distributes Pornographic Material of Himself or Herself

In the mid-1970s, the federal government and state governments determined a need to focus their legislation "on the use of children as the subjects of pornographic material." Previously, states had focused on obscenity in general, but this period was the first time the statutes were targeting the involvement of minors in the commercial production and trade of child pornography. Congress passed the Protection of Children Against Sexual Exploitation Act to address the interstate nature of this pornography. At that time, "only six States then had statutes proscribing the use of children in the production of pornographic material and no Federal law [existed that] dealt directly with 'the abuse of children that is inherent in the production of such materials.'" As a result of the federal legislation, many states followed suit and enacted their own statutes. The General Assembly enacted Maryland's first child pornography statute in 1978.

[In] *New York v. Ferber*, 458 U.S. 747 (1982)[, the United States Supreme Court] held "that the First Amendment permits a state to proscribe the distribution of sexual materials involving minors without regard to an obscenity standard." As to the dangers of child pornography, the Supreme Court stated: "The distribution of photographs and films depicting sexual activity by juveniles is intrinsically related to the sexual abuse of children in at least two ways. First, the materials produced are a permanent record of the children's participation and the harm to the child is exacerbated by their circulation. Second, the distribution network for child pornography must be closed if the production of material which requires the sexual exploitation of children is to be effectively controlled."

With this historical backdrop, we now turn to an analysis of the statute. The 1978 child pornography statute as amended, CR § 11-207(a)(4)(i), prohibits a "person" from knowingly distributing "any matter, visual representation, or performance . . . that depicts a minor engaged as a subject in . . . sexual conduct." Sexual conduct is defined in CR § 11-101(d) as (1) human masturbation; (2) sexual intercourse; or (3) whether alone or with another individual or animal, any touching of or contact with: (i) the genitals, buttocks, or pubic areas of any individual; or (ii) breasts of a female individual."

S.K. contends this case is about whether CR § 11-207(a)(4) permits the prosecution of a minor for transmitting a visual representation of herself engaged in consensual, legal sexual conduct. S.K. argues the answer is no, stating the statute was intended to protect, not prosecute, minors victimized and exploited in the production of sexually explicit videos.

S.K. argues there are two points of ambiguity in CR § 11-207(a) and thus a plain meaning interpretation of the statute is inapplicable. One point of ambiguity is the phrase "engaged as a subject in" sexual conduct and the other point is the dichotomy between the "person" knowingly distributing the sexually explicit child pornography and the "minor" victim who is portrayed in the sexual conduct. S.K. believes "subject" is defined as "one who is under the rule of another or others." Thus, the phrase "engages as a subject in" connotes a legislative intent to proscribe the distribution of a visual representation of a minor who is unable to consent to the sexual conduct by force or age. As S.K was a sixteen-year-old minor, she was legally able to consent to engage in sexual conduct, and thus cannot be "subjected" to the apparently consensual sexual conduct. *See Garnett v. State*, 332 Md. 571, 577 (1993) (recognizing the age of consent to sexual relations in Maryland as sixteen). Further, S.K. argues that [under] CR § 11-207(a), the "person" whose action is being criminalized and the person being prosecuted cannot be the minor.

We do not find any ambiguity in this text and, therefore it is our duty to interpret the law as written and apply its plain meaning to the facts before us. We turn first to whether one individual can be both a person and a minor, as contemplated by CR § 11-207 or whether, as S.K. argues, the statute creates a dichotomy that requires the person and minor be different individuals. Under the definitional section of the Criminal Law Article, a minor "means *an individual* under the age of 18 years" and a person is defined as "*an individual*, sole proprietorship, partnership, firm, association . . . or other entity." CL § 1-101(g), (h) (emphasis added). Evident from these definitions, minors and persons are both individuals. However, a "person" is the broader concept; whereas, minors are a limited subset of persons, demarcated by age. Quite clearly, the term "person" encompasses both minors and adults.

As to the [other] potential area of ambiguity S.K. raises, we . . . [find] that a minor is "engaged as a subject" under the statute "if she or he is a participant in, or the object of, such conduct." S.K. interprets the phrase "engaged as a subject in" to mean under authority or control and proffers that the statute applies only when the minor is unable to consent to the sexual conduct. This interpretation would certainly create a major loophole with respect to child pornography laws. For example, a prosecutor would have to establish, particularly with respect to foreign-produced child pornography, that the child was younger than the age of consent in the particular country where the image or video was produced, as the child depicted would likely not be identifiable to testify as to the issue of consent.

This case presents a unique challenge. On the one hand, there is no question that the State has an overwhelming interest in preventing the spread of child pornography and has been given broad authority to eradicate the production and distribution of child pornography. On the other hand, S.K., albeit unwisely, engaged in the same behavior as many of her peers. Here, S.K is prosecuted as a "child pornographer" for sexting and, because she is a minor, her actions fell directly within the scope of the statute. The General Assembly has consistently expanded the scope of the statute to assist in the eradication of any form of child pornography. As written, the statute in its plain meaning is all encompassing, making no distinction whether a minor or an adult is distributing the matter.

Therefore, based on this intent and the unambiguous language, we believe S.K.'s conduct falls within the purview of the statute. In affirming this adjudication, however, we recognize that there may be compelling policy reasons for treating teenage sexting different from child pornography.[23] In response to this case, legislation was introduced in the 2019 Legislative Session that was not passed but in light of these policy concerns, such legislation ought to be considered by the General Assembly in the future.[24]

[The court then held that S.K.'s conduct also violated Maryland's obscenity statute.]

Judgment of the Court of Special Appeals is affirmed in part and reversed in part; costs to be paid by Petitioner/Cross-Respondent.

HOTTEN, J., dissents.

The text of Crim. Law § 11-207(a)(4)(i) provides that: "A *person* may not: knowingly promote, advertise, solicit, distribute, or possess with the intent to distribute any matter, visual representation, or performance: that depicts a *minor* engaged as a subject in sadomasochistic abuse or sexual conduct[.]" (emphasis added). The Majority provides that a "person" and "minor" are one and the same individual, such that S.K. is delinquent "for transmitting a visual representation of herself engaged in consensual, legal sexual conduct."

I assert that a plain reading of the text could lead to a conclusion that "person" and "minor" are two different people.

Grammatical convention provides that one purpose of a colon is to "introduce[] an element or series of elements that illustrates or amplifies the information that preceded the colon. . . . [One can] [t]hink [of a colon] as a flashing arrow that points to the information following it." *Colon*, GRAMMARLY, https://www.grammarly.com/blog/colon-2/, *available at* https://perma.cc/D5KK-FMXX (last visited Aug. 27, 2019). Therefore, the noun "person," which precedes the colon, applies equally to all of § 11-207(a)'s subsections; reading "person" and "minor" to be the same individual would create redundancy in the statute. The statute's format is such that a "person" is a separate entity from the "minor."

Therefore, I conclude that the plain language of Crim. Law § 11-207(a)(4)(i) does not permit S.K. to be delinquent for transmitting a visual representation of herself.

---

[23] *See* Dr. JoAnne Sweeny, *Sexting Freedom of Expression: A Comparative Approach*, 102 Kentucky Law Journal 103 (2014) for a comparison of the ramifications of sexting compared with child pornography. Dr. Sweeny proposes that sexting and child pornography are different for crucial reasons. Unlike traditional pornography, the majority of these images are taken with consent and only discovered by an adult viewing the teens' phone or nonconsensual sharing. The harm at issue when sexting is not the taking or sharing of the image, but instead what happens when other peers may review the image. This is unlike child pornography where the child victim is subjected to abuse or exploitation. Dr. Sweeny also posits the "haunting" rationale does not apply to sexting as in child pornography, the haunting is the "existence of the images themselves or the fact that the sexual acts were photographed." Finally, the "drying up the market" rationale does not fully apply as these images are often only passed around teen to teen.

[24] In response to Court of Special Appeals' decision, Delegate C.T. Wilson, from Charles County, introduced House Bill 1049 in the 2019 Legislative Session which would have decriminalized the distribution or manufacturing of child pornography by a person younger than eighteen. *See* Fiscal and Policy Note for House Bill 1049. During a hearing on the bill before the House Judiciary Committee, Delegate Wilson testified that he introduced the bill because he disagreed with the decision of the State's Attorney for Charles County to pursue S.K. under the child pornography statute for her sexting incident. He acknowledged that as drafted the language of his bill was too broad but he urged the Committee to address the issue of teenage sexting by amending and passing House Bill 1049. After the March 6, 2019 hearing, the Committee took no further action.

[Moreover, to the extent the statute is ambiguous], "the job of this Court is to resolve the ambiguity in light of the legislative intent[.]" The legislative purpose in enacting the child pornography statute was to address child pornography trafficking and to prevent the sexual exploitation and abuse of minors. [T]he State sought to protect children from *exploitation and abuse* as opposed to enacting laws that criminalized consensual sexual activity among minors. Reading the statute in a contrary fashion subverts legislative intent.

In the case at bar, S.K. was not being exploited by someone else. She made a video depicting consensual sexual conduct. The General Assembly did not seek to subject minors who recorded themselves in non-exploitative sexual encounters to prosecution, as reflected by the language of Crim. Law § 11-207(a). Rather, the statute contemplates *protecting* children from the *actions of others* that bear negatively upon them.

In *State v. Gray*, 189 Wash. 2d 334 (Wash. 2017) [cited by the majority], three judges dissented, contending that the legislative intent for the statute at issue was to protect children and that such an intent should exempt children from prosecution under the law. Relevant to the case at bar, the dissenting judges wrote:

> For more than 80 years, the United States Supreme Court, federal courts, and Washington courts have held that when the legislature enacts a statute designed for the protection of one class — here, children depicted in sexually explicit conduct — it shows the legislature's intent to protect members of that class from criminal liability for their own depiction in such conduct. *E.g., Gebardi v. United States*, 287 U.S. 112, 119 (1932). [I]f the legislature wanted us to apply a different rule of statutory interpretation — one that would permit members of the protected class to be charged, prosecuted, convicted, and imprisoned for up to 10 years for sexually explicit, exploitative depictions of their own bodies — it was the legislature's duty to explicitly say that they were departing from the general rule of statutory interpretation. The legislature did not say so here. Its silence must be construed as an endorsement of the general rule.

189 Wash. 2d at 349-50 (McCloud, J., dissenting). The *Gray* dissent is applicable to the case at bar, demonstrating that the Majority's interpretation of the statutory language "punishes the most vulnerable participant — the depicted child — no matter what personal pressures or personal struggles . . . compelled the child to do it." 189 Wash. 2d at 350, 402 P.3d at 262.

The Court of Special Appeals recognized that self-produced pornography can cause "significant 'physiological, emotional, and mental' harm to the minor[,]" including withdrawal from others, depression, anxiety, and low self-esteem. *In Re: S.K.*, 237 Md. App. 458, 473 n.6 (2018). S.K.'s mother testified that "[w]hen all this hit, sort of hit the fan back [in] December that was when everything, her grades went downhill. She, she did not, didn't go to school the whole month of December because of this." S.K.'s mother further testified that when S.K. learned that the video was being circulated to others at school, S.K. called her mother "from school in tears[.]" It is clear that S.K. suffered immense distress after learning that the digital file had been circulated among peers — such distress that she could not fathom going back to school for an entire month. She suffered from the very emotional and mental harms that the Court of Special Appeals referenced. It therefore seems counterintuitive to further subject S.K. to prosecution under a statute that was designed to protect her.

For purposes of resolving delinquent behavior or conduct, the mission of the juvenile court in Maryland includes achievement of a respectful, sensitive, holistic approach to the child — balancing the components of rehabilitation, treatment and public safety with attention and care — in an effort to resolve the delinquent conduct. The General Assembly enacted Crim. Law § 11-207 to protect minors, not to subject them to prosecution "for their own harm[.]"[3]

Based on a statutory interpretation of Crim. Law § 11-207, in conjunction with the rehabilitative nature of juvenile proceedings, I conclude that S.K.'s conduct does not fall within the purview of the statute.

---

**Post-Case Follow-Up**

In *In re S.K.*, the majority held that Maryland's child pornography statute applied to a minor who shared a pornographic video of herself with her friends. The court appeared uncertain about whether this was the right result as a matter of policy, noting that "we recognize that there may be compelling policy reasons for treating teenage sexting different from child pornography." Nevertheless, the court found that the text of the statute applied to S.K.'s conduct. As discussed in the opinion, a majority of states have passed legislation to specifically address teen sexting, although a sizeable minority of states — 21 at the time of the decision in *In re S.K.* in August 2019 — have not. Among the states that have passed legislation on the subject, there have been a number of different approaches, including adopting "separate offenses applied to minors, affirmative defenses for minors, and lower penalties if the minor is found delinquent."

---

## In re S.K.: *Real Life Applications*

1. Following the opinion in *In re S.K.*, multiple bills were filed by state representatives to amend Maryland's child pornography statute. Below are key excerpts of two of the bills. When reading the excerpts, note that plain text formatting denotes language from the statute as it currently exists, the **BOLD AND CAPITALIZED** portions indicate proposed additions to existing law, and the ~~strikethrough~~ text indicates proposed deletions from existing law.

---

[3] The goal of the juvenile justice system is to reform, not punish, juveniles. *See* Cts. & Jud. Proc. § 3-8A-01(b).

Given the collateral consequences of juvenile adjudication within the broader scheme of rehabilitation, we must proceed cautiously with findings of delinquency. In the instant matter, the retributive nature of the juvenile adjudication by the State is evident by the significant stigma and trauma to S.K., which is exacerbated by the juvenile court's delinquency findings. Rather than provide remedies to assist and protect, the State generated conditions on S.K. that were retributive, including GPS monitoring, which the juvenile court unequivocally denied.

I also find the failure to exercise prosecutorial discretion towards a 16-year-old minor who was visibly distressed by dissemination of — what she believed to be — a confidential file shared with two friends highly problematic. The State had the discretion to file charges, and ultimately charged S.K. as a juvenile with three counts, one of which was dismissed for lack of evidence. The rigor with which the State sought to prosecute S.K. is at odds with the rehabilitative nature of juvenile proceedings.

Senate Bill 45
Introduced by State Senator Jeffrey D. Waldstreicher

11-207

(a) A person may not:

(1) cause, induce, solicit, or knowingly allow **ANOTHER WHO IS** a minor to engage as a subject in the production of obscene matter or a visual representation or performance that depicts **ANOTHER WHO IS** a minor engaged as a subject in sadomasochistic abuse or sexual conduct;

(2) photograph or film **ANOTHER WHO IS** a minor engaging in an obscene act, sadomasochistic abuse, or sexual conduct;

(3) use a computer to depict or describe **ANOTHER WHO IS** a minor engaging in an obscene act, sadomasochistic abuse, or sexual conduct;

(4) knowingly promote, advertise, solicit, distribute, or possess with the intent to distribute any matter, visual representation, or performance:

(i) that depicts **ANOTHER WHO IS** a minor engaged as a subject in sadomasochistic abuse or sexual conduct; or

(ii) in a manner that reflects the belief, or that is intended to cause another to believe, that the matter, visual representation, or performance depicts **ANOTHER WHO IS** a minor engaged as a subject of sadomasochistic abuse or sexual conduct; or

(5) use a computer to knowingly compile, enter, transmit, make, print, publish, reproduce, cause, allow, buy, sell, receive, exchange, or disseminate any notice, statement, advertisement, or minor's name, telephone number, place of residence, physical characteristics, or other descriptive or identifying information for the purpose of engaging in, facilitating, encouraging, offering, or soliciting unlawful sadomasochistic abuse or sexual conduct of or with **ANOTHER WHO IS** a minor.

House Bill 931
Introduced by Delegate C.T. Wilson (the same delegate mentioned
in footnote 24 of the court's opinion)

11-207

(a) A person may not:

(1) cause, induce, solicit, or knowingly allow a minor to engage as a subject in the production of obscene matter or a visual representation or performance that depicts a minor engaged as a subject in sadomasochistic abuse or sexual conduct;

(2) photograph or film a minor engaging in an obscene act, sadomasochistic abuse, or sexual conduct;

(3) use a computer to depict or describe a minor engaging in an obscene act, sadomasochistic abuse, or sexual conduct;

(4) knowingly promote, advertise, solicit, distribute, or possess with the intent to distribute any matter, visual representation, or performance:

i. that depicts a minor engaged as a subject in sadomasochistic abuse or sexual conduct; or

ii. in a manner that reflects the belief, or that is intended to cause another to believe, that the matter, visual representation, or performance depicts a minor

## Sex Offender Registries

Criminal sentences for many sex offenses include an unusual penalty: a requirement to register as a sex offender. Although registries for other offenses are not entirely unheard of — for example, California has a registry for drug offenders, see Cal. Health & Safety Code § 11590 — sex offender registration carries unique legal and social consequences.

Most state sex offender registration laws were passed in the 1990s. As originally conceived, these laws were not meant to be punitive. Rather, they were intended as a way to prevent future offenses. The theory was that a registry of people convicted of serious sex offenses involving children would help police investigations and inform concerned parents. In the years since, sex offense registration laws have expanded in a number of ways. Registries have become more than just a list of offenders. Registration status now carries a number of legal restrictions — prohibitions on living in certain places, for example. The number and kinds of offenses that trigger the registration requirement have also expanded significantly. By 2006, approximately 30 states required juvenile offenders to register. In addition, because information is much more accessible than it was in the 1990s (when access to the Internet was much more limited), a sex offender's status is now easily and widely known — not just to concerned parents and the police, but to anyone who types the registrant's name into Google.

All of these developments have led some prominent early supporters of sex offender registry laws to call for reforms. Perhaps most notable in this group is Patty Wetterling. The

~~engaged as a subject of sadomasochistic abuse or sexual conduct; or~~

(5) use a computer to knowingly compile, enter, transmit, make, print, publish, reproduce, cause, allow, buy, sell, receive, exchange, or disseminate any notice, statement, advertisement, or minor's name, telephone number, place of residence, physical characteristics, or other descriptive or identifying information for the purpose of engaging in, facilitating, encouraging, offering, or soliciting unlawful sadomasochistic abuse or sexual conduct of or with a minor.

**(b) A PERSON AT LEAST 18 YEARS OLD MAY NOT KNOWINGLY PROMOTE, ADVERTISE, SOLICIT, DISTRIBUTE, OR POSSESS WITH THE INTENT TO DISTRIBUTE ANY MATTER, VISUAL REPRESENTATION, OR PERFORMANCE:**

**(1) THAT DEPICTS A MINOR ENGAGED AS A SUBJECT IN SADOMASOCHISTIC ABUSE OR SEXUAL CONDUCT; OR**

**(2) IN A MANNER THAT REFLECTS THE BELIEF, OR THAT IS INTENDED TO CAUSE ANOTHER TO BELIEVE, THAT THE MATTER, VISUAL REPRESENTATION, OR PERFORMANCE DEPICTS A MINOR ENGAGED AS A SUBJECT OF SADOMASOCHISTIC ABUSE OR SEXUAL CONDUCT.**

Imagine that you are a legislative aide working for a member of the Maryland House of Delegates. Your boss is considering whether to support one or both of these proposed bills, and she has asked for your opinion. Would you recommend that your boss support one or both of the proposed bills? If you would recommend that your boss support both bills, which proposal do you think is better and why? If you would recommend that she support neither of the proposed bills, why not?

2. In footnote 3 of the court's opinion in *In re S.K.*, the court noted that at S.K.'s delinquency proceeding, A.T. testified that K.S. "distributed the video throughout the school." It does not appear that K.S. was charged with distributing child pornography, however. Nor does it appear that the police conducted an investigation to try to find out who else at the school may have distributed the video.

Imagine you were the prosecutor who received the report from the school resource officer, Eugene Caballero. Assume for purposes of this question that your boss has instructed you to file charges against S.K., but that it is up to you to decide whether to pursue charges against anyone else at the school. Would you have considered charging K.S. with distribution of child pornography? Would you have asked the police to conduct a thorough investigation to try to determine which other student(s) distributed the video?

first federal sex offense registry law was named after her son, Jacob Wetterling, who was abducted and murdered in 1989. "While she still supports the idea of registries, Wetterling thinks they have gone too far and should drop juveniles and many other categories of offenders." Eli Leher, *Rethinking Sex-Offender Registries*, National Affairs (Winter 2016). For more on the inclusion of juveniles on sex offense registries, see Amy E. Halbrook, *Juvenile Pariahs*, 65 Hastings L.J. 1 (2013).

# Chapter Summary

- The crime of rape includes the elements of (1) sexual intercourse (2) without consent of the victim. There is a great deal of variation when it comes to other aspects of the offense, however. Of particular doctrinal importance is the jurisdictional split regarding the elements of force and resistance, and *mens rea*.

- Until the 1970s, rape included a very strict requirement of physical force (or the threat of force) and "utmost resistance" by the victim. Today, every state has rejected the utmost resistance requirement. A majority of states have eliminated the requirement of resistance by the victim entirely. A minority of states have retained the requirement of some resistance by the victim. Force is still an element of the crime of rape in a majority of jurisdictions. Jurisdictions that require force are split into roughly two camps. Under the intrinsic force approach, the force inherent in the sexual act itself meets the requirement. Under the extrinsic force approach, there must be proof of the use of force or the threat of force beyond that inherent in the act of nonconsensual sex.

- Because of the strict force and resistance requirements, *mens rea* with respect to the victim's lack of consent was a non-issue in pre-1970s rape cases. Changes to the elements of force and resistance have also led to changes to the *mens rea* required for the crime, in some jurisdictions. Today, the majority of jurisdictions require proof that the defendant acted with a culpable mental state with respect to the victim's nonconsent. Jurisdictions with a *mens rea* requirement are further split with respect to the exact mental state required. Some require the government to prove that the defendant acted with knowledge that the victim was not consenting; others require only recklessness or negligence. In a significant minority of states, there is no *mens rea* requirement with respect to the victim's consent. There is an overlap between jurisdictions that have no *mens rea* requirement and those that have retained the force and resistance elements of the crime.

■ Statutory rape criminalizes sex with minors, with the age of consent ranging from 16 to 18 depending on the state. Statutory rape was a strict liability offense with respect to the victim's age at common law. Today, states are very closely split on this issue. In a slight majority of states, statutory rape remains a strict liability crime. This means that a defendant's mistaken belief as to the victim's age is never a defense. A sizeable minority of states have adopted a *mens rea* requirement of some kind with respect to the victim's age. The *mens rea* required differs in each state but the most common approach appears to be a negligence standard, under which a defendant's mistake as to the victim's age must be reasonable.

■ Every state criminalizes the production, distribution, and possession of child pornography, as does the federal government. The application of child pornography laws to teenagers who share pornographic images of themselves with one another has become a hotly contested topic in many courts and state legislatures. In many states, courts have held that child pornography statutes can be applied to teenagers for sharing images of themselves. In these states, a teenager who shares a pornographic image of him- or herself can be convicted of distribution of child pornography (or, in a juvenile proceeding, adjudicated delinquent) — possibly triggering a requirement to register as a sex offender. A sizeable minority of states have passed new laws to specifically address the issue of teen sexting, with approaches ranging from creating an affirmative defense to creating a separate misdemeanor offense for teen sexting.

## Applying the Concepts

1. Amy, a 25-year-old high school teacher, had sexual intercourse with one of her students, Adam. Amy mistakenly believed that Adam was 17 years old. In fact, Adam was 19. The age of consent in the jurisdiction where this occurred is 18 and statutory rape is treated as a strict liability crime. Can Amy be convicted of statutory rape?

2. The following factual summary comes from *People v. Denbo*, 868 N.E.2d 347, 348 (Ill. App. Ct. 2007): "Defendant put her hand into R.H.'s vagina during otherwise consensual sexual relations. R.H. pushed defendant twice — harder the second time — intending to signify that she no longer consented to the sexual penetration. Defendant removed her hand from R.H.'s vagina on the second push."

   Defendant is charged with rape. Can she be convicted?

3. These facts come from *State v. Barela*, 2015 UT 22, ¶¶ 4-8:

   Barela had sex with K.M. at a Massage Envy studio, where Barela was employed as a massage therapist and K.M. was a client. K.M. had received one previous massage from Barela at the studio. And when she arrived on the date in question, she had not requested Barela as her therapist. K.M. removed all of her clothing for the massage. During the massage she was covered only by a sheet and blanket.

That much is undisputed. But as to other details of the events leading to the sexual encounter, the jury heard two very different stories. In Barela's version of the encounter, K.M. became aroused and initiated sexual contact by humping the table and grabbing Barela's crotch. The two then began having sex, in which K.M. showed active engagement by giving him oral sex, rolling over on the table, and playing with her breasts.

In contrast, K.M. told the jury that she was receiving a massage from Barela when he unexpectedly started massaging her inner thigh. She testified that she felt "very uncomfortable" because she had never had a massage therapist do that in previous massages, and she "didn't know how to respond." Then, "before [she] knew it," Barela pulled her to the end of the table, dropped his pants and penetrated her vagina with his penis. K.M. testified that "everything happened very fast" and that Barela may have touched or penetrated her vagina with his finger, but that she wasn't sure. She testified that Barela went from rubbing her thigh to penetrating her vagina within "a matter of seconds."

K.M. testified that she had not "flirt[ed]" with Barela, and did not say or do anything to suggest that she wanted to have sex with him. She also testified that she did not physically resist or verbally tell Barela "no"; she said nothing at all. Instead, she clung to the blanket and "just froze." She said she felt fearful because she was alone, and because the only other person in the massage parlor was a male receptionist. She repeatedly stressed that "everything happened very fast." She elaborated that she "checked out," "kind of withdrew," and "was scared." When asked to explain what "checked out" meant, K.M. said she just "kind of froze."

K.M. testified that she heard Barela make an alarmed (and profane) exclamation, and then saw him looking at semen in his hand. Then he told her "this concludes your massage" and left the room. K.M. got up as "quickly as [she] could," wiped herself with a towel, and got dressed. She testified that her main concern was "getting out of Massage Envy" as quickly as she could. Barela met her in the hallway, where he offered her water, which she accepted. She "checked out as normal," told the receptionist the massage was "fine," paid her bill (including a tip), and took a mint.

a. At the close of evidence, Barela's attorney requests the following jury instruction: "To convict Barela, the People must prove that (1) he engaged in sexual intercourse with K.M.; (2) without the consent of K.M.; and (3) he knew of or recklessly disregarded K.M.'s lack of consent."

   The prosecutor objects to number (3) of Barela's instruction. Should the court give Barela's proposed instruction?

b. Assume for purposes of this question that the jury convicts Barela, and he appeals. Should the appellate court uphold Barela's conviction?

## Criminal Law in Practice

1. Jurisdictions are split on a number of key questions for the offenses covered in this chapter. For your jurisdiction, answer the following questions:

   a. What approach does your state take to the force and resistance elements of the crime of rape? Look up the relevant statute in your state to see if it includes a force and/or resistance requirement. If it does, has the highest court in your state issued an opinion interpreting how the requirement should be defined? If you are in one of the states where any of the opinions in the rape section of the chapter was issued — Idaho, Massachusetts, or Maine — look up the law in a neighboring state. (Note that some states use a different term — e.g., sexual assault in the first degree — for the crime of rape.)

b. Has your state resolved the question of what *mens rea*, if any, is required with respect to the victim's lack of consent for the crime of rape? As with the previous question, if you are in one of the states where any of the opinions in the rape section of the chapter was issued — Idaho, Massachusetts, or Maine — look up the law in a neighboring state.

c. Is the crime of statutory rape a strict liability offense with respect to the age of the victim in your state? If not, what *mens rea* standard has your state adopted on this issue? If you are located in Maryland, look up the answer for a neighboring state.

d. Does your state have a law that specifically addresses the application of the child pornography laws to teen sexting? If so, what does the law provide? If not, are you able to determine if there have been any bills proposed to address the issue?

# Attempts

As the old saying goes, the best laid plans of mice and men often go awry. This is true of both legal and criminal undertakings. Not surprisingly, a person whose criminal endeavor fails is not necessarily free of criminal liability. This is because it is a crime to attempt to commit some other crime. It makes sense that the law would punish people who try, but fail, to commit a crime. But the practice of punishing criminal attempts is relatively new. Attempt was not widely recognized as a general offense until the 1800s. Today, every jurisdiction punishes criminal attempts.

Attempts are **inchoate offenses**, meaning that they provide for punishment before harm has occurred. The law of attempts is, in effect, an add-on to the rest of the criminal code, making it a crime to commit attempted larceny, attempted robbery, attempted drug possession, attempted murder, and so on. It "is an adjunct crime, it cannot exist by itself, but only in connection with another crime." *Cox v. State*, 311 Md. 326, 330 (2006). As such, the legal principles that govern attempts are the same regardless of the target offense.

In general, to convict a defendant of an **attempt** to commit a crime, the government must prove that she intended to commit the completed offense and that she engaged in a legally sufficient overt act. But, as the material that follows shows, courts remain split on some aspects of the law of attempts, particularly when it comes to the conduct necessary to give rise to attempt liability. The "simple intuitive appeal of the idea that attempts are to be punished belies the complexity and confusion that surround their adjudication."
Gideon Yaffe, *Criminal Attempts*, 124 Yale L.J. 92, 95 (2014).

## A. *MENS REA*: INTENT

To be guilty of an attempt to commit a crime, the defendant must have acted with the intent or purpose of committing that target crime.

# Key Concepts

- What is the *mens rea* required for attempts?
- What is the line between preparatory acts and conduct that is sufficient to constitute an attempt?
- What are the differences between the dangerous proximity to success test and the substantial step test?
- When, if ever, can abandonment serve as a defense in an attempt prosecution?

Recall that, for many offenses, a person acts intentionally either when he acts purposely, meaning that it is his conscious object to cause a result, *or* when he acts knowingly, meaning he is aware a result is practically certain to follow from his conduct. In the law of attempts, intent is limited to the purpose variant. In other words, "[i]n the context of an 'attempt' crime, specific intent means that the defendant consciously intended the completion of acts comprising the choate offense." *State v. Sutton*, 340 S.C. 393, 397 (2000).

The *mens rea* requirement for attempted crimes is rarely the central point of dispute in an attempt prosecution. In part for that reason, and also because the *mens rea* of intent is covered elsewhere in this book in the context of other offenses, we do not focus on the issue in this chapter. But before turning to the next section, it is important to highlight one important principle, unique to the law of attempts, that results from its *mens rea* requirement.

As an add-on offense, the law of attempts can be applied to nearly any crime — attempted larceny, attempted drug possession, attempted murder, and so on. But, because of attempt's *mens rea* requirement, it *cannot* be applied to crimes that impose liability for causing a result by accident — most notably, depraved heart murder, reckless manslaughter, and negligent homicide. Courts are in nearly universal agreement that, when it comes to crimes that punish people for causing "an unintended result, an attempt to commit that crime is not a legally cognizable offense." *People v. Aponte*, 886 N.Y.S.2d 547, 548 (2011). One court summarized the reason for this rule in the context of an involuntary (reckless) manslaughter prosecution:

> The illogic of attempted involuntary manslaughter is easily demonstrated. Involuntary manslaughter is a homicide unintentionally caused. Attempt liability requires that the defendant entertain the intent required for the substantive crime. Thus, the crime of attempted involuntary manslaughter requires a logical impossibility, namely, that the actor in his attempt intend that an unintended death result. Such an anomaly the legislature could scarcely have intended. Accordingly, we hold that attempted [involuntary] manslaughter . . . is not a crime cognizable under our law.

*State v. Almeda*, 189 Conn. 303, 309 (1983). This rule means that there is no such thing as attempted depraved heart murder, attempted reckless manslaughter, or attempted negligent homicide. For similar reasons, there is no crime of attempted felony murder. In the words of *Aponte* and *Almeda*, these are not "legally cognizable offenses" because they would "require[] a logical impossibility, namely, that the actor in his attempt intend that an unintended death result."

Notice the practical implications of this rule. Imagine that, as in *People v. Roe*, 74 N.Y.2d 20 (1989) (presented in Chapter 5), the defendant "load[s] a mix of 'live' and 'dummy' shells at random into the magazine" of a shotgun, points it at his friend, says "Let's play Polish roulette," and pulls the trigger. If, as in *Roe*, the gun discharges and the bullet strikes and kills the victim, the defendant is guilty of second-degree murder — specifically, the depraved heart form of second-degree murder. If, however, the gun does not fire and the victim lives, the defendant cannot be prosecuted for attempted second-degree murder because there is simply no such crime as "attempted depraved heart murder."

Though this rule has been adopted in virtually every jurisdiction, it has its share of critics, who argue that it treats equally blameworthy individuals very differently. Defenders of the rule respond that it does not treat equally blameworthy individuals differently because a person who recklessly causes death is, in fact, more blameworthy than one who acts recklessly but does not cause death. Whatever the merits of that debate, practical considerations may help to explain the rule.

If attempted reckless manslaughter or attempted negligent homicide were crimes, then homicide law would sweep much more broadly than it does today. In theory, every drunk driver could be convicted of "attempted negligent homicide" if it were a cognizable offense. Instead of punishing every drunk driver as an attempted killer, legislatures have established a variety of separate offenses to punish people for reckless or negligent conduct that endangers others. The crime of driving under the influence is an example of this. Similarly, many states have an offense called "reckless endangerment," that in its most common formulation "prohibits creating a 'substantial risk' (or 'danger') of 'serious' injury to another person." Michael T. Cahill, *Attempt, Reckless Homicide, and the Design of Criminal Law*, 78 U. Colo. L. Rev. 879, 925 (2007).

Whatever one thinks about the wisdom of the current rule, it is relatively straightforward, even if possibly counterintuitive: An attempt to cause an unintended result is not a cognizable offense. Again, the doctrinal reason for this is that intending for an unintended result to occur is a logical impossibility. And, in order to be guilty of attempting to commit a crime, a person must act with the *purpose* of committing the acts and causing the result that comprises the target offenses.

# B. *ACTUS REUS*

The criminal law does not punish people for their thoughts alone. One scholar has colorfully explained this principle by observing that "[i]ndividuals can spend their days beseeching the gods for suffering to be inflicted upon their enemies, or plotting elaborate schemes to exact revenge upon them, but such mental activities are not properly within the ambit of the criminal law." Richard L. Lippke, *Harm Matters: Punishing Failed Attempts*, 14 Ohio St. J. Crim. L. 629, 631 (2017). All jurisdictions agree that fantasizing, or even beginning to plan or prepare to commit a crime, does not constitute an attempt. When, exactly, planning or preparation crosses the line and becomes an attempt is a much trickier question. Indeed, one court has lamented that, in some cases, "the facts may reveal that the line of demarcation [between mere planning and an attempt] is not a line at all but a murky 'twilight zone.'" *United States v. Williamson*, 42 M.J. 613, 617 n.2 (N-M Ct. Crim. App. 1995).

Formulating a rule that can distinguish preparation from conduct sufficient to constitute an attempt is difficult in part because the law of attempts applies to so many different types of cases. Because attempt is an adjunct crime that only exists in connection with other offenses, the standard for the *actus reus* of an attempt must be capable of governing all crimes, from attempted murder to attempted drug possession. Compounding this problem is the "competition among policy considerations [that] exists in this realm of the law. On the one hand, there exists a policy not to punish or convict innocent persons for evil or criminal thoughts alone; on the other hand a countervailing policy exists to allow law enforcement to prevent criminal conduct before it reaches the point of completion." *People v. Reid*, 383 S.C. 285, 293 (Ct. App. 2009).

Over the years, courts and commentators have devised a number of different possible tests for determining when planning ends and attempt begins. Currently, most jurisdictions apply either the dangerous proximity to success test or the substantial step test. Both tests are presented below.

Regardless of which test a jurisdiction applies, if the defendant successfully completes the target crime, then she cannot also be convicted of attempt. Specifically, under the merger doctrine, a person cannot be convicted of *both* a completed crime and attempting to commit *that same crime*.

## 1. Dangerous Proximity to Success

The **dangerous proximity to success test**, developed by Justice Oliver Wendell Holmes, dates back to the late 1800s and early 1900s. It asks, in effect, how close the defendant came to completing the crime. Under this test, a defendant has committed an attempt only if he "comes so close or near to the object crime that the danger of success is very great." *State v. Reid*, 383 S.C. 285, 294 (Ct. App. 2009). It is a forward-looking test that focuses not on what the defendant has already done but "upon how much remains to be done before the defendant would have succeeded in his goals." *Id.* The next two cases explain this test in greater detail, and show how it is applied by courts.

**Case Preview**

### *People v. Rizzo*

In the next case, the defendant and three partners were driving around New York City searching for a payroll carrier that they planned to rob. Two members of the group were armed and, the court found, "[t]here [was] no doubt that [they] had the intention to commit robbery, if [they] got the chance." Nevertheless, the court held that the evidence did not establish that the group was close enough to completing the crime to satisfy the dangerous proximity to success test.

As you read the decision, consider the following questions:

1. How does the court describe the dangerous proximity to success test?
2. The defendant had taken significant steps toward robbing the payroll carrier, and the court found that there was "no doubt" he would have gone through with the crime if he had the chance. Yet the court held that he had not committed an attempt. Why do you think the defendant's actions were insufficient to satisfy

the dangerous proximity test? Does the test focus primarily on what the defendant has already done, or do other considerations control its application?

3. What more would have been necessary to satisfy the dangerous proximity test and make the defendant guilty of attempted robbery? If, for example, the target of the robbery had been two blocks from the defendant's car at the time of the arrest, would that have changed the outcome of the case?

---

## People v. Rizzo
### 246 N.Y. 334 (1927)

CRANE, J.

The police of the city of New York did excellent work in this case by preventing the commission of a serious crime. It is a great satisfaction to realize that we have such wide-awake guardians of our peace. Whether or not the steps which the defendant had taken up to the time of his arrest amounted to the commission of a crime, as defined by our law, is, however, another matter. He has been convicted of an attempt to commit the crime of robbery in the first degree, and sentenced to state's prison. There is no doubt that he had the intention to commit robbery, if he got the chance. An examination, however, of the facts is necessary to determine whether his acts were in preparation to commit the crime if the opportunity offered, or constituted a crime in itself, known to our law as an attempt to commit robbery in the first degree.

Charles Rizzo, the defendant, appellant, with three others, Anthony J. Dorio, Thomas Milo, and John Thomasello, on January 14th planned to rob one Charles Rao of a pay roll valued at about $1,200 which he was to carry from the bank for the United Lathing Company. These defendants, two of whom had firearms, started out in an automobile, looking for Rao or the man who had the pay roll on that day. Rizzo claimed to be able to identify the man, and was to point him out to the others, who were to do the actual holding up. The four rode about in their car looking for Rao. They went to the bank from which he was supposed to get the money and to various buildings being constructed by the United Lathing Company. At last they came to One Hundred and Eightieth street and Morris Park avenue. By this time they were watched and followed by two police officers. As Rizzo jumped out of the car and ran into the building, all four were arrested. The defendant was taken out from the building in which he was hiding. Neither Rao nor a man named Previti, who was also supposed to carry a pay roll, were at the place at the time of the arrest. The defendants had not found or seen the man they intended to rob. No person with a pay roll was at any of the places where they had stopped, and no one had been pointed out or identified by Rizzo. The four men intended to rob the pay roll man, whoever he was. They were looking for him, but they had not seen or discovered him up to the time they were arrested.

Does this constitute the crime of an attempt to commit robbery in the first degree? The Penal Law, § 2, prescribes: "An act, done with intent to commit a crime, and tending but failing to effect its commission, is 'an attempt to commit that crime.'"

Any act in preparation to commit a crime may be said to have a tendency towards its accomplishment. The procuring of the automobile, searching the streets looking for the desired victim, were in reality acts tending toward the commission of the proposed crime. The law, however, had recognized that many acts in the way of preparation are too remote to constitute the crime of attempt. The line has been drawn between those acts which are remote and those which are proximate and near to the consumation. The law must be practical, and therefore considers those acts only as tending to the commission of the crime which are so near to its accomplishment that in all reasonable probability the crime itself would have been committed, but for timely interference. The cases which have been before the courts express this idea in different language, but the idea remains the same. The act or acts must come or advance very near to the accomplishment of the intended crime.

In *Hyde v. U.S.*, 225 U.S. 347 [1912], it was stated that the act amounts to an attempt when it is so near to the result that the danger of success is very great. "There must be dangerous pro[xim]ity to success."

The method of committing or attempting crime varies in each case, so that the difficulty, if any, is not with this rule of law regarding an attempt, which is well understood, but with its application to the facts.

How shall we apply this rule of immediate nearness to this case? The defendants were looking for the pay roll man to rob him of his money. This is the charge in the indictment. Robbery is defined in section 2120 of the Penal Law as "the unlawful taking of personal property from the person or in the presence of another, against his will, by means of force, or violence, or fear of injury, immediate or future, to his person"; and it is made robbery in the first degree by section 2124 when committed by a person aided by accomplices actually present.

To constitute the crime of robbery, the money must have been taken from Rao by means of force or violence, or through fear. Did the acts above described come dangerously near to the taking of Rao's property? Did the acts come so near the commission of robbery that there was reasonable likelihood of its accomplishment but for the interference? Rao was not found; the defendants were still looking for him; no attempt to rob him could be made, at least until he came in sight; he was not in the building at One Hundred and Eightieth street and Morris Park avenue. There was no man there with the pay roll for the United Lathing Company whom these defendants could rob. Apparently no money had been drawn from the bank for the pay roll by anybody at the time of the arrest. In a word, these defendants had planned to commit a crime, and were looking around the city for an opportunity to commit it, but the opportunity fortunately never came. Men would not be guilty of an attempt at burglary if they had planned to break into a building and were arrested while they were hunting about the streets for the building not knowing where it was. Neither would a man be guilty of an attempt to commit murder if he armed himself and started out to find the person whom he had planned to kill but could not find him. So here these defendants were not guilty of an attempt to commit robbery in the first degree when they had not found or reached the presence of the person they intended to rob.

For these reasons, the judgment of conviction of this defendant appellant must be reversed and a new trial granted.

A very strange situation has arisen in this case. [T]he four defendants . . . were all tried together upon the same evidence, and jointly convicted, and all sentenced to state's prison for varying terms. Rizzo was the only one of the four to appeal to the Appellate Division and to this court. His conviction was affirmed by the Appellate Division by a divided court, two of the justices dissenting, and we have now held that he was not guilty of the crime charged. If he were not guilty, neither were the other three. As the others, however, did not appeal, there is no remedy for them through the courts; their judgments stand, and they must serve their sentences. This, of course, is a situation which must in all fairness be met in some way. Two of these men were guilty of the crime of carrying weapons, pistols, contrary to law, for which they could be convicted. Two of them, John Thomasello and Thomas Milo, had also been previously convicted, which may have had something to do with their neglect to appeal. However, the law would fail in its function and its purpose if it permitted these three men whoever or whatever they are to serve a sentence for a crime which the courts subsequently found and declared had not been committed. We therefore suggest to the district attorney of Bronx county that he bring the cases of these three men to the attention of the Governor, to be dealt with as to him seems proper in the light of this opinion.

The judgment of the Appellate Division and that of the county court should be reversed, and a new trial ordered.

---

**Post-Case Follow-Up**

In *Rizzo*, the court held that to satisfy the dangerous proximity to success test, the defendant must come "so near to [the] accomplishment [of the crime] that in all reasonable probability the crime would have been committed but for timely interference." Because Rizzo and his partners were arrested before they were able to locate the contemplated victim, the test was not met and Rizzo's conviction for attempted robbery was overturned. As the court explained, in order to commit the crime, the group first needed to find the payroll carrier — "no attempt to rob him could be made, at least until he came in sight." As a result, it is possible that the group would not have been able to commit the crime even if the police had not intervened. They might have driven around all day without ever finding the payroll carrier. Note that this test is forward looking. It is primarily concerned with the odds that the defendant would have been able to complete the crime, not with the steps the defendant had already taken toward its commission.

---

In the jurisdictions that continue to adhere to the dangerous proximity test, *Rizzo* remains an influential decision. In the next case, the court relied on *Rizzo* to help determine whether or not a would-be drug buyer had committed attempted possession of cocaine.

---

| Case Preview | ## *People v. Acosta* |
|---|---|

In *People v. Acosta*, the court found there was sufficient evidence to sustain the defendant's conviction for attempted possession of cocaine. The court's opinion sheds additional light on the dangerous proximity test.

As you read the decision, consider the following questions:

1. What is the court's rationale for distinguishing the decision in *Warren*, where the court overturned the defendants' convictions for attempted drug possession on the grounds that they had not come very near to the accomplishment of the crime?
2. Although the court relies on *Rizzo*, it does not compare the facts to those of *Rizzo*. If you were to compare the facts of *Rizzo* to those of *Acosta*, what facts do you think would account for the different outcome in each case?

---

## *People v. Acosta*
### 80 N.Y.2d 665 (1993)

KAYE, J.

By jury verdict, defendant was convicted of conspiracy and attempted possession of cocaine. The latter charge — the only one at issue on this appeal — centers on the events of March 21, 1988.

Evidence at trial revealed that, commencing in November 1986, officers of the Manhattan North Narcotics Division began investigating the activities of defendant, his brother Miguel and others. Their investigation techniques included the use of an undercover officer to infiltrate the organization, stakeouts and court-authorized wiretaps. In July 1987 the undercover met with Miguel at a Manhattan apartment and purchased cocaine. At that time, Miguel introduced defendant to the officer, telling her that they "work together."

A wiretap on defendant's telephone at his Bronx apartment revealed that for several days prior to March 21, 1988, he was negotiating with Luis Rojas to purchase kilogram quantities of cocaine.[1] On March 21, at 11:37 A.M., Rojas called defendant and asked, "are you ready?" Defendant replied "come by here" and Rojas responded, "I'm going over." At 11:42, defendant called "Frank," an associate, and told him that he "spoke to the man" who would be "coming over here * * *. Right now."

About a half hour later, around 12:15 P.M., officers staking out defendant's six-floor apartment building saw a man pull up in a car, remove a black and white plastic bag from the trunk, and enter the building. The bag's handles were stretched, indicating that the contents were heavy. At 12:30, the man emerged from the building,

---

[1] These conversations were routinely conducted in code words such as "tickets" or "tires" which the prosecution expert testified represented kilos of cocaine. Many such conversations were recorded in the weeks leading up to defendant's arrest.

carrying the same plastic bag which still appeared to be heavy. He placed the bag back in the trunk and drove off.

Minutes later, at 12:37 P.M., defendant called Frank, stating that he "saw the man" but "those tickets * * * were no good; they weren't good for the game man." Frank wondered whether "they got more expensive, the seats" and defendant explained that they were the "same price and all" but they were "not the same seats * * * some seats real bad, very bad, very bad." Defendant elaborated: "two pass tickets together on the outside stuck together, like a thing, like a ticket falsified. Then I told him to take it away, no, I don't want any problems and anything you see." Frank asked if defendant was told when the tickets would arrive, and defendant responded "No because who came was someone, somebody else, the guy, the messenger." Defendant acknowledged that he "want[s] to participate in the game but if you can't see it, you're going to come out upset."

At 12:50 P.M., Rojas called defendant and said something inaudible about "my friend." Defendant responded, "Oh yes, but he left because (inaudible) it doesn't fit me. * * * You told me it was the same thing, same ticket." Rojas rejoined, "No. We'll see each other at six."

Finally, at 1:26 P.M., defendant telephoned Hector Vargas, who wanted to know "what happened?" Defendant said, "Nothing. I saw something there, what you wanted, but I returned it because it was a shit there." Hector wanted to know, "like how?" but defendant simply responded, "No, no, a weird shit there." Vargas suggested that he might be able to obtain something "white and good."

The following day, defendant again called Vargas to discuss "the thing you told me about, you know what I'm referring to." Defendant recommended that Vargas "go talk to him, talk to him personally and check it out." Defendant thought that "it would be better if you took the tickets, at least one or whatever."

At trial, in motions before and after the verdict, defendant argued that the foregoing evidence was insufficient to establish that he attempted to possess cocaine on March 21. The trial court rejected those arguments and sentenced defendant, upon the jury's guilty verdict, to a prison term of 25 years to life, the maximum permitted by law.[2] On appeal, a sharply divided Appellate Division reversed and vacated the attempted possession conviction. One of the dissenting Justices granted the People leave to appeal and we now reverse.

A person knowingly and unlawfully possessing a substance weighing at least four ounces and containing a narcotic drug is guilty of criminal possession of a controlled substance in the first degree. Under the Penal Law, "[a] person is guilty of an attempt to commit a crime when, with intent to commit a crime, he [or she] engages in conduct which tends to effect the commission of such crime." While the statutory formulation of attempt would seem to cover a broad range of conduct — anything "tend[ing] to effect" a crime — case law requires a closer nexus between defendant's acts and the completed crime.

In *People v. Rizzo*, 246 N.Y. 334, 337, we observed that in demarcating punishable attempts from mere preparation to commit a crime, a "line has been drawn

---

[2] Defendant was sentenced to a concurrent term of 8 ⅓ to 25 years on the conspiracy charge, also the maximum.

between those acts which are remote and those which are proximate and near to the consummation." In *Rizzo*, this Court drew that line at acts "very near to the accomplishment of the intended crime." Though apparently more stringent than the Model Penal Code "substantial step" test . . . in this State we have adhered to *Rizzo*'s "very near" or "dangerously near" requirement.

A person who orders illegal narcotics from a supplier, admits a courier into his or her home and examines the quality of the goods has unquestionably passed beyond mere preparation and come "very near" to possessing those drugs. Indeed, the only remaining step between the attempt and the completed crime is the person's acceptance of the proffered merchandise, an act entirely within his or her control.

Our decision in *People v. Warren*, 66 N.Y.2d 831 is thus readily distinguishable. In that case, an informant and an undercover officer posing as a cocaine seller met defendants in a hotel room and reached an agreement for the sale of about half a pound. The actual exchange, however, was to occur hours later, in another part of town, after repackaging and testing. We concluded that since "several contingencies stood between the agreement in the hotel room and the contemplated purchase," defendants did not come "very near" to accomplishment of the intended crime. The same cannot be said here.

[T]he Appellate Division [did not] dispute[] the proposition that a person who arranges for the delivery of drugs and actually examines them has come sufficiently close to the completed crime to qualify as an attempt. Rather, the Appellate Division [concluded that] the evidence was insufficient to establish that defendant in fact met with a drug courier and examined his wares.

A jury, of course, concluded from the evidence presented that defendant attempted to possess cocaine on March 21, 1988. In examining the record for legal sufficiency, "the evidence must be viewed in a light most favorable to the People * * * to determine whether there is a valid line of reasoning and permissible inferences from which a rational jury could have found the elements of the crime proved beyond a reasonable doubt."

Applying these governing standards, we conclude that the evidence was legally sufficient to support the jury's finding that defendant met with a drug courier in his home on March 21. About a half-hour after defendant's supplier, Rojas, told defendant that he would be coming over, the police saw a man enter the apartment building with a weighted-down plastic bag and emerge 15 minutes later with the same heavy bag. Contemporaneously with the unidentified man's departure, defendant reported to an associate that he met with a messenger but that he rejected the offer because the "seats" were "very bad" and the "tickets" looked "falsified." When Rojas immediately called defendant asking about his "friend," defendant explained that "he left" and complained that Rojas misrepresented that the "same ticket" would be brought. And shortly thereafter, defendant called Vargas and told him that he "saw something there, what you wanted, but I returned it because it was a shit there."

On the evidence presented, a rational jury could have found beyond a reasonable doubt that defendant, with the intent to possess more than four ounces of a controlled substance,[4] met with Rojas' courier and examined cocaine, but rejected it because he was dissatisfied with the quality.

---

[4] A kilogram weighs 35 ounces.

As background, the jury knew from defendant's many earlier conversations about "tickets" and his meeting with the undercover that he was involved with drugs. Further, the jury knew that in the days immediately preceding March 21 defendant was negotiating with Rojas to buy kilos of cocaine and that on March 21 Rojas said that he was coming over. The unidentified man's visit to the apartment building with the parcel — coinciding to the minute with defendant's conversations — was fully consistent with defendant's several later admissions that he had met with a courier but rejected his merchandise. [In addition,] the evidence revealed that even after rejecting the March 21 offer, defendant continued making efforts to obtain cocaine.

Accordingly, the order of the Appellate Division should be reversed, the conviction for attempted criminal possession of a controlled substance in the first degree reinstated, and the case remitted to that court for [further proceedings].

**Post-Case Follow-Up**

The court holds that Acosta had "come 'very near' to possessing" cocaine because "the only remaining step between the attempt and the completed crime [was his] acceptance of the proffered merchandise, an act entirely within [Acosta's] control." In light of the holding in *Rizzo*, this outcome might strike some readers as strange since Acosta ultimately decided not to buy the cocaine. To better appreciate the court's holding, it can help to imagine how the dangerous proximity test would apply if the police had entered Acosta's apartment in the middle of the potential drug sale, before Acosta had the opportunity to sample the product and decide whether or not to go through with the purchase. If the police had arrested Acosta at that moment, there is no doubt he would have been guilty of attempted possession of cocaine. In the words of *Rizzo*, once Acosta was in the same room with the seller and the merchandise, "in all reasonable probability the crime would have been committed but for timely interference." Of course, in *Acosta*, the police did not enter the apartment and make an arrest during the transaction. But that does not change the analysis. The fact remains that "[a] person who orders illegal narcotics from a supplier, admits a courier into his or her home and examines the quality of the goods has unquestionably passed beyond mere preparation and come 'very near' to possessing those drugs." The moment the seller arrived at Acosta's apartment with the cocaine, Acosta (who at that time intended to buy the drugs) was guilty of attempted cocaine possession under the dangerous proximity test. Once he committed the crime, he could not un-commit it simply by rejecting the drugs.

## Rizzo *and* Acosta: *Real Life Applications*

**1.** At around midnight, a police officer stopped Luna, who was driving a pickup truck, for a traffic violation. During a consensual search of the truck, the officer found equipment that could be used to manufacture hashish, including PVC pipe, PVC glue, couplings, fittings, adapters, Teflon tape, Pyrex bowls, a butane burner, rubbing alcohol, a metal spigot, and 299 bottles of butane. At trial, the government presented expert testimony that these items were "all one needed" to manufacture hashish through the "butane extraction method," except for "grocery bags full of marijuana." (The police found a small amount of marijuana for personal use in Luna's truck. Luna, who was homeless, was living out of his truck at the time he was arrested.) Hashish and marijuana are classified as controlled substances in the jurisdiction where this occurred. Do you think this evidence would be sufficient to convict Luna of attempt to manufacture a controlled substance in a jurisdiction that applies the dangerous proximity rule? Why or why not?

2. Late one night, a police officer responded to a 911 call. The 911 caller, Victoria, reported that she had heard strange noises outside her home and that she thought she had seen a man with a shotgun near her house. When the officers arrived, they found Naradzav wandering around the neighborhood near Victoria's house. The officer asked Naradzav if he had any weapons. Naradzav replied that he did, and pointed to his shotgun, which was resting on a snowbank a few feet away. The police handcuffed Naradzav and retrieved the weapon, which was loaded with four rounds of ammunition. The police searched Naradzav and found a handwritten note on his person that contained a step-by-step plan for breaking into Victoria's residence and killing Victoria and her husband in front of their children. (Victoria was a casual acquaintance of Naradzav's.) Do you think this evidence would be sufficient to convict Naradzav of attempt to murder Victoria and her husband in a jurisdiction that applies the dangerous proximity test? Why or why not?

## 2. Substantial Step

Rooted in the Model Penal Code, the **substantial step test** is now the majority test for the *actus reus* of attempts. It has been codified in at least 25 states and adopted by every federal circuit court. At its core, the substantial step test requires the defendant to commit an act that is "strongly corroborative of the actor's criminal purpose." Model Penal Code § 5.01(2). In contrast to the dangerous proximity test, the substantial step test assesses guilt by looking backward at what the defendant has already done.

The substantial step test was designed out of a belief that the dangerous proximity test and others like it allowed some blameworthy individuals to escape punishment and put police officers in a difficult position. Under the dangerous proximity test, arresting a would-be criminal too soon can result in an acquittal, but waiting to make an arrest can increase the risk of harm to innocent bystanders. *People v. Rizzo* was cited by the Model Penal Code's drafters as an example of this problem. Recall that in *Rizzo* the court praised the police for doing "excellent work in this case by preventing the commission of a serious crime," and yet the court felt compelled to reverse the conviction under the dangerous proximity test. To address this concern, the drafters of the Model Penal Code proposed the less stringent substantial step test.

**Case Preview**

## United States v. Jackson

In *Jackson*, the court applied the substantial step test in an attempted robbery case. In its opinion affirming the defendants' convictions, the court described the substantial step test in detail and compared it to the dangerous proximity test.

As you read the decision, consider the following questions:

**1.** What is the definition of the substantial step test?
**2.** What are the differences between the substantial step test and the dangerous proximity test? Which test do you think is likely to be easier for the prosecutor to meet in a typical case?
**3.** Do you think the outcome in *Jackson* would have been the same under the dangerous proximity test?

## United States v. Jackson
### 560 F.2d 112 (2d Cir. 1977)

BRYAN, J.

Robert Jackson, William Scott, and Martin Allen appeal from judgments of conviction entered on November 23, 1976 in the United States District Court for the Eastern District of New York after a trial before Chief Judge Jacob Mishler without a jury.

Count one of the indictment alleged that between June 11 and June 21, 1976 the appellants conspired to commit an armed robbery of the Manufacturers Hanover Trust branch located at 210 Flushing Avenue, Brooklyn, New York. Counts two and three each charged appellants with an attempted robbery of the branch on June 14 and on June 21, 1976, respectively. Count four charged them with possession of two unregistered sawed-off shotguns on June 21, 1976.

After a suppression hearing on July 23, 1976 and a one-day trial on August 30, 1976, Chief Judge Mishler filed a memorandum of decision finding each defendant guilty on all four counts.

Appellants' principal contention is that the court below erred in finding them guilty on counts two and three. While they concede that the evidence supported the conspiracy convictions on count one, they assert that, as a matter of law, their conduct never crossed the elusive line which separates "mere preparation" from "attempt." For the reasons which follow, we affirm the convictions of all three appellants on all four counts.

The Government's evidence at trial consisted largely of the testimony of Vanessa Hodges, an unindicted co-conspirator, and of various FBI agents who surveilled the Manufacturers Hanover branch on June 21, 1976.

On June 11, 1976, Vanessa Hodges was introduced to appellant Martin Allen by Pia Longhorne, another unindicted co-conspirator. Hodges wanted to meet someone who would help her carry out a plan to rob the Manufacturers Hanover branch located at 210 Flushing Avenue in Brooklyn, and she invited Allen to join her. Hodges proposed that the bank be robbed the next Monday, June 14th, at about 7:30 A.M. She hoped that they could enter with the bank manager at that time, grab the weekend deposits, and leave. Allen agreed to rob the bank with Hodges, and told her he had access to a car, two sawed-off shotguns, and a .38 caliber revolver.

The following Monday, June 14, Allen arrived at Longhorne's house about 7:30 A.M. in a car driven by appellant Robert Jackson. A suitcase in the back seat of the car contained a sawed-off shotgun, shells, materials intended as masks, and handcuffs to bind the bank manager. While Allen picked up Hodges at Longhorne's, Jackson filled the car with gas. The trio then left for the bank.

When they arrived, it was almost 8:00 A.M. It was thus too late to effect the first step of the plan, viz., entering the bank as the manager opened the door. They rode around for a while longer, and then went to a restaurant to get something to eat and discuss their next move. After eating, the trio drove back to the bank. Allen and Hodges left the car and walked over to the bank. They peered in and saw the bulky weekend deposits, but decided it was too risky to rob the bank without an extra man.

Consequently, Jackson, Hodges, and Allen drove to Coney Island in search of another accomplice. In front of a housing project on 33rd Street they found appellant William Scott, who promptly joined the team. Allen added to the arsenal another sawed-off shotgun obtained from one of the buildings in the project, and the group drove back to the bank.

When they arrived again, Allen entered the bank to check the location of any surveillance cameras, while Jackson placed a piece of cardboard with a false license number over the authentic license plate of the car. Allen reported back that a single surveillance camera was over the entrance door. After further discussion, Scott left the car and entered the bank. He came back and informed the group that the tellers were separating the weekend deposits and that a number of patrons were now in the bank. Hodges then suggested that they drop the plans for the robbery that day, and reschedule it for the following Monday, June 21. Accordingly, they left the vicinity of the bank and returned to Coney Island where, before splitting up, they purchased a pair of stockings for Hodges to wear over her head as a disguise and pairs of gloves for Hodges, Scott, and Allen to don before entering the bank.

Hodges was arrested on Friday, June 18, 1976 on an unrelated bank robbery charge, and immediately began cooperating with the Government. After relating the events on June 14, she told FBI agents that a robbery of the Manufacturers branch at 210 Flushing Avenue was now scheduled for the following Monday, June 21. The three . . . male robbers [Jackson, Scott, and Allen], according to Hodges, would be heavily armed with hand and shoulder weapons and expected to use a brown four-door sedan equipped with a cardboard license plate as the getaway car.

At the request of the agents, Hodges called Allen on Saturday, June 19, and asked if he were still planning to do the job. Allen said that he was not going to rob the bank that Monday because he had learned that Hodges had been arrested and he feared that federal agents might be watching. Hodges nevertheless advised the agents that she thought the robbery might still take place as planned with the three men proceeding without her.

At about 7:00 A.M. on Monday, June 21, 1976, some ten FBI agents took various surveilling positions in the area of the bank. At about 7:39 A.M. the agents observed a brown four-door Lincoln, with a New York license plate on the front and a cardboard facsimile of a license plate on the rear, moving in an easterly direction on Flushing Avenue past the bank, which was located on the southeast corner of Flushing and Washington Avenues. The Lincoln circled the block and came to a stop at a fire hydrant situated at the side of the bank facing Washington Avenue, a short distance south of the corner of Flushing and Washington.

A [man] got out of the passenger side rear door of the Lincoln, walked to the corner of Flushing and Washington, and stood on the sidewalk in the vicinity of the bank's entrance. He then walked south on Washington Avenue, only to return a short time later with a container of coffee in his hand. He stood again on the corner of Washington and Flushing in front of the bank, drinking the coffee and looking around, before returning to the parked Lincoln.

The Lincoln pulled out, made a left turn onto Flushing, and proceeded in a westerly direction. It stopped . . . midway between Flushing and Park Avenues, and remained there for several minutes. During this time Jackson was seen working in the front of the car, which had its hood up.

The Lincoln was next sighted several minutes later in the same position it had previously occupied on the south side of Flushing Avenue between Waverly and Washington. The front license plate was now missing. The vehicle remained parked there for close to thirty minutes. Finally, it began moving east on Flushing Avenue once more, in the direction of the bank.

At some point near the bank as they passed down Flushing Avenue, the appellants detected the presence of the surveillance agents. The Lincoln accelerated down Flushing Avenue and turned south on Grand Avenue again. It was overtaken by FBI agents who ordered the appellants out of the car and arrested them. The agents then observed a black and red plaid suitcase in the rear of the car. The zipper of the suitcase was partially open and exposed two loaded sawed-off shotguns, a toy nickel-plated revolver, a pair of handcuffs, and masks. A New York license plate was seen lying on the front floor of the car. All of these items were seized.

In his memorandum of decision, Chief Judge Mishler concluded that . . . on June 14 and again on June 21, the defendants took substantial steps, strongly corroborative of the firmness of their criminal intent, toward commission of the crime of bank robbery and found the defendants guilty on each of the two attempt counts. These appeals followed.

[To commit an attempt, a defendant must intend to commit a crime and] engage in conduct which constitutes a substantial step toward commission of the crime, conduct strongly corroborative of the firmness of the defendant's criminal intent.

This [rule is derived from] the sensible definition of an attempt proffered by the American Law Institute's Model Penal Code. That definition, Model Penal Code § 5.01 (Proposed Official Draft 1962), [defines substantial step as follows]:

(2) Conduct shall not be held to constitute a substantial step . . . unless it is strongly corroborative of the actor's criminal purpose. Without negativing the sufficiency of other conduct, the following, if strongly corroborative of the actor's criminal purpose, shall not be held insufficient as a matter of law:

    (a) lying in wait, searching for or following the contemplated victim of the crime;

    (b) enticing or seeking to entice the contemplated victim of the crime to go to the place contemplated for its commission;

    (c) reconnoitering the place contemplated for the commission of the crime;

    (d) unlawful entry of a structure, vehicle or enclosure in which it is contemplated that the crime will be committed;

    (e) possession of materials to be employed in the commission of the crime, which are specially designed for such unlawful use or which can serve no lawful purpose of the actor under the circumstances;

    (f) possession, collection or fabrication of materials to be employed in the commission of the crime, at or near the place contemplated for its commission, where such possession, collection or fabrication serves no lawful purpose of the actor under the circumstances;

    (g) soliciting an innocent agent to engage in conduct constituting an element of the crime.

The draftsmen of the Model Penal Code recognized the difficulty of arriving at a general standard for distinguishing acts of preparation from acts constituting an attempt. They found general agreement that when an actor committed the "last proximate act," i.e., when he had done all that he believed necessary to effect a particular result which is an element of the offense, he committed an attempt. They also concluded, however, that while the last proximate act is sufficient to constitute an attempt, it is not necessary to such a finding. The problem then was to devise a standard more inclusive than one requiring the last proximate act before attempt liability would attach, but less inclusive than one which would make every act done with the intent to commit a crime criminal.

The draftsmen considered and rejected the . . . dangerous proximity doctrine[,] a test given impetus by Mr. Justice Holmes whereby the greater . . . probability of the offense, and the nearer the act to the crime, the stronger is the case for calling the act an attempt.

The formulation upon which the draftsmen ultimately agreed required, in addition to criminal purpose, that an act be a substantial step in a course of conduct designed to accomplish a criminal result, and that it be strongly corroborative of criminal purpose in order for it to constitute such a substantial step. The following differences between this test and [the dangerous proximity test] were noted: "[T]his formulation shifts the emphasis from what remains to be done the chief concern of the proximity tests to what the actor has already done. The fact that further major steps must be taken before the crime can be completed does not preclude a finding that the steps already undertaken are substantial. It is expected, in the normal case, that this approach will broaden the scope of attempt liability." Model Penal Code s 5.01, Comment at 47 (Tent. Draft No. 10, 1960).

The draftsmen concluded that, in addition to assuring firmness of criminal design, the requirement of a substantial step would preclude attempt liability, with its accompanying harsh penalties, for relatively remote preparatory acts. At the same time, however, . . . it would permit the apprehension of dangerous persons at an earlier stage than the [dangerous proximity test] without immunizing them from attempt liability.

In the case at bar, . . . on June 14 the appellants, already agreed upon a robbery plan, drove to the bank with loaded weapons. In order to carry the heavy weekend deposit sacks, they recruited another person. Cardboard was placed over the license, and the bank was entered and reconnoitered. Only then was the plan dropped for the moment and rescheduled for the following Monday. On that day, June 21, the defendants performed essentially the same acts. Since the cameras had already been located there was no need to enter the bank again, and since the appellants had arrived at the bank earlier, conditions were more favorable to their initial robbery plan than they had been on June 14.

[T]he criminal intent of the appellants was beyond dispute. The question remaining then is the substantiality of the steps taken on the dates in question, and how strongly this corroborates the firmness of their obvious criminal intent. This is a matter of degree.

On two separate occasions, appellants reconnoitered the place contemplated for the commission of the crime and possessed the paraphernalia to be employed in the commission of the crime loaded sawed-off shotguns, extra shells, a toy revolver, handcuffs, and masks which was specially designed for such unlawful use and which could serve no lawful purpose under the circumstances. Under the Model Penal Code formulation, . . . either type of conduct, standing alone, was sufficient as a matter of law to constitute a "substantial step" if it strongly corroborated their criminal purpose. Here both types of conduct coincided on both June 14 and June 21, along with numerous other elements strongly corroborative of the firmness of appellants' criminal intent.[8]

The judgments of conviction are affirmed.

**Post-Case Follow-Up**

A substantial step is an act that is "strongly corroborative of the actor's criminal purpose." The Model Penal Code provides a nonexclusive list of types of conduct that, "*if* strongly corroborative of the actor's criminal purpose," can constitute a substantial step. In *Jackson*, the court found that the defendants had taken at least two substantial steps toward commission of

---

[8] After securing the extra man they needed on June 14, the gang returned to the bank with their weapons ready and the car's license plate disguised for the getaway. Hodges' testimony was that they were ready to rob the bank at that time, but eventually postponed the robbery because conditions did not seem favorable. The fact that they then made further preparations by buying the stockings and gloves, an afterthought according to Hodges, does not undercut the firmness of their criminal intent when they were at the bank on June 14. By only postponing execution of the plan, appellants did not renounce their criminal purpose but reaffirmed it. They reflected further upon the plan and embellished it by acquiring the stockings and gloves.

On June 21, the firmness of appellants' criminal intent was again evident. The very fact that they showed up at the bank that day after discovering that the agents had arrested Hodges suggests that they were determined to execute their plan. Moreover, they once again had the necessary weapons, the car prepared for escape, and gave every indication that they were ready to strike.

the crime: They "reconnoitered the place contemplated for the commission of the crime and possessed the paraphernalia to be employed in the commission of the crime." Because these acts were "strongly corroborative of the firmness of appellants' criminal intent," the court upheld their convictions.

---

**Case Preview**

## United States v. Gladish

The substantial step test is less stringent than the dangerous proximity test, but it still does not punish merely preparatory steps. In *Gladish*, the court reversed the defendant's conviction for attempt to entice a minor to engage in sexual activity, finding that he had not taken a substantial step toward commission of the crime.

As you read the decision, consider the following questions:

1. What do you think distinguishes this case from the *Goetzke* case, cited by the court, where the defendant's conviction was upheld?
2. Although the court reversed the defendant's conviction for attempt to entice a person under 18 to engage in a sexual activity, the defendant was also convicted of attempt to transfer obscene material to a person under 16, a conviction that he did not challenge on appeal. Why do you think the defendant did not challenge that conviction on appeal?

---

## United States v. Gladish
### 536 F.3d 646 (7th Cir. 2008)

POSNER, J.

A jury convicted the defendant of having violated two federal statutes: 18 U.S.C. § 1470, which prohibits knowingly transferring or attempting to transfer obscene material to a person under 16, and 18 U.S.C. § 2422(b), which, so far as bears on this case, forbids knowingly attempting to persuade, induce, entice, or coerce a person under 18 to engage either in prostitution or in any sexual activity for which one could be charged with a criminal offense. Section 1470 imposes a maximum sentence of 10 years in prison; section 2422(b) imposes a minimum sentence of 10 years and a maximum of life. The judge sentenced the defendant to 10 years for the violation of section 1470 and 13 years . . . for the violation of section 2422(b), the sentences to run concurrently. The defendant challenges only his conviction for violating section 2422(b).

The defendant, a 35-year-old man, was caught in a sting operation in which a government agent impersonated a 14-year-old girl in an Internet chat room called "Indiana regional romance." The defendant visited the chat room and solicited "Abagail" (as the agent called herself) to have sex with him. The defendant lived in southern Indiana; "Abagail" purported to live in the northern part of the state. She agreed to have sex with the defendant and in a subsequent chat he discussed the possibility of traveling to meet her in a couple of weeks, but no arrangements were made. He was then arrested.

The defendant of course did not succeed in getting "Abagail" to have sex with him, and if he had, he would not have been guilty of a completed violation of section 2422(b) because the agent who called herself "Abagail" was not a minor. The question (the only one we need answer to resolve the appeal) is whether the defendant is guilty of having *attempted* to get an underage girl to have sex with him. To be guilty of an attempt you must intend the completed crime and take a "substantial step" toward its completion.

In tort law, unsuccessful attempts do not give rise to liability. The criminal law, because it aims at taking dangerous people out of circulation before they do harm, takes a different approach. A person who demonstrates by his conduct that he has the intention and capability of committing a crime is punishable even if his plan was thwarted. The "substantial step" toward completion is the demonstration of dangerousness. You are not punished just for saying that you want or even intend to kill someone, because most such talk doesn't lead to action. You have to do something that makes it reasonably clear that had you not been interrupted or made a mistake — for example, the person you thought you were shooting was actually a clothier's manikin — you would have completed the crime. That something marks you as genuinely dangerous — a doer and not just one of the "hollow men" of T.S. Eliot's poem, incapacitated from action because

> Between the conception
>
> And the creation
>
> Between the emotion
>
> And the response
>
> Falls the Shadow.

In the usual prosecution based on a sting operation for attempting to have sex with an underage girl, the defendant after obtaining the pretend girl's consent goes to meet her and is arrested upon arrival, as in *United States v. Gagliardi*, 506 F.3d 140, 150 (2d Cir. 2007); *United States v. Spurlock*, 495 F.3d 1011, 1012-13 (8th Cir. 2007), and *United States v. Tykarsky*, 446 F.3d 458, 469 (3d Cir. 2006). It is always possible that had the intended victim been a real girl the defendant would have gotten cold feet at the last minute and not completed the crime even though he was in position to do so. But there is a sufficient likelihood that he would have completed it to allow a jury to deem the visit to meet the pretend girl a substantial step toward completion, and so the visit is conduct enough to make him guilty of an attempt and not merely an intent.

Travel is not a sine qua non of finding a substantial step in a section 2422(b) case. It can be taking other . . . steps, such as . . . buying a bus or train ticket, especially one that is nonrefundable. "[T]he defendant's initiation of sexual conversation, writing insistent messages, and attempting to make arrangements to meet" were described as a substantial step in *United States v. Goetzke*, 494 F.3d 1231, 1237 (9th Cir. 2007). We won't try to give an exhaustive list of the possibilities.

But we disagree with the government's suggestion that the line runs between "harmless banter" and a conversation in which the defendant unmistakably proposes sex. In all the cases cited to us by the government or found by our independent research there was more than the explicit sex talk that the government quotes from the defendant's chats with "Abagail."

[T]he fact that the defendant in the present case said to a stranger whom he thought a young girl things like . . . "ill kiss your inner thighs" . . . , while not "harmless banter," did not indicate that he would travel to northern Indiana to do these things to her in person; nor did he invite her to meet him in southern Indiana or elsewhere. His talk and his sending her a video of himself masturbating (the basis of his unchallenged conviction for violating 18 U.S.C. § 1470) are equally consistent with his having intended to obtain sexual satisfaction vicariously.

We are surprised that the government prosecuted him under section 2422(b). Treating speech (even obscene speech) as the "substantial step" would abolish any requirement of a substantial step. It would imply that if $X$ says to $Y$, "I'm planning to rob a bank," $X$ has committed the crime of attempted bank robbery, even though $X$ says such things often and never acts. The requirement of proving a substantial step serves to distinguish people who pose real threats from those who are all hot air; in the case of Gladish, hot air is all the record shows. So he is entitled to an acquittal on the section 2422(b) count, the effect of which will be to reduce his sentence from 13 years to 10 years.

The defendant's conviction of violating 18 U.S.C. § 2422(b) is reversed with instructions to acquit. The sentence for violating section 1470 will stand.

*Gladish* provides another illustration of the substantial step test in action. The substantial step test is not as stringent as the dangerous proximity test but, as the decision in *Gladish* demonstrates, it still requires an act that is sufficiently corroborative of the defendant's criminal purpose. The court describes this concept in less formal terms than the Model Penal Code by explaining that "[t]he requirement of proving a substantial step serves to distinguish people who pose real threats from those who are all hot air."

## Jackson *and* Gladish: *Real Life Applications*

1. The substantial step test requires conduct to be "strongly corroborative of the actor's purpose" in order to convict. As the drafters of the Model Penal Code noted, this is an inherently imprecise and heavily fact dependent standard because the question of "[w]hether a particular act is a substantial step is obviously a matter of degree." Herbert Wechsler et al., *The Treatment of Inchoate Crime in the Model Penal Code of the American Law Institute: Attempt, Solicitation, and Conspiracy*, 61 Colum. L. Rev. 571, 593 (1961). An act that constitutes a substantial step in one case may be considered insufficient in another

if the surrounding circumstances are such that the conduct is not strongly corroborative of a criminal purpose.

With this in mind, consider the following two cases. Imagine that in each
case the jury convicted the defendant and the case is on appeal. What arguments
do you think each side will make as to why the conduct does or does not qualify
as a substantial step? How do you think the court should rule?

a. Monhalland was convicted of attempting to receive an explosive in interstate
commerce, a federal offense. The evidence showed that Monhalland had
asked an undercover government agent what the price of a box of dynamite
would be while viewing a stick of simulated dynamite. Later, Monhalland
asked the agent "what he would take for" dynamite that the agent claimed he
possessed. A price was never discussed and no evidence was presented that
Monhalland had enough money to pay for the explosives.

b. McPherson was convicted of attempt to manufacture methamphetamine in
1993. The evidence showed that McPherson had paid $12,000 to buy a rec-
ipe that would yield about $100,000 worth of the drug within two weeks
after the manufacturing process began. He ordered the necessary chemicals
and equipment, although he had not yet received and assembled all of it.
McPherson had not yet hired a chemist, which was a necessary step to starting the manufacturing process. But he was actively searching for a chemist
and had arranged to meet with one shortly before his arrest.

## C. "IMPOSSIBLE" ATTEMPTS

In most attempt cases, it is possible that the defendant could have successfully completed the crime if he had not been caught by the police or impeded by other circumstances. In *People v. Rizzo*, for example, the court overturned the defendant's
conviction on the ground that he was not "near to" completing the crime. But, of
course, it is certainly *possible* that if the police had not intervened Rizzo and his
partners would have eventually found and robbed the payroll carrier.

In so-called **"impossible" attempt** cases, the defendant was destined to fail
from the start. In *United States v. Gladish*, for example, the defendant sent an
obscene video to someone he thought was a 14-year-old girl but who turned out to
be an undercover police officer. He did every act necessary to commit the crime of
knowingly transferring obscene material to a person under 16 but he failed because
he was mistaken about the age of the person he was communicating with. Or consider the hypothetical case of a defendant who decides to kill a victim by shooting
her while she is sleeping. Late one night, the defendant goes to the victim's house
and fires a gun through her bedroom window. The bullet strikes the victim in the
head. Unknown to the defendant, the would-be victim was already dead when the
defendant pulled the trigger, having passed away in her sleep of natural causes an
hour earlier. As in *Gladish*, the defendant in this hypothetical performed the last
act necessary to commit the crime of murder, but failed, because he mistakenly
thought the victim was alive when in fact she was dead. In both of these examples,

the defendants cannot be convicted of the completed offenses because they have not met every element of the offense. In *Gladish*, the recipient of the obscene video was not actually underage; in the hypothetical case, the defendant did not cause the victim's death.

Can the defendants in these examples be convicted of *attempted* crimes? Or does the fact that it was "factually impossible" for them to succeed give them a defense? The short answer is that factual impossibility is *not* a defense to an attempt prosecution. This rule is described in more detail in the next case.

**Case Preview**

### State v. McElroy

In *McElroy*, the defendant possessed a substance that he thought was an illegal drug, namely "speed." In fact, an analysis of the substance by a police chemist found that the pills in the defendant's possession "were not amphetamines or dangerous drugs of any kind proscribed by statute." The defendant was prosecuted for attempted drug possession. On appeal, he argued that his conviction should be overturned because it was "impossible" for him to complete the crime of drug possession. Consistent with the rule followed in nearly every jurisdiction today, the court rejected the defendant's argument and affirmed his conviction.

As you read the decision, consider the following questions:

1. What is the difference between factual impossibility, which is not a defense, and so-called legal impossibility, which is a defense?
2. If the defendant possessed the substance, why was he guilty of attempted drug possession rather than the completed crime of drug possession?

### State v. McElroy
#### 128 Ariz. 315 (1981)

CAMERON, J.

Defendant was found guilty by the court sitting without a jury of the crime of attempted possession of dangerous drugs. The crime was treated as a misdemeanor, and defendant was placed on probation.

We must answer only one question on appeal: May the defendant be charged with attempted possession of dangerous drugs when it was impossible for him to complete the crime of possession of dangerous drugs because the drugs were not, in fact, [illegal to possess]?

The facts necessary for a determination of this matter on appeal are as follows. At approximately 1:00 A.M. on 8 December 1978, the Yuma County Sheriff's Office received a call to investigate the presence of two suspicious persons near a residence on Highway 95 in Yuma County, Arizona. The two persons told the officer who came to investigate that they were hitchhiking. The defendant asked a deputy sheriff for a ride into Yuma. The deputy agreed and, pursuant to standard procedure, patted the defendant down for weapons. During the search, the deputy found a plastic bag in defendant's shirt. The deputy took the bag, looked at it, and found it contained white pills. The defendant stated that the pills were "speed" or amphetamines, and that he had purchased them earlier at a bar. Later the deputy found another plastic bag with more white pills in the back seat of the patrol vehicle after placing defendant in the back seat.

A field test showed positive for amphetamines, the defendant was advised of his *Miranda* rights, and defendant again stated that the pills were "speed." Later analysis by a chemist indicated that the pills were not amphetamines or dangerous drugs of any kind proscribed by statute.

Trial was held before the court without a jury. After the State's case, the defendant moved for a directed verdict which was denied. Defendant did not present any evidence at trial. The court found defendant guilty and defendant appealed.

The defendant was charged with "attempt" to possess dangerous drugs.

Where the act, if completed, would still not be a criminal act, then it is said to be legally impossible to commit and is a valid defense to the charge of attempt. For example, in *Foster v. Commonwealth*, 96 Va. 306, 31 S.E. 503 (1898), the defendant was under 14 years of age and by law was conclusively presumed to be incapable of committing rape. The court held that because of his age it was legally impossible for him to be convicted of rape, and he could not "as a plain legal deduction" be convicted of attempted rape. Where the crime is impossible to complete because of some physical or factual condition unknown to the defendant, the impossibility is factual rather than legal. The courts have held that factual impossibility is not a valid defense. For example, the California Supreme Court has held that a person attempting to possess heroin, when in fact the substance was talcum powder, was nevertheless guilty of attempted possession of heroin. The court stated:

> " 'If there is an apparent ability to commit the crime in the way attempted, the attempt is indictable, although, unknown to the person making the attempt, the crime cannot be committed, because the means employed are in fact unsuitable, or because of extrinsic facts, such as the nonexistence of some essential object, or an obstruction by the intended victim or by a third person.' " *People v. Siu*, 126 Cal. App. 2d 41, 44 (1954).

Our Court of Appeals has stated in upholding a conviction for attempt to receive stolen property where the property was not in fact stolen:

> "We therefore hold that . . . impossibility is not a bar to prosecution for an attempt to receive stolen property. The rationale for this conclusion is that but for factors unknown to appellant, he committed acts which would have been sufficient to complete the substantive crime and exhibited the requisite intent. (footnote omitted)" *State v. Vitale*, 23 Ariz. App. 37, 44 (1975).

We believe . . . that factual impossibility is not a defense to the crime of attempt.

There can be no doubt that the defendant could never have been convicted of possession of dangerous drugs. However, if the pills were what defendant thought them to be, he could have been convicted of possession of drugs. The defendant believed he had the ability to accomplish the crime of possession, and the fact that the pills were not dangerous drugs does not erase his attempt to possess. Mere intent alone does not amount to an "attempt," but intent plus conduct toward the commission of a crime may be an attempt. In the instant case, defendant's conduct indicated not only intent, but an attempt to complete the crime of possession. We find no error.

Affirmed.

---

**Post-Case Follow-Up**

The court holds that "[w]here a crime is impossible to complete because of some physical or factual condition unknown to the defendant," it is no defense to an attempt prosecution. This is the rule followed in nearly every jurisdiction today. Applying this rule, the court in *McElroy* held that even though "[t]here can be no doubt that the defendant could never have been convicted of possession of dangerous drugs," he was nonetheless guilty of attempted drug possession.

---

## The Abolished Defense of Hybrid Legal Impossibility

The law of impossible attempts was not always as straightforward as it is today. For many years, courts in a number of jurisdictions extended the legal impossibility doctrine to cases where the defendant's goal was illegal "but commission of the offense was impossible due to a factual mistake by her regarding the legal status of some factor relevant to her conduct" — for example, where a defendant "receives unstolen property believing it was stolen." *People v. Thousand*, 465 Mich. 149, 159 (2001). This strange interpretation of legal impossibility, sometimes referred to as hybrid legal impossibility, led "the doctrine of impossibility [to] become mired in fine distinctions" and was "'a source of utter frustration,' plunging the . . . courts into a 'morass of confusion.'" *United States v. Everett*, 700 F.2d 900, 905 (3d Cir. 1983).

The confusion caused by these cases was due to the fact

### Legal Impossibility

While factual impossibility is no defense to an attempt prosecution, as the *McElroy* court notes, legal impossibility can be a "valid defense to the charge of attempt." Legal impossibility "occurs when the law does not even 'proscribe the goal that the defendant sought to achieve.'" *United States v. Hsu*, 155 F.3d 189, 199 n.16 (3d Cir. 1998). Thus, "a hunter cannot be convicted of attempting to shoot a deer if the law does not prohibit shooting deer in the first place," even if the hunter mistakenly thought that shooting deer was against the law. *Id.* at 199 n.16.

To illustrate the point further, imagine that Dan is a regular consumer of an energy drink called *Extreme Hyphy Energy*, and he has two cases of the beverage in his garage. One day, to his great disappointment, Dan reads that the Food and Drug Administration (FDA) has banned the sale of *Extreme Hyphy Energy* because it contains a dangerously high level of caffeine. Dan misunderstands the article and mistakenly believes the FDA has made it a crime to merely possess the *Extreme Hyphy Energy* drink. The next day, Dan is driving to work, drinking a can of *Extreme Hyphy Energy*, when a police officer pulls him over for speeding. When the officer arrives at Dan's car, Dan immediately confesses to the "crime" of possessing the energy drink. Can Dan be convicted of attempting to possess an illegal drug?

No. Because it is not a crime to possess the energy drink, the legal impossibility doctrine applies.

Although legal impossibility is often referred to as a "defense," it is really just an application of the principle that the crime of attempt "cannot exist by itself, but only in connection with another crime." *Cox v. State*, 311 Md. 326, 330 (2006). If it is not a crime to possess *Extreme Hyphy Energy*, then Dan's knowing possession of the drink is neither an attempted crime nor a completed crime. The legal impossibility defense addresses a circumstance that arises rarely, if ever, in the real world but quite often in legal texts. If a police officer were to encounter a person who confessed to possessing an energy drink that was not against the law to possess, the officer would be exceedingly unlikely to make an arrest and a prosecutor would be even less likely to try to bring charges. Nevertheless, the rule that legal impossibility is a defense is considered to be an important part of the black letter law of criminal attempts.

In summary, in almost every jurisdiction today, the law of impossible attempts is as follows: Factual impossibility is never a defense and legal impossibility — meaning "when an actor engages in conduct that he believes is criminal, but is not actually prohibited by law" — is always a defense. *People v. Thousand*, 465 Mich. 149, 159 (2001).

> that "it is possible to view virtually any example of 'hybrid legal impossibility' as an example of 'factual impossibility,'" and vice-versa. Fortunately, "the great majority of jurisdictions have now recognized that [hybrid] legal and factually impossibility are 'logically indistinguishable' and have abolished [hybrid legal] impossibility as a defense." *United States v. Hsu*, 155 F.3d 189, 199 (3d Cir. 1998). See also Gideon Yaffee, *Criminal Attempts*, 124 Yale L.J. 92, 133 (2014) ("[T]he doctrine is a disaster, and, thankfully, has almost disappeared in the United States.").
>
> Because hybrid legal impossibility has been almost entirely abandoned, lawyers and law students no longer have to devote energy to studying this "confused mass of law." *State v. Moretti*, 52 N.J. 182 (1968). But the doctrine is still sometimes mentioned in the literature on impossible attempts, so it is worth being aware of its existence.

## D. ABANDONMENT (RENUNCIATION)

In general, once a person commits a crime, she cannot uncommit it. For example, "[o]ne cannot, as a legal matter, undo or wipe away one's liability for a theft by returning the stolen item, even if one does so before anyone realizes it has gone missing. Such post-theft restitution of the stolen property might influence a prosecutor to exercise discretion and forgo bringing a case, or might be a basis (formalized or not) for mitigating the offender's sentence, but it does not create a full and outright defense to liability." Michael T. Cahill, *Defining Inchoate Crime: An Incomplete Attempt*, 9 Ohio St. J. Crim. L. 751, 753 (2012). The same is true of virtually every other crime, from burglary to drug possession.

Attempt, however, is different. In a significant number of states, **abandonment** (also known as **renunciation**) can be a defense to an attempt prosecution. Not all states recognize abandonment as a defense. Until the arrival of the Model Penal Code, most "American courts . . . consistently and firmly maintained that 'once the elements of attempt are complete, abandonment of criminal purpose is no defense.'" Paul R. Hoeber, *The Abandonment Defense to Criminal Attempt and Other Problems of Temporal Individuation*, 74 Cal. L. Rev. 377, 381-82 (1986).

The Model Penal Code's drafters decided to recognize abandonment as a defense, an approach that has been followed in at least 22 states. In these jurisdictions, a defendant who went far enough in his effort to complete the elements of an attempt before having second thoughts and deciding not to go through with the crime *may* be able to escape conviction based on the abandonment defense. But the elements of the abandonment defense are demanding. As a result, the defense is only rarely successful.

The renunciation defense requires the defendant to have abandoned his attempt to commit the target offense and for his abandonment to have been both complete and voluntary. In the typical case involving the renunciation defense, there is persuasive evidence that the defendant stopped his effort to commit the crime. Disputes center around whether the defendant's decision to abandon the criminal attempt was complete and voluntary, as in the case that follows.

## Case Preview

### *State v. Riley*

In *Riley*, the court discusses and applies the abandonment defense in a decision upholding an attempted robbery conviction.

As you read the decision, consider the following questions:

1. What does it mean for abandonment of an attempt to be "complete"?
2. What does it mean for abandonment of an attempt to be "voluntary"?
3. What evidence demonstrated that the defendant's abandonment in this case was neither complete nor voluntary?

## *State v. Riley*
### 159 Conn. App. 462 (2015)

SHELDON, J.

The defendant, Winston Anthony Riley, appeals from the judgment of conviction, rendered after a jury trial, of attempt to commit robbery in the first degree in violation of General Statutes §§ 53a-49. Following the jury's guilty verdict on th[is] . . . charge[],[1] the defendant was sentenced by the court to a total effective term of six years incarceration. The defendant appeals on [the] ground[] . . . that there

---

[1] The defendant was also convicted of threatening in the second degree in violation of General Statutes § 53a-62(a)(1) and carrying a dangerous weapon in violation of General Statutes § 53-206(a). The defendant does not challenge the conviction of those charges here. The defendant was acquitted of reckless endangerment in the first degree under General Statutes § 53a-63(a).

was insufficient evidence to support the jury's rejection of his defense of renunciation[3] beyond a reasonable doubt. We affirm the judgment of the trial court.

The following facts, which the jury reasonably could have found, are relevant to this appeal. On March 18, 2012, the defendant drove to the Mohegan Sun Casino in Montville in order to make up an $800 gambling loss from the prior day. Upon his arrival at the casino, the defendant attempted to withdraw money from an automated teller machine, but could not do so because his wife had transferred money out of their account. After returning to his car and falling asleep for a period of time, the defendant woke up and decided to commit a robbery. The defendant thus slipped a knife up the sleeve of his sweatshirt and began to walk around the parking garage.

Louise Carty, an eighty-three year old woman, was at the casino on March 18, 2012, to play the penny slots. As she was entering the elevator in the Winter Parking Garage, Carty noticed that a man, later identified as the defendant, was following her inside. After the elevator door closed, the man, whom Carty was never able to identify, "all of a sudden pull[ed] a knife out of his pocket and head[ed] toward me." In response, Carty screamed, "No, no, no," and shoved the man, causing him to jump away from her. Carty then grabbed the man's sweatshirt by the sleeve and pursued him off the elevator. The man never took or demanded money or property from Carty or verbally threatened her.

At trial, the defendant sought to defend himself by raising the defense of renunciation under General Statutes § 53a-49(c).[4] In support of that defense, he testified as follows. First, he admitted that he was the man who had accosted Carty in the elevator. Having initially intended to rob her, he admittedly followed her into the elevator, pulled a knife out of his sleeve to confront her and took two or three steps toward her after the elevator doors closed. The defendant described as follows what happened in the elevator as he began to approach Carty:

"[Defense Counsel]: What was your intention at that moment?

"[The Defendant]: My intentions as I approached her, as I took, like, the second or third step to her, I'm, like, oh, my God, this could by my grandmother; what am I doing?

"[Defense Counsel]: So, when you thought that, what were you going to do about that; were you going to do anything about your thought?

"[The Defendant]: I immediately said I'm sorry. I basically curled the knife toward myself, and I was, like, I'm sorry, I'm sorry. She then grabbed me."

Carty, by contrast, testified that, although she heard the man mumble something after she shoved him, she could not make out what he said and did not hear him say that he was sorry. After she and the man exited the elevator, the man hustled away

---

[3] The defendant does not argue that the state failed to prove beyond a reasonable doubt the elements of attempted robbery. The crime of attempt requires proof beyond a reasonable doubt that the defendant . . . intentionally took a substantial step in a course of conduct planned to culminate in his commission of that substantive crime.

[4] "When the actor's conduct would otherwise constitute an attempt . . . it shall be a defense that he abandoned his effort to commit the crime or otherwise prevented its commission, under circumstances manifesting a complete and voluntary renunciation of his criminal purpose." General Statutes § 53a-49(c).

from Carty while she told others in the vicinity that the man had tried to knife her. Additional facts will be set forth as necessary.

The defendant . . . claims that the state failed to disprove beyond a reasonable doubt that he renounced his criminal purpose under § 53a-49(c). According to the defendant, the state did not successfully rebut his testimony that he changed his mind as he took his second or third step toward Carty, then curled his knife back toward himself and apologized, because both Carty's testimony and a casino surveillance video of the incident supported his version of events. We disagree with the defendant's claim on the merits, concluding that the evidence in this case was sufficient to disprove his defense of renunciation beyond a reasonable doubt.

The standard of review employed in a sufficiency of the evidence claim is well settled. We apply a two part test. First, we construe the evidence in the light most favorable to sustaining the verdict. Second, we determine whether upon the facts so construed and the inferences reasonably drawn therefrom the finder of fact reasonably could have concluded that the cumulative force of the evidence established guilt beyond a reasonable doubt.

Before evaluating the defendant's claim, it is first necessary to examine the defense of renunciation. At common law, renunciation was not universally recognized as a defense to the crime of attempt. The Model Penal Code, however, included the defense of renunciation in its 1962 proposed official draft.

Two main reasons have been advanced for allowing the defense of renunciation to the crime of attempt. First, an actor's renunciation of his criminal purpose prior to the completion of a substantive crime suggests that he did not have a firm purpose to commit the crime, and thus tends to negate his dangerousness. Second, the availability of the defense can provide the actor with the motivation to desist from his criminal effort, "thereby diminishing the risk that the substantive crime will be committed."

Connecticut first codified renunciation as an affirmative defense to the crime of attempt in 1969, basing it in substance on the Model Penal Code.

Section 53a-49(c) . . . provides in relevant part that "[w]hen the actor's conduct would otherwise constitute an attempt . . . it shall be a defense that he abandoned his effort to commit the crime or otherwise prevented its commission, under circumstances manifesting a complete and voluntary renunciation of his criminal purpose."

[In Connecticut, the government carries the burden to] disprove the [renunciation] defense beyond a reasonable doubt whenever it is raised at trial.

A defendant is deemed to have raised the defense of renunciation, and thus to have met his *burden of going forward* with respect to that defense, whenever the evidence presented at trial, if construed in the light most favorable to the defendant, is sufficient to raise a reasonable doubt in support of each essential element of the defense. The defendant, however, has no *burden of proof* with respect to the defense of renunciation. Instead, the state has the burden of disproving that defense beyond a reasonable doubt whenever it is duly raised at trial.

In order to meet its burden of proof as to the defense of renunciation, the state need only disprove one of its . . . essential elements beyond a reasonable doubt.

The parties in the present case do not dispute that the defendant abandoned his effort to commit the substantive crime[] of robbery . . . against Carty. Thus, the only contested issue in this case was whether the defendant's abandonment of his effort to commit those crimes against Carty and the resulting prevention of their commission took place under circumstances manifesting a complete and voluntary renunciation of the defendant's criminal purpose.

As to the . . . "complete and voluntary" element [of the renunciation defense], General Statutes § 53a-50 provides the following further explanation: "[R]enunciation of criminal purpose is not voluntary if it is motivated, in whole or in part, by circumstances, not present or apparent at the inception of the actor's course of conduct, which increase the probability of detection or apprehension or which make more difficult the accomplishment of the criminal purpose. Renunciation is not complete if it is motivated by a decision to postpone the criminal conduct or to transfer the criminal effort to another but similar objective or victim." See also Model Penal Code and Commentaries, supra, § 5.01, comment 8, p. at 356 ("An 'involuntary' abandonment occurs when the actor ceases his criminal endeavor because he fears detection or apprehension, or because he decides he will wait for a better opportunity, or because his powers or instruments are inadequate for completing the crime. There has been no doubt that such an abandonment does not exculpate the actor from attempt liability otherwise incurred. A 'voluntary' abandonment occurs when there is a change in the actor's purpose that is not influenced by outside circumstances. This may be termed repentance or change of heart. Lack of resolution or timidity may suffice.").

The defendant claims that he decided not to rob Carty when he took his second or third step toward her in the elevator, but before she screamed and grabbed him. On cross-examination, the defendant denied that his change of mind resulted from Carty grappling with him or the elevator door opening. Although the state played the video recording of the incident when it cross-examined the defendant, he denied that it showed him moving toward Carty without stopping and turning away before she grabbed him and pushed him away.

The state presented the following evidence to prove that the defendant's prevention of the crime[] of robbery . . . against Carty was not complete and voluntary. First, Carty testified that she screamed when she saw the defendant pull out the knife, and kept on screaming, "No, no, no." According to Carty, she "kind of" shoved the defendant, then heard him mumble something, although later she said that she never touched the defendant.

Second, the state presented video evidence that afforded the jury a substantial basis for rejecting the defendant's claim as to the sequence of events here at issue. A review of the video recording shows the following. Carty entered the elevator, followed by the defendant. After the doors closed, as the defendant and Carty were standing on opposite sides of the elevator from one another, the defendant pulled a knife from his sleeve and approached Carty. The defendant then took three steps toward Carty, who did not appear to notice him until he was taking his third step, at which point she immediately raised her hands, grabbed his right hand (holding the knife) and his left wrist/forearm, and pushed him away, causing the defendant to take a step backward. The defendant and Carty briefly struggled before the defendant raised his arms in an apparent attempt to free himself from her grasp, then briefly broke free and turned away from her toward the opening elevator doors. At that point, as the defendant was slightly in front of and to the left of Carty, she grabbed a piece of his sweatshirt, near the elbow of his right sleeve, and held onto it as the defendant walked off the elevator in front of her. The surveillance video does not have sound and does not clearly show the defendant's or Carty's mouth moving. The video also does not clearly show the defendant curling his knife back toward himself before Carty raised her hands and pushed him.

Construing this evidence in the light most favorable to the state, we conclude that it was sufficient to support the jury's conclusion that the defendant's abandonment of his criminal purpose was not complete and voluntary. The jury reasonably could have concluded, based on Carty's testimony alone, that she screamed as soon as she saw him coming at her with the knife, and that the defendant, upon hearing her scream and feeling her resist him physically, abandoned his criminal effort to rob her under circumstances that were neither voluntary nor complete. The jury reasonably could have concluded that the defendant decided that the screaming Carty would "increase the probability of [his] detection or apprehension," because her actions could draw attention to him. Moreover, the jury reasonably could have concluded that Carty's screaming at and wrestling with the defendant—both circumstances that were not apparent at the inception of the defendant's criminal conduct—led the defendant to "postpone [his] criminal conduct or to transfer the criminal effort to another but similar objective or victim," such as a more cooperative victim. The video evidence corroborates Carty's version of events. The video shows the defendant turning away from Carty only *after* she sought to defend herself against him by grabbing him and shoving him away. The jury thus reasonably could have viewed the video as supporting the state's version of events—that the defendant did not abandon his criminal effort until it became clear to him that Carty would not be a passive victim.

Considering the totality of the evidence in the light most favorable to the state, as we must, we conclude that there was ample evidence for the jury to find that the state disproved beyond a reasonable doubt that the defendant abandoned his criminal effort under circumstances manifesting a complete and voluntary renunciation of his criminal purpose.

The judgment is affirmed.

---

**Post-Case Follow-Up**

Although Riley abandoned his attempt to rob Carty, the court found the evidence sufficient to establish that his abandonment was neither complete nor voluntary. Riley's abandonment was not voluntary because it may have been motivated by a fear of being caught following Carty's screams, rather than by a genuine renunciation of his criminal purpose. Nor was Riley's abandonment a complete renunciation of his criminal purpose, since Carty's resistance may have "led [Riley] to 'postpone [his] criminal conduct or to transfer the criminal effort to another but similar objective or victim,' such as a more cooperative victim." As a result, the court found that the jury's decision to reject Riley's renunciation defense was supported by substantial evidence. The decision demonstrates how hard it is for defendants to succeed in a renunciation defense. The defendant must fully renounce his criminal purpose, not just postpone it, and his decision must be voluntary and not motivated by a fear of being caught by the police or difficulty in completing the crime.

---

# Riley: *Real Life Applications*

1. Recall the case of *People v. Acosta*, presented above at page 350. There, the court affirmed Acosta's conviction for attempt to possess a controlled substance in a jurisdiction that applies the dangerous proximity test. The evidence showed that Acosta "order[ed] illegal narcotics from a supplier, admit[ted] a courier into his . . . home and examine[d] the quality of the goods" before deciding not to go through with the purchase because the drugs were not of good enough quality. In a portion of the opinion that was not included in the excerpt above, the court held that Acosta did not meet the requirements for the renunciation defense, despite his decision not to purchase the drugs. What aspect of the renunciation defense do you think was not met in Acosta's case?

2. Johnson was drinking with his friend at a bar one night when the pair got into an argument. The argument escalated into a fistfight, which Johnson lost. Angry, Johnson walked to his house (about a mile away) to get his shotgun. Johnson returned to the bar with the weapon. Instead of walking inside, however, Johnson crawled under a pickup truck parked across the street. At trial, Johnson testified that he planned to wait until his friend left the bar and then shoot him to "pay him back."

   About a half an hour later, the pickup truck's owner — whom Johnson did not know — arrived and was startled to discover a man lying underneath his vehicle. Johnson explained the situation to the owner of pickup truck, who gave Johnson a beer and invited him to sit and talk in the pickup truck.

   Johnson and the pickup truck's owner sat in the car for about an hour, drinking beers and conversing. At some point during the conversation, Johnson told the truck's owner that he had "changed his mind" about shooting his friend. Johnson then removed the shells from his shotgun and put them in his pocket. Shortly before the bar closed, a police officer approached the vehicle to investigate. The officer found Johnson and the truck's owner drinking beers together. Johnson, who made a full statement to the police officer, was charged with attempted murder.

   At trial, Johnson raises the defense of renunciation. Imagine you are Johnson's attorney and that you are preparing for closing argument. Briefly sketch out your closing argument on the renunciation defense.

---

## Should Attempts Be Punished Less Harshly Than Completed Crimes?

Although sentencing rules vary significantly from one jurisdiction to the next, the law often assigns greater penalties for a completed crime than an attempt to commit that same crime. Is this the right approach?

Some commentators believe that results should not play a role in criminal punishment. Stephen Morse, for example, argues that "intentional action and forbearance are the only aspects of human conduct that potentially can be fully guided consciously, explicitly, and effectively by moral or legal rules." Stephen J. Morse, *Reason, Results, and Criminal Responsibility*, 2004 U. Ill. L. Rev. 363, 365. For this reason, "[i]mposing blame and punishment for anything other than intentional action and forbearance is both unfair and, in most cases, useless." *Id.* Applying this principle to attempts, Morse argues "that the law should not distinguish the culpability of agents who commit last-act attempts" — meaning attempts where a defendant performed the last act necessary to cause the anticipated harm — "from those who complete their crimes." *Id.* at 386.

Do you agree that harm is irrelevant to blameworthiness? Can you think of reasons apart from blameworthiness that the law might take harm into account in grading offenses and meting out punishment?

## Chapter Summary

■ To convict a defendant of an attempt to commit a crime, the prosecutor must prove that she acted with the intent — in this context, meaning purpose — of completing the acts necessary to commit the crime. Because a person cannot intend to bring about an unintended result, crimes like "attempted involuntary manslaughter" or "attempted negligent homicide" are not cognizable offenses.

■ Jurisdictions are split on the conduct required to commit an attempt. A slight majority of jurisdictions apply the "substantial step" test, which is derived from the Model Penal Code. Among states that do not use the substantial step test, the "dangerous proximity to success" test is the most prominent.

■ The dangerous proximity to success test is a forward-looking test. It asks the fact finder to look at how close the defendant got to completing the crime. To satisfy the dangerous proximity test, the prosecutor must prove that the defendant came "so near to [the] accomplishment [of the crime] that in all reasonable probability the crime would have been committed but for timely interference." *People v. Rizzo*, 246 N.Y. 334 (1927).

■ The substantial step test is a backward-looking test. It asks the fact finder to focus exclusively on the defendant's actions. The substantial step test is satisfied if the defendant committed an act that is "strongly corroborative of the actor's criminal purpose." Model Penal Code § 5.01(2).

■ In almost every jurisdiction today, so-called factual impossibility is not a defense to an attempt prosecution. This means that a defendant cannot escape punishment in an attempt prosecution by arguing that the "crime [was] impossible to complete because of some physical or factual condition unknown to the defendant." *State v. McElroy*, 128 Ariz. 315 (1981).

■ By contrast, legal impossibility is considered a viable defense to an attempt prosecution. Legal impossibility refers to circumstances where the act the defendant committed or tried to commit is not against the law. Calling legal impossibility a defense is something of a misnomer. It is simply an application of the principle that the crime of attempt "cannot exist by itself, but only in connection with another crime." *Cox v. State*, 311 Md. 326, 330 (2006).

■ States are split on whether abandonment (also referred to as renunciation) is a defense to an attempt prosecution. In jurisdictions that recognize the defense, it applies only if the defendant's decision to abandon the attempt was both complete and voluntary.

## Applying the Concepts

1. Derrick's favorite football team won the Super Bowl. To celebrate, Derrick shot a gun in the air from the top of his apartment building in a densely populated area. Derrick realized that firing a gun into the air was dangerous, but he decided to do it anyway. Derrick's bullet almost struck Vivian, who was standing

in a crowd about a block from Derrick's building. The bullet whizzed by Vivian's head but, luckily, she was not hit by it. The prosecutor charges Derrick with attempted involuntary manslaughter. At trial, a government expert is prepared to testify that if the bullet had struck Vivian, it would certainly have killed her. Can Derrick be convicted?

   **a.** Yes, but only in a substantial step jurisdiction.
   **b.** Yes, in either a substantial step or a dangerous proximity jurisdiction.
   **c.** No, because the impossibility defense applies in this case.
   **d.** No, because attempted involuntary manslaughter is not a crime.

2. Dan, who lives in Boise, Idaho, decides to take a road trip to visit his friend in Denver, Colorado. Dan brings an eighth of an ounce of marijuana with him on the trip. About half an hour outside of Denver, Dan is pulled over for speeding by a Colorado Highway Patrol Officer. Under Colorado law, it is legal to possess an ounce or less of marijuana. Dan mistakenly thinks that it is only legal to possess marijuana under Colorado law if it was purchased in Colorado. In fact, it is legal to possess an ounce or less of marijuana in Colorado regardless of where the marijuana was purchased. The officer asks to search Dan's car. In response, Dan says to the officer, "I've got some marijuana in the car. I bought it in Idaho, so I know it is not legal to possess here in Colorado. Please don't arrest me." Assume that Colorado applies the substantial step test for attempts. Has Dan committed a crime under Colorado law?

   **a.** Yes, Dan is guilty of attempted possession of a controlled substance.
   **b.** Yes, Dan is guilty of possession of a controlled substance.
   **c.** No, because this is a case of legal impossibility.
   **d.** No, because Dan did not come sufficiently near to completing the crime.

3. In *United States v. Jackson*, the court upheld the defendants' convictions under the substantial step test. Would the outcome have been the same or different if *Jackson* had been decided in a jurisdiction that followed the dangerous proximity test? Review the facts of *Jackson* and write a short paragraph analyzing whether the defendants could have been convicted under the dangerous proximity test.

4. A helpful exercise for better understanding the law of attempts can be to think about a crime step by step and apply the substantial step and dangerous proximity tests at each stage. The fact pattern that follows describes an attempt to possess marijuana in four steps. For each step, separately apply the dangerous proximity and substantial step tests and decide whether you think each test has been met. In addition, rate how certain you are of the outcome at each step on a scale of one to ten, with ten being most certain. For example, if you think the defendant's actions would constitute an attempt and you are absolutely certain of that outcome, then the rating would be a ten. By contrast, if you believe the case is a close one that could easily go either way but because you are forced to choose, you conclude that the defendant's actions constitute an attempt, the rating would be a one.

■ Devon tells her friend Kris that she has always wanted to try marijuana. Devon asks Kris if Kris knows anyone who sells marijuana. (Marijuana is illegal to possess in the state where Devon and Kris live.)

■ Kris gives Devon the phone number of a man named Stan, who Kris believes sells marijuana. Devon texts Stan, "I got your number from Kris. I'd like to make a purchase, if you have anything available. Can we talk?"

■ Stan calls Devon and briefly describes the strains of marijuana he has for sale and the prices. Devon asks Stan to come to Devon's house with an eighth of an ounce of marijuana the next day and Stan agrees.

■ The next day, Stan texts Devon, "I'm on my way with the stuff." Stan drives to Devon's house with an eighth of an ounce of marijuana. One block from Devon's house, Stan is pulled over by the police for speeding. Stan agrees to let the police search his car and phone. The police find the marijuana and the text messages to Devon. The police go to Devon's house and arrest Devon for attempted possession of marijuana.

## Criminal Law in Practice

1. As discussed in this chapter, jurisdictions are split on the test that they apply for the conduct element of attempt offenses and on whether or not abandonment can be a defense to an attempt prosecution.

   a. Look up the test that your state applies for the conduct element of the crime of attempt. Does your state apply the substantial step test, the dangerous proximity test, or a different test entirely? (If you live in New York, where *Rizzo* and *Acosta* were decided, look up the law in a neighboring state of your choosing.)

   b. Look up whether your state recognizes the defense of abandonment to an attempt prosecution. If so, how closely do the requirements for the defense align with the Model Penal Code's definition that has been adopted by Connecticut, as discussed in *State v. Riley*? (If you live in Connecticut, where *Riley* was decided, look up the law in a neighboring state of your choosing.)

2. In some cases, there may be compelling evidence of an attempt to commit a crime but less clarity about exactly *which* crime the defendant was planning to commit. Imagine that you are a prosecutor in a substantial step jurisdiction and that you must decide whether to charge the individual in the fact pattern that follows with attempted robbery or attempted armed robbery. You can find the definition of the crime of robbery in Chapter 3. In this jurisdiction, armed robbery is defined as follows: A person commits the offense of armed robbery when, with intent to commit theft, he or she takes property of another from the person or the immediate presence of another by use of an offensive weapon, or any replica, article, or device having the appearance of such weapon.

A security guard at a pharmacy noticed the defendant, Rainey, pull his car into an unusual location in the pharmacy's parking lot. The license plate on Rainey's car was obscured by a piece of paper. The guard watched Rainey exit the vehicle wearing a surgical mask, a hooded sweatshirt, and a hat. The guard called 911 and reported her concern that Rainey may be planning to rob the store.

Rainey entered the pharmacy. The security guard stayed on the phone with the 911 operator and monitored Rainey from security cameras in a back room. Rainey walked around the store for several minutes before approaching the counter. Rainey, who was still wearing a surgical mask, asked an employee about the price of cigarettes.

Just then, a police officer who was responding to the 911 call entered the pharmacy and placed Rainey under arrest. The officer searched Rainey's car and found that the license plate was obscured by an insurance bill. Rainey gave the officer permission to look inside the car. A search of the car revealed a police scanner and a note inside the glove box that read "I have a gun and there is someone outside listening to a police scanner so do not activate the alarm. Hand over the money from the register and be fast." The police did not find a weapon (or any items resembling a weapon) in Rainey's car or on his person.

As you consider what charge to bring — attempted robbery or attempted armed robbery — it may be helpful to recall some basic principles of prosecutorial discretion discussed in Chapter 2. In order to charge someone with a crime, the prosecutor must have probable cause (meaning a reasonable ground for belief in guilt) that the crime was committed. This is a much lower standard than the burden of proof for a conviction, which is proof beyond a reasonable doubt. When a prosecutor has probable cause to believe a crime has been committed, she *may* charge the defendant with that crime, but she may also exercise her prosecutorial discretion to charge the defendant with a less serious crime (or to decline to bring charges entirely).

3. Now that we have covered attempts, it is worth briefly reconsidering the crime of burglary. One of the sidebars in Chapter 3 (see page 138) asks, "What purpose does burglary as a distinct offense serve?" As discussed there, the drafters of the Model Penal Code considered eliminating the crime of burglary on the grounds that it is arguably superfluous to modern criminal codes. Whether or not burglary *currently* serves a useful purpose, there is no doubt that it filled a very important potential gap at common law. As noted briefly at the beginning of this chapter, attempt was not a widely recognized offense until the 1800s. When the offense was first recognized, most jurisdictions applied the so-called last act test, which was significantly narrower than the dangerous proximity test. (As the name implies, the test required the defendant to perform the last act necessary to commit the crime in order to be guilty of attempt.) Without the crime of attempt, burglary makes a lot more sense. In a world where a defendant who was caught breaking into a house to commit larceny could not be prosecuted for attempted larceny, burglary was indispensable. In light of the modern law of attempts, do you think burglary still serves an important purpose? If so, what is it? (Be sure to reread the sidebar referenced above to help you in considering this question.)

# Accomplice Liability

Not surprisingly, it is against the law to help someone else commit a crime. A person who helps someone else commit a crime is an accomplice. But "aiding and abetting is not a separate substantive offense." *People v. Robinson*, 475 Mich. 1, 6 (2006). Instead, a person who helps someone else commit a crime is guilty of the crime that she helped to commit. For example, a defendant who serves as a lookout to a drug sale is guilty of distribution of a controlled substance as an accomplice. In this way, accomplice liability is vicarious or "'derivative,' that is, it results from an act by the perpetrator to which the accomplice contributed." *People v. Prettyman*, 14 Cal. 4th 248 (1996).

Although there is no separate crime of "aiding and abetting" or "being an accomplice," accomplice liability is governed by distinct legal requirements. In order to apply accomplice liability rules, it can be helpful to distinguish between principals and accomplices. A principal is the person who carries out the crime — the person who enters the bank and takes the money by threatening force, for example. An accomplice (also sometimes called an aider and abettor) assists the principal in some way.

To convict a defendant of committing a crime as an **accomplice**, the government must prove three things: (1) that a crime was committed, (2) that the defendant intended to facilitate the commission of that crime, and (3) that the defendant did some act to assist in the commission of that crime.

## A. PROOF THAT A CRIME WAS COMMITTED

The first step to convicting a defendant as an accomplice is to prove that a crime was committed. This follows from the fact that accomplice liability is derivative. An accomplice's assistance can give rise to criminal liability only if the principal committed or attempted to commit a

## Key Concepts

- What is the difference between knowing and intentional assistance for purposes of accomplice liability?
- What level of assistance is necessary to satisfy accomplice liability's *actus reus* element?
- How do courts apply accomplice liability principles to compound offenses?
- What is the natural and probable consequences doctrine?

**379**

crime. As a result, if what the principal did is not a crime, then helping the principal do that thing is not a crime, either.

Consider a person who sells difficult-to-obtain chemicals to a buyer, believing that the buyer plans to manufacture methamphetamine. In fact, the buyer never planned to manufacture methamphetamine and uses the chemicals for a completely lawful purpose. In this case, the buyer has not committed any crime. As a result, even if the seller had acted with the intent of assisting in the manufacture of methamphetamine, she could not be prosecuted for manufacturing methamphetamine (or any other crime) as an accomplice. This is because "for a defendant to be found guilty under an aiding and abetting theory, someone other than the defendant must be proven to have attempted or committed a crime; i.e., absent proof of a predicate offense, conviction on an aiding and abetting theory cannot be sustained." *People v. Perez*, 35 Cal. 4th 1219, 1227 (2005).

Accomplice liability requires proof that the principal committed a crime. But does the government have to actually *convict* the principal in order to successfully prosecute an accomplice? At one time, the answer was yes. In earlier years, an accomplice could not be convicted of a crime unless the government had first won a conviction against the principal. This restriction has been universally abandoned. Today, "the principal offender need not be convicted of the underlying offense in order to sustain the conviction of an accomplice." *Taylor v. Commw.*, 31 Va. App. 54, 60 (1999). Instead, the government "must prove that the underlying offense has been committed by the principal offender" at the *accomplice's* trial. *Id.*

Notice that this state of affairs means that it is possible for a jury to convict a defendant of committing a crime as an accomplice even if the alleged principal has already been acquitted. See *Standefer v. United States*, 447 U.S. 10, 11 (1980) (holding that "a defendant accused of aiding and abetting in the commission of a federal offense may be convicted after the named principal has been acquitted of that offense"). This is not necessarily as strange as it might seem. In some cases, the government can have very strong evidence that a person helped to commit a crime as an accomplice even though the evidence against the principal is very weak or nonexistent. For example, imagine that the police catch the getaway driver to a robbery a few blocks from the scene of the crime, but the principal flees on foot and escapes. In a case like this, the principal to the robbery might never be caught at all. Even so, the accomplice could still be prosecuted. Likewise, if a suspected principal is arrested, tried, and acquitted, the acquittal will not prevent the getaway driver from being prosecuted for robbery as an accomplice. So long as, *at the accomplice's trial*, the government is able to prove that a crime was committed, the first requirement for accomplice liability is satisfied.

## B. *MENS REA*: INTENT

To be convicted of a crime as an accomplice, the defendant must have acted with the intent — in this context, meaning purpose — of facilitating the commission of the target crime. Put in more practical terms, to be guilty of a crime as an accomplice, "the alleged aider and abettor must want to make the principal's venture succeed." *United States v. Giovannetti*, 919 F.2d 1223, 1229 (7th Cir. 1990).

Courts sometimes express the required mental state for accomplice liability as encompassing "a twofold requirement: that the accessory have the intent to aid the principal and that in so aiding he intend to commit the offense with which he is charged." *State v. Harrison*, 178 Conn. 689, 694 (1979). Often, this "dual intent" characterization of the *mens rea* for accomplice liability has little practical significance. After all, ordinarily, a person who intends to assist someone in an endeavor also intends for the person she is helping to succeed in that endeavor. But the distinction can be an important one in some cases.

**Case Preview**

## *Hicks v. United States*

To commit a crime as an accomplice, the defendant must intend to assist the principal in committing the crime. In *Hicks*, the United States Supreme Court considered whether the trial court properly instructed the jury on this requirement. The defendant, John Hicks, was convicted of murdering Andrew J. Colvard as an accomplice. The evidence showed that Hicks was present when Stand Rowe shot and killed Colvard. All three men were on horseback. A few moments before Rowe shot Colvard, witnesses saw Hicks "take off his hat, . . . hit his horse on the neck or shoulder with it, [and] say to Colvard, 'Take off your hat, and die like a man.'"

As you read the decision, consider the following questions:

1. What was problematic about the trial court's jury instruction regarding intent?
2. If Hicks did not intend to encourage Rowe to shoot Colvard, what other reason might he have had for saying to Colvard, "Take off your hat, and die like a man"?

---

**Exhibit 8.1** **Fort Worth Daily Gazette Story About Colvard's Murder**

> **Killed Without Provocation.**
> PRYOR CREEK, I. T., Feb. 23.—Last Saturday, as John Hicks and Stan Roe, two Indians, and Jack Colvard (white) were returning home from a dance, Hicks rode up and took Colvard's hat off. remarking at the same time "Hold your head up, Jack, and die like a man." They then stepped back a few paces, took aim, and shot Colvard dead. It was done without any provocation. They were all drunk. Stan Roe is a noted outlaw. There is no reward offered for them. Colvard leaves four motherless children. His life was insured for $27,500.

## Hicks v. United States
### 150 U.S. 442 (1893)

Shiras, J.

In the circuit court of the United States for the western district of Arkansas, John Hicks, an Indian, was jointly indicted with Stand Rowe, also an Indian, for the murder of Andrew J. Colvard, a white man, by shooting him with a gun on the 13th of February, 1892. Rowe was killed by the officers in the attempt to arrest him, and Hicks was tried separately, and found guilty, in March, 1893. We adopt the statement of the facts in the case made in the brief for the government as correct, and as sufficient for our purposes:

> It appears that on the night of the 12th of February, 1892, there was a dance at the house of Jim Rowe, in the Cherokee Nation; that Jim Rowe was a brother to Stand Rowe, who was indicted jointly with the defendant; that a large number of men and women were in attendance; that the dance continued until near sunrise the morning of the 13th; that Stand Rowe and the defendant were engaged in what was called "scouting," viz. eluding the United States marshals who were in search of them with warrants for their arrest, and were armed for the purpose of resisting arrest. They appeared at the dance, each armed with a Winchester rifle. They were both Cherokee Indians. The deceased, Andrew J. Colvard, was a white man, who had married a Cherokee woman. He had been engaged in the mercantile business in the Cherokee country until a few months before the homicide. He came to the dance on horseback on the evening of the 12th. A good deal of whisky was drank during the night by the persons present, and Colvard appears to have been drunk at some time during the night. Colvard spoke Cherokee fluently, and appears to have been very friendly with Stand Rowe and the defendant, Hicks.
>
> Some time after sunrise on the morning of the 13th, about 7 o'clock, [four witnesses], all of whom had been at the dance the night before, and had seen there Colvard, Stand Rowe, and the defendant [at the dance], were standing on the porch of [a] house . . . about 414 steps west from the house of Jim Rowe, and saw Stand Rowe, coming on horseback in a moderate walk, with his Winchester rifle lying down in front of him, down a "trail," which led into the main traveled road. Stand Rowe halted within five or six feet of the main road, and the men on the porch saw Mr. Colvard and the defendant, Hicks, riding together down the main road from the direction of Jim Rowe's house.
>
> As Colvard and Hicks approached the point where Stand Rowe was sitting on his horse, Stand Rowe rode out into the road and halted. Colvard then rode up to him in a lope or canter, leaving Hicks, the defendant, some 30 or 40 feet in his rear. The point where the three men were together on their horses was about 100 yards from where the four witnesses stood on the porch. The conversation between the three men on horseback was not fully heard by the four men on the porch, and all that was heard was not understood, because part of it was carried on in the Cherokee tongue; but some part of this conversation was distinctly heard and clearly understood by these witnesses. They saw Stand Rowe twice raise his rifle and aim it at Colvard, and twice he lowered it. They heard Colvard say, "I am a friend to both of you." They saw and heard the defendant, Hicks, laugh aloud when Rowe directed his rifle towards Colvard. They saw Hicks take off his hat, and hit his horse on the neck or shoulder with it. They heard Hicks say to Colvard, "Take off your hat, and die like a man." They

saw Stand Rowe raise his rifle for the third time point it at Colvard, and fire it. They saw Colvard's horse wheel and run back in the direction of Jim Rowe's house, 115 or 116 steps. They saw Colvard fall from his horse. They went to where he was lying in the road, and found him dead. They saw Stand Rowe and John Hicks ride off together after the shooting.

Hicks testified in his own behalf, denying that he had encouraged Rowe to shoot Colvard, and alleging that he had endeavored to persuade Rowe not to shoot.

The language attributed to Hicks, and which he denied having used, cannot be said to have been entirely free from ambiguity. It was addressed, not to Rowe, but to Colvard. Hicks testified that Rowe was in a dangerous mood, and that he did not know whether he would shoot Colvard or Hicks. The remark made—if made—accompanied with the gesture of taking off his own hat, may have been an utterance of desperation, occasioned by his belief that Rowe would shoot one or both of them. That Hicks and Rowe rode off together after seeing Colvard fall was used as a fact against Hicks. Hicks testified that he did it in fear of his life; that Rowe had demanded that he should show him the road which he wished to travel. Hicks further testified—and in this he was not contradicted—that he separated from Rowe a few minutes afterwards, on the first opportunity, and that he never afterwards had any intercourse with him, nor had he been in the company of Rowe for several weeks before the night of the fatal occurrence.

[In this appeal, Hicks challenges] that portion of the charge wherein the judge sought to instruct the jury as to the evidence relied on as showing that Hicks aided and abetted Rowe in the commission of the crime. The [jury was instructed in relevant part] as follows: "[I]f the facts show that [the defendant] either aided or abetted or advised or encouraged Stand Rowe, he is made a participant in the crime as thoroughly and completely as though he had with his own hand fired the shot which took the life of the man killed. If the deliberate and intentional use of words was the effect to encourage one man to kill another, he who uttered these words is presumed by the law to have intended that effect, and is responsible therefor."

We agree with the counsel for [Hicks] in thinking that this instruction was erroneous. It omitted to instruct the jury that the acts or words of encouragement and abetting must have been used by the accused with the intention of encouraging and abetting Rowe. So far as the instruction goes, the words may have been used for a different purpose, and yet have had the actual effect of inciting Rowe to commit the murderous act. Hicks, indeed, testified that the expressions used by him were intended to dissuade Rowe from shooting. But the jury were left to find Hicks guilty . . . because the effect of his words may have had the result of encouraging Rowe to shoot, regardless of Hicks' intention.

[The part of the jury instruction regarding the intentional use of words was] defective in confounding the intentional use of the words with the intention as respects the effect to be produced. Hicks no doubt intended to use the words he did use, but did he thereby intend that they were to be understood by Rowe as an encouragement to act? However this may be, we . . . think [the instruction] of the learned judge [was erroneous because it may have led the jury to wrongly believe] that the mere use of certain words would suffice to warrant the jury in finding Hicks guilty, regardless of the intention with which they were used.

The judgment of the court below is reversed, and the cause remanded, with directions to set aside the verdict and award a new trial.

**Post-Case Follow-Up**

Hicks was retried and acquitted following the Supreme Court's decision. The case highlights the *mens rea* required for accomplice liability: an intent to help the principal commit the offense. As the Supreme Court explained in *Hicks*, it is not enough that the defendant intentionally commit an act that actually encourages or assists the principal. Instead, the defendant must act "with the intention of encouraging and abetting" the defendant.

## Hicks: *Real Life Applications*

1. The Supreme Court overturned John Hicks's conviction because the jury instructions were "defective in confounding the intentional use of the words with the intention as respects the effect to be produced." As noted in the Post-Case Follow-Up, the jury acquitted Hicks at his second trial. Review the facts of Hicks's case as described in the Supreme Court's opinion.
   a. Imagine that you were the prosecutor at Hicks's retrial. Prepare a brief closing argument arguing why the evidence proves that Hicks acted with the required *mens rea* to be convicted of murder as an accomplice.
   b. Now, imagine that you were Hicks's defense attorney at his retrial. Prepare a brief closing argument arguing why the evidence is insufficient to prove your client's guilt beyond a reasonable doubt.
   c. When a case is retried, each side is free to conduct additional investigation and call witnesses who were not called at the first trial. Can you think of any additional investigative steps that either the prosecutor or the defense might have taken to try to help clarify what Hicks intended when he told Colvard to take off his hat "and die like a man"?

### Intent and Legitimate Retail Sales and Services

In the accomplice liability setting, the *mens rea* of intent is used narrowly to mean purpose; knowledge that one's actions will assist in the commission of a crime is not enough. Of course, in most cases, evidence that a person knowingly helped someone else commit a crime will be very persuasive evidence that they acted with the requisite intent. In the retail sales and services setting, things can become much more complicated. In a decision presented later in this chapter, *Rosemond v. United States*, the Supreme Court posited the hypothetical case of "a gun owner who sells a firearm to a criminal, knowing but not caring how the gun will be used." 572 U.S. 65, 77 n.8 (2014). One could also imagine an Uber driver who knows, but does not care, that a client has hailed a ride to purchase drugs. Can our hypothetical Uber driver be convicted of drug possession as an accomplice? In theory, the answer should be no, because the driver did not act with the requisite intent. In practice, policing intent in these kinds of cases often presents challenges.

As Judge Learned Hand put it, the question in these cases is "whether the seller of goods, in themselves innocent, becomes a conspirator with — or, what is in substance the same thing, an abettor of — the buyer because he knows that the buyer means to use the goods to commit a crime." *United States v. Falcone*, 109 F.2d 579, 581 (2d Cir. 1940). The United States Supreme Court has never addressed the question of what kind of evidence "would suffice to show that such a third party has the intent necessary to be convicted of aiding and abetting." *Rosemond*, 572 U.S. at 77 n.8. Many courts employ the so-called stake in the venture test, however. Learned Hand described this concept in *Falcone* as follows: "It is not enough that [the defendant] does not forego a normally lawful activity, of the fruits of which he knows that others will make an unlawful use; he must in some sense promote their venture himself, make it his own, have a stake in its outcome." *Falcone*, 109 F.2d at 581.

Under what circumstances can jurors infer that the seller of a legitimate good has a stake in a criminal venture? The most frequently cited examples include when there is evidence of "inflated charges" for the services, when the "volume of business with the buyer is grossly disproportionate to any legitimate demand, or when sales for illegal use amount to a high proportion of the seller's total business." *People v. Lauria*, 251 Cal. App. 2d 471, 478-79 (1967).

It bears noting that while the "stake in the venture" concept has many adherents, courts "have not spoken uniformly about the standard for determining guilt" in this setting. Benton Martin & Jeremiah Newhall, *Technology and the Guilty Mind: When Do Technology Providers Become Criminal Accomplices?*, 105 J. Crim. L. & Criminology 95, 124 (2015).

## C. *ACTUS REUS*: ASSISTANCE

Intending to assist in the commission of a crime is not enough to make someone an accomplice. Accomplice liability also requires that the defendant actually provide assistance. As the two cases that follow demonstrate, it does not take much assistance to satisfy the conduct element of accomplice liability.

**Case Preview**

### *In re Wilson*

Does standing by while a friend commits a crime make one an accomplice to that crime? In *In re Wilson*, the evidence showed that Wilson, a juvenile, was present while his friends pulled a rope across a road, thereby endangering passing cars. There was no evidence that Wilson provided any active assistance or encouragement to his friends. Nevertheless, the trial court found that Wilson had committed the crime of reckless endangerment as an accomplice. The Washington Supreme Court reversed, in the opinion that follows.

As you read the decision, consider the following questions:

1. If mere presence is insufficient to make one an accomplice to a crime, what more is required?
2. The court notes in passing that providing encouragement is considered to be a form of assistance within the law of accomplice liability. What sort of encouragement do you think would suffice?

---

## *In re Wilson*
### 91 Wash. 2d 487 (1979)

HICKS, J.

At issue in this case is whether a juvenile's continued presence at the scene of a purported crime without more, though with knowledge of the ongoing activities, is sufficient to sustain a conviction as an accomplice to the crime of reckless endangerment. RCW 9A.36.050.[2]

The juvenile court found the evidence sufficient to support a determination that petitioner, Ronald E. Wilson, had given support and encouragement to other youths engaged in activities constituting reckless endangerment. Consequently, Wilson was found guilty. The Court of Appeals, Division One, affirmed by per curiam opinion. We granted the petition for review and we reverse.

The verbatim report of proceedings consists of a mere 31 pages, from which the following sketchy details can be elicited concerning the activities of a group of youths on the evening of August 29, 1976. Weatherstripping was pulled from office building windows, fashioned into a rope of sorts, tied around a tree and strung across a road to a fairway on an adjacent golf course. From time to time this "rope" was pulled taut across the road.

[T]he state's eyewitness . . . testified:

> When we went outside, we saw several kids on top of the fairway. Down on the highway was a rope that was tied to a tree, and strung across the highway up onto the fairway. At certain times, the rope would be pulled when cars were coming down the street. It looked like it could cause an accident.

The eyewitness called the police and while awaiting their arrival, she remained outside to observe activities on the hill. She testified as follows:

---

[2] RCW 9A.36.050 reads as follows:

"(1) A person is guilty of reckless endangerment when he recklessly engages in conduct which creates a substantial risk of death or serious physical injury to another person.
"(2) Reckless endangerment is a gross misdemeanor."

Q. Approximately how long was it before the police arrived?

A. I would say anywhere to about fifty minutes to an hour. It was a long time before they arrived.

Q. During the time when you were watching and waiting for the police, was the rope or whatever material that was strung across the road held in the air?

A. It was pulled twice while we were out there watching. At one time it was pulled when there was no cars coming down the road. On the second time, it was pulled when headlights were coming around the corner. The rope was dropped before the car got to the area where the rope was.

[As to petitioner's involvement in the offense, t]he eyewitness . . . testified that the rope was pulled taut once [while] petitioner was on the hill [standing near the people who were pulling the rope].

Based on the record presented, we are somewhat skeptical that the State established the underlying crime of reckless endangerment; nevertheless, . . . assuming that the activities described above constitute reckless endangerment, we do not believe Wilson's presence, knowledge of the theft [of the weatherstripping], and personal acquaintance with active participants is sufficient to support a finding of abetting.

As the judge was ruling at the conclusion of the juvenile court hearing, defense counsel inquired:

[DEFENSE COUNSEL:] Your Honor, are you indicating that the conduct is not stopping the other people from doing what they were doing?

THE COURT: No. His participation in going to the scene, being with his friend, standing and being involved in the whole atmosphere of what was going on. That the actual touching and pulling the rope was not necessary for him to really contribute to what was happening. He should, when he recognized what was going on, leave. Then there wouldn't have been any problem.

The court found the allegation of reckless endangerment correct as to aiding and abetting. The court dismissed the petition as to the second count alleging third-degree theft. The court deferred a finding of delinquency conditioned on Wilson's completion of 15-hours community service.

In its affirmance of the juvenile court, the Court of Appeals stated:

It is not a crime to be indifferent to criminal activity and although it would have been praiseworthy for appellant to make an effort to prevent these delinquent acts the law does not require him to do this. However once he has knowledge of the theft and the stretching of the rope across the road, his continued presence at the scene of the ongoing crime can be reasonably inferred to "encourage" the crime.

We believe the language employed by the Court of Appeals establishes an overly broad rule, and we accepted discretionary review to consider the matter.

[A] person is not an accomplice unless he or she . . . "solicits, commands, encourages, or requests" the commission of a crime, or aids in the planning or commission thereof. Washington case law has consistently stated that physical presence and assent alone are insufficient to constitute aiding and abetting. Presence at the scene of an ongoing crime may be sufficient if a person is "ready to assist." We fail to find evidence in the record indicative of Wilson's readiness to "assist."

[As we have stated in a previous case]:

> One does not aid and abet unless, in some way, he associates himself with the undertaking, participates in it as in something he desires to bring about, and seeks by his action to make it succeed. Mere knowledge or physical presence at the scene of a crime neither constitutes a crime nor will it support a charge of aiding and abetting a crime.

The juvenile court held and the Court of Appeals confirmed that in the context of the juvenile activity described above, Wilson's knowing presence was a sufficient act to permit the court to find him to be an accomplice to the crime of reckless endangerment. This cannot be.

Reversed.

---

**Post-Case Follow-Up**

*In re Wilson* illustrates the universally followed principle that "physical presence and assent alone" do not make someone an accomplice. In other words, a person does not become an accomplice by standing by and watching a friend commit a crime. This is true even if the person watching her friend commit a crime secretly hopes to see the crime carried out. Instead, accomplice liability requires assistance, which can include physical assistance or encouragement.

---

As *In re Wilson* shows, being physically present while someone else commits a crime does not, standing alone, make one an accomplice. In the next case, we will see what more is required.

---

**Case Preview**

## *State v. Wilson*

Decided by the Washington Supreme Court just two years after *In re Wilson* (and, coincidentally, also involving a defendant with the last name Wilson), *State v. Wilson* considers how much assistance is sufficient to give rise to accomplice liability.

As you read the decision, consider the following questions:

1. What distinguishes the facts in this case from those of *In re Wilson*?
2. In what way did the defendant in this case assist in the marijuana sale?

---

## *State v. Wilson*
### 95 Wash. 2d 828 (1981)

ROSELLINI, J.

The appellant was found guilty as an accomplice in the delivery of a controlled substance. The prosecution arose out of the following occurrences, as testified to by the State's witnesses.

On August 27, 1979, an agent of the Washington State Patrol Drug Assistance Unit, one Faust, went with an informant, Wimberly, to the appellant's rented home in Soap Lake. The appellant, who had previously been introduced to Faust by Wimberly, met the two at the door and invited them in. The appellant's wife and baby were present, as was his brother, Paul Wilson. In the appellant's presence, the agent asked Paul if he could buy an ounce of sensamilion [sic] (marijuana). Paul told him that he could and quoted a price of $100 per ounce. The agent remarked that the price was high, and at that point the appellant told the agent that it was very good "pot" and well worth the money. The agent agreed to pay $100 and Paul brought the marijuana from under the couch on which he was sitting and delivered it to the agent.

The appellant . . . contends that there was no evidence to support the verdict on the charge of aiding and abetting the delivery of a controlled substance, for which reason the court erred in denying the appellant's motions to dismiss. Our attention is directed to *State v. Peasley*, 80 Wash. 99 (1914), wherein this court said that mere . . . acquiescence is not sufficient to constitute aiding and abetting . . . and the recent case of *In re Wilson*, 91 Wash. 2d 487, 588 P.2d 1161 (1979), where we held that a person's physical presence at the scene of an offense, with knowledge of what was taking place, would not, standing alone, support a charge of aiding and abetting a crime.

It is . . . suggested that the appellant took no active part in the sale of marijuana to the agent, but was "merely present" at the transaction. The theory is that the agent admittedly came to the house intending to make a purchase and that he would have done so had there been no encouraging remarks from the appellant.

---

### Accessory After the Fact

A person who intentionally helps someone commit a crime can be convicted of committing that crime as an accomplice. By contrast, a person who provides assistance *after* the commission of a crime is not an accomplice. But, depending on the kind of assistance provided, she could be prosecuted for the crime of accessory after the fact (called hindering in some states).

Generally speaking, an accessory after the fact is a person who helps someone who has already committed a crime try to escape arrest or prosecution. Under one fairly representative definition of accessory after the fact, the offense requires that "(1) someone other than the accused, that is, a principal, must have committed a specific, completed felony; (2) the accused must have harbored, concealed, or aided the principal; (3) with knowledge that the principal committed the felony or has been charged or convicted of the felony; and (4) with the intent that the principal avoid or escape from arrest, trial, conviction, or punishment." *People v. Partee*, 8 Cal. 5th 860, 866-67 (Cal. 2020). The elements of the crime vary from state to state, however. For example, in many states the offense covers assistance to principals who have committed both misdemeanors and felonies.

None of the authorities cited by the appellant holds that, where it is made an offense to sell a substance, the state of mind of the person to whom the substance is sold is material in determining the culpability of the seller or other participants. Rather, the cases cited are concerned with the degree of participation which amounts to aiding and abetting.

In *State v. Peasley, supra,* this court held that it was error to instruct the jury that the accused should be found guilty if money was stolen by any of his codefendants with his . . . assent. The court said:

> To assent to an act implies neither contribution nor an expressed concurrence. It is merely a mental attitude which, however culpable from a moral standpoint, does not constitute a crime, since the law cannot reach opinion or sentiment however harmonious it may be with a criminal act.

Here, the evidence was that the appellant [made] remarks [that were] calculated to induce the buyer to make the purchase [of marijuana].

[I]n *In re Wilson, supra,* we said that a person is not an accomplice merely because he was present at the scene and knew that a crime was being committed. There, a number of juveniles were charged with "reckless endangerment" for stringing an improvised rope across a highway and manipulating it in a manner which constituted a possible hazard to automobile traffic. The accused was seen in the group of young men but was not seen participating in the activity.

We said that in order to establish abetting, the State must show . . . encourage[-ment] on the part of the accused. Quite apart from the evidence that the appellant consented to the keeping of marijuana in his home for the purpose of sale, the . . . encourage[ment] was manifest in the appellant's attempt to persuade an apparently reluctant prospect to make a purchase. The fact that the sale would have been completed, even without such encouragement, does not change the nature of the appellant's conduct.

Finding no error, we affirm the judgment of the trial court.

---

**Post-Case Follow-Up**

Mere presence at the scene of a crime does not make one an accomplice. But, as *State v. Wilson* shows, accomplice liability does not require all that much beyond presence — any assistance, however small, suffices. Notably, assistance includes encouragement. In this case, Wilson provided encouragement by telling the prospective buyer "that it was very good 'pot' and well worth the money." As a result, the court upheld the defendant's conviction for delivery of a controlled substance (called distribution of a controlled substance in most jurisdictions) as an accomplice. The fact that the buyer would have made the purchase anyway is immaterial because accomplice liability does not include a causation requirement. So long as the alleged accomplice actually provided any assistance or encouragement, accomplice liability's *actus reus* requirement will be satisfied.

---

# In re Wilson *and* State v. Wilson: *Real Life Applications*

**1.** In *In re Wilson*, the court stated that presence at the scene of a crime plus readiness to assist "*may*" be sufficient to make one an accomplice. Can you think of a circumstance where a person would be considered an accomplice by virtue of being present at the scene of a crime and ready to assist, even if it turned out that her assistance was not necessary?

**2.** Constance lived with her husband Michael in a small town in Maine. The couple lived near Constance's mother, Norma. For years, Constance and Michael had feuded with Norma. One night, after an especially terrible argument with Norma, Constance said to Michael, "I wish we could just get rid of her permanently." Michael replied, "If you're serious, I could take care of that."

   Over the next few days, Michael talked openly with Constance about developing a plan to kill Norma. Whenever Michael would bring up the subject, Constance would say, "I can't bring myself to be involved but I won't give you any problem." That weekend, Michael and Constance hired a babysitter to attend a party at the home of a friend who lived near Norma. On the way to the party, Michael said to Constance, "I'm going to leave the party for a little while to take care of some business." Michael then opened the car glove box, revealing a handgun and a box of bullets. Constance said to Michael, "I understand. If you aren't finished in time to come back before the babysitter needs to go home, I can go back on my own and drive the babysitter back to her house."

   About an hour after getting to the party, Michael walked five minutes to Norma's house, where he shot and killed Norma. Michael returned to the party in time to drive back home with Constance. On the way home, Michael said to Constance, "Thanks again for offering to go back home alone and take the babysitter back to her place. I'm glad it wasn't necessary."

   Constance is convicted of murder as an accomplice. On appeal, her defense attorney argues that there was insufficient evidence that she provided assistance to Michael in his commission of the crime. Imagine you are one of the judges on the appellate panel that hears the case. How would you rule and why?

# D. THE WITHDRAWAL DEFENSE

Fourteen states recognize withdrawal as a defense to accomplice liability, but the requirements for the defense are fairly demanding. To succeed, the defendant must "terminate[] his complicity prior to the commission of the offense and (i) wholly deprive[] it of effectiveness in the commission of the offense; or (ii) give[] timely warning to the law enforcement authorities or otherwise make[] proper effort to prevent the commission of the offense." Model Penal Code § 2.06(6)(c). Perhaps in part because this is a difficult standard to meet, the defense appears to be very rarely employed. As one court put it, "there appears to be a paucity of authority" regarding the defense. *State v. Formella*, 158 N.H. 114, 118 (2008). The published cases that have discussed the issue have held that the first prong of the defense requires an accomplice to have *at least* "ma[d]e some affirmative act, such as an overt expression of disapproval to the principles," and to have done so "far enough in advance to allow the others involved in the crime to follow suit." *Id.* at 118-19. This sort of advance disapproval may suffice for a defendant who provided only encouragement, but much more is required if the defendant provided tangible assistance. This is because the more assistance the defendant has provided, the more he will need to do in order to "wholly deprive[]" that assistance of any "effectiveness in the commission of the offense." Model Penal Code § 2.06(6)(c).

## E. APPLYING ACCOMPLICE LIABILITY TO COMPOUND OFFENSES

Applying the law of accomplice liability to a crime like delivery of marijuana, as in *State v. Wilson*, is relatively straightforward. If the government can prove that the defendant assisted in the sale and intended to assist in the sale, then the defendant is guilty of delivery of marijuana as an accomplice. The task of applying accomplice liability principles can become much trickier when the defendant is accused of acting as an accomplice to a crime that involves more than one criminal act. (The United States Supreme Court has described this sort of crime as a "compound" crime in the accomplice liability setting.)

To see why compound offenses can pose challenges, recall the distinction between larceny and robbery (covered in Chapter 3). Larceny is the trespassory taking and carrying away of the personal property of another with the intent to permanently deprive. Robbery is, in essence, an aggravated larceny. "To elevate larceny to robbery, the taking must be accomplished by force or fear and the property must be taken from the victim or his presence." *People v. Gomez*, 43 Cal. 4th 249, 254 (2008).

Now, imagine a hypothetical defendant, Adam, who agrees to serve as the getaway driver for a theft that his friend Dave plans to commit. Dave tells Adam that he plans to break into a store after hours when no one is there and steal money from the cash register. Adam drives Dave to the store and waits outside in the car. Dave breaks in and, to his surprise, discovers that an employee is still inside. Dave pulls out a gun that (unknown to Adam) Dave had brought with him, and forces the employee to hand over money from the cash register. Dave runs outside to the car and Adam drives away. Dave never tells Adam that an employee was in the store. Dave is guilty of robbery. Is Adam also guilty of robbery as an accomplice? Or is Adam guilty of larceny as an accomplice because Adam only intended to help with a non-violent theft? The Supreme Court addressed how to apply accomplice liability principles to situations like this in *Rosemond v. United States*.

## Case Preview

# *Rosemond v. United States*

A federal statute makes it a crime to use or carry a firearm "during and in relation to any crime of violence or drug trafficking crime." 18 U.S.C. § 924(c). If a defendant serves as an accomplice to a drug sale — which is a drug trafficking crime — is he *also* guilty of violating § 924(c) as an accomplice if the principal is secretly carrying a firearm?

As you read the decision, consider the following questions:

1. What was problematic about the trial court's jury instructions?
2. Do you think the opinion is clear about whether purpose or knowledge is sufficient to make one an accomplice to a violation of 18 U.S.C. § 924(c)?

---

# *Rosemond v. United States*
### 572 U.S. 65 (2014)

Justice KAGAN delivered the opinion of the Court**

A federal criminal statute, § 924(c) of Title 18, prohibits "us[ing] or carr[ying]" a firearm "during and in relation to any crime of violence or drug trafficking crime." In this case, we consider what the Government must show when it accuses a defendant of aiding or abetting that offense.

## I

This case arises from a drug deal gone bad. Vashti Perez arranged to sell a pound of marijuana to Ricardo Gonzales and Coby Painter. She drove to a local park to make the exchange, accompanied by two confederates, Ronald Joseph and petitioner Justus Rosemond. One of those men apparently took the front passenger seat and the other sat in the back, but witnesses dispute who was where. At the designated meeting place, Gonzales climbed into the car's backseat while Painter waited outside. The backseat passenger allowed Gonzales to inspect the marijuana. But rather than handing over money, Gonzales punched that man in the face and fled with the drugs. As Gonzales and Painter ran away, one of the male passengers — but again, which one is contested — exited the car and fired several shots from a semiautomatic handgun. The shooter then re-entered the vehicle, and all three would-be drug dealers gave chase after the buyers-turned-robbers. But before the three could catch their quarry, a police officer, responding to a dispatcher's alert, pulled their car over. This federal prosecution of Rosemond followed.[1]

---

** Justice Scalia joins all but footnotes 7 and 8 of this opinion.
[1] The Government agreed not to bring charges against the other four participants in the narcotics deal in exchange for their giving truthful testimony against Rosemond.

The Government charged Rosemond with, *inter alia*, violating § 924(c) by using a gun in connection with a drug trafficking crime. Section 924(c) provides that "any person who, during and in relation to any crime of violence or drug trafficking crime[,] . . . uses or carries a firearm," shall receive a five-year mandatory-minimum sentence, with seven- and ten-year minimums applicable, respectively, if the firearm is also brandished or discharged. 18 U.S.C. § 924(c)(1)(A). Section 2 [of Title 18] . . . is the federal aiding and abetting statute: It provides that "[w]hoever commits an offense against the United States or aids, abets, counsels, commands, induces or procures its commission is punishable as a principal."

[T]he Government prosecuted the § 924(c) charge on two alternative theories. The Government's primary contention was that Rosemond himself used the firearm during the aborted drug transaction. But recognizing that the identity of the shooter was disputed, the Government also offered a back-up argument: Even if it was Joseph who fired the gun as the drug deal fell apart, Rosemond aided and abetted the § 924(c) violation.

The District Judge accordingly instructed the jury on aiding and abetting law. He first explained, in a way challenged by neither party, the rudiments of § 2. Under that statute, the judge stated, "[a] person who aids or abets another to commit an offense is just as guilty of that offense as if he committed it himself." And in order to aid or abet, the defendant must [intentionally] "seek[] by some act to help make the crime succeed." The judge then turned to applying those general principles to § 924(c) — and there, he deviated from an instruction Rosemond had proposed. According to Rosemond, a defendant could be found guilty of aiding or abetting a § 924(c) violation only if he "intentionally took some action to facilitate or encourage the use of the firearm," as opposed to the predicate drug offense. But the District Judge disagreed, instead telling the jury that it could convict if "(1) the defendant knew his cohort used a firearm in the drug trafficking crime, and (2) the defendant knowingly and actively participated in the drug trafficking crime." In closing argument, the prosecutor contended that Rosemond easily satisfied that standard, so that even if he had not "fired the gun, he's still guilty of the crime." After all, the prosecutor stated, Rosemond "certainly knew [of] and actively participated in" the drug transaction. "And with regards to the other element," the prosecutor urged, "the fact is a person cannot be present and active at a drug deal when shots are fired and not know their cohort is using a gun. You simply can't do it."

The jury convicted Rosemond of violating § 924(c) (as well as all other offenses charged). The verdict form was general: It did not reveal whether the jury found that Rosemond himself had used the gun or instead had aided and abetted a confederate's use during the marijuana deal. As required by § 924(c), the trial court imposed a consecutive sentence of 120 months of imprisonment for the statute's violation.

The Tenth Circuit affirmed, rejecting Rosemond's argument that the District Court's aiding and abetting instructions were erroneous.

We granted certiorari to resolve the Circuit conflict over what it takes to aid and abet a § 924(c) offense.

## II

The federal aiding and abetting statute, 18 U.S.C. § 2, states that a person who furthers — more specifically, who "aids, abets, counsels, commands, induces or procures" — the commission of a federal offense "is punishable as a principal." That provision derives from (though simplifies) common-law standards for accomplice liability. And in so doing, § 2 reflects a centuries-old view of culpability: that a person may be responsible for a crime he has not personally carried out if he helps another to complete its commission.

We have previously held that under § 2 "those who provide . . . aid to persons committing federal crimes, with the intent to facilitate the crime, are themselves committing a crime." Both parties here embrace that formulation, and agree as well that it has two components. As at common law, a person is liable under § 2 for aiding and abetting a crime if (and only if) he (1) takes an affirmative act in furtherance of that offense, (2) with the intent of facilitating the offense's commission. See *Hicks v. United States*, 150 U.S. 442, 449 (1893) (an accomplice is liable when his acts of assistance are done "with the intention of encouraging and abetting" the crime).

The questions that the parties dispute, and we here address, concern how those two requirements — affirmative act and intent — apply in a prosecution for aiding and abetting a § 924(c) offense. Those questions arise from the compound nature of that provision. Recall that § 924(c) forbids "us[ing] or carr[ying] a firearm" when engaged in a "crime of violence or drug trafficking crime." The prosecutor must show the use or carriage of a gun; so too he must prove the commission of a predicate (violent or drug trafficking) offense. For purposes of ascertaining aiding and abetting liability, we therefore must consider: When does a person act to further this double-barreled crime? And when does he intend to facilitate its commission? We address each issue in turn.

### A

Consider first Rosemond's account of his conduct (divorced from any issues of intent). Rosemond actively participated in a drug transaction, accompanying two others to a site where money was to be exchanged for a pound of marijuana. But as he tells it, he took no action with respect to any firearm. He did not buy or borrow a gun to facilitate the narcotics deal; he did not carry a gun to the scene; he did not use a gun during the subsequent events constituting this criminal misadventure. His acts thus advanced one part (the drug part) of a two-part incident — or to speak a bit more technically, one element (the drug element) of a two-element crime. Is that enough to satisfy the conduct requirement of this aiding and abetting charge, or must Rosemond, as he claims, have taken some act to assist the commission of the other (firearm) component of § 924(c)?

The common law imposed aiding and abetting liability on a person (possessing the requisite intent) who facilitated any part — even though not every part — of a criminal venture. As a leading treatise, published around the time of § 2's enactment, put the point: Accomplice liability attached upon proof of "[a]ny participation in a general felonious plan" carried out by confederates. 1 F. Wharton, Criminal Law

§ 251, p. 322 (11th ed. 1912) (emphasis added). Indeed, as [another] treatise under-scored, a person's involvement in the crime could be not merely partial but mini-mal too: "The quantity [of assistance was] immaterial," so long as the accomplice did "*something*" to aid the crime. R. Desty, A Compendium of American Criminal Law § 37a, p. 106 (1882) (emphasis added). After all, the common law maintained, every little bit helps — and a contribution to some part of a crime aids the whole.

That principle continues to govern aiding and abetting law under § 2: As almost every court of appeals has held, "[a] defendant can be convicted as an aider and abettor without proof that he participated in each and every element of the offense." In proscribing aiding and abetting, Congress used language that "comprehends all assistance rendered by words, acts, encouragement, support, or presence" — even if that aid relates to only one (or some) of a crime's phases or elements. The division of labor between two (or more) confederates thus has no significance: A strategy of "you take that element, I'll take this one" would free neither party from liability.[6]

Under that established approach, Rosemond's participation in the drug deal here satisfies the affirmative-act requirement for aiding and abetting a § 924(c) vio-lation. As we have previously described, the commission of a drug trafficking (or violent) crime is — no less than the use of a firearm — an "essential conduct element of the § 924(c) offense." In enacting the statute, "Congress proscribed both the use of the firearm *and* the commission of acts that constitute" a drug trafficking crime. Rosemond therefore could assist in § 924(c)'s violation by facilitating either the drug transaction or the firearm use (or of course both). In helping to bring about one part of the offense (whether trafficking drugs or using a gun), he necessarily helped to complete the whole. And that ends the analysis as to his conduct. It is inconsequen-tial . . . that his acts did not advance each element of the offense; all that matters is that they facilitated one component.

Rosemond [argues] that our approach would conflate two distinct offenses — allowing a conviction for abetting a § 924(c) violation whenever the prosecution shows that the defendant abetted the underlying drug trafficking crime. [Rosemond's fears are misplaced] because, as we will describe, an aid-ing and abetting conviction requires not just an act facilitating one or another element, but also a state of mind extending to the entire crime. And under that rule, a defendant may be convicted of abetting a § 924(c) violation only if his intent reaches beyond a simple drug sale, to an armed one. Aiding and abetting law's intent component — to which we now turn — thus preserves the distinction between assisting the predicate drug trafficking crime and assisting the broader § 924(c) offense.

---

[6] Consider a hypothetical. Suppose that as part of a kidnapping scheme, one accomplice lures the victim into a car under false pretenses; another drives the vehicle; a third allows the use of her house to hold the victim captive; and still a fourth keeps watch outside to divert potential witnesses. None would have personally com-pleted, or even assisted with, all elements of the offense. But (if they had the requisite intent) all would be liable under § 2.

*B*

Begin with (or return to) some basics about aiding and abetting law's intent requirement, which no party here disputes. As previously explained, a person aids and abets a crime when (in addition to taking the requisite act) he intends to facilitate that offense's commission. An intent to advance some different or lesser offense is not, or at least not usually, sufficient: Instead, the intent must go to the specific and entire crime charged — so here, to the full scope (predicate crime plus gun use) of § 924(c).[7] And the canonical formulation of that needed state of mind — later appropriated by this Court and oft-quoted in both parties' briefs — is Judge Learned Hand's: To aid and abet a crime, a defendant must not just "in some sort associate himself with the venture," but also "participate in it as in something that he wishes to bring about" and "seek by his action to make it succeed." *Nye & Nissen v. United States*, 336 U.S. 613, 619 (1949) (quoting *Peoni*, 100 F.2d, at 402).

We have previously found that intent requirement satisfied when a person actively participates in a criminal venture with full knowledge of the circumstances constituting the charged offense. [I]n *Bozza v. United States*, 330 U.S. 160, 165 (1947), we upheld a conviction for aiding and abetting the evasion of liquor taxes because the defendant helped operate a clandestine distillery "know[ing]" the business was set up "to violate Government revenue laws." And several Courts of Appeals have similarly held — addressing a fact pattern much like this one — that the unarmed driver of a getaway car had the requisite intent to aid and abet armed bank robbery if he "knew" that his confederates would use weapons in carrying out the crime. So for purposes of aiding and abetting law, a person who actively participates in a criminal scheme knowing its extent and character intends that scheme's commission.[8]

The same principle holds here: An active participant in a drug transaction has the intent needed to aid and abet a § 924(c) violation when he knows that one of his confederates will carry a gun. In such a case, the accomplice has decided to join in the criminal venture, and share in its benefits, with full awareness of its scope — that the plan calls not just for a drug sale, but for an armed one. In so doing, he has chosen (like the abettors in . . . *Bozza* or the driver in an armed robbery) to align himself with the illegal scheme in its entirety — including its use of a firearm. And he has determined (again like those other abettors) to do what he can to "make [that scheme] succeed." He thus becomes responsible, in the typical way of aiders and abettors, for the conduct of others. He may not have brought the gun to the drug deal himself, but because he took part in that deal knowing a confederate would do so, he intended the commission of a § 924(c) offense — *i.e.,* an armed drug sale.

---

[7] Some authorities suggest an exception to the general rule when another crime is the "natural and probable consequence" of the crime the defendant intended to abet. See, *e.g.,* 2 LaFave § 13.3(b), at 356 (citing cases); but see *id.,* § 13.3 ("Under the better view, one is not an accomplice to a crime merely because . . . that crime was a natural and probable consequence of another offense as to which he is an accomplice"). That question is not implicated here, because no one contends that a § 924(c) violation is a natural and probable consequence of simple drug trafficking. We therefore express no view on the issue.

[8] We did not deal in these cases, nor do we here, with defendants who incidentally facilitate a criminal venture rather than actively participate in it. A hypothetical case is the owner of a gun store who sells a firearm to a criminal, knowing but not caring how the gun will be used. We express no view about what sort of facts, if any, would suffice to show that such a third party has the intent necessary to be convicted of aiding and abetting.

For all that to be true, though, the § 924(c) defendant's knowledge of a firearm must be advance knowledge — or otherwise said, knowledge that enables him to make the relevant legal (and indeed, moral) choice. When an accomplice knows beforehand of a confederate's design to carry a gun, he can attempt to alter that plan or, if unsuccessful, withdraw from the enterprise; it is deciding instead to go ahead with his role in the venture that shows his intent to aid an *armed* offense. But when an accomplice knows nothing of a gun until it appears at the scene, he may already have completed his acts of assistance; or even if not, he may at that late point have no realistic opportunity to quit the crime. And when that is so, the defendant has not shown the requisite intent to assist a crime involving a gun. As even the Government concedes, an unarmed accomplice cannot aid and abet a § 924(c) violation unless he has "foreknowledge that his confederate will commit the offense with a firearm." For the reasons just given, we think that means knowledge at a time the accomplice can do something with it — most notably, opt to walk away.[9]

Both parties here find something to dislike in our view of this issue. Rosemond argues that a participant in a drug deal intends to assist a § 924(c) violation only if he affirmatively desires one of his confederates to use a gun. The jury, Rosemond concedes, could infer that state of mind from the defendant's advance knowledge that the plan included a firearm. But according to Rosemond, the instructions must also permit the jury to draw the opposite conclusion — that although the defendant participated in a drug deal knowing a gun would be involved, he did not specifically want its carriage or use. That higher standard, Rosemond claims, is necessary to avoid subjecting persons of different culpability to the same punishment. Rosemond offers as an example an unarmed driver assisting in the heist of a store: If that person spent the drive "trying to persuade [his confederate] to leave [the] gun behind," then he should be convicted of abetting shoplifting, but not armed robbery.

We think not. What matters for purposes of gauging intent, and so what jury instructions should convey, is that the defendant has chosen, with full knowledge, to participate in the illegal scheme — not that, if all had been left to him, he would have planned the identical crime. Consider a variant of Rosemond's example: The driver of a getaway car wants to help rob a convenience store (and argues passionately for that plan), but eventually accedes when his confederates decide instead to hold up a national bank. Whatever his original misgivings, he has the requisite intent to aid and abet *bank* robbery; after all, he put aside those doubts and knowingly took part in that more dangerous crime. The same is true of an accomplice who knowingly joins in an armed drug transaction — regardless whether he was formerly indifferent or even resistant to using firearms. The law does not, nor should it, care whether he participates with a happy heart or a sense of foreboding. Either way, he has the same culpability, because either way he has knowingly elected to aid in the commission of a peculiarly risky form of offense.

The Government, for its part, thinks we take too strict a view of when a defendant charged with abetting a § 924(c) violation must acquire that knowledge. As

---

[9] Of course, if a defendant continues to participate in a crime after a gun was displayed or used by a confederate, the jury can permissibly infer from his failure to object or withdraw that he had such knowledge. In any criminal case, after all, the factfinder can draw inferences about a defendant's intent based on all the facts and circumstances of a crime's commission.

noted above, the Government recognizes that the accused accomplice must have "foreknowledge" of a gun's presence. But the Government views that standard as met whenever the accomplice, having learned of the firearm, continues any act of assisting the drug transaction. According to the Government, the jury should convict such a defendant even if he became aware of the gun only after he realistically could have opted out of the crime.

But that approach, we think, would diminish too far the requirement that a defendant in a § 924(c) prosecution must intend to further an *armed* drug deal. Assume, for example, that an accomplice agrees to participate in a drug sale on the express condition that no one brings a gun to the place of exchange. But just as the parties are making the trade, the accomplice notices that one of his confederates has a (poorly) concealed firearm in his jacket. The Government would convict the accomplice of aiding and abetting a § 924(c) offense if he assists in completing the deal without incident, rather than running away or otherwise aborting the sale. But behaving as the Government suggests might increase the risk of gun violence — to the accomplice himself, other participants, or bystanders; and conversely, finishing the sale might be the best or only way to avoid that danger. In such a circumstance, a jury is entitled to find that the defendant intended only a drug sale — that he never intended to facilitate, and so does not bear responsibility for, a drug deal carried out with a gun. A defendant manifests that greater intent, and incurs the greater liability of § 924(c), when he chooses to participate in a drug transaction knowing it will involve a firearm; but he makes no such choice when that knowledge comes too late for him to be reasonably able to act upon it.[10]

## III

Under these principles, the District Court erred in instructing the jury, because it did not explain that Rosemond needed advance knowledge of a firearm's presence. Recall that the court stated that Rosemond was guilty of aiding and abetting if "[he] knew his cohort used a firearm in the drug trafficking crime." In telling the jury to consider merely whether Rosemond "knew his cohort used a firearm," the court did not direct the jury to determine *when* Rosemond obtained the requisite knowledge. So, for example, the jury could have convicted even if Rosemond first learned of the gun when it was fired and he took no further action to advance the crime.

Accordingly, we vacate the judgment below and remand the case for further proceedings consistent with this opinion.

*It is so ordered.*

[The dissenting opinion of Justice Alito, joined by Justice Thomas, has been omitted.]

---

[10] Our holding is grounded in the distinctive intent standard for aiding and abetting someone else's act — in the words of Judge Hand, that a defendant must not just "in some sort associate himself with the venture" . . . but also "participate in it as in something that he wishes to bring about" and "seek by his action to make it succeed." For the reasons just given, we think that intent standard cannot be satisfied if a defendant charged with aiding and abetting a § 924(c) offense learns of a gun only after he can realistically walk away — i.e., when he has no opportunity to decide whether "he wishes to bring about" (or make succeed) an *armed* drug transaction, rather than a simple drug crime. And because a defendant's prior knowledge is part of the intent required to aid and abet a § 924(c) offense, the burden to prove it resides with the Government.

**Post-Case Follow-Up**

In *Rosemond*, the Supreme Court addressed the application of accomplice liability principles to an offense that involves multiple criminal acts. With respect to the conduct required to be an accomplice, the Court held that providing assistance to any component of the offense suffices. The *mens rea*, by contrast, requires "a state of mind extending to the *entire crime*." The defendant must intend to assist in the criminal venture — it must be "something that he wishes to bring about." Once intent with respect to the criminal venture is established, the defendant is an accomplice to at least some crime. In *Rosemond*, the defendant was at least an accomplice to the attempted sale of the marijuana. For Rosemond to be guilty of the additional crime of using or carrying a firearm in furtherance of a drug crime, the Court held that "advance knowledge" that one of his confederates would carry a gun is required.

## Rosemond: *Real Life Applications*

1. Pierre lived in Columbia, Missouri. Pierre's friends Laurent and Jermaine were thieves who made most of their money stealing expensive jewelry from people's houses when they were not at home. Laurent and Jermaine were always in search of potential targets.

   One day, Pierre told Laurent and Jermaine that he thought his neighbor Bernard might make a good target. Bernard sold illegal drugs for a living. As a result, Bernard typically stored large amounts of cash in a safe in his house. In addition, Pierre knew that Bernard often left his garage door open. Finally, Pierre believed that Bernard would be unlikely to report a theft to the police, given Bernard's line of work. The only problem was that to get into the safe, Laurent and Jermaine would need Bernard's assistance.

   After hearing Pierre's pitch, Laurent and Jermaine decided to break into Bernard's house. They asked Pierre to help them plan the robbery and Pierre agreed. Pierre could see Bernard's bedroom from his house. One night, Pierre watched Bernard turn off his bedroom lights and texted Laurent and Jermaine to let them know that Bernard had gone to sleep. Thirty minutes later, Laurent and Jermaine broke into Bernard's house through the garage. They went to Bernard's bedroom, pointed a gun at Bernard's face, and then woke him up. At gunpoint, Bernard opened up his safe and gave Laurent and Jermaine the $2,000 inside of it.

   Contrary to Pierre's assumption, Bernard decided to report the incident to the police. Bernard watched Laurent and Jermaine drive away from his house and wrote down the license place, which he gave to the police. The police arrested Laurent, Jermaine, and Pierre.

Pierre was charged with first-degree robbery as an accomplice. Under Missouri law, first-degree robbery occurs where a person commits a robbery with the use of "a deadly weapon." Second-degree robbery occurs where a person steals property through the use or threat of force but without a deadly weapon. In a statement to the police, Laurent said that he and Jermaine never specifically discussed the use of a gun with Pierre. Laurent told the police that Pierre knew that they would need to force Bernard to open the safe. In addition, Laurent said that Pierre knew Laurent owned a gun and that Laurent had used the gun in a previous robbery. Assume that Laurent's statement to the police is admissible at Pierre's trial.

**a.** At trial, Pierre requests a jury instruction that, in order to be convicted of first-degree robbery, the government must prove that he had advance knowledge that one of his confederates would use a deadly weapon to commit the robbery. In support, Pierre cites the Supreme Court's decision in *Rosemond*. You are the trial judge. Would you grant Pierre's request?

**b.** Assume that the trial judge grants Pierre's request. You are the prosecutor. Do you believe there is enough evidence to prove beyond a reasonable doubt that Pierre had the requisite advance knowledge?

## F. THE NATURAL AND PROBABLE CONSEQUENCES DOCTRINE

The Supreme Court observed in footnote 7 of its opinion in *Rosemond* that some jurisdictions extend accomplice liability to crimes that are "the 'natural and probable consequence' of the crime the defendant intended to abet." The Court found that the natural and probable consequences doctrine was "not implicated" in *Rosemond*, however, because "no one contends that a § 924(c) violation is a natural and probable consequence of simple drug trafficking." In cases where the natural and probable consequences doctrine is at issue, it can sometimes extend accomplice liability well beyond its normal application.

Under the **natural and probable consequences doctrine**, "a defendant may be held criminally responsible as an accomplice not only for the crime he or she intended to aid and abet (the target crime), but also for any other crime that is the 'natural and probable consequence' of the target crime." *People v. Prettyman*, 14 Cal. 4th 248, 261 (1996). "This 'in for a penny, in for a pound' basis of liability has been roundly criticized by academic and judicial commentators for at least half a century," on the ground that it extends guilt beyond the accomplice's culpability. Wesley M. Oliver, *Limiting Criminal Law's "In for a Penny, in for a Pound" Doctrine*, 103 Geo. L.J. Online 8, 9 (2013). The Model Penal Code and a majority of jurisdictions reject the natural and probable consequences rule. But it has been adopted in a substantial minority of jurisdictions (20, according to a 2008 survey), often by judicial decision. John F. Decker, *The Mental State*

*Requirement for Accomplice Liability in American Criminal Law*, 60 S.C. L. Rev. 237, 312-56 (2008).

**Case Preview**

## *People v. Montes*

In the next case, the court applies the natural and probable consequences doctrine to uphold a defendant's conviction for attempted murder.

As you read the decision, consider the following questions:

1. What is the legal standard for determining whether one crime is the "natural and probable consequence" of another crime?
2. Why was the natural and probable consequences rule satisfied in this case?

## *People v. Montes*
### 74 Cal. App. 4th (1999)

BEDSWORTH, J.

Juan Alexander Montes was convicted of attempted murder, assault with a semi-automatic firearm, assault with a deadly weapon, exhibiting a firearm, street terrorism, and attendant firearm use and gang enhancements. On appeal, he contends the evidence is insufficient to support some of the counts and the trial court's aiding and abetting instructions were flawed. We affirm.

One night, Montes and several other members of the Orange Krazy Mexicans gang (OKM) were hanging out in the parking lot of a fast food restaurant when Jorge Garcia pulled in with Eduardo Flores and two females. Garcia expected trouble because he used to belong to a gang called the Varrio Pelones Locos (VPL), a rival of OKM. In fact, two months earlier, Montes and another OKM member had confronted Garcia and Flores at the very same restaurant. During that meeting, Montes hit Flores in the head with a stick.

This time Montes greeted Garcia by dousing his car with soda and yelling, "Fuck VPL." Then, after Garcia parked and exited his car, Montes and his cohorts quickly surrounded him. Garcia pulled a switchblade, but Montes had a three-foot chain, which Garcia described as "kind of thick" and bigger than a wallet chain. Doubling the chain over, Montes struck Garcia on his right shoulder as the other OKM'ers closed in on him.

To save Garcia, Flores yelled something about a gun, which caused the OKM'ers to retreat to their car. Flores then retrieved a pipe from Garcia's car and threw it towards the OKM'ers. After that, Flores and Garcia got in their car and prepared to drive away. However, before they could do so, OKM member Arturo Cuevas retrieved a gun from a nearby vehicle, ran up to Garcia and shot him several times.

Detective Gary Nelson, the prosecution's gang expert, testified members of criminal street gangs such as OKM are expected to back each other up in confrontational situations. This entails using "whatever weapons are handy" to protect a fellow gang member and establish dominance over another gang. Nelson believed the circumstances of this case fit the classic pattern of how "a gang crime escalates from merely yelling something, throwing something, to shooting."

Instructing the jury on aiding and abetting, the trial court stated Montes could be convicted of attempted murder if that offense was a natural and probable consequence of (1) assault with a semiautomatic firearm, (2) simple assault, or (3) breach of the peace for fighting in public. Montes claims the latter two offenses were improperly included as predicate offenses because there is no evidence that he knew Cuevas was armed. We reject this claim.

In *People v. Prettyman* (1996) 14 Cal. 4th 248, the [California] Supreme Court reiterated the well-established principle that ". . . a defendant may be held criminally responsible as an accomplice not only for the crime he or she intended to aid and abet (the target crime), but also for any other crime that is the 'natural and probable consequence' of the target crime." The court noted that decisions applying this rule "most commonly involved situations in which a defendant assisted or encouraged a confederate to commit an assault with a deadly weapon or with potentially deadly force, and the confederate not only assaulted but also murdered the victim. In those instances, the courts generally had no difficulty in upholding a murder conviction, reasoning that the jury could reasonably conclude that the killing of the victim was a 'natural and probable consequence' of the assault that the defendant aided and abetted."

On the other hand, it is rarely, if ever, true that "an aider and abettor can become liable for the commission of a very serious crime committed by the aider and abettor's confederate [where] the target offense contemplated by his aiding and abetting [was] trivial." "Murder, for instance, is *not* the natural and probable consequence of trivial activities. To trigger application of the natural and probable consequences doctrine, there must be a close connection between the target crime aided and abetted and the offense actually committed."

Under the circumstances presented in this case, the targeted offenses of simple assault and breach of the peace for fighting in public were not trivial. They arose in the context of an ongoing rivalry between OKM and VPL during which the two gangs acted violently toward each other. This feud spilled over on the night in question when Montes and his gang confronted Garcia in the parking lot. From the start, the confrontation was punctuated by threats and weaponry. And when it was clear the chain-wielding Montes and his gang were too much for Garcia, Flores shouted something about a gun, which in turn prompted Cuevas to obtain a firearm and shoot Garcia.

As gang expert Nelson explained, these facts represent a textbook example of how a gang confrontation can easily escalate from mere shouting and shoving to gun fire. There can be little question that the target offenses of assault and breach of the peace were closely connected to the shooting. Nonetheless, relying on *People v. Butts* (1965) 236 Cal. App. 2d 817, Montes insists he cannot be held responsible for Cuevas' conduct because he did not know Cuevas had a gun.

In *Butts,* defendants Otwell and Butts were involved in a brawl with a group of strangers. Although the altercation began as a fistfight, Otwell eventually pulled a knife and fatally stabbed one of his foes. The court decided Butts could not be held responsible for the killing under aiding and abetting principles because there was "no evidence that [he] advised and encouraged use of a knife, that he had advance knowledge of Otwell's wrongful purpose to use a knife or that he shared Otwell's criminal intent to resort to a dangerous weapon." In other words, Butts was off the hook for the stabbing because he was aware only of a fistfight, not a knife fight.

[*Butts* is distinguishable from this case.] [For the natural and probable consequences doctrine to apply,] "[t]he only requirement is that defendant share the intent to facilitate the *target* criminal act and that the crime committed be a foreseeable consequence of the target act."

*Butts* is . . . more than three decades old, a remnant of a different social era, when street fighters commonly relied on fists alone to settle disputes. Unfortunately, as this case illustrates, the nature of modern gang warfare is quite different. When rival gangs clash today, verbal taunting can quickly give way to physical violence and gun fire. No one immersed in the gang culture is unaware of these realities, and we see no reason the courts should turn a blind eye to them. Given the great potential for escalating violence during gang confrontations, it is immaterial whether Montes specifically knew Cuevas had a gun. [T]he circumstances in this case were such that it was reasonably foreseeable the initial confrontation would quickly escalate to gun fire. We therefore uphold Montes' convictions.

The judgment is affirmed.

---

**Post-Case Follow-Up**

For the natural and probable consequences doctrine to apply, the government must first establish that the defendant is guilty of committing an offense as an accomplice. In the language of the natural and probable consequences doctrine, that offense — the one that the defendant intended to assist in committing — is referred to as the target offense. Under the natural and probable consequences rule, in addition to the target offense, the defendant can also be convicted of "any other crime that is the 'natural and probable consequence' of the target crime." To be considered a natural and probable consequence, the crime must be "a foreseeable consequence of the target act."

---

## Montes: *Real Life Applications*

**1.** Now that we have read more about the natural and probable consequences rule, do you think the Supreme Court was correct that the natural and probable consequences rule was "not implicated" in *Rosemond*? If so, what differentiates the facts of *Montes* from those of *Rosemond* as it relates to the natural and probable consequences rule?

2. Return to the facts from Question 1 in the *Rosemond Real Life Applications.* If Missouri were to apply the natural and probable consequences doctrine, do you think that Pierre should be convicted on that theory? If so, do you think this means that the natural and probable consequences rule and *Rosemond* are incompatible with one another?

## Chapter Summary

- Accomplice liability addresses the circumstance of a person who helps someone else commit a crime — serving as the getaway driver in a robbery, for example. An accomplice is convicted of the crime that she helped to commit (e.g., robbery). There is no separate crime of "being an accomplice" or "aiding and abetting."

- To convict someone of committing a crime as an accomplice, the prosecutor must prove (1) that a crime was committed, (2) that the defendant intended to facilitate commission of that crime, and (3) that the defendant did some act to assist in the commission of the crime.

- Although accomplice liability principles require proof that a crime was committed, it is *not* necessary for prosecutors to convict the principal of the crime in order to successfully prosecute an accomplice.

- Accomplice liability's *mens rea* element requires proof that the defendant intended to help the principal commit the offense. Generally speaking, knowledge alone is not enough.

- To be guilty of committing a crime as an accomplice, the defendant must also have actually provided some assistance. Physical presence at the crime is not enough, but any assistance, however small, will suffice. This includes words of encouragement.

- Applying accomplice liability principles to compound offenses can become tricky. For example, imagine that Adam drives Dave to a drug sale with the intent of helping Dave sell drugs; to Adam's surprise, Dave brings a gun with him to the sale. Adam is guilty of distribution of a controlled substance as an accomplice, but can he also be convicted of possessing a firearm in furtherance of a drug trafficking crime? In *Rosemond v. United States*, 572 U.S. 65 (2014), the Supreme Court held that to be guilty of possessing a firearm in furtherance of a drug trafficking crime as an accomplice, the defendant must intend to assist in the commission of a drug trafficking crime and have at least "advance knowledge" that one of his confederates would carry a gun.

- Under the natural and probable consequences doctrine, an accomplice can be convicted of any crimes that are the "natural and probable consequence" of the crime the defendant intended to assist. The natural and probable consequences doctrine is often criticized and a majority of states have rejected it. But it is the law in a sizeable minority of states.

## Applying the Concepts

1. An off-duty police officer observed a man wearing a ski mask exit the passenger side of a car and run into a convenience store while carrying a gun. A driver, Dave, remained inside the car. The off-duty officer called the police station and an on-duty officer who was nearby immediately drove to the scene. The on-duty officer arrived just as the man wearing the ski mask was leaving the store. The on-duty officer drove in front of Dave's car, blocking it in. The man in the ski mask ran away and was able to escape arrest. The police arrested Dave on charges of robbery as an accomplice.

   At the police station, Dave waived his *Miranda* rights and agreed to talk with the police. Dave admitted that he drove to the convenience store to help in a robbery but he refused to tell the police who the man in the ski mask was. The police continued their investigation. They interviewed the convenience store owner, who told the police that the robber had threatened him with a gun and stolen $200 in cash. The police found evidence in Dave's phone that suggested the person who was wearing the ski mask was a man named Bob. The police arrested Bob and charged him with robbery.

   Bob's case went to trial before Dave's case. The jury found Bob not guilty of the robbery. Two weeks after Bob's acquittal, Dave's case goes to trial. What will be the most likely result?

2. Adam is friends with Dan, who makes his living illegally selling marijuana. Although it is legal to possess marijuana in the jurisdiction where Adam and Dan live, it is only legal to sell it with a license from the state, which Dan does not have. One day, Adam and Dan decide to go see a movie together. Adam and Dan walk to the movie. On the way to the movie, Dan receives a text message from one of his clients asking to buy an eighth of an ounce of marijuana. Dan tells Adam he needs to make a quick stop on the way to the movie "to take care of some business." Adam does not object. Dan stops by his client's apartment and sells him an eighth of an ounce of marijuana. Adam waits outside during the transaction.

   Unknown to Dan, his client had recently become an informant for the police after being arrested for possessing cocaine. As soon as Dan completes the sale, he is arrested by an officer who was waiting inside of the client's apartment. A different officer arrests Adam outside of the building. Adam is charged with distribution of marijuana as an accomplice.

   Is Adam more likely to be acquitted or to be found guilty?

3. Jackson and his friend Chris were hanging out on Jackson's porch at around 8:30 P.M. one night. Jackson's next-door neighbor, Stanley, left his house to run an errand.

   Ten minutes later, Jackson and Chris saw a man named Tiny walking toward them. Tiny, who lived a few blocks from Jackson, was known as a bully around the neighborhood. The only thing small about Tiny was his name. Tiny was 6'5" and weighed 300 pounds. Tiny walked up to Jackson and Chris and said, "Did you guys see Stanley leave his house a few minutes ago? Stanley owes me some money. I'm going to break into his house and steal some of his stuff to teach him a lesson. If you see Stanley coming back, I want you to whistle so I can get out of there."

Jackson and Chris told Tiny that they did not want to help him out. Tiny walked closer to Jackson and Chris and said, "You don't understand. I wasn't *asking* you to help me out. I was *telling* you to help me out." Tiny then gave Chris and Jackson a menacing look while pounding his fist into his hand in a threatening manner.

Chris said, "OK, I'll do what you say."

"Good," said Tiny, and he walked over to Stanley's driveway. Tiny was pleasantly surprised to find that one of the windows to Stanley's house was unlocked. Tiny opened the unlocked window and pulled himself into Stanley's house. Less than a minute later, Chris saw Stanley's car coming down the street. Chris whistled loudly. Tiny heard Chris's whistle and ran out of Stanley's house through the back door, and escaped by hopping over Stanley's fence. Stanley ran out of his car and into his house. Stanley looked around his house and although it did not appear that anything was missing, he called the police anyway. Assume that Tiny committed burglary when he broke into Stanley's house. Is Chris guilty of committing burglary as an accomplice?

4.  Johnny Utah was an FBI agent working undercover as part of a bank robbery investigation. The robbers wore masks of former Presidents of the United States and had robbed several banks without getting caught. The primary suspects were a group of surfers: Bodhi, Roach, Grommet, and Nathaniel (collectively "Bodhi's group"). Utah's undercover assignment was to pose as a surfer. Utah had been posing as a surfer for approximately three months and had successfully befriended Bodhi's group.

During the investigation, Utah's FBI partner Detective Pappas spent much of his time following Bodhi and observing his actions. One day, Pappas followed Bodhi and Grommet to National Bank. Pappas saw Bodhi and Grommet pace in front of the bank and talk with one another for 5 minutes, at which point the two went inside the bank where they stayed for 20 minutes. After emerging from the bank, Bodhi and Grommet returned to their car and took pictures of the bank for approximately 2 to 3 minutes before departing. Based on his observations, Pappas believed that Bodhi and Grommet might have been scoping out National Bank as a target for a possible robbery.

Pappas called Utah and told him what he'd observed. Pappas and Utah decided to park across the street from National Bank the next day to keep an eye out for Bodhi's group. After waiting in the car for approximately four hours, Utah observed Roach's vehicle pull up beside National Bank and park in a 15-minute "loading" zone. Bodhi and Grommet exited the car while Roach stayed inside the car in the driver's seat. Worried that Bodhi and Grommet might be planning to rob the bank, Utah immediately got out of his car, held up his badge and a gun, and yelled, "Don't move!" Bodhi and Grommet took one look at Utah and ran. Utah chased after the pair on foot.

While Utah took off after Bodhi and Grommet, Roach remained in his car. Pappas arrested Roach.

a. Assume that Bodhi and Grommet committed the crime of attempted robbery. Can Roach be convicted of attempted robbery as an accomplice?

b. Assume for purposes of this question that shortly after Bodhi and Grommet took off running, Bodhi pulled out a gun and fired it at Utah. The bullet struck Utah in the leg. If Bodhi committed the crime of attempted murder, could Roach be convicted of attempted murder as an accomplice?

## Criminal Law in Practice

1. Many states have decided not to adopt the natural and probable consequences doctrine. Look up whether your state applies the natural and probable consequences doctrine. (If you live in California, where *People v. Montes* was decided, you should look up the answer for a neighboring state of your choice.)

2. A legislator in your state has filed a bill to limit application of the natural and probable consequences doctrine. The bill's text reads as follows:

   A person cannot be convicted of murder or attempted murder as an aider and abettor under a natural and probable consequences theory unless the prosecutor proves that one of the following is true:
       the person was the actual killer; or
       the person (who was not the actual killer) was a "major participant" in the target crime and acted with reckless indifference to life; or
       the victim was a peace officer engaged in the performance of their duties.

   a. You are an aide to a state legislator. Would you advise your boss to vote in favor of this bill?

   b. Look back at the facts of *People v. Montes* on page 402 of this chapter. Under this proposed bill, could Montes have been convicted of attempted murder?

3. Consider the following facts, which come from *Regan v. State*, 2015 WY 62, ¶¶ 3-9:

   On October 26, 2012, Regan and his roommate Shayne Trujillo drove from Denver[, Colorado] to Gillette[, Wyoming]. A six-year veteran of the Gillette Police Department, Officer Troy Cyr, pulled them over after they stopped at a yield sign because there was no traffic on the roadway to yield to, and because the officer could not tell whether the vehicle had a rear license plate. Regan was the driver and owner. When Officer Cyr approached his window, he immediately smelled raw marijuana and requested that a drug dog be dispatched. Officer Vos arrived on the scene, spoke to Officer Cyr, and explained to Regan and Trujillo why he was there. He also smelled marijuana before retrieving his dog, Jordy, from his patrol vehicle. Jordy alerted at the front passenger door, signaling that it had detected the odor of a controlled substance in the car.

Officer Vos then directed Trujillo to get out of the car, looked inside, and saw two glass jars containing what he recognized as marijuana on the passenger floorboard. After further inspection of the vehicle's interior, he discovered a plastic grocery bag, Ziploc sandwich bags, and a large white plastic bin in the passenger and cargo portions of the vehicle. Each contained clumps of a green leafy substance that he recognized as marijuana. The total weight of the marijuana was approximately one and a half pounds. Vos also found paraphernalia commonly associated with the sale of marijuana and $1,000 in cash in the glove box.

The officers arrested Regan and Trujillo and took them to the Gillette police station, where Regan voluntarily consented to an interview. Officer Greg Brothers interviewed Regan, who gave the following account. While still in Denver, Regan saw Trujillo load marijuana into his vehicle. He told Officer Brothers that he had expressly rejected Trujillo's offer to join in Trujillo's plan to make money distributing marijuana because "it wasn't worth the risk."

When they arrived in Gillette, Trujillo directed Regan to three different locations, and at each one Trujillo got out of the car and delivered marijuana. Regan remained in the vehicle at each stop. He gave the interviewing officer detailed descriptions of each location and the amount of marijuana Trujillo delivered at each stop. He showed him the locations on a map, and then helped officers identify them in an unmarked police car.

Trujillo confirmed to officers that over a pound of marijuana in the car belonged exclusively to him, and that no one else had anything to do with it.

**a.** Regan is charged with possession of marijuana with the intent to distribute as an accomplice.

You are Regan's trial attorney. The prosecutor has offered a plea deal in which your client would plead guilty to simple possession of marijuana, with a recommended sentence of one year of probation. Assume that if Regan were to be convicted of possession of marijuana with the intent to distribute, his likely sentence would be four years of probation. Would you recommend that your client accept this deal?

**b.** If you were the prosecutor in this case, would you have charged Regan with possession of marijuana with the intent to distribute as an accomplice?

# Conspiracy

Conspiracy is a controversial offense, and one that can sometimes raise especially difficult legal problems. At its core, conspiracy makes it a crime to enter into an agreement to commit some other crime. Conspirators do not have to carry out their plan, or even come close to carrying out their plan, to be guilty of the crime of conspiracy — conspiracy criminalizes the making of the plan itself.

Although conspiracy is a crime in every jurisdiction, some commentators have argued that the offense should be abolished or significantly narrowed. Critics of the crime of conspiracy contend that punishing people for a mere agreement to commit a crime risks punishing people for their words alone or for "associating with others who are found culpable." Phillip E. Johnson, *The Unnecessary Crime of Conspiracy*, 61 Cal. L. Rev. 1137, 1139 (1973). On occasion, some judges have expressed sympathy with these criticisms. But legislators have not been convinced, so the crime remains part of the criminal code in every jurisdiction.

## A. OVERVIEW AND ELEMENTS OF THE OFFENSE

A person commits the crime of **conspiracy** if he (1) agrees with another person to commit a crime, and (2) does so with the intent to agree and the intent that the contemplated crime be committed. In some jurisdictions, and at common law, these are the only elements of the crime of conspiracy. Today, some jurisdictions also require proof of a third element: an overt act. An **overt act** is any act in furtherance of the conspiracy done by any member of the conspiracy.

## Key Concepts

- What are the elements of the crime of conspiracy?
- What kind of evidence is sufficient to prove a defendant entered into a criminal agreement in a conspiracy prosecution?
- What principles guide courts in conspiracy cases that involve large numbers of participants engaged in an ongoing venture?
- Under what circumstances is a conspirator liable for crimes committed by her co-conspirators in jurisdictions that have adopted the rule articulated in *Pinkerton v. United States*, 328 U.S. 640 (1946)?

The fundamentals of each element of the offense are well established and relatively straightforward. First, conspiracy requires that the defendant have entered into a criminal agreement — that is, an agreement to commit one or more crimes — with one or more other persons. The agreement does not need to be a formal one; in fact, it is possible for a defendant to be part of the same conspiratorial agreement with someone she has never met. As the California Supreme Court put it, the parties to a conspiracy "need not *expressly* agree at all: To prove an agreement, it is not necessary to establish the parties met and expressly agreed; rather, a criminal conspiracy may be shown by direct or circumstantial evidence that the parties positively or tacitly came to a mutual understanding to accomplish the act and unlawful design." *People v. Johnson*, 57 Cal. 4th 250, 264 (2013).

The *mens rea* for conspiracy is twofold: an intent to agree, and an intent that the target offense that is the object of the conspiracy be committed. In the context of conspiracy, intent means that it was the defendant's conscious object; "mere knowledge of or acquiescence in the conspiracy is not a sufficient basis for a finding of guilt." *United States v. Guillette*, 547 F.2d 743, 750 (2d Cir. 1976). Not surprisingly, in most cases, if the prosecutor is able to prove that the defendant entered into an agreement, she will also be able to prove the requisite mental state.

In addition to an intentional agreement, some jurisdictions require an overt act. The overt act element is easily met in almost every case. An overt act is any act that is performed in furtherance of the agreement — literally *any* outward act that is done in furtherance of the criminal objective can qualify, no matter how preliminary. Moreover, the overt act can be committed by *any* member of the conspiracy. This is an especially notable and unusual feature since it means that the defendant does not need to have personally performed an overt act for this element to be met.

## Conspiracy, Attempts, and Accomplice Liability

Conspiracy shares some traits with both attempts and accomplice liability.

Like attempts, the crime of conspiracy is an inchoate offense — it punishes preparatory acts, rather than completed conduct. But conspiracy sweeps more broadly than the law of attempts because it applies much earlier in the criminal process. Recall that to be guilty of an attempt to commit a crime, the defendant must have either taken a substantial step toward the commission of that crime or have come dangerously close

By criminalizing the mere agreement to commit a crime, conspiracy can apply to very preliminary acts. Indeed, in its broadest application, the crime of conspiracy can "come[] close to punishing thoughts and speech alone." Laurent Sacharoff, *Conspiracy as Contract*, 50 U.C. Davis L. Rev. 405, 407 (2016). Consider a hypothetical example. Two friends, Dan and Kris, are college students majoring in chemistry. One night while having dinner on campus they discuss their financial troubles. Dan, who had been re-watching the television series *Breaking Bad*, suggests to Kris that they try manufacturing and selling methamphetamine to make some money. Kris replies, "That sounds like a great idea to me. Let's do it." The friends discuss the idea some more and agree to pursue it. After getting home from dinner, Kris searches online for information about the process for manufacturing methamphetamine. Notice that at this point, neither Dan nor Kris could be convicted of attempt to manufacture methamphetamine — the conduct is too preliminary, even under the relatively forgiving substantial step test for attempts (which was covered in Chapter 7). Likewise, neither Dan nor Kris would be guilty of committing a crime as an accomplice. But both could be convicted of conspiracy to manufacture methamphetamine. Why? Because Dan and Kris have agreed to commit a crime, with the intent to agree and to carry out the criminal act. Kris's online search was done in furtherance of the agreement, and so constitutes an overt act. As a result, each of the elements of the crime of conspiracy has been met for both Dan and Kris.

In our hypothetical, Dan and Kris are both guilty of conspiracy under the letter of the law. But it is rare to see a prosecution in these kinds of circumstances in practice. For one thing, conspirators usually try to hide their plans from law enforcement; even the most careless conspirator is not likely to be caught immediately after entering into a criminal agreement. And, in the unlikely event the police learn of a conspiracy at its earliest stages, they have a strong incentive not to intervene right away. After all, the earlier the police intervene, the harder it will be for the prosecutor to convince a jury that the alleged criminal plan was serious, and not just loose talk among friends. For similar reasons, although conspiracy is an inchoate offense — meaning that it punishes preparatory acts that have not yet caused any harm — in many conspiracy prosecutions, the defendants will have carried out their plan. This is because conspirators are much more likely to get caught by the police after they have committed the target offense than during the planning stages. Still, in theory and occasionally in real life, a person can be convicted of conspiracy based on agreeing to a vague criminal plan that never comes remotely close to fruition.

In cases where conspirators are caught after they have already committed their planned crime, they will be guilty of *both* conspiracy and the target offense. Imagine that our hypothetical Dan and Kris continue with their plan and actually begin to manufacture methamphetamine. If the police catch them, Dan and Kris can be convicted of *both* manufacture of methamphetamine (the target offense of the conspiracy) *and* conspiracy to manufacture methamphetamine. This is because in most jurisdictions (and in contrast to the law of attempts), the crime of conspiracy does *not* merge with the target offense.

to success (depending on the jurisdiction). Conspiracy requires only an *agreement* to commit the crime and, in some jurisdictions, an overt act. The California Supreme Court has compared conspiracy and attempts this way: "Criminal activity exists along a continuum. At its conclusion is the commission of a completed crime. The principle of attempt recognizes that some measure of criminal culpability may attach before a defendant actually completes the intended crime. Conspiracy law attaches culpability at an earlier point along the continuum than attempt. The crime of conspiracy punishes the agreement itself and does not require the commission of the substantive offense that is the object of the conspiracy." *People v. Johnson*, 57 Cal. 4th 250, 258 (2013).

Conspiracy is also similar to accomplice liability in that it punishes group criminality. In order for someone to be an accomplice or to commit the crime of conspiracy, at least one other party must be involved. While many conspiracy cases will also give rise to accomplice liability, it is possible to be guilty of a crime as an accomplice without also being guilty of the crime of conspiracy. Spontaneous encouragement can make one an accomplice to a crime. But spontaneous encouragement alone does not give rise to conspiracy liability because conspiracy requires an agreement to commit a crime. Another important difference between accomplice liability and conspiracy is that an accomplice is guilty of whatever crime he helped the principal commit. An accomplice to robbery is guilty of robbery; there is no crime of being an accomplice. Conspiracy, by contrast, is itself a stand-alone crime.

## Case Preview

### *United States v. Brown*

The elements of conspiracy are easily stated, but they can often be quite difficult to apply in practice. One reason for this is that conspiracy punishes the agreement to commit a crime, but people rarely memorialize their criminal agreements. As one court put it: "Whereas an agreement in a business con-text may be manifested with precision, namely, through a contract, a correspondence, or conspicuous dialogue, an agreement in the criminal realm typically would result from more clandestine and ambiguous activity." *People v. Reyes*, 31 N.Y.3d 930, 932 (2018). This means that prosecutors often must rely on circumstantial evidence to prove an agreement. In the next case, the court considers whether the circumstantial evidence presented by the government was sufficient to prove the defendant agreed to commit a crime.

As you read the decision, consider the following questions:

1. What is the evidence that Brown agreed to commit a crime?
2. Do you agree with the court's conclusion that this evidence was sufficient to sustain Brown's conviction?

### *United States v. Brown*
#### 776 F.2d 397 (2d Cir. 1985)

FRIENDLY, J.

This is another case, *see United States v. Peterson*, 768 F.2d 64 (2 Cir. 1985), where the federal narcotics laws have been invoked with respect to the New York City Police Department's Operation Pressure Point in Harlem. Here, as in *Peterson*, Officer William Grimball, acting under cover as an addict, procured a "joint" of heroin, and a backup team promptly pounced on those thought to have been involved in the sale.

The indictment, in the District Court for the Southern District of New York, contained two counts. Count One charged appellant Ronald Brown and a codefendant, Gregory Valentine, with conspiring to distribute and to possess with intent to distribute heroin in violation of 21 U.S.C. § 846. Count Two charged them with distribution of heroin in violation of 21 U.S.C. §§ 812, 841(a)(1), 841(b)(1)(A), and 18 U.S.C. § 2. After a three day trial, the jury convicted Brown on Count One but was unable to reach a verdict on Count Two.[1] This appeal followed.

Officer Grimball was the Government's principal witness. He testified that early in the evening of October 9, 1984, he approached Gregory Valentine on the corner of 115th Street and Eighth Avenue and asked him for a joint of "D."[2] Valentine asked

---

[1] Valentine was a fugitive at the time of trial.
[2] The officer explained that a "joint" is a street term for a Harlem quarter, or $40 worth of heroin, and that "D" is a street term for heroin.

Grimball whom he knew around the street. Grimball asked if Valentine knew Scott. He did not. Brown "came up" and Valentine said, "He wants a joint, but I don't know him." Brown looked at Grimball and said, "He looks okay to me." Valentine then said, "Okay. But I am going to leave it somewhere and you [meaning Officer Grimball] can pick it up." Brown interjected, "You don't have to do that. Just go and get it for him. He looks all right to me." After looking again at Grimball, Brown said, "He looks all right to me" and "I will wait right here."

Valentine then said, "Okay. Come on with me around to the hotel." Grimball followed him to 300 West 116th Street, where Valentine instructed him, "Sit on the black car and give me a few minutes to go up and get it." Valentine requested and received $40, which had been prerecorded, and then said, "You are going to take care of me for doing this for you, throw some dollars my way?," to which Grimball responded, "Yeah."

Valentine then entered the hotel and shortly returned. The two went back to 115th Street and Eighth Avenue, where Valentine placed a cigarette box on the hood of a blue car. Grimball picked up the cigarette box and found a glassine envelope containing white powder, stipulated to be heroin. Grimball placed $5 of prerecorded buy money in the cigarette box, which he replaced on the hood. Valentine picked up the box and removed the $5. Grimball returned to his car and made a radio transmission to the backup field team that "the buy had went down" and informed them of the locations of the persons involved. Brown and Valentine were arrested. Valentine was found to possess two glassine envelopes of heroin and the $5 of prerecorded money. Brown was in possession of $31 of his own money; no drugs or contraband were found on him. The $40 of marked buy money was not recovered, and no arrests were made at the hotel.

[At trial, Officer Grimball testified as an expert witness that] the typical drug buy in the Harlem area involved two to five people. As a result of frequent police sweeps, Harlem drug dealers were becoming so cautious that they employed "people who act as steerers and the steerer's responsibility is basically to determine whether or not you are actually an addict or a user of heroin and they are also used to screen you to see if there is any possibility of you being a cop looking for a bulge or some indication that would give them that you are not actually an addict. And a lot of the responsibility relies [sic] on them to determine whether or not the drug buy is going to go down or not."

## SUFFICIENCY OF THE EVIDENCE

In considering the sufficiency of the evidence, we begin with some preliminary observations. One is that, in testing sufficiency, "the relevant question is whether, after viewing the evidence in the light most favorable to the prosecution, *any* rational trier of fact could have found the essential elements of the crime beyond a reasonable doubt." *Jackson v. Virginia*, 443 U.S. 307, 319 (1979) (emphasis in original).

The second observation is that since the jury convicted on the conspiracy count alone, the evidence must permit a reasonable juror to be convinced beyond a reasonable doubt not simply that Brown had aided and abetted the drug sale but that he had agreed to do so. On the other hand, the jury's failure to agree on the aiding and abetting charge [(Count Two)] does not operate against the Government; even an acquittal on that count would not have done so.

A review of the evidence against Brown convinces us that it was sufficient, . . . although barely so. Although Brown's mere presence at the scene of the crime and his knowledge that a crime was being committed would not have been sufficient to establish Brown's knowing participation in the conspiracy, the proof went considerably beyond that. Brown was not simply standing around while the exchanges between Officer Grimball and Valentine occurred. He came on the scene shortly after these began and Valentine immediately explained the situation to him. Brown then conferred his seal of approval on Grimball, a most unlikely event unless there was an established relationship between Brown and Valentine. Finally, Brown took upon himself the serious responsibility of telling Valentine to desist from his plan to reduce the risks by not handing the heroin directly to Grimball. A rational mind could take this as bespeaking the existence of an agreement whereby Brown was to have the authority to command, or at least to persuade. Brown's remark, "Just go and get it for him," permits inferences that Brown knew where the heroin was to be gotten, that he knew that Valentine knew this, and that Brown and Valentine had engaged in such a transaction before.

The mere fact that these inferences were not ineluctable does not mean that they were insufficient to convince a reasonable juror beyond a reasonable doubt. When we add to the inferences that can be reasonably drawn from the facts to which Grimball testified the portion of his expert testimony about the use of steerers in street sales of narcotics, . . . we conclude that the Government offered sufficient evidence . . . for a reasonable juror to be satisfied beyond a reasonable doubt not only that Brown had acted as a steerer but that he had agreed to do so.

Affirmed.

OAKES, J. (dissenting):

While it is true that this is another $40 narcotics case, it is also a conspiracy case, and by the majority's own admission one resting on "barely" sufficient evidence. But evidence of what? An agreement — a "continuous and conscious union of wills upon a common undertaking," in the words of Note, *Developments in the Law — Criminal Conspiracy*, 72 Harv. L. Rev. 920, 926 (1959)? Not unless an inference that Brown agreed to act as a "steerer" may be drawn from the fact that he said to Valentine (three times) that Grimball "looks okay [all right] to me," as well as "[j]ust go and get it for him." [I]ndeed, Brown was apprehended after leaving the area of the crime with only thirty-one of his own dollars in his pocket, and no drugs or other contraband. He did not even stay around for another Valentine sale, though the majority infers, speculatively, that Brown and Valentine had engaged in "such a transaction before."

When . . . numerous other inferences could be drawn from the few words of conversation in which Brown is said to have engaged, I cannot believe that there is proof of *conspiracy*, or Brown's membership in it, beyond a reasonable doubt.

This case may be unique. It . . . supports Justice Jackson's reference to the history of the law of conspiracy as exemplifying, in Cardozo's phrase, the "'tendency of a principle to expand itself to the limits of its logic.'" *Krulewitch v. United States*, 336 U.S. 440, 445 (1949) (Jackson, J., concurring). But it also illustrates Cardozo's phrase at work in two other respects — the use of "expert" testimony to prove guilt and the proposition that inconsistent verdicts on different counts are immaterial. Both are carried here to their logical extremes. And the convergence of these three threads in the case of the street sale to Officer Grimball seems to me, again to borrow a phrase from Justice Jackson's *Krulewitch* concurrence, to "constitute[ ] a serious threat to fairness in our administration of justice." *Id.* at 446. If today we uphold a conspiracy to sell narcotics on the street, on this kind and amount of evidence, what conspiracies might we approve tomorrow? The majority opinion will come back to haunt us, I fear.

Although, according to the majority, . . . the evidence was "sufficient . . . although barely so," and the verdict is both inconsistent and very probably a compromise, the court permits this conspiracy conviction to stand. I fear that it thereby promotes the crime of conspiracy — "that darling of the modern prosecutor's nursery," *Harrison v. United States*, 7 F.2d 259, 263 (2d Cir. 1925) (L. Hand, J.) — to a role beyond that contemplated even by Sgt. Hawkins of *Pleas of the Crown* fame. *See* Note, *Developments in the Law — Criminal Conspiracy, supra,* at 923 & n. 14; P. Winfield, *The Chief Sources of English Legal History* 325-26 (1925). Precisely because this is another $40 narcotics case, I would draw the line. This case effectively permits prosecution of everyone connected with a street sale of narcotics to be prosecuted on two counts — a conspiracy as well as a substantive charge. And evidence showing no more than that a defendant was probably aware that a narcotics deal was about to occur will support a conspiracy conviction, our previous cases to the contrary notwithstanding.

Accordingly, I dissent.

---

**Post-Case Follow-Up**

To commit the crime of conspiracy, the government must prove that the defendant agreed with another person to commit an offense and that the defendant did so with an intent to agree to commit an offense and an intent that the offense be committed. In *Brown*, the defendant argued on appeal that there was insufficient evidence that he agreed to commit a crime. The Court of Appeals disagreed, concluding that the evidence was sufficient to allow a jury to conclude "not only that Brown had acted as a steerer but that he had agreed to do so." As a result, the court upheld Brown's conviction.

---

## Brown: *Real Life Applications*

**1.** Put yourself in the shoes of Brown's trial attorney. You are preparing your closing argument. How you would explain Brown's actions to the jury? What inference(s) would you suggest the jury draw from Brown's conversation with Valentine?

**2.** In *Brown*, the investigation was conducted by New York City police officers, but Brown was prosecuted in federal — not state — court. Imagine you were a federal prosecutor with the discretion to decide whether to bring charges against

Brown in federal court, where drug sentences are often much longer than in state court. Would you have done so? Or would you have referred the case back to the local District Attorney to prosecute it in state court? What factors would influence your decision?

---

### The Two or More Parties Requirement: Unilateral versus Bilateral Approach

Because an agreement necessarily requires more than one party, a person cannot commit the crime of conspiracy by herself. But what if one of the parties to the criminal plan is only feigning agreement? Does the crime of conspiracy require that all parties to the agreement be sincere? Today, this question arises most often in the context of undercover policing. An undercover officer might "agree" to commit a crime with a suspect as part of his investigation. The suspect's agreement is sincere, but the officer's is not. In this circumstance, can the suspect be convicted of conspiracy?

Jurisdictions are split between two different approaches to this issue — the bilateral approach and the unilateral approach.

Under the **bilateral approach**, which is the common law rule, there must be at least two sincere parties to the agreement. This means that if there are two conspirators, and one is only pretending to agree to the criminal plan (for example, because she is an undercover police officer), then the sincere party *cannot* be convicted. Arguments in favor of the bilateral approach include that it prevents against overreach by undercover officers and that it is more consistent with the chief justification for criminalizing conspiracy — that group criminality presents unique risks that warrant early intervention. As the Supreme Court put it in explaining the unique risks of criminal agreements, "[c]oncerted action both increases the likelihood that the criminal object will be successfully attained and decreases the probability that the individuals involved will depart from their path of criminality. Group association for criminal purposes often, if not normally, makes possible the attainment of ends more complex than those which one criminal could accomplish." *Callanan v. United States*, 364 U.S. 587, 593 (1961).

The **unilateral approach** is the modern rule, and it is the rule adopted by the Model Penal Code. Under the unilateral approach, a defendant can be convicted of conspiracy even if she was the only sincere party to the agreement. This means that if the defendant agrees to commit a crime with an undercover officer whose agreement is not sincere, the defendant can still be convicted of conspiracy. The rationale for the unilateral approach is that the defendant's culpability should not turn on whether the other party was sincere, but rather on the defendant's own conduct and mental state.

### Wharton's Rule

Although conspiracy criminalizes an agreement to commit a crime, in most jurisdictions there is a narrow exception that applies to offenses that by their nature can only be committed by two or more people. This exception, known as **Wharton's rule**, "prohibits prosecution of a conspiracy to commit a particular crime when the commission of that crime *requires* the participation of more than one person." *People v. Laws*, 155 Ill. 2d 208, 211 (1993). Although that quotation reflects the most common statement of Wharton's rule, it does not fully capture its meaning. As the Supreme Court of Illinois explained:

> As generally stated, the Rule can be misleading. The Rule does not prohibit prosecution of a conspiracy simply because the substantive crime involves the participation of two or more actors. It prohibits only such prosecution when the cooperative conduct inherent in the substantive crime is indistinguishable from the element of agreement in the alleged conspiracy.
>
> For example, the crimes of dueling, bigamy, adultery, and incest are the classic Wharton's Rule offenses. Commentators have added to that list the crimes of pandering, gambling, the buying and selling of contraband goods, and the giving and receiving of bribes. What is common to those crimes is a general congruence of the elemental agreement among the criminal actors and the completed substantive offense. Such congruency is crucial to the proper application of Wharton's Rule.

*Id.* at 213-14.

To understand how Wharton's rule operates, and to appreciate its importance, consider the case of a single drug sale. To complete a drug sale, the buyer and the seller must agree on the transaction — specifically, they will have to agree to the exchange of drugs for money. This is a criminal agreement. Technically, the buyer has entered into an agreement with the seller for the distribution of drugs. But if this sort of buyer-seller agreement could give rise to conspiracy liability, then every drug buyer would be guilty of conspiracy to distribute drugs by virtue of his purchase. If drug users could be convicted of conspiracy to distribute drugs simply for buying drugs, it would undermine the law's treatment of drug possession as a less serious offense than distribution. Wharton's rule prevents this outcome. Under the terminology of Wharton's rule, "the cooperative conduct inherent" between the parties to a drug sale, "is indistinguishable from the criminal agreement" that would be alleged in a conspiracy between the buyer and the seller. *Id.* at 213. For this reason, the sale of drugs *standing alone* cannot serve as the basis for a conspiracy prosecution between the buyer and seller under Wharton's rule.

Likewise, bribery *standing alone* cannot serve as the basis for a conspiracy prosecution between the person paying the bribe and the person receiving the bribe; an illegal bet *standing alone* cannot serve as the basis of a conspiracy prosecution between the person who places the bet and the person who takes the bet; and so on. What these crimes have in common — along with pandering (also known as prostitution), incest, bigamy, and the outdated common law crimes of adultery and dueling — is that, by their very nature, they cannot be committed without an agreement between two parties. The drug buyer and seller must agree to the sale; the bettor and the bookmaker must agree to the bet; the sex worker and the client must agree to the act of prostitution. Wharton's rule says that these kinds of agreements — those "inherent in the substantive crime" — cannot serve as the basis of a conspiracy prosecution.

Importantly, as the Illinois Supreme Court noted, Wharton's rule "does *not* prohibit prosecution of a conspiracy simply because the substantive crime involves the participation of two or more actors." *Id.* As a result, although a drug buyer-seller relationship *alone* does not qualify as a conspiratorial agreement, a drug buyer and seller who work together on an ongoing basis can still be prosecuted as co-conspirators in some cases. Courts have held, for example, that sales on credit or consignment (also called fronting) can establish a conspiratorial agreement between buyer and seller. Imagine that Distributor gives $2,500 worth of cocaine to Street Dealer on a consignment basis. Street Dealer sells the cocaine in smaller portions to users at a 20 percent markup. Once the sales are complete, Street Dealer pays Distributor the $2,500 and pockets the remaining money as profit. In this hypothetical, the consignment arrangement effectively makes Distributor and Street Dealer partners in business. As one court put it, "[w]ith fronting, the seller becomes the buyer's creditor, adding a dimension to the relationship that goes beyond" the mere sale of drugs. *United States v. Colon*, 549 F.3d 565, 569 (7th Cir. 2008). Because the consignment agreement between our hypothetical Distributor and Street Dealer goes beyond that inherent in the sale of drugs, Wharton's rule would not prohibit it from serving as the basis for a conspiracy prosecution.

## B. MULTIPARTY AND ONGOING CONSPIRACIES

Many criminal agreements involve a small group of participants who plan to commit a specific crime — two or three friends might agree to rob a convenience store together, for example. The crime of conspiracy can be relatively straightforward in these kinds of cases. If the friends agreed to rob the store with the requisite intent, and at least one of them committed an overt act in furtherance of the crime (such as buying ski masks), then each of them has committed the crime of conspiracy.

Other criminal agreements are much more wide-ranging. Consider a market-based criminal activity like drug distribution. Because drug crimes occur within a marketplace, drug conspiracies are often much more sprawling than robbery conspiracies. Selling drugs is an ongoing business enterprise, not a discrete crime or even a series of crimes. As a result, people engaged in the illegal drug business typically collaborate with one another more closely and regularly in comparison to people who are planning to rob a bank. Like any ongoing business venture, most participants in a drug distribution scheme work at it on a daily basis. Similarly, it often takes a large number of participants to make the drug operation work, and so each person's role may be quite specialized. Just as a clerk working at a supermarket might never meet the store's owner or top manager, a retail-level drug seller who works within a drug ring might never speak to the leader of the enterprise.

In this context, it can sometimes become almost maddeningly difficult for courts (and law students) to identify the outer boundaries of the crime of conspiracy. Part of the difficulty stems from the fact that conspiracy can be an ongoing offense. As a result, an "agreement to commit an offense does not become several conspiracies because it continues over a period of time." *Braverman v. United States*, 317 U.S. 49, 52 (1942). Likewise, "a single continuing agreement to commit several offenses" gives rise to a single count of conspiracy; not multiple counts of conspiracy. *Id.* This is so because conspiracy punishes the criminal agreement, and a single agreement can be ongoing and can embrace multiple target offenses. As the Supreme Court has put it, "[w]hether the object of a single agreement is to commit one or many crimes, it is in either case that agreement which constitutes the conspiracy which the statute punishes. The one agreement cannot be taken to be several agreements and hence several conspiracies because it envisages the violation of several statutes rather than one." *Id.* at 53. While these basic principles are well established, they can be quite difficult to apply to ongoing market-based criminal enterprises. Is the low-level employee of a drug ring guilty of a single count of conspiracy to distribute drugs with all of the other members of the enterprise, including the managers who he has never even met? Or is the employee guilty of multiple counts of conspiracy with smaller groups of people (e.g., only the people he worked with directly)?

On these questions the law, frankly, remains somewhat murky. This is due in part to the fact that the answer in any particular case can often depend on idiosyncratic details of how the criminal enterprise is arranged. The lack of clarity may also be partly because conspiracy prosecutions against a large number of individuals are comparatively infrequent, even in the drug setting. Even if, in theory, a prosecutor could charge every member of a 50-person drug ring with conspiracy in a single case, the case would be very difficult for the prosecutor to manage and for the jury to make sense of. It is typically much easier for the prosecutor to charge members of a 50-person drug ring in smaller groups, or to omit conspiracy charges altogether for some participants. And, of course, the vast majority of criminal cases are resolved by a plea agreement, not a trial. The prosecutor might decide to seek the cooperation of some members of the drug ring in order to make a stronger case against other members of the drug ring. For all of these reasons, courts do not have to grapple with disputes about how the crime of conspiracy applies to wide-ranging criminal enterprises nearly as often as one might imagine. But in the small slice of cases where these issues are presented, applying the law can be quite challenging.

**Case Preview**

## *United States v. Ulbricht*

How does the law of conspiracy apply to ongoing criminal conduct that involves a large number of participants? In the next case, *United States v. Ulbricht*, a federal trial court considered this question in the context of the prosecution of Ross Ulbricht, the operator of a website called Silk Road. According to the court, Silk Road was somewhat like an illicit version of "eBay: a seller would electronically post a good or service for sale; a buyer would electronically purchase the item; the seller would then ship or otherwise provide to the buyer the purchased item; the buyer would provide feedback; and the site operator (*i.e.*, Ulbricht) would receive a portion of the seller's revenue as a commission." The government alleged that thousands of illegal transactions took place on Silk Road, with Ulbricht receiving money for each sale. Ulbricht moved to dismiss the conspiracy charges against him, leading the court to consider "whether the conduct alleged here can serve as the basis of a criminal conspiracy — and, if so, when, how, and with whom." To answer these questions, the court reviewed and applied some of the core legal principles that guide complex conspiracy cases.

As you read the decision, consider the following questions:

1. If there is a dispute over whether there is a single conspiracy involving many parties or multiple conspiracies, what principle(s) do courts apply to resolve the issue?
2. The opinion discusses how the "chain" and "hub-and-spoke" metaphors are often used to conceptualize large conspiracies. What is the difference between a chain conspiracy and a hub-and-spoke conspiracy, and what is the significance of these metaphors in the law of conspiracy?
3. Do you think the chain and hub-and-spoke metaphors are helpful and accurate guides for conceptualizing conspiracy cases that involve a large number of alleged participants?

---

## United States v. Ulbricht
### 311 F. Supp. 3d 540 (S.D.N.Y. 2014)

FORREST, J.

On February 4, 2014, a Grand Jury sitting in the Southern District of New York returned [an] Indictment charging Ross Ulbricht ("the defendant" or "Ulbricht") on four counts for participation in a narcotics trafficking conspiracy (Count One), a continuing criminal enterprise ("CCE") (Count Two), a computer hacking conspiracy (Count Three), and a money laundering conspiracy (Count Four). Pending before the Court is the defendant's motion to dismiss all counts. For the reasons set forth below, the Court Denies the motion in its entirety.

The Government alleges that Ulbricht engaged in narcotics trafficking, computer hacking, and money laundering conspiracies by designing, launching, and administering a website called Silk Road ("Silk Road") as an online marketplace for illicit goods and services. These allegations raise novel issues as they relate to the Internet and the defendant's role in the purported conspiracies.

A conspiracy claim is premised on an agreement between two or more people to achieve an unlawful end. The Government alleges that by designing, launching, and administering Silk Road, Ulbricht conspired with narcotics traffickers and hackers to buy and sell illegal narcotics and malicious computer software and to launder the proceeds using Bitcoin. There is no allegation that Ulbricht conspired with anyone prior to his launch of Silk Road. Rather, the allegations revolve around the numerous transactions that occurred on the site following its launch.

The Government alleges that Silk Road was designed to operate like eBay: a seller would electronically post a good or service for sale; a buyer would electronically purchase the item; the seller would then ship or otherwise provide to the buyer the purchased item; the buyer would provide feedback; and the site operator (*i.e.*, Ulbricht) would receive a portion of the seller's revenue as a commission. Ulbricht, as the alleged site designer, made the site available only to those using Tor, software and a network that allows for anonymous, untraceable Internet browsing; he allowed payment only via Bitcoin, an anonymous and untraceable form of payment.

Following the launch of Silk Road, the site was available to sellers and buyers for transactions. Thousands of transactions allegedly occurred over the course of nearly three years — sellers posted goods when available; buyers purchased goods when desired. As website administrator, Ulbricht may have had some direct contact with some users of the site, and none with most. This online marketplace thus allowed the alleged designer and operator (Ulbricht) to be anywhere in the world with an Internet connection (he was apprehended in California), the sellers and buyers to be anywhere, the activities to occur independently from one another on different days and at different times, and the transactions to occur anonymously.

A number of legal questions arise from conspiracy claims premised on this framework. In sum, they address whether the conduct alleged here can serve as the basis of a criminal conspiracy — and, if so, when, how, and with whom.

While this is a case of first impression as to the charged conduct, the fact that the alleged conduct constitutes cognizable crimes requires no legal contortion and is not surprising.

## I. THE INDICTMENT

Rule 7(c)(1) of the Federal Rules of Criminal Procedure provides that an indictment "must be a plain, concise, and definite written statement of the essential facts constituting the offense charged." It need not contain any other matter not necessary to such statement.

As with all motions to dismiss an indictment, the Court accepts as true the allegations set forth in the charging instrument for purposes of determining the sufficiency of the charges.

The Indictment here alleges that Ulbricht designed, created, operated, and owned Silk Road, "the most sophisticated and extensive criminal marketplace on the Internet." Silk Road operated using Tor, software and a network that enables users to access the Internet anonymously — it keeps users' unique identifying Internet Protocol ("IP") addresses obscured, preventing surveillance or tracking. All purchases occurred on Silk Road using Bitcoin, an anonymous online currency.

Silk Road allegedly functioned as designed — tens of thousands of buyers and sellers are alleged to have entered into transactions using the site, violating numerous criminal laws. Over time, thousands of kilograms of heroin and cocaine were allegedly bought and sold, as if the purchases were occurring on eBay or any other similar website.

Count One charges that, from in or about January 2011 up to and including October 2013, the defendant engaged in a narcotics trafficking conspiracy. To wit, "the defendant . . . designed [Silk Road] to enable users across the world to buy and sell illegal drugs and other illicit goods and services anonymously and outside the reach of law enforcement." The defendant allegedly "controlled all aspects of Silk Road, with the assistance of various paid employees whom he managed and supervised." "It was part and object of the conspiracy" that the defendant and others "would and did deliver, distribute, and dispense controlled substances by means of the Internet" and "did aid and abet such activity" in violation of the law. The controlled substances allegedly included heroin, cocaine, and lysergic acid diethylamide ("LSD"). The defendant allegedly "reaped commissions worth tens of millions of dollars, generated from the illicit sales conducted through the site." According to the Indictment, the defendant "pursued violent means, including soliciting the murder-for-hire of several individuals he believed posed a threat to that enterprise."

## II. THE LAW OF CONSPIRACY

### A. *Elements of a Conspiracy*

"The essence of the crime of conspiracy . . . is the *agreement* to commit one or more unlawful acts." Put differently, a conspiracy is the "'combination of minds for an unlawful purpose.'"[2]

A meeting of the minds is required in order for there to be an agreement. Two people have to engage in the "act of agreeing" in order for this requirement to be met. The conspirators must agree to the object, or unlawful end, of the conspiracy. While the coconspirators need not agree to every detail, they must agree to the "essential nature" of the plan.

To be convicted of a conspiracy, . . . "[t]he government must prove that the defendant agreed to commit a *particular offense* and not merely a vague agreement to do something wrong."

The crime of conspiracy requires that a defendant both know the object of the crime and that he knowingly and intentionally join the conspiracy.

### B. *Types of Conspiracies*

Conspiracies come in myriad shapes and sizes: from a small conspiracy involving two people to achieve a limited end to a large one involving numerous participants and with an expansive scope. Similarly, a defendant may participate in a single conspiracy or multiple conspiracies. Most questions as to size and number are left to trial. Here, the Court addresses these issues only insofar as they inform whether and how the Government might ultimately prove the conspiracies alleged in the Indictment.

"Whether the government has proven the existence of the conspiracy charged in the indictment and each defendant's membership in it, or, instead, has proven several independent conspiracies is a question of fact for a properly instructed jury." Where an indictment charges a single conspiracy and the evidence later shows multiple conspiracies, the court will only set aside a jury's guilty verdict due to the variance if the defendant can show "substantial prejudice, *i.e.* that the evidence proving the conspiracies in which the defendant did *not* participate prejudiced the case against him in the conspiracy in which he *was* a party."

---

[2] There is no overt act requirement to establish a violation of a drug conspiracy prosecuted under 21 U.S.C. § 846.

### 1. Overview of Single Conspiracies

"[A]cts that could be charged as separate counts of an indictment may instead be charged in a single count if those acts could be characterized as part of a single continuing scheme." In determining whether a single conspiracy involving many people exists, the question is whether there is a "mutual dependence" among the participants. The Government must show that each alleged member of the conspiracy agreed to participate "'in what he knew to be a collective venture directed towards a common goal.'"

A "'single conspiracy is not transformed into multiple conspiracies merely by virtue of the fact that it may involve two or more spheres or phases of operation, so long as there is sufficient proof of mutual dependence and assistance.'" Neither changing membership nor different time periods of participation by various coconspirators precludes the existence of a single conspiracy, "especially where the activity of a single person was 'central to the involvement of all.'"

### 2. Types of Single Conspiracies

Courts often conceptualize single conspiracies using either a "chain" or a "hub-and-spoke" metaphor.

#### (a) Chain Conspiracies

A chain conspiracy refers to a situation in which there are numerous conspiring individuals, each of whom has a role in a "chain" that serves the conspiracy's object. For example, in a narcotics conspiracy, a chain may be comprised of producers, exporters, wholesalers, middlemen, and dealers. The success of each "link" in the chain depends on the success of the others, even though each individual conspirator may play a role that is separated by great distance and time from the other individuals involved.

This form of conspiracy "is dictated by a division of labor at the various functional levels." "An individual associating himself with a 'chain' conspiracy knows that it has a 'scope' and that for its success it requires an organization wider than may be disclosed by [one's] personal participation."

#### (b) Hub-and-Spoke Conspiracies

In a hub-and-spoke (or "wheel") conspiracy, one person typically acts as a central point while others act as "spokes" by virtue of their agreement with the central actor. Put another way, in a hub-and-spoke conspiracy, "members of a 'core' group deal with a number of contacts who are analogized to the spokes of a wheel and are connected with each other only through the core conspirators."

To prove a single conspiracy in such a situation, the Government must show that there was a "rim" around the spokes, such that the "spokes" became coconspirators with each other. To do so, the Government must prove that "each defendant . . . participated in the conspiracy with the common goal or purpose of the other defendants."

In the absence of such a "rim," the spokes are acting independently with the hub; while there may in fact be multiple separate conspiracies, there cannot be a single conspiracy. *See Dickson v. Microsoft Corp.*, 309 F.3d 193, 203 (4th Cir. 2002) ("A rimless wheel conspiracy is one in which various defendants enter into separate agreements with a common defendant, but where the defendants have no connection with one another, other than the common defendant's involvement in each transaction.").

### C. *The Buyer-Seller Exception*

Of course, not all narcotics transactions occur within a conspiracy. A conspiracy to distribute narcotics does not arise between a buyer and seller simply because they engage in a narcotics transaction. That is, the mere purchase and sale of drugs does not, without more, amount to a conspiracy to distribute narcotics. "It is sometimes said that the buyer's agreement to buy from the seller and the seller's agreement to sell to the buyer cannot 'be the conspiracy to distribute, for it has no separate criminal object.'"

## III. DISCUSSION OF CONSPIRATORIAL AGREEMENT

The Indictment alleges that Ulbricht designed Silk Road specifically to enable users to anonymously sell and purchase narcotics and malicious software and to launder the resulting proceeds. On this motion to dismiss, the Court's task is a narrow one — it is not concerned with whether the Government will have sufficient evidence to meet its burden of proof as to each element of the charged conspiracies at trial. Instead, the Court is concerned solely with whether the nature of the alleged conduct, if proven, legally constitutes the crimes charged.

The Court has set forth [four] questions that concern the potential existence of a conspiratorial agreement in this case. Each question is now taken up in turn.

*Question One:* Can there be a legally cognizable "agreement" between Ulbricht and one or more coconspirators to engage in narcotics trafficking, computer hacking, and money laundering by virtue of his and their conduct in relation to Silk Road? If so, what is the difference between what Ulbricht is alleged to have done and the conduct of designers and administrators of legitimate online marketplaces through which illegal transactions may nevertheless occur?

The "gist" of a conspiracy charge is that the minds of two or more people met — that they agreed in some manner to achieve an unlawful end. For the reasons explained below, the design and operation of Silk Road *can* result in a legally cognizable conspiracy.

According to the Indictment, Ulbricht purposefully and intentionally designed, created, and operated Silk Road to facilitate unlawful transactions. Silk Road was nothing more than code unless and until third parties agreed to use it. When third parties engaged in unlawful narcotics transactions on the site, however, Ulbricht's design and operation gave rise to potential conspiratorial conduct. The subsequent sale and purchase of unlawful narcotics and software on Silk Road may, as a matter of law, constitute circumstantial evidence of an agreement to engage in such unlawful conduct. *See United States v. Svoboda*, 347 F.3d 471, 477 (2d Cir. 2003) ("A conspiracy need not be shown by proof of an explicit agreement but can be established by showing that the parties have a tacit understanding to carry out the prohibited conduct.").

Additionally, the Indictment charges that Ulbricht obtained significant monetary benefit in the form of commissions in exchange for the services he provided via Silk Road. He had the capacity to shut down the site at any point; he did not do so. The defendant allegedly used violence in order to protect the site and the proceeds it generated.

Ulbricht argues that his conduct was merely as a facilitator—just like eBay, Amazon, or similar websites.[6]

[I]n this case, the charges in the Indictment go further than Ulbricht acknowledges. The Indictment alleges that Ulbricht engaged in conduct that makes Silk Road different from other websites that provide a platform for individual buyers and sellers to connect and engage in transactions: Silk Road was specifically and intentionally designed for the purpose of facilitating unlawful transactions. The Indictment does not allege that Ulbricht is criminally liable simply because he is alleged to have launched a website that was—unknown to and unplanned by him—used for illicit transactions. If that were ultimately the case, he would lack the *mens rea* for criminal liability. Rather, Ulbricht is alleged to have knowingly and intentionally constructed and operated an expansive black market for selling and purchasing narcotics and malicious software and for laundering money. This separates Ulbricht's alleged conduct from the mass of others whose websites may—without their planning or expectation—be used for unlawful purposes.

> *Question Two:* As a matter of law, *who* are Ulbricht's alleged coconspirators and potential coconspirators? That is, whose "minds" can have "met" with Ulbricht's in a conspiratorial agreement? What sort of conspiratorial structure frames the allegations: one large single conspiracy or multiple small conspiracies?

Ulbricht's alleged coconspirators are "several thousand drug dealers and other unlawful vendors." If these individuals possessed the requisite intent, there is no legal reason they could not be members of the conspiracies charged in the Indictment.

A more complicated question is whether any or all of Ulbricht's coconspirators also conspired with each other, so as to create a potentially vast single conspiracy. In this regard, the Government may argue that the conspiracy was a "chain" conspiracy or that it was a "hub-and-spoke" conspiracy (in which case it would be necessary for the Government to prove the existence of a "rim"). Each approach has its own complexities regarding the (largely anonymous) inter-conspirator relationships on the Internet. While this is not an issue the Government need address at this stage, it will be relevant as the proof comes in at trial.

Of course, ultimately, the form of the conspiracy is not as important as a determination that at least one other person joined in the alleged conspiratorial agreement with Ulbricht. With respect to the narcotics conspiracy charge, to prove that the drug types and quantities alleged in the Indictment were the objects of a conspiracy Ulbricht knowingly and intentionally joined, the Government will have to prove either a single such conspiratorial agreement or an aggregation of conspiracies.

---

[6] While the defendant refers to Amazon and eBay as similar, there are certain important factual differences between them. For instance, Amazon has warehouses which may fulfill certain orders. Silk Road is not alleged to have ever possessed products for fulfillment.

While, as explained, proof of participants' intent could involve numerous complexities, these are issues for trial and not for this stage.

> *Question Three:* As a matter of law, *when* could any particular agreement have occurred between Ulbricht and his alleged coconspirators? Need each coconspirator's mind have met simultaneously with Ulbricht's? Did Ulbricht, simply by designing and launching Silk Road, make an enduring showing of intent?

The issue here is one of temporal proximity. For the sake of illustration, assume that Ulbricht launched Silk Road on Day 1. [C]an Ulbricht have agreed to a conspiracy on Day 1 with an alleged coconspirator who, at that time, had not even contemplated engaging in an unlawful transaction, and determined to do so only on, for example, Day 300?

One way of thinking about this issue is to look to the basic contract principles of offer and acceptance. On Day 1, according to the Indictment, Ulbricht "offers" to work with others to traffic illegal narcotics, engage in computer hacking, and launder money. He makes this offer by creating and launching a website specifically designed and intended for such unlawful purposes. Ulbricht's continued operation of the site evinces an enduring intent to be bound with those who "accept" his offer and utilize the site for its intended purpose. It is as though the defendant allegedly posted a sign on a (worldwide) bulletin board that said: "I have created an anonymous, untraceable way to traffic narcotics, unlawfully access computers, and launder money. You can use the platform as much as you would like, provided you pay me a percentage of your profits and adhere to my other terms of service." Each time someone "signs up" and agrees to Ulbricht's standing offer, it is possible that, as a matter of law, he or she may become a coconspirator.

To put this another way, the fact that Ulbricht's active participation may occur at a different point in time from the agreement by his coconspirator(s) does not render the conspiracy charges legally defective. Courts have long recognized that members of a conspiracy may be well removed from one another in time. The law has similarly recognized that coconspirators need not have been present at the outset of a conspiracy in order to be found criminally responsible; they may join at some later point. A lapse in time — in particular in a narcotics chain conspiracy, where a manufacturer creates a substance months prior to a wholesale or retailer selling it, not knowing (and perhaps never knowing) who, precisely, will ultimately distribute it — does not *ipso facto* render the alleged conspiracy defective as a matter of law. Similarly, the law long ago accepted that coconspirators may not know each other's identity. The alleged conduct here is another step along this established path.

> *Question Four:* As a matter of law, is it legally necessary, or factually possible, to pinpoint *how* the agreement between Ulbricht and his coconspirators was made?

Another issue raised by this case is whether a conspiratorial agreement may be effected through what are primarily automated, pre-programmed processes. This is not a situation in which Ulbricht is alleged to have himself approved or had a hand in each individual transaction that occurred on Silk Road during the nearly three-year period covered by the Indictment. Instead, he wrote (or had others write) certain code that automated the transaction. Yet, as a legal matter, this automation does not preclude the formation of a conspiratorial agreement. Indeed, whether an agreement occurs electronically or otherwise is of no particular legal relevance.

It is well-established that the act of agreeing, or having a meeting of the minds, may be proven through circumstantial evidence. There is no requirement that any words be exchanged at all in this regard, so long as the coconspirators have taken knowing and intentional actions to work together in some mutually dependent way to achieve the unlawful object. Though automation may enable a particular transaction to take place, it is the individuals behind the transaction that take the necessary affirmative steps to utilize that automation. Automation is effected through a human design; here, Ulbricht is alleged to have been the designer of Silk Road, and as a matter of law, that is sufficient.[9]

The defendant argues that [the controlled substances conspiracy charge] must be dismissed because he is not alleged to have distributed or possessed any controlled substance. No such allegation is required. The law of conspiracy recognizes that members of a conspiracy may serve different roles. *See United States v. Garcia-Torres*, 280 F.3d 1, 4 (1st Cir. 2002) ("[A] drug conspiracy may involve ancillary functions (e.g., accounting, communications, strong-arm enforcement), and one who joined with drug dealers to perform one of those functions could be deemed a drug conspirator."). There are numerous examples of participants in narcotics conspiracies who did not themselves intend physically to possess or distribute narcotics; an individual may have been a middleman, the protective muscle, the lookout, a decoy, a person with information or contacts, etc. — in any event, the individual may nonetheless be found to be part of the conspiratorial enterprise. *See, e.g., United States v. Pitre*, 960 F.2d 1112, 1121-22 (2d Cir. 1992) (affirming conviction of defendant where evidence revealed that defendant was acting as a lookout and was carrying a beeper to facilitate narcotics transactions).

For the reasons set forth above, the defendant's motion to dismiss is Denied in its entirety.

So Ordered.

**Post-Case Follow-Up**

In *Ulbricht*, the court denied the defendant's motion to dismiss the conspiracy charges against him. In doing so, the court relied on a number of legal principles that are often important in complex conspiracy cases. On the element of the criminal agreement, Ulbricht took issue with the fact that he was alleged to have conspired with people he never met simply by virtue of their use of his website. The court found that this was not fatal to the charges, explaining that "the law long ago accepted that coconspirators may not know each other's identity." Although the court allowed the charges to go forward, it did not decide the question of whether the government had alleged

---

[9] Acceptance of the terms of service, the payment of commissions, placing Bitcoins in escrow, and other intervening steps involved in the transactions that allegedly occurred on Silk Road could, in this regard, perhaps constitute evidence that Silk Road users entered into an unlawful conspiracy with Ulbricht (and others). It will be for the Government to prove which conduct in fact occurred, and how, at trial.

a single large conspiracy or multiple smaller ones. "In determining whether a single conspiracy involving many people exists," the court explained, "the question is whether there is a mutual dependence among the participants. The Government must show that each alleged member of the conspiracy agreed to participate in what he knew to be a collective venture directed towards a common goal." The court left the resolution of the "complexities" of applying this rule to Ulbricht's case for the jury to consider at trial.

---

## Ulbricht: *Real Life Applications*

1. Imagine that you are the judge in Ulbricht's case. The case goes to trial, and the jury finds Ulbricht guilty of all of the charges and conduct described in the opinion above. It is now up to you to decide on Ulbricht's sentence. In real life, federal sentencing law (including the Federal Sentencing Guidelines and any applicable mandatory minimum penalty provisions) would restrain the judge's sentencing decision in Ulbricht's case. For purposes of this hypothetical, however, assume that you have free rein to impose whatever sentence you believe is just.
    a. What sentence would you impose in Ulbricht's case? What three factors would be most important to you in reaching your decision?
    b. To what extent, if any, would you consider the legal distinction between single and multiple conspiracies in reaching your sentence? Specifically, would it make a difference to you if Ulbricht was found guilty of a single conspiracy with thousands of Silk Road users or thousands of counts of conspiracy with each Silk Road user?

2. Consider the facts of *United States v. Caldwell*, 589 F.3d 1123 (10th Cir. 2009). The government charged three people — Michael Caldwell, David Anderson, and Samuel Herrera — with conspiracy to distribute at least 100 kilograms of marijuana, a quantity that triggers a mandatory minimum sentence of 5 years under federal law.

    Over a two-year period, Caldwell sold marijuana on consignment for Herrera. Once a month, Herrera distributed two kilograms of marijuana to Caldwell on consignment. Caldwell then resold the marijuana to users at a retail level.

    Anderson, who was a friend of Caldwell's, eventually became another one of Herrera's main customers. About one year after Caldwell began selling marijuana for Herrera, Anderson asked Caldwell if he knew of a reliable drug supplier. Caldwell arranged a meeting between Anderson and Herrera. Even though Caldwell was present at the initial meeting, during which Herrera sold approximately 4.5 kilograms of marijuana to Anderson on consignment, Caldwell received no economic benefit from the introduction. From that point on, Anderson and Herrera dealt with one another "one on one" — that is, no subsequent drug transactions between Anderson and Herrera involved Caldwell. Anderson received monthly supplies of approximately four to nine kilograms of marijuana from Herrera, generally on consignment. All told, Anderson sold between 163 and 327 kilograms of marijuana for Herrera on consignment.

The jury convicted all three men of participating in a single conspiracy to distribute at least 100 kilograms of marijuana. Caldwell appeals. He argues that the evidence was insufficient to prove a *single* tripartite conspiracy between himself, Anderson, and Herrera. Instead, Caldwell argues there were two separate conspiracies — one between himself and Herrera, and one between Anderson and Herrera.

You are a clerk working for one of the appeals court judges hearing the case. Would you recommend to the judge that she affirm the conviction or overturn it?

## The Significance of the Single versus Multiple Conspiracies Question

When a criminal enterprise involves multiple participants, what is the practical significance (if any) of the distinction between a single conspiracy involving all of the participants and multiple conspiracies involving smaller groups of the participants? In other words, what does it matter if the defendant is guilty of a single conspiracy with 20 other people or of multiple conspiracies with smaller groups of those same 20 people? In some cases, the answer matters a great deal, and in others not much at all.

In a conspiracy case involving a single defendant who led the criminal enterprise, the distinction may *not* make much practical difference. Consider *Ulbricht.* The prosecutor alleged that Ulbricht conspired with a large number of other people, but the only defendant in the case was Ulbricht. In a case like this, "there is no danger of any spill over effect, from one conspiracy to another, since the defendant is alleged to have participated in all conspiratorial conduct." *United States v. Pauling,* 256 F. Supp. 3d 329, 335 (S.D.N.Y. 2017). On this view, whether Ulbricht is guilty of a single conspiracy with all of the users of Silk Road or thousands of separate counts of conspiracy with each user may be immaterial; "he's either guilty or he's not guilty." *Id.*

The calculus can be much different when the government prosecutes more than one alleged conspirator in a single case. Imagine that a prosecutor alleges that 20 people are guilty of participating in a single drug conspiracy and prosecutes all 20 alleged participants together in one case. One of the 20 defendants, Dan, is alleged to have been a very low-level participant. The only evidence against Dan is that he drove one of the other defendants, Steph, to a single drug deal. In a case like this, it is possible that Dan is not guilty of conspiring with all of the other 20 defendants even if he might be guilty of conspiring with Steph. Prosecuting Dan in a single trial with all of the other defendants could be unfair to Dan because "there is a legitimate concern that a defendant who operated on the periphery of a large, overarching conspiracy will be unfairly grouped in with a larger conspiracy than he intended to join." *United States v. Richardson,* 532 F.3d 1279, 1291 (11th Cir. 2008).

There are other circumstances where the single conspiracy/multiple conspiracies distinction has practical significance. In federal drug cases, for example,

"Congress has enacted a tiered scheme of mandatory minimum sentences based on [the] quantity" of drugs involved in the conspiracy. *Pauling*, 256 F. Supp. 3d at 335. Under this scheme, a five-year mandatory minimum sentence could apply to a defendant convicted of a single conspiracy involving 501 grams of cocaine, but not to a defendant convicted of two conspiracies involving 250 and 251 grams of cocaine. As a result, in federal drug cases that involve a mandatory minimum sentence, "it is imperative that the boundaries between conspiracies be well defined," even if there is a single defendant. *Id.*

Ultimately then, the practical importance (if any) of the single conspiracy/multiple conspiracies distinction depends on a number of different factors and varies from case to case.

## C. VICARIOUS LIABILITY FOR CONSPIRATORS: THE *PINKERTON* RULE

In many jurisdictions, a conspiracy conviction has the potential to result in convictions for additional offenses under the so-called ***Pinkerton* rule**. The rule, adopted by the United States Supreme Court in the 1946 case *Pinkerton v. United States*, provides that a defendant who has committed the crime of conspiracy can also be convicted of any crimes committed by her co-conspirators that were (1) reasonably foreseeable to her and (2) done in furtherance of the illegal agreement. Some courts interpret *Pinkerton* as including a third requirement: that the crimes be within the scope of the conspiracy.

To understand how the rule applies, consider the following hypothetical: Don and Cass agree to rob a bank. Don's role will be to enter the bank and commit the robbery, with Cass serving as the getaway driver. Don leaves it to Cass to plot out the robbery and make all of the necessary arrangements. Without telling Don, Cass steals a Buick to use as the getaway car. Cass is caught and arrested by the police a few blocks from the car theft. In this example, Don is no doubt guilty of conspiracy to commit robbery. What about Cass's theft of the Buick? Don would not be considered to be an accomplice to Cass's car theft — as covered in Chapter 8, accomplice liability requires an intent to assist in the crime, and Don did not intend to assist in the theft of the Buick. But under *Pinkerton*, Don is *also* guilty of larceny for Cass's car theft. This is because it was (1) reasonably foreseeable that Cass would steal a vehicle to use as a getaway car; (2) the theft of the car was in furtherance of the conspiracy; and (3) the theft was within the scope of the agreement, which left it to Cass to plan the robbery.

The *Pinkerton* rule has been heavily criticized over the years on the grounds that it creates a form of vicarious liability that is unsound as a matter of principle, and illegitimate as a matter of statutory interpretation. Many states have rejected *Pinkerton* for these reasons. However, it remains the law at the federal level and has been adopted by 30 states and the District of Columbia, according to a 2018 survey of state criminal laws. Paul H. Robinson & Tyler Scot Williams, Mapping American Criminal Law: Variations Across the 50 States 121 (2018).

### Case Preview

## *State v. Walton*

In the next case, the Connecticut Supreme Court considered whether to adopt *Pinkerton* liability. The court's decision outlines the requirements for convicting a defendant of a crime under *Pinkerton* and the rationale for the *Pinkerton* rule.

As you read the decision, consider the following questions:

**1.** What is the rationale for the *Pinkerton* rule?
**2.** Do you think that the *Pinkerton* rule is a good one? Why or why not?

## *State v. Walton*
### 227 Conn. 32 (1993)

BORDEN, J.

The principal issue in these consolidated appeals is the extent to which we should recognize the principle of vicarious liability of a conspirator articulated in *Pinkerton v. United States*, 328 U.S. 640 (1946). Scott Walton appeals from the judgment of conviction of one count of possession of narcotics with intent to sell by a person who is not drug-dependent, in violation of General Statutes § 21a-278(b), and one count of conspiracy to distribute narcotics, in violation of General Statutes §§ 53a-48(a) and 21a-277(a). Robert Walton and Aubrey Johnson [were also convicted] of one count each of conspiracy to distribute narcotics, in violation of General Statutes §§ 21a-277(a) and 53a-48.

The jury could reasonably have found the following facts. The defendants were engaged in the trafficking of street drugs, during which the bulk of the drugs was stored in a three-family house located at 284-86 Enfield Street, Hartford. From late September, 1988, through January, 1989, Hartford police department detectives Michael Manzi and Jose Morales conducted a total of approximately fifteen undercover surveillances of the house. During each surveillance, there was a group of young males in front of the house. As a car or pedestrian would stop in front of the house, one of the group would run to the car or person and exchange small packets of street drugs for money. Among this group were the three defendants and a codefendant, Rodney Kelley.[3]

Manzi saw Robert Walton on approximately nine of the fifteen surveillance occasions. Robert Walton would give signals to drug customers in cars, such as pointing to his nose or giving a "high five" sign, approach the cars, hand drugs through the windows and take money from the customers. During the surveillances, he approached drug customers and made drug sales approximately thirty-five times.

---

[3] Rodney Kelley was also tried jointly with the three defendants and with two other codefendants, Lenwood Huff, Jr., and Janet Franklin. The trial court granted Huff's and Franklin's motions for judgments of acquittal at the close of the state's case. The jury acquitted Kelley.

On approximately twelve occasions, Johnson engaged in the same drug activity as Robert Walton.

Scott Walton, who lived on the second floor of the house with his mother, who owned the building, engaged in the same drug activity as Robert Walton and Johnson on approximately twelve occasions. In addition, Scott Walton would follow Kelley, Robert Walton and Johnson to cars to oversee the drug sales. Scott Walton was often on the porch of the house, and went in and out of the front door more often than the other three. Individuals would walk up to Scott Walton on the porch and converse with him, and when they returned to the street, he would enter the house.

The detectives who had conducted surveillances secured a search warrant for the house and, together with approximately ten other detectives, executed the warrant on January 21, 1989. In the television room were the three defendants, Rodney Kelley and Franklin. The sofas and chairs were arranged in a circle around a coffee table, so that all six of the people could reach the coffee table from where they were sitting. On the coffee table was a white, upright, open, plastic shopping bag containing: (1) approximately $2000 in cash; (2) a clear, open, plastic bag containing twelve grams of 84.7 percent pure cocaine, which was in the process of being packaged for distribution; and (3) several one ounce plastic bags containing cocaine. Also on the coffee table were numerous one ounce size plastic bags, the smaller of which weighed between three grams and six and one-half grams, containing 70.8 percent to 79.8 percent pure cocaine. There were forty-three bags of cocaine in all. The street value of the cocaine on the coffee table was approximately $30,000.

The detectives searched the television room and the persons in it. They found a loaded .45 caliber automatic pistol under the cushion where Scott Walton had been sitting. On Johnson's person, the detectives found a paging beeper, which is frequently used to facilitate drug sales over the phone, and $1700 in cash. On Robert Walton, they found two $100 bills; on Scott Walton, $350 in cash; and on Kelley, $200 in cash.

We first consider Scott Walton's challenge to his conviction of one count of possession of narcotics with intent to sell by a person who is not drug-dependent. He claims that the trial court, by instructing the jury regarding that offense in accordance with the vicarious liability principles of *Pinkerton v. United States,* supra, "wrongly expanded the liability of a conspirator." We disagree.

This claim arises in the following context. In the first count of the information filed against him, the state charged that "at the City of Hartford on or about the 21st day of January, 1989, at approximately 1:15 P.M., at or near the first floor of 286 Enfield Street . . . Scott Walton did possess a narcotics [sic] substance, to wit: cocaine, with the intent to sell, and that the said Scott Walton was not, at that time, a drug dependent person, in violation of Section 21a-278(b) of the General Statutes."

In the second count, the state charged Scott Walton with conspiracy to distribute narcotics in violation of General Statutes §§ 21a-277(a) and 53a-48(a). This count alleged that "at the City of Hartford, on or about the 1st day of December, 1988, thru [sic] the 21st day of January, 1989 . . . Scott Walton did, with the intent that conduct constituting the crime of Distribution of Narcotics be committed, agree with one or more persons, to wit: Lenwood Huff, Janet Franklin, Rodney Kelley, Aubrey Johnson, Robert Walton and others unknown, to engage in and cause the performance of such conduct, and that one or more of the conspirators committed an overt act in pursuance of the conspiracy."

The trial court instructed the jury that, even if the state failed to prove beyond a reasonable doubt that Scott Walton had possessed narcotics with the intent to sell, as charged in the first count, he could be convicted under the first count if the jury found "beyond a reasonable doubt: (1) that he was a member of a conspiracy as charged in the second count; (2) that another member of that same conspiracy did possess narcotics with intent to sell at the time and place charged in the first count of the information; and, (3) that that possession was within the scope of the conspiracy[,] in furtherance of its purpose and a foreseeable part of its execution."

The defendants excepted to this instruction. The jury convicted all three defendants of conspiracy, and also convicted Scott Walton of possession of narcotics with intent to sell by a person who is not drug-dependent.[10]

The trial court's instruction on vicarious criminal liability derives from *Pinkerton v. United States*. In that case, the United States Supreme Court held that a conspirator may be held liable for criminal offenses committed by a coconspirator that are within the scope of the conspiracy, are in furtherance of it, and are reasonably foreseeable as a necessary or natural consequence of the conspiracy. *Pinkerton* liability is now a recognized part of federal criminal conspiracy jurisprudence. As the Second Circuit Court of Appeals recently stated, "*Pinkerton* is not a broad principle of vicarious liability that imposes criminal responsibility upon every co-conspirator for whatever substantive offenses any of their confederates commit. On the contrary, in the very decision in which the principle was articulated, co-conspiratory liability was carefully confined to substantive offenses that are (a) committed 'in furtherance of the conspiracy,' and (b) 'reasonably foresee[able]' by the co-conspirator sought to be held responsible 'as a necessary or natural consequence of the unlawful agreement.'"

*Pinkerton* liability has also been adopted by the majority of state jurisdictions that have considered the issue.

We note initially that the question of whether *Pinkerton* liability should be recognized in this state is not foreclosed by our penal code.

We do not believe that the *Pinkerton* principle is inconsistent with any other principle of criminal liability stated in the code. The issue, therefore, is whether the principle should be recognized as a matter of policy under the circumstances of this case. We conclude that the principles of *Pinkerton* appropriately apply under the facts of this case. Several considerations lead us to this conclusion.

First, the rationale of *Pinkerton* . . . is essentially that, because the conspirator played a necessary part in setting in motion a discrete course of criminal conduct, he should be held responsible, within appropriate limits, for the crimes committed as a natural and probable result of that course of conduct. We endorse this rationale, at least as applied to the facts of the present case.

---

[10] We cannot determine from the general verdict of the jury whether it convicted Scott Walton of possession of narcotics with intent to sell upon the basis of evidence that he in fact so possessed narcotics or upon the basis of evidence that one of his coconspirators so possessed narcotics. There was evidence to support either theory. For purposes of this claim, however, we will assume that the basis of the jury's verdict was the latter.

Second, . . . holding Scott Walton vicariously liable under the circumstances of this case is consistent with holding him liable for conspiracy by virtue of an overt act committed by a coconspirator. At least if, as in this case, the substantive offense was a principal object of the conspiracy and was proven by one of the overt acts alleged, the rationale of the court in *Pinkerton* is apt: "An overt act is an essential ingredient of the crime of conspiracy. . . . If that can be supplied by the act of one conspirator, we fail to see why the same . . . [act] in furtherance of the conspiracy [is] likewise not attributable to the others for the purpose of holding them responsible for the substantive offense."

Some commentators have criticized the *Pinkerton* principle. The principal basis of that criticism is that "'law would lose all sense of just proportion' if one might, by virtue of his one crime of conspiracy, be 'held accountable for thousands of additional offenses of which he was completely unaware and which he did not influence at all.'" In an appropriate case, that criticism might well be valid. We do not believe, however, that it applies to this case, in which we have applied the *Pinkerton* principle to a situation in which the jury reasonably could have found that Scott Walton was in control of the operation, the crime was a principal object of the conspiracy, and the crime was one of the overt acts alleged as part of the conspiracy.

Scott Walton argues that recognizing the *Pinkerton* principle would be contrary to the scheme of our penal code because "[t]he fact that the General Assembly enacted separate statutes for accessory liability and for conspiracy clearly means that they are not to be collapsed into one." We disagree.

Recognition of the *Pinkerton* principle in an appropriate case is not inconsistent with the notion of accessory liability, and does not mean, as the defendant argues, that the two are "collapsed into one."

The judgment[ is] affirmed.

BERDON, J., dissenting.

By incorporating the principles articulated in *Pinkerton v. United States*, 328 U.S. 640 (1946), the majority creates a new type of accomplice liability not envisioned by the legislature when it adopted General Statutes §§ 53a-8 and 53a-48, which separately delineate criminal liability for the acts of another and conspiracy, respectively. Under *Pinkerton*, a conspirator may be convicted of substantive offenses committed by a coconspirator if the offenses were within the scope of the conspiracy, were in furtherance of the conspiracy and reasonably could be foreseen as a necessary or natural consequence of the agreement. In devising our penal code, the legislature specifically limited the crime of conspiracy to pertain only to the conduct that was the subject of the agreement between the coconspirators and the overt act in furtherance of that agreement.

This court does not have the authority to create a new form of accomplice liability. "To permit mere guilt of conspiracy to establish the defendant's guilt of the substantive crime without any evidence of further action on the part of the defendant, would be to expand the basis of accomplice liability beyond the legislative design."

The holding in *Pinkerton* offends the most basic principles of criminal law, which "has its foundation in personal and individual guilt . . . and any doctrine of vicarious criminal liability is repugnant to common law concepts."

Accordingly, I would reverse the conviction in regard to Scott Walton.

**Post-Case Follow-Up**

In *Walton*, the court followed the majority of states and recognized the *Pinkerton* rule as a basis for criminal liability. Under *Pinkerton*, a defendant who is convicted of the crime of conspiracy is held responsible for his co-conspirators' crimes that are (1) reasonably foreseeable, (2) in furtherance of the conspiracy, and in some jurisdictions (3) within the scope of the conspiracy.

## Walton: *Real Life Applications*

1.  The dissent in *Walton* argued that "[b]y incorporating the principles articulated in *Pinkerton v. United States*, 328 U.S. 640 (1946), the majority creates a new type of accomplice liability not envisioned by the legislature." Imagine that you are a legislative aide to a representative in the Connecticut legislature. The legislature is considering a bill that would expressly abolish *Pinkerton* liability in the state, effectively overturning the *Walton* court's decision. Would you recommend to your boss that she vote in favor of the bill or against it? Why or why not?

2.  Whitted and Harris planned to buy a large quantity of cocaine together from James. Whitted and Harris agreed to meet James in a parking lot to make the exchange of money for cocaine. Unfortunately for Whitted and Harris, James was an undercover police officer. The pair were arrested shortly after they arrived at the parking lot to make the deal. The police searched Harris and found a gun in the waistband of his pants. (No gun was found on Whitted's person.) An officer who interviewed Harris at the police station asked Harris whether Whitted knew about the gun. Harris replied, "I didn't tell Whitted I was bringing it. But it's common sense that I might bring a gun with me to a deal like this."

    Assume that by bringing a gun to the drug deal, Harris committed the crime of possession of a firearm in furtherance of a drug trafficking crime. In a jurisdiction that has adopted the rule in *Pinkerton*, could Whitted also be convicted of the crime of possession of a firearm in furtherance of a drug trafficking crime?

## Chapter Summary

- The crime of conspiracy consists of two elements: (1) an agreement to commit a crime entered into (2) with the intent to agree and the intent that the contemplated crime be committed. In some jurisdictions, there is a third element — an overt act. An overt act is any act by any of the conspirators that is done in furtherance of the agreement.

- Because a person cannot enter into an agreement with himself, it takes at least two people to commit the crime of conspiracy. There is a jurisdictional split on the question of whether the crime of conspiracy requires two *sincere* parties, however. This issue arises most often in the context of undercover policing. If an undercover officer "agrees" to rob a bank with a defendant, can the defendant be convicted of conspiracy even though the officer's agreement was insincere? In jurisdictions that follow the unilateral approach (which is the modern rule contained in the Model Penal Code), the defendant is guilty of conspiracy; the fact that there was never an actual agreement because of the officer's intent is irrelevant. In jurisdictions that follow the bilateral approach (which is the common law rule), the defendant cannot be convicted of conspiracy because there must be at least two persons who sincerely agree to commit the crime.

- Under Wharton's rule, an agreement to commit a crime that requires the cooperation of two or more people does not, standing alone, constitute an agreement for purposes of the crime of conspiracy. For example, the sale of an illegal drug requires a buyer and a seller to agree to the sale. If the sale agreement could give rise to a conspiracy prosecution, then every drug buyer would be guilty of conspiracy to distribute the drugs they purchased. In jurisdictions that follow Wharton's rule, the sale of drugs alone does not result in a conspiracy between buyer and seller.

- It can be particularly difficult to apply the offense of conspiracy to ongoing criminal enterprises that involve many participants. Even if it is clear that all of the participants are guilty of the crime of conspiracy, there may be a great deal of uncertainty about how to define the conspiratorial groups. Consider the case of a low-level employee of a drug sales ring. Even if there were no doubt that he conspired to distribute drugs, the question of *who* he is guilty of conspiring with — does his conspiratorial group include the head of the operation or only other lower-level participants? — can sometimes be open to debate among the parties. In these circumstances, most courts rely on an interdependence or mutual dependence test. As the *Ulbricht* court put it, "the question is whether there is a mutual dependence among the participants." The *Ulbricht* court also explained that courts often conceptualize complex conspiracy cases "using either a 'chain' or a 'hub-and-spoke' metaphor." The application of these principles is typically quite fact-bound.

- Under the *Pinkerton* rule, which is derived from a 1946 Supreme Court decision, a defendant who has committed the crime of conspiracy can also be convicted of any crimes committed by her co-conspirators that were (1) reasonably foreseeable to the defendant and (2) done in furtherance of the illegal agreement. Some courts interpret *Pinkerton* as including a third requirement: that the crimes be within the scope of the conspiracy. Although *Pinkerton* remains the law at the federal level and has been adopted by many states, many other states have not adopted the *Pinkerton* rule.

## Applying the Concepts

1. Do you think the crime of conspiracy is a useful offense, or is it superfluous in light of the law of attempts and accomplice liability?

2. Consider the facts of *People v. Rizzo*, 246 N.Y. 334 (1927), presented in Chapter 7:

   > Charles Rizzo, the defendant, appellant, with three others, Anthony J. Dorio, Thomas Milo, and John Thomasello, on January 14th planned to rob one Charles Rao of a pay roll valued at about $1,200 which he was to carry from the bank for the United Lathing Company. These defendants, two of whom had firearms, started out in an automobile, looking for Rao or the man who had the pay roll on that day. Rizzo claimed to be able to identify the man, and was to point him out to the others, who were to do the actual holding up. The four rode about in their car looking for Rao. They went to the bank from which he was supposed to get the money and to various buildings being constructed by the United Lathing Company. At last they came to One Hundred and Eightieth street and Morris Park avenue. By this time they were watched and followed by two police officers. As Rizzo jumped out of the car and ran into the building, all four were arrested. The defendant was taken out from the building in which he was hiding. Neither Rao nor a man named Previti, who was also supposed to carry a pay roll, were at the place at the time of the arrest. The defendants had not found or seen the man they intended to rob. No person with a pay roll was at any of the places where they had stopped, and no one had been pointed out or identified by Rizzo. The four men intended to rob the pay roll man, whoever he was. They were looking for him, but they had not seen or discovered him up to the time they were arrested.

   If Rizzo had been charged with conspiracy to commit robbery, should the jury have convicted him?

3. The police obtained a wiretap warrant for Acosta's cell phone in a drug investigation. On March 21, at 11:37 A.M., they recorded a call from Acosta to Rojas to purchase one kilogram of cocaine. Acosta told Rojas, "OK. I'm ready, come by here now."

   At 11:42 A.M., Acosta called Frank and said, "I just spoke to the man. He's coming over here right now."

   At 12:15 P.M., the police observed Rojas park near Acosta's apartment. Rojas removed a black and white plastic bag from the trunk and entered Acosta's apartment building. At 12:30 P.M., Rojas emerged from the building carrying the same black and white plastic bag.

   At 12:37 P.M., Acosta called Frank and said, "I just saw the man. But the stuff he had, it wasn't any good. So I told him to take it away. We're going to have to wait to get different stuff."

   The next day, the police obtain warrants to arrest Acosta and Rojas and search their homes. Inside Acosta's home, the police find 250 grams (.25 kilograms) of cocaine. Inside Rojas's home, they find 4 kilograms of cocaine.

The prosecutor charges Frank with conspiracy to possess 5.25 kilograms of cocaine with the intent to distribute. The prosecutor alleges that Frank conspired with Acosta and Rojas to possess 1 kilogram of cocaine, and that Frank is responsible under the *Pinkerton* rule for the .25 kilograms found in Acosta's home and the 4 kilograms found in Rojas's home.

    a. Has Frank committed the crime of conspiracy? If so, is he guilty of conspiring with both Acosta and Rojas, or only with Acosta?

    b. Can Frank be held responsible under *Pinkerton* for the .25 kilograms of cocaine found in Acosta's home?

    c. Can Frank be held responsible under *Pinkerton* for the 4 kilograms of cocaine found in Rojas's home?

## Criminal Law in Practice

1. It is sometimes difficult to conceptualize the boundaries between accomplice liability and conspiracy. Look back at the facts of *State v. Wilson*, 95 Wash. 2d 828 (1981), presented in Chapter 8 on page 389. The defendant in that case was convicted of delivery of a controlled substance as an accomplice. Do you think he could be convicted of conspiracy to deliver a controlled substance? If not, why not?

2. Can you think of a hypothetical set of facts in which a defendant would be guilty of the crime of conspiracy and yet not be guilty of committing a crime as an accomplice?

3. Many states have decided not to adopt the rule established in *Pinkerton v. United States*, 328 U.S. 640 (1946). Does your state apply the *Pinkerton* rule? If so, was the rule adopted by statute or by court decision? If not, is there a court decision that expressly rejected the idea of adopting the rule? (If you live in Connecticut, you have already seen the answers to these questions for your state in *State v. Wilson*, 227 Conn. 32 (1993), so you should look up the answers for a neighboring state of your choice.)

4. Alfred Anaya was one of "the most sought-after" custom car installers in Southern California. Brendan I. Koerner, *Alfred Anaya Put Secret Compartments in Cars, So the DEA Put Him in Prison*, Wired, Mar. 19, 2013. He had been named one of the top 100 installers in the nation by *Mobile Electronics*. Anaya sometimes installed secret compartments for his customers; "these secret stash spots — or traps, as they're known in automotive slang — have become a popular luxury item among the wealthy and shady alike." *Id.* Some of Anaya's clients were involved in the drug trade, and Anaya was prosecuted for conspiracy as a result. The Tenth Circuit Court of Appeals described the evidence against Anaya as follows:

Evidence at trial revealed an extensive drug trafficking organization ("DTO") that bought marijuana, cocaine, and meth in California and transported the drugs for sale in Kansas. Californians Esteban Magallon-Maldonado and Cesar Bonilla-Montiel headed the DTO, which included around twenty individuals. Curtis Crow ran the DTO operations in Kansas. The evidence included intercepted calls and records of hotel, airline, and car rental costs incurred by the DTO for drug transportation. The DTO used several vehicles that had been modified to include hidden compartments to transport drugs. Mr. Anaya built the hidden compartments. He lived in California during this time.

Mr. Bonilla-Montiel learned from a friend that Mr. Anaya installed compartments in cars that were difficult for police to discover and open. The DTO employed Mr. Anaya to build compartments in their vehicles. Mr. Bonilla-Montiel credited Mr. Anaya with enabling the DTO's drug loads to travel without detection from California to Kansas.

In late 2008, a secret compartment that Mr. Anaya had installed in the DTO's Ford F150 truck jammed after being stuffed with $800,000. Mr. Bonilla-Montiel and Mr. Magallon-Maldonado testified that they took the vehicle to Mr. Anaya's residence in California, where he worked on cars. Mr. Bonilla-Montiel also brought the DTO's Honda Ridgeline truck to determine whether Mr. Anaya could install a compartment in it.

Mr. Anaya could not open the compartment in the F150 using the series of buttons that he had programmed to open it, so he took it apart. When the compartment opened and Mr. Anaya could see large amounts of money inside, he said, "I don't want to see this; I don't want any problems." He immediately got out of the car. He accepted $1,500 as payment for opening and repairing the F150 compartment. He continued to build compartments for the DTO, including the compartment in the Ridgeline.

Mr. Bonilla-Montiel asked Mr. Anaya to install a compartment in the Ridgeline that was large enough to hold "at least 10 kilos" and showed him a red brick to indicate the approximate size of a kilo. While Mr. Anaya was building the compartment in the Ridgeline, the DTO used the compartment he installed in the F150 to transport six kilos of cocaine and five pounds of meth. Police stopped the F150 during this time as it was travelling with drugs from California to Kansas, but they could not find or open Mr. Anaya's compartment and released the F150 and its drivers. Mr. Crow sold the drugs from the F150 to two of the DTO's top distributors for approximately $70,000-$80,000.

In 2009, officers began surveillance of DTO operations, including a wiretap that intercepted calls to and from Mr. Anaya between January 30, 2009, and November 29, 2009. During this time, the officers witnessed DTO members dropping off and picking up many vehicles from Mr. Anaya's residence and Mr. Anaya meeting with known drug dealers.

On February 19, 2009, officers saw a white Toyota Sequoia arrive at Mr. Anaya's home. Mr. Bonilla-Montiel testified that he and Mr. Magallon-Maldonado drove the Sequoia to Mr. Anaya's home to pick up the Ridgeline. After Mr. Anaya showed them how to work the Ridgeline's hidden compartment, they paid him $5,000 in $10 and $20 bills and took the Ridgeline. Mr. Crow and other DTO members loaded the Ridgeline's compartment with 100 pounds of marijuana. Another DTO member, Jaime Rodriguez, drove it from California to Kansas. Mr. Crow then left the Ridgeline, still loaded with marijuana, at DTO member Noah Adams's house in Kansas for safekeeping.

Mr. Bonilla-Montiel, Mr. Magallon-Maldonado, and Mr. Crow arranged for Mr. Anaya to install a hidden compartment between the back seats of the Toyota Sequoia for "4 kilos or to store money." Mr. Anaya charged them $4,500 for the work on the Sequoia. Mr. Anaya warned Mr. Crow not to show anyone how to open the compartment or where it was located because the police had apprehended previous cars with his compartments. Mr. Crow later unloaded cocaine from the compartment in the Sequoia. Mr. Bonilla-Montiel and other DTO members transported cocaine and proceeds from marijuana sales between California and Kansas in the Sequoia.

On April 5, 2009, police officers stopped several DTO members during a return trip to California. Officers found $106,000 in heat-sealed packets in the Sequoia's hidden compartment and noted that someone had insulated the "sophisticated" compartment to mask the smell of drugs.

On April 4-6, 2009, officers intercepted calls between Mr. Bonilla-Montiel and Mr. Anaya, during which Mr. Anaya said that he could put "three speakers" in the Camry for $2,500. Mr. Bonilla-Montiel testified "three speakers" was their code term for three kilos or three pounds of meth. Once Mr. Anaya completed the compartment in the Camry, DTO members used the car to transport two pounds of meth from California to Kansas in the hidden compartment.

On April 24, 2009, officers stopped the Camry and found the two pounds of meth concealed in the compartment. Mr. Crow and Mr. Bonilla-Montiel then began to fear that Mr. Anaya was involved with the police. They traded the Ridgeline for an Altima and did no further business with Mr. Anaya.

On November 18, 2009, police executed a search warrant at Mr. Anaya's home and shop. Officers found more than 15 removed airbags, insulation, electrical devices required to build the hidden compartments, rifles, shotguns, pistols, bulletproof vests, and various ammunition. They found stereo wires but no speakers. Mr. Anaya confessed that he had built hidden compartments in cars for more than ten years.

a. Assume that Anaya is convicted of conspiracy to distribute drugs with Esteban Magallon-Maldanado, Cesar Bonilla-Montiel, Curtis Crow, Jaime Rodriguez, and Noah Adams. He appeals, arguing the evidence was insufficient to convict him. Should the court affirm his conviction? If so, should the court affirm Anaya's conviction with respect to every co-conspirator listed above, or only some of them?

b. Imagine you are the federal prosecutor assigned to Anaya's case. The head of your office has given you the discretion to decide what charge(s), if any, to bring against Anaya. What charge(s), if any, would you bring? If you were to offer a plea deal to Anaya, what would the terms of the offer be?

c. The Tenth Circuit's recitation of the facts states that "Cesar Bonilla-Montiel headed the" drug trafficking organization, and that Bonilla-Montiel testified against Anaya at his trial. The reason Bonilla-Montiel testified against Anaya is that the prosecutor made a deal with Bonilla-Montiel. Under the deal, Bonilla-Montiel received a sentence that was half as long as the sentence Anaya ultimately received. Why do you think the prosecutor made a plea deal with Bonilla-Montiel if he was one of the heads of the organization? Do you think it is fair that Anaya received a sentence twice as long as Bonilla-Montiel's?

# Revisiting the Elements of Crimes and Interpreting Criminal Statutes

As discussed in Chapter 2, there are literally thousands of different criminal offenses today — over 4,000 at the federal level alone according to one estimate. Criminal law casebooks and courses necessarily focus on only a small number of the most significant offenses. For this reason, it is important to better understand the general principles that shape other criminal statutes. These general principles were introduced in Chapter 2, and we have now seen them in action in the context of specific offenses.

As we have seen, every crime is made up of one or more elements. Most elements fall into one of four categories: (1) acts (*actus reus*), (2) mental state (*mens rea*), (3) causation (results elements), and (4) attendant circumstances. In most cases, criminal lawyers do not spend much energy thinking about which category a particular element falls into. Their concern is whether or not the element is met in the case at hand. After all, to win a conviction, the prosecutor must prove every element of the charged crime(s) beyond a reasonable doubt. The defense attorney will try to raise a reasonable doubt as to one or more elements. Labeling each element as an act or a mental state element is often beside the point. But the task can sometimes be an important one. This is because there are some fixed legal principles that apply to each type of element — particularly in the areas of act and mental state elements.

In this chapter, we revisit general principles regarding

## Key Concepts

- How does the principle that the act (*actus reus*) element is typically satisfied only by a voluntary act impact the interpretation of criminal statutes with more than one act element?
- What is the relationship between *mens rea* and mistakes of fact?
- Most of the time, criminal statutes are clear about the *mens rea* (if any) required for each element. When there is ambiguity, how do courts determine what mental state (if any) should apply?

acts and mental states. We also explore some of the principles that govern the interpretation of criminal statutes.

## A. ACT (*ACTUS REUS*)

## 1. Revisiting *Actus Reus*

It is often said that the *actus reus* of a crime can only be satisfied by a voluntary act, meaning a volitional act by the defendant; or, in limited circumstances, by the failure to act when there is a duty to act. Although legal principles regarding voluntary acts and omissions can be important in some cases, they are effectively irrelevant in the context of many offenses and in the overwhelming majority of prosecutions.

Consider, for example, burglary (discussed in Chapter 3). Under the common law definition, burglary is the breaking and entering of the dwelling of another at night with the intent to commit a felony therein. Two of these elements — breaking and entering — would be categorized as act elements. Pursuant to the black letter law of voluntary acts, the breaking and entering elements will be met only if they were the result of the defendant's willed bodily movement. But, of course, it is difficult to imagine many circumstances in which a defendant's breaking and entering of a dwelling could be anything other than voluntary. A sleepwalker is unlikely to leave her house, walk to someone else's, and break into it. Moreover, in the very unlikely event that a person did involuntarily break into and enter someone else's house by sleepwalking or otherwise, the absence of an intent to commit a felony inside is likely to be a more effective defense, as a practical matter. Notice also that the law of omissions has no application whatsoever to the crime of burglary. The act elements of burglary are *specific* actions — breaking and entering — that are impossible to achieve by the failure to take action. This is not to say that the act elements of a crime like burglary are unimportant. But disputes about them center on questions like whether the defendant's conduct qualified as *breaking* and *entering* as those elements are defined under the law of burglary, and not on whether the defendant's physical acts were voluntary.

Disputes about the law of voluntary acts and omissions arise in just a few kinds of settings — and even then, only rarely. To better appreciate why this is so, recall the definition of an involuntary act and the legal principles regarding omissions. As discussed in Chapter 2, a voluntary act means a volitional act; a willed bodily movement. By contrast, an involuntary act is any act resulting from "a reflex or convulsion; a bodily movement during unconsciousness or sleep; conduct during hypnosis or resulting from hypnotic suggestion; or a bodily movement that otherwise is not a product of the effort or determination of the actor, either conscious or habitual." Model Penal Code § 2.01. In limited circumstances, a person's failure to act (i.e., an omission) can satisfy the act element of a crime. For an omission to satisfy the act element of a crime, there must be a legal duty to act. A legal duty arises in only a few circumstances: (1) special relationships, including parents to their children or spouses to one another; (2) a contractual obligation, such as a nursing home's contractual duty to care for its residents; (3) the assumption of care, meaning that a person who starts rendering aid has a duty to continue; (4) failing to provide assistance after putting someone in harm's way; or (5) when a statute expressly creates a duty to act—for example, the federal statute that makes it a crime to fail to pay one's taxes (26 U.S.C. § 7203) or the federal statute that makes it a crime for a person who has been convicted of certain sex offenses to fail to register under the Sex Offender Registration and Notification Act (18 U.S.C. § 2250).

With these principles in mind, consider one of the most common settings in which issues regarding voluntary acts and omissions can arise: homicide offenses (covered in Chapter 5). Unlike the crime of burglary, which requires specific acts (breaking and entering), a prosecution for murder or manslaughter can rest on literally any voluntary act or culpable omission that causes death. In comparison to the acts of breaking and entering, it is much more plausible to imagine scenarios in which someone's involuntary act causes death. For example, a driver who has a muscle spasm, swerves into oncoming traffic, and kills another motorist has acted involuntarily. This is because the spasm that caused the accident was not is the product of the driver's effort or determination. The same would be true of a driver who has an unexpected seizure, resulting in a deadly crash. In each hypothetical, the driver's act led to someone else's death, but because the acts were involuntary, the driver has not committed a homicide offense.

What about a driver who *knows* he is prone to seizures and drives anyway? If this driver has a seizure, loses control of the car, and kills a pedestrian, does the voluntary act principle mean that he cannot be convicted of a homicide offense? The short answer is no. To see why, focus on the nature of the act element of a homicide offense—it is *any* voluntary act that *causes* death. The driver's seizure is surely an involuntary act. But before his seizure, the driver committed a voluntary act by getting behind the wheel. Because this hypothetical driver knew he was prone to seizures, it was reasonably foreseeable that an accident like this might occur. For this reason, the act of driving would be every bit as much a proximate cause of the death as the seizure itself, and therefore can be a basis for homicide liability. This was the holding in a well-known New York case that is often cited in casebooks and treatises, *People v. Decina*, 2 N.Y.2d 133 (1956). Whether the seizure-prone driver could ultimately be convicted of a homicide and, if so, what degree, would depend on the driver's mental state with respect to the level of risk involved in driving. But for purposes of *actus reus* of a homicide offense, the act of driving would be a voluntary act that proximately caused death. (By contrast, in the case of a driver who has an *unexpected* seizure, the voluntary act of driving would not foreseeably result in a seizure-induced crash, and so it would not be a proximate cause of the accident.)

Homicide cases are relatively more likely to raise voluntary act and omission issues because the *actus reus* of the offense is so open-ended. (Although even in the homicide setting, very few cases raise voluntary act or omissions issues.) But sometimes offenses that target specific conduct can also be amenable to raising voluntary act issues.

Consider a location-based crime like public intoxication. In some states it is a crime to appear in an intoxicated condition in public. In comparison to the act elements of burglary (breaking and entering), it is easier to imagine circumstances in which the act of appearing in public is not voluntary. For example, a person might get drunk inside his home and be carried into public by someone else — an unlikely event, but not unimaginable. In fact, this happened in *Martin v. State*, 17 So. 2d 427 (Ala. Ct. App. 1944), another case that is included in many criminal law casebooks and treatises. Martin was drunk inside his home. The police arrested him and took him outside, "where he allegedly committed the proscribed act[]" of being drunk in public. *Id.* The court overturned Martin's conviction on the ground that "an accusation of drunkenness in a designated public place cannot be established by proof that the accused, while in an intoxicated condition, was involuntarily and forcibly carried to that place by the arresting officer." *Id.* Put another way, because Martin's appearance in public was not the result of a volitional act, the act element of the offense was not satisfied.

## 2. Interpreting Criminal Statutes in Light of Voluntary Act Principles

One of the most important ways that general legal principles about voluntary acts and omissions impact criminal law is through the interpretation of criminal statutes. Consistent with these principles, courts generally interpret the act element(s) of criminal statutes to implicitly require a voluntary act or a culpable omission (i.e., the failure to act despite a recognized legal duty). It is for this reason that the court in *Martin v. State*, described immediately above, held that a statute making it a crime for an intoxicated person to "appear[] in any public place" required a voluntary act. 17 So. 2d 427 (Ala. Ct. App. 1944). Appearing in a place can be accomplished through a voluntary or an involuntary act. Nevertheless, the court held that "a voluntary appearance is presupposed" by the statute. *Id.* Although courts often interpret every act element of a criminal statute to require a voluntary act, the question is not always so clear.

Disputes about voluntary act principles are infrequent, but one setting where they have arisen with some regularity is in prosecutions for possessing contraband in a jail. Like the crime of public intoxication, drug possession in a jail includes a location-based element. Perhaps more important, many of the people who go to jail do not walk in the door voluntarily — they are arrestees, who are brought into jail by the police. If an arrestee who is in possession of drugs is transported to jail, can he be convicted of the crime of possession of a controlled substance in a jail? Or do statutes criminalizing possession of a controlled substance in a jail, in the words of *Martin v. State*, presuppose "a voluntary appearance"? Courts across the country are split on the question of how to interpret statutes criminalizing drug possession in a jail, in light of voluntary act principles.

## Case Preview

# State v. Barnes

In *Barnes*, the court addresses whether the crime of possession of marijuana in a penal institution requires the defendant's presence in jail to have been due to a voluntary act.

As you read the decision, consider the following questions:

1. The majority agrees that "guilt of a criminal offense ordinarily requires proof that the defendant voluntarily committed a physical act." Given that, why does the court hold that "a defendant may be found guilty of possession of a controlled substance in a local confinement facility even though he was not voluntarily present in the facility in question"?
2. What key issue(s) lead the dissent to disagree with the majority's holding?

# State v. Barnes
### 229 N.C. App. 556 (2013)

ERVIN, J.

Defendant Christopher L. Barnes appeals from a judgment sentencing him to a term of six to eight months imprisonment based upon his convictions for simple possession of a controlled substance and possession of a controlled substance in a penal institution or local confinement facility.

At approximately 2:00 A.M. on 21 January 2011, Officer Melvin Smith of the Goldsboro Police Department observed Defendant drive his vehicle onto Ash Street in Goldsboro without operating his headlights. As a result, Officer Smith stopped Defendant's vehicle. Upon approaching Defendant, Officer Smith noticed a strong smell of alcohol about his person. As a result of Defendant's performance on these field sobriety tests, the smell of alcohol about Defendant's person, and Defendant's red and glassy eyes, Officer Smith determined that Defendant was "appreciably impaired" as the result of his consumption of alcohol and arrested him for driving while subject to an impairing substance.

After being placed under arrest, Defendant was handcuffed with his hands behind his back, searched for weapons, and transported to the Wayne County jail. Upon his arrival at the jail, Defendant requested to use the restroom. As part of his attempt to honor Defendant's request, Officer Smith changed the positioning of Defendant's handcuffs so as to place Defendant's hands in front of his body. In addition, Officer Smith placed himself in a position to observe Defendant's effort to use the restroom without seeing his private parts. [Afterwards, Officer Smith returned] Defendant to the location at which breath samples were taken from individuals who had been placed under arrest for driving while impaired. After Defendant was seated in a chair at that location, a bag containing a substance ultimately determined to be marijuana fell from his pants leg.

[T]he jury returned verdicts convicting Defendant of simple possession of marijuana and possession of marijuana in a penal institution or local confinement facility. Defendant noted an appeal to this Court from the trial court's judgment.[2]

Defendant argues that the trial court erred by denying his motion to dismiss the possession of a controlled substance in a local confinement facility charge.

N.C. Gen. Stat. § 90-95(e)(9) provides that "[a]ny person who violates [N.C. Gen. Stat. §] 90-95(a)(3) on the premises of a penal institution or local confinement facility shall be guilty of a Class H felony." N.C. Gen. Stat. § 90-95(a)(3) . . . punishes the possession of a controlled substance.

Defendant argues that he did not "voluntarily enter the Wayne County Detention Center."[5] In essence, Defendant argues that, even if he had the requisite mental state needed to support a conviction for committing the offense made punishable by N.C. Gen. Stat. § 90-95(e)(9), his dismissal motion still should have been granted because he did not voluntarily bring controlled substances into a local confinement facility. According to the argument advanced by Defendant and accepted by our dissenting colleague, the offense of possession of less than a half ounce of marijuana, which would have otherwise been a Class 3 misdemeanor, *see* N.C. Gen. Stat. § 90-95(d)(4), cannot be transformed into a felony by the conduct of the officers who arrested him and brought him into a local confinement facility against his wishes. As a result, Defendant essentially contends, and our dissenting colleague agrees, that the record does not reflect the occurrence of the voluntary act necessary to support his conviction for committing a criminal offense.

As a general proposition, the term *"actus reus"* refers to "[t]he wrongful deed that comprises the physical components of a crime." *Black's Law Dictionary* 37 (7th ed. 1999). According to the *actus reus* requirement, guilt of a criminal offense ordinarily requires proof that the defendant voluntarily committed a physical act. As a result, regardless of "[w]hether the offense charged be a specific-intent or a general-intent crime, in order to convict the accused the State must prove that he voluntarily did the forbidden act." *State v. Caddell*, 287 N.C. 266, 296 (1975). After considering the specific language of the statute under which Defendant was convicted and the decisions reached in the majority of jurisdictions which have considered this issue, however, we are convinced, contrary to Defendant's contention, that a defendant may be found guilty of possession of a controlled substance in a local confinement facility even though he was not voluntarily present in the facility in question.

The first problem with this aspect of Defendant's challenge to the trial court's decision to deny his dismissal motion is that it has no support in the relevant statutory language. The offense punishable by N.C. Gen. Stat. § 90-95(e)(9) revolves

---

[2] In addition to the offenses discussed in the text, Defendant was also charged with and convicted of driving while impaired. We have not set forth the procedural facts relating to this charge in our opinion given that Defendant has not advanced any argument concerning this charge in his brief before this Court.

[5] Although Defendant never specifically mentions the term *actus reus* and describes his argument as resting upon the State's failure to show that he possessed the "intent" required for a finding of guilt, we believe that it is fair to interpret Defendant's argument as an assertion that . . . he did not enter the Wayne County jail while possessing marijuana voluntarily.

around the possession of a controlled substance in a penal institution or local confinement facility rather than around the intentional bringing or introduction of a controlled substance into such a facility. A reviewing court should, of course, take the statutory language defining the offense for which a defendant was convicted and the purpose which the General Assembly sought to accomplish by enacting that language seriously in determining the showing necessary to support a finding of guilt. [N]othing in the relevant statutory language requires proof that Defendant voluntarily introduced a controlled substance into the penal institution or confinement facility. In addition, given that the offense made punishable by N.C. Gen. Stat. § 90-95(e)(9) was obviously intended to assist in controlling the amount of controlled substances brought into and consumed in prisons or jails, we have difficulty seeing how the purpose underlying N.C. Gen. Stat. § 90-95(e)(9) is served by treating defendants who simply possess controlled substances at the time of their arrest and have those substances on their persons when taken into a jail or prison differently from defendants who consciously intend to bring controlled substances into such facilities. As a result, the position espoused by the Defendant is unsupported by the language of and contrary to the purpose underlying N.C. Gen. Stat. § 90-95(e)(9).

In addition, Defendant's position is inconsistent with the result reached in the majority of decisions from other jurisdictions that have addressed the issue of whether a defendant can be convicted of possessing a controlled substance in a confinement facility after having been involuntarily brought into the facility following an arrest. *See State v. Canas*, 597 N.W.2d 488, 496 (Iowa 1999) (upholding the defendant's conviction because "the defendant in [that case] had the option of disclosing the presence of the drugs concealed in his person before he entered the jail and became guilty of the additional offense of introducing controlled substances into a detention facility"); *Brown v. State*, 89 S.W.3d 630, 632-33 (Tex. Crim. App. 2002) (*en banc*) (upholding the defendant's conviction on the grounds that the "voluntary act" requirement had no relation to the defendant's mental state and that the necessary "voluntary act" had occurred as long as the defendant's physical movements were not involuntary); *State v. Winsor*, 110 S.W.3d 882, 886 (Mo. Ct. App. 2003) (upholding the defendant's conviction on the grounds that the existence of the required "voluntary act" hinged upon the voluntariness of the defendant's possession of the controlled substance rather than the voluntariness of his presence in the jail); *but see State v. Tippetts*, 180 Or. App. 350, 354 (2002) (overturning the defendant's conviction on the grounds that he had not committed the required "voluntary act," which the court defined as an act "performed or initiated by the defendant"); *State v. Cole*, 142 N.M. 325, 328 (2007) (overturning the defendant's conviction on the grounds that, rather than bringing contraband into the jail himself, "law enforcement brought him and the contraband in his possession into the facility").[9]

The majority of decisions which have addressed the issue before us in this case have essentially held that, while guilt of an offense stemming from possession of a

---

[9]Interestingly, the New Mexico Court of Appeals has held in a number of unpublished decisions that, when a prisoner who has been granted work release brings unlawful controlled substances back to the facility after work, he can be convicted of bringing contraband into the prison facility despite having no alternative except to enter the unit in which he is confined because the defendant "was in prison where he knew the contraband was prohibited" and elected to return to the facility with forbidden substances anyway. *See State v. Rueda*, 2009 WL 6593952, at *2.

controlled substance in a confinement facility does require the defendant to commit a voluntary act, the necessary voluntary act occurs when the defendant knowingly possesses the controlled substance. We find this logic convincing. As a result, we conclude that the voluntary act necessary for guilt of the offense made punishable by N.C. Gen. Stat. § 90-95(e)(9) occurs when the defendant knowingly possesses a controlled substance and that the recognition of a requirement that a defendant make a decision to intentionally bring controlled substances into a confinement facility would be, in reality, the adoption of a specific intent or *mens rea* requirement rather than the effectuation of the *actus reus* requirement.[11]

The ultimate logic underlying the position taken in the decisions from other courts that have refrained from adopting the majority view and the position espoused by Defendant and our dissenting colleague appears to rest upon a sense that it is simply unfair to punish a defendant who chooses to possess a controlled substance and is then arrested and taken into custody without voluntarily surrendering the controlled substances in his possession as severely as a defendant who deliberately chooses to introduce controlled substances into a penal institution or confinement facility. Although we understand the equitable appeal of such logic, we also believe that a defendant who is arrested with controlled substances in his possession has options other than simply taking the controlled substances with him into the confinement facility. For example, the defendant always has an opportunity to disclose the existence of these controlled substances to the arresting officer before he ever reaches the jail. As the Ohio Supreme Court has noted, while the defendant "was made to go to the detention facility, . . . he did not have to take the drugs with him." Thus, we simply do not find the logic that appears to underlie the decisions requiring a finding that the defendant voluntarily decide to introduce controlled substances into a penal institution or local confinement facility as a precondition for a determination that the defendant committed an offense like that made punishable pursuant to N.C. Gen. Stat. § 90-95(e)(9) persuasive.[12]

As a result, for the reasons set forth above, . . . the fact that Defendant was involuntarily brought to the Wayne County Jail at a time when he possessed marijuana does not preclude his conviction for possession of a controlled substance in a local confinement facility.

[In a portion of the opinion that is omitted from this excerpt, the court reversed Barnes's conviction for simple possession of a controlled substance on the grounds that it is a lesser-included offense of possession of a controlled substance in a penal local confinement facility.]

---

[11] Although certain of the opinions from other jurisdictions that uphold convictions resting on facts similar to those present here note that the defendant was warned that taking a controlled substance into the jail would constitute a separate offense, we do not believe that the absence of such a warning in this case is of any consequence given that ignorance of the law is no excuse for a failure to comply with its terms and given that legislatures and courts do not, in most instances, make the criminality of specific instances of conduct dependent on the provision of information by law enforcement officers.

[12] This Court is not oblivious to the fact that our decision may have the effect of requiring a defendant who is arrested while in possession of a controlled substance to admit to the commission of a criminal offense in order to avoid liability for committing a more serious one. However, aside from the fact that Defendant did not advance an argument in reliance upon Fifth Amendment principles in his brief, we agree with the Supreme Court of California that effectively forcing such a choice upon the defendant does not violate the state and federal constitutional right against compulsory self-incrimination.

Thus, for the reasons set forth above, we conclude that, while the trial court did not err by denying Defendant's motion to dismiss the possession of a controlled substance in a local confinement facility charge, it erred by entering judgment against Defendant based upon his convictions for both possession of a controlled substance in a local confinement facility and simple possession of the same controlled substance. As a result, we find no error in Defendant's conviction for possession of a controlled substance in a confinement facility, vacate Defendant's conviction for simple possession of a controlled substance, and remand this case to the Wayne County Superior Court for resentencing.

McGEE, J., dissenting.

I respectfully dissent from the majority's conclusion that the trial court did not err in denying Defendant's motion to dismiss the charge of possession of marijuana in a confinement facility.

It is well-established that, to hold a defendant criminally liable for an offense, the State must show an *actus reus. See* 4 William Blackstone, Commentaries \*19, \*20-21.

> An involuntary act, as it has no claim to merit, so neither can it induce any guilt: the concurrence of the will, when it has its choice either to do or to avoid the fact in question, being the only thing that renders human actions either praiseworthy or culpable. Indeed, to make a complete crime cognizable by human laws, there must be both a will and an act.

*Id.* The common law is clearly in force in this State. *See* N.C. Gen. Stat. § 4-1 (2011).

> All such parts of the common law as were heretofore in force and use within this State . . . and which has not been otherwise provided for in whole or in part, not abrogated, repealed, or become obsolete, are hereby declared to be in full force within this State.

*Id.*

Our Supreme Court has long recognized the rule that criminal liability requires a voluntary act.

The present issue must therefore be analyzed while bearing in mind these settled principles. "[C]riminal liability requires that the activity in question be voluntary." Wayne R. LaFave, Substantive Criminal Law § 6.1, at 425 (2nd ed.). "The deterrent function of the criminal law would not be served by imposing sanctions for involuntary action, as such action cannot be deterred." *Id.* at 425-26. "In the overwhelming majority of criminal cases, the voluntary nature of defendant's acts is not at issue." *Id.* at 426, n.24. Where an officer transports a defendant into a confinement facility, the voluntary nature of the defendant's acts is at issue.

Defendant was initially handcuffed with his hands behind his back, and an officer transported Defendant to the confinement facility. A bag containing marijuana fell out of Defendant's pants while he was inside the facility. Defendant was convicted of possessing marijuana in a confinement facility.

The amount of marijuana found was approximately one seventh of one ounce. Possession of one seventh of one ounce of marijuana is a Class 3 misdemeanor. The maximum sentence for a Class 3 misdemeanor for a Level II offender like Defendant is fifteen days of community or intermediate punishment. In contrast, possession of one seventh of one ounce of marijuana in a confinement facility is a Class H felony, for which Defendant was sentenced to six to eight months in prison.

No case in this State analyzes the precise issue of whether a defendant who is brought to a confinement facility in handcuffs voluntarily possesses marijuana in the facility. Cases from other jurisdictions, including Oregon, Washington, and New Mexico, yield persuasive reasoning on similar facts.

In *State v. Tippetts*, 180 Or. App. 350 (2002), the defendant was charged with introducing "contraband into a correctional facility" in violation of Or. Rev. Stat. § 162.185. The defendant in *Tippetts* was found with marijuana in his pants pocket during a search inside the jail. The State argued the "earlier voluntary act of possession" was sufficient to hold the defendant "criminally liable for the later involuntary act of introducing the marijuana into the jail." The Court of Appeals of Oregon disagreed. The "[d]efendant, however, did not initiate the introduction of the contraband into the jail or cause it to be introduced in the jail. Rather, the contraband was introduced into the jail only because the police took [the] defendant (and the contraband) there against his will."

In *State v. Eaton*, 168 Wash. 2d 476 (2010) (en banc), the defendant received an enhanced sentence for possessing drugs in a jail. The Supreme Court of Washington stated that as "a general rule, every crime must contain two elements: (1) an actus reus and (2) a mens rea. Actus reus is defined as [t]he wrongful deed that comprises the physical components of a crime[.]" "Once [the defendant] was arrested, he no longer had control over his location. From the time of arrest, his movement from street to jail became involuntary: involuntary not because he did not wish to enter the jail, but because he was forcibly taken there by State authority. He no longer had the ability to choose his own course of action." The Supreme Court of Washington concluded the defendant did not voluntarily possess the drugs in the jail and affirmed the decision of the Court of Appeals of Washington.

Cases from other jurisdictions are not binding on this Court and, likewise, the apparent majority or minority nature of a foreign rule is not binding either. Nevertheless, cases from other jurisdictions can be persuasive, and I find the reasoning in the above cases to be convincing. Most importantly, the reasoning comports with our State's long-established principle that criminal liability requires a voluntary act. *See, e.g., State v. Bush*, 164 N.C. App. 254, 265 (2004) ("[T]he absence of consciousness not only precludes the existence of any specific mental state, but also excludes the possibility of *a voluntary act without which there can be no criminal liability*.") (emphasis added)).

In the present case, Defendant was handcuffed with his hands behind his back, and an officer transported Defendant to the confinement facility. Eventually, a bag containing marijuana fell out of Defendant's pants while Defendant was inside the facility. The facts demonstrate, and the majority does not disagree that, from the time Defendant was arrested, Defendant had no control over his location. Rather, the officer controlled Defendant's location. The officer took Defendant to the confinement facility. Defendant had no ability to choose his own course of action regarding his location. To hold Defendant criminally liable for possession of marijuana inside a confinement facility under these facts violates the common law requirement to show an *actus reus*.

I would hold that the State failed to offer evidence to show that Defendant acted voluntarily in bringing marijuana to the confinement facility and possessing marijuana inside. Without showing that Defendant acted voluntarily and thereby satisfying the common law requirement to show an *actus reus*, the State cannot hold Defendant criminally liable for possession of marijuana in a local confinement facility.

---

## Post-Case Follow-Up

Does the crime of possession of a controlled substance in a jail require the defendant's presence at the jail to have been the result of a voluntary act? As the opinion in *Barnes* reveals, the majority of jurisdictions to decide the issue have held that presence as the result of a voluntary act is not required. These courts have reasoned that, "while guilt of an offense stemming from possession of a controlled substance in a confinement facility does require the defendant to commit a voluntary act, the necessary voluntary act occurs when the defendant knowingly possesses the controlled substance." By contrast, in a minority of jurisdictions, courts have held that the offense requires the defendant to have acted voluntarily in entering the jail. The dispute shows that while there is widespread agreement that at least one of the acts proscribed by a criminal statute must be voluntary, there is disagreement about whether *every* act element of an offense must be voluntary. In the context of the crime of possessing a controlled substance in jail, most courts have taken the view that so long as one of the act elements (possession of a controlled substance) was voluntary, the other act element (presence in a jail) need not be.

---

## Barnes: *Real Life Applications*

1. You are an Assistant District Attorney in Alabama prosecuting a defendant charged with possession of a controlled substance in a prison.

   The defense requests the following jury instruction: "To convict, the defendant's presence in the jail must have been the result of a voluntary act. A voluntary act is a volitional act. An involuntary act is any act resulting from a reflex or convulsion; a bodily movement during unconsciousness or sleep; conduct during hypnosis or resulting from hypnotic suggestion; or a bodily movement that otherwise is not a product of the effort or determination of the actor, either consciousness or habitual."

   In support of the proposed instruction, the defendant cites *Martin v. State*, 17 So. 2d 427 (Ala. Ct. App. 1944), the decision described above at page 446. Because this is an Alabama case, *Martin* is binding precedent and the trial court is required to follow it.

   What argument(s) would you make to distinguish *Martin*?

2. You are an aide to a state legislator in Oregon. As discussed in *Barnes*, Oregon is one of the states in which courts have held that the crime of possession of

a controlled substance in jail does not apply to a person who was brought to the jail by the police. See *State v. Tippetts*, 180 Or. App. 350 (2002). Your boss is thinking of introducing a bill that would expressly overturn the holding in *Tippetts* and adopt the position taken by the majority in *Barnes*.

    **a.** Draft a proposed statute that would accomplish your boss's goal.

    **b.** Although your boss is thinking of introducing a bill to overturn the holding in *Tippetts*, she wants to consider counterarguments before she makes a final decision. She is especially interested in whether overturning *Tippetts* would help to further the goal of keeping illegal drugs out of correctional facilities. In *Barnes*, the majority argued that applying the statute to defendants who are brought to jail by the police is consistent with the legislative purpose of keeping controlled substances out of jails. Your boss asks you to write a brief memo discussing any possible counterarguments to this position. Can you think of any?

---

## B. MENTAL STATE (*MENS REA*)

## 1. Revisiting Mental States

Mental states are at the center of criminal law. Although strict liability crimes exist, a culpable mental state (or *mens rea*) is usually considered to be "an indispensable element of a criminal offense." *United States v. U.S. Gypsum Co.*, 438 U.S. 422, 437 (1978). This is in part due to "the background rules of the common law, in which the requirement of some *mens rea* for a crime is firmly embedded." *Staples v. United States*, 511 U.S. 600, 605 (1994). The criminal law's focus on mental states is also driven by the theories of punishment, which support linking punishment severity to *mens rea*. Most would consider a person who commits a bad act on purpose to be more blameworthy than a person who acts recklessly, for example. Similarly, a person who is willing to commit a bad act on purpose is arguably in greater need of deterrence than a person who acts recklessly.

    In its early development, the term *mens rea* was understood quite broadly — "based on general moral blameworthiness, the conception was an exceedingly vague one." Francis Bowes Sayre, *Mens Rea*, 45 Harv. L. Rev. 974, 994 (1932). As the common law developed, the *mens rea* required for different offenses "inevitably came to differ from those of another." *Id*. This history gave rise to both the elemental meaning of *mens rea* that the law employs today and the handful of mental states that recur throughout the criminal code. These mental states are intent, purpose, knowledge, recklessness, and negligence. To be sure, criminal statutes sometimes incorporate other mental states. In the area of homicides, for example, intentional killings are further divided into those that were willful, deliberate, and premeditated and those that were not. In addition, and as discussed further below, the historical development of mental state terms has left some ambiguity and variation for some terms.

By this point, we have seen each of the mental states (intent, purpose, knowledge, recklessness, and criminal negligence) in action in the context of specific offenses. This section revisits and reviews some of the important general principles of *mens rea*.

## Intent

Intent is one of the oldest and more frequently used mental states. Despite (or perhaps because of) this, there can sometimes be uncertainty about its meaning. At a minimum, a person acts intentionally when it is her purpose (i.e., her conscious object or desire) to perform an act or cause a result. This definition of intent is equivalent to the more modern mental state of purpose. Often, intent *also* encompasses the more modern mental state of knowledge, which is "when [a person] knows that the result is practically certain to follow from his conduct, whatever his desire may be as to that result." *U.S. Gypsum Co.*, 438 U.S. at 445 (citation omitted). The distinction between the purpose and knowledge variants of intent carries little practical significance in most cases. After all, a person who knows that her conduct is practically certain to achieve a particular result typically wants for that result to occur. Occasionally, however, the distinction is a critically important one. And, for some offenses, courts or legislatures define intent to mean *only* the purpose variant of the term.

Let's look at examples of each approach to the mental state of intent. For the broad approach to defining intent, consider the crime of murder, covered in Chapter 5. Murder is the killing of another human being with malice aforethought, a term that includes cases where a person acts with an intent to kill. In this setting, a killing is intentional if either the perpetrator's conscious object was to cause the victim's death or if he knew that it was practically certain that his conduct would cause the victim's death. A frequently employed hypothetical demonstrates the practical application of this rule. Imagine that Don attaches a bomb to his boss Victor's house. Don knows that Victor lives with his wife, Betty. Don sets off the bomb one night when Victor and Betty are at home sleeping, killing them both. Don's conscious object when he set off the bomb was to kill only Victor. Indeed, Don hoped that Betty would somehow miraculously escape harm, but he knew that the explosion was practically certain to

## Specific Intent Crimes and General Intent Crimes

We have seen passing references to the terms "specific intent crime" and "general intent crime" in a few of the cases we have encountered in this book so far. For example, in *State v. Barnes*, presented earlier in this chapter, the court noted that a voluntary act is typically required "[w]hether the offense charged be a specific-intent or a general-intent crime." 229 N.C. App. 556, 563 (2013).

What do these terms mean? And what is the legal significance of whether an offense falls into one category or the other? The terms are over 150 years old, so one might think there are clear answers to these questions. Sadly, there are not. The terms have long been criticized by courts and scholars alike "as confusing and perhaps incoherent"; nevertheless, "[t]he terminology persists." Eric A. Johnson, *Understanding General and Specific Intent: Eight Things I Know for Sure*, 13 Ohio St. J. Crim. L. 521, 521 (2016). On the bright side, it is rarely necessary to determine which category an offense belongs to because the distinction has little practical significance in most cases. In addition, although the exact meaning of the terms and the reason for them remains disputed, there is fairly widespread agreement about their most important characteristics.

The main consequence of an offense being categorized as a specific or a general intent crime concerns the affirmative defense of voluntary intoxication. The defense of voluntary intoxication is addressed in detail in Chapter 11. For present purposes, it is enough to state the basic rule, which is that a defendant can introduce evidence of her intoxication to show that she did not form (or was incapable of forming) the requisite mental state *only* as a defense to a specific intent crime, and not to a general intent crime. In some jurisdictions, the classification of a crime as specific or general intent impacts other defenses and doctrines. But these effects vary.

So, what makes an offense a specific or a general intent crime? A crime will qualify as a specific intent crime in two circumstances. The first is if the crime requires an intent to "do some further act" in addition to the prohibited conduct. *People v. Hood*, 1 Cal. 3d 444, 457 (1969). For example, recall that the common law definition of burglary is the breaking and entering of a dwelling of another at night with the intent to commit a felony therein. The requirement that the defendant intend to commit a felony inside the dwelling "is the 'intent to do a further act' that makes burglary a specific-intent offense." Johnson, *supra*, at 528.

Second, a crime will fall into the specific intent category if an element of the offense requires proof that the defendant acted with the purpose to "achieve some additional consequence" beyond the prescribed act. *Hood*, 1 Cal. 3d at 457. Under this rule, "an offense will qualify as a specific-intent offense if it requires proof that the defendant intended to bring about the social harm at which the statute is targeted." Johnson, *supra*, at 527. Larceny, for example, is "targeted at the social harm of permanent deprivation of property," and it requires proof that the defendant "intended to deprive the owner of the stolen property permanently." *Id*. at 524-25. As a result, it is classified as a specific intent crime.

kill Betty. Don has intentionally killed both Victor and Betty, as that term is defined for purposes of the crime of murder. This outcome makes intuitive sense to most people — it would seem odd in these circumstances if Don were guilty of a lesser homicide offense for the death of Betty than for the death of Victor.

For an example of the narrow approach to the mental state of intent, consider accomplice liability, addressed in Chapter 8. In *Hicks v. United States*, 150 U.S. 442 (1893), the Supreme Court held that to be an accomplice to a crime a person must act "with the intention of encouraging and abetting" someone else in the commission of that crime. In this setting, courts equate intent with purpose. Knowledge that one's actions would assist in the commission of a crime is not enough. This distinction is an especially important one in the case of legitimate retail sales and services, a topic that is addressed in Chapter 8 on pages 384-85. As discussed there, most courts have held that a person who sells legitimate goods with knowledge that the buyer plans to use the goods to commit a crime does not become an accomplice to that crime. Instead, a conviction requires proof that the seller "in some sense promote the[ criminal] venture himself, make it his own, have a stake in its outcome." *United States v. Falcone*, 109 F.2d 579, 581 (2d Cir. 1940). In other words, an accomplice must act with the conscious object — the purpose, in the terminology of the Model Penal Code — of assisting the commission of the crime.

When a statute includes intent as a mental state, how do we know whether the term is being used in the broad sense (meaning acting with purpose or knowledge) or the narrow sense (meaning acting only with purpose)? For many crimes, longstanding precedent provides the answer; case law establishes that intent is defined narrowly in the context of accomplice liability, for example. Where the question has not already been settled, courts must rely on tools of statutory interpretation to resolve the issue. In *United States v. Tobin*, for example, the United States Court of Appeals for the First Circuit considered a federal statute that criminalized making or causing "the telephone of another repeatedly or continuously to ring, with *intent* to harass any person at the called number." 552 F.3d 29, 30 (1st Cir. 2009). The issue presented in the case was whether the statute required that the defendant act with the *purpose* to harass, or if *knowledge* that the victim would feel harassed was sufficient. The court began its analysis by briefly summarizing the basis for the dispute:

> Although the word "intent" can often mean with "knowledge" that a particular result will follow, it sometimes instead requires a "purpose" to bring about a specific end. To avoid this confusion, the ALI Model Penal Code chose to avoid the term "intent," identifying knowledge or purpose as the more exact identifiers. Legislatures, however, have remained attached to the term.

> Any crime that does not have one of these two qualities is classified as a general intent crime. The following crimes that we have covered are considered specific intent crimes for purposes of the bar exam: burglary, larceny, robbery, embezzlement, extortion, first-degree premeditated murder, attempts, and conspiracy.

*Id.* at 32-33. Because the meaning of the term intent, standing alone, was "inconclusive," the court considered the structure of the statute and the legislative history. *Id.* at 32. Neither interpretive tool provided insight on the question of whether Congress meant for the statute to cover knowing harassment, or only purposeful harassment. The court resolved the ambiguity by focusing on culpability principles:

> We are therefore cast back on more general considerations. For most crimes "intent" in the sense of knowledge is enough; for example, when a defendant points a gun at the victim's head and pulls the trigger, the knowledge that death will result is ordinarily sufficient. But the distinction sometimes matters; this can be especially so for conduct which may be defensible only if done for a benevolent purpose (a doctor swabbing a wound may foreseeably cause considerable pain) or where bad purpose magnifies the harm (*e.g.*, racially motivated crimes).
>
> There is nothing inherently wicked or even suspect about multiple phone calls, even when the repeated phone calls and resultant ringing are annoying or distressing to someone who refuses to answer. Imagine repeated calls to warn that a fire is sweeping the neighborhood. Or, suppose repeated calls to sell a product or to solicit a contribution — where ringing is suffered rather than taking the phone off the hook for all calls. Nothing in [the statute] suggests that it was designed to mediate such difficult problems.

*Id.* at 33-34. For this reason, the court held that in the context of that statute, intent "require[d] a 'purpose' to harass"; knowledge was not enough. *Id.* at 34.

In most cases, the distinction between the broad meaning of intent (purpose or knowledge) and the narrow meaning (purpose) will be unimportant. This is because people who know that their acts will produce a particular result usually also intend for that result to occur. In addition, courts have already definitively resolved the issue for many offenses, like homicide. But, as *Tobin* shows, courts can sometimes struggle to determine precisely what mental state is required when a statute uses the *mens rea* term intent.

## Purpose

As already discussed, the drafters of the Model Penal Code avoided the ambiguity of the *mens rea* of intent by replacing it with two distinct mental states: purpose and knowledge. The Model Penal Code defines purpose as follows:

> A person acts purposely with respect to a material element of an offense when:
>     (i) if the element involves the nature of his conduct or a result thereof, it is his conscious object to engage in conduct of that nature or to cause such a result; and
>     (ii) if the element involves the attendant circumstances, he is aware of the existence of such circumstances or he believes or hopes that they exist.

Model Penal Code § 2.02(2)(a). The mental state of purpose matches the narrow definition of intent discussed above. Returning to the example of accomplice liability, if a retail employee sells a legitimate product to a customer who plans to use the product to commit a crime, the employee has acted purposely only if it was her conscious object to assist in the commission of the crime. By contrast, an employee who knew the customer was going to use an item to commit a crime but was indifferent to that fact has not acted purposely.

### Knowledge

The Model Penal Code provides the following definition of the mental state of knowledge:

> A person acts knowingly with respect to a material element of an offense when:
>     (i) if the element involves the nature of his conduct or the attendant circumstances, he is aware that his conduct is of that nature or that such circumstances exist; and
>     (ii) if the element involves a result of his conduct, he is aware that it is practically certain that his conduct will cause such a result.

Model Penal Code § 2.02(2)(b). As with purpose, this definition is nearly uniformly followed, even in jurisdictions that have not adopted other provisions of the Model Penal Code. We have already seen examples distinguishing knowledge from purpose in the sections immediately above.

To appreciate the difference between knowledge and the next most culpable mental state, recklessness, consider the crime of drug possession, which was covered in Chapter 4. Drug possession requires proof that the defendant had knowledge that she possessed a controlled substance. As the court put it in *United States v. Louis*, 861 F.3d 1330, 1333 (11th Cir. 2017), presented in Chapter 4, this means that the government must "prove that the defendant knew 'the substance [wa]s a controlled substance.'"

Imagine that Derrick, a college student, needs to stay up all night to finish a final paper for one of his classes. Derrick's roommate, Steve, offers Derrick a "caffeine pill." Although caffeine pills can be dangerous in large amounts, caffeine is not a controlled substance. Derrick, who avoids using illegal drugs, asks Steve how he knows that the pill contains caffeine and not something else. Steve replies that he got the pill from a friend whom he trusts "completely." Derrick believes Steve's explanation of how he got the pill, but because Derrick doesn't know anything about Steve's friend he thinks there might still be some risk that the pill contains something other than caffeine. Nevertheless, he accepts the pill. It turns out that the pill is Adderall, which *is* a controlled substance and illegal to possess without a prescription. Because Derrick was not aware that the pill was Adderall, he did not knowingly possess a controlled substance. And, because an element of the crime of drug possession is knowing possession of a controlled substance, Derrick has not committed the crime of drug possession. By contrast, if the *mens rea* for drug possession were recklessness, and not knowledge, there would be an argument that Derrick could be convicted. This is because Derrick was aware of some risk that the pill contained a controlled substance, and consciously disregarded that risk. Of course, recklessness requires not just conscious disregard of any risk, but of a substantial and unjustifiable risk. If the risk Derrick took regarding the content of the pill rose to that level, then he would have acted recklessly.

As discussed in Chapter 4, many (but not all) jurisdictions have adopted the willful blindness (or deliberate ignorance) doctrine, which is as "an alternate theory on which the government may prove knowledge." *United States v. Pérez-Meléndez*, 599 F.3d 31, 41 (1st Cir. 2010). Under the willful blindness doctrine, a person is considered to have acted with knowledge if she was (1) aware of a high probability of a fact and (2) deliberately avoided gaining positive knowledge of that fact. Some courts also include a third requirement — the defendant's motive for deliberately avoiding positive knowledge was to preserve a defense in the event of a prosecution. The theory behind the willful blindness rule is that a person can "'know' of facts of which he is less than absolutely certain." *United States v. Jewell*, 532 F.2d 697, 700 (9th Cir. 1978). Because willful blindness is the equivalent of knowledge, it would not apply to the above hypothetical case of Derrick. First, although Derrick thought that it was possible the caffeine pill *might* contain something else, he was not aware of a *high probability* that the pill was a controlled substance. Second, Derrick did not deliberately avoid learning the truth. Indeed, he tried to find out the truth by asking Steve about the origins of the pill, and he believed Steve's explanation that he got it from a friend who represented that the pill contained caffeine. Although Derrick remained concerned that the pill might have something else in it, he did not *deliberately* avoid learning the truth. For these reasons, as already discussed, Derrick was at worst reckless. The prototypical willful blindness case is much different. In *Jewell*, for example, the defendant was on a trip to Mexico when a stranger asked him if he wanted to drive a car across the border for $100. The defendant was very suspicious, but he didn't ask the stranger any questions about what was in the car. In addition, the defendant inspected the car and he noticed a void where it seemed like a secret compartment could be placed, but he decided not to inspect further. In a case like *Jewell*, the defendant has acted with knowledge under the willful blindness doctrine. Jewell was aware of more than just *a risk* that drugs were in the car, but of a *high probability* of that fact. He did not just *disregard* that risk, he *deliberately* avoided taking steps that might help him confirm the truth.

## Recklessness

Historically, recklessness and criminal negligence were often considered to be synonymous. Today, most jurisdictions use the Model Penal Code's definition of recklessness, or have adopted one that is very similar. Under the Model Penal Code,

> A person acts recklessly with respect to a material element of an offense when he consciously disregards a substantial and unjustifiable risk that the material element exists

or will result from his conduct. The risk must be of such a nature and degree that, considering the nature and purpose of the actor's conduct and the circumstances known to him, its disregard involves a gross deviation from the standard of conduct that a law-abiding person would observe in the actor's situation

Model Penal Code § 2.02(2)(c).

The case of *State v. Janklow*, 2005 SD 25, covered in Chapter 5, provides an example of the *mens rea* of recklessness in action. In that case, Janklow (then a United States Congressman) was driving his car on county Highway 13 in South Dakota after giving a political speech. Highway 13 intersects with Highway 14. Highway 13 has a stop sign at the intersection; Highway 14 does not. About three miles north of the intersection, Janklow passed a car while going significantly over the speed limit of 55 miles per hour. Janklow failed to stop at the stop sign, and he collided with a motorcycle, killing the driver. A prosecution expert testified that Janklow's car was traveling at 71 miles per hour at the point of impact. The court upheld Janklow's conviction for involuntary manslaughter (called reckless manslaughter in some jurisdictions). There was evidence that Janklow's conduct presented a substantial risk of death. Janklow did more than just commit a traffic infraction. He "was speeding prior to the collision" and instead of stopping at the intersection, he drove through it above the speed limit. Finally, there was also evidence that Janklow consciously disregarded the substantial risk — "[t]he State presented evidence that Janklow was familiar with this intersection and was aware of the stop sign." For these reasons, the court held that "[t]here was sufficient evidence from which the jury could conclude that Janklow was aware of, yet disregarded, the risk of an accident occurring as a result of his conduct."

### Negligence

Criminal negligence and recklessness are distinguished from one another primarily by the actor's awareness of risk. Recklessness requires conscious disregard of a substantial and unjustifiable risk. By contrast,

> A person acts negligently with respect to a material element of an offense when he *should be aware* of a substantial and unjustifiable risk that the material element exists or will result from his conduct. The risk must be of such a nature and degree that the actor's failure to perceive it, considering the nature and purpose of his conduct and the circumstances known to him, involves a gross deviation from the standard of care that a reasonable person would observe in the actor's situation.

Model Penal Code § 2.02(2)(d) (emphasis added). As with recklessness, most jurisdictions have either adopted this definition or one that is very similar.

### Strict Liability

Strict liability refers to the imposition of criminal punishment in the absence of a culpable mental state. Strict liability offenses are both controversial and uncommon.

At common law, there was only one significant strict liability offense: statutory rape, which was covered in Chapter 6. The crime of statutory rape, which criminalizes sex with a minor, remains a strict liability offense in slightly more than half of all states. In these jurisdictions, no *mens rea* is required with respect to the age of the victim. As a result, a person can be convicted of statutory rape even if he took every possible step to assure himself that the victim was above the age of consent, including reviewing the victim's identification.

Apart from statutory rape, most strict liability crimes fall into the category of so-called public welfare offenses (also sometimes called regulatory offenses). Two main features define public welfare offenses. First, they "regulate potentially harmful or injurious items." *Staples v. United States*, 511 U.S. 600, 607 (1994). Because these offenses target conduct in heavily regulated industries that implicates public health or safety, courts have concluded that legislators might have a good reason to impose strict liability. For example, the Supreme Court has "reasoned that as long as a defendant knows that he is dealing with a dangerous device of a character that places him 'in responsible relation to a public danger,' he should be alerted to the probability of strict regulation, and we have assumed that in such cases Congress intended to place the burden on the defendant to 'ascertain at his peril whether [his conduct] comes within the inhibition of the statute.'" *Id.* The second defining feature of public welfare offenses is that "penalties commonly are relatively small, and conviction does no grave damage to an offender's reputation." *Morissette v. United States*, 342 U.S. 246, 256 (1952). An example of a strict liability public welfare offense would be a statute "criminalizing the shipment of adulterated or misbranded drugs" and imposing a relatively small penalty. *Staples*, 511 U.S. at 606 (citing *United States v. Dotterweich*, 320 U.S. 277, 281 (1943)).

## 2. *Mens Rea* and Mistakes of Fact

The relationship between a defendant's mistaken belief and *mens rea* is a recurring issue that warrants special attention.

We first encountered this issue in the larceny case *Commonwealth v. Liebenow*, 470 Mass. 151 (2014), presented in Chapter 3. In that case, the defendant was charged with larceny. As you'll recall, one of the elements of larceny is that the defendant intended to permanently deprive someone else of her personal property. At a bench trial, the defendant testified that he lacked the requisite intent "because he honestly, albeit mistakenly, believed that the property" he had taken from a construction site was abandoned. The judge (sitting as fact finder at the bench trial) rejected the defense on the ground that it "require[ed] proof that the defendant's belief was objectively reasonable." The Supreme Judicial Court of Massachusetts reversed. The court held that "[a] defendant's honest belief that the property he took was abandoned constitutes a[] . . . defense to larceny." This is true regardless of whether the defendant's mistaken belief was reasonable. Because larceny requires proof that the defendant *intended* to permanently deprive someone else of her property, a defendant who honestly believed that the property was abandoned has not acted with the mental state required for the crime, period.

The strict liability crime of statutory rape provides another relevant data point. In *Garnett v. State*, 332 Md. 571 (1993), presented in Chapter 6, the defendant was charged with statutory rape. At trial, the defendant sought to introduce evidence that the victim "and her friends had previously told [him] that she was 16 years old, and that he had acted with that belief." The trial court excluded the evidence on the ground that it was immaterial. The Court of Appeals of Maryland upheld the trial court's ruling. Because statutory rape is a strict liability crime in Maryland, the prosecutor does not need to prove the defendant had any particular *mens rea* with respect to the victim's age. As a result, "mistake of age" was no defense.

Why was the mistake of fact in *Garnett* treated differently than the mistake in *Liebenow*? The answer is in the "rather simple rule" that a mistake of fact "is a defense when it negates a required mental element of the crime." *Liebenow*, 470 Mass. at 160. When *intent* is an element of a crime, as in larceny, a defendant's honest mistake can negate the required mental state, regardless of whether the mistake was reasonable. By contrast, because a *strict liability* crime has no required mental state, even a reasonable mistake is no defense. This principle also holds true for the other frequently used mental states. In the case of *criminal negligence*, the mental state is negated by a mistake of fact only if the mistake was reasonable. An honest mistake is not enough. This is because negligence is an objective standard — it applies when a person should have been aware of a substantial and unjustifiable risk. As a result, in a state that has adopted a *mens rea* of negligence for the crime of statutory rape, a defendant's mistaken belief about the victim's age would negate the requisite mental state only if it were reasonable.

Because the significance of a mistake of fact is whether or not it negates a mental state element of the crime, the doctrine is not technically a defense. Rather, "evidence of an actor's mistaken belief relates to whether the State has failed to prove an essential element of the charged offense beyond a reasonable doubt." *State v. Sexton*, 160 N.J. 93, 106 (1999). Nevertheless, "[a]s a practical matter, lawyers and judges . . . continue to consider a mistake of fact as a defense." *Id*. This is because in order to effectively raise the issue of a mistake of fact, the defendant must typically put forward some affirmative evidence about his mistaken belief. Consider again, for example, the facts of *Liebenow*. The defendant was caught removing two lengths of steel pipe that did not belong to him from a construction site. Without any contrary evidence, many fact finders would be readily convinced beyond a reasonable doubt that Liebenow intended to steal the pipes from their owner. After all, it is natural to infer that someone who takes steel pipes from a construction site intended to deprive someone else of his property. For a fact finder to seriously entertain the possibility that Liebenow did not act with the requisite intent because he mistakenly believed that the pipes were abandoned, there is going to have to be some evidence to support the claim.

Technically, mistake of fact principles "simply confirm what is stated elsewhere" — that the government must prove the mental state element(s) of the charged crime beyond a reasonable doubt. Paul H. Robinson & Jane A. Grall, *Element Analysis in Defining Criminal Liability: The Model Penal Code and Beyond*,

35 Stan. L. Rev. 681, 726 (1983). Nevertheless, judges will give a separate mistake of fact instruction to the jury in any case where the issue is raised and the law supports the requested instruction. Indeed, in practice, these instructions are often the most important component of mistake of fact jurisprudence. This is because a favorable instruction can very be helpful to a trial attorney in making her closing argument to the jury. If supported by the law, the judge will give a mistake of fact jury instruction tailored to the mental state at issue in the case. California's model jury instruction, for example, includes alternative formulations that can be used depending on the *mens rea* of the offense. The model mistake of fact instruction provides in relevant part: "The defendant is not guilty of <<insert crime[s]>> if (he/she) did not have the intent or mental state required to commit the crime because (he/she) [reasonably] did not know a fact or [reasonably and] mistakenly believed a fact." *Cal. Crim. Jury Instr.* 3406 (brackets indicating alternative formulations in original). When a mistake of fact instruction is given, the defense lawyer can rely on that instruction during closing argument to explain why her client's mistaken belief means he did not act with the requisite mental state. This is usually much more effective than drawing the jury's attention to instructions regarding the elements of the crime, since those instructions do not explain the legal significance of a defendant's factual mistake.

In contrast to a mistake of fact, a defendant's mistaken belief about whether or not his conduct was against the law — a mistake of law — is generally not a defense. This is because of the principle, covered in Chapter 11, that ignorance of the law is no excuse.

## 3. *Mens Rea* and Statutory Interpretation

The *mens rea* element(s) of an offense do not exist in isolation. Instead, they modify other elements of the offense. Usually, the relevant statute will clearly identify which *mens rea* terms attach to which elements. But a surprising number of statutes leave some doubt about the *mens rea* required for one or more elements. As one commentator has observed, "Congress is notoriously careless about defining the mental state element of criminal offenses." Dan M. Kahan, *Is* Chevron *Relevant to Federal Criminal Law?*, 110 Harv. L. Rev. 469, 477 (1996). When a statute is ambiguous, it is up to courts to resolve the ambiguity. To do this, courts rely on canons of interpretation.

To better understand the task of interpreting *mens rea* terms in criminal statutes, consider the abridged version of Nebraska's arson statute that served as a vehicle for introducing the elements of crime in Chapter 2. That statute provided: "A person commits arson in the first degree if he or she intentionally damages a building . . . by starting a fire . . . when another person is present in the building at the time and . . . the actor knows that fact[.]" Neb. Rev. Stat. § 28-502. There are two *mens rea* terms in this statute — intent and knowledge. It is clear from the text that the mental state term *intentionally* modifies the results element of *damaging a building*. It is also clear that the mental state of *knowledge* applies to the *presence of another person in the building*. As a result, to violate this statute a person must intend to damage a building *and* she must know that someone else is present in that building. This statute is relatively clearly written. And yet one could still imagine a potential area of ambiguity with respect to the *mens rea* required by this statute. Consider, what mental state (if any) is required for the element of *starting a fire*? The statute does not expressly say. Faced with language like this, most courts would interpret the term *intentionally* to modify both the element of damaging a building and the element of starting a fire. This is because the element of starting a fire comes after the term intentionally, and nothing in the statute indicates a legislative intent to adopt a different *mens rea* for the elements of damaging a building and starting a fire. In this particular case, an issue like this is unlikely to result in litigation. After all, a person's mental state for causing damage and starting a fire will almost always be identical — it would be bizarre for a person to *intentionally* damage property by *accidentally* starting a fire. Still, this example highlights how even clearly written statutes can sometimes contain at least an arguable ambiguity when it comes to the *mens rea* required for one or more element.

The task of statutory interpretation is particularly challenging when a statute contains no *mens rea* term whatsoever. General principles of statutory construction suggest that if a statute does not include a *mens rea* term, it should be interpreted to provide for strict liability. This is because courts do not usually add language to a statute that is not there. On the other hand, in most jurisdictions there is a strong presumption against strict liability offenses. This presumption, based on the central role of *mens rea* in criminal culpability, is codified in some jurisdictions. It is in part for this reason that, as discussed above, strict liability offenses are typically limited to statutory rape and public welfare offenses.

Although approaches to interpreting the *mens rea* terms in criminal statutes can vary from state to state, two sources are particularly influential: United States Supreme Court precedent and the Model Penal Code.

The Model Penal Code includes relatively straightforward guidance when it comes to interpreting *mens rea* terms in statutes. First, the Model Penal Code addresses ambiguities like the one described in the Nebraska arson statute with the following rule: "When the law defining an offense prescribes the kind of culpability that is sufficient for the commission of an offense, without distinguishing among the material elements thereof, such provision shall apply to all the material elements of the offense, unless a contrary purpose plainly appears." Model Penal Code § 2.02(4). Under this rule, the term *intentionally* in Nebraska's arson statute would apply to both the element of damaging a home and to starting a fire.

Second, the Model Penal Code provides an interpretive rule for statutes that do not include any *mens rea* terms at all: "When the culpability sufficient to establish a material element of an offense is not prescribed by law, such element is established if a person acts purposely, knowingly or recklessly with respect thereto." Model Penal Code § 2.02(3). Under this rule, if a statute is silent regarding *mens rea*, the mental state of recklessness serves as a default. There is a provision like this one in about half of all state criminal codes. Darryl K. Brown, *Criminal Law Reform and the Persistence of Strict Liability*, 62 Duke L.J. 285, 289 n.8 (2012).

In jurisdictions that have *not* adopted these provisions of the Model Penal Code—a group that includes the federal government—resolving ambiguities about the *mens rea* required in a criminal statute can be especially difficult. The United States Supreme Court has offered some guidance in a series of decisions that are also often relied on by courts in states that have not adopted the Model Penal Code's *mens rea* provisions. These cases provide that where a federal criminal statute is silent regarding *mens rea*, "some indication of congressional intent, express or implied, is required to dispense with *mens rea* as an element of a crime." *Staples v. United States*, 511 U.S. 600, 606 (1994). Congressional intent to create a strict liability offense may be implied for crimes that fall into the category of public welfare offenses, for the reasons discussed above. The next case is the Supreme Court's most recent treatment of how to interpret criminal statutes that are silent with respect to *mens rea*.

## Case Preview

## *Elonis v. United States*

In *Elonis*, the United States Supreme Court considered what mental state, if any, applies to a federal statute that makes it a crime to "transmit[] in interstate or foreign commerce any communication containing any threat to kidnap any person or any threat to injure the person of another." 18 U.S.C. § 875(c). The statute does not include any *mens rea* term. But the Court held by a vote of 8-1 that the statute requires at least recklessness with respect to whether a communication is a threat. *Elonis* clarified the meaning of a federal statute that has gained increasing relevance in the digital age, but that is not why it is being presented here. The significance of *Elonis* for our purposes is twofold. First, the decision illustrates how federal courts interpret criminal statutes that are silent with respect to *mens rea*, an approach that is also influential in many states. Second, *Elonis* provides a useful vehicle for thinking about the meaning of frequently used *mens rea* terms in greater depth.

As you read the decision, consider the following questions:

1. What is the difference between the interpretive rule the Court adopts in this case and the rule provided in the Model Penal Code regarding statutory interpretation described above?

2. The Court holds that "negligence is not sufficient to support a conviction" under the statute but declines to decide whether recklessness, purpose, or knowledge is required. In a concurring opinion, Justice Alito argues that the statute should only require recklessness. Can you think of any arguments that knowledge or purpose should be required?

## *Elonis v. United States*
### 575 U.S. 723 (2015)

Chief Justice ROBERTS delivered the opinion of the Court.

Federal law makes it a crime to transmit in interstate commerce "any communication containing any threat . . . to injure the person of another." 18 U.S.C. § 875(c). Petitioner was convicted of violating this provision under instructions that required the jury to find that he communicated what a reasonable person would regard as a threat. The question is whether the statute also requires that the defendant be aware of the threatening nature of the communication.

### I.

### A

Anthony Douglas Elonis was an active user of the social networking Web site Facebook. Users of that Web site may post items on their Facebook page that are accessible to other users, including Facebook "friends" who are notified when new content is posted. In May 2010, Elonis's wife of nearly seven years left him, taking with her their two young children. Elonis began "listening to more violent music" and posting self-styled "rap" lyrics inspired by the music. Eventually, Elonis changed the user name on his Facebook page from his actual name to a rap-style nom de plume, "Tone Dougie," to distinguish himself from his "on-line persona." The lyrics Elonis posted as "Tone Dougie" included graphically violent language and imagery. This material was often interspersed with disclaimers that the lyrics were "fictitious," with no intentional "resemblance to real persons." Elonis posted an explanation to another Facebook user that "I'm doing this for me. My writing is therapeutic."

Elonis's co-workers and friends viewed the posts in a different light. Around Halloween of 2010, Elonis posted a photograph of himself and a co-worker at a "Halloween Haunt" event at the amusement park where they worked. In the photograph, Elonis was holding a toy knife against his co-worker's neck, and in the caption Elonis wrote, "I wish." Elonis was not Facebook friends with the co-worker and did not "tag" her, a Facebook feature that would have alerted her to the posting. But the chief of park security was a Facebook "friend" of Elonis, saw the photograph, and fired him.

In response, Elonis posted a new entry on his Facebook page:

> "Moles! Didn't I tell y'all I had several? Y'all sayin' I had access to keys for all the f***in' gates. That I have sinister plans for all my friends and must have taken home a couple. Y'all think it's too dark and foggy to secure your facility from a man as mad as me? You see, even without a paycheck, I'm still the main attraction. Whoever thought the Halloween Haunt could be so f***in' scary?"

This post became the basis for Count One of Elonis's subsequent indictment, threatening park patrons and employees.

Elonis's posts frequently included crude, degrading, and violent material about his soon-to-be ex-wife.

After viewing some of Elonis's posts, his wife felt "extremely afraid for [her] life." A state court granted her a three-year protection-from-abuse order against Elonis (essentially, a restraining order). Elonis referred to the order in another post on his "Tone Dougie" page, [which was part of the basis for] Count Two of the indictment:

> "Fold up your [protection-from-abuse order] and put it in your pocket
> Is it thick enough to stop a bullet?
> Try to enforce an Order
> that was improperly granted in the first place
> Me thinks the Judge needs an education
> on true threat jurisprudence
> And prison time'll add zeros to my settlement . . .
> And if worse comes to worse
> I've got enough explosives
> to take care of the State Police and the Sheriff's Department."

At the bottom of this post was a link to the Wikipedia article on "Freedom of speech." Elonis's reference to the police was the basis for Count Three of his indictment, threatening law enforcement officers. [Elonis was also charged with two additional counts in connection with one post suggesting he was thinking about going to an elementary school and "initiat[ing] the most heinous school shooting ever imagined" and a second post in which Elonis imagined committing violent acts against an FBI agent who had visited his house.]

### B

A grand jury indicted Elonis for making threats to injure patrons and employees of the park, his estranged wife, police officers, a kindergarten class, and an FBI agent, all in violation of 18 U.S.C. § 875(c). At trial, Elonis testified that his posts emulated the rap lyrics of the well-known performer Eminem, some of which involve fantasies about killing his ex-wife. In Elonis's view, he had posted "nothing . . . that hasn't been said already." The Government presented as witnesses Elonis's wife and co-workers, all of whom said they felt afraid and viewed Elonis's posts as serious threats.

Elonis requested a jury instruction that "the government must prove that he intended to communicate a true threat." The District Court denied that request. The jury instructions instead informed the jury that

> "A statement is a true threat when a defendant intentionally makes a statement in a context or under such circumstances wherein a reasonable person would foresee that the statement would be interpreted by those to whom the maker communicates the statement as a serious expression of an intention to inflict bodily injury or take the life of an individual."

The Government's closing argument emphasized that it was irrelevant whether Elonis intended the postings to be threats — "it doesn't matter what he thinks." A jury convicted Elonis on four of the five counts against him, acquitting only on the charge of threatening park patrons and employees. Elonis was sentenced to three years, eight months' imprisonment and three years' supervised release.

Elonis renewed his challenge to the jury instructions in the Court of Appeals, contending that the jury should have been required to find that he intended his posts to be threats. The Court of Appeals disagreed, holding that the intent required by Section 875(c) is only the intent to communicate words that the defendant understands, and that a reasonable person would view as a threat.

We granted certiorari.

## II.

### A

An individual who "transmits in interstate or foreign commerce any communication containing any threat to kidnap any person or any threat to injure the person of another" is guilty of a felony and faces up to five years' imprisonment. 18 U.S.C. § 875(c). This statute requires that a communication be transmitted and that the communication contain a threat. It does not specify that the defendant must have any mental state with respect to these elements. In particular, it does not indicate whether the defendant must intend that his communication contain a threat.

### B

The fact that the statute does not specify any required mental state, however, does not mean that none exists. We have repeatedly held that "mere omission from a criminal enactment of any mention of criminal intent" should not be read "as dispensing with it." *Morissette v. United States*, 342 U.S. 246, 250 (1952). This rule of construction reflects the basic principle that "wrongdoing must be conscious to be criminal." *Id.*, at 252. As Justice Jackson explained, this principle is "as universal and persistent in mature systems of law as belief in freedom of the human will and a consequent ability and duty of the normal individual to choose between good and evil." *Id.*, at 250. The "central thought" is that a defendant must be "blameworthy in mind" before he can be found guilty, a concept courts have expressed over time through various terms such as *mens rea*, scienter, malice aforethought, guilty knowledge, and the like. Although there are exceptions, the "general rule" is that a guilty mind is "a necessary element in the indictment and proof of every crime." We therefore generally "interpret [ ] criminal statutes to include broadly applicable scienter requirements, even where the statute by its terms does not contain them."

*Morissette*, for example, involved an individual who had taken spent shell casings from a Government bombing range, believing them to have been abandoned. During his trial for "knowingly convert[ing]" property of the United States, the judge instructed the jury that the only question was whether the defendant had knowingly taken the property without authorization. This Court reversed the defendant's conviction, ruling that he had to know not only that he was taking the casings, but also that someone else still had property rights in them. He could not be found liable "if he truly believed [the casings] to be abandoned."

When interpreting federal criminal statutes that are silent on the required mental state, we read into the statute "only that *mens rea* which is necessary to separate wrongful conduct from 'otherwise innocent conduct.'" *Carter v. United States*,

530 U.S. 255, 269, (2000). In some cases, a general requirement that a defendant *act* knowingly is itself an adequate safeguard. For example, in *Carter*, we considered whether a conviction under 18 U.S.C. § 2113(a), for taking "by force and violence" items of value belonging to or in the care of a bank, requires that a defendant have the intent to steal. We held that once the Government proves the defendant forcibly took the money, "the concerns underlying the presumption in favor of scienter are fully satisfied, for a forceful taking—even by a defendant who takes under a good-faith claim of right—falls outside the realm of . . . 'otherwise innocent'" conduct. *Id.,* at 269-270. In other instances, however, requiring only that the defendant act knowingly "would fail to protect the innocent actor." *Id.,* at 269. A statute similar to Section 2113(a) that did not require a forcible taking or the intent to steal "would run the risk of punishing seemingly innocent conduct in the case of a defendant who peaceably takes money believing it to be his." *Ibid.* In such a case, the Court explained, the statute "would need to be read to require . . . that the defendant take the money with 'intent to steal or purloin.'" *Ibid.*

## C

Section 875(c), as noted, requires proof that a communication was transmitted and that it contained a threat. The "presumption in favor of a scienter requirement should apply to *each* of the statutory elements that criminalize otherwise innocent conduct." The parties agree that a defendant under Section 875(c) must know that he is transmitting a communication. But communicating *something* is not what makes the conduct "wrongful." Here "the crucial element separating legal innocence from wrongful conduct" is the threatening nature of the communication. The mental state requirement must therefore apply to the fact that the communication contains a threat.

Elonis's conviction, however, was premised solely on how his posts would be understood by a reasonable person. Such a "reasonable person" standard is a familiar feature of civil liability in tort law, but is inconsistent with "the conventional requirement for criminal conduct—*awareness* of some wrongdoing." Having liability turn on whether a "reasonable person" regards the communication as a threat—regardless of what the defendant thinks—"reduces culpability on the all-important element of the crime to negligence," and we "have long been reluctant to infer that a negligence standard was intended in criminal statutes." Under these principles, "what [Elonis] thinks" does matter.

The Government is at pains to characterize its position as something other than a negligence standard, emphasizing that its approach would require proof that a defendant "comprehended [the] contents and context" of the communication. The Government gives two examples of individuals who, in its view, would lack this necessary mental state—a "foreigner, ignorant of the English language," who would not know the meaning of the words at issue, or an individual mailing a sealed envelope without knowing its contents. But the fact that the Government would require a defendant to actually know the words of and circumstances surrounding a communication does not amount to a rejection of negligence. Criminal negligence standards often incorporate "the circumstances known" to a defendant.

ALI, Model Penal Code § 2.02(2)(d) (1985). Courts then ask, however, whether a reasonable person equipped with that knowledge, not the actual defendant, would have recognized the harmfulness of his conduct. That is precisely the Government's position here: Elonis can be convicted, the Government contends, if he himself knew the contents and context of his posts, and a reasonable person would have recognized that the posts would be read as genuine threats. That is a negligence standard.

\* \* \*

In light of the foregoing, Elonis's conviction cannot stand. The jury was instructed that the Government need prove only that a reasonable person would regard Elonis's communications as threats, and that was error. Federal criminal liability generally does not turn solely on the results of an act without considering the defendant's mental state. That understanding "took deep and early root in American soil" and Congress left it intact here: Under Section 875(c), "wrongdoing must be conscious to be criminal." *Morissette*, 342 U.S., at 252, 72 S. Ct. 240.

There is no dispute that the mental state requirement in Section 875(c) is satisfied if the defendant transmits a communication for the purpose of issuing a threat, or with knowledge that the communication will be viewed as a threat. In response to a question at oral argument, Elonis stated that a finding of recklessness would not be sufficient. Neither Elonis nor the Government has briefed or argued that point, and we accordingly decline to address it. Given our disposition, it is not necessary to consider any First Amendment issues.

Both Justice Alito and Justice Thomas complain about our not deciding whether recklessness suffices for liability under Section 875(c). Justice Alito contends that each party "argued" this issue but they did not address it at all until oral argument, and even then only briefly.

Justice Alito also suggests that we have not clarified confusion in the lower courts. That is wrong. Our holding makes clear that negligence is not sufficient to support a conviction under Section 875(c), contrary to the view of nine Courts of Appeals. There was and is no circuit conflict over the question Justice Alito and Justice Thomas would have us decide — whether recklessness suffices for liability under Section 875(c). No Court of Appeals has even addressed that question. We think that is more than sufficient "justification," *post*, at 2014 (opinion of Alito, J.), for us to decline to be the first appellate tribunal to do so.

We may be "capable of deciding the recklessness issue," *post*, at 2014 (opinion of Alito, J.), but following our usual practice of awaiting a decision below and hearing from the parties would help ensure that we decide it correctly.

The judgment of the United States Court of Appeals for the Third Circuit is reversed, and the case is remanded for further proceedings consistent with this opinion.

*It is so ordered.*

Justice ALITO, concurring in part and dissenting in part.

In *Marbury v. Madison*, 1 Cranch 137, 177 (1803), the Court famously proclaimed: "It is emphatically the province and duty of the judicial department to say what the law is." Today, the Court announces: It is emphatically the prerogative of this Court to say only what the law is not.

The Court's disposition of this case is certain to cause confusion and serious problems. Attorneys and judges need to know which mental state is required for conviction under 18 U.S.C. § 875(c), an important criminal statute. This case squarely presents that issue, but the Court provides only a partial answer. The Court holds that the jury instructions in this case were defective because they required only negligence in conveying a threat. But the Court refuses to explain what type of intent was necessary. Did the jury need to find that Elonis had the *purpose* of conveying a true threat? Was it enough if he *knew* that his words conveyed such a threat? Would *recklessness* suffice? The Court declines to say. Attorneys and judges are left to guess.

There is no justification for the Court's refusal to provide an answer. If the Court thinks that we cannot decide the recklessness question without additional help from the parties, we can order further briefing and argument. In my view, however, we are capable of deciding the recklessness issue, and we should resolve that question now.

Section 875(c) provides in relevant part:

"Whoever transmits in interstate or foreign commerce any communication containing . . . any threat to injure the person of another, shall be fined under this title or imprisoned not more than five years, or both."

Thus, conviction under this provision requires proof that: (1) the defendant transmitted something, (2) the thing transmitted was a threat to injure the person of another, and (3) the transmission was in interstate or foreign commerce.

At issue in this case is the *mens rea* required with respect to the second element—that the thing transmitted was a threat to injure the person of another. This Court has not defined the meaning of the term "threat" in § 875(c), but in construing the same term in a related statute, the Court distinguished a "true 'threat'" from facetious or hyperbolic remarks. *Watts v. United States*, 394 U.S. 705, 708, 89 S. Ct. 1399, 22 L. Ed. 2d 664 (1969) (*per curiam*). In my view, the term "threat" in § 875(c) can fairly be defined as a statement that is reasonably interpreted as "an expression of an intention to inflict evil, injury, or damage on another." Webster's Third New International Dictionary 2382 (1976). Conviction under § 875(c) demands proof that the defendant's transmission was in fact a threat, *i.e.*, that it is reasonable to interpret the transmission as an expression of an intent to harm another. In addition, it must be shown that the defendant was at least reckless as to whether the transmission met that requirement.

Why is recklessness enough? My analysis of the *mens rea* issue follows the same track as the Court's, as far as it goes. I agree with the Court that we should presume that criminal statutes require some sort of *mens rea* for conviction. To be sure, this presumption marks a departure from the way in which we generally interpret statutes. We "ordinarily resist reading words or elements into a statute that do not appear on its face." But this step is justified by a well-established pattern in our criminal laws. "For several centuries (at least since 1600) the different common law crimes have been so defined as to require, for guilt, that the defendant's acts or omissions be accompanied by one or more of the various types of fault (intention, knowledge, recklessness or—more rarely—negligence)." 1 W. LaFave, Substantive Criminal

Law § 5.5, p. 381 (2003). Based on these "background rules of the common law, in which the requirement of some *mens rea* for a crime is firmly embedded," we require "some indication of congressional intent, express or implied, . . . to dispense with *mens rea* as an element of a crime."

For a similar reason, I agree with the Court that we should presume that an offense like that created by § 875(c) requires more than negligence with respect to a critical element like the one at issue here. As the Court states, "[w]hen interpreting federal criminal statutes that are silent on the required mental state, we read into the statute 'only that *mens rea* which is necessary to separate wrongful conduct from "otherwise innocent conduct."'" Whether negligence is morally culpable is an interesting philosophical question, but the answer is at least sufficiently debatable to justify the presumption that a serious offense against the person that lacks any clear common-law counterpart should be presumed to require more.

Once we have passed negligence, however, no further presumptions are defensible. In the hierarchy of mental states that may be required as a condition for criminal liability, the *mens rea* just above negligence is recklessness. Negligence requires only that the defendant "should [have] be[en] aware of a substantial and unjustifiable risk," ALI, Model Penal Code § 2.02(2)(d), while recklessness exists "when a person disregards a risk of harm of which he is aware." And when Congress does not specify a *mens rea* in a criminal statute, we have no justification for inferring that anything more than recklessness is needed. It is quite unusual for us to interpret a statute to contain a requirement that is nowhere set out in the text. Once we have reached recklessness, we have gone as far as we can without stepping over the line that separates interpretation from amendment.

There can be no real dispute that recklessness regarding a risk of serious harm is wrongful conduct. In a wide variety of contexts, we have described reckless conduct as morally culpable. Someone who acts recklessly with respect to conveying a threat necessarily grasps that he is not engaged in innocent conduct. He is not merely careless. He is aware that others could regard his statements as a threat, but he delivers them anyway.

Accordingly, I would hold that a defendant may be convicted under § 875(c) if he or she consciously disregards the risk that the communication transmitted will be interpreted as a true threat. Nothing in the Court's non-committal opinion prevents lower courts from adopting that standard.

Justice THOMAS, dissenting.

We granted certiorari to resolve a conflict in the lower courts over the appropriate mental state for threat prosecutions under 18 U.S.C. § 875(c). Save two, every Circuit to have considered the issue — 11 in total — has held that this provision demands proof only . . . that a defendant knew he transmitted a communication, knew the words used in that communication, and understood the ordinary meaning of those words in the relevant context. The outliers are the Ninth and Tenth Circuits, which have concluded that proof of an intent to threaten was necessary for conviction.

Rather than resolve the conflict, the Court casts aside the approach used in nine Circuits and leaves nothing in its place. Lower courts are thus left to guess at the appropriate mental state for § 875(c).

Enacted in 1939, § 875(c) provides, "Whoever transmits in interstate or foreign commerce any communication containing any threat to kidnap any person or any threat to injure the person of another, shall be fined under this title or imprisoned not more than five years, or both." Because § 875(c) criminalizes speech, the First Amendment requires that the term "threat" be limited to a narrow class of historically unprotected communications called "true threats." To qualify as a true threat, a communication must be a serious expression of an intention to commit unlawful physical violence, not merely "political hyperbole"; "vehement, caustic, and sometimes unpleasantly sharp attacks"; or "vituperative, abusive, and inexact" statements. It also cannot be determined solely by the reaction of the recipient, but must instead be "determined by the interpretation of a *reasonable* recipient familiar with the context of the communication," lest historically protected speech be suppressed at the will of an eggshell observer. There is thus no dispute that, at a minimum, § 875(c) requires an objective showing: The communication must be one that "a reasonable observer would construe as a true threat to another." And there is no dispute that the posts at issue here meet that objective standard.

The only dispute in this case is about the state of mind necessary to convict Elonis for making those posts. On its face, § 875(c) does not demand any particular mental state. But because we read criminal statutes "in light of the background rules of the common law, in which the requirement of some *mens rea* for a crime is firmly embedded," we require "some indication of congressional intent, express or implied, . . . to dispense with *mens rea* as an element of a crime." Absent such indicia, we ordinarily apply the "presumption in favor of scienter" to require only "proof . . . that the defendant [must] posses[s] knowledge with respect to the *actus reus* of the crime."

Under this "conventional *mens rea* element," "the defendant [must] know the facts that make his conduct illegal," but he need not know *that* those facts make his conduct illegal.

To "know the facts that make his conduct illegal" under § 875(c), a defendant must know that he transmitted a communication in interstate or foreign commerce that contained a threat. Knowing that the communication contains a "threat"—a serious expression of an intention to engage in unlawful physical violence—does not, however, require knowing that a jury will conclude that the communication contains a threat as a matter of law. Instead, . . . a defendant prosecuted under § 875(c)

## The Rule of Lenity

When there is ambiguity about the *mens rea* required for an element of a crime, courts are guided by principles regarding mental states and statutory interpretation. But ambiguity can infect other terms in criminal statutes as well. There are a number of important canons of construction that courts consider when interpreting both criminal and civil statutes. Under the plain meaning rule, for example, when a statute's language is clear, courts must give effect to its plain meaning.

When the plain meaning of a criminal statute is uncertain, courts sometimes turn to the rule of lenity. The rule of lenity is a canon of statutory interpretation that is specific to criminal statutes. This rule "requires ambiguous criminal laws to be interpreted in favor of the defendants subject to them." *United States v. Santos*, 553 U.S. 507, 514 (2008) (plurality opinion). The rule of lenity both "vindicates the fundamental principle that no citizen should be held accountable for a violation of a statute whose commands are uncertain" and "places the weight of inertia upon the party that can best induce Congress to speak more clearly" — the government. *Id.*

To appreciate how the rule of lenity works, consider the federal money laundering statute's prohibition against knowingly conducting financial transactions involving the "proceeds" of certain unlawful activity. Does the term "proceeds" encompass *all* receipts of unlawful activity, or only the *profits* of unlawful activity? In *United States v. Santos*, the Court relied on the rule of lenity to adopt the narrower reading of the statute. The plurality found that, "[f]rom the face of the statute, there is no more reason to think that 'proceeds' means 'receipts' than there is to think that 'proceeds' means 'profits.'" *Id.* at 514. In this circumstance, the rule of lenity provided that "the tie must go to the defendant." *Id.*

The rule of lenity is not as powerful a tool for defendants as it might seem. This is in large part because courts typically only turn to the rule of lenity in cases where other canons of interpretation do not provide an answer. In other words, the rule of lenity "applies only when, after consulting traditional canons of statutory construction, we are left with an ambiguous statute." *United States v. Shabani*, 513 U.S. 10, 17 (1994).

must know only the words used in that communication, along with their ordinary meaning in context.

[This approach] divides those who know the facts constituting the *actus reus* of this crime from those who do not. For example, someone who transmits a threat who does not know English — or who knows English, but perhaps does not know a threatening idiom — lacks the [*mens rea*] required under § 875(c). Likewise, the hapless mailman who delivers a threatening letter, ignorant of its contents, should not fear prosecution. A defendant like Elonis, however, who admits that he "knew that what [he] was saying was violent" but supposedly "just wanted to express [him]self," acted with the [*mens rea*] required under § 875(c).

Elonis . . . suggests that an intent-to-threaten element is necessary in order to avoid the risk of punishing innocent conduct. But there is nothing absurd about punishing an individual who, with knowledge of the words he uses and their ordinary meaning in context, makes a threat. For instance, a high-school student who sends a letter to his principal stating that he will massacre his classmates with a machine gun, even if he intended the letter as a joke, cannot fairly be described as engaging in innocent conduct.

There is always a risk that a criminal threat statute may be deployed by the Government to suppress legitimate speech. But the proper response to that risk is to adhere to our traditional rule that only a narrow class of true threats, historically unprotected, may be constitutionally proscribed.

I respectfully dissent.

---

**Post-Case Follow-Up**

In *Elonis*, the Court holds that, "[w]hen interpreting federal criminal statutes that are silent on the required mental state, we read into the statute 'only that *mens rea* which is necessary to separate wrongful conduct from 'otherwise innocent conduct.'" Applying this rule, the majority finds that the federal interstate threats statute requires more than negligence to convict, but does not resolve the question of what *mens rea* — recklessness, knowledge, or purpose — is required. The Supreme Court's approach to statutes that are silent regarding *mens rea* differs somewhat from the Model Penal Code's approach. The MPC makes recklessness the default mental state whenever a statute does not include a mental state.

---

# Elonis: *Real Life Applications*

1. Imagine that you represent Anthony Douglas Elonis in his retrial following the Supreme Court's decision. The court instructs the jury that to find Elonis guilty, "the government must prove it was Elonis's purpose to communicate a true threat, that Elonis knew his words communicated a true threat, or that Elonis acted recklessly with regard to whether his words communicated a true threat." In her closing argument, the prosecutor says to the jury, "It is irrelevant whether Elonis intended his posts to be threatening. The victims perceived them as a threat and that is all that matters." You object on the grounds that this misstates the law, as provided by the court's jury instruction. Write a brief, one-paragraph argument in support of your objection.

2. You are serving as a law clerk for a military judge who is set to preside over the trial of Gifford, a 29-year-old infantry specialist stationed in South Korea. Gifford is charged with violating a lawful general military order that provides: "Service members who are 21 years of age and over may not distribute or give alcohol to anyone under 21 years of age for the purpose of consumption." A violation of the order carries a maximum penalty of dishonorable discharge and confinement for up to two years. The prosecution alleges that Gifford hosted a social event in his barracks where he provided alcohol to fellow soldiers who were under 21 years of age.

   In anticipation of pretrial motions, the judge has asked you to write a short memo regarding the *mens rea* required with respect to the age of the recipients of the alcohol under this statute. The judge anticipates that the prosecutor is likely to argue in favor of strict liability while the defense attorney is likely to argue that at least recklessness is required. Briefly summarize the arguments in favor of each side, keeping in mind that military courts are bound by United States Supreme Court precedent.

---

# C. REVISITING CAUSATION AND ATTENDANT CIRCUMSTANCES

Before concluding this chapter, a few words about the other two types of elements (results and attendant circumstances) are in order.

Results elements are those that require the defendant to have caused a specific result. Most crimes do not include a results element. Consider larceny, for example, which is defined as the trespassory taking and carrying away of the personal property of another with the intent to permanently deprive. None of these elements demands a particular result flow from the defendant's conduct; though the defendant must *intend* to permanently deprive the victim of property, *actual* permanent deprivation is not required. Indeed, only two of the offenses covered in the preceding chapters have a results element — arson and homicide offenses. The common law definition of arson, covered in Chapter 3, requires the *burning* of a dwelling house, meaning an act that *causes* a house to burn. Homicide offenses, covered in

Chapter 5, require the defendant to have *caused* the victim's death (with the exception of felony murder, where a causal relationship between the felony and the death is required). Causation issues arise most often in the context of homicide offenses. And, for that reason, the legal principles regarding causation were already covered in Chapter 5. Because those same principles apply to the results elements of other offenses, there is no need to address them further in this chapter.

Attendant circumstances elements are more prevalent than results elements. These are elements that require some objective situation to exist that is distinct from the defendant's acts or any results that those acts may cause. We have seen a number of crimes with elements that would be best described as attendant circumstances elements. Common law burglary, for example, is the breaking and entering of a dwelling of another at nighttime with the intent to commit a felony therein. *Dwelling of another*, *nighttime*, and *felony* are all attendant circumstances — they are objective circumstances that must exist that are distinct from the defendant's acts. Larceny's elements of *trespassory* and *personal property of another* would also be classified as attendant circumstances elements. As a final example, the crime of statutory rape requires that the victim be a minor, an attendant circumstance distinct from the act element of the offense. As discussed in Chapter 2, in contrast to *actus reus*, *mens rea*, and results elements, attendant circumstances elements are not governed by any generally applicable legal principles. There is nothing like the voluntary act requirement, the rules of causation, or the definitions of mental states that guide courts in interpreting attendant circumstances elements. Instead, the legal issues that arise with respect to attendant circumstances elements are either specific to the particular offense (e.g., whether the building in a burglary prosecution was a *dwelling*) or concern the *mens rea* required for the element (e.g., what *mens rea*, if any, is required with respect to the victim's age in a prosecution for statutory rape).

## Chapter Summary

- Every crime has its own *actus reus* element(s). For example, burglary includes two act elements — breaking and entering. Although each crime has its own act element(s), courts typically interpret the act element(s) of criminal statutes to implicitly mean a voluntary act or a culpable omission.
- A voluntary act is a willed bodily movement. An involuntary act is an act that is not a product of the effort or determination of the actor, such as a reflex or convulsion, a bodily movement during sleep, or conduct during hypnosis.
- There is widespread agreement among courts that at least one of the act elements of a crime must be voluntary. Although courts also typically interpret all of the *actus reus* elements of a crime to require a voluntary act, in some cases some courts have held that only one of the act elements requires a voluntary act. For example, in the context of the crime of possessing a controlled substance in jail, many courts have held that as long as the possession of a controlled substance was a voluntary act, the defendant's presence in a jail need not be due to a voluntary act.

- A handful of mental states recur throughout criminal codes: intent, purpose, knowledge, recklessness, and negligence. The *mens rea* of an offense does not exist in isolation; it modifies other elements of the crime. When no *mens rea* is required for an element or crime, this is called strict liability.

- When a defendant's mistake about a fact impacts his *mens rea*, this is sometimes referred to as a mistake of fact defense. A mistake of fact will be an effective defense if, and only if, the mistake negates a required *mens rea* element of the crime. Because it goes to an element of the crime, a mistake of fact is not a true affirmative defense, although courts and attorneys often describe it as a defense.

- If a statute is silent or ambiguous with respect to the *mens rea* required for a particular element, courts must resolve the issue. Under the Model Penal Code, recklessness is the default mental state. At the federal level, courts will read into a statute the mental state that is necessary to separate wrongful conduct from otherwise innocent conduct, unless it appears there is a legislative intent to provide for strict liability.

## Applying the Concepts

1. Write down a list of the offenses that have been covered in your course. For each offense, identify the *actus reus* element(s) of the offense.

2. Now, identify the *mens rea* element(s) of the offenses on your list. Do any of the offenses appear to have ambiguity about the mental state required for one or more elements of the offense?

3. A federal statute makes it a crime to "to use the services of the Postal Service or other interstate conveyance as part of a scheme to sell drug paraphernalia." The statute defines drug paraphernalia as "any equipment, product, or material of any kind which is primarily intended or designed for use" with illegal drugs. Applying the principles of the *Elonis* decision, what mental state, if any, do you think a defendant should have to have with respect to whether an item constitutes "drug paraphernalia" to be convicted?

4. Assume that a state that follows the Model Penal Code has a statute exactly like the federal drug paraphernalia statute from Question 3. Applying the Model Penal Code provision regarding the interpretation of mental states in statutes, what mental state, if any, must a defendant have with respect to whether an item constitutes "drug paraphernalia" to be convicted?

5. A federal statute makes it a misdemeanor to "take any migratory bird." The statute defines take as "pursue, hunt, shoot, wound, kill, trap, capture, or collect." The statute is silent regarding what mental state, if any, is required by the offense. Devin, the supervisor of an oil drilling operation, is convicted of violating this statute after dead birds were found in his oil drilling equipment. At trial,

the defense asks that the jury be instructed that the government must prove that Devin intended to take the migratory birds in order to be convicted. The prosecutor argues that the statute is a strict liability crime, and no *mens rea* is required. What is the best argument in favor of the prosecutor's position?

## Criminal Law in Practice

1. About half of all states have adopted the Model Penal Code's default rule regarding *mens rea* or one like it — namely that, "[w]hen the culpability sufficient to establish a material element of an offense is not prescribed by law, such element is established if a person acts purposely, knowingly or recklessly with respect thereto." Model Penal Code § 2.02(3).

   a. Look up whether the state you are in has adopted this provision of the Model Penal Code.
   b. If so, can you find a case issued by a state court in your state where the provision was outcome determinative?
   c. If not, can you find any precedent — either case law or a statute — that guides courts in interpreting the *mens rea* provisions of criminal statutes?

2. Does your state have a statute criminalizing possession of a controlled substance in a jail? If so, has any court in your state addressed the question of whether a person's presence in the jail must be voluntary to violate the statute? (If you are in North Carolina, where the opinion in *Barnes* was issued, look up the law in a neighboring state.)

3. As discussed in the section on mistakes of fact, as a practical matter, jury instructions are often the most important component of mistake of fact jurisprudence. Look up whether your state has a pattern (or model) jury instruction on mistakes of fact. If so, does it appear to differ in any way from the doctrine regarding mistakes of fact as described in this chapter?

# Affirmative Defenses

Even if the government proves every element of the charged crime beyond a reasonable doubt, the defendant will not necessarily be convicted. In some circumstances, a defendant whose conduct would normally constitute a crime can win acquittal by relying on an affirmative defense. For example, a defendant in a murder prosecution might admit that she intentionally killed the victim, but argue that she should be acquitted nonetheless based on the affirmative defense of self-defense.

Affirmative defenses are typically based on either a **justification** or an **excuse** theory. Although this distinction is mostly of interest to theorists, it can be a helpful framework for understanding some of the differences between the various defenses as well as what they have in common. The Model Penal Code explains the concepts this way: "To say that someone's conduct is 'justified' ordinarily connotes that the conduct is thought to be right, or at least not undesirable; to say that someone else's conduct is 'excused' ordinarily connotes that the conduct is thought to be undesirable but that for some reason the actor is not to be blamed for it." Model Penal Code, Introduction to Art. 3, at 3 (1985). As you read about each defense in this chapter, it might be useful to consider whether you think it is best categorized as a justification defense or an excuse defense, or if you think the defense does not fall neatly into these categories.

This chapter covers the major affirmative defenses: self-defense, duress, necessity, insanity, intoxication, entrapment, and public authority. We will also examine the principle that ignorance of the law is generally not a defense.

## Key Concepts

- What are the legal elements of the major affirmative defenses?
- Do you think each defense is properly defined, or should some of them be expanded or more narrowly defined?
- Should prosecutors take the existence of a possible affirmative defense into account when exercising their discretion? And if so, how?

## A. SELF-DEFENSE, DEFENSE OF OTHERS, AND DEFENSE OF PROPERTY

In certain circumstances, the law grants people the right to use force to defend themselves, others, and property. This section examines the requirements for these affirmative defenses.

### 1. Self-Defense

You do not need to be a lawyer to know that people have the right to use physical force to defend against an attacker. Indeed, self-defense is so deeply rooted in our law that some "Founding era sources call defending life a natural right." Eugene Volokh, *Medical Self-Defense, Prohibited Experimental Therapies, and Payment for Organs*, 120 Harv. L. Rev. 1813, 1819 (2007). Forty-four state constitutions recognize a "right to lethal self-defense." *Id.* In the context of its Second Amendment jurisprudence, the Supreme Court has suggested there is a right to self-defense under the federal constitution, describing it as "a basic right, recognized by many legal systems from ancient times to the present day." *McDonald v. City of Chicago*, 561 U.S. 742, 767 (2010) (quoting *District of Columbia v. Heller*, 554 U.S. 570, 599 (2008)).

Self-defense is a defense in every jurisdiction, with a core definition that is well established and universally followed. Legally, self-defense comes in two different varieties: deadly and non-deadly self-defense.

An individual is entitled to use **non-deadly force in self-defense** if she reasonably believes it is necessary to defend against the imminent use of unlawful physical force.

To use **deadly force in self-defense**, a person must meet all of the requirements for non-deadly force *and* reasonably believe that the imminent threat she faces is a deadly one — that is, a threat of death or great bodily harm. In a majority of jurisdictions, self-defense statutes also expressly allow an individual to use deadly force to defend against serious felonies, including kidnapping, rape, and robbery.

The discussion that follows addresses each element of self-defense in turn, followed by the case of *People v. Goetz*, which considers the defense in greater detail.

---

### Affirmative Defenses and the Burden of Proof

To convict someone of a crime, the prosecution must prove his guilt beyond a reasonable doubt. While many aspects of criminal law vary from state to state, this rule does not. That is because the Supreme Court has held that due process requires the government to prove every element of a crime beyond a reasonable doubt to win a conviction.

When a defendant raises an affirmative defense, does the prosecutor have the burden of disproving that defense beyond a reasonable doubt? Or does the burden of proof for an affirmative defense rest with the defendant? The answer is, it depends. The Constitution does not require states to allocate the burden to disprove an affirmative defense to the government. As a result, legislatures are free to allocate the burden of proof for affirmative defenses more or less as they see fit.

This has led to a wide range of approaches to allocating the burden of proof for an affirmative defense. A significant number of states place the burden on the

## *Reasonable Belief*

The objective reasonable belief standard governs all self-defense claims. It applies to every element of the defense. This means that the defendant must reasonably believe a threat is imminent, must reasonably believe that the threat is unlawful, and so on.

The reasonable belief standard incorporates two requirements. First, the defendant must actually—subjectively—have believed that he needed to use force to defend against an imminent unlawful attack. Second, that belief must have been reasonable—that is, a reasonable person in the defendant's situation would have believed that force was necessary to defend against an imminent unlawful attack. A person who honestly but *unreasonably* believes he needs to use force to defend himself will not qualify for self-defense. (As discussed further below, in some jurisdictions, a defendant in this circumstance may qualify for what is called imperfect self-defense.)

government to disprove most affirmative defenses beyond a reasonable doubt. But "most states, at least occasionally, shift the burden of persuasion for affirmative defenses to a criminal defendant." Ben W. Studdard & Michael A. Arndt, *Georgia's Safe Harbor Ruling for Affirmative Defenses in Criminal Cases Should Be Revisited*, 68 Mercer L. Rev. 35, 46-47 (2016). Typically, when the defendant bears the burden of proving an affirmative defense, she must do so by a preponderance of the evidence.

The requirement that a defendant's belief be reasonable does *not* mean that she must have been right. In other words, a mistaken belief can still be reasonable. Imagine a defendant who shot and killed a person who she believed was pointing a gun at her. If it turns out that the defendant was mistaken and the person was pointing a toy gun, that will not necessarily preclude a self-defense claim. The elements of self-defense could still be satisfied if a reasonable person in the defendant's position would have made the same mistake.

Although the reasonable belief standard is an objective one, most courts permit juries to consider at least some of the defendant's characteristics when applying it. Physical characteristics present the clearest example. A reasonable five foot tall, 100-pound, elderly person is likely to perceive the nature of some threats differently than a reasonable person in her 20s. Consider a 40-year-old attacker of average weight and height who threatens to punch a victim in the face. A reasonable victim of average weight and height in his 20s would be unlikely to view this as a deadly threat. From the perspective of a 90-year-old victim in poor health, it might be reasonable to conclude that this threat carries the risk of death or great bodily injury. While there is widespread agreement that the reasonable person standard should incorporate physical characteristics in the self-defense setting, courts have struggled over where to draw the line. Should other personal characteristics, like life experiences, be taken into account when applying the reasonable person standard? This question is examined below in the *People v. Goetz* case.

## *Imminent Threat*

The right to use force in self-defense requires a reasonable belief that a threat is imminent. An imminent threat is defined as an "'immediate danger, such as must be instantly met, such as cannot be guarded against by calling for the assistance of others or the protection of the law.'" *State v. Norman*, 324 N.C. 253 (1989).

In most cases, this requirement is uncontroversial and easy enough to apply. Typically, if a person faces a threat of physical violence sometime in the future, it is not necessary to use force in self-defense. If someone walks up to you at a bar and threatens to attack you the next day, for example, you can call the police. There is no need to resort to self-help in the form of physical violence.

The imminence requirement becomes more difficult in cases where a person uses force against an aggressor who has engaged in a pattern of threats and violence. The clearest, and most controversial, example of this involves victims of domestic violence. A battered partner might suffer repeated violence on an ongoing basis from her abuser. If the battered partner uses force to defend against a specific, immediate threat, then the imminence requirement will be satisfied. But if a battered partner takes the life of her abuser at a time when she is not facing a specific threat, the imminence requirement may prevent her from successfully claiming self-defense.

*Norman*, a case from the late 1980s, illustrates the point. In that case, Norman "shot her husband three times in the back of the head as he lay sleeping in his bed" and sought to present a self-defense claim at trial. Her self-defense theory was based on a "long history of physical and mental abuse by her husband," which the North Carolina Supreme Court summarized in its opinion. 324 N.C. at 254. The court's recitation of the facts describes a particularly disturbing pattern of abuse by the decedent against the defendant:

> At the time of the killing, the thirty-nine-year-old defendant and her husband had been married almost twenty-five years and had several children. The defendant testified that her husband had started drinking and abusing her about five years after they were married. His physical abuse of her consisted of frequent assaults that included slapping, punching and kicking her, striking her with various objects, and throwing glasses, beer bottles and other objects at her. The defendant described other specific incidents of abuse, such as her husband putting her cigarettes out on her, throwing hot coffee on her, breaking glass against her face and crushing food on her face.
>
> The defendant's evidence also tended to show other indignities inflicted upon her by her husband. Her evidence tended to show that her husband did not work and forced her to make money by prostitution, and that he made humor of that fact to family and friends. He would beat her if she resisted going out to prostitute herself or if he was unsatisfied with the amounts of money she made. He routinely called the defendant "dog," "bitch" and "whore," and on a few occasions made her eat pet food out of the pets' bowls and bark like a dog. He often made her sleep on the floor. At times, he deprived her of food and refused to let her get food for the family. During those years of abuse, the defendant's husband threatened numerous times to kill her and to maim her in various ways.
>
> The defendant said her husband's abuse occurred only when he was intoxicated, but that he would not give up drinking.
>
> In the early morning hours on the day before his death, the defendant's husband, who was intoxicated, went to a rest area off I-85 near Kings Mountain where the defendant was engaging in prostitution and assaulted her. While driving home, he was stopped by a patrolman and jailed on a charge of driving while impaired. After the

defendant's mother got him out of jail at the defendant's request later that morning, he resumed his drinking and abuse of the defendant.

The defendant's evidence also tended to show that her husband seemed angrier than ever after he was released from jail and that his abuse of the defendant was more frequent. That evening, sheriff's deputies were called to the Norman residence, and the defendant complained that her husband had been beating her all day and she could not take it anymore. The defendant was advised to file a complaint, but she said she was afraid her husband would kill her if she had him arrested. The deputies told her they needed a warrant before they could arrest her husband, and they left the scene.

The deputies were called back less than an hour later after the defendant had taken a bottle of pills. The defendant's husband cursed her and called her names as she was attended by paramedics, and he told them to let her die. A sheriff's deputy finally chased him back into his house as the defendant was put into an ambulance. The defendant's stomach was pumped at the local hospital, and she was sent home with her mother.

While in the hospital, the defendant was visited by a therapist with whom she discussed filing charges against her husband and having him committed for treatment. Before the therapist left, the defendant agreed to go to the mental health center the next day to discuss those possibilities.

The next day, the day she shot her husband, the defendant went to the mental health center to talk about charges and possible commitment, and she confronted her husband with that possibility. She testified that she told her husband later that day: "J.T., straighten up. Quit drinking. I'm going to have you committed to help you." She said her husband then told her he would "see them coming" and would cut her throat before they got to him.

The defendant also went to the social services office that day to seek welfare benefits, but her husband followed her there, interrupted her interview and made her go home with him. He continued his abuse of her, threatening to kill and to maim her, slapping her, kicking her, and throwing objects at her. At one point, he took her cigarette and put it out on her, causing a small burn on her upper torso. He would not let her eat or bring food into the house for their children.

That evening, the defendant and her husband went into their bedroom to lie down, and he called her a "dog" and made her lie on the floor when he lay down on the bed. Their daughter brought in her baby to leave with the defendant, and the defendant's husband agreed to let her baby-sit. After the defendant's husband fell asleep, the baby started crying and the defendant took it to her mother's house so it would not wake up her husband. She returned shortly with [a] pistol and killed her husband. She pointed the pistol at the back of her sleeping husband's head, but it jammed the first time she tried to shoot him. She fixed the gun and then shot her husband in the back of the head as he lay sleeping. After one shot, she felt her husband's chest and determined that he was still breathing and making sounds. She then shot him twice more in the back of the head.

The defendant testified at trial that she was too afraid of her husband to press charges against him or to leave him. She said that she had temporarily left their home on several previous occasions, but he had always found her, brought her home and beaten her. Asked why she killed her husband, the defendant replied: "Because I was scared of him and I knowed when he woke up, it was going to be the same thing, and I was scared when he took me to the truck stop that night it was going to be worse than he had ever been. I just couldn't take it no more. There ain't no way, even if it means going to prison. It's better than living in that. That's worse hell than anything."

The defendant and other witnesses testified that for years her husband had frequently threatened to kill her and to maim her. When asked if she believed those threats, the defendant replied: "Yes. I believed him; he would, he would kill me if he got a chance. If he thought he wouldn't a had to went to jail, he would a done it."

*Id.* at 255-58. The trial court refused to instruct the jury on self-defense, finding that Norman had not presented evidence that she faced an *imminent* threat at the time of the killing. She was convicted of voluntary manslaughter, sentenced to six years imprisonment, and appealed.

The trial court properly refused to let Norman present her self-defense claim to the jury, the North Carolina Supreme Court held, because "no evidence was introduced tending to show that at the time of the killing the defendant reasonably believed herself to be confronted by circumstances which necessitated her killing her husband to save herself from *imminent* death or great bodily harm." *Id.* at 260. The court explained that the law requires an imminent threat in order to ensure that "force will be used only where it is necessary and as a last resort in the exercise of the inherent right of self-preservation." *Id.* at 261. Accordingly, the court upheld the defendant's conviction.

In part because of decisions like *Norman*, some commentators argue that self-defense should not include an imminence requirement. For example, Alafair Burke has argued that the imminence requirement is nothing more than "an imperfect proxy to ensure that a defendant's use of force is necessary." Alafair S. Burke, *Rational Actors, Self-Defense, and Duress: Making Sense, Not Syndromes, Out of the Battered Woman*, 81 N.C. L. Rev. 211, 279 (2002). "[A] better standard would require that the use of force be necessary," not that it be imminent. *Id.* In the typical case, of course, "the avoided threat would need to be imminent in order for self-protection to be necessary." *Id.* at 280. But in some cases, such as those involving an abusive partner, a reasonable person in the actor's situation might believe it is necessary to use force, even if a threat is not imminent. As an example, Professor Burke asked readers to "consider a woman who remained in a violent domestic relationship because she tried multiple times to leave only to be tracked down. Suppose, in addition, that after the most recent and most aggressive separation assault, the batterer stated that if she ever tried to leave again, he would track her down and this time kill her, himself, and their children. If the woman were to kill her husband in his sleep, a necessity-based theory of justification would permit the woman to present a claim of self-defense for jury decision." *Id.* at 282. For a contrary view and argument in favor of the imminence requirement, see Kimberly Kessler Ferzan, *Defending Imminence: From Battered Women to Iraq*, 46 Ariz. L. Rev. 213, 217 (2004) (arguing that "self-defense is best understood as a limited right to respond to aggression" and that "when one seeks to pull at the thread of imminence, the fabric of self-defense itself unravels").

Whatever the merits of arguments against the imminence requirement, they have not swayed legislatures to revise self-defense statutes. For now at least, imminence remains an element of self-defense. A number of jurisdictions do, however, permit defendants to present expert testimony on battered spouse syndrome to assist the jury "[i]n evaluating the reasonableness of the defendant's belief in imminent danger." *State v. Janes*, 121 Wash. 2d 220, 240 (1993).

## Unlawful Force

The unlawful force element requires the defendant to have reasonably believed the threat against them was unlawful. This element prevents a defendant from claiming self-defense if they use force against a police officer to try to stop a lawful arrest, for example.

As with the other elements of self-defense, the relevant question is not whether the threat the defendant faced was *actually* unlawful but whether a reasonable person in the defendant's position would have perceived the threat as unlawful. Consider, for example, a person who wakes up in the middle of the night to the sound of someone breaking down his door. He grabs a gun from his nightstand and fires it into the hallway in an attempt to ward off the intruder. If it turns out that the intruder was actually a police officer executing a no-knock warrant, that fact alone will not defeat a self-defense claim. So long as the homeowner reasonably believed he was faced with an imminent, unlawful, and deadly attack at the time he acted, he would be entitled to claim self-defense.

## Deadly Force

A person who uses deadly force in self-defense must meet an additional requirement. Deadly force in self-defense is permitted only if the defendant reasonably believed that the imminent, unlawful threat she faced was a deadly threat or, in many jurisdictions, a threat that she would be the victim of a serious felony.

Although the definition of deadly force varies slightly across jurisdictions, it generally means force that is likely to cause death or serious bodily injury. Notice that under this definition, it is possible for a defendant to have killed his attacker without using deadly force. Imagine for example, that the defendant is attacked at a bar. The defendant pushes his attacker, and the attacker unexpectedly falls onto a sharp object and dies. In this hypothetical, the defendant did not use deadly force because a push is not likely to cause death or seriously bodily injury. As a result, even though the attacker died, the defendant would not be required to show that he faced a deadly threat to successfully claim self-defense.

In 19 states, the right to use deadly force in self-defense applies *only* in cases where the defendant reasonably believed he faced a deadly threat. Paul H. Robinson & Tyler Scot Williams, Mapping American Criminal Law: Variations Across the 50 States 143 (2018).

In the remaining states, a person may also use deadly force to defend against certain enumerated felonies. Although the list of felonies varies from state to state, it usually includes at least rape, kidnapping, and robbery. In practice, statutes that permit the use of deadly force to defend against serious felonies do not add much to the right of self-defense in most cases. After all, a person who reasonably believes she is facing an imminent threat of kidnapping, rape, or robbery will typically *also* reasonably believe she is facing a deadly threat. Of course, there are sometimes cases where the victim of a robbery, kidnapping, or rape may not fear for her life; in these circumstances the right to use deadly force in self-defense will depend on whether the jurisdiction extends the defense to serious felonies.

**EXHIBIT 11.1**   Bernhard Goetz in New York Supreme Court

**Case Preview**

### *People v. Goetz*

The next case examines the elements of self-defense with a particular focus on the meaning of the reasonable belief standard. In *Goetz*, the defendant fired multiple shots at a group of teenagers on a subway in New York City after they approached him and either asked for or demanded money. The case generated a great deal of media coverage, with some news outlets dubbing Bernhard Goetz the "Subway Vigilante." In the decision below, the Court of Appeals of New York discussed the reasonable belief standard for self-defense claims, including the extent to which a defendant's past life experiences can factor into the assessment.

As you read the court's opinion, consider the following questions:

1. The court discusses the reasons for using an objective standard to measure self-defense claims. Do you agree that an objective standard is preferable, or do you think a subjective standard would be better?
2. What kinds of facts does the court say can be considered when applying the reasonable person standard in the context of a self-defense claim?

---

### *People v. Goetz*
#### 68 N.Y.2d 96 (1986)

WACHTLER, J.

A Grand Jury has indicted defendant on attempted murder, assault, and other charges for having shot and wounded four youths on a New York City subway train after one or two of the youths approached him and asked for $5. The lower courts, concluding that the prosecutor's charge to the Grand Jury on the defense of justification was erroneous, have dismissed the attempted murder, assault and weapons possession charges. We now reverse and reinstate all counts of the indictment.

## I.

The precise circumstances of the incident giving rise to the charges against defendant are disputed, and ultimately it will be for a trial jury to determine what occurred. We feel it necessary, however, to provide some factual background to properly frame the legal issues before us. Accordingly, we have summarized the facts as they appear from the evidence before the Grand Jury. We stress, however, that we do not purport to reach any conclusions or holding as to exactly what transpired or whether defendant is blameworthy. The credibility of witnesses and the reasonableness of defendant's conduct are to be resolved by the trial jury.

On Saturday afternoon, December 22, 1984, Troy Canty, Darryl Cabey, James Ramseur, and Barry Allen boarded an IRT express subway train in The Bronx and headed south toward lower Manhattan. The four youths rode together in the rear portion of the seventh car of the train. Two of the four, Ramseur and Cabey, had screwdrivers inside their coats, which they said were to be used to break into the coin boxes of video machines.

Defendant Bernhard Goetz boarded this subway train at 14th Street in Manhattan and sat down on a bench towards the rear section of the same car occupied by the four youths. Goetz was carrying an unlicensed .38 caliber pistol loaded with five rounds of ammunition in a waistband holster. The train left the 14th Street station and headed towards Chambers Street.

It appears from the evidence before the Grand Jury that Canty approached Goetz, possibly with Allen beside him, and stated "give me five dollars." Neither Canty nor any of the other youths displayed a weapon. Goetz responded by standing up, pulling out his handgun and firing four shots in rapid succession. The first shot hit Canty in the chest; the second struck Allen in the back; the third went through Ramseur's arm and into his left side; the fourth was fired at Cabey, who apparently was then standing in the corner of the car, but missed, deflecting instead off of a wall of the conductor's cab. After Goetz briefly surveyed the scene around him, he fired another shot at Cabey, who then was sitting on the end bench of the car. The bullet entered the rear of Cabey's side and severed his spinal cord.

All but two of the other passengers fled the car when, or immediately after, the shots were fired. The conductor, who had been in the next car, heard the shots and instructed the motorman to radio for emergency assistance. The conductor then went into the car where the shooting occurred and saw Goetz sitting on a bench, the injured youths lying on the floor or slumped against a seat, and two women who had apparently taken cover, also lying on the floor. Goetz told the conductor that the four youths had tried to rob him.

While the conductor was aiding the youths, Goetz headed towards the front of the car. The train had stopped just before the Chambers Street station and Goetz went between two of the cars, jumped onto the tracks and fled. Police and ambulance crews arrived at the scene shortly thereafter. Ramseur and Canty, initially listed in critical condition, have fully recovered. Cabey remains paralyzed, and has suffered some degree of brain damage.*

On December 31, 1984, Goetz surrendered to police in Concord, New Hampshire, identifying himself as the gunman being sought for the subway shootings in New York nine days earlier. Later that day, after receiving *Miranda* warnings, he made two lengthy statements, both of which were tape recorded with his permission. In the statements, which are substantially similar, Goetz admitted that he had been illegally carrying a handgun in New York City for three years. He stated that he had first purchased a gun in 1981 after he had been injured in a mugging. Goetz also revealed that twice between 1981 and 1984 he had successfully warded off assailants simply by displaying the pistol.

According to Goetz's statement, the first contact he had with the four youths came when Canty, sitting or lying on the bench across from him, asked "how are you," to which he replied "fine." Shortly thereafter, Canty, followed by one of the other youths, walked over to the defendant and stood to his left, while the other two youths remained to his right, in the corner of the subway car. Canty then said "give me five dollars." Goetz stated that he knew from the smile on Canty's face that they wanted to "play with me." Although he was certain that none of the youths had a gun, he had a fear, based on prior experiences, of being "maimed."

When Canty again requested money, Goetz stood up, drew his weapon, and began firing, aiming for the center of the body of each of the four. Goetz recalled that the first two he shot "tried to run through the crowd [but] they had nowhere to run." Goetz then turned to his right to "go after the other two." One of these two "tried to run through the wall of the train, but * * * he had nowhere to go." The other youth (Cabey) "tried pretending that he wasn't with [the others]" by standing still, holding on to one of the subway hand straps, and not looking at Goetz. Goetz nonetheless fired his fourth shot at him. He then ran back to the first two youths to make sure they had been "taken care of." Seeing that they had both been shot, he spun back to check on the latter two. Goetz noticed that the youth who had been standing still was now sitting on a bench and seemed unhurt. As Goetz told the police, "I said '[y]ou seem to be all right, here's another,'" and he then fired the shot which severed Cabey's spinal cord. Goetz added that "if I was a little more under self-control * * * I would have put the barrel against his forehead and fired." He also admitted that "if I had had more [bullets], I would have shot them again, and again, and again."

## II.

After waiving extradition, Goetz was brought back to New York and arraigned on a felony complaint charging him with attempted murder and criminal possession of a weapon. The matter was presented to a Grand Jury in January 1985, with the prosecutor seeking an indictment for attempted murder, assault, reckless endangerment, and criminal possession of a weapon.

---

* Barry Allen, shot in the back by Goetz, also survived. See Anne Groer, *Troubles Follow 4 Subway Victims*, Orlando Sentinel, Apr. 26, 1987. [Footnote by casebook author.]

[T]he . . . Grand Jury filed a 10-count indictment, containing four charges of attempted murder, four charges of assault in the first degree, one charge of reckless endangerment in the first degree, and one charge of criminal possession of a weapon in the second degree.

On October 14, 1985, Goetz moved to dismiss the charges . . . alleging, among other things, that the evidence before the . . . Grand Jury was not legally sufficient to establish the offenses charged and that the prosecutor's instructions to th[e] Grand Jury on the defense of justification were erroneous and prejudicial to the defendant so as to render its proceedings defective.

In an order dated January 21, 1986, Criminal Term granted Goetz's motion to the extent that it dismissed all counts of the . . . indictment, other than the reckless endangerment charge, with leave to resubmit these charges to [another] Grand Jury. The court, after inspection of the Grand Jury minutes, first rejected Goetz's contention that there was not legally sufficient evidence to support the charges. It held, however, that the prosecutor, in a supplemental charge elaborating upon the justification defense, had erroneously introduced an objective element into this defense by instructing the grand jurors to consider whether Goetz's conduct was that of a "reasonable man in [Goetz's] situation." The court . . . concluded that the statutory test for whether the use of deadly force is justified to protect a person should be wholly subjective, focusing entirely on the defendant's state of mind when he used such force. It concluded that dismissal was required for this error because the justification issue was at the heart of the case.

On appeal by the People, a divided Appellate Division affirmed Criminal Term's dismissal of the charges.

## III.

Penal Law § 35.15(1) sets forth the general principles governing [the] uses of force [in self-defense]: "[a] person may * * * use physical force upon another person when and to the extent he *reasonably believes* such to be necessary to defend himself or a third person from what he *reasonably believes* to be the use or imminent use of unlawful physical force by such other person" (emphasis added).[3]

Section 35.15(2) sets forth further limitations on these general principles with respect to the use of "deadly physical force": "A person may not use deadly physical force upon another person under circumstances specified in subdivision one unless (a) He *reasonably believes* that such other person is using or about to use deadly physical force[4] or (b) He *reasonably believes* that such other person is committing or attempting to commit a kidnapping, forcible rape, forcible sodomy or robbery" (emphasis added).

Because the evidence before the second Grand Jury included statements by Goetz that he acted to protect himself from being maimed or to avert a robbery, the prosecutor correctly chose to charge the justification defense in section 35.15 to the

---

[3] Subdivision (1) contains certain exceptions to this general authorization to use force, such as where the actor himself was the initial aggressor.

[4] Section 35.15(2)(a) further provides, however, that even under these circumstances a person ordinarily must retreat "if he knows that he can with complete safety as to himself and others avoid the necessity of [using deadly physical force] by retreating."

Grand Jury. The prosecutor properly instructed the grand jurors to consider whether the use of deadly physical force was justified to prevent either serious physical injury or a robbery, and, in doing so, to separately analyze the defense with respect to each of the charges. He elaborated upon the prerequisites for the use of deadly physical force essentially by reading or paraphrasing the language in Penal Law § 35.15. The defense does not contend that he committed any error in this portion of the charge.

When the prosecutor had completed his charge, one of the grand jurors asked for clarification of the term "reasonably believes." The prosecutor responded by instructing the grand jurors that they were to consider the circumstances of the incident and determine "whether the defendant's conduct was that of a reasonable man in the defendant's situation." It is this response by the prosecutor — and specifically his use of "a reasonable man" — which is the basis for the dismissal of the charges by the lower courts.

As expressed repeatedly in the Appellate Division's plurality opinion, because section 35.15 uses the term "*he* reasonably believes," the appropriate test, according to that court, is whether a defendant's beliefs and reactions were "reasonable *to him*." Under that reading of the statute, a jury which believed a defendant's testimony that he felt that his own actions were warranted and were reasonable would have to acquit him, regardless of what anyone else in defendant's situation might have concluded. Such an interpretation defies the ordinary meaning and significance of the term "reasonably" in a statute, and misconstrues the clear intent of the Legislature, in enacting section 35.15, to retain an objective element as part of any provision authorizing the use of deadly physical force.

Penal statutes in New York have long codified the right recognized at common law to use deadly physical force, under appropriate circumstances, in self-defense. These provisions have never required that an actor's belief as to the intention of another person to inflict serious injury be correct in order for the use of deadly force to be justified, but they have uniformly required that the belief comport with an objective notion of reasonableness.

In *Shorter v. People*, 2 N.Y. 193, we emphasized that deadly force could be justified under the statute even if the actor's beliefs as to the intentions of another turned out to be wrong, but noted there had to be a reasonable basis, viewed objectively, for the beliefs. We explicitly rejected the position that the defendant's own belief that the use of deadly force was necessary sufficed to justify such force regardless of the reasonableness of the beliefs.

Interpreting the statute to require only that the defendant's belief was "reasonable to *him*," as done by the plurality below, would hardly be different from requiring only a genuine belief; in either case, the defendant's own perceptions could completely exonerate him from any criminal liability.

We cannot lightly impute to the Legislature an intent to fundamentally alter the principles of justification to allow the perpetrator of a serious crime to go free simply because that person believed his actions were reasonable and necessary to prevent some perceived harm. To completely exonerate such an individual, no matter how aberrational or bizarre his thought patterns, would allow citizens to set their own standards for the permissible use of force. It would also allow a legally competent defendant suffering from delusions to kill or perform acts of violence with impunity, contrary to fundamental principles of justice and criminal law.

We can only conclude that the Legislature retained a reasonableness require-ment to avoid giving a license for such actions.

Statutes or rules of law requiring a person to act "reasonably" or to have a "rea-sonable belief" uniformly prescribe conduct meeting an objective standard mea-sured with reference to how "a reasonable person" could have acted.

The defense contends that our . . . opinion in *People v. Miller*, 39 N.Y.2d 543 [sup-ports his position that self-defense claims should be measured under a subjective standard]. In *Miller*, we held that a defendant charged with homicide could intro-duce, in support of a claim of self-defense, evidence of prior acts of violence commit-ted by the deceased of which the defendant had knowledge. The defense, as well as the plurality below, place great emphasis on the statement in *Miller* that "the crucial fact at issue [is] the state of mind of the defendant." This language, however, in no way indicates that a wholly subjective test is appropriate. To begin, it is undisputed that section 35.15 does contain a subjective element, namely that the defendant believed that deadly force was necessary to avert the imminent use of deadly force or the commission of certain felonies. Evidence that the defendant knew of prior acts of violence by the deceased could help establish his requisite beliefs. Moreover, such knowledge would also be relevant on the issue of reasonableness, as the jury must consider the circumstances a defendant found himself in, which would include any relevant knowledge of the nature of persons confronting him.

Goetz also argues that the introduction of an objective element will preclude a jury from considering factors such as the prior experiences of a given actor and thus, require it to make a determination of "reasonableness" without regard to the actual circumstances of a particular incident. This argument, however, falsely presupposes that an objective standard means that the background and other relevant character-istics of a particular actor must be ignored. To the contrary, we have frequently noted that a determination of reasonableness must be based on the "circumstances" facing a defendant or his "situation." Such terms encompass more than the physical move-ments of the potential assailant. As just discussed, these terms include any relevant knowledge the defendant had about that person. They also necessarily bring in the physical attributes of all persons involved, including the defendant. Furthermore, the defendant's circumstances encompass any prior experiences he had which could provide a reasonable basis for a belief that another person's intentions were to injure or rob him or that the use of deadly force was necessary under the circumstances.

The prosecutor's instruction to the . . . Grand Jury that it had to determine whether, under the circumstances, Goetz's conduct was that of a reasonable man in his situation was thus essentially an accurate charge. It is true that the prosecutor did not elaborate on the meaning of "circumstances" or "situation" and inform the grand jurors that they could consider, for example, the prior experiences Goetz related in his statement to the police. We have held, however, that a Grand Jury need not be instructed on the law with the same degree of precision as the petit jury. This lesser standard is premised upon the different functions of the Grand Jury and the petit jury: the former determines whether sufficient evidence exists to accuse a person of a crime and thereby subject him to criminal prosecution; the latter ultimately determines the guilt or innocence of the accused, and may convict only where the People have proven his guilt beyond a reasonable doubt.

The prosecutor more than adequately fulfilled [his] obligation here. His instructions were not as complete as the court's charge on justification should be [at trial], but they sufficiently apprised the Grand Jury of the existence and requirements of that defense to allow it to intelligently decide that there is sufficient evidence tending to disprove justification and necessitating a trial. The Grand Jury has indicted Goetz. It will now be for the petit jury to decide whether the prosecutor can prove beyond a reasonable doubt that Goetz's reactions were unreasonable and therefore excessive.

Accordingly, the order of the Appellate Division should be reversed, and the dismissed counts of the indictment reinstated.

---

**Post-Case Follow-Up**

To succeed in a self-defense claim, the defendant's beliefs must "comport with an objective notion of reasonableness." The law employs an objective standard for self-defense claims because a subjective standard would risk "allow[ing] citizens to set their own standards for the permissible use of force." The reasonable person standard does not, however, "mean[] that the background and other relevant characteristics of a particular actor must be ignored." In the self-defense setting, the reasonable person standard is assessed based on the defendant's circumstances, which includes his physical attributes. Some jurisdictions, like New York, also hold that a defendant's relevant "prior experiences" may be taken into account. In *Goetz*, this meant the jury could consider the fact that the defendant previously had been mugged in its application of the reasonable person standard. In practical terms, then, the jury would be tasked with assessing self-defense based on the reasonable person who had previously been mugged.

---

## Goetz: *Real Life Applications*

1. The procedural posture of the case in *Goetz* is different from most of the cases in this book. *Goetz* did not involve an appeal following a conviction. Instead, the appeal in *Goetz* involved a challenge to the validity of the grand jury's indictment. Because the court held that the indictment should be reinstated, the case was remanded for trial. Imagine you are Goetz's attorney and that you are preparing for your closing argument. Assume that the facts established at trial are identical to those described in the Court of Appeals's opinion above. What would your argument in favor of self-defense be?

2. Look back at the facts of *State v. Norman*, described above at pages 482-84. Assume for purposes of this question that the North Carolina Supreme Court reversed Norman's conviction on the grounds that the trial court should have granted her request to instruct the jury on self-defense. The case is being retried and Norman's attorney has requested that the jury be instructed as follows: "A

person is justified in the use of deadly force against an aggressor when and to the extent it appears to her and she reasonably believes that such conduct is necessary to defend herself or another against such aggressor's imminent use of unlawful deadly force. *In determining whether the defendant's belief was reasonable, you must consider how a reasonably prudent battered spouse would perceive the facts and circumstances known to her.*" The prosecutor objects to the italicized portion of Norman's proposed jury instruction, arguing that it would effectively transform the "reasonable person" standard into a subjective test.

You are the trial court judge. How would you rule on Norman's proposed jury instruction?

3. In 2005, Vega and Baker left a strip club in Las Vegas, Nevada at about 5:30 in the morning. Surveillance footage from the strip club showed that Vega and Baker walked toward their car, which was in the strip club parking lot. As the pair walked in the center of one of the lanes of the parking lot, a black SUV pulled out of a parking space and drove toward them at a normal rate of speed. Vega and Baker moved out of the way of the black SUV, and Baker appeared to make an obscene gesture at the SUV. The black SUV proceeded to leave the parking lot, and Vega and Baker continued to walk to their car. Baker then appeared to make a second gesture in the direction of the SUV.

About 20 seconds later, the black SUV drove back into the parking lot. As this happened, Vega and Baker ran toward their car. The black SUV pulled up next to Vega and Baker, who by now were standing by their car. The passenger door of the SUV opened up and a man named Liu began to step out of it. As Liu exited the SUV, Vega fired multiple shots in the direction of the SUV. One of shots hit Liu, killing him. All of this was recorded by the strip club's surveillance camera.

The police separately interviewed Vega and Baker. Both men told the police that they thought someone in the SUV had a gun, and that Vega had fired in self-defense. Specifically, they told the police that after Baker made the obscene gesture, Baker thought that he saw one of the men inside the SUV display a gun. Baker immediately said to Vega, "One of them has a gun!" Both Vega and Baker told the police that when the SUV drove back into the lot, they were afraid that they were about to be shot.

The driver of the SUV, who emerged uninjured, told the police that neither he nor Liu were carrying a gun at the time of the incident. But, the driver said, Liu was carrying a knife. The driver told the police that he drove back into the parking lot because he thought that Vega and Baker wanted to engage in a fistfight. The driver told the police that he had never seen Vega or Baker before their encounter in the strip club parking lot.

Imagine you are the prosecutor. Based on this evidence, would you charge Vega with a homicide offense? Or would you decline to file charges in light of Vega's apparent self-defense claim? If you were to bring charges against Vega, would you charge him with first-degree murder, second-degree murder, or voluntary manslaughter?

## Race, Reasonableness, and Self-Defense

Is there a risk that racial stereotypes might influence jurors in deciding self-defense claims? If so, is there is way to guard against this?

In her article *Race and Self-Defense: Toward a Normative Conception of Reasonableness*, Cynthia Lee argued that there is reason to think jurors may rely on racial stereotypes in assessing the reasonableness of a defendant's actions. Among other examples, Professor Lee cited the *Goetz* case. After the opinion reinstating the indictment (presented above), Bernhard Goetz's case went to trial. The jury acquitted Goetz of attempted murder, even though "[a]s a textbook criminal law hypothetical, Goetz's self-defense claim should have been rejected for several reasons" — including that "Goetz admitted his intent was to murder the youths, to hurt them, and make them suffer as much as possible." Cynthia Kwei Yung Lee, *Race and Self-Defense: Toward a Normative Conception of Reasonableness*, 81 Minn. L. Rev. 367, 419, 420 (1996). Notably, Goetz's attorney seemed to play on "the Black-as-criminal stereotype" throughout the trial; he described the victims in his opening statement "as 'savages,' 'predators,' 'vultures,' and the 'gang of four,' conjuring up images of gang members preying on society." *Id.* at 422. In a case like *Goetz*, "[t]he jurors may have imagined themselves in Goetz's situation and felt that they too would have been afraid of four Black youths asking them for five dollars." *Id.* at 423. But, of course, that should be insufficient to make out a self-defense claim.

## Imperfect Self-Defense

In most jurisdictions, self-defense is an either-or proposition. But a number of states recognize a more limited version of self-defense for people who use deadly force based on an honest but *unreasonable* belief that they are facing a deadly threat. This defense, called **imperfect self-defense**, does not absolve the defendant of guilt entirely. Instead, where it applies, it mitigates a killing that would otherwise qualify as murder to voluntary manslaughter.

To appreciate how this defense works, consider the facts of *Goetz*. Imagine that after hearing the evidence at Bernhard Goetz's trial, the jury concluded that Goetz sincerely believed that he was faced with an unlawful, imminent threat of deadly force or of a robbery, but that Goetz's belief was unreasonable. In this hypothetical, Goetz would have no defense in the majority of jurisdictions, and he would be guilty of attempted murder as a result. But in the jurisdictions that recognize imperfect self-defense, the defense would apply and Goetz would be guilty of attempted voluntary manslaughter.

The rationale for imperfect self-defense is that "a defendant who commits a homicide while honestly, though unreasonably, believing that he is threatened with death or serious bodily harm" does not act with the type of culpability (i.e., malice aforethought) to warrant a murder conviction. *State v. Faulkner*, 301 Md. 482, 500 (1984). On the other hand, because the defendant's belief was unreasonable, he "is not entitled to full exoneration." *Id.* Imperfect self-defense balances these considerations by grading these kinds of killings as voluntary manslaughter.

## The Initial Aggressor Rule

A person who was the initial aggressor in an encounter loses the right to use force in self-defense. An initial aggressor is "the person who first acts in such a manner that creates a reasonable belief in another person's mind that physical force is about to be used on that other person." *State v. Jones*, 320 Conn. 22, 53-54 (2015). Under this definition, a person who makes a verbal threat of force is an initial aggressor. By contrast, "mere use of offensive words, without more, is insufficient to qualify a defendant as the initial aggressor." *Id.* at 54.

The initial aggressor rule proceeds from the premise that a person "who first attacks or threatens to attack another, is not justified in using force to protect himself from the counterattack that he provoked." *State v. Anthony*, 319 S.W.3d 524, 526 (Mo. Ct. App. 2010). This rule is also consistent with self-defense's unlawful force requirement. After all, if a person is the first aggressor, then the other party has a lawful a right to use force in self-defense.

An initial aggressor can regain her right to self-defense by withdrawing from the encounter and effectively communicating that fact to the other person. If, despite the initial aggressor's withdrawal, the other party "continues or threatens the use of unlawful physical force," the initial aggressor can act in self-defense. *People v. Toler*, 9 P.3d 341, 350 (Colo. 2000).

In addition, under the escalation principle, "an initial aggressor at the nondeadly level may yet claim self-defense if the other party escalated the fight to the deadly level." *Watkins v. State*, 79 Md. App. 136, 137 (1989). If, for example, a defendant acts as the initial aggressor by pushing his adversary and his adversary responds by pulling out a gun, the adversary's sudden escalation gives the defendant the right to use deadly force in self-defense, even though he was the initial aggressor.

## *Duty to Retreat?*

If a person can avoid using deadly force against his attacker by retreating, must he do so? Jurisdictions are divided on this question. The common law rule imposes a **duty to retreat** before using deadly force, subject to certain conditions discussed below. A majority of jurisdictions today reject the common law rule in favor of what is sometimes called the **"stand your ground"** rule, under which there is no duty to retreat before using deadly force. Note that this jurisdictional split concerns the use of *deadly* force in self-defense; all jurisdictions agree that there is *no* duty to retreat before using *non-deadly* force.

### Duty to Retreat Jurisdictions

In jurisdictions that recognize a duty to retreat, "a person may not use deadly physical force in self-defense if he knows that he can avoid the necessity of using that force with complete safety by retreating." *Douglas v. State*, 2018 AR 89, ¶ 8. Two components of this rule are worth particular attention. First, the duty to retreat employs a subjective standard. The defendant must subjectively *know* that he can

To reduce the risk that racial bias might influence jurors' views about reasonableness in self-defense cases, Professor Lee made a number of proposals, including a model supplemental jury instruction to expressly "remind jurors that they should not rely upon stereotypes to support a finding that the defendant's use of force was reasonable." *Id.* at 482. The first paragraph of Professor Lee's proposed instruction reads: "It is natural to make assumptions about the parties and witnesses in any case based on stereotypes. Stereotypes constitute well-learned sets of associations or expectations correlating particular traits with members of a particular social group. You should try not to make assumptions about the parties and witnesses based on their membership in a particular racial group." *Id.*

Do you agree with Professor Lee's argument that stereotypes about race might influence juries when assessing reasonableness in self-defense cases? If so, do you agree with her proposed supplemental jury instruction? In addition to racial stereotypes about victims in self-defense cases, do you think stereotypes about the *defendant's* race have the potential to influence juries in self-defense cases?

retreat with complete safety. If a defendant mistakenly thinks that he cannot retreat with complete safety, he is not required to retreat under this rule. This is true even if the defendant's mistaken belief is unreasonable. Second, the duty to retreat only arises if the defendant knows he can retreat with *complete* safety. Together, these two aspects of the duty to retreat mean that it applies only in limited circumstances since it is very unusual for a person to face an imminent, deadly attack and yet also be able to flee from the attacker with complete safety.

The duty to retreat is also subject to an important exception, sometimes called the **castle doctrine**. "Premised on the common law principle that a man's home is his castle, indeed his ultimate sanctuary, the castle doctrine permits a person who is without fault and is attacked within his dwelling or its curtilage to stand his ground and defend himself, even if a retreat could be safely accomplished." *Gainer v. State*, 40 Md. App. 382, 388 (1978). Put in practical terms, this exception means that a person who is facing an imminent deadly attack in his home or yard (i.e., the home's curtilage) does not have to retreat, *even if* he knows he can do so with complete safety.

Proponents of the retreat rule argue that it respects the value of human life and that it is an application of the principle that taking a life in self-defense is only justified if it is truly necessary. The rule's proponents also argue that the duty to retreat decreases homicides in practice, including homicides of bystanders who can be killed accidentally during violent altercations. On this point, a few empirical studies have found that states that have rejected the duty to retreat have seen an increase in homicides as a result. Critics of these studies argue that they do not show how many of the additional homicides that result from stand your ground laws are legally justified. See Cynthia V. Ward, *"Stand Your Ground" and Self-Defense*, 42 Am. J. Crim. L. 89, 125-28 (2015) (reviewing empirical evidence on the impact of stand your ground laws and homicide rates).

### Stand Your Ground Jurisdictions

A majority of states have rejected the common law duty to retreat in favor of a stand your ground rule. More than 30 states have some form of a stand your ground rule, either by court decision or statute. The move toward stand your ground laws is a relatively recent trend, driven in part by lobbying efforts by the National Rifle Association. See Erica Goode, *N.R.A.'s Influence Seen in Expansion of Self-Defense Laws*, N.Y. Times, Apr. 12, 2012.

In most jurisdictions that follow the stand your ground approach, the rule is simple and straightforward. By rejecting the duty to retreat, these jurisdictions permit a defendant to claim self-defense even if he knew he could have safely retreated without using deadly force. A few states have adopted statutes that go much further, however, by granting not just an affirmative defense but "*immunity* from criminal prosecution and civil suit to individuals who use force under Stand Your Ground laws." American Bar Association, National Task Force on Stand Your Ground Laws: Report and Recommendations 1 (2015).

Stand your ground laws became a subject of intense political focus in 2013, partly due to the prosecution in Florida of George Zimmerman for killing Trayvon

Martin, a 17-year-old high school student. Zimmerman successfully claimed self-defense based in part on Florida's stand your ground statute. Proponents of stand your ground laws argue that people who reasonably believe they are faced with an imminent, deadly threat should not be required to retreat, even if they can do so with complete safety. Stand your ground opponents cite the arguments in favor of the duty to retreat mentioned above — namely, that limiting deadly self-defense to cases where it is truly necessary better respects the value of human life. In addition, the data suggests that stand your ground laws are unevenly enforced, with one study concluding that "the race of the victim was the dominant fact that determined the outcome in Florida Stand Your Ground cases." *Id.* at 25.

## 2. Defense of Others

Closely related to self-defense, the law recognizes a defense when a person uses force to protect a third party. This defense was mentioned in passing in *People v. Goetz* and mirrors self-defense. In *Goetz*, the court quoted a New York statute that provides that "[a] person may * * * use physical force upon another person when and to the extent he reasonably believes such to be necessary to defend himself or *a third person* from what he reasonably believes to be the use or imminent use of unlawful physical force by such other person." As that statute suggests, in most jurisdictions, a person can use force in defense of a third party if she reasonably believes that force is necessary to protect the third party from the imminent use of unlawful physical force. The legal requirements for defense of others are identical to self-defense in every respect, with the only difference being that force is being used to defend a third party. As a result, as with self-defense, in order to use *deadly* force in defense of a third party, the defendant must reasonably believe that the threat the third party faced was a deadly one.

## 3. Defense of Property and Dwellings

There are two defenses related to the use of force to protect property: defense of personal property and defense of a dwelling. Both defenses are used relatively infrequently, likely because most cases that could give rise to a defense of property claim also implicate self-defense.

### *Defense of Personal Property*

A person may use non-deadly force in defense of personal property if he reasonably believes it is necessary to stop imminent, unlawful interference with the property. This standard permits defendants to take immediate steps to reclaim property that is in the process of being stolen or that has just been stolen. It does not, however, allow defendants to use force to reclaim previously stolen property. As the Nevada Supreme Court observed in denying O.J. Simpson's appeal of his robbery conviction for taking memorabilia that he claimed had been stolen from him, "a good faith belief that the property at issue is one's own" does not give a person the right to use force to retake the property. *Simpson v. State*, 126 Nev. 756 (2010). Instead, the right to use force to reclaim stolen property applies only if the defendant "acts immediately after the dispossession has occurred, or in hot pursuit of the person who has dispossessed the property." *Doby v. United States*, 550 A.2d 919, 920 (D.C. 1988).

The defense does not permit the use of deadly force. This means that if deadly force is the only way to prevent the theft of property, the law requires the property owner to suffer the loss. The reason for this rule is that "[t]he preservation of life and limb from grievous harm is of more importance to society than the protection of property." *People v. Ceballos*, 12 Cal. 3d 470, 483 (1974).

### Defense of a Dwelling

A person may use force if she "reasonably believes such conduct is necessary to prevent another's unlawful entry into a dwelling." *People v. Morris*, 162 Ill. App. 1046, 1054 (1987). Unlike the defense of personal property, a person can use deadly force in defense of a dwelling. Deadly force is permitted in defense of a dwelling if, in addition to the requirements already noted, the occupant reasonably believes the intruder intends to commit a felony inside.

There is relatively little case law addressing this defense. This may be because in most cases where it could be at issue, a defendant can rely on self-defense instead of defense of a dwelling. After all, when an intruder unlawfully enters a dwelling, it will often be reasonable for the occupant to believe that the intruder presents an imminent threat of force. In theory, however, the defense of a dwelling gives occupants of a home a slightly broader right to use force than self-defense does in some cases. Most notably, "one does *not* have to fear great bodily harm or death to justify the use of deadly force to defend against the commission of a felony in one's home." *State v. Pendleton*, 567 N.W.2d 265, 268 (Minn. 1997). As a result, a defendant who reasonably believes that deadly force is necessary to prevent an intruder from entering her home to commit a non-deadly felony (such as a non-violent burglary) would be entitled to use deadly force in defense of her dwelling even if she would *not* meet the requirements for self-defense.

## B. DURESS

Like self-defense, duress provides a defense for people who commit a crime in the face of a physical threat. Unlike self-defense, duress governs threats that are designed to induce someone to commit a crime. (Sometimes courts and commentators refer to this defense as the compulsion or coercion defense, although duress is the most frequently used name for the defense.)

Although there is a relatively wide range of statutory definitions for **duress**, jurisdictions can be split into roughly two camps on the issue. The majority of jurisdictions follow the common law rule for duress, which requires a showing that the defendant committed a criminal act in response to what she reasonably believed to be a "present, imminent and pending" threat "of such a nature as to induce a well grounded apprehension of death or serious bodily injury" to herself or a third party if the act was not done. *State v. Toscano*, 74 N.J. 421, 432-33 (1977).

A sizeable minority of states have adopted the Model Penal Code test for duress, which provides that duress is a defense "if the defendant engaged in conduct because he was coerced to do so by the use of, or threat to use, unlawful force against his person or the person of another, which a person of reasonable firmness in his situation would have been unable to resist." *Id.* at 442.

Under either jurisdictional approach, duress cannot be used as a defense to a homicide offense. Some states do, however, allow duress to be used as a defense to the predicate felony in a felony murder prosecution. In those states, if the defense is successful and the defendant is acquitted of the predicate felony, then he cannot be convicted of felony murder.

**Case Preview**

## State v. Toscano

The next case, *State v. Toscano*, considers the common law definition of duress in comparison to the Model Penal Code rule. The defendant, a chiropractor, was convicted of conspiracy to defraud an insurance company for falsifying a medical report. He attempted to claim duress at trial, but the trial court granted the prosecution's motion to exclude the defense on the grounds that Toscano could not meet the common law requirements for duress. On appeal, the New Jersey Supreme Court decided to adopt the Model Penal Code's definition of duress and reversed. The court had the power to change New Jersey's definition of duress because New Jersey had not codified criminal defenses at the time of the decision. In contrast to criminal offenses, which are almost entirely statutory, a number of states and the federal government continue to leave some or all criminal defenses uncodified, thereby permitting courts to reinterpret existing defenses as they see fit.

As you read the decision, consider the following questions:

1. The court indicates that Toscano would not qualify for a defense under the common law approach to duress but that he might satisfy the Model Penal Code version. Before you read the case, take a look back at the common law and Model Penal Code definitions of duress above. What do you think are the key differences between the two definitions?
2. Which approach to the duress defense — the common law version or the Model Penal Code version — do you think is preferable and why?

# *State v. Toscano*
## 74 N.J. 421 (1977)

PASHMAN, J.

Defendant Joseph Toscano was convicted of conspiring to obtain money by false pretenses in violation of N.J.S.A. 2A:98-1. Although admitting that he had aided in the preparation of a fraudulent insurance claim by making out a false medical report, he argued that he had acted under duress. The trial judge ruled that the threatened harm was not sufficiently imminent to justify charging the jury on the defense of duress. After the jury returned a verdict of guilty, the defendant was fined $500.

We granted certification to consider the status of duress as an affirmative defense to a crime. We hold that duress is an affirmative defense to a crime other than murder, and that it need not be based upon an alleged threat of immediate bodily injury. Under the standard announced today, we find that this defendant did allege sufficient facts to warrant charging the jury on his claim of duress. Accordingly, we reverse his conviction and remand for a new trial.

On April 20, 1972, the Essex County Grand Jury returned a 48-count indictment alleging that eleven named defendants and two unindicted co-conspirators had defrauded various insurance companies by staging accidents in public places and obtaining payments in settlement of fictitious injuries.

Dr. Joseph Toscano, a chiropractor, was named as a defendant in . . . two counts alleging a conspiracy to defraud the Kemper Insurance Company (Kemper). Prior to trial, seven of the eleven defendants pleaded guilty to various charges. Among those who pleaded guilty was William Leonardo, the architect of the alleged general conspiracy and the organizer of each of the separate incidents.[1] [T]he evidence . . . reveal[ed] a characteristic modus operandi by Leonardo and his cohorts which is helpful in understanding the fraudulent scheme against Kemper. Typically, they would stage an accident or feign a fall in a public place.[2] A false medical report for the "injured" person, together with a false verification of employment and lost wages, would then be submitted to the insurer of the premises. The same two doctors were used to secure the medical reports in every instance except that involving the claim against Kemper. Likewise, the confirmations of employment and lost wages were secured from the same pool of friendly employers. The insurance companies made cash payments to resolve the claims under their "quick settlement" programs, usually within a few weeks after the purported accidents. Leonardo took responsibility for dividing the funds to the "victims" of the accidents, to the doctors and employers, taking a substantial portion for himself.

---

[1] Defendant moved to sever his trial from those of [the] other defendants on the ground that he participated in the alleged general conspiracy on only one occasion. [The trial court denied the motion.] In addition to this refusal to sever, defendant raises several other errors supposedly committed by the trial judge, including a prejudicial charge to the jury and failure to grant a motion for acquittal. Because of our holding that the issue of duress was erroneously withheld from the jury, we do not reach those questions.

[2] The mishaps occurred in supermarkets, discount stores, movie theaters and a factory. On two occasions, Leonardo and others deliberately caused an accident while road testing a used car from a dealer. There were three incidents in 1968, five in 1969, three in 1970 and one in 1971.

Michael Hanaway, an unindicted co-conspirator who acted as the victim in a number of these staged accidents, testified that defendant was drawn into this scheme largely by happenstance. On January 6, 1970, Hanaway staged a fall at E. J. Korvette's in Woodridge, New Jersey under the direction of Leonardo and Frank Neri, another defendant who pleaded guilty prior to trial. Dr. Miele, one of the two doctors repeatedly called upon by Leonardo to provide fraudulent medical reports, attested to Hanaway's claimed injuries on a form supplied by the insurer. Hanaway was subsequently paid $975 in settlement of his claim by the Underwriters Adjusting Company on behalf of Korvette's insurer.

In the meantime, however, the same trio performed a similar charade at the R.K.O. Wellmont Theater in Montclair, New Jersey. Kemper, which insured the R.K.O. Theater, was immediately notified of Hanaway's claim, and Dr. Miele was again enlisted to verify Hanaway's injuries on a medical report. However, because the R.K.O. accident occurred on January 8, 1970 only two days after the Korvette's incident Dr. Miele confused the two claims and mistakenly told Kemper's adjuster that he was treating Hanaway for injuries sustained at Korvette's. When Hanaway learned of the claims adjuster's suspicions, he informed William Leonardo who, in turn, contacted his brother Richard (a co-defendant at trial) to determine whether Toscano would agree to verify the treatments.

The State attempted to show that Toscano agreed to fill out the false medical report because he owed money to Richard Leonardo for gambling debts. Defendant sharply disputed [this] assertion[] and maintained that he capitulated to William Leonardo's demands only because he was fearful for his wife's and his own bodily safety. Since it is not our function here to assess these conflicting versions, we shall summarize only those facts which, if believed by the jury, would support defendant's claim of duress.

Defendant first met Richard Leonardo in 1953 as a patient and subsequently knew him as a friend. Defendant briefly encountered the brother, William, in the late 1950's at Caldwell Penitentiary when Toscano served as a prison guard. Although William was an inmate, the doctor did not know him personally. Through conversations with some police officers and William's brother and father, however, he did learn enough about William to know of his criminal record.[4] In particular, Richard told him many times that William was "on junk," that he had a gang, that "they can't keep up with the amount of money that they need for this habit," and that he himself stayed away from William.

Thus, when William first called the defendant at his office, asking for a favor, he immediately cut off the conversation on the pretext that he was with a patient. Although William had not specifically mentioned the medical form at that time, defendant testified that he was "nauseated" by "just his name." A few days later, on a Thursday evening, he received another call in his office. This time Leonardo asked defendant to make out a report for a friend in order to submit a bill to a claims adjuster. He was more insistent, stating that defendant was "going to do it," but defendant replied that he would not and could not provide the report. Once again

---

[4] [O]ther testimony at trial supported [Toscano's] characterization of William Leonardo as a violent, erratic individual. Hanaway stated that Leonardo "opened Frank Neri's skull with a bat" and often did "off-the-wall things."

the doctor ended the conversation abruptly by claiming, falsely, that he was with other persons.

The third and final call occurred on Friday evening. Leonardo was "boisterous and loud" repeating, "You're going to make this bill out for me." Then he said: "Remember, you just moved into a place that has a very dark entrance and you leave there with your wife. . . . You and your wife are going to jump at shadows when you leave that dark entrance." Leonardo sounded "vicious" and "desperate" and defendant felt that he "just had to do it" to protect himself and his wife. He thought about calling the police, but failed to do so in the hope that "it would go away and wouldn't bother me any more."

In accordance with Leonardo's instructions, defendant left a form in his mailbox on Saturday morning for Leonardo to fill in with the necessary information about the fictitious injuries. It was returned that evening and defendant completed it. On Sunday morning he met Hanaway at a pre-arranged spot and delivered a medical bill and the completed medical report. He received no compensation for his services. He heard nothing more from Leonardo after that Sunday.

Shortly thereafter, still frightened by the entire episode, defendant moved to a new address and had his telephone number changed to an unlisted number in an effort to avoid future contacts with Leonardo. He also applied for a gun permit but was unsuccessful. His superior at his daytime job with the Newark Housing Authority confirmed that the quality of defendant's work dropped so markedly that he was forced to question defendant about his attitude. After some conversation, defendant explained that he had been upset by threats against him and his wife. He also revealed the threats to a co-worker at the Newark Housing Authority.

After defendant testified, the trial judge granted the State's motion to exclude any further testimony in connection with defendant's claim of duress, and announced his decision not to charge the jury on that defense. He based his ruling on . . . the common law rule that a successful claim of duress required a showing of a "present, imminent and impending" threat of harm.

The trial judge's formulation of the law of duress appears in harmony with . . . the common law rule.

Since New Jersey has no applicable statute defining the defense of duress, we are guided only by common law principles which conform to the purposes of our criminal justice system and reflect contemporary notions of justice and fairness.

At common law the defense of duress was recognized only when the alleged coercion involved a use or threat of harm which is "present, imminent and pending" and "of such a nature as to induce a well grounded apprehension of death or serious bodily harm if the act is not done."

It was commonly said that duress does not excuse the killing of an innocent person even if the accused acted in response to immediate threats. Aside from this exception, however, duress was permitted as a defense to prosecution for a range of serious offenses, see, e.g., *D'Aquino v. United States*, 192 F.2d 338, 358 (9 Cir. 1951) (treason; capital offense); *Gillars v. United States*, 182 F.2d 962, 976 (D.C. Cir. 1950) (treason); *Shannon v. United States*, 76 F.2d 490 (10 Cir. 1935) (kidnapping).

[Under the common law rule,] neither threats of slight injury nor threats of destruction to property are coercive enough to overcome the will of a person of ordinary courage. [Similarly, under the common law rule], the defense of duress has not been allowed because of the lack of immediate danger to the threatened person. When the alleged source of coercion is a threat of "future" harm, courts have generally found that the defendant had a duty to escape from the control of the threatening person or to seek assistance from law enforcement authorities. Assuming a "present, imminent and impending" danger, however, there is no requirement that the threatened person be the accused. [C]oncern for the well-being of another, particularly a near relative, can support a defense of duress if the other requirements are satisfied.

The insistence under the common law on a danger of immediate force causing death or serious bodily injury may be ascribed to its origins in early cases dealing with treason, to the proclivities of a "tougher-minded age," or simply to judicial fears of perjury and fabrication of baseless defenses. We do not discount the latter concern as a reason for caution in modifying this accepted rule, but we are concerned by its obvious shortcomings and potential for injustice. Under some circumstances, the commission of a minor criminal offense should be excusable even if the coercive agent does not use or threaten force which is likely to result in death or "serious" bodily injury. Similarly, it is possible that authorities might not be able to prevent a threat of future harm from eventually being carried out. Warnings of future injury or death will be all the more powerful if the prospective victim is another person, such as a spouse or child, whose safety means more to the threatened person than his own wellbeing. Finally, as the drafters of the Model Penal Code observed, "long and wasting pressure may break down resistance more effectively than a threat of immediate destruction."

The drafters of the Model Penal Code and the [proposed] New Jersey Penal Code . . . focus[ed] on whether the standard imposed upon the accused was one with which "normal members of the community will be able to comply." Thus, they . . . substantially departed from the existing statutory and common law limitations [to the duress defense] requiring that the result be death or serious bodily harm [or] that the threat be immediate and aimed at the accused. While these factors would be given evidential weight, the failure to satisfy one or more of these conditions would not justify the trial judge's withholding the defense from the jury.

For reasons suggested above, a per se rule based on immediate injury may exclude valid claims of duress by persons for whom resistance to threats or resort to official protection was not realistic. While we are hesitant to approve a rule which would reward citizens who fail to make such efforts, we are not persuaded that capitulation to unlawful demands is excusable only when there is a "gun at the head" of the defendant. We believe that the better course is to leave the issue to the jury with appropriate instructions from the judge.

[U]nder both [the Model Penal Code and the proposed New Jersey Penal Code] defendant would have had his claim of duress submitted to the jury. Defendant's testimony provided a factual basis for a finding that Leonardo threatened him and his wife with physical violence if he refused to assist in the fraudulent scheme. Moreover, a jury might have found from other testimony adduced at trial that Leonardo's threats induced a reasonable fear in the defendant. Since he asserted that he agreed to complete the false documents only because of this apprehension, the requisite elements of the defense were established. Under the model code provisions, it would have been solely for the jury to determine whether a "person of reasonable firmness in his situation" would have failed to seek police assistance or refused to cooperate, or whether such a person would have been, unlike defendant, able to resist.

Exercising our authority to revise the common law, we have decided to adopt this approach as the law of New Jersey. Henceforth, duress shall be a defense to a crime other than murder if the defendant engaged in conduct because he was coerced to do so by the use of, or threat to use, unlawful force against his person or the person of another, which a person of reasonable firmness in his situation would have been unable to resist.*

Defendant's conviction of conspiracy to obtain money by false pretenses is hereby reversed and remanded for a new trial.

---

**Post-Case Follow-Up**

In *Toscano*, the New Jersey Supreme Court decided to jettison the common law definition of duress in favor of the Model Penal Code's version. As the court's discussion of the two tests reveals, the Model Penal Code's definition of duress is more forgiving than that of the common law. The common law approach limits the duress defense to *imminent* threats of force that are likely to produce at least *serious* bodily harm. Under the Model Penal Code's definition of the defense, a defendant can succeed in a duress defense even if he acted in response to a non-imminent and non-deadly threat. He is entitled to the defense if he can show that a person of reasonable firmness in his situation would have been unable to resist the threat.

---

Under both jurisdictional approaches to duress, the defense is not available "to a person who intentionally or recklessly places himself in a situation in which it is probable that he will be subjected to duress." *State v. Heinemann*, 282 Conn. 281, 301 (2007). In *Toscano*, for example, the prosecution had "attempted to show that Toscano agreed to fill out the false medical report because he owed money to Richard Leonardo for gambling debts." Toscano "sharply disputed" this at his trial, and "maintained that he capitulated to William Leonardo's demands only because he was fearful for his wife's and his own bodily safety." Assume that Toscano was retried and that the jury believed the prosecution's evidence about his alleged gambling debts. In that case, the jury might well reject Toscano's defense on the ground that by incurring the gambling debt, he had intentionally or recklessly placed himself in a situation where he would be subjected to duress. Similarly, consider the example of drug smuggling, which is one of the types of cases where the duress defense is most often raised. Drug smuggling operators are exceedingly unlikely to personally transport drugs across the U.S. border because of the risk of getting caught. Instead, they recruit couriers — sometimes called "drug mules" — to bring

---

* "Subsequent to the *Toscano* decision, the Legislature codified duress as an affirmative defense" with a definition that matches the one adopted by the *Toscano* court. *State v. B.H.*, 183 N.J. 171, 187 (2005). [Footnote by casebook author.]

drugs across the border (and to transport drugs within the interior of the United States). Drug smugglers will sometimes threaten a prospective courier or her family in order to induce her to carry drugs into the United States. Duress can provide a defense to the courier in this kind of circumstance, so long she did not recklessly place herself in this situation. Imagine, for example, a defendant who agrees to smuggle drugs in exchange for money on one occasion. Afterwards, the drug smuggling operators ask her to do it again. When she declines, the smuggling operators threaten to harm her and her family unless she continues to smuggle drugs. If the defendant reluctantly agrees, she will not be able to rely on the duress defense because she was at fault for placing herself in a situation where she could be subject to duress.

## Toscano: *Real Life Applications*

1. Because the New Jersey legislature had not codified its defenses at the time *Toscano* was decided, the New Jersey Supreme Court had the power to decide how to define the duress defense. Imagine that shortly after the *Toscano* decision was issued, the New Jersey legislature is considering whether to adopt a statute to define the duress defense. Further imagine that two bills have been proposed: one that uses the common law definition of duress and one that uses the Model Penal Code's definition of duress.

   You are a legislative aide whose boss is trying to decide which of the two proposed bills she should support. She is also open to the possibility of introducing her own bill with a different definition of duress (e.g., a definition that combines elements of the common law and Model Penal Code definitions). She has asked for you advice on the matter. Would you recommend that she support the common law bill, the Model Penal Code bill, or that she propose a new definition of duress? If the latter, what definition of duress would you recommend?

2. Tremaine Speer is appealing his conviction for attempted aggravated robbery. Speer argues that the trial court erred by refusing to instruct the jury on the defense of duress. The evidence introduced was as follows:

   > At trial, the prosecution presented evidence that the victim negotiated with an acquaintance named Jamar Dickey to sell his used Honda for $600. After the victim met Dickey at an automotive parts store on the evening in question and completed the vehicle transaction, Dickey agreed to drive him and his family home in the Honda. When Dickey made an unplanned stop at a convenience store and went inside, Speer emerged from behind a dumpster in the parking lot, pointed a gun at the victim, and demanded his money. As the victim hesitated, Speer shot the victim in the stomach. After a brief altercation with Speer, the victim fled on foot and collapsed less than a block from the convenience store.
   >
   > Testifying on his own behalf, Speer did not dispute that he demanded the victim's money at gunpoint or that he shot the victim in the process but asserted instead that the shooting was accidental and that the robbery was part of a plot in which he participated only under duress. Speer testified that the man identified as Dickey, an acquaintance whom Speer had met through friends several months

before, threatened him with a gun earlier in the day and also threatened to find and harm his brother if he declined to cooperate in the robbery. He described in considerable detail the entire day he spent with Dickey, including various times in which he was out of Dickey's presence and in control of both Dickey's gun and a car. In particular he described positioning himself to carry out the robbery by driving himself, with the weapon in his possession, to the alley behind the convenience store, while Dickey was meeting the victim at the automotive parts store to consummate the sale.

At the close of evidence Speer requested that the jury be instructed on the affirmative defense of duress. The trial court, however, denied the instruction, finding that Speer had failed to present evidence from which the jury could make the factual findings necessary to satisfy the defense.

*People v. Speer*, 255 P.3d 1115, 1118 (Colo. 2011). You are a law clerk for one of the appellate judges who will be hearing Speer's appeal. Would you recommend affirming or reversing the trial court? Would your answer change depending on which definition of the defense of duress your jurisdiction has adopted?

## C. NECESSITY

Necessity and duress are both aimed at a similar situation: a defendant who commits a crime in order to avoid a greater harm. The fundamental difference between duress and necessity is that the necessity defense (also sometimes called the "choice of evils" defense) applies when the harm the defendant is trying to avoid is the result of forces beyond his control, as opposed to the result of a threat. The Supreme Court has explained the difference this way: "[D]uress cover[s] the situation where the coercion had its source in the actions of other human beings" and necessity "cover[s] the situation where physical forces beyond the actor's control render[] illegal conduct the lesser of two evils." *United States v. Bailey*, 444 U.S. 394, 409-10 (1980).

One of the most famous necessity defense cases, *The Queen v. Dudley and Stephens*, 14 QBD 273 DC (1884), was presented at the very beginning of this book. Recall that in *Dudley and Stephens*, four sailors were stranded at sea. After 20 days, two of the sailors killed an already nearly dead shipmate and ate his remains. Four days later, the surviving sailors were unexpectedly rescued. Although *Dudley and Stephens* is still read in Criminal Law courses today because it raises challenging issues about the theories of punishment, the court's holding that necessity is never a defense to intentionally taking another's life remains good law. This limitation is also present in the duress defense, of course. Also as in the duress defense, the defense of necessity is unavailable if the defendant was at fault for the threat.

The elements of the **necessity** defense are that the defendant committed the offense to prevent a significant evil, that there was no adequate reasonable alternative to committing the offense, and that the harm caused by the offense was not disproportionate to the harm avoided.

Imagine, for example, that the defendant sees his neighbor's house on fire while his neighbor is not at home. The defendant calls 911, but while he is waiting for the firefighters to arrive, he sees the neighbor's dog barking behind a downstairs window. The defendant smashes the window in order to let the pet jump out. This would constitute vandalism in most jurisdictions, but the defendant in this hypothetical will not be convicted of it because of the necessity defense. The defendant committed the act of vandalism to avoid a significant evil (imminent harm to the pet), there was no reasonable adequate alternative (the firefighters might have arrived too late to save the dog), and the harm caused by the vandalism (damage to the window) was not disproportionate to the harm avoided (the possible death of the dog).

## Case Preview

### *Allen v. State*

The defendant in *Allen* was prosecuted for driving with a suspended license. The trial court excluded his necessity defense on the grounds that he had reasonable alternatives to breaking the law. A divided Alaska Court of Appeals reversed. As the decision highlights, the necessity defense often turns on the extent to which the defendant had a reasonable alternative to breaking the law. After all, if there was a reasonable alternative, then breaking the law was not truly necessary.

As you read the decision, consider the following questions:

1. Which element of the necessity defense is at the heart of the disagreement between the majority and the dissent?
2. Do you think that this case is distinguishable from *Nelson*, cited by the dissent?
3. If you were the prosecutor, would you have brought criminal charges in this case?

---

### *Allen v. State*
#### 123 P.3d 1106 (Alaska Ct. App. 2005)

MANNHEIMER, J.

Dominic Allen appeals his convictions for driving with a suspended license and violating the conditions of his release (based on the same act of unlicensed driving). Allen contends that his trial judge should have instructed the jury on his proposed defense of necessity. For the reasons explained here, we agree with Allen and we therefore conclude that he is entitled to a new trial.

On the evening of April 24, 2003, a state trooper pulled Allen over for driving with his headlights off. (Allen was driving with only his parking lights on.) Allen's mother, Sharon Allen, was a passenger in the car. The trooper determined that Allen's driver's license was suspended, and so he arrested Allen for driving with a suspended license.

At the time, Allen was on bail release from another criminal charge. Allen was later charged with violating the condition of his release that required him to obey all laws.

Before trial, Allen's attorney notified the State that he intended to assert the affirmative defense of necessity under AS 11.81.320. On the first day of trial, the State asked the trial judge to preclude Allen from discussing this proposed defense in front of the jury until Allen made an offer of proof demonstrating that there was some evidence to support the defense.

In response, Allen's attorney asserted that the defense was prepared to present the following evidence: On the evening in question, Allen's mother (Sharon Allen) had initially been driving the car, but she had to pull over because she began to suffer fatigue and double vision. Although Allen knew that he was not supposed to drive, he believed that his mother needed medical attention, so (with his mother now in the passenger seat) Allen started driving to Big John's Liquors, approximately one-half mile down the road, where there was a telephone. Shortly after Allen began driving, he was stopped by the state trooper.

[T]he defense attorney called Allen's mother to the stand (outside the presence of the jury) in support of the proposed necessity defense.

Sharon Allen testified that she picked her son up from a class that night. As she was driving to Sterling, Allen told her to pull the car over because she was weaving. Mrs. Allen stated that she was suffering from fatigue and double vision at the time, recurring symptoms that stemmed from her being doused with gasoline three years earlier. She testified that, after she pulled over, Allen took the wheel and drove to Big John's to use the telephone to "find a ride for [her]." Mrs. Allen further testified that, although her physical ailments were recurring, Allen had not previously seen her in this condition, and he was scared about her health.

During cross-examination by the prosecutor, Sharon Allen conceded that, during the time her son was driving to Big John's, they must have passed Good Time Charlie's, a strip club. Mrs. Allen further conceded that they did not stop at the strip club. She explained that the only telephone she knew about was at Big John's, that she was not a "bar person," and that she "wouldn't have considered going in [Good Time Charlie's]."

In addition to presenting this testimony, Allen's attorney also offered to prove that Allen believed that his mother needed medical attention, that he wanted to transport her to Big John's because that was the nearest place he knew of where there was a telephone, and that Allen believed there was no adequate alternative to his driving the car to Big John's.

When the trial judge, Magistrate David S. Landry, suggested that Allen might have walked the half-mile to Big John's, Allen interjected, "And leave my mother in the car? Is that what you would do, Your Honor?"

Magistrate Landry refused to instruct the jury on the defense of necessity, and he precluded Allen from presenting any evidence in support of this defense. Magistrate Landry concluded that Allen had an adequate, reasonable alternative to breaking the law: he could have walked to Good Time Charlie's (which was closer than Big John's) and used the telephone there.

To establish the defense of necessity, a defendant must show (1) that they committed the charged offense to prevent a significant evil, (2) that there was no adequate, reasonably available alternative to committing the offense, and (3) that the harm caused by the charged offense was not disproportionate to the harm the defendant avoided by breaking the law.

[The defense is] judged from the perspective of a reasonable person in the defendant's position. Thus, the question is what the defendant reasonably believed at the time, even if it later turns out that the defendant's belief was partially or wholly mistaken.

In Allen's case, the trial judge precluded him from presenting a necessity defense because the judge concluded that Allen had an adequate, reasonably available alternative to driving to Big John's Liquors — to wit, leaving his mother in the car and walking to Good Time Charlie's.

Here, Allen asserted that he drove to Big John's Liquors because he knew that a telephone was available there. Moreover, Allen asserted that even if a telephone had been available at Good Time Charlie's, it would have been unreasonable for Allen to walk to this telephone and leave his mother alone in the car when he reasonably believed that she was in need of speedy medical attention. Allen presented evidence (or an offer of proof) on these issues, and we conclude that this evidence created a jury question on both issues. That is, jurors who viewed this evidence in the light most favorable to Allen could properly find in Allen's favor on these issues. For this reason, it was error for the trial judge to refuse to instruct the jury on the defense of necessity.

The judgment of the district court is Reversed. Allen is entitled to a new trial.

STEWART, J., dissenting.

[T]he Alaska Supreme Court [has] described the necessity defense as having three elements: (1) the defendant's violation of the law must have been done to prevent a significant evil, (2) there must have been no adequate alternative method to prevent this evil, and (3) the harm caused by the defendant's violation of the law must not have been disproportionate to the foreseeable harm that the defendant was trying to avoid. An objective determination must be made as to whether the defendant's value judgment was correct, given the facts as he reasonably perceived them.

The necessity defense is an affirmative defense; a defendant must present some evidence of that defense before the defendant is entitled to a jury instruction on the necessity defense. "Some evidence" is evidence which, viewed in the light most favorable to the defendant, is sufficient to allow a reasonable juror to find in the defendant's favor on each element of the defense.

I conclude that the record did not support Allen's request for a necessity instruction. Allen was required to present some evidence that he reasonably believed that he had no adequate alternative to driving with his suspended license.

In *Nelson v. State*, the Alaska Supreme Court ruled, as a matter of law, that Nelson was not entitled to [raise] a necessity defense where the record showed that he had adequate alternatives available to breaking the law. Nelson drove his vehicle off the road and got it stuck. He then took heavy equipment from a nearby state highway facility to retrieve his vehicle. The court said that, according to the record, there were several alternatives available to Nelson that did not involve breaking the law.

Thus, a court faced with a request for a jury instruction on a necessity defense should consider whether there was an "adequate" legal alternative available to the defendant. In other words, does the law allow a person in the defendant's position to break the law rather than pursuing the alternative?

As the majority describes, Allen was less than half a mile from Big John's Liquors when he started breaking the law by driving. I see nothing in the record that shows that Allen was at risk because of the weather or that Allen was disabled. I conclude that the record shows Allen had an adequate alternative; he could have walked less than one-half of a mile for his phone call.

**Post-Case Follow-Up**

The necessity defense requires the defendant to show that he committed a crime in order to avoid a significant evil, that there was no adequate, reasonable alternative to committing the offense, and that the harm caused by the charged offense was not disproportionate to the harm the defendant avoided by breaking the law. All of this is measured using an objective standard. It is not uncommon for trial courts to deny requests to present a necessity defense on the ground that the defendant had adequate alternatives available to him as a matter of law. In this case, however, the Court of Appeals concluded that the question of whether walking a half a mile to the nearest pay phone was a reasonable alternative should have been left to the jury to decide. As a result, the court reversed the defendant's conviction, allowing him to present his defense on retrial.

## Allen: *Real Life Applications*

1. Lewis, age 42, is an inmate at a prison in California. He has served 16 years of a 33-year sentence for a carjacking conviction. One day, a prison guard discovered Lewis smoking marijuana in his cell. In addition to the marijuana cigarette that Lewis was smoking, the guard found about a third of an ounce of marijuana in Lewis's cell. Lewis is charged with possession of a controlled substance in a prison.

   Before trial, Lewis files a motion seeking to present a necessity defense. Specifically, Lewis wants to argue at trial that he possessed the marijuana out of medical necessity. Lewis plans to introduce evidence that would show that, in 2010, he was the victim of two prison attacks that left him with chronic neck and back pain. Lewis has also been diagnosed with severe bilateral carpal tunnel syndrome and degenerative joint disease. Although prison doctors acknowledged Lewis was suffering from these conditions, his treatment consisted exclusively of over-the-counter-strength medications like Tylenol, Aleve, and ibuprofen.

Starting two years before he was found with marijuana, Lewis filed 12 requests for medical care with the prison. In these requests, Lewis explained that the medications he was receiving did not address his extreme pain and he requested additional medical evaluation. The prison denied all of Lewis's requests. Lewis did not pursue an administrative appeal of the denials or file a petition for habeas corpus challenging his medical care. One month before the incident, Lewis was put into an administrative segregation unit because there were no cells available that could accommodate his disability. While in the unit, Lewis was denied his back and neck brace, exacerbating his pain.

Desperate for pain relief, Lewis obtained the marijuana because he had heard that it might be effective at relieving chronic pain.

**a.** You are the trial court judge. Would you allow Lewis to present his necessity defense to the jury?

**b.** Assume for purposes of this question that the trial court judge denied Lewis's motion and has precluded his necessity defense. You are the prosecutor, and the trial is now two weeks away. Your supervisor has told you that you have the discretion to make a plea offer to Lewis, take the case to trial, or dismiss the charges entirely. It may be relevant to your decision to know that the prison has already imposed a number of administrative penalties against Lewis for his possession of the marijuana, including the loss of a total of one year of good-time credits (effectively extending the time he will serve for his original prison sentence by one year).

You anticipate that if Lewis is convicted of possession of a controlled substance in a prison at trial, the court is likely to sentence him to two years in prison (to run consecutively to his original sentence).

If you were to make a plea offer to Lewis, the offer would be that Lewis would plead guilty to possession of a controlled substance and, in exchange, you would drop the charge of possession of a controlled substance *in a prison*, which is a more serious offense. You anticipate that under this deal, the judge would likely sentence Lewis to one year in prison (to run consecutively to his original sentence).

Would you (a) take the case to trial, (b) offer Lewis the plea deal described above, or (c) drop the charges entirely?

## D. INSANITY

The insanity defense attracts attention out of proportion to its practical importance. Public opinion surveys suggest that people believe the insanity defense is used in a large number of cases. In fact, it is only very rarely employed. Studies indicate that less than 1 percent of criminal defendants who take their case to trial "try to use the insanity defense and, of these, only one-quarter use it successfully. A thirty-six state survey found an average of 33.4 insanity acquittals per state, per year, from 1970 to 1995." Elizabeth Nevins-Saunders, *Not Guilty as Charged: The*

*Myth of* Mens Rea *for Defendants with Mental Retardation*, 45 U.C. Davis L. Rev. 1419, 1454 (2012). Even though very few defendants raise an insanity defense, a significant number of criminal defendants suffer from mental illness. Estimates differ due in part to differences in the definition of mental illness employed but, as an example, a 2006 Bureau of Justice Statistics survey found that 56 percent of state prisoners, 45 percent of federal prisoners, and 64 percent of jail inmates have a mental health issue. See Margaret Wilkinson Smith, Note, *Restore, Revert, Repeat: Examining the Decompensation Cycle and the Due Process Limitations on the Treatment of Incompetent Defendants*, 71 Vand. L. Rev. 319, 320-21 (2018) (discussing data on the prevalence of mental illness among jail and prison inmates in the United States).

Two factors help to explain the disconnect between the relatively large number of criminal defendants who suffer from mental illness and the small number who attempt to rely on the insanity defense at trial. First, succeeding in an insanity defense can often turn out to be a pyrrhic victory. This is because in most states, a verdict of not guilty by reason of insanity results in automatic commitment to a mental institution, often with no limit on the duration of the commitment. Indeed, empirical studies suggest that insanity "acquittees actually spend almost double the amount of time that defendants convicted of similar charges spend in prison settings and often face a lifetime of post-release judicial oversight." Michael L. Perlin, *"Wisdom Is Thrown into Jail": Using Therapeutic Jurisprudence to Remediate the Criminalization of Persons with Mental Illness*, 17 Mich. St. U. J. Med. & L. 343, 356 (2013). As a result, even if a defendant might have a viable insanity defense, it is not necessarily in her best interest to raise it. In cases where a defendant is facing the death penalty or life in prison, a verdict of not guilty by reason of insanity may be a clearly preferable result. But a defendant who is facing, say, a ten-year sentence could very well spend more time in confinement (albeit in a mental health facility) if she successfully raises an insanity defense than she would if she were convicted.

Second, as the material that follows shows, the insanity defense is not an easy one to meet. The fact that the defendant was suffering from mental illness at the time he committed a crime is not itself exculpatory. Indeed, a defendant can be very seriously mentally ill and yet not meet the legal definition of insanity.

The insanity defense may be infrequently used. But legislatures across the country continually revisit it. Over the years, high profile cases involving the insanity defense have led voters and lawmakers to call for it to be narrowed or reformed. (High profile insanity cases also likely explain the public's misperception about how often the defense is used.) As one court put it, the insanity defense "is frequently reformulated in response to a public outcry." *People v. Serravo*, 823 P.2d 128, 134 n.8 (Colo. 1992). As a result of all this legislative tinkering, there is a good deal of variation when it comes to the legal standard for insanity. Very roughly speaking, however, there are three tests for insanity: the *M'Naghten* test, the irresistible impulse test, and the Model Penal Code test.

# 1. The *M'naghten* Test

Although the insanity defense is hundreds of years old, modern insanity doctrine dates to an 1843 case, *M'Naghten*, which involved the attempted assassination of the British prime minister. The defendant, Daniel M'Naghten, suffered from paranoid delusions and believed the prime minister was leading a plot to kill him. In response, M'Naghten shot and killed a person whom he believed to be the prime minister. As it turned out, the victim was the prime minister's secretary. The case led the Queen's Bench to establish what is now known as the *M'Naghten* test for insanity.

The ***M'Naghten* test** is as follows: "[T]o establish a defence on the ground of insanity, it must be clearly proved that, at the time of the committing of the act, the party accused was labouring under such a defect of reason, from disease of the mind, as not to know the nature and quality of the act he was doing; or, if he did know it, that he did not know he was doing what was wrong." *M'Naghten's Case*, 8 Eng. Rep. 718, 722 (1843).

Technically, *M'Naghten* is a two-pronged test. A defendant can meet the test by showing that either (1) he did not know the nature and quality of the act he was doing, *or* (2) he did not know what he was doing was wrong, meaning the defendant did not know the difference between right and wrong.

*M'Naghten*'s first prong adds very little to the test. It applies in cases where the defendant's delusions are so strong that she literally does not know what she is doing — for example, a person who thinks she is chopping down a tree when she is actually striking a human being. It is unclear how often, if ever, this prong is actually relied upon in real-world cases. Cases that involve hallucinations that are severe enough to meet *M'Naghten*'s first prong are rare. Moreover, it seems that a defendant who is legally insane under *M'Naghten*'s first prong would also necessarily meet its second prong. As the Supreme Court has observed, "if a defendant did not know what he was doing when he acted, he could not have known that he was performing the wrongful act charged as a crime." *Clark v. Arizona*, 548 U.S. 735, 753-54 (2006). Despite the near uselessness of *M'Naghten*'s first prong in the real world, it remains a part of the black letter formulation of the *M'Naghten* test for insanity.

In practice, *M'Naghten*'s second prong is by far the more important of the two. It applies when, because of the defendant's mental disease or defect, he did not know what he was doing was wrong. In *M'Naghten* itself, for example, the defendant believed that he had to kill the prime minister in order to prevent the prime minister from killing him. Although the defendant knew the nature and quality of what he was doing (firing a gun at another person), he did not know what he was doing was wrong in the eyes of society and the law. Importantly, *M'Naghten*'s second prong does *not* mean a defendant with a mental disease can act according to his own moral standards. For example, a defendant suffering from a mental disease who attempts to assassinate a member of Congress in the hope of overthrowing the capitalist system still knows her acts are considered wrong in the eyes of society and the law and so will be considered legally sane under the *M'Naghten* test.

**EXHIBIT 11.2** Modern Insanity Doctrine Dates to *M'Naghten's Case*

PORTRAIT OF DANIEL M'NAUGHTEN.

*THE MARKETS.*

## 2. The Irresistible Impulse Test

The irresistible impulse test was "formulated in response to medical dissatisfaction with *M'Naghten*" — in particular, with "*M'Naghten's* sole emphasis upon cognition." John Reid, *Understanding the New Hampshire Doctrine of Criminal Insanity*, 69 Yale L.J. 367, 368 (1960). To remedy this arguable deficiency in *M'Naghten*, the irresistible impulse test focuses on volition. The irresistible impulse test is not concerned with whether a defendant knew what he was doing was wrong but with whether the defendant was unable to control his actions.

The **irresistible impulse test** is met if the defendant can establish that, due to a mental disease or defect, he suffered from "an uncontrollable impulse to commit the offense charged. This impulse must be such as to override the [defendant's] reason and judgment . . . to the extent that the accused is deprived of the power to choose between right and wrong." *Smith v. United States*, 36 F.2d 548, 549 (D.C. Cir. 1929).

The irresistible impulse test is sometimes described as a "'policeman at the elbow'" standard, meaning that the impulse to commit the crime must be so strong that the defendant would be unable to resist it even if a police officer were present and ready to make an arrest. *People v. Jackson*, 245 Mich. App. 17, 20 (2001). A defendant who would have been unable to resist the impulse to commit the crime in the presence of the arresting officer is one who has "has been completely deprived of the power to conform his conduct to the dictates of the law." *Id.* at 21.

Under the irresistible impulse test, a person can be considered legally insane even if he knew the nature of his act and knew that what he was doing was wrong. For example, a person who was compelled to kill in response to voices in his head, despite knowing what he was doing was wrong, could satisfy the irresistible impulse test but not the *M'Naghten* test. This is because "his reasoning powers were so far dethroned by his diseased mental condition as to deprive him of the will power to resist the insane impulse to perpetrate the deed, though knowing it to be wrong." *Smith*, 36 F.2d at 549. (By contrast, if the person in this hypothetical had believed he was hearing the voice of *God*, he might be able to satisfy the *M'Naghten* test since by acting according to God's instructions, he might not have known what he was doing was wrong.)

## 3. The Model Penal Code Test

The **Model Penal Code test** for insanity combines and expands on both the *M'Naghten* and the irresistible impulse tests. It provides that "[a] person is not responsible for criminal conduct if at the time of such conduct as a result of mental disease or defect he lacks substantial capacity either to appreciate the criminality [wrongfulness] of his conduct or to conform his conduct to the requirements of the law." Model Penal Code § 4.01(1) (brackets in original).

In effect, the Model Penal Code test combines an expanded version of the second prong of *M'Naghten* with an expanded version of the irresistible impulse test. Under the resulting rule, a defendant can establish an insanity defense by showing that he lacked the substantial capacity to either (1) appreciate the criminality or wrongfulness of his conduct, *or* (2) conform his conduct to the requirements of the law. The first prong of this test is sometimes referred to as the cognitive prong, and the second prong is sometimes referred to as the volitional prong.

Notice how the test compares to *M'Naghten* and the irresistible impulse test. First, the *M'Naghten* test requires a showing that the defendant did not *know* that what he was doing was wrong. The Model Penal Code grants the defense to a person who *lacked the substantial capacity to appreciate* the criminality or wrongfulness of his conduct. As the Connecticut Supreme Court observed, "the Model Penal Code test focuses on the defendant's actual *appreciation of*, rather than merely his *knowledge of*, the wrongfulness of his conduct. The drafters of the Model Penal Code purposefully adopted the term 'appreciate' in order to account for the defendant whose 'detached or abstract awareness' of the wrongfulness of his conduct 'does not penetrate to the affective level.'" *State v. Wilson*, 242 Conn. 605, 613-14 (1997) (citation omitted). Quoting the chief reporter for the Model Penal Code, Herbert Wechsler, the court explained that to *appreciate* the wrongfulness of conduct is "to grasp it in a way that makes it meaningful in the life of the individual, not as a bare abstraction put in words." *Id.* at 614 (citation omitted).

Second, the irresistible impulse test requires an uncontrollable impulse to commit the crime, one that *deprives the defendant of the power to choose* between right and wrong. The Model Penal Code test requires only proof that the defendant *lacked the substantial capacity to conform his conduct* to the requirements of the law. The phrase "substantial capacity" means that, in contrast to the irresistible impulse test, the "defendant need not prove that he totally lacks the capacity for self-control." *People v. Jackson*, 245 Mich. App. 17, 20 (2001).

## 4. The Current State of the Law

Although all three of the insanity tests described above are considered to be part of the criminal law canon, only *M'Naghten* and the Model Penal Code test are widely followed. Roughly half of all states today apply the *M'Naghten* definition of insanity or a modified version of it. Four of these states *also* apply the irresistible impulse test, meaning that a defendant is considered legally insane if he meets either test. Another 20 states follow the Model Penal Code's test or a modified version of it. (One state, New Hampshire, applies its own test, known as the New Hampshire test or the *Durham* test.) Finally, four states have abolished the insanity defense entirely. See Beatrice R. Maidman, *The Legal Insanity Defense: Transforming the Legal Theory into a Medical Standard*, 96 B.U. L. Rev. 1831, 1840 (2016) (summarizing the different state approaches to insanity).

**Case Preview**

## *State v. Worlock*

*M'Naghten*'s second prong asks fact finders to consider whether the defendant was able to distinguish between right and wrong. This raises the question: What does it mean for a person to know that what he was doing was "wrong"? If a defendant knows that the law forbids his conduct but he nevertheless believes that it is justified — for example, because he believes God has commanded him to act — does he know what he is doing is wrong within the meaning of *M'Naghten*? After 175 years, courts have not agreed upon a single definition of "wrong" for purposes of *M'Naghten*'s test. The case below discusses the problem and reviews some of the points of agreement and disagreement among courts when it comes to this issue.

As you read the court's opinion, consider the following questions:

1. Why does the court find that the trial court did not need to instruct the jury on the meaning of "wrong"?
2. The court states that the defendant's belief that his conduct was justified under his personal code of morality did not meet the definition of insanity under *M'Naghten*. Why not?

# *State v. Worlock*
### 117 N.J. 596 (1990)

POLLOCK, J.

The primary issue in this case concerns the adequacy of the jury charge on the defense of insanity, which the Appellate Division sustained in an unreported opinion. We granted certification and likewise find the charge to be sufficient. [W]e affirm [the defendant's] convictions for murder and for possession of a weapon for an unlawful purpose.

The following summary is substantially consistent with defendant's version of the facts. Defendant, Carlyle Worlock, and his two victims, Guy Abrahamsen and Shawn Marchyshyn, had an unstable friendship in which Abrahamsen would periodically subject defendant to ridicule and physical abuse. On the night before the killing, the three young men went from Jackson Township to Seaside Heights, where, at defendant's expense, they spent the night smoking marijuana, drinking beer, and "partying" with two women "picked up" by Abrahamsen and Marchyshyn. After returning to Marchyshyn's apartment the following morning, Abrahamsen asked defendant for his pants. The ostensible reason for the request was that defendant's pants were dirty and Abrahamsen wanted to launder them. Apparently, however, the request was a ruse to obtain defendant's wallet, which contained, among other things, approximately $130 and a photograph of defendant dressed in a sadomasochistic costume at a gay parade in Hollywood. Defendant viewed the theft of his wallet as an act of betrayal, and feared that Abrahamsen could "destroy" him by disclosing the photograph.

"Burning and angry," defendant retrieved a semi-automatic .22 caliber rifle that he had hidden in a nearby wooded area because of a premonition that Abrahamsen "would do something like this." While brooding, he decided to "let this guy [Abrahamsen] have it." Defendant proceeded to the vicinity of Marchysyn's apartment, where he waited for the victims.

Shortly thereafter, defendant saw Abrahamsen and Marchyshyn exit from a taxi cab. He knew that neither of them had any money, so the sight of the cab confirmed the suspicion that Abrahamsen had taken his money. According to a defense psychiatrist, defendant was "devastated" by the realization that Abrahamsen had stolen his wallet. Concealing the rifle in a cloth, defendant moved to the far side of the building and "wait[ed] in ambush." As they approached, he moved to within fifteen feet of them and quickly fired twelve rounds.

As defendant testified, "I aimed at Guy, and I * * * hit Shawn." The first bullet struck Marchyshyn in the chest and killed him. Three other bullets hit Abrahamsen, one in each arm and one in the back. Defendant fired a second burst of bullets, hitting Abrahamsen with six more shots as he opened the screen door of a ground-floor apartment. According to the occupants of the apartment, Abrahamsen stumbled into the family room and collapsed on the floor.

Defendant stated that he then tried to "divorce [himself] from the act," ran into the woods, changed his clothes, and went to a pizza parlor. While eating pizza, he saw several police officers "scouting" around, and he asked "what's happening?". Defendant testified that he then walked to the home of Abrahamsen's girlfriend, and told her that he had shot Abrahamsen. According to her, however, defendant said only that Abrahamsen had been shot. She left with two of her friends, one of whom called the police.

Defendant next went to his parents' house. They told him that the police were looking for him. On leaving the house, defendant noticed a police car parked nearby, and decided to "give himself in." After defendant identified himself, Officer Barry Wohl handcuffed him, read him his *Miranda* rights, and told him that he was wanted "as a material witness involving an investigation."

At police headquarters, defendant again received *Miranda* warnings, signed a consent-to-questioning form, and confessed to shooting Abrahamsen and Marchyshyn. Defendant explained, however, that the shooting of Marchyshyn was an accident, stating that "Shawn got in the way."

On September 21, 1983, an Ocean County Grand Jury indicted defendant for the capital murder of Abrahamsen and Marchyshyn.

At trial, the principal issue was whether defendant was legally insane when he shot Abrahamsen and Marchyshyn.

The test for criminal insanity is set forth in N.J.S.A. 2C:4-1, which provides:

> A person is not criminally responsible for conduct if at the time of such conduct he was laboring under such a defect of reason, from disease of the mind as not to know the nature and quality of the act he was doing, or if he did know it, that he did not know what he was doing was wrong. Insanity is an affirmative defense which must be proved by a preponderance of the evidence.

Under the statute, as at common law, a defendant is presumed sane and bears the burden of proving insanity as an affirmative defense. Underlying that presumption is the belief that people are capable of choosing between right and wrong. A defendant who lacks that capacity is excused from criminal responsibility, but is subject to institutionalization as long as he is a danger to himself or others.

The insanity defense is consistent with the fundamental purpose of the criminal law as a means of protecting public safety. For a defendant who can choose between right and wrong, criminal sanctions serve as punishment for him or her and as a deterrent to others. If the defendant cannot understand the wrongfulness of his or her conduct, he or she will not understand the reason for the punishment, and that punishment will not serve as a deterrent to anyone. From that perspective, an insane defendant is neither responsible nor blameworthy. The insanity defense, therefore, serves to distinguish those who should be punished from those who lack sufficient capacity to merit punishment. In brief, the insanity defense separates "the sick from the bad."

The insanity test codified in N.J.S.A. 2C:4-1 traces its origins to the rules set forth in *M'Naghten's Case*, 8 Eng. Rep. 718 (H.L. 1843). There Daniel M'Naghten shot and killed Edward Drummond, secretary to Robert Peel, the Prime Minister of England. M'Naghten was charged with murder, and the jury returned a verdict of not guilty by reason of insanity. In responding to the ensuing public outcry, the House of Lords posed to its Law Lords five abstract questions concerning the defense of insanity. In a combined answer to the second and third questions, Chief Justice Tindal stated that

> to establish a defense on the ground of insanity, it must be clearly proved that, at the time of the committing of the act, the party accused was labouring under such a defect of reason, from disease of the mind, as not to know the nature and quality of the act he was doing; or, if he did know it, that he did not know he was doing what was wrong.

Directed at the defendant's ability to "know," the *M'Naghten* test is essentially one of cognitive impairment. Sometimes described as the "right and wrong" test, its purpose is to determine whether the defendant had sufficient mental capacity to understand what he was doing when he committed the crime.

With the advance of modern psychiatry, some critics, viewing the *M'Naghten* Rule as too restrictive, have suggested alternative tests of legal insanity. One alternative, sometimes described as the New Hampshire or *Durham* test, would excuse the defendant for an act that was a "product of mental disease." Another alternative, the "irresistible impulse" test, focuses on volitional, rather than cognitive, impairment. It attempts to determine whether a defendant, due to mental illness, lacked the ability to control his criminal impulses.

The most successful alternative, one that combines elements of the *M'Naghten* and irresistible-impulse tests, is contained in section 4.01 of the Model Penal Code. That section provides:

> A person is not responsible for criminal conduct if at the time of such conduct as a result of mental disease or defect he lacks substantial capacity either to appreciate the criminality [wrongfulness] of his conduct or to conform his conduct to the requirements of law.

By 1980, the Model Penal Code test had been accepted in more than half the states and in most federal circuits.

Notwithstanding those alternative formulations, New Jersey has consistently followed the *M'Naghten* Rule from its inception.

The insanity defense is a legal standard incorporating moral considerations often established by medical testimony. Notwithstanding advances in psychiatry, mental states remain inscrutable, especially when an abnormal state is in issue. Generally, the determination of a defendant's ability to distinguish between right and wrong depends on psychiatric testimony. Such testimony provides insight into a defendant's mental condition and enables the fact-finder to differentiate defendants who can choose between right and wrong from those who cannot. Ultimately, the insanity defense requires satisfaction of a legal, not a medical, standard. As applied, the "right and wrong" test blends legal, medical, and ethical concepts. Perhaps for this reason, courts have generally admitted any credible medical testimony on the insanity defense.

Defendant urges that the trial court committed plain error by failing to charge expressly that "wrong" as used in N.J.S.A. 2C:4-1 includes moral wrong. Although other jurisdictions have considered the issue, it is one of first impression in this state.

The issue harks back to an ambiguity in the first question posed by the House of Lords in the *M'Naghten* case:

> What is the law respecting alleged crimes committed by persons afflicted with insane delusion in respect of one or more particular subjects or persons: as, for instance where at the time of the commission of the alleged crime the accused knew he was acting contrary to law, but did the act complained of with a view, under the influence of insane delusion, of redressing or revenging some supposed grievance or injury, or of producing some supposed public benefit?

In reply, Chief Justice Tindal stated that

> assuming * * * the inquir[y is] confined to those persons who labour under such partial delusions only, and are not in other respects insane, we are of the opinion that * * * he is nevertheless punishable according to the nature of the crime committed, if he knew at the time of committing such crime that he was acting contrary to law; by which expression we understand your Lordships to mean the law of the land.

Without more, that reply would suggest that "wrong" means legal, not moral, wrong.

In addition to his previously-quoted answer to the second and third questions posed by the House of Lords, however, the Chief Justice explained that "[i]f the accused was conscious that the act was one which he ought not to do, and if that act was at the same time contrary to the law of the land, he is punishable." This elaboration suggests that "wrong" means both moral and legal wrong, an apparent conflict with the answer to the first question. The confusion is compounded because "wrong" is undefined in the opinion. At trial, moreover, the court charged the jury that M'Naghten was entitled to an acquittal if, at the time he shot Drummond, he did not know "that he was violating the laws both of God and man," thereby suggesting that "wrong" meant both legal and moral wrong.

Time has not resolved the ambiguity. Although a subsequent English decision has interpreted "wrong" to mean legal wrong, the High Court of Australia, which purports to follow *M'Naghten*, has decided that "wrong" includes moral wrong. The Model Penal Code proposed both alternatives, leaving to each state the determination whether to use "wrongfulness" or "criminality" in the insanity test.

Throughout the country, states have divided on the issue. Several states hold that a defendant is sane if he knows that his conduct is unlawful. The supporting rationale is that a standard based on morality would be too amorphous to be useful and that "[u]ntil a moral standard becomes law it is an unreliable test for sanity." Because murder contravenes all legal and moral standards, moreover, "[t]here is no practical distinction between moral and legal right or wrong in a murder case."

Other jurisdictions hold that "wrong" encompasses both legal and moral wrong. In these jurisdictions, defendants must prove that they were incapable of knowing that their acts were both morally and legally wrong. The only generally-recognized instance in which a "moral" wrong standard has provided an insanity defense is when the defendant has killed under the delusion that he or she was acting pursuant to a "command from God."

In [*People v.*] *Schmidt*, [216 N.Y. 324 (1915),] Judge Cardozo stated that juries generally should be allowed to consider whether a defendant who claimed that he acted on a command from God was capable of perceiving that his act was morally wrong. As Judge Cardozo explained:

A mother kills her infant child to whom she has been devotedly attached. She knows the nature and quality of her act; she knows that the law condemns it; but she is inspired by an insane delusion that God has appeared to her and ordained the sacrifice. It seems a mockery to say that, within the meaning of the statute, she knows that the act is wrong. * * * We find nothing either in the history of the [*M'Naghten*] rule, or in its reason or purpose, or in judicial exposition of its meaning, to justify a conclusion so abhorrent.

Finding that it was not error to leave "wrong" undefined, the court stated that "there are times and circumstances in which the word 'wrong,' as used in the statutory test of responsibility, ought not to be limited to legal wrong."

Long-standing New Jersey law also supports the premise that a defendant's ability to appreciate society's morals may be relevant to the determination of his sanity.

It may distort the analysis, however, to focus on whether the wrong was legal or moral. In the vast majority of cases, if the defendant was capable of understanding that he was acting contrary to law, he would also have sufficient capacity to understand that he was acting contrary to the morals of society. Law is largely the crystallization of societal morals. Rarely would an allegedly illegal act not also be wrongful morally. Thus, "wrong" as used in the insanity defense will generally incorporate notions of both legal and moral wrong.

The "right and wrong" test does not focus on the actual knowledge of the defendant, but rather on his ability to perceive the wrongfulness of his conduct. Under the test, a defendant is excused from criminal liability if at the time of the commission of the offense, he or she lacked the capacity to distinguish right from wrong. Only that defendant whose mind is impaired to the extent that he or she lacks the ability to comprehend that his or her conduct is wrong may successfully invoke the insanity defense.

Because the insanity inquiry focuses on the defendant's ability to comprehend whether his or her actions would ordinarily be disapproved by society, the concept of moral wrong must be judged by societal standards, not the personal standard of the individual defendant. As a general rule, it will not be sufficient, therefore, that a defendant's personal moral code justified a killing otherwise prohibited by law and societal morals.

The critical question here is whether the trial court should have expressly defined "wrong" to include moral wrong.

Defendant . . . contends that the trial court committed plain error by not telling the jury that "wrong" encompasses both legal and moral wrong. According to defendant, that omission misled the jury because Dr. Robert Sadoff, a psychiatric expert for the prosecution, testified that defendant was sane and therefore he knew the killings were unlawful. On direct examination, Dr. Sadoff testified:

A. My opinion, number one, is that Mr. Worlock did not have a defect of reason. He does not have a disease of the mind. He has personality disorders which are not mental illnesses or diseases of the mind.

   Secondly, that he did know the nature and quality of his act, and he did know what he was doing was wrong.

Q. What is the difference, Doctor, between feeling justified and knowing the difference between right and wrong?

A. The difference is that a person may believe that he is doing something right for him at a particular time, while at the same time he knows that it is wrong in that it is frowned upon and prohibited by society and that there is a law against such behavior. Despite that knowledge, he may still believe in his own mind that what he is doing is justified. The difference is, in terms of belief and knowledge, he knew but he believed that it was right for him.

Defendant asserts Dr. Sadoff's testimony is tantamount to the instruction of an "erroneous legal theory to the jury." The testimony is erroneous, according to defendant, because it misled the jury to believe that defendant was sane if he appreciated that the killings were against the law.

First, Dr. Sadoff's testimony does not include an "erroneous legal theory." "Wrongfulness" in the insanity defense takes account of both legal and moral wrong. Dr. Sadoff's testimony addresses both concepts. His statement that a defendant's act may be "frowned upon and prohibited by society," when contrasted with the immediately-following statement "and there is a law against such behavior," conveys both moral and legal considerations. Thus, we find no merit in defendant's claim that, in light of Dr. Sadoff's testimony, the trial court committed plain error in failing to define "wrong" for the jury.

Second, the record does not support defendant's claim that the trial court should have instructed the jury that "wrong" includes both legal and moral wrong. Such an instruction is necessary only if the distinction is critical to the facts on which a defendant bases the insanity defense. Here, defendant claims not that he killed Abrahamsen and Marchyshyn because the killings comported with societal morals, but because he was "infuriated" that they had stolen his wallet. He did not kill the victims because of his inability to distinguish "right" from "wrong." He killed them because he "hated" Abrahamsen and Marchyshyn "got in the way." Defendant openly admitted at trial that at the time he killed the victims, he knew his acts were illegal and that they were wrong under societal morals. On this record, we cannot fault the trial court for failing to define more specifically the word "wrong."

The most that can be said for defendant is that he believed the killings were justified under his personal code of morality. He viewed society with contempt, stating: "[t]o me, they're the folly-ridden mass, they're controlled by their popular beliefs." As defendant testified, "the law is not for me. The law is for subservient people." His moral code was based on "indulgence instead of abstinence" and "might makes right." Although defendant believed that under his own moral code he was justified in killing Abrahamsen and Marchyshyn, that belief does not nullify his appreciation that the killings were wrong according to law and the morals of society. Belief in an idiosyncratic code of morality does not constitute the defense of criminal insanity. If the insanity defense were so readily available, the life of each member of society would be imperilled by the whims of every other member.

The judgment of the Appellate Division is affirmed.

**Post-Case Follow-Up**

The *M'Naghten* test focuses on whether the defendant knew his conduct was wrong. As the opinion in *Worlock* explains, courts remain divided on the question of whether this means legal or moral wrong, or both. All courts agree, however, that the test is not satisfied simply because "a defendant's personal moral code justified a killing otherwise prohibited by law and societal morals." Instead, the defendant must be unable to perceive that his conduct was wrong as judged by law or social morals or both.

## Worlock: *Real Life Applications*

1. You are a member of your state's legislature, which is thinking of revising its insanity statute. Which test for insanity (*M'Naghten*, irresistible impulse, or the Model Penal Code test) would you favor adopting, and why?

2. The prosecution of John Hinckley for the attempted assassination of Ronald Reagan is one of the most well-known and impactful insanity defense cases in recent history. Hinckley was found not guilty by reason of insanity. The verdict led Congress to revise the federal definition of insanity in order to limit the number of cases where it might apply.

   The facts and history of Hinckley can be easily located online. See, e.g., *United States v. Hinckley*, 200 F. Supp. 3d 1 (D.D.C. 2016). First, look up the facts that formed the basis of Hinckley's not guilty by reason of insanity defense. Under which of the three tests for insanity that we have covered, if any, do you think Hinckley would have a successful insanity defense? Now, look up a description of the Insanity Defense Reform Act of 1984, which is the law that was passed following the Hinckley case. What changes did it make to the federal insanity defense?

---

**EXHIBIT 11.3** Ronald Reagan Waves Just Before Being Shot by John Hinckley

# E. INTOXICATION

If a person is drunk or high when she commits a crime, can she claim intoxication as a defense? Generally, the answer is no. Intoxication as such is never a defense to a crime. An intoxicant might lower a person's inhibitions, leading her to commit a crime that she never would have committed while sober. But this "neither exonerates nor excuses criminal conduct." *Commonwealth v. Bridge*, 495 Pa. 568, 572 (1981).

This simple and straightforward rule is complicated by the fact that, in a small slice of cases, a person might become so drunk or high that it affects her *mens rea*. For example, imagine a defendant who got drunk at a bar, took someone else's cell phone home with her, and is charged with larceny. If she knew that she was taking someone else's phone but decided to do it anyway because she was drunk and her inhibitions were lowered, intoxication will be no defense. If, however, the defendant was *so* drunk that she mistakenly thought the phone belonged to her, then she did not act with the *mens rea* necessary to commit larceny (an intent to permanently deprive someone else of property). In that limited sense, intoxication *can*, subject to some limitations, serve as a "defense." This is not a defense in the same sense as self-defense, insanity, or duress — the defendant's intoxication does not justify or excuse her otherwise criminal conduct. Instead, evidence of the defendant's intoxication is introduced to rebut the prosecutor's claim that the defendant acted with the mental state required to commit the crime.

The traditional rule, which is followed in most jurisdictions today, is that a defendant can introduce evidence of her **voluntary intoxication** to show that she did not form (or was incapable of forming) the requisite mental state *only* as a defense to a so-called specific intent crime. As discussed in Chapter 10 on pages 455-57, a crime is considered to be a specific intent crime if the defendant acted either with the intent to do some further act in addition to the prescribed conduct or with the intent to achieve some additional consequence or result beyond the prohibited act. Examples include larceny (an intent to permanently deprive the owner of property); common law burglary (an intent to commit a felony in a dwelling); and attempted crimes (an intent to commit the target crime). By contrast, a defendant charged with a so-called general intent crime is *not* permitted to introduce evidence of his intoxication to negate the *mens rea* required for the crime. Critics of this distinction argue, among other things, that it is an unnecessarily complicated rule that relies on an outdated understanding of mental states. Nevertheless, most jurisdictions continue to follow this rule.

Intoxication can serve as a defense in one more, very unusual, circumstance. In the case of **involuntary intoxication** — meaning where a person took an intoxicant by accident or had an unexpected reaction to a prescribed medicine — a defendant can raise temporary insanity as an affirmative defense. To do this, however, the defendant must show that, as a result of the involuntary intoxication, he was temporarily in a state of mind that would satisfy the jurisdiction's definition of insanity at the time of the offense. Not surprisingly, cases where a defendant is able to successfully claim temporary insanity as a result of involuntary intoxication are exceedingly uncommon.

In sum, three rules emerge with respect to intoxication. First, intoxication as such is *never* a defense, meaning that a defendant can never claim as a defense that he committed a crime because his inhibitions were lowered. Second, a defendant who was voluntarily or involuntarily intoxicated can introduce evidence of his intoxication in order to show that he did not act with the intent required for a specific intent crime. He is not, however, permitted to do the same if he is charged with a general intent crime. Third, a defendant who was involuntarily intoxicated can raise temporary insanity as a defense if, as a result of the intoxication, he was legally insane when he committed the crime.

**Case Preview**

## *State v. Jama*

The next case highlights the barriers facing defendants who seek to rely on intoxication as a defense. The defendant in this case was prosecuted for indecent exposure. He hoped to argue to the jury that he did not act with the required mental state because he was intoxicated, but the trial court excluded the defense on the grounds that indecent exposure is a general intent crime. In addition, the defendant sought to present an involuntary intoxication–based claim of temporary insanity. The trial court excluded this defense on the grounds that the defendant did not make a prima facie showing that he was legally insane at the time of the offense.

As you read the decision, consider the following questions:

1. Why does the court hold that indecent exposure is a general intent crime?
2. Why does the court hold that the proposed defense of temporary insanity due to involuntary intoxication was properly excluded?

## *State v. Jama*
### 908 N.W.2d 372 (Minn. Ct. App. 2018)

CLEARY, J.

On July 5, 2015, appellant approached a family gathering in the front yard of a residence in Minneapolis, exposed his penis, and danced provocatively. Multiple family members, including three children under the age of 16, witnessed appellant's exposure. During the incident, witnesses attempted to stop appellant from exposing himself, videotaped appellant's conduct, called 911, and eventually removed him from the area in front of their home. When the police arrived, they encountered appellant in the street in front of the residence and arrested him.

Appellant was charged with one count of indecent exposure in violation of Minn. Stat. § 617.23, subd. 2(1) (2014). Prior to the presentation of evidence, the defense made a series of motions stating its intent to rely on the statutory defense of voluntary intoxication and the common-law defense of involuntary intoxication.

The district court determined that because indecent exposure is a general-intent crime, appellant was not entitled to an instruction on the statutory defense of voluntary intoxication. But the court ruled that the common-law defense of involuntary intoxication would still be available to appellant, provided he could make a prima facie showing on each element of the defense.

At trial, witnesses testified that appellant exposed himself within five feet of their group during the incident. Video evidence of the incident was played for the jury. Multiple witnesses testified that appellant appeared to be intoxicated and nonresponsive. The arresting officer testified that appellant appeared to be "intoxicated and/or drugged." No tests were conducted to determine what, if any, substances appellant ingested prior to the incident.

Appellant testified that, prior to the incident, he smoked what he believed to be shisha—a flavored tobacco consumed through a hookah—with some men he met that day. He testified that after smoking the substance, he felt dizzy and disoriented. His reaction to the substance intensified and he vomited, blacked out, and woke up in the jail hours later—with no recollection of the incident. Appellant testified that he never experienced a similar reaction to shisha in the past and was not under the influence of any other drugs or alcohol that day. At the conclusion of his testimony, appellant rested and requested that the jury receive the involuntary-intoxication instruction. The district court denied appellant's request for this instruction, finding that appellant failed to make a prima facie showing on . . . the defense. Appellant was found guilty and convicted of gross misdemeanor indecent exposure in violation of Minn. Stat. § 617.23, subd. 2(1). This appeal follows.

Appellant argues that indecent exposure is a specific-intent crime, and therefore he was entitled to an instruction on the statutory defense of voluntary intoxication. We disagree.

Minnesota law provides:

> An act committed while in a state of voluntary intoxication is not less criminal by reason thereof, but when *a particular intent or other state of mind is a necessary element to constitute a particular crime*, the fact of intoxication may be taken into consideration in determining such intent or state of mind.

Minn. Stat. § 609.075 (2014) (emphasis added). "[T]he phrase 'particular intent' as used in Minn. Stat. § 609.075, unambiguously refers to specific-intent crimes, not general-intent crimes."

Under the Minnesota indecent-exposure statute, any person who commits any of the following acts "in the presence of a minor under the age of 16" is guilty of a gross misdemeanor:

> (1) willfully and lewdly exposes the person's body, or the private parts thereof; (2) procures another to expose private parts; or (3) engages in any open or gross lewdness or lascivious behavior, or any public indecency other than behavior specified in this subdivision.

Appellant argues that the inclusion of the word "willful" in the indecent exposure statute . . . make[s] indecent exposure a specific-intent crime. We disagree.

A specific-intent crime "requires an intent to cause a particular result." The indecent exposure statute prohibits "willful" acts of "open or gross lewdness." "Willful" generally means a "bad purpose or evil intent in statutes involving moral turpitude." Willful is the "one term referring to the actor's mental state" in the statute and "is not among the terms used to denote a specific intent." We conclude that indecent exposure is a general-intent crime because the statute simply prohibits willful conduct: voluntary . . . indecent or lewd exposures with no intent to cause a particular result.

Because indecent exposure is a general-intent crime, appellant was not entitled to the instruction and the district court did not err in refusing to instruct the jury on the statutory defense of voluntary intoxication.

Appellant [next] argues that the district court erred in refusing to instruct the jury [on the defense of involuntary intoxication]. We disagree.

The defense of involuntary intoxication has been accepted in Minnesota since the supreme court's decision in *City of Minneapolis v. Altimus*, 306 Minn. 462 (1976). *Altimus* set out four types of involuntary intoxication: (1) compelled intoxication; (2) pathological intoxication; (3) innocent intoxication; and (4) intoxication as the result of a medically prescribed drug. Appellant pursued a theory of innocent-involuntary intoxication. Innocent-involuntary intoxication occurs "when intoxication results from an innocent mistake by the defendant about the character of the substance taken, as when another person has tricked him into taking the liquor or drugs." The defendant bears the burden of making a "prima facie showing that he is entitled to a jury instruction on the defense of involuntary intoxication, included in which is the defense of mental illness." To be entitled to the instruction, appellant needed to establish that (1) he "was innocently mistaken as to the nature of the substance taken"; (2) the "intoxication was caused by the intoxicating substance in question and not by some other intoxicant"; and (3) he was temporarily mentally ill at the time of the offense. A prima facie showing is one that is "[s]ufficient to establish a fact or raise a presumption unless disproved or rebutted."

Appellant presented evidence in the form of his own testimony that he went to the home of two men he had never met before, smoked a substance in a hookah he believed to be shisha, and blacked out. Through the testimony of other witnesses, he established that he appeared to be intoxicated during the incident. The district court found that appellant failed to make a prima facie case for the defense. Upon review of the record, the district court did not abuse its discretion in determining that appellant failed to make the required showing.

[To establish that he was temporarily insane,] appellant was required to make a prima facie showing that "at the time of committing the alleged criminal act," he "was laboring under such a defect of reason, from [mental illness or cognitive impairment], as not to know the nature of [the] act, or that it was wrong." Appellant presented evidence that he blacked out, and was non-communicative and unsteady on his feet. The state presented evidence that police found appellant "leaning up against a vehicle with his stomach, as if he was hiding something" with his zipper "halfway down." The district court found that, because appellant "hid his privates" when the uniformed police officer approached and "put himself back together and put his genitals back in his pants," he knew his behavior to be criminal and therefore there was no mental defect.

The supreme court has endorsed "a district court's rejection of a mental-illness defense based in part on a defendant's behavior before and after crimes, such as planning and concealment, flight from authorities, disposal of evidence, and expressing awareness of consequences." In *Roberts*, the supreme court affirmed a district court's rejection of a mental-illness defense based in part on evidence that the defendant "refused to identify himself and resisted arrest" and "indicated an awareness of the consequences of his behavior." Here, the evidence indicated that appellant was aware of the potential consequences of his behavior and attempted to conceal evidence of his crime when the police arrived. Even when viewed in the light most favorable to appellant, this evidence demonstrates that he knew his actions were wrong and attempted to conceal his wrongdoing when confronted by police. The district court did not abuse its discretion in concluding appellant failed to make a prima facie case that he was temporarily mentally ill at the time of the act.

Appellant failed to make a prima facie showing on the elements of the involuntary intoxication defense and thus the district court did not err in refusing to instruct the jury on that defense.

Affirmed.

**Post-Case Follow-Up**

Minnesota follows most jurisdictions by providing that "the fact of intoxication may be taken into consideration" by the jury in determining the defendant's intent, but *only* for specific intent crimes. Because the court found that indecent exposure is a general intent crime under Minnesota law, the defendant was not permitted to argue to the jury that he did not act with the required mental state as a result of his intoxication. Minnesota also follows the majority of jurisdictions by permitting an involuntarily intoxicated defendant to claim temporary insanity. To do this, however, the defendant must meet the jurisdiction's test for insanity, which is typically very difficult to do. In this case, the court held that the defendant had not made out a prima facie case that he was legally insane under Minnesota's definition of insanity (which tracks the *M'Naghten* test).

## Jama: *Real Life Applications*

1. Minnesota's indecent exposure statute divides the crime into three degrees: misdemeanor, gross misdemeanor, and felony. The difference between misdemeanor indecent exposure and gross misdemeanor indecent exposure (the degree that Jama was convicted of) is the presence of a minor under the age of 16.

   Imagine that you were the prosecutor in Jama's case. Before trial, Jama's attorney contacts you with a proposed plea deal. Under the proposal, Jama would plead guilty to the reduced charge of misdemeanor indecent exposure. Would you be inclined to agree to this deal? Or would you go to trial in order to try to win a conviction on the more serious charge of gross misdemeanor indecent exposure? To what extent, if any, would Jama's intoxication factor into your decision?

# F. ENTRAPMENT

To what degree should the criminal law allow government agents to induce people to commit crimes? This question is at the heart of the entrapment defense. Under the approach adopted by a majority of jurisdictions, the **entrapment** defense "has two related elements: government inducement of the crime, and a lack of predisposition on the part of the defendant to engage in the criminal conduct." *Matthews v. United States*, 485 U.S. 58, 63 (1988). To succeed in the defense, the defendant must show that a government agent induced him to carry out a crime that he was not predisposed to commit. The defendant's predisposition (or lack of it) is "the principal element in the defense of entrapment." *Id.*

**Case Preview**

## United States v. Russell

The entrapment defense arises in the context of undercover policing. The defense applies where an undercover police officer induces a defendant to commit a crime that the defendant was not predisposed to commit. In the next case, *Russell*, the Supreme Court discussed the predisposition test for entrapment. The decision describes the requirements of the entrapment defense along with the rationale for the defense.

As you read the decision, consider the following questions:

1. What test for entrapment does the Court adopt?
2. What kind of evidence might show that a person is predisposed to commit a crime?
3. What is the point of disagreement between the majority and the dissenting Justices?

## United States v. Russell
### 411 U.S. 423 (1973)

Mr. Justice REHNQUIST delivered the opinion of the Court.

Respondent Richard Russell was charged in three counts of a five-count indictment returned against him and codefendants John and Patrick Connolly. After a jury trial in the District Court, in which his sole defense was entrapment, respondent was convicted on all three counts of having unlawfully manufactured and processed methamphetamine ("speed") and of having unlawfully sold and delivered that drug. He was sentenced to concurrent terms of two years in prison for each offense, the terms to be suspended on the condition that he spend six months in prison and be placed on probation for the following three years. On appeal, the United States Court of Appeals for the Ninth Circuit, one judge dissenting, reversed the conviction solely for the reason that an undercover agent supplied an essential chemical for manufacturing the methamphetamine which formed the basis of respondent's conviction. We granted certiorari and now reverse that judgment.

There is little dispute concerning the essential facts in this case. On December 7, 1969, Joe Shapiro, an undercover agent for the Federal Bureau of Narcotics and Dangerous Drugs, went to respondent's home on Whidbey Island in the State of Washington where he met with respondent and his two codefendants, John and Patrick Connolly. Shapiro's assignment was to locate a laboratory where it was believed that methamphetamine was being manufactured illicitly. He told the respondent and the Connollys that he represented an organization in the Pacific Northwest that was interested in controlling the manufacture and distribution of methamphetamine. He then made an offer to supply the defendants with the chemical phenyl-2-propanone, an essential ingredient in the manufacture of methamphetamine, in return for one-half of the drug produced. This offer was made on the condition that Agent Shapiro be shown a sample of the drug which they were making and the laboratory where it was being produced.

During the conversation, Patrick Connolly revealed that he had been making the drug since May 1969 and since then had produced three pounds of it. John Connolly gave the agent a bag containing a quantity of methamphetamine that he represented as being from "the last batch that we made." Shortly thereafter, Shapiro and Patrick Connolly left respondent's house to view the laboratory which was located in the Connolly house on Whidbey Island. At the house, Shapiro observed an empty bottle bearing the chemical label phenyl-2-propanone.

By prearrangement, Shapiro returned to the Connolly house on December 9, 1969, to supply 100 grams of propanone and observe the manufacturing process. When he arrived he observed Patrick Connolly and the respondent cutting up pieces of aluminum foil and placing them in a large flask. There was testimony that some of the foil pieces accidentally fell on the floor and were picked up by the respondent and Shapiro and put into the flask.[3] Thereafter, Patrick Connolly added all of the necessary chemicals, including the propanone brought by Shapiro, to make two batches of methamphetamine. The manufacturing process having been completed the following morning, Shapiro was given one-half of the drug and respondent kept the remainder. Shapiro offered to buy, and the respondent agreed to sell, part of the remainder for $60.

About a month later, Shapiro returned to the Connolly house and met with Patrick Connolly to ask if he was still interested in their "business arrangement." Connolly replied that he was interested but that he had recently obtained two additional

---

[3] Agent Shapiro did not otherwise participate in the manufacture of the drug or direct any of the work.

bottles of phenyl-2-propanone and would not be finished with them for a couple of days. He provided some additional methamphetamine to Shapiro at that time. Three days later Shapiro returned to the Connolly house with a search warrant and, among other items, seized an empty 500-gram bottle of propanone and a 100-gram bottle, not the one he had provided, that was partially filled with the chemical.

There was testimony at the trial of respondent and Patrick Connolly that phenyl-2-propanone was generally difficult to obtain. At the request of the Bureau of Narcotics and Dangerous Drugs, some chemical supply firms had voluntarily ceased selling the chemical.

At the close of the evidence, and after receiving the District Judge's standard entrapment instruction,[4] the jury found the respondent guilty on all counts charged. On appeal, the respondent conceded that the jury could have found him predisposed to commit the offenses but argued that on the facts presented there was entrapment as a matter of law. The Court of Appeals agreed, although it did not find the District Court had misconstrued or misapplied the traditional standards governing the entrapment defense. Rather, the court in effect expanded the traditional notion of entrapment, which focuses on the predisposition of the defendant, to mandate dismissal of a criminal prosecution whenever the court determines that there has been "an intolerable degree of governmental participation in the criminal enterprise." In this case the court decided that the conduct of the agent in supplying a scarce ingredient essential for the manufacture of a controlled substance established that defense.

This new defense was held to rest on either of two alternative theories. One theory is based on two lower court decisions which have found entrapment, regardless of predisposition, whenever the government supplies contraband to the defendants. The second theory, a nonentrapment rationale, is based on a recent Ninth Circuit decision that reversed a conviction because a government investigator was so enmeshed in the criminal activity that the prosecution of the defendants was held to be repugnant to the American criminal justice system. The court below held that these two rationales constitute the same defense, and that only the label distinguishes them. In any event, it held that "both theories are premised on fundamental concepts of due process and evince the reluctance of the judiciary to countenance 'overzealous law enforcement.'"

This Court first recognized and applied the entrapment defense in *Sorrells v. United States*, 287 U.S. 435 (1932). In *Sorrells*, a federal prohibition agent visited the defendant while posing as a tourist and engaged him in conversation about their common war experiences. After gaining the defendant's confidence, the agent asked for some liquor, was twice refused, but upon asking a third time the defendant finally capitulated, and was subsequently prosecuted for violating the National Prohibition Act.

---

[4] The District Judge stated the governing law on entrapment as follows: "Where a person already has the willingness and the readiness to break the law, the mere fact that the government agent provides what appears to be a favorable opportunity is not entrapment." He then instructed the jury to acquit respondent if it had a "reasonable doubt whether the defendant had the previous intent or purpose to commit the offense . . . and did so only because he was induced or persuaded by some officer or agent of the government." No exception was taken by respondent to this instruction.

Mr. Chief Justice Hughes, speaking for the Court, held that as a matter of statutory construction the defense of entrapment should have been available to the defendant. Under the theory propounded by the Chief Justice, the entrapment defense prohibits law enforcement officers from instigating a criminal act by persons "otherwise innocent in order to lure them to its commission and to punish them." Thus, the thrust of the entrapment defense was held to focus on the intent or predisposition of the defendant to commit the crime. "If the defendant seeks acquittal by reason of entrapment he cannot complain of an appropriate and searching inquiry into his own conduct and predisposition as bearing upon that issue."

Mr. Justice Roberts concurred but was of the view "that courts must be closed to the trial of a crime instigated by the government's own agents." The difference in the view of the majority and the concurring opinions is that in the former the inquiry focuses on the predisposition of the defendant, whereas in the latter the inquiry focuses on whether the government "instigated the crime."

In 1958[, in *Sherman v. United States*,] the Court again considered the theory underlying the entrapment defense and expressly reaffirmed the view expressed by the *Sorrells* majority. In *Sherman* the defendant was convicted of selling narcotics to a Government informer. As in *Sorrells*, it appears that the Government agent gained the confidence of the defendant and, despite initial reluctance, the defendant finally acceded to the repeated importunings of the agent to commit the criminal act. On the basis of *Sorrells*, this Court reversed the affirmance of the defendant's conviction.

In affirming the theory underlying *Sorrells*, Mr. Chief Justice Warren for the Court, held that "to determine whether entrapment has been established, a line must be drawn between the trap for the unwary innocent and the trap for the unwary criminal."

In the instant case, respondent asks us to reconsider the theory of the entrapment defense as it is set forth in the majority opinions in *Sorrells* and *Sherman*. His principal contention is that the defense should rest on constitutional grounds. He argues that the level of Shapiro's involvement in the manufacture of the methamphetamine was so high that a criminal prosecution for the drug's manufacture violates the fundamental principles of due process.

While we may some day be presented with a situation in which the conduct of law enforcement agents is so outrageous that due process principles would absolutely bar the government from invoking judicial processes to obtain a conviction, the instant case is distinctly not of that breed. Shapiro's contribution of propanone to the criminal enterprise already in process was scarcely objectionable. The chemical is by itself a harmless substance and its possession is legal. While the Government may have been seeking to make it more difficult for drug rings, such as that of which respondent was a member, to obtain the chemical, the evidence described above shows that it nonetheless was obtainable. The law enforcement conduct here stops far short of violating that "fundamental fairness, shocking to the universal sense of justice," mandated by the Due Process Clause of the Fifth Amendment.

The illicit manufacture of drugs is not a sporadic, isolated criminal incident, but a continuing, though illegal, business enterprise. In order to obtain convictions for illegally manufacturing drugs, the gathering of evidence of past unlawful conduct frequently proves to be an all but impossible task. Thus in drug-related offenses law enforcement personnel have turned to one of the only practicable means of detection: the infiltration of drug rings and a limited participation in their unlawful present practices. Such infiltration is a recognized and permissible means of investigation; if that be so, then the supply of some item of value that the drug ring requires must, as a general rule, also be permissible. For an agent will not be taken into the confidence of the illegal entrepreneurs unless he has something of value to offer them. Law enforcement tactics such as this can hardly be said to violate "fundamental fairness" or "shocking to the universal sense of justice[.]"

Respondent also urges, as an alternative to his constitutional argument, that we broaden the nonconstitutional defense of entrapment in order to sustain the judgment of the Court of Appeals. This Court's opinions in *Sorrells v. United States* and *Sherman v. United States* held that the principal element in the defense of entrapment was the defendant's predisposition to commit the crime. Respondent conceded in the Court of Appeals, as well he might, "that he may have harbored a predisposition to commit the charged offenses." Yet he argues that the jury's refusal to find entrapment under the charge submitted to it by the trial court should be overturned and the view[] of Justice[] Roberts in *Sorrells*, which [would] make the essential element of the defense turn on the type and degree of governmental conduct, be adopted as the law.

We decline to overrule these cases. *Sorrells* is a precedent of long standing that has already been once reexamined in *Sherman* and implicitly there reaffirmed. Since the defense is not of a constitutional dimension, Congress may address itself to the question and adopt any substantive definition of the defense that it may find desirable.

Critics of the rule laid down in *Sorrells* and *Sherman* have . . . pointed to what they conceive to be the anomalous difference between the treatment of a defendant who is solicited by a private individual and one who is entrapped by a government agent. Questions have been likewise raised as to whether "predisposition" can be factually established with the requisite degree of certainty. Arguments such as these, while not devoid of appeal, have been twice previously made to this Court, and twice rejected by it, first in *Sorrells* and then in *Sherman*.

We believe that at least equally cogent criticism has been made of the concurring views in these cases. Commenting in *Sherman* on Mr. Justice Roberts' position in *Sorrells* that "although the defendant could claim that the Government had induced him to commit the crime, the Government could not reply by showing that the defendant's criminal conduct was due to his own readiness and not to the persuasion of government agents," Mr. Chief Justice Warren quoted the observation of Judge Learned Hand in an earlier stage of that proceeding: "'Indeed, it would seem probable that, if there were no reply [to the claim of inducement], it would be impossible ever to secure convictions of any offences which consist of transactions that are carried on in secret.'"

Nor does it seem particularly desirable for the law to grant complete immunity from prosecution to one who himself planned to commit a crime, and then committed it, simply because government undercover agents subjected him to inducements which might have seduced a hypothetical individual who was not so predisposed. We are content to leave the matter where it was left by the Court in *Sherman*:

"The function of law enforcement is the prevention of crime and the apprehension of criminals. Manifestly, that function does not include the manufacturing of crime. Criminal activity is such that stealth and strategy are necessary weapons in the arsenal of the police officer. However, 'A different question is presented when the criminal design originates with the officials of the Government, and they implant in the mind of an innocent person the disposition to commit the alleged offense and induce its commission in order that they may prosecute.'"

Those cases establish that entrapment is a relatively limited defense. It is rooted, not in any authority of the Judicial Branch to dismiss prosecutions for what it feels to have been "overzealous law enforcement," but instead in the notion that Congress could not have intended criminal punishment for a defendant who has committed all the elements of a proscribed offense, but was induced to commit them by the Government.

*Sorrells* and *Sherman* both recognize "that the fact that officers or employees of the Government merely afford opportunities or facilities for the commission of the offense does not defeat the prosecution." Nor will the mere fact of deceit defeat a prosecution, for there are circumstances when the use of deceit is the only practicable law enforcement technique available. It is only when the Government's deception actually implants the criminal design in the mind of the defendant that the defense of entrapment comes into play.

Respondent's concession in the Court of Appeals that the jury finding as to predisposition was supported by the evidence is, therefore, fatal to his claim of entrapment. He was an active participant in an illegal drug manufacturing enterprise which began before the Government agent appeared on the scene, and continued after the Government agent had left the scene. He was, in the words of *Sherman*, not an "unwary innocent" but an "unwary criminal." The Court of Appeals was wrong, we believe, when it sought to broaden the principle laid down in *Sorrells* and *Sherman*. Its judgment is therefore

*Reversed.*

---

## Outrageous Government Conduct and Stash House Stings

In *United States v. Russell*, the majority opinion stated that "we may some day be presented with a situation in which the conduct of law enforcement agents is so outrageous that due process principles would absolutely bar the government from invoking judicial processes to obtain a conviction" but concluded Richard Russell's case was "distinctly not of that breed." 411 U.S. 423, 431-32 (1973). Based

---

Mr. Justice DOUGLAS, with whom Mr. Justice BRENNAN concurs, dissenting.

A federal agent supplied the accused with one chemical ingredient of the drug known as methamphetamine ("speed") which the accused manufactured and for which act he was sentenced to prison. His defense was entrapment, which the Court of Appeals sustained and which the Court today disallows. Since I have an opposed view of entrapment, I dissent.

In my view, the fact that the chemical ingredient supplied by the federal agent might have been obtained from other sources is quite irrelevant. Supplying the chemical ingredient used in the manufacture of this batch of "speed" made the United States an active participant in the unlawful activity. As stated by Mr. Justice Brandeis, dissenting in *Casey v. United States*:

"I am aware that courts—mistaking relative social values and forgetting that a desirable end cannot justify foul means—have, in their zeal to punish, sanctioned the use of evidence obtained through criminal violation of property and personal rights or by other practices of detectives even more revolting. But the objection here is of a different nature. It does not rest merely upon the character of the evidence or upon the fact that the evidence was illegally obtained. The obstacle to the prosecution lies in the fact that the alleged crime was instigated by officers of the Government; that the act for which the Government seeks to punish the defendant is the fruit of their criminal conspiracy to induce its commission. The Government may set decoys to entrap criminals. But it may not provoke or create a crime and then punish the criminal, its creature."

Federal agents play a debased role when they become the instigators of the crime, or partners in its commission, or the creative brain behind the illegal scheme. That is what the federal agent did here when he furnished the accused with one of the chemical ingredients needed to manufacture the unlawful drug.

Mr. Justice STEWART, with whom Mr. Justice BRENNAN and Mr. Justice MARSHALL join, dissenting.

In *Sorrells v. United States* and *Sherman v. United States* the Court took what might be called a "subjective" approach to the defense of entrapment. In that view, the defense is predicated on an unexpressed intent of Congress to exclude from its criminal statutes the prosecution and conviction of persons, "otherwise innocent," who have been lured to the commission of the prohibited act through the Government's instigation. The key phrase in this formulation is "otherwise innocent," for the entrapment defense is available under this approach only to those who would not have committed the crime but for the Government's inducements. Thus, the subjective approach focuses on the conduct and propensities of the particular defendant in each individual case: if he is "otherwise innocent," he may avail himself of the defense; but if he had the "predisposition" to commit the crime, or if the "criminal design" originated with him, then—regardless of the nature and extent of the Government's participation—there has been no entrapment. And, in the absence of a conclusive showing one way or the other, the question of the defendant's "predisposition" to the crime is a question of fact for the jury. The Court today adheres to this approach.

on this language, some courts have recognized a defense for outrageous government conduct, distinct from the entrapment defense.

Unlike traditional affirmative defenses, which are considered by the jury at trial, the outrageous government conduct defense bars the prosecution altogether. Motions to dismiss based on the outrageous government conduct defense are very rarely successful, however. This is because "[t]he standard of police action that would warrant the judge dismissing the case is extremely high." Katherine Tinto, *Fighting the Stash House Sting*, Champion 16, 17 (October 2014). Indeed, "[t]he Supreme Court has never affirmed the dismissal of an indictment based on a finding of outrageous government conduct, nor has the Court articulated a set of guidelines for lower courts to use in determining what government conduct would be sufficiently 'outrageous' to successfully invoke the defense." Marc D. Esterow, *Lead Us Not into Temptation: Stash House Stings and the Outrageous Government Conduct Defense*, 8 Drexel L. Rev. Online 1, 6 (2016).

The outrageous government conduct defense has become increasingly relevant as a result of so-called stash house sting cases. In a stash house sting, an undercover agent creates a fictional drug stash house and then tries to recruit people to help rob it. The tactic has become a favorite of the Bureau of Alcohol, Tobacco, Firearms, and Explosives (ATF). "Since 2003, the ATF has more than quadrupled the use of these controversial sting operations as part of a crime-fighting strategy meant to target armed and violent criminals. Over 1,000 individuals have been prosecuted as a result of stash house stings, and operations have taken place in major metropolitan cities all across the United States." Esterow, *supra*, at 5.

In the typical stash house sting, "an undercover officer, or informant working at the police's direction, recruits one or more suspects to rob a location where drug dealers allegedly keep large amounts of drugs, money, or weapons. The undercover officer or informant frequently poses as a disgruntled drug dealer, with both inside knowledge of the stash house and the desire to 'rip off' former employers, competitors, or customers. After meeting with the suspects on one or more occasions, and after the suspects agree to commit the robbery, the suspects are arrested, often at an arranged meeting place or in a vehicle, supposedly on their way to commit the agreed upon crimes. Defendants caught in these operations are charged with a range of crimes, including conspiracy and firearms and narcotics offenses." Tinto, *supra*, at 16. Because the stash house is fictional, "the government has 'virtually unfettered ability' to guarantee a lengthy sentence" by telling targets that an amount of drugs that triggers a mandatory minimum sentence is inside the stash house. *Id.*

Do you think that courts should prohibit prosecutions in these cases based on the outrageous government conduct defense?

The concurring opinion of Mr. Justice Roberts in the *Sorrells* case, and that of Mr. Justice Frankfurter in the *Sherman* case, took a different view of the entrapment defense. In their concept, the defense is not grounded on some unexpressed intent of Congress to exclude from punishment under its statutes those otherwise innocent persons tempted into crime by the Government, but rather on the belief that "the methods employed on behalf of the Government to bring about conviction cannot be countenanced." Thus, the focus of this approach is not on the propensities and predisposition of a specific defendant, but on "whether the police conduct revealed in the particular case falls below standards, to which common feelings respond, for the proper use of governmental power." Phrased another way, the question is whether — regardless of the predisposition to crime of the particular defendant involved — the governmental agents have acted in such a way as is likely to instigate or create a criminal offense. Under this approach, the determination of the lawfulness of the Government's conduct must be made — as it is on all questions involving the legality of law enforcement methods — by the trial judge, not the jury.

In my view, this objective approach to entrapment advanced by the Roberts opinion in *Sorrells* and the Frankfurter opinion in *Sherman* is the only one truly consistent with the underlying rationale of the defense. Indeed, the very basis of the entrapment defense itself demands adherence to an approach that focuses on the conduct of the governmental agents, rather than on whether the defendant was "predisposed" or "otherwise innocent." I find it impossible to believe that the purpose of the defense is to effectuate some unexpressed congressional intent to exclude from its criminal statutes persons who committed a prohibited act, but would not have done so except for the Government's inducements. For, as Mr. Justice Frankfurter put it, "the only legislative intention that can with any show of reason be extracted from the statute is the intention to make criminal precisely the conduct in which the defendant has engaged." Since, by definition, the entrapment defense cannot arise unless the defendant actually committed the proscribed act, that defendant is manifestly covered by the terms of the criminal statute involved.

Furthermore, to say that such a defendant is "otherwise innocent" or not "predisposed" to commit the crime is misleading, at best. The very fact that he has committed an act that Congress has determined to be illegal demonstrates conclusively that he is not innocent of the offense. He may not have originated the precise plan or the precise details, but he was "predisposed" in the sense that he has proved to be quite capable of committing the crime. That he was induced, provoked, or tempted to do so by government agents does not make him any more innocent or any less predisposed than he would be if he had been induced, provoked, or tempted by a private person — which, of course, would not entitle him to cry "entrapment." Since the only difference between these situations is the identity of the tempter, it follows that the significant focus must be on the conduct of the government agents, and not on the predisposition of the defendant.

The purpose of the entrapment defense, then, cannot be to protect persons who are "otherwise innocent." Rather, it must be to prohibit unlawful governmental activity in instigating crime. As Mr. Justice Brandeis stated in *Casey v. United States*: "This prosecution should be stopped, not because some right of Casey's has been denied, but in order to protect the Government. To protect it from illegal conduct of its officers. To preserve the purity of its courts." If that is so, then whether the particular defendant was "predisposed" or "otherwise innocent" is irrelevant; and the important question becomes whether the Government's conduct in inducing the crime was beyond judicial toleration.

This does not mean, of course, that the Government's use of undercover activity, strategy, or deception is necessarily unlawful. Indeed, many crimes, especially so-called victimless crimes, could not otherwise be detected. Thus, government agents may engage in conduct that is likely, when objectively considered, to afford a person ready and willing to commit the crime an opportunity to do so.

But when the agents' involvement in criminal activities goes beyond the mere offering of such an opportunity, and when their conduct is of a kind that could induce or instigate the commission of a crime by one not ready and willing to commit it, then — regardless of the character or propensities of the particular person induced — I think entrapment has occurred. For in that situation, the Government has engaged in the impermissible manufacturing of crime, and the federal courts should bar the prosecution in order to preserve the institutional integrity of the system of federal criminal justice.

What the agent did here was to meet with a group of suspected producers of methamphetamine, including the respondent; to request the drug; to offer to supply the chemical phenyl-2-propanone in exchange for one-half of the methamphetamine to be manufactured therewith; and, when that offer was accepted, to provide the needed chemical ingredient, and to purchase some of the drug from the respondent.

In this case, the chemical ingredient was available only to licensed persons, and the Government itself had requested suppliers not to sell that ingredient even to people with a license. Yet the Government agent readily offered, and supplied, that ingredient to an unlicensed person and asked him to make a certain illegal drug with it. The Government then prosecuted that person for making the drug produced *with the very ingredient* which its agent had so helpfully supplied. This strikes me as the very pattern of conduct that should be held to constitute entrapment as a matter of law.

It is the Government's duty to prevent crime, not to promote it. Under the objective approach that I would follow, this respondent was entrapped, regardless of his predisposition or "innocence."

In the words of Mr. Justice Roberts:

"The applicable principle is that courts must be closed to the trial of a crime instigated by the government's own agents. No other issue, no comparison of equities as between the guilty official and the guilty defendant, has any place in the enforcement of this overruling principle of public policy."

I would affirm the judgment of the Court of Appeals.

**Post-Case Follow-Up**

Justice Rehnquist's opinion in *Russell* explains the rationale for the "subjective" test for entrapment. The subjective test considers the defendant's state of mind to determine whether he was "predisposed" to commit the offense. The federal courts and a majority of states continue to apply this test today. Under this test, a defendant who is induced by government agents to commit a crime is not entitled to the entrapment defense if he was predisposed to commit the offense prior to being induced by the government agents.

## Russell: *Real Life Applications*

1. Consider the facts summarized by the court in *State v. J.D.W.*, 910 P.2d 1242 (Utah Ct. App. 1995):

> J.D.W. and a friend went to the Layton Hills Mall to buy a musical compact disc. While there, they were approached by officer Dave Wakefield of the Davis Metro Narcotics Strike Force. Wakefield asked if they were interested in a smoke. J.D.W.'s friend asked "smoke what?" and Wakefield made a gesture simulating smoking marijuana. Wakefield told them that he had some marijuana and hashish and that if they were interested they could go outside and look at it. J.D.W. and his friend thereupon followed Wakefield outside. Once outside, J.D.W.'s friend stopped while J.D.W. and Wakefield continued on a short distance further. Wakefield presented J.D.W. a baggy containing marijuana. J.D.W. took the baggy, "separated the buds from the shake" and smelled the contents. Wakefield also offered J.D.W. the hashish, but J.D.W. refused it. J.D.W. asked how much the marijuana cost. Wakefield told him that it was $35. J.D.W. only had a $100 bill and offered to go get change. Wakefield told J.D.W. that he could make change, whereupon J.D.W. paid Wakefield, who then gave J.D.W. the marijuana and the change. Wakefield then arrested J.D.W. for possession of a controlled substance.

   **a.** You are assigned to represent J.D.W. Do you think he has a viable entrapment defense? Why or why not?

   **b.** Imagine you are the District Attorney in the county where this occurred. The Chief of Police has let you know of plans to conduct additional similar undercover operations. Would you support these efforts? If not, would you decline to prosecute suspects who were arrested in these stings?

# G. IGNORANCE OF THE LAW IS NO EXCUSE AND THE PUBLIC AUTHORITY DEFENSE

In general, a person who commits a crime while under the mistaken belief that her conduct is not against the law can still be convicted. In other words, her ignorance of the criminal law is no excuse. This rule and the exception to it provided by the public authority defense are the subject of this section.

## 1. Ignorance of the Law Is No Excuse (Mistake of Law)

In 2014, the police arrested Guy Lanchester in Key West, Florida for possession of cocaine. In response to the arrest, Lanchester said to the police, "I don't understand . . . I thought cocaine wasn't illegal in Florida." Ben Candea, *Key West Man Tells Cops He Didn't Think Cocaine Was Illegal in Florida*, ABCNews.com, Feb. 28, 2014.

Assume that Lanchester's belief was genuine. Is his **mistake of law** a defense? The answer, not surprisingly, is no. This principle is captured by the maxim, which dates to Roman law, that **ignorance of the law is no excuse**. The rationale for this rule is that to uphold the rule of law, it must be uniformly applied. The rule also reflects the fact that criminal statutes do not ordinarily make the defendant's knowledge of the law an element of the offense. In most cases, the rule is intuitive. It is easy enough to see why the law will not permit a defendant like Lanchester to escape punishment on the grounds that he thought it was legal to possess cocaine in Florida.

The complexity of modern criminal law can make the rule that ignorance of the law is no defense more controversial in some cases, however. Consider the following hypothetical case. Dave goes to a store in Denver, Colorado to buy some marijuana for recreational use. There is a sale going on, so Dave decides to buy the maximum amount that the store will sell him — one ounce. In addition to the one ounce of marijuana that Dave buys at the store, he already has a quarter of an ounce of marijuana in his car. The police pull Dave over, search his car, and arrest him for possession of more than one ounce of marijuana. Even though marijuana is legal to possess under Colorado state law, the law limits possession to one ounce or less; possession of more than one ounce is still a crime. If Dave was ignorant of this detail of Colorado's marijuana legalization law, will he have a defense to a prosecution for possession of marijuana? No. Once again, ignorance of the law — here, Dave's mistaken understanding of Colorado's marijuana laws — is no excuse.

Now, imagine that Dave is operating a marijuana business in Colorado. Dave hires a lawyer to advise him on complying with state and federal law. Dave's lawyer advises him that as long as he scrupulously follows state law, he cannot be prosecuted under federal law. Dave's lawyer is wrong. In fact, Dave's compliance with state law is not a defense to a prosecution under the federal Controlled Substances Act. If Dave is arrested and prosecuted under federal law, will he have a defense based on his attorney's advice? Again, the answer is no. The principle that ignorance of the law is no excuse applies even if a defendant is acting pursuant to an attorney's misadvice.

As these examples show, the rule that ignorance of the law is no excuse means that a person's misunderstanding about the legality of her actions is generally not a defense in a criminal case. This is true even if the defendant's mistake seems to be a reasonable one, or if the defendant has tried to comply with the law by consulting with an attorney.

While a person's mistaken belief that the law does not criminalize her actions is no defense, a person's misunderstanding about the legal status of a fact that affects her *mens rea* can be a defense under mistake of fact principles covered elsewhere in this book, including in Chapter 10. To appreciate this distinction, consider the facts of *State v. Varszegi*, 635 A.2d 816 (Conn. App. Ct. 1993). In *Varszegi*, the defendant was the landlord of a commercial property. The lease contained a clause that authorized the landlord to enter and seize the tenant's personal property if the tenant defaulted on the lease. The tenant defaulted and the landlord entered the premises and seized some of the tenant's property, based on his belief that the property now legally belonged to him. As it turned out, the default section of the lease was invalid under state property law principles. As a result, the landlord did not truly have a legal right to the property. He was charged with larceny. Can the defendant in a case like this argue in his defense that he is not guilty because he thought the property belonged to him? Yes. To understand why, recall that larceny requires proof that the defendant intended to permanently deprive another person of her property. As a result, "[a] defendant who acts under the subjective belief that he or she has a lawful claim on property lacks the required felonious intent to steal." *Id.* at 818. This is true whether the defendant thought he had a lawful claim to the property because he mistook it for his own or because, as in *Varszegi*, he honestly misunderstood the legal impact of a lease provision of a contract.

The principle that ignorance of the law is no excuse does not change the outcome in a case like *Varszegi*. The reason is simple. The defendant in *Varszegi* did not claim to be mistaken about the criminal law. He did not claim, for example, that he thought theft was legal or that he thought the crime of larceny included an exception for landlords whose tenants owed them rent. If he had, the principle that ignorance of the law is no excuse would have applied. Instead, the defendant genuinely thought that the personal property belonged to him. He was mistaken about whether or not he owned the property (a question of property law that affects his *mens rea*), *not* about what conduct the criminal law permits or forbids. In other words, *Varszegi* was a case involving a mistake of fact, which "is a defense when it negates a required mental element of the crime," not a mistake of criminal law. *Commw. v. Liebenow*, 470 Mass. 151, 160 (2014). And, because larceny requires an intent to permanently deprive someone else of her property, the "defendant's honest belief that the property that he took" belonged to him was a defense — just as in *Liebenow*, presented in Chapter 3 and discussed again in Chapter 10. *Id.* at 161.

## 2. Public Authority Defense

The **public authority** defense (also sometimes called the entrapment by estoppel defense) provides a limited exception to the rule that ignorance of the law is no excuse. Specifically, a defendant who reasonably believes her conduct to be lawful based on the advice of a public official is entitled to this defense.

The public authority defense applies in two circumstances. The first is where a public official in charge of enforcing a law has made an official statement regarding that law. This can occur in the context of regulated industries. In some regulated industries, it is not uncommon for industry participants to seek guidance from a public official about whether a proposed business practice is legal. In response to these sorts of inquiries, an agency will sometimes release an official statement on the meaning of a particular provision of the law. Imagine, for example, that the Securities and Exchange Commission (SEC) issues a formal statement providing guidance about whether the SEC believes that a particular stock trading practice is legal under the Securities and Exchange Act. The guidance provides that, in the opinion of the SEC, the stock trading practice is legal. In reliance on this guidance, Dan engages in the stock trading practice. If Dan were to be prosecuted for having engaged in the stock trading practice, he could raise his reliance on the SEC's guidance as a defense under the public authority doctrine. In contrast to the case of a person who relies on the advice of a private attorney, the public authority defense recognizes that people are entitled to rely on official guidance about the meaning of a law from the person or entity that is responsible for enforcing that law.

The second circumstance where the public authority defense can arise is in the context of the police use of informants. Police officers sometimes enlist private individuals to work for them as informants. If an officer tells one of her informants that she can commit a crime in order to help gather information, this can give rise to a public authority defense in the event of a later prosecution. Of course, an informant who commits a crime pursuant to an officer's clear directions is very unlikely to be prosecuted for the act. As a result, public authority defense cases tend to involve either ambiguity in the officer's instructions, a dispute about the instructions, or both.

**Case Preview**

### *United States v. Burt*

The next case provides an example of the type of situation where the public authority defense most often arises. In *Burt,* the defendant claimed that she believed she had been granted the authority to transport undocumented immigrants across the border as part of her work as an informant for a border patrol agent. The trial court nevertheless refused to instruct the jury on the public authority defense. In the opinion that follows, the Ninth Circuit reversed Burt's conviction on the ground that she should have been allowed to present her defense to the jury.

As you read the decision, consider the following questions:

1. The court outlines the elements of the public authority defense in footnote 1. What are the elements of the defense?
2. If you were a juror, would you find that the defendant has met the requirements of the public authority defense based on the facts as stated in this opinion?

---

## United States v. Burt
### 410 F.3d 1100 (9th Cir. 2005)

BRIGHT, J.

The government filed a two-count indictment charging appellant Marnie Ann Burt with conspiracy to transport illegal aliens and transportation of illegal aliens. Burt requested jury instructions on her apparent public authority defense. The district court refused to give Burt's requested jury instructions, and the jury found Burt guilty on both counts. Burt appeals and argues the district court erred in refusing to instruct the jury on her public authority defense. Burt presented sufficient evidence to justify jury instructions on her public authority defense. We reverse and remand for a new trial.

On May 22, 2003, Border Patrol Agents Mike Van Edwards and Brian Brown arrested Burt for transporting illegal aliens. Burt told the agents that she had information regarding a plan to transport illegal aliens in a semi-trailer that coming weekend. The agents were interested in this information. Agent Brown decided not to recommend that Burt be prosecuted, and Agent Van Edwards contends he told Burt she would not be prosecuted. Burt agreed to come back the next day to meet with the agents regarding her knowledge of the semi-trailer plan. Burt contends that the agents told her that a warrant would be issued for her arrest if she did not attend the meeting.

The next day, May 23, 2003, Agent George Scott interviewed Burt. Agents Brown, Van Edwards, and Mark Friend were also present at the interview. Agent Scott was the only person who took notes during the interview. Burt contends she appeared at the meeting to avoid prosecution. Agent Scott contends he told Burt that she was not a confidential informant, that she should not do anything illegal, and that she should contact him with any information. Burt claims that the agents instructed her to get information and told her not to do anything illegal. Burt contends, however, that the agents told her that she would not be doing anything illegal as long as she was gathering information for the agents. Burt never contacted the agents after the interview.

On May 28, 2003, border patrol agents arrested Burt for transporting illegal aliens in a van. Burt told the agents that she was working for Agent Van Edwards. Shortly after Agent Scott heard that Burt had been arrested, he destroyed his notes of the May 23 meeting.

The government filed an indictment, charging Burt with conspiracy to transport illegal aliens and transportation of illegal aliens. At trial, Burt testified that she believed she was properly collecting information for the agents. At the close of evidence, Burt's counsel and the district court discussed Burt's requested jury instructions, which included the model Ninth Circuit public authority instruction. The following exchange took place:

> MR. KAUFMANN [Burt's counsel]: . . . I have requested the Court give the public authority defense instruction pursuant to [the Ninth Circuit's Model Criminal Jury Instruction] 6.10, and I have included the public authority defense as my Defendant's Requested Instruction No. 2. I know we have argued this ad nauseam, so I'm not going to bother the Court with the other arguments. I'm going to try to incorporate them by reference herein and tell the Court once again, much to my consternation, that it's a question for the jury and not for the Court.
>
> THE COURT: I'm going to refuse Defendant's Requested Instruction No. 2 on public authority. . . .[1]

The jury found Burt guilty of both counts in the indictment.

Burt filed a motion for a new trial, challenging the district court's decision not to give her requested instructions. The district court denied Burt's motion. The district court sentenced Burt to concurrent terms of thirty-six months in prison on both charges, to be followed by thirty-six months of supervised release. Burt filed a timely notice of appeal, and this appeal followed.

We review the district court's refusal to give a defendant's jury instructions based on a question of law de novo. We review the district court's findings on whether a defendant's theories are factually supported for an abuse of discretion. A defendant is entitled to instructions relating to a defense theory for which there is any foundation in the evidence, even though the evidence may be weak, insufficient, inconsistent, or of doubtful credibility. A mere scintilla of evidence supporting a defendant's theory, however, is not sufficient to warrant a defense instruction.

Burt contends that the district court erred in refusing to give her requested apparent public authority jury instruction. Burt argues that a jury with appropriate instructions should decide whether her belief, that her conduct on May 28 was for the sole purpose of gathering information for the agents, was reasonable.

The district court erred in refusing to give Burt's requested jury instructions on the public authority defense. At trial, Burt testified that the agents told her that as long as she was gathering information for the agents her actions would not be illegal. Burt also noted that the agents gave her no instructions on how to conduct herself. Agent Scott testified at the evidentiary hearing that Burt "should not be committing an offense if she's working for me." A jury could believe Burt and interpret Agent

---

[1] The Ninth Circuit Model Criminal Jury Instruction 6.10 Public Authority or Government Authority Defense reads:

> If a defendant engages in conduct violative of a criminal statute at the request of a government enforcement officer, with the reasonable belief that the defendant is acting as an authorized government agent to assist in law enforcement activity, then the defendant may not be convicted of violating the criminal statute, because the requisite criminal intent is lacking. The government must prove beyond a reasonable doubt that the defendant did not have a reasonable belief that [he] [she] was acting as an authorized government agent to assist in law enforcement activity at the time of the offense charged in the indictment.

Scott's statement to mean that if Burt was working for Scott her actions would not be illegal. In addition, Agent Scott destroyed his notes from his interview with Burt, which was the only contemporaneous record of the interview. The magistrate judge correctly noted that "[w]hen government agents destroy evidence, they place their own credibility in serious jeopardy."

Although Burt's evidence may not be strong, Burt has presented sufficient evidence to justify jury instructions on her public authority defense. The evidence, taken in its best light for Burt, could indicate that Burt's participation in the May 28 transportation of illegal aliens served the purpose of Burt gathering information about the crime, which could be reported to the agents. Burt's arrest, however, terminated her opportunity to make such a report. A jury could have determined, based on the evidence presented, that on May 28 Burt reasonably believed that she was working for the agents. Burt was, therefore, entitled to instructions relating to her public authority defense, and the district court erred in refusing to instruct the jury on the defense.

Accordingly, we Reverse and Remand for a new trial.

**Post-Case Follow-Up**

The public authority defense applies where the defendant commits a crime based on "the reasonable belief that [she] is acting as an authorized agent to assist in law enforcement activity." In *Burt*, the court found that the defendant was entitled to a jury instruction on the defense based on her testimony that border patrol agents told her that as long as she was gathering information for them, her actions would not be illegal.

## Burt: *Real Life Applications*

1. From 2010 to 2011, James operated a medical marijuana dispensary in San Diego, California. Although the dispensary complied with California law, the Drug Enforcement Administration raided James's dispensary and arrested James in late 2011. James was charged with possession of marijuana with the intent to distribute.

   James sought to raise a public authority defense based on a Department of Justice memorandum issued in 2009. The memo was issued by the Deputy Attorney General and sent to every federal prosecutor in the country. The memo stated, in relevant part: "As a general matter, federal prosecutors should not focus federal resources in your States on individuals whose actions are in clear and unambiguous compliance with existing state laws providing for the medical use of marijuana."

   Should the trial court permit James to present a public authority defense?

## Chapter Summary

- A person can use non-deadly force in self-defense if she reasonably believes it is necessary to defend against the imminent use of unlawful physical force. To use deadly force in self-defense, a person must also reasonably believe that the imminent threat she faces is a deadly one or, in some jurisdictions, that she is about to become the victim of a kidnapping, rape, or robbery. The reasonableness inquiry is an objective one, but it accounts for relevant physical attributes of the parties (height, weight, physical strength, etc.). Jurisdictions are split on the question of whether a defendant's prior experiences — for example, being the victim of a prior robbery — should be considered under the reasonableness standard.

- The definition of the duress defense varies across jurisdictions, but most states generally follow either the common law rule or the Model Panel Code rule. Under the common law rule, the defendant must have committed the crime in response to what she reasonably believed to be an imminent threat of death or serious bodily injury to herself or a third party. Under the Model Penal Code, the defendant must have engaged in conduct because he was coerced to do so by the use of, or threat to use, unlawful force against his person or the person of another, which a person of reasonable firmness in his situation would have been unable to resist.

- The defense of necessity arises when the defendant committed a crime in order to avoid a significant evil if there was no reasonable alternative to committing the offense, and the harm caused by the charged offense was not disproportionate to the harm the defendant avoided by breaking the law. The major difference between necessity and duress is that duress applies when the defendant's crime came in response to a threat by another person; necessity concerns situations where forces beyond the actor's control make committing a crime the lesser of two evils.

- Although there is a good deal of variation in the legal definition of insanity across jurisdictions, there are three notable approaches. Under the *M'Naghten* test, a defendant is considered insane if either (1) he did not know the nature and quality of the act he was doing, *or* (2) he did not know what he was doing was wrong, meaning he did not know the difference between right and wrong. Under the irresistible impulse test, a defendant is considered insane if he committed the crime as a result of an irresistible impulse that deprived him of the power to choose between right and wrong. Finally, the Model Penal Code test provides that a defendant is considered insane if he lacked the substantial capacity either (1) to appreciate the criminality (wrongfulness) of his conduct, or (2) to conform his conduct to the requirements of the law.

- If the defendant was intoxicated when she committed a crime, it may provide her with a defense in certain limited circumstances. The fact that a defendant's inhibitions were lowered as a result of intoxication is never a defense. But a defendant who is being prosecuted for a specific intent crime can introduce evidence of her intoxication if it is relevant to show that she did not act with the *mens rea* required for the crime. This sort of intoxication evidence is not admissible in prosecutions for general intent crimes. In addition, if a person commits a crime while in a state of involuntary intoxication, she can raise temporary insanity as an affirmative defense. To succeed, she will have to show that, as a result of involuntary intoxication, she was temporarily placed in a state of mind that meets the jurisdiction's test for insanity.

■ If the police induce a defendant to commit a crime she was not already predisposed to commit, she can claim entrapment as a defense. This is a subjective test that focuses on the defendant's predisposition to commit the crime.

■ A person's misunderstanding about the legality of her actions is generally not a defense in a criminal case because ignorance of the law is no excuse. The public authority defense provides for an exception to this rule if government officials responsible for enforcing the relevant law have led the defendant to reasonably believe her conduct is legally authorized. This defense can arise in two circumstances: first, if an agency responsible for enforcing the law issues an opinion letter or other guidance stating that certain conduct does not violate the relevant law, and second, if a government agent tells an informant that she is permitted to commit a crime in order to help with an undercover sting operation.

## Applying the Concepts

1. Nate was driving one day when he was lawfully stopped by a police officer. The police officer asked for permission to search the car, which Nate granted. Inside the glove compartment, the officer found one and a half ounces of marijuana. The officer placed Nate under arrest.

   As the officer was handcuffing Nate, Nate said, "I thought it was legal to possess marijuana in this state."

   "Yeah, but not this much marijuana," replied the police officer. The officer's statement was correct. In the state where this occurred, it is legal to possess an ounce of marijuana or less. Possession of more than one ounce of marijuana remains a felony, however.

   What defense(s), if any, will Nate be able to raise at trial?

2. Jackson and his friend Chris were hanging out on Jackson's porch at around 8:30 P.M. one night. Jackson's next-door neighbor, Stanley, left his house to run an errand.

   Ten minutes later, Jackson and Chris saw a man named Tiny walking toward them. Tiny, who lived a few blocks from Jackson, was known as a bully around the neighborhood. The only thing small about Tiny was his name. Tiny was 6′5″ and weighed 300 pounds. Tiny walked up to Jackson and Chris and said, "Did you guys see Stanley leave his house a few minutes ago? Stanley owes me some money. I'm going to break into his house and steal some of his stuff to teach him a lesson. If you see Stanley coming back, I want you to whistle so I can get out of there."

Jackson and Chris told Tiny that they did not want to help him out. Tiny walked closer to Jackson and Chris and said, "You don't understand. I wasn't *asking* you to help me out. I was *telling* you to help me out." Tiny then gave Chris and Jackson a menacing look while pounding his fist into his hand in a threatening manner.

Chris said, "OK, I'll do what you say. Just don't hurt us."

"Good," said Tiny, and he walked over to Stanley's driveway. Tiny broke into Stanley's house through a partially open window, took some jewelry from inside, and fled the scene. Chris is prosecuted for burglary and larceny as an accomplice. What defense(s), if any, might Chris have?

3. Doug went to a dive bar one night. At the bar, Doug accidentally knocked Victor's beer to the ground, causing the glass to shatter. Victor, who was quite large, said to Doug, "I'm going to punch you in the face for what you just did." Doug shoved Victor and began to run away toward the bar exit. As a result of Doug's push, Victor slipped awkwardly, hit his head on the corner of the bar, and fell to the ground. Victor landed chest-first onto on a shard of glass from his spilt beer. Victor died instantly. If Doug is prosecuted for a homicide offense, will he be able to successfully claim self-defense?

4. One night, Derrick found out that his best friend Lawrence had been secretly dating his ex-girlfriend Sara. Derrick bought a six-pack of beer to drown his sorrows. After drinking all six beers, Derrick decided to walk to Lawrence's house, which was just a quarter mile away.

When Derrick got to Lawrence's house, he saw that Lawrence's car was not in the driveway and the lights were off. Derrick decided to break into Lawrence's house in order to try to access Lawrence's computer and post embarrassing messages to social media from Lawrence's account. Assume that this would constitute the felony of computer trespass in the jurisdiction where this occurred.

Derrick picked up a rock from the ground then walked up to Lawrence's house and used the rock to smash a downstairs window. Derrick began to climb through the window. Derrick had half his body through the window when a police officer drove by and noticed what was going on. The officer pulled over and arrested Derrick.

In a prosecution for burglary, Derrick seeks to rely on evidence that he was intoxicated in his defense. What is the most likely outcome?

5. As discussed at the very beginning of this chapter, affirmative defenses are typically based on either a justification or an excuse rationale. If you were to categorize each of the affirmative defenses covered in this chapter as a justification defense, an excuse defense, or something else (a hybrid, or neither), how would you categorize them?

## Criminal Law in Practice

1. Look up your state's test for the insanity defense. Does your state recognize the insanity defense? If so, what test has your state adopted? (If you are in New Jersey, where the *Worlock* case presented in this chapter was decided, choose a neighboring state for this exercise.)

2. Look up your state's test for the duress defense. Does your state recognize the duress defense? If so, what test has your state adopted? (If you are in New Jersey, where the *Toscano* case presented in this chapter was decided, choose a neighboring state for this exercise.)

3. Review the facts of the *Goetz Real Life Applications* Question 3 on page 493, involving Vega. In the original question, you were asked questions from the perspective of the prosecutor. Imagine now that you are Vega's attorney.

   a. The prosecutor has charged Vega with first-degree murder. If your client is convicted of that offense, he will be sentenced to a minimum of 25 years, with the possibility of a sentence of life without the possibility of parole. Shortly after the charges are filed, the prosecutor calls you with a plea offer. Under the proposed deal, Vega would plead guilty to voluntary manslaughter. The prosecutor would agree to make a non-binding sentencing recommendation of two years in prison, but the judge would be free to impose any sentence in the range of zero to six years. Would you advise your client to accept this offer?

   b. Assume for purposes of this question that Vega rejects the plea offer and the case is going to trial. You will be meeting with your investigator tomorrow. What additional evidence would you most like your investigator to try to gather before the trial?

# Table of Cases

*Principal cases are italicized.*

# Index